Principles of International Politics

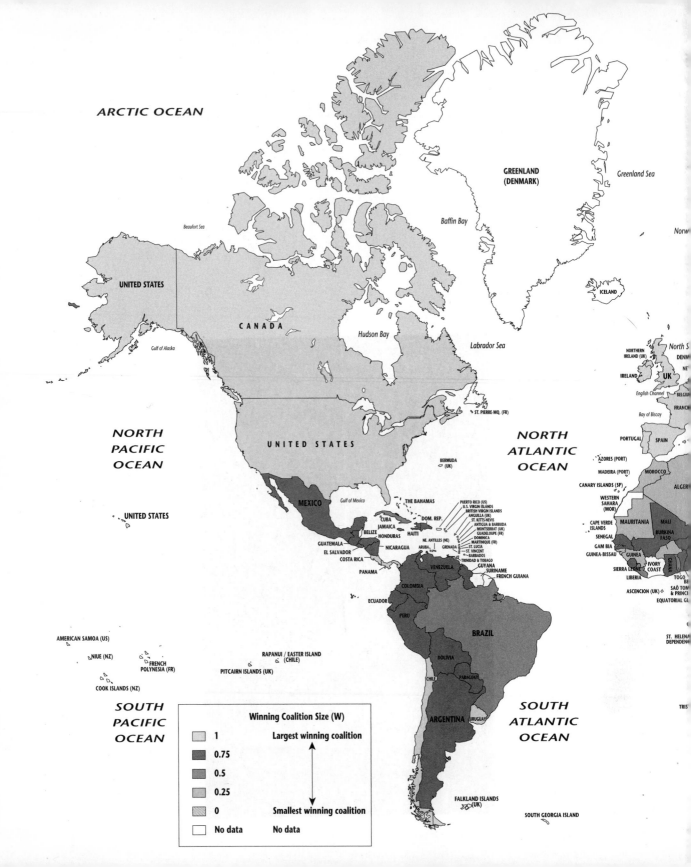

ARCTIC OCEAN

GREENLAND
(DENMARK)

Greenland Sea

Beaufort Sea

Baffin Bay

Norw

ICELAND

UNITED STATES

C A N A D A

Hudson Bay

Labrador Sea

North S

NORTHERN
IRELAND (UK)

DENM
NE

IRELAND   UK

Gulf of Alaska

BELGIU

English Channel

FRANC

NORTH
PACIFIC
OCEAN

St. Pierre-MQ. (FR)

NORTH
ATLANTIC
OCEAN

Bay of Biscay

UNITED STATES

PORTUGAL   SPAIN

BERMUDA
(UK)

AZORES (PORT)

MADEIRA (PORT)

MOROCCO

CANARY ISLANDS (SP)

UNITED STATES

MEXICO   *Gulf of Mexico*

THE BAHAMAS

CUBA

PUERTO RICO (US)
U.S. VIRGIN ISLANDS
BRITISH VIRGIN ISLANDS
ANGUILLA (UK)
ST. KITTS-NEVIS
ANTIGUA & BARBUDA
MONTSERRAT (UK)
GUADELOUPE (FR)
DOMINICA
MARTINIQUE (FR)
ST. LUCIA
ST. VINCENT
BARBADOS
TRINIDAD & TOBAGO

WESTERN
SAHARA
(MOR)

ALGER

JAMAICA
BELIZE

HAITI
DOM. REP.

CAPE VERDE
ISLANDS

MAURITANIA   MALI

GUATEMALA
HONDURAS

BURKINA
FASO

EL SALVADOR
NICARAGUA

NE. ANTILLES (NE)

SENEGAL

GAM BIA

COSTA RICA

ARUBA
GRENADA

GUINEA-BISSAU   GUINEA   GHA

PANAMA

VENEZUELA
GUYANA
SURINAME
FRENCH GUIANA

SIERRA LEONE
IVORY
COAST

TOGO
BE

LIBERIA

ASCENCION (UK)

SAÓ TOMÓ
& PRINCI

COLOMBIA

EQUATORIAL GU

ECUADOR

PERU

BRAZIL

ST. HELENA
DEPENDEN

AMERICAN SAMOA (US)

BOLIVIA

NIUE (NZ)

FRENCH
POLYNESIA (FR)

RAPANUI / EASTER ISLAND
(CHILE)

PITCAIRN ISLANDS (UK)

CHILE

PARAGUAY

COOK ISLANDS (NZ)

SOUTH
PACIFIC
OCEAN

ARGENTINA   URUGUAY

SOUTH
ATLANTIC
OCEAN

TRIS

Winning Coalition Size (W)

1   Largest winning coalition

0.75

0.5

0.25

0   Smallest winning coalition

No data   No data

FALKLAND ISLANDS
(UK)

SOUTH GEORGIA ISLAND

Principles of International Politics

Fourth Edition

BRUCE BUENO DE MESQUITA

New York University

and

Hoover Institution at Stanford University

CQ PRESS

A Division of SAGE
Washington, D.C.

CQ Press
2300 N Street, NW, Suite 800
Washington, DC 20037

Phone: 202-729-1900; toll-free, 1-866-4CQ-PRESS (1-866-427-7737)

Web: www.cqpress.com

Cover design: Matthew Simmons
Composition: C&M Digitals (P) Ltd.
Photo credits:
AP Images: 2, 109, 202, 224 (right), 247, 274
Corbis: 389
Getty Images: 179, 224 (left)
The Granger Collection: 361
Reuters: 24, 44, 83, 148, 316

♾ The paper used in this publication exceeds the requirements of the American National Standard for Information Sciences—Permanence of Paper for Printed Library Materials, ANSI Z39.48-1992.

Printed and bound in the United States of America

13   12   11   10   09   1   2   3   4   5

Library of Congress Cataloging-in-Publication Data

Bueno de Mesquita, Bruce,
Principles of international politics / Bruce Bueno de Mesquita.—4th ed.
    p. cm.
  Includes bibliographical references and index.
  ISBN 978-0-87289-598-0 (alk. paper)
  1. International relations. I. Title.

JZ1242.B84 2009
327.101—dc22

                                              2009010934

To the memory of my teachers. They showed me what life lived with dignity is, and they taught me to reflect on how our world works. Though I can no longer turn to them for counsel, still I listen for their whispers on the wind.

About the Author

Bruce Bueno de Mesquita is Julius Silver Professor of Politics and Director of the Alexander Hamilton Center for Political Economy at New York University and a senior fellow at the Hoover Institution at Stanford University. He is an expert on international conflict, foreign policy formation, the peace process, and nation building. He is the author of fifteen books, including *The Predictioneer's Game* (Random House 2009); *The Logic of Political Survival* (with Alastair Smith, Randolph M. Siverson, and James D. Morrow; MIT Press, 2003); *The Strategy of Campaigning* (with Kiron Skinner, Serhiy Kudelia, and Condoleezza Rice; University of Michigan Press, 2007); and *The War Trap* (Yale University Press, 1981). He is the managing partner of Mesquita & Roundell, LLC, a consultancy. In 2007, he won the DMZ Peace Prize for contributing to the advancement of peace on the Korean Peninsula. He received the Lifetime Achievement Award from the Conflict Processes section of the American Political Science Association and the Distinguished Scholar Award from the Foreign Policy section of the International Studies Association in 2008. He and Alastair Smith won the American Political Science Association's 2008 Franklin Burdette/Pi Sigma Alpha Award for the best paper presented at the 2007 annual meeting for their work "Political Survival and Endogenous Institution Change" (*Comparative Political Studies,* February 2009). He is a former Guggenheim Fellow, recipient of the Karl Deutsch Award, and a member of the American Academy of Arts and Sciences and the Council on Foreign Relations.

Brief
Contents

Contents

Contents

Maps, Tables, and Figures

MAPS

TABLES

FIGURES

Preface

The fourth edition of *Principles of International Politics* represents a substantial departure from earlier incarnations of the text. I take a more focused approach, spending far less space contesting alternative theories and far more developing the logic and evidence behind the strategic perspective. The changes are the consequence of the thoughtful feedback that many of you who have taught from or studied from this book have offered me. Because of your insights, this new edition is not merely a rearrangement and update of material. It has been rewritten from the ground up. This edition is, in essence, a nontechnical explanation of the selectorate theory as it applies to international affairs, ranging across such topics as the causes of war, the effects of foreign aid and military intervention on nation building, and the impact of domestic politics on trade and international organizations. I believe we now know enough and have amassed sufficient evidence and compelling logic to conclude that we can safely move beyond structural theories and much received wisdom to examine what is actually consistent with logic and with the current state of evidence. This book places international politics firmly within the realm of domestic, comparative politics.

The great attraction in writing this textbook is that through its pages I gain the opportunity to give students their first exposure to international affairs and to shape how they think about international events for the rest of their lives. Today's students are our future leaders in government, business, and academia and so must be well informed, not only about the facts of history but also about ideas that will guide their thinking. I have tried here to present students with a view of international relations grounded in the scientific method, anchored in history and current events, and focused on a unified theoretical theme. I have used theory to explore important policy questions and challenge intuition and, most of all, I have urged all of us to rely on logic and evidence rather than opinion or personal predilections in forming and evaluating foreign policy.

International relations often is studied as a subject divorced from daily politics or as a scattershot sampling of competing ideas and conjectures. It frequently is presented as a mysterious subject that depends on wisdom without the assistance of science, rather than as a subject amenable to the scientific method. And all too often it is treated as if events were unpredictable when they can be predicted and explained through the judicious application of analytic tools, logic, and empirical rigor. This book gives students those tools.

THE APPROACH

Principles of International Politics is unique in its theoretical focus; its attention to logical, empirical, and analytic rigor; and its historical sweep. Central among my convictions is that international politics is a product of the normal pulls and tugs of domestic affairs, that leaders (not nations) make policy decisions and do so to maximize their prospects of staying in office. Their decisions, therefore, are strategic, taking into account expected responses by adversaries and supporters and designed to maximize the leader's (not the state's) welfare. I call this view the strategic perspective. The quest for personal political power guides policy choices, and the cumulative effect of policy choices gives rise to what we call the international system. Therefore, domestic politics, foreign policy, and international politics are inextricably linked. We cannot make sense of international relations without considering all three.

As the theoretical backbone, the strategic perspective—especially in its selectorate guise—is always at the core of each explanation and comparison within the book, whether I discuss contemporary terrorism, trade and currency policies, or the emergence of the modern sovereign state during the High Middle Ages. I explain why terrible leaders who bankrupt their countries, steal foreign aid, and oppress their citizens persist in office for a long time, whereas leaders who provide peace and prosperity are frequently ousted. The empirical regularities known as the democratic peace are explained, as is the role of power in the initiation and escalation of disputes. The book explores at length trade sanctions, pressures for trade protectionism, the links of these sanctions and pressures to domestic political considerations, and issues of international law, international organizations, and the role that "We, the People" play in shaping foreign aid policies and their unfortunate consequences for many of the world's poorest people. I suggest why Saddam Hussein could sensibly oppose UN inspectors looking for weapons of mass destruction in 2002 and 2003 even though Iraq had none, and why it was in his interest to heighten George W. Bush's confidence in the mistaken belief that Iraq had such weapons. Students learn why and how unwanted trade wars can occur and the conditions in which economic sanctions are likely to be effective or ineffective. I take them through a careful examination of globalization, with clear arguments about who the winners and losers are likely to be from free trade. I explore paths to war and peace, as well as questions about the functioning of international organizations and international law. Nation building, military intervention, and innumerable other topics are related to the volume's theoretical framework.

The fourth edition sets out competing arguments and evaluates both their logical coherence and empirical reliability, frequently combining historical examples with nontechnical summaries of statistical evidence. It sets out an assessment of constructivist, realist, and liberal theories, all the while employing the strategic perspective to compare and contrast to these other perspectives. Through these comparisons I seek to bring coherence to a topic that is often seen as overwhelming. In this new edition I have tried to make even the most demanding concepts readily accessible and interesting to beginning students by offering many illustrative applications in each chapter and by writing in a more easily understood style. A key component of the book's new accessibility is to concentrate the technical material at the beginning of the book, where it is interwoven through a series of examples. Readers are thus exposed from the start, and in an intuitive way, to selectorate theory and a set of other game-theoretic tools that they then see applied to and developed in the subsequent issues discussed in the book. At the same time, I have attempted to make the book meaty enough so that students will want to return to it long after they have completed the introductory course. This should be a book to keep and use as a ready reference guide to seemingly puzzling developments in the international arena.

METHODOLOGY

My primary purpose in writing this book is to provide students with a better understanding of international relations. The book teaches students how to use sophisticated analytic tools, making them accessible, easily understood, and easily applied to today's problems and crises. These "tools" include spatial models, the median voter theorem (and how it relates to estimating security), win sets, expected utility calculations, and noncooperative game theory. Each of these methods is illustrated with a single, extended example concerned with the international dispute over Iran's nuclear ambitions. In this way, students immediately get to see how analytic methods can help tease out subtle implications of alternative approaches to major foreign policy problems, and they can even experiment with ways to solve such problems. Although the ideas are sophisticated, they require only skills possessed by beginning college students to be understood. I have worked from the assumption that readers have had no prior exposure to international relations, statistics, or model building. Additionally, to ensure that the methods are easy to understand and apply and that their relevance is apparent, the book has been classroom tested in a host of different institutions, from large state schools to small private colleges and two-year community colleges. I have incorporated feedback from students into every aspect of the presentation.

Students are taught to look beneath international problems to find the small set of key factors that contribute to cooperation or conflict. They gain exposure to problems of collective action and the difficulties of monitoring and sanctioning international misconduct, as well as to the problems that arise in trying to coordinate international interactions and deal with the distribution of valuable, scarce resources. In each case, they are also guided toward means to resolve these problems, learning to recognize the difference between cheap talk and meaningful statements, between commitment problems and ways to design institutions to ensure commitment, and between wishful thinking and reality.

ORGANIZATION AND PEDAGOGY

The book is organized so that the Introduction and eleven subsequent chapters follow a natural sequence for use in either a semester or quarter system. The fourth edition builds on the objectives of its predecessors while adding substantial new material. The Introduction and first chapter set out the strategic perspective, while chapters 2 and 3 provide all the analytic tools needed to think deeply about international affairs. These chapters combine well with the book's two appendixes, which provide a common base of historical knowledge and a shared philosophical vantage point among readers. Chapter 4 examines structural theories of war while chapter 5 reprises that subject from the strategic vantage point. In addition to its thorough examination of realist and liberal theories, the book also offers extended discussion and evaluation of the constructivist approach and suggests ways to link constructivism with the strategic perspective. Terrorism, nation building, military intervention, and strategic uses of foreign aid are given much more thorough treatment than in previous editions, including new theoretical insights and empirical evidence. The problems and opportunities presented by globalization and its relationship to trade and currency policy receive a detailed treatment, as do issues of compliance and commitment in the context of international law, international organization, and international norms of conduct. Students are given a basic introduction to important ideas in economics, especially supply and demand, comparative versus absolute advantage, and the meaning of a production possibility frontier. Every chapter is full of timely examples, reflections on historical developments from various theoretical perspectives, and carefully explained insights from the most recent research.

Because historical examples, concepts, and techniques are interspersed throughout, always in mutual support of each other, the book can readily be taught from a variety of perspectives. The instructor can emphasize events, ideas, hypotheses, historical analysis, formal analysis, or statistical analysis as suits his or her style, needs, and preferences.

To facilitate learning, the fourth edition features a number of pedagogical features and enhancements. Each chapter begins with an outline of the major ideas and arguments of the chapter (called "Overview") and ends with a summary that highlights the major points, helping to set up the discussion and bring it to a logical conclusion. Because the book introduces students to many new and important concepts, students will find those "key concepts" boldfaced in the text and listed at the end of each chapter with page references for ease of review. There is also a well-refined glossary of key terms and ideas at the end of the book so that students can spend their time learning ideas rather than memorizing terms. The book also has two indexes (subject and author), both of which serve as valuable guides for students who want to explore the field further or begin to do bibliographic or original research.

As in previous editions, the theoretical arguments and historical and contemporary examples are accompanied by an array of figures, charts, tables, maps, and images. These include substantial, contextual captions that allow the illustrations and figures to stand alone as summary statements of important ideas. In addition, "Try This" boxes found throughout each chapter pose puzzles that students can solve by applying concepts introduced in the book. (Some of these are picked up in the student workbook, *Applying the Strategic Perspective*, as problem sets.) Everything has been designed to stimulate students' interest and understanding and encourage students to continue their investigation of international relations.

A UNIQUE TEACHING AND LEARNING PACKAGE

More than ever, students and adopters will find excellent support for these diverse approaches in the ancillary materials that accompany the text, including the student workbook, the companion Web site for students, and the instructor's resources that are available for download. The superb student workbook—*Applying the Strategic Perspective*—thoroughly revamped for the fourth edition by Leanne C. Powner, provides detailed coverage and more extensive problem sets than in earlier editions. New problems early in the chapters help beginning students work through some of the nuts-and-bolts aspects of the strategic perspective—everything from learning to create and interpret symbolic expressions to helping identify independent and dependent variables. At the end of each chapter, students who wish to do so are able to stretch their capabilities with more complex problems in the "Extensions" section.

Students will find a host of resources available to them on the companion Web site at http://bdm.cqpress.com. Brief chapter summaries and questions for review help guide student learning by identifying and clarifying key concepts in each chapter. An interactive "Flashcard" feature enables students to study and review key terms and tells them where each is located in the text. Online quizzes feature multiple-choice and true/false questions to allow students to self-test and report scores to instructors. Exercises for each chapter provide students and instructors with opportunities to practice basic problems either alone or in class. Finally, "Walk Throughs" allow students to explore difficult problems in an interactive setting, helping them see how to conceptualize and solve significant international relations problems tackled in the text and the supporting materials.

The Web site continues to support the Policy Forecaster, software similar to that used by the U.S. government in making major foreign policy decisions and by large corporations in dealing with significant policy choices. Simplified for easy use and interpretation, students can use the Forecaster to explain and predict current international problems, whether these involve issues of international political economy, security studies, or anything else.

A full set of instructor's resources is available for download at www.cqpress.com/prof/Ancillaries-Download.html. These include:

- A comprehensive test bank with more than 400 multiple-choice and short essay questions created by Anna Getmansky. The test bank is available in Word and Word Perfect formats as well as fully loaded in Respondus, a flexible and easy-to-use test-generation software that allows instructors to build, customize, and integrate exams into course management systems.
- A set of 280 PowerPoint lecture slides and a full set of "Walk Throughs" from the Web, written and edited by Anna Getmansky for the fourth edition, for use in lectures and to help ease class preparation.
- All of the tables and figures from the fourth edition textbook and workbook in .pdf format and PowerPoint slides for classroom presentation.
- An instructor's manual with "at a glance" lists of topics and methods, discussion of key topics and arguments, lists of important points to bring up in class, discussion questions, and links to relevant topics in the book.

ACKNOWLEDGMENTS

Principles of International Politics is my effort to explain a way of looking at international relations and reshape how the subject is taught. If it succeeds in doing so, the credit belongs to those who have helped me along the way. A textbook provides a unique opportunity to express thanks, not only to those who helped with the book at hand but also to those whose teaching, inspiration, and guidance have shaped the way I think. It is my pleasure to take this opportunity to thank them here.

This book was inspired by Kenneth Organski, my teacher, mentor, and friend. Without his urging, it surely would not have been written. To be fair, Ken tricked me into writing the book, but that is another story. This was to have been a joint effort by Ken and me, but the tragic terminal illness of his daughter and then his own sudden death precluded that collaboration. How I wish I had his wisdom, insight, and elegant turn of phrase to share with you throughout this book. He is missed by all who loved him, and all who knew him loved him.

William Riker's shadow will be found on every page of this book. The principles of international politics are every bit as much an expression of his understanding of politics as they are of mine. Never have I known a more profound thinker. His was truly the intellect of a once-in-a-century man. I hope my effort does some small justice to his memory.

My parents, Abraham and Clara Bueno de Mesquita, survived Hitler, fled their homelands, and spent fruitful, successful, and rewarding lives in demanding times. They ensured that my sisters, Mireille Bany and Judy Berton, and I had every opportunity for fulfillment. Their lessons and their aspirations inspire me still. Every day I hear their wisdom as whispers on the wind.

Teachers leave incredible marks on our lives. I wish to express my gratitude to my most important classroom teachers, too many of whom are no longer with us: Henry Morton (Queens College), Richard Park (University of Michigan), Solomon Resnik (Queens College), Donald Stokes (University of Michigan), Phyllis Taylor (third grade), Lionel M. Yard (Stuyvesant High School), and many others inspired me to want to teach. To touch the lives of students as they have done is one of life's remarkable accomplishments.

I have benefited from the counsel of many colleagues who, of course, cannot be held accountable for my failure to heed all of their advice. Certainly the advice I did take has improved my effort in shaping this fourth edition. While I cannot mention everyone who counseled me through the original development and subsequent revisions of *Principles of International Politics,* I especially want to thank D. Scott Bennett, William Clark, Mark Crescenzi, Andrew Enterline, Andrew Farkas, Erik Gartzke, Alan Lamborn, David Leblang, Douglas Lemke, the much-missed Joseph Lepgold, Rose McDermott, the much-missed Fiona McGillivray, Cliff Morgan, James Morrow, Jeffrey Ritter, Alexander Rosenberg, Shanker Satyanath, Randolph Siverson, Kiron Skinner, Alastair Smith, Andrew Sobel, Alan Stam, Richard Stoll, Douglas Van Belle, Suzanne Werner, and John H. P. Williams. Each provided me with much valued guidance. The reviewers of the fourth edition—Jeff Cavanaugh, Mississippi State University; Feryal Cherif, University of California–Riverside; David Clark,

SUNY–Binghamton; and Glenn Palmer, Penn State University—provided especially insightful and useful guidance. Their comments inspired many of the changes you see here. Additionally, Ethan Bueno de Mesquita provided invaluable assistance in the development of the fourth edition's treatment of terrorism. Some among those who gave generously of their time and counsel have been students of mine; I have been the student of all of them. Although they are too numerous to name, I thank all of my students, who, over the years, have suffered through my efforts to identify and explain the principles of international politics as I see them.

CQ Press has been an author's dream publisher. Randolph Siverson first suggested this project to Brenda Carter, director of CQ's college group. I thank him for doing so. Brenda persuaded me that CQ was the right way to go, and I have never regretted the decision. I told her at the outset that I hoped to write a text with a point of view and that I was more interested in making my viewpoint clear than in writing a "garden variety" text. She and the rest of the CQ Press team never wavered from their commitment to that vision. My editor for the first edition, Charisse Kiino, did absolutely everything right to make the original book turn out as well as possible and much better than I could have done on my own. She has continued to be a source of inspired support. This edition has been overseen by its development editor Elise Frasier; Lorna Notsch, who took on production responsibilities; and Julie F. Nemer, who copyedited the manuscript and significantly improved its clarity and accuracy. This superb threesome has provided inspired ideas for conveying information and concepts through maps and figures; they have helped me to tighten arguments, write more clearly and succinctly, clarify ideas, and ensure internal logical consistency across the volume. They are second to none in the quality of their advice, editing, creative insight, and in the tremendous charm and good humor that they have brought to this project. I cannot imagine working with better people. Robin Bourjaily proofread the text, and Pat Ruggiero created the indexes. Wow, what a team. Thank you all.

The Wilf Family Department of Politics at New York University (NYU) and the Hoover Institution at Stanford University provide me with all the support one could hope for when researching and writing a book. I thank both NYU and the Hoover Institution for their continued support.

My final and greatest debt belongs to my family, who has been a constant source of support and patience. My wife, Arlene, put in long hours helping with proofreading, making it possible to complete this project on schedule and still make it to the opera on time. She also tolerated innumerable working "vacations" so that I could complete the manuscript on schedule. I cannot sing her praises sufficiently. I am most grateful not only to Arlene but also to Erin, Jason, Ethan, Rebecca, Gwen, Adam and my grandchildren Nathan, Clara, Abraham, and Hannah for making life fulfilling.

Introduction
Foundations of International Relations

- We begin the study of international politics by outlining an approach to the field that differs from traditional ones; we focus on leaders and their constituents, not states.

- Leaders of states are motivated by personal, not national, interests. Their foreign policy choices are constrained by domestic politics as much as they are by forces external to the nation.

- Yet, whatever their policy preferences, leaders must coordinate their foreign policy actions with other leaders.

- The study of international relations may best be understood as the interaction of power, perception, and preferences.

- Four basic categories of problems arise: coordination, distribution, monitoring, and sanctioning.

OVERVIEW

Writing in 1933, two noted scholars, James Russell and Quincy Wright, observed that:

> Students of international relations are concerned with the description, prediction, and control of the external behavior of states, particularly of their more violent types of behavior such as intervention, hostilities, and war. It is clear that mere description of a diplomatic or military event has little meaning by itself and that such an event can neither be predicted nor controlled unless account is taken of the circumstances which preceded it *within* each of the states involved. (1933, 555 [emphasis added])

Motivated by a desire to learn how to predict and control world events in order to diminish threats to human welfare, Russell and Wright articulated a mission for the scientific study of international affairs. This book shares their ambition. It is committed to understanding, predicting, and improving international affairs in all of its guises through the careful application of logic and evidence to world events. By the time you complete this book you will know how to predict the unfolding of current events. You will have acquired the skills and insights that will allow you to explain why things occur as they do and to think about how to change the future course of events for the better. This book is no mere exercise in ivory tower thinking. It is intended to help you improve the world as well as your understanding of it.

The domestic challenges Barack Obama faced upon entering office included high unemployment, a fractured housing market, a broken auto industry, and unstable financial markets. Here he speaks before signing the $787 billion economic stimulus bill, as Vice President Joe Biden listens at right, at the Denver Museum of Nature and Science in February 2009.

Russell and Wright's view that we must look within **states*** to understand the interactions that take place among them continues to occupy a distressingly small place in many courses, in most textbooks, in most research and, most important, in how most policymakers think about foreign affairs. Instead of distinguishing the **self-interests** of individual leaders from the interests of the states they lead, most of us assume that those sets of interests overlap—that in making foreign policy decisions leaders will do what is best for their nation,

---

* Although it is sometimes useful to distinguish among the terms *state*, *nation*, and *country*, unless the context dictates otherwise, I use them interchangeably for presentational convenience.

that they will act in the so-called **national interest,** the aggregated preferences of a substantial majority of the citizenry.

This is a demanding assumption. The conflation of a nation's interests with the interests of a leader—if we think of states and leaders as essentially the same thing—leads us to think of nations as **unitary actors,** that is, as if all the interests of the citizenry and leadership can be represented by a single decision maker in each state. This has important implications. It means that states and not some other entity, namely leaders, are the best unit of analysis for understanding world events. A state's internal structure or composition is not likely to be seen as relevant to its actions in international affairs; instead, we'll care mostly about how a state responds to external threats to its survival and about the degree to which it holds power or influence relative to other states. Domestic politics within countries and the differences in such institutional arrangements as whether a state is a presidential democracy, parliamentary democracy, military junta, monarchy, or authoritarian dictatorship seem irrelevant to what happens in the international arena.

On the contrary, the main point of departure in this book is to take **domestic politics,** that is, the full range of political decisions about matters internal to the state, seriously in thinking about international relations. To do so, I substitute the **strategic perspective,** introduced at greater length in Chapter 1, for the standard unitary state actor perspective. The strategic perspective acknowledges that people, not states, make policy. They do so with their own interests front and center in their calculations of what to do and what not to do. From the strategic point of view, the state is merely a metaphor for the collection of groups and individuals living within a sovereign territory.

The central insight of the strategic perspective is that leaders want first and foremost to stay in office. This means that they choose which policies to support and which actions to take with an eye toward enhancing their personal political survival prospects whether their choices are good for their citizen-subjects or not. The strategic perspective recognizes that a leader's job security often is distinct from the state's security. The leader's job security always depends, at least in part, on avoiding foreign entanglements that are likely to lead to the incumbent's overthrow either by foreign or domestic political rivals. By grasping this essential political fact, including attentiveness to domestic threats arising from a leader's foreign policy choices, and its sometimes surprising implications, we derive a better understanding of international relations than has proven possible from unitary actor modes of thinking.

To put the strategic perspective into context, this chapter summarizes the evolution of the study of international affairs over the past century and highlights some of its key principles and concepts. This allows me to introduce briefly some important ideas about how people think about international relations. Those ideas reflect the mainstream unitary actor perspective. It also allows me to demonstrate how events, especially during the past century, have shaped thinking and understandably led researchers to look for general principles based on a handful of important but unrepresentative events. Like army generals whose strategy for today's war is overly colored by what worked in yesterday's war, the leading theories of international affairs are explanations—but not the only explanations—of yesterday's biggest problems. They capture partial truths that reflect principles that work some of the time but that too often fail to account for events other than those used to identify the principles in the first place. This chapter, like this entire book, emphasizes the use of logic, rather than past events, to determine general principles and uses broad-based evidence across large swaths of history to evaluate the extent to which these logically grounded principles are, indeed, general and capable of informing our understanding both of past events and future events. I believe those general principles reside in looking within states, as urged by Russell and Wright three-quarters of a century ago, and so that is exactly what I will do.

We start by focusing on three basic principles:

1. The actions that leaders take to influence events in the international arena are motivated by their personal welfare and, especially, by a desire to stay in office. Leaders' concerns for the national interest are subordinate to personal interests. If the two coincide, then so much the better; if they do not, leaders do what they believe is best for themselves even when doing so harms most citizens and, in that sense, the national interest.

2. International relations cannot be separated from domestic politics. Every foreign policy action is undertaken in the shadow of the domestic political consequences the action is expected to produce. Therefore, if a foreign policy is expected to achieve beneficial consequences for a nation in the long term but in the short term will result in the ouster of the leader, then that policy will not be pursued.

3. Relations between nations and between leaders are driven by strategic considerations. As such, foreign policy decisions are designed to influence international affairs and the leader's well-being. To be effective in this, foreign policies must be chosen with an eye toward the reaction they will create among friends and adversaries. The reaction expected from a policy choice is compared with the reaction anticipated from other policy options. Leaders pick the policy they believe will produce the best outcome for them, knowing that, at the same time, domestic and foreign rivals are choosing policies to enhance their own well-being.

These three principles indicate that international affairs are best understood through the use of game theory. Game theory is a means to evaluate strategic interactions in which the choices of any individual are contingent on expectations about the choices of other individuals or groups. It provides an explicit, logically consistent, straightforward way to understand how people make choices, knowing that they must anticipate as best as they can how others will react and knowing also that others are trying to anticipate everyone else's actions. Chapters 2 and 3 provide a primer on decision theory, game theory, and associated tools of rational decision making. These are the techniques you will need to know to work through the arguments, examples, and problems in this book. You should feel confident about your ability to master these techniques—the tools are well within your reach.

The first principle of this book draws attention away from a focus on nations and puts it more squarely on leaders; leadership; and domestic social, political, and economic circumstances. The most important aspect of international affairs is the way in which national leaders translate their self-interest into foreign policy decisions and actions. The reason I focus on decision makers and their choices is quite simple. Nations do not make decisions. Nations do not feel secure and wealthy, or threatened and poor. Nations do not make agreements or wage war; they do not obey laws or break them. People do these things. They may do them in the name of the nation they lead or represent, but it is individuals who choose goals, actions, and strategies. It is individual citizens and leaders who bear the costs of failure and enjoy the benefits of success for the actions taken in the name of their state.[†]

Because leaders, not states, make choices, we are compelled to explore questions about the extent to which we can speak meaningfully about any nation having a collective, national interest. We will see that the idea of a national interest works well as rhetoric but not so well when it comes to saying which policies promote it and which do not. It may be surprising to realize that at the end of the day leaders determine what is in the national interest based on their own desires and beliefs and not based on any reasonable, objective view of what the national interest might be. The reason for this, as we will see, is that in many—maybe most—circumstances, it is not possible to identify a national interest, if that term means something like "the policies desired by a large majority of people living in a country."

TRY THIS

Here is a preliminary problem to get you thinking about the national interest. Let's define the *American national interest* as a set of policies preferred by a majority of Americans. Suppose 60 percent of Americans wants to tighten control to restrict further the number of immigrants entering the country, with two-thirds of those Americans also favoring trade restrictions to prevent American manufacturing and other jobs from going overseas (fair trade) and with one-third of those Americans supporting unfettered trade in goods and services (free trade). Suppose 40 percent wants to change American immigration law to expand the number of people who can enter the country as legal immigrants and to provide the means for many who entered illegally to be treated as legal immigrants. Imagine that half of the second group of people support free trade in goods and services and half support fair trade laws to protect American workers from overseas competition.

What is in the national interest? Is it possible for a majority to favor expanding access to legal entry into the United States and to favor freer trade? to expand legal entry but impose more protections against foreign competition? to restrict immigration and favor freer trade? to restrict immigration and favor more trade protectionism? Defend your answer based on the information provided, not on your personal point of view.

The focus on leadership forces us to think about why seemingly successful and effective leaders get turned out of office, whereas some manifestly terrible leaders keep their jobs for

---

† A policy is a *failure* from a given individual's perspective when the policy yields results that are worse for that individual than the results expected had the policy not been pursued. Likewise, we may think of *success* as a policy outcome that improves on what was expected had the policy not been pursued.

a very long time. Take, for example, Winston Churchill. As Britain's prime minister during World War II, he sustained Britain as one of the last bastions of democracy in Europe during the darkest days of the war before ultimately guiding it to a valiant victory against Nazi Germany. Yet, in the final days of the war, the British electorate voted Churchill out of office. In contrast, such dictators as Kim Jong-il in North Korea, Fidel Castro in Cuba, Robert Mugabe in Zimbabwe, the late Saddam Hussein of Iraq, and countless others past and present manage to remain in office for decades even as they impoverish and even murder many of their citizens. Even defeat in war, it seems, is not sufficient reason to overthrow some dictators (Bueno de Mesquita and Siverson 1995; Bueno de Mesquita et al. 2003; Chiozza and Goemans 2004). This certainly is a puzzle that raises questions about leadership, morality, and the motives behind and consequences of foreign policy.

The second principle also deviates from current thinking about international affairs. The dominant view today tends to see international politics as shaped by elements outside the control of any one nation or leader. It says that how nations interact with one another is predicated on factors such as how balanced or skewed the distribution of power is. Those nations endowed with great wealth and weaponry are thought by many to shape international affairs by influencing who does what to whom and when. Henry Kissinger, Richard Nixon's noted national security advisor and later his and Gerald Ford's secretary of state, for example, argues that: "History so far has shown us only two roads to international stability: domination or equilibrium. We do not have the resources for domination, nor is such a course compatible with our values. So we are brought back to a concept maligned in much of America's intellectual history—the balance of power" (1992, 239). What Kissinger means by the "balance of power" comes down to his understanding of what makes some nations more influential than others:

> Throughout history the political influence of nations has been roughly correlative to their military power. While states might differ in their moral worth and prestige of their institutions, diplomatic skill could augment but never substitute for military strength. In the final reckoning weakness has invariably tempted aggression and impotence brings abdication of policy in its train. . . . The balance of power . . . has in fact been the precondition of peace. (Kissinger 1979, 195)

This is why people speak of superpowers, such as the United States today, as imposing their will on weak states. Those who are less well endowed allegedly must simply go along. They have no choice. Yet in 1776 when the American colonies were seemingly weak and the United Kingdom was the greatest power in the world, it was the colonies that prevailed in the American Revolution against Britain. Two centuries later, when Vietnam was weak and the United States was one of two superpowers, it was Vietnam that prevailed and not the United States. As these examples illustrate, it is not always true, and perhaps not even generally true, that "weakness has invariably tempted aggression and impotence brings abdication of policy in its train." The strategic perspective does not give much credit to power by itself as a determinant of outcomes in international affairs. Instead, it weighs power and motivations together to evaluate foreign policy choices and their expected results.

In this book, I make clear that the links between domestic politics and international affairs lead to a full-blown theory of international relations capable of explaining many of the prominent puzzles about international cooperation and international competition. We look at some of these puzzles later in this introduction. Furthermore, I show that if we ignore the interdependencies between domestic politics and international relations, we are dooming ourselves to gross misunderstandings of how the world actually works. If political leaders act as if foreign policy is "high" politics not subject to the "low" politics of domestic maneuvering and horse trading (Morgenthau 1978), then they are likely to make serious errors that could endanger us all. We see an example of this in our discussion of the Iraq War later in the chapter.

The third governing principle views the unfolding of international relations as a function of reasoned decision making. The perspectives that have dominated thinking since the end of World War II—in particular, realism and liberalism and their variants—give little attention to individual choices. They see nations as reacting to changes in the international environment like pin balls responding to the tilt of the machine and the obstructions they happen to encounter as they bounce their way through the pinball maze. Consequently, these perspectives miss the essence of political maneuvering that is, I maintain, at the heart of international affairs.

Because so much that follows differs from standard accounts of international affairs, I pause here to introduce the central themes of the three most important alternatives to the strategic perspective: neorealism, liberalism, and constructivism. These approaches will come up from time to time throughout the remainder of this book, so it is important to understand their essential features. Then I turn to the history of the field to help you better understand how and why people think about international affairs as they do.

NEOREALISM

Neorealism (Waltz 1979), discussed in much greater detail in Chapter 4, makes four core assumptions:

1. International politics is anarchic.
2. States, as rational unitary entities, are the central actors in international politics.
3. States seek to maximize their security above all else; they consider other factors only after security is assured.
4. States seek to increase their power so long as doing so does not place their security at risk.

These assumptions establish neorealism's view that what happens inside states, that is, domestic politics, is irrelevant to the fundamentals of international affairs. Of course, neorealists understand that this is a simplification of reality. It is one that many find useful but that the strategic perspective rejects as an oversimplification. There is plenty of time to discuss the limitations of neorealism. Here I just focus on its essence and some of its important strengths.

Neorealism's most important innovation is to suggest that nations are interested in maximizing their security rather than maximizing their power (Waltz 1979). The focus on security implies that nations are concerned with relative gains in their competition with other states (Grieco 1988a, 1988b; Powell 1991; Snidal 1991). It does a nation no good to gain new resources if, in the process, others gain even more, leaving the first nation relatively worse off. Kenneth Waltz, the founder of neorealism, explains his emphasis on relative gains as follows:

> When faced with the possibility of cooperating for mutual gain, states that feel insecure must ask how the gain will be divided. They are compelled to ask not "Will both of us gain?" but "Who will gain more?" If an expected gain is to be divided, say, in the ratio of two to one, one state may use its disproportionate gain to implement a policy intended to damage or destroy the other. Even the prospect of large absolute gains for both parties does not elicit their cooperation so long as each fears how the other will use its increased capabilities. (1979, 105)

The neorealist perspective sees the world as naturally in a state of war, a condition that is avoided only by the skillful pursuit of national security by each and every nation. It gives scant attention to the prospect that states (or governments) can cooperate with one another. It suggests a world devoid of anyone who can be trusted to protect a state's security interests except the state itself. Thus, neorealists view international politics as essentially a self-help system. Alliances, international organizations, and all other means of cooperation between states are just (usually short-term) conveniences for states to protect and enhance their own security. They will break from such arrangements at the drop of a hat if doing so will improve their security.

LIBERALISM

Liberal theories emerged as a counterweight to the neorealist perspective. Unlike realist approaches, **liberalism** draws attention to the frequent and often long-standing occurrences of international cooperation. Indeed, a desire to explain such cooperation is its first point of departure from neorealism. Furthermore, for liberal theories, structural **hierarchy,** which implies the presence of an actor that can authoritatively enforce agreements between states (rather than anarchy, a system in which states must be able to help themselves because they cannot count on anyone else), is the central organizing principle of international politics. The presence of a hegemonic state (an overwhelmingly dominant power) helps enforce norms of conduct and maintain regimes. Norms are generally observed patterns of conduct.

For example, most nations most of the time respect the territorial boundaries of their neighbors. They do so, according to liberal theorists (and constructivists too, as explained next) because this is an accepted norm of conduct. Thus, even though territorial integrity cannot be enforced easily as a matter of law, it is generally enforced as a matter of shared values, or norms. Regimes are sets of international laws, rules, and organizations designed to promote coordination among nations with shared interests (Krasner 1983; see also Chapter 11). Norms and regimes combine to provide the behavioral basis by which the international system's hierarchical structure promotes cooperation and supports the assumed natural inclination of nations to maximize their wealth.

Robert Keohane and Joseph Nye's (1977) theory of interdependence is the most prominent liberal theory. It draws attention to the international political economy (as do I in Chapter 10) rather than focusing exclusively on problems related to security. Liberalism and neorealism quite naturally focus on different variables. For the structural theory of liberalism, power distributions are not as important as distributions of shared interests produced, for instance, by trade regimes or cultural norms. Trade regimes are agreements and relevant enforcing institutions or organizations designed to regulate and enforce specific trade policies. Their function is to promote cooperation among participants and, in fact, they are often successful in doing so.

Cultural norms, or shared values, may also promote cooperation by making clear what sorts of behavior are unacceptable and open to punishment. Of course, the feasibility of punishment for violating norms or regime expectations depends to a large degree on the assumption that the international system is hierarchical rather than anarchic. Theories that share the liberal perspective are more likely to treat international law as a serious constraint on national action (as discussed in Chapter 11), even when the law is contrary to a nation's self-interest, than are theories such as neorealism that subscribe to anarchy.

CONSTRUCTIVISM

Neorealism and liberalism assume state objectives. In the former case, security is the assumed objective; in the latter case, wealth and cooperation. **Constructivism,** in contrast, is a theoretical perspective that focuses on explaining how certain types of objectives come into being or change. Constructivism began primarily as an attempt to theorize about the formation of identity, that is, how we see ourselves (Keck and Sikkink 1998; Risse-Kappen, Ropp, and Sikkink 1999; Wendt 1999). For constructivists, individual preferences and identity are formed or altered by legitimation, role redefinition, and reflection.

A nation's leaders might, for instance, agree to an international treaty on human rights even though they routinely violate the human rights of their subjects (Cherif 2005). By doing so, constructivists hypothesize that the leadership seeks to legitimate themselves in the eyes of the international community. However, as these leaders engage in the rhetorical endorsement of human rights, they may find themselves under international pressure to participate in the shared norms of conduct implied by the treaty they ratified (Risse-Kappen, Ropp, and Sikkink 1999). Eventually, faced with a contradiction between their rhetoric and behavior and confronted with international pressure to abide by the norm of conduct to which they give rhetorical support, the leaders become persuaded to change their behavior and respect the norm of conduct to which they agreed.

Constructivism does not view decision makers as primarily strategic. Rather, leaders are thought initially to adopt a course of action for strategic reasons—to obtain legitimacy—but then to become caught up in socially accepted norms of conduct, reinforced by external pressure and persuasion until they have altered their own sense of self and their own subjective view of their interests. They become socialized to a new way of behaving even if the changed behavior jeopardizes their own political welfare.

Unfortunately, much of the empirical research to evaluate this theory's conjectures is poorly designed to do so. Thus far, constructivists have tended to select cases based on prior knowledge of how the dependent variable turned out rather than drawing cases at random to see whether their independent variables—related to norms, pressure, and persuasion—tend to produce systematically the predicted effect (that is, altered international values and improved behavior). Thus, their research designs tend to unintentionally contain an antifalsification bias.

Recent efforts to evaluate constructivism in a manner more consistent with the scientific method tend not to find much support for constructivist hypotheses. For example, Thomas König and Brooke Luetgert (2005) have investigated apparent preference changes in negotiations within the European Union. The pair provides an empirical examination of the competing views on preference change during the Nice intergovernmental conference that took place in December 2000. They "study whether and how the contracting parties changed their positions on eight key reform topics over time—did they act strategically or did they adapt their positions through a process of deliberation, social interaction and persuasion?" (König and Luetgert 2005, 2). They note that constructivism leads to the expectation that preferences will converge among the members as they adopt shared norms and are subjected to pressures and persuasion. Nevertheless, König and Luetgert report that, "The results refute the claims of constructivists predicting that positions converge and increase the capacity to act due to common norms, rhetoric action or persuasion" (2005, 6). For the constructivist account see, for instance, J. Checkel (2003) and J. Jupille, J. Caporaso, and J. Checkel (2003).

Similarly, Feryal Cherif (2005) finds insignificant evidence that human rights behavior improves over time in response to signing international treaties and being subjected to international pressure that obliges the member states to adhere to specific rules of conduct with regard to women's rights. Constructivists sometimes argue that the metamorphosis of preferences and behaviors takes time, as external pressure and personal redefinition gradually take hold. But Cherif's study—which surveys a fifteen-year period—shows that this has not proven to be true, at least with regard to women's political participation.

Although several empirical studies raise questions about the accuracy of the constructivist account, there is still too little research to reach a firm conclusion, so constructivism remains a troubled but still plausible alternative (or complementary) explanation of at least some facets of international affairs, especially in the domain of international law and international organizations. Therefore, we return to a consideration of constructivism when we take up those these topics in Chapter 11.

With this background information under our belts, let's discuss the origins and development of those perspectives in international relations.

A BRIEF HISTORY OF INTERNATIONAL RELATIONS THINKING

Woodrow Wilson was president of the United States during the First World War. Before that—and importantly here—he was a professor of political science. Many of his ideas about international affairs were formed while he was a professor of American politics at Princeton University. A lasting part of his legacy is an approach to foreign affairs that is closely associated with him. Wilson's idealism, the dominant approach to international affairs before World War II, painted a rosy picture of states cooperating with one another in promoting peace, democracy, and prosperity. Today, more sophisticated forms of Wilsonian idealism exist in modern-day liberal theories (Keohane 1986; Keohane and Nye 1972; Oneal and Russett 1997; Russett 1993) and constructivist theories (Keck and Sikkink 1998; Risse, Ropp, and Sikkink 1999; Wendt 1999). They paint an encouraging picture of international cooperation based on shared norms and values across many states and their leaders.

During the decade of the 1930s, a new breed of theorists, called realists, observed that the Russian Revolution in 1917, naval arms races both in Europe and between European powers and Japan in the 1920s and 1930s, and regional conflicts throughout the world seemed incompatible with idealist expectations. They noted that deliberation through the League of Nations, Wilson's grand instrument for promoting international peace, was insufficient to sustain peace. By the end of World War II, hard-nosed realist approaches had largely supplanted Wilsonian idealism. Consequently, even as the United Nations replaced the League as a deliberative peace-keeping body, states began organizing into regional alliances for mutual defense and tough realist tactics replaced idealist expectations during the cold war.

Today, realist ideas, in their turn, face significant challenges. These challenges reflect: (1) the insufficiency of realist theories to anticipate or explain the peaceful ending of the cold war and the accompanying implosion of the Soviet Union and the unraveling of its Eastern European empire (Gaddis 1992); (2) the discovery that several of the most important realist propositions suffer from logical inconsistencies (Milner 1998; Powell 1994, 1999); (3) the discovery that key logically consistent realist propositions turn out to be falsified by the record of history; and (4) the growing evidence that the causes of and solutions to international conflict can be better understood, as urged by Russell and Wright, by looking within states (Bueno de Mesquita et al. 2003; Fearon 1994; Smith 1996;).

Realism in its newer, more sophisticated neorealist version continues to dominate thinking among policymakers and international relations scholars (Maliniak et al. 2007).[‡] Realism evolved from research conducted in the 1950s on European politics in the aftermath of the Thirty Years War (1618–1648). That war was resolved with the Treaty of Westphalia, which is often credited with establishing the modern sovereign state. Article 64 of the treaty establishes territoriality and the right of the state to choose its own religion (a central matter in the war, which was between Catholic and Protestant European monarchies) as well as the right to noninterference by other states in any of these matters. Under article 65, sovereign rights are further spelled out, especially with regard to foreign policy. This article establishes that no supernational authority (then, the Catholic Church or the Holy Roman Empire) can make or negate alliances made between sovereigns for the purpose of protecting their respective nation's security. In a similar manner, article 67 establishes that sovereign states can determine their own domestic policies, free from external pressures and "with full Jurisdiction within the inclosure of their Walls and their Territorys."[§]

The Treaty of Westphalia emphasized territoriality over personal loyalties as the foundation for international relations. It was primarily in this emphasis on the institutional importance of borders that the treaty broke with the feudal past. Borders became a critical institutional feature that defined where sovereign authority was exercised. Even today, border disputes are a prominent source of conflict in international relations (Huth 1996; Vasquez 1993, 1995; Senese 1995, 1997) because shifts in their location expand or contract sovereign authority. One way that rulers can expand their authority is to usurp the sovereign claims of another ruler by snatching some territory and redefining the location of the state's perimeter. This is exactly what Saddam Hussein attempted to do in 1990 when his army invaded neighboring Kuwait. Likewise, just such a concern with territory and sovereignty is at the heart of the ongoing Israeli-Palestinian conflict; the current struggles between the government of Sri Lanka and the Tamil Tigers, a Sri Lankan insurgency; and the battles between Shiite and Sunni Muslim factions in present-day Iraq. The significance of territoriality and defined borders that were relevant to forging the resolution of the Thirty Years War remain ever so relevant today.

The idea of territoriality has other significant implications. An important one concerns the central role that states play in international affairs. Because each state's territorial borders define a domain within which its rulers have sovereign authority over the use of force (Krasner 1999; Spruyt 1994), international law has come to view all states as legally equivalent entities. This, in turn, is a factor behind the realist concept of the state as a unitary actor. It is why inter*national* relations focus on states and not multinational corporations, ethnic groups, or other ways of dividing up the international pie.

[‡] There are important differences between realism and neorealism; however, for most of our discussions, these distinctions are secondary. Therefore, I use *neorealism* and *realism* interchangeably except when it makes a substantive difference. To avoid ambiguity, unless stated otherwise, I am always referring to neorealist theory, primarily as devised by Kenneth Waltz (1979), when I reference realism or neorealism.

[§] For more information on this and other historical events, see Appendix A in this book.

The Thirty Years War enveloped most of Europe, making it a reasonable candidate to be described as the first world war or, at least, the first comprehensive European war. To understand how realist thinking may lead foreign policy decision makers astray, it is worth reflecting on the extent to which the historical circumstances of the 1600s led to realism's melding of the interests of leaders and the state. Louis XIV (1638–1715), king of France, is believed to have declared: "L'etat cest moi" (I am the state). This statement provides the quintessential example of the blending of state and leader interests. His outlook embodies the idea that there should be no separation of powers, that the state's interests and the leader's interests are one and the same. In such a world, treating states as unitary actors (the king) makes perfectly good sense.

The Louis "absolutist" outlook also meshed well during the 1930s and 1940s with the totalitarianism of Hitler's Nazi regime in Germany and Stalin's regime in the Soviet Union. The rise of these totalitarian regimes led those seeking an alternative to idealism's explanation for international affairs to develop realist theories about power and neorealist theories about national security and international stability. In doing so, they drew an equivalence between seemingly absolutist leaders and "the state," putting their attention on how factors such as the distribution of power across states promoted stability and security (as in the neorealist view) or created competition for advantages in power (as in the earlier realist perspective).

The equivalence that was drawn between absolutist leaders and "the state," however, masked institutional differences both within and across monarchies, juntas, rigged-election autocracies, and various forms of democracy. Central among these differences are the extent to which leaders are accountable to a small inner circle of supporters or to a broad constituency and the extent to which leaders insulate themselves from accountability to their core constituency (the aristocracy, members of the military or civil service, or a broad electorate) by having a larger or smaller pool of substitutes available to replace disloyal backers (Bueno de Mesquita et al. 2003).

Contemporary international politics is characterized by interactions among various types of autocrats, between autocrats and democrats, and between pairs of democrats. The differences in the extent to which leaders are accountable to the national interest as a result of domestic political arrangements mean that international interactions—whether over war and peace, the spread of freedom and human rights, or trade and commerce—vary more today in their consistency with realist thought than they did in the past. This breakdown in consistency is not merely a concern for academics. It profoundly influences the course of current international affairs.

For example, many writers complain that American foreign policy reflects the arrogance of power in which the rich and powerful do whatever they want and the poor and downtrodden are powerless to do anything about it. Implicitly, they attribute policy failure to some allegedly unique American policy flaw (Forsythe 1992; Rueschmeyer, Stephens, and Stephens 1992) and see malevolent intentions behind many foreign policy choices. I believe malevolence and arrogance are incorrect explanations of policy failures and policy decisions in the American context or any other context. Instead, I contend that many disastrous foreign policy outcomes are the product of realism's promotion of misguided thinking about how foreign objectives are formed, implemented, and attained. After all, this idea of American arrogance and malevolence ignores the ability of the voters to throw the rascals out (Chomsky 2003; Mearsheimer and Walt 2007). If American policies have bad consequences in the world, it is more likely that those consequences are serving the interests of a broad swath of American voters rather than just advancing the well-being of a tiny group of rich or powerful individuals. In a realist view, however, there are no voters because the state is unitary. Realism cannot accommodate meaningful differences in important policies from Jimmy Carter to Ronald Reagan to George H. W. Bush to Bill Clinton to George W. Bush to Barack Obama. If we want to fix bad policies, then, we must confront their actual causes and not the rhetoric of arrogance and malevolence that ignores the role of "We the People" as protestors and voters.

Until there is a generation of policymakers whose assessment of foreign policy is outside the realist box, we are likely to continue to experience too many major foreign policy errors. The real world and the realist world overlap too infrequently for realist thinking to be an effective guide to policymaking. In Louis XIV's world, the declaration "L'etat c'est moi" made perfectly good sense; it does not make sense anymore. Let us look at the Iraq War to illustrate how realist thinking reaches beyond the ivory tower to contribute to international—and domestic—turmoil, misery, and policy failure. The idea here is not to blame realist theorists, many of whom did not support the Bush administration's Iraq policy but, rather, to highlight the translation of realist ideas into action by policymakers.

Iraq and the Realist View

The Iraq War is widely regarded as a failure. This is true despite a decisive American military victory in 2003 against Saddam Hussein's regime. Why is it a failure? A major reason is that the key to a lasting peace and to a civil society in Iraq rests on the so far unsuccessful effort to reconstruct that country's social, political, and economic foundations. It does not rest solely on the ability to depose Saddam Hussein.

At least in the years 2003–2007, American leaders who were concerned about advancing Iraq's reconstruction seem to have believed, in solid realist fashion, that American power was, by itself, enough to ensure that Iraq would follow the policy path prescribed by the United States. The United States, after all, as the world's most powerful state, was supposed to be a reliable guarantor of Iraq's stability and security. National stability and security are the primary goals of states according to neorealist thinking.

It must have been very difficult for realist thinkers such as President George W. Bush and his most important foreign policy advisers, including Vice President Richard Cheney, Secretary of State Condoleezza Rice, and Secretary of Defense Donald Rumsfeld, to anticipate that Iraq's leaders would pay more attention to managing their relations with contending

Iraqi factions such as those led by Muqtada al-Sadr (the anti-American cleric) and Grand Ayatollah Ali Sistani (the more moderate religious leader) than to implementing the policies promoted by the United States. Realist theory leaves little room for such a focus on domestic threats to political survival. For realists, the relevant survival threat is to the state's survival and the relevant source of the threat is powerful states, such as the United States. Realism was a useful way (but not the only useful way) for Saddam Hussein to have thought about the United States, but it is not such a useful way for Iraq's current leaders or American leaders to think about one another. As we will see, the strategic perspective offers an explanation both for the interplay between the United States and Iraq under Saddam Hussein and under the post-Hussein government.

It appears that only in spring 2007 did American leaders grasp the nonrealist foreign policy insight that to achieve their goals they would need to reestablish the basic day-to-day security on the streets in Iraq's cities. Domestic threats, not foreign threats, were the key problem in Iraq. In summer and fall 2007, the U.S. government committed about 30,000 additional troops to Iraq in an effort to diminish suicide bombings and other forms of street violence. Military might, a crucial instrument in the realist arsenal, was the tool chosen to advance this objective. The idea was that the military surge would produce enough pacification for the Iraqi government to adopt the policies promoted by the United States, including the distribution of oil revenues to all segments of the population and the promotion of political reconciliation among competing Shiite and Sunni religious factions.

The military surge succeeded in diminishing violence in Iraq. Yet, contrary to expectations within the realist framework, Iraq's political leaders made little progress in implementing the policies and programs promoted by the United States. Those programs surely would be beneficial to most Iraqis, but it is not evident that they would be beneficial to the short-term job security (not to mention personal security) of Iraq's leaders. Their survival depends on keeping the right gun- and bomb-toting militias on their side. Apparently, many Iraqi leaders believe keeping Muqtada al-Sadr content is more important to their welfare than keeping the American president happy. Domestic political considerations trump American pressure in Iraq, realism's unitary actor perspective notwithstanding. Displeasing the United States did not jeopardize Iraq's leadership nearly as much as would the betrayal of key domestic factions whose support has proven essential to the leadership. The realist focus on Iraq's subservience to American hegemony simply proved to be less important than the strategic calculations of Iraq's leaders about which group represents the greatest threat to their hold on power. Here we can see that the debate between different theoretical perspectives truly is not a mere academic, ivory tower debate. It is a debate about avoiding policy failure and promoting better outcomes in the international community.

The strategic perspective, in contrast to realist theories, focuses our attention on leaders, not states, as the object of study. In doing so, it argues that relations among nations are produced by the normal pulls and tugs of domestic affairs, taking into account the domestic and international constraints under which leaders in contending states operate. That the strategic perspective implies important policy changes is evident from the extent to which so many foreign policy developments, from the collapse of the Soviet Union and the end of the cold war to the morass in Iraq, are at least as much the product of domestic politics as of international competition. To fix such problems, we have to think about the motivations and incentives of leaders and of rival politicians and about how we can alter their behavior based on responding to their motivations and incentives rather than worrying so much about the balance of power between states.

SOLVING INTERNATIONAL RELATIONS PUZZLES

What are the fundamental puzzles in international relations, and how might the principles that guide this book help us better understand their solutions? These puzzles involve everything that influences how states and national leaders interact. We are concerned, for example, with the horrors of war and with the costs and benefits of trade. We are interested in how and why nations sometimes manage to cooperate with one another, yet sometimes compete even at the level of deadly conflict. We are curious about the formation of bilateral alliances and multilateral negotiations. We wish to understand international organizations that exist to regulate international commerce, global warming, and international peace, such as the United Nations, the Kyoto Protocols, the World Trade Organization (WTO), and the International Court of Justice.

We are interested in international law, such as the law of the sea, the Universal Declaration of Human Rights, and the international copyright conventions, which regulate the use of natural resources found under the world's oceans, seek to protect individual rights, and seek to protect intellectual property rights, respectively. We are intrigued by uncodified norms and customs of behavior between states that facilitate cooperation and dampen conflict. Some of these norms of conduct occasionally get written down as laws of behavior—agreements on the treatment of prisoners of war, for example—but oftentimes rely instead on mutual understandings rather than signed agreements. For many centuries, people could move freely across national borders without passports. Indeed, before World War I passports were not widely required for international travel. Custom, rather than law, guided decisions on whether to permit or block people from crossing national frontiers. We want to know how resources influence actions, but we also want to know whether resources shape choices more or less than do individual desires and beliefs.

Each of these subjects, and many others, are explored in the chapters that follow. These issues are generally discussed in terms of four broad categories of problems: coordination, distribution, monitoring, and sanctioning. **Coordination** entails finding ways for states or leaders to act together in pursuit of common objectives. **Distribution** concerns the allocation of scarce goods among citizens, leaders, and states. **Monitoring** involves detecting situations in which one or another leader or state has cheated on an agreement. **Sanctioning** concerns punishing cases of cheating. These four generic issues are at the core of cooperation and competition, and they arise in one form or another throughout this book. Much of what is challenging about international affairs revolves around how to cope with various combinations of these four issues.

The traditional issues in international relations can be understood as various combinations of coordination, distribution, monitoring, and sanctioning. For example, why do nations go to war? Some argue that wars are fought to gain territory, to acquire wealth, to impose policies, or to spread values. Each of these is an argument involving distributional issues between rivals. Whether allies can be counted on to help out in time of war is a question of both coordination and monitoring. Sanctions encourage compliance, as do rewards (distribution)—sanctions function as the "stick" and rewards are the "carrot." The production of parts, such as automobile components, electronics, or textiles, in one place and their assembly in another generally involve difficulties in coordinating decisions across multiple governments. How this coordination is achieved is an important problem in international trade relations. Protecting endangered whales or wild salmon as they swim from the territorial waters of one state to the territorial waters of another or even as they swim in the open ocean involves problems of both coordination and distribution. What is more, it can be very difficult to monitor the exploitation of resources (for example, commercial fish or hydroelectric power) that can move from jurisdiction to jurisdiction. Whether one country's fishermen have overfished in international waters can be difficult to detect.

International treaties provide a common means of addressing these problems and represent an important feature of international efforts at cooperation. Trade disputes and even wars are sometimes the product of failed efforts to reach cooperative understandings. A common source of dispute between neighboring states involves disagreements over the benefits derived from river systems that flow across national borders. If the upstream country dams a river, for example, the downstream country (or countries) may be deprived of vital energy, drinking water, food from fish and fowl, recreation areas, and so forth, all of which can precipitate conflict. Indeed, water supply is a major issue influencing relations between Israel and Syria over control of the Golan Heights and was—until it was resolved with the help of the United Nations—one significant source of conflict between India and Pakistan over Kashmir.

Through the remainder of this Introduction, we look at how power, preferences, and perceptions combine with leaders' self-interests to shape international questions of coordination, distribution, monitoring, and sanctioning. In doing so, we clarify how states—that is, the leaders of their governments—relate to one another and establish how we might better predict and influence the course of international relations.

Power, Preferences, and Perceptions: The Three Pillars of International Relations

International relations as a subject is primarily about the choices and actions that political leaders take in the name of their nation to influence how their state relates to other states.

Interstate relations are motivated by leaders' preferences for certain goals over other goals. These preferences are tempered by the power to pursue those goals and by perceptions or beliefs about the costs and benefits associated with seeking out one goal over another. The preferences, power, and perceptions of leaders are not the only factors in play. Ultimately, foreign leaders, like all political leaders, must judge the preferences, power, and perceptions of the people whose support they need or whose opposition they must avoid to retain office. This is true whether the support or opposition comes from domestic or foreign interests.

Usually threats to power and authority arise from among competing elites who desire to hold office. Such competition is at the heart of succession crises in hereditary monarchies, in authoritarian dictatorships, and in political democracies. But threats to a leader's authority can also come from ordinary people. Mass riots and grassroots revolutions sometimes lead to the overthrow of governments. Mass support may also play a role in preserving a particular regime. In August 1991, for instance, hundreds of thousands of Russian citizens intent on deflating a coup in progress gathered in Moscow's Red Square. Those who gathered there believed that they could help shape the course of events. They acted on this *perception* by mobilizing the *power* they had in numbers to display their *preference* for continuing with the reforms of the existing government and not going back to the days of dictatorial rule. Although such events are probably less common than elite infighting, they can be at least as devastating to a leader's prospects of political or even physical survival. Thus, international relations is about how the power, preferences, and perceptions of different people—leaders, their rivals, and ordinary citizens—shape the actions of states toward one another.

Power. Success in influencing relations between states depends on the ability of a particular state to muster the relevant political, economic, and military resources that persuade or coerce another state into actions it would rather not take. Ultimately, power is about mobilizing resources to alter the behavior of others.

Simply put, **power** is an instrument for promoting and achieving goals. As such, it is a mistake to think of the quest for national power as the ultimate goal of foreign policy leaders or of the nation they represent. Rather, power is the servant of ambitious leaders prepared to take risks to advance the objectives they hold dear. Thus, although power provides the wherewithal to take action, the preferences of political leaders, as well as those of their opponents and their backers, are what motivate action.

Preferences. Foreign policy goals and the ways nations interact with one another are reflections of the **preferences,** or desires, of key foreign policy leaders and those **constituents** whose support they require to stay in office. The preferences of constituents are important because if a leader's preferences are sufficiently inconsistent with the wants and desires of his or her core constituents, then the leader runs the risk of being overthrown. Such a risk emanates from two sources. First, opponents capable of jeopardizing a leader's authority may arise from within the state, as is true when there is a revolution, coup, or electoral defeat. In addition, opponents may arise from outside the state, as when Adolf Hitler overthrew the Third French Republic in June 1940 and was overthrown, in turn, by the successful invasion of Germany by Russian, American, and other allied armies in 1945. Being overthrown, of course, means that a leader loses control over the selection of national goals and over the mobilization of the resources needed to enforce national actions. This is an outcome every decision maker wants to avoid because it contradicts his or her own self-interest.

Perceptions. Leaders' **perceptions** about reality also affect foreign policy decision making. Leaders may misjudge the amount of resources or degree of power they can mobilize on behalf of their nation or miscalculate the level of political support that will follow from their pursuit of articulated preferences. They may hold a worldview or ideology that limits how they perceive the actions and intentions of rivals. They may frame problems

> ### TRY THIS
>
> Give several examples of internal challengers who want to replace the president of the United States or the prime minister in China. What foreign threats do these leaders face? How about the leader of Iraq? Israel? India? What foreign threats challenge their ability to lead effectively? Can you name a political leader who was overthrown or politically defeated by domestic opponents of his or her foreign policy? Draw up a list of leaders who were ousted by foreign adversaries.

to emphasize possible gains (as any individual does when buying a lottery ticket), or they may emphasize possible losses (as when citizens insist that a government remove all risks associated with nuclear energy, driving cars, and flying in airplanes). Perceptions may lead policymakers to take greater risks than they had intended or to forgo opportunities they did not realize they had. Rivals know this and so have incentives to mislead their adversaries and, sometimes, even their friends. Thus, national leaders must be ever vigilant, sifting through information to judge best which of the threats, offers of assistance, or other actions by friend and foe alike are mere bluffs and which are credible dangers (or benefits) to the society they lead and, especially, to their own interest.

ORGANIZATIONAL FEATURES OF THIS BOOK

This is a book about ideas. The facts of history and of current events help illustrate and support or refute the contending ideas about foreign policy and international relations. By learning how to marry ideas to facts, we can all become experts at evaluating the foreign policies that shape the international relations of our time. This marriage of ideas and facts is demanding. The paths to improving the world are strewn with obstacles to be overcome. Among the obstacles are the difficulties involved in thinking really carefully, logically, and dispassionately about why things are as they are. Political passion is best reserved for thinking about how to improve matters after you have worked out what are the true impediments to improvement; the world cannot be made better by wishful thinking or by ideas taken on faith alone. This book provides the tools, skills, and ideas to help you to make things better if you are willing to confront the real obstacles to change with an open mind. These tools and skills will help you evaluate the merits of the principles set out in this chapter as well as those that guide alternative perspectives.

After developing the strategic perspective in Chapter 1, I go on in Chapters 2 and 3 to introduce the major analytic building blocks applied throughout this book. Chapter 2 provides a primer on the logic and uses of social choice theory, while Chapter 3 introduces the essentials of game theory. Chapters 2 and 3 maintain a running example based on the issues surrounding Iran's potential quest to develop nuclear weapons. The running example is intended to help clarify how to use social choice and game theory reasoning in addressing the pressing international problems of this or any time.

Chapter 4 examines the causes of war according to those who treat the state as a rational (self-interested) unitary actor. It investigates hypotheses about war from two prominent theories—neorealism and the power transition theory—looking closely at the logical implications of the assumptions made in these theories. The chapter then investigates how well these theories' predictions fit the record of history. Chapter 5 examines the logical consistency and empirical reliability of predictions about war derived from the strategic perspective. Here I also identify situations in which unitary actor analyses and the strategic approach lead to the same expectations about war and situations in which they differ. We will see that when they differ the strategic outlook tends to be right more often than the unitary actor approach. Chapter 6 turns our attention to the democratic peace, that is, the idea that democracies rarely if ever fight wars with one another. In that chapter, we strive to understand why democracies behave well toward one another and yet show no reluctance to engage in wars of colonial or imperial expansion and domination. Chapter 7 examines issues regarding the causes of terrorism and the difficulties, opportunities, and consequences of efforts to resolve terrorist threats.

Chapters 8 and 9 are important transitional chapters. They look at the crossroads between international conflict and international cooperation by discussing two central instruments behind the rhetoric of nation building. Chapter 8 investigates the impact that different types of military interveners (such as the United Nations, the United States, and other democracies) have on the prospects of spreading democracy. Chapter 9 examines the impact that foreign aid has on democratization and on alleviating poverty or suffering. I believe you will be surprised—and depressed—by some of the conclusions; Chapter 9 might be an especially good place for you to think about how the problems discussed there might be overcome to improve what happens in the international arena. Chapter 10 provides an economics primer and then explores trade policy and other aspects of foreign affairs that are associated with globalization. Once again, you may be surprised by the conclusions—although this time there may be cause for optimism instead of depression. Chapter 11 turns to an investigation of international organizations, alliances, and international law. Two important appendices follow. The first contains a summary of world history from 1453 to the present; the second offers a discussion of the scientific method and its application to improving our understanding of international relations. I recommend reading these two appendices before plunging into the book. Although they are not essential for following the main discussion, they do provide a shared understanding of the essential features of history and of the development of knowledge.

SUMMARY

International relations is concerned with any aspect of politics that influences how nations relate to one another. Because it shapes the choices of foreign policy leaders, domestic politics strongly influences relations between states. Policymakers must strike a balance between the needs of vital domestic interests and the external pressures imposed by foreign interests. How leaders determine the appropriate trade-off between domestic and foreign concerns depends on the risks they are willing to take and on their perceptions of how choices influence their own self-interest.

In this book, I stress that to speak of a nation's policies or a nation's interests in any other than metaphoric terms is problematic. To avoid this, I focus on the decision-making elements that shape foreign policy choices and their link to the international system. In doing so, I highlight the importance of calculating the costs and benefits of alternative courses of action and estimating the likelihood that one or another approach to a problem will succeed or fail. This approach differs markedly from other approaches to studying international affairs.

The problems of international politics fall into four broad categories—distribution, coordination, monitoring, and sanctioning—and various combinations thereof (Morrow 1994b). The application of power in pursuit of preferred outcomes, colored by perceptions about how others will react to alternative courses of action, serves to both generate and resolve these problems. Because actions are tempered by expectations about the reactions they will elicit, foreign policy decision making is inherently strategic. As we proceed in our study of international relations, we will develop the skills to effectively evaluate policy choices within an environment where no one is always able to get whatever he or she wants. As the Rolling Stones aptly taught us, "You can't always get what you want—but if you try sometimes, you just might find, you get what you need."

SUGGESTED READINGS

Most chapters provide citations to relevant literature in the text. In this chapter, I have avoided citations that might break the flow of the introductory material, so I offer a few suggested readings now. Readers who want to delve more deeply into any subject touched on in the chapters that follow would do well to start with the cited works that are listed in the Bibliography at the end of the book.

- On linkages between domestic politics and international relations: James Rosenau (1963, 1969); Robert Putnam (1988); Alex Mintz (1993); James Fearon (1994); Kenneth Schultz (1998); and Bruce Bueno de Mesquita, Alastair Smith, Randolph M. Siverson, and James D. Morrow (2003).
- Early works on strategic interaction in international affairs: Thomas Schelling (1960); Graham Allison (1972); Steven Brams (1985); and Robert Powell (1990).
- On foreign policy and leadership survival: Bruce Bueno de Mesquita and Randolph M. Siverson (1995); Suzanne Werner (1996); Hein Goemans (2000); and Bruce Bueno de Mesquita, Alastair Smith, Randolph M. Siverson, and James D. Morrow (2003).

KEY CONCEPTS

constituents 18	neorealism 7
constructivism 9	perceptions 19
coordination 16	power 18
distribution 16	preferences 18
domestic politics 3	sanctioning 16
hierarchy 8	self-interests 2
liberalism 8	state 2
monitoring 16	strategic perspective 3
national interest 3	unitary actors 3

The Strategic Perspective

When Foreign Policy Collides with Domestic Politics

- The strategic perspective alerts us that foreign policy is part of normal domestic politics and that national leaders face a difficult problem in balancing the interests of constituents and the desires of foreign rivals. Satisfying domestic interests may put stress on foreign relations and satisfying foreign interests may provoke domestic challenges to the political leadership. This duality of pressures is the fundamental difference between international relations and all other politics.

- Rather than speaking of governments in categorical terms such as democracy, monarchy, and autocracy, we use two crucial domestic factors to differentiate them: the size of the selectorate (those with a say in choosing leaders) and the size of the winning coalition (those in the selectorate whose support is essential to keep a leader in office).

- Considered together, these two factors allow us to locate all governments in a two-dimensional institutional space and to understand and predict how the leaders of those governments will act and react.

- Polities that rely on a large winning coalition emphasize producing public goods over private rewards for coalition members. They produce greater prosperity, more efficient governance, and low raters of corruption; their leaders stay in office for a relatively short time.

- Polities that rely on a small winning coalition and a large selectorate, such as autocracies with rigged elections, tend to produce high degrees of kleptocracy, poor public policies, and high levels of corruption and rent-seeking; their leaders last in office for a very long time.

- States with large-winning-coalition systems are more likely to enjoy not only prosperity but also peace, especially with one another, while states with small-winning-coalition systems tend not only to be poor but also to experience lots of wars with other states, as well as undergoing revolutions, civil wars, and coups d'etat.

- States with large-winning-coalition systems differ from states with small-winning-coalition regimes in their use of foreign aid, military intervention, warfare, and a host of other critical choices in international affairs.

OVERVIEW

Why do some political systems seem to give leaders an incentive to rob and pillage their own citizens, whereas other domestic political arrangements encourage leaders to be attentive to the quality of their economic and military policies? What kinds of political arrangements make leaders indifferent to whether they produce peace and prosperity or war and famine? In this chapter, I develop a strategic theory that shows how two domestic political institutions shape the motivations of leaders and the actions they take on behalf of their nation. We take as a starting point the fact that policymakers must surely weigh the personal and national costs and benefits that flow both from domestic and foreign pressures in choosing their international actions. Without balancing the two sources of pressure, they are unlikely to remain in power. How they do this balancing is the topic of this chapter.

While exploring the strategic perspective, we will also begin to see why prominent structural theories are insufficient to understand international relations. We will see both the important limitations and strengths of constructivist theories, especially when coupled with a strategic approach. The remainder of this book is dedicated to probing the contention that a strategic perspective offers a better accounting of the key features of international affairs than its alternatives.

Robert Mugabe has ruled Zimbabwe since 1980. Although facing increasing domestic and international criticism, he continues to rule through close affiliations with his ruling party, the ZANU Alliance, and the military. Here, Mugabe (right) talks to Central Intelligence Organisation (CIO) Director General Happyton Bonyongwe (left) and Army Commander General Constantine Chiwenga (center) on his arrival at Harare International Airport, July 4, 2008.

INTERNATIONAL POLITICS: DOMESTIC POLITICS WITH A TWIST

International relations are the product of the cumulative impact of the foreign policies of the nations of the world. As a subject, they are viewed typically as radically different from any other aspect of politics. Yet it is the contention of many who study foreign policy, myself included, that domestic and international politics are inseparable and have much in common. There is, however, at least one critical difference between the two. In the arena of purely domestic affairs, political leaders need not worry that their actions will prompt a foreign country to jeopardize their hold on power.* Domestic politics involves the selection by leaders of policies (including

---

* Indeed, even this claim may exaggerate the difference between domestic politics and international relations. There are probably few, if any, purely domestic issues. Even the seemingly most mundane domestic political question may have international ramifications. Corporate tax breaks in Arizona, for example, may be sufficient to persuade companies to locate factories there instead of in Mexico or South Africa or Sri Lanka.

foreign policies) and actions designed to keep them in office. In international affairs, leaders must worry that their foreign policies not only may mobilize domestic opposition capable of overthrowing them but also may irritate a foreign rival, sparking attack and possible defeat. That distinction is central to the principles of international politics.

A foreign policy that is popular at home may prove to be disastrous abroad. Conversely, a foreign policy designed to deter a foreign adversary or intended to satisfy the demands of a foreign foe may irritate domestic opponents or lose the support of domestic backers. This difficulty can arise whether the government in question is autocratic or democratic, although who and how powerful the domestic **constituents,** that is, the people whose interests a leader is expected to serve, are will surely vary depending on the nature of the regime. I offer two examples, one

> ## TRY THIS
>
> Give examples of political leaders who were overthrown by their own citizens during a war or right after a military defeat. Then identify some leaders who were removed from office by a foreign power after experiencing a military defeat at the hands of that power. Finally, give examples of leaders who were not deposed either by their own citizens or by their foreign rivals, even following military defeat.

from autocratic Afghanistan and the other from democratic Israel, to illustrate how the tension between domestic and foreign pressures may be resolved differently depending on internal political arrangements.

The Afghan Taliban's Problem in 2001

The former leaders of the Taliban government in Afghanistan saw the tension between domestic pressures and foreign opposition in action following the terrorist attacks against the United States on September 11, 2001. Afghanistan's Taliban leaders drew important support from Osama bin Laden and others in Al Qaeda's terrorist network, and Al Qaeda had turned Afghanistan into their home base. For the Taliban to break with them would surely have aroused an active effort by Al Qaeda and its allies to depose the Afghan rulers and replace them with others more likely to cooperate. Yet the United States and its key allies were visibly banding together after September 11, 2001, threatening to overthrow the Taliban government unless it broke with Osama bin Laden.

The Taliban chose to gamble that the American threat was less dangerous than the risks associated with breaking with Al Qaeda. Apparently, Afghanistan's leaders did not believe that the United States and its allies would take decisive action to overthrow them if they failed to turn over Osama bin Laden and other terrorist figures. More precisely, the Taliban apparently believed the consequences for them of betraying bin Laden were worse than the consequences of shunning U.S. pressures. They were wrong if they believed the United States would not act, but they may have been right in fearing Al Qaeda more than the United States and its allies. After all, as of this writing in 2009, the most senior Afghan Taliban leaders are still alive and waging a campaign against the U.S.-backed government in Kabul. Perhaps if they had betrayed Al Qaeda, they would not only be out of power today but might also have been killed by Al Qaeda loyalists. We will never know.

Of course, sometimes the belief that a rival will not take decisive action proves correct. The United States did not take such steps after the bombing by terrorists of the World Trade Center in February 1993 or following the Iraqi-sponsored attempt on George H. W. Bush's life during his trip to Kuwait in April 1993. The U.S. government took only modest steps following the destruction of American embassies in Kenya and Tanzania in 1998 and after the attack on the U.S. Navy ship, the USS *Cole,* in Aden, Yemen, in October 2000. Whether Al Qaeda is swifter and surer in imposing punishment on those it sees as traitors is difficult to know. We get to observe such information only selectively. What is clear is that the Afghanistan-based Al Qaeda leadership commanded greater responsiveness from the Taliban government than did their foreign, American rival.

The Israeli Prime Minister's Problem

Consider, now, the problems Israeli prime ministers face when contemplating building new Israeli settlements on land claimed by the Palestinians. If the prime minister draws significant electoral support from religious groups, as most do, he or she knows that he or she must advance that constituency's interest in building settlements to stay in office. This electoral support is especially important for prime ministers from Israel's Likud Party or from Kadima, two significant conservative political parties that rely on backing from religious groups. But, by permitting the construction of settlements in certain areas, the prime minister raises the risk of war with the Palestinians and their allies in the region. Although Israel has been successful in many of its military campaigns to date, one can never be certain of a war's outcome, as the Israelis learned painfully following their unsuccessful war with Hezbollah in the summer 2006.

Israel is a small country that has lost thousands of its young men and women to war and hundreds to terrorism. Palestine is a nascent, even smaller country that has lost even larger numbers in recent years in its struggle against Israel. This is a high price indeed for each side. Such a price will cause a democratically elected prime minister to think twice before pursuing policies that risk such losses in the future. Israeli leaders are, in a sense, backed into a difficult corner whatever they do. If they tear down settlements, they may diminish conflict with the Palestinians but at the price of losing the domestic support they need to carry out such a settlement policy. If they fail to tear down settlements, they risk cross-border violence with Palestinian groups such as Hamas and Islamic Jihad, but they retain the domestic political support that they must have to stay in power.

Certainly the balancing act that foreign policy leaders such as Israel's prime minister and Afghanistan's rulers must perform—trying to achieve their goals while holding on to power—is more difficult than the comparable act of their purely domestic politics counterparts (a city mayor, for example).

Who and What to Study in International Affairs

In the strategic perspective, to borrow a phrase, all politics is domestic. The two examples underscore the real risks that leaders face as they navigate the domestic pressures of foreign policy decisions and illustrate that no leader is fully insulated against the repercussions of his or her decisions. The examples also demonstrate that understanding exactly who the domestic constituents are—and what they have at stake—is crucial. Let's set the stage for that discussion.

Politics is the domain of competition among groups and individuals for special advantages, particularly over control of power and wealth. Such political competition involves the risk of punishment as well as the opportunity for rewards for one's actions. In international politics, leaders continually risk being punished by foreign adversaries and domestic foes. And in international affairs, there are few institutions comparable to domestic police forces and courts that effectively regulate how nations relate to one another. Unlike domestic affairs, international relations involves only a few commonly accepted means of regulating behavior and even fewer and weaker means to enforce accepted rules and norms of action and punish violations of them. These few means of enforcement are reflected in international law and in international organizations. Research shows that they tend to be especially ineffective when the stakes are high and national leaders are disinclined to abide by common norms of action. This is one important reason why most studies of international relations draw attention to the state as the fundamental actor on the international stage. In this examination of international politics, however, although we pay attention to states, we also are attentive to domestic interest groups, individuals, and, when appropriate, nonstate actors such as multinational corporations and environmental groups. All these participants in international politics are capable of shaping the policies followed by states and of altering the course of international affairs. That is why an alternative is needed to the unitary actor, state-centered approach favored by most students and practitioners of international politics.

All political leaders must figure out how to answer a straightforward question: What are they to do if they want to keep their jobs and their heads? This is no idle question. The answer to it goes to the very heart of politics. If you were king, president, or dictator, what might you try to accomplish? How would you allocate scarce resources to best perform your job and to prevent yourself from being removed from office? What would your friends try to do? Are the answers different depending on whether your friends aspire to be king, president, or dictator?

One seemingly obvious answer to this question is that all leaders need to seek peace and prosperity for their country. Peace and prosperity, after all, enhance the national well-being. Don't they also promote the popularity and longevity of the leadership? As it turns out, peace and prosperity are good for all leaders, but they are not necessary or even equally important for all leaders. Kings and dictators have no need for peace and prosperity to retain power. To be sure, neither peace nor prosperity harms them; they just are not essential. Presidents, at least in democracies, can hold on to office a lot longer if they preside over peace and prosperity than if they do not, but they rarely hold on to power as long as kings and dictators, even when the latter create war, poverty, and misery for most of their subjects.

If peace and prosperity were equally the recipe for political success in all states, then the structuralist, unitary actor perspective, which contends that states seek to maximize wealth (liberalism) or security (neorealism); the constructivist point of view, which maintains that leaders converge on common norms of conduct in response to external and internal pressures; and the strategic perspective, which says that leaders promote their own welfare through internal and external maneuvering, would all be compatible. Yet such a viewpoint is not correct.

Leaders do not benefit equally from peace and prosperity. In fact, leaders in democracies find it essential to pursue national peace and prosperity, whereas autocrats do not. Democratic leaders who fail to provide peace and prosperity for their constituents are ousted from office with alacrity, whereas autocrats, despite gross failures to provide for the welfare of ordinary citizens, stay in office for a long time. Even in the absence of term limits, few democratic leaders last as long as autocrats. Over the past 200 years, democratic leaders have remained in office for an average of about 3.7 years; in contrast, autocrats have remained in office an average of 8.6 years. Figure 1.1 shows the risk of losing office over time depending on whether a leader heads a democracy or an autocracy. The vertical axis plots what are called hazard rates. For our purposes, we need focus only on relative magnitudes; higher numbers mean a higher risk of being thrown out of office, while lower numbers mean the leader is more secure. As we can see, democrats and autocrats start out almost alike in their risk of being deposed. In fact, the risk is higher for newly installed dictators than for newly elected democrats. But by the end of the first year in office, the risk of losing power is vastly different. Democrats have settled in at an ongoing high risk and autocrats have settled in at a low and decreasing danger that over time they will be overthrown.

Autocratic leaders suffer relatively few punishments for creating famine, sickness, and misery at home or military defeat abroad. They seem relatively unconcerned with whether or not peace and prosperity are achieved. That is why, as we see in the coming chapters, different types of government adopt different approaches to trade, foreign investment, economic assistance, human rights, sanctions, military intervention, peacekeeping, and even warfare. To understand these differences, we need a perspective that recognizes that the institutional framework within which leaders operate is important in shaping what they do and whether they remain in office or get overthrown. The strategic perspective gives us such a way of thinking about international affairs.

How to Study International Affairs

Strategic models and the empirical assessments that follow from them allow us to evaluate policy choices as parts of behavior induced by domestic institutions. Our models assume that foreign policies are chosen for their compatibility with the motives of national leaders

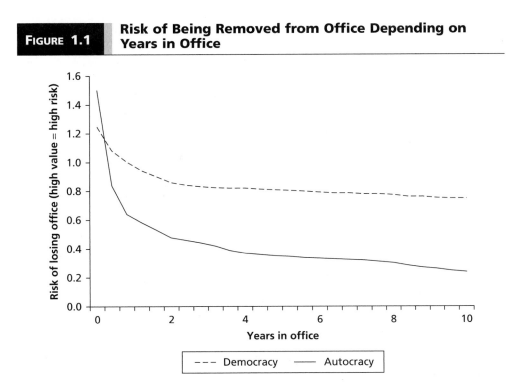

FIGURE 1.1   **Risk of Being Removed from Office Depending on Years in Office**

who want, first and foremost, to stay in power. These leaders' motivations may not be—and often are not—compatible with their nation's interest if we construe the national interest as what a majority of citizens think is best for their nation. Domestic institutional structures (such as the competitiveness of leadership selection or the extent of government account-ability and transparency) help shape the interplay of leaders, elites, and ordinary citizens, resulting in policies that create the contours of the international environment, contours that in structuralist realist approaches are taken as given rather than as factors to be explained.

By drawing attention to leaders, we uncover new ways to think about international affairs and we discover empirical regularities that cannot be true if the conventional wisdom of realist approaches is right. For instance, we know that leaders make decisions about when to go to war depending on where they are in the election cycle, what the electoral rules are under which they operate, and other aspects of domestic political circumstances (Gaubatz 1991; Fordham 1998, 2002; Smith 2004). Autocrats are not subjected to these constraints; their war-timing decisions seem more dependent on things such as the weather and terrain than on domestic political arrangements.

War timing is not the only feature of war that differs across regime types. James Fearon (1994), Alastair Smith (1998), and others suggest that democratic leaders are more likely than autocrats to carry out the foreign policy threats they make because of their domestic political-audience costs; that is, democrats suffer from a decline in their chances of being reelected if they fail to act on their most important, threatening international pronouncements. Saying "there will be dire consequences" is apparently less consequential when the threatener is an autocrat instead of a democrat.

Kenneth Schultz (1998, 2001) shows another feature that follows from having a domestic audience, especially in a democracy, where there is at least one opposition party eager to oust the incumbents and take their place. He demonstrates that the existence of a domestic political opposition limits democratic foreign policy adventurism in ways not experienced by nondemocrats. That is, democrats are less likely to adopt risky foreign policies than are autocrats whose countries are otherwise comparable in terms of their military or economic power to shake up the world. As we will see, democrats are much more likely to win the wars they start than are autocrats, not just because they are better at fighting wars (they may or may not be) but because, as reasoning such as Schultz's highlights, they cannot afford to lose if they hope to get reelected.

Schultz's reasoning offers a compelling explanation for the appearance, and disappearance, of a bipartisan American foreign policy. The argument, briefly, goes as follows. Typically, American foreign policy is thought of as nonpartisan and as driven by efforts to advance the national interest. Rarely, however, is there much effort to explain why partisanship should not be as important in foreign policy decisions as it is in the routine domestic choices of political leaders. In defense of a nonpartisan foreign policy, we must acknowledge that we infrequently observe deep divisions between the major American political parties when it comes to the "big" question in foreign policy—the question of war or peace. From this observation, casual observers leap to the inference that, at least on the big questions, foreign policy is, indeed, bipartisan or nonpartisan.

But there is an alternative explanation for the observed cooperation of the major political parties during times of war or international crisis that is, I believe, far more compelling. The American political system, being democratic, constrains leaders to rely on large voter coalitions for support. This means that elected officials are held accountable by their constituents for the policies they deliver. If they hope to be reelected—and they, or their political party, almost always do—then they must pursue policies that satisfy their voters. But their political opponents also hope to be elected. They want to depose the local representative or senator or president and win that job for themselves. To do so, they need to persuade enough voters to switch from the incumbent to them in the next election. Similarly, those already in office but not in the majority must be concerned to back policies that their voters like enough to reelect them. The president and his foreign policy advisors understand this very well. The members in the majority party in the House of Representatives and the Senate likewise understand this very well.

If the incumbent party and its leaders select a foreign policy that is unpopular or that is believed will be unsuccessful, then they can anticipate that the other party's leaders and candidates will see an opportunity to win votes by opposing the majority party's foreign policy. When a foreign policy idea is discussed, the early trial balloons that measure public opinion provide a useful means for the incumbent party to discover whether there is likely to be significant opposition. Such opposition is a signal that the opposition party (or opposition parties in many proportional representation parliamentary systems) believes it can gain an electoral advantage by speaking out against the policy being contemplated. This early opposition does not occur if the party that is out of power believes the president's approach to a foreign problem is likely to be popular and successful. Thus, the president tries to choose foreign policies, especially when it comes to highly visible policies such as war and peace, that are likely to succeed and that, therefore, are likely not to prompt a well-organized opposition by the minority party.

If the president miscalculates or the policy unexpectedly backfires, there is opposition from the rival party. Bipartisan support falls away. This is exactly what happened with the U.S. policy toward Iraq between 2003 (when the policy commanded the overwhelming support of Republican and Democratic members of Congress) and the run-up to the 2008 election. The bipartisan policy became distinctly partisan as the results in Iraq failed to match expectations. Most of the time, however, war policies prove fairly successful or war is avoided in anticipation that it will prove costlier politically than is justified by the expected benefits. The result of such selectivity in choosing policies is that we observe little partisanship on questions of war and peace, not because of nonpartisanship but because these policies are chosen to avoid opening the way to electoral success by the party not in power (Fearon 1994; Smith 1996; Schultz 2001).

None of the insights discussed so far can be true from a realist perspective because from that point of view differences in the domestic features of states are irrelevant to fundamental actions in the international arena. But it is just such observations as these that make it necessary to look within states to understand international affairs.

Next, I introduce the **selectorate theory** of politics, an example of the strategic perspective. It shows how variations in the size of a polity's political institutions help explain many facets of international interactions, ranging from warfare capabilities to the uses of foreign aid and military intervention to encourage or stymie democratization to the so-called democratic peace. The selectorate theory also suggests why it is that democracies are willing to fight wars of imperial and colonial expansion and are even more prepared than autocrats to overthrow foreign rivals. We look at other examples of the strategic perspective later in this chapter.

SELECTORATE THEORY: AN EXAMPLE OF THE STRATEGIC PERSPECTIVE

The selectorate theory represents one version of the strategic perspective. In selectorate theory, leaders build a coalition of supporters among the selectorate. The **selectorate** consists of those who have at least a nominal say in choosing leaders and are eligible to become members of a winning coalition. The **winning coalition** is the subset of the selectorate without whose support an incumbent cannot be sustained in office. Leaders attempt to retain the loyalty of their supporters by giving them more benefits than any domestic political opponent can credibly promise to deliver. Rewards come in two varieties: private goods and public goods. **Private goods** are rewards that benefit only those who get them, that is, members of the leader's essential coalition of supporters. Examples might include privileged access to government contracts, exploitation of a black market, or protection against prosecution. **Public goods** are government policies and programs that all people benefit from whether they are in the leader's inner circle or not. Examples of public goods include national defense, free speech and free assembly, public parks, equal protection under the law, and free access to education.

Leaders pay for private and public benefits by taxing people's labor, exploiting natural resource wealth (for example, oil or diamonds), and by receiving foreign economic assistance. Any revenues that do not have to be spent on maintaining the loyalty of the incumbent's essential backers represents money that can be spent, saved, or invested at the leadership's discretion. The more discretionary resources a leader has, the better his or her chances of surviving in office. We will see why as we proceed.

When domestic institutions constrain a leader to require a broad base of support, as is true in most democracies, private rewards are an inefficient way to retain power (de Tocqueville 2000; Lake and Baum 2001; Bueno de Mesquita et al. 2003). Democratic leaders would have to spread these rewards across so many people that each would receive too little for the benefits to influence their loyalty to the incumbent. In such a situation, it is more efficient for leaders to rely on public goods as their best means to retain office. When political institutions compel a leader to depend on many supporters, so that a bundle of public goods is the reward for retaining the incumbent, the institutions of governance induce weak loyalty to the incumbent. After all, everyone benefits from public goods whether he or she supports the incumbent or not. Conversely, when a leader needs backing only from a few people to stay in power, the few are expected to be loyal both because they are well rewarded with private benefits and because they face a high risk of losing those privileges if a challenger topples the incumbent regime. Thus it is that resource allocations—including provisions for national defense—are induced in significant part by domestic political institutions rather than just by international compulsions, culture, or the luck of the draw in leaders.

All political systems have two institutional characteristics that describe how they retain and select their leaders. The selectorate (S), as mentioned earlier, is the set of people in the polity who can take part in choosing a leader. The winning coalition (W) is the subset of the selectorate whose support the leader must retain to remain in office (see Figure 1.2). Selectorates and winning coalitions may range in size from small to large, subject to the limitation that the winning coalition cannot be larger than the selectorate. For analytical convenience, I treat all selectors as having equal weight, allowing us to characterize the sizes of both the winning coalition and selectorate as numbers or fractions of the population of the state in question. The winning coalition is the set of those selectors whose support the current leader must maintain. If the size of this coalition falls below W, then the leader is vulnerable to being removed and replaced by a challenger who can create a coalition of his or her own of at least size W from the selectorate.

FIGURE 1.2   The Selectorate and the Winning Coalition

The sorts of governments that people generally describe as democracies share in common that they have large selectorates and large winning coalitions, although the exact size of each varies with the extent of suffrage and the precise rules by which leaders are elected. One-party autocracies have smaller winning coalitions than democracies, although their selectorates may be large. Monarchies and military dictatorships have both small selectorates and small winning coalitions. (See Figure 1.3.)

Let's look at a few real-world examples. In Figure 1.4, we can see the estimated sizes of the winning coalition and selectorate for ten countries in 2006, based on country expert surveys done by my colleagues and me as part of a pilot project that we conducted of these ten countries for the years 1955–2006. The figure illustrates some of the considerable variation in the size of these two institutions across countries and across ordinary classifications of regimes as autocratic (e.g., Syria and North Korea) or democratic (e.g., Russia and Venezuela). For example, China and Egypt both have winning coalitions with a size that is close to 0 percent of the adult population, yet Egypt has a larger selectorate than China relative to their adult populations. This means that both regimes are heavily oriented toward private goods but that leaders have more discretion and better prospects for remaining in power in Egypt than in China. In fact, those expectations are consistent with the facts. China enforces age-based retirement on even its most senior leaders, thereby limiting their terms; Egypt does not. Both are highly corrupt societies, but China ranks 72nd (out of 180) on Transparency International's 2008 Corruption Index[†] and Egypt ranks 115th (lower values mean better behavior). Syria and Nigeria differ markedly from one another according to Figure 1.4. Nigeria has a smaller selectorate than Syria (controlling for the difference in the size of their populations) but depends on a much larger winning coalition. This means, according to

TRY THIS

Choose some more pairs of countries from Figure 1.4. Work out the loyalty norm for each (that is, W/S), and then find out online how corrupt the country was said to be by Transparency International around 2006. Also see how long, on average, leaders have lasted in these countries (remembering that I have shown you only one year of data on coalition size and selectorate size), and see whether it is related to W/S.

[†] Transparency International, www.transparency.org/policy_research/surveys_indices/cpi.

FIGURE 1.3 **Coalition Size (*W*) in Relation to Selectorate Size (*S*) and Standard Polity Types**

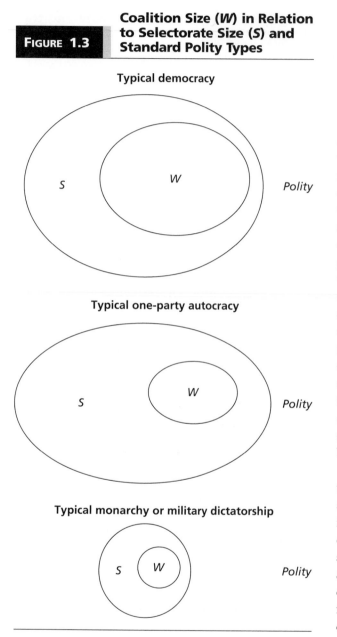

Typical democracy

Typical one-party autocracy

Typical monarchy or military dictatorship

selectorate theory, that the loyalty norm is stronger in Syria than in Nigeria (*W/S* is smaller in Syria). That makes corruption more likely and leadership survival more robust. Again, that's true. Although Nigeria is a very corrupt society, ranking 121st out of 180 in 2008, Syria is worse; it ranks 147th.

If we were to plot any one of these countries across the years from 1955 through 2006, we would also see that even when its regime type remained the same in name year after year, the size of the selectorate and the coalition varied greatly. One of the benefits of selectorate theory is that it allows us to avoid using loose labels like *democracy* or *autocracy* and to instead locate each and every government at a specific spot in the figure. When we are able to resist treating all democracies as if they had one and the same form of government even though their electoral rules make them look quite different from one another or understand more clearly the various forms of autocracy, junta, or monarchy, we are less likely to make misleading assumptions about the behavior of those states. In fact, we can make precise predictions about foreign and domestic policy choices by knowing the size of *W* and *S*, two variables that in principle can be measured with a high degree of accuracy.

Figure 1.4 highlights another important distinction. The selectorate theory makes predictions about actions based on the size of *W* and *S*, each itself determined by specific electoral rules and procedures (including there being no such rules). The size of the winning coalition, *W*, and the selectorate, *S*, are basic features of every society and, indeed, every organization. They do not vary without fundamental institutional changes. For example, changes in how much popular support a leader gets, say in an electoral context, has no bearing on the size of the winning coalition. To illustrate this point, take a look at Russia's location in Figure 1.4. Its winning coalition is estimated to be about 25 percent of the electorate. Yet Russia's president, Dimitri Medvedev, won 70 percent of the vote in Russia's 2008 presidential election,

| FIGURE 1.4 | **Distribution of Winning Coalition Size _W_ and Selectorate Size _S_ for Ten States in 2006: Pilot Study Illustration** |

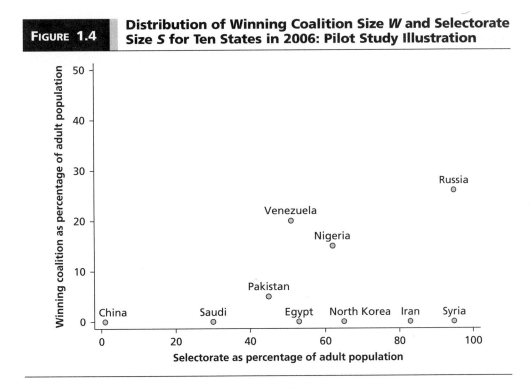

and United Russia, his supporting party, won a comparable share of seats in the Duma (the Russian parliament). Still, assuming an update of expert surveys would see Russian institutions as being much as they were in 2006, W is estimated to be 25 percent of S. That is because Medvedev needed only half the members of parliament to support him and, in a two-party race, each candidate needed only half the voters to support him to be elected, making the maximum minimal winning coalition in Russia 25 percent [0.5 (voters per seat) × 0.5 (number of seats)]. With more than two parties (and there were more than two parties contesting the 2008 election, although for many the opportunity to campaign was suppressed), the actual minimal winning coalition required for power was smaller. Leaders may get more support than they need, but they only need to reward those in their coalition, not everyone who votes for them. Furthermore, from the perspective of other world leaders who need to interact with Medvedev (as a stand-in really for Vladimir Putin) and formulate foreign policy with regard to Russia, understanding this basic dynamic is a powerful tool.

To illustrate the point further, consider two additional political systems. Whether an American president wins in a landslide (as Reagan did in 1984 and Clinton did in 1996) or squeaks by (as Bush did in 2000 and as John Kennedy did in 1960), the size of S in any election year is fixed by American enfranchisement rules and the size of W is fixed by the constitutional

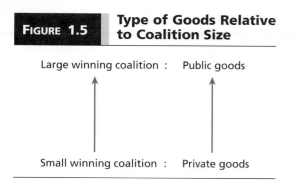

| FIGURE 1.5 | **Type of Goods Relative to Coalition Size** |

Large winning coalition : Public goods

Small winning coalition : Private goods

As the size of the winning coalition increases, the mix of goods distributed to the coalition shifts from private to public.

requirements for election to the presidency and state rules on how to aggregate votes. Similarly, whether or not the entire North Korean population comes out to cheer for Kim Jong-il, his winning coalition (those getting private rewards), according to the experts surveyed, is between 9 and 250 people out of a selectorate that has been several million strong (or, more appropriately, weak).

Public and Private Goods: Who Gets Rewarded as *W* and *S* Change?

All political systems, as noted, produce both public goods and private benefits; it is the mix of the two that varies with selection institutions. As the size of the winning coalition increases, leaders shift that mix away from the provision of private benefits and toward the provision of public goods (see Figure 1.5). This is not because those who depend on a large coalition are necessarily more civic-minded. Rather, a larger winning coalition means more supporters to please, spreading out private benefits and making public goods a more efficient way for the leader to retain the support of his winning coalition. That is why leaders who answer to a large winning coalition will predominantly produce public goods to hold their loyalty.

The Value of Being Needed when *W/S* Is Small

Let's look at a numerical example to clarify the choice between favoring public or private rewards as a function of coalition size. Assume a leader has $1 billion in revenue and governs a polity with a selectorate made up of 100,000 people, of which 1,000 make up the winning coalition. In this case, there is only a 1 percent chance that any member of the current winning coalition will also be a member of a successor winning coalition, given that the odds of being in a successor coalition are the ratio *W/S,* which in this case is 1,000/100,000, or 1/100. If all the revenue is spent on private rewards to the 1,000 members of the winning coalition, then each can expect to receive $1 million ($1 billion/1,000 coalition members). If a member of the incumbent's coalition defects, then he or she has a 1 percent chance of receiving $1 million from the new regime and a 99 percent chance of receiving no private goods whatsoever from that regime. The expected value of the prospective defector's share of the private goods to be dispensed by the successor regime is only $10,000 (that is, $1 million × 0.01, where 0.01 is the probability of getting private benefits, which is equal to *W/S*). It is easy to see that as long as the incumbent beats that expectation and provides **public policies** that are not much worse than those proposed by the challenger, the would-be defector can be kept happy and loyal. The incumbent can keep the difference between the $1 million per supporter that could be distributed and the something above $10,000 per supporter that needs to be distributed. If the incumbent's challenger offers especially attractive public policies, then the incumbent can give up some of the "slush fund" to his or her supporters to purchase their continued loyalty. No wonder so many dictators have fat Swiss bank accounts!

Leaders have a natural preference for providing private goods as a means of retaining power. This follows directly from the expected value of the calculation we have just discussed. The risk to supporters of exclusion from private goods if they defect makes it possible for incumbents always to beat their challengers if the competition is over private goods alone. Challengers recognize their inherent disadvantage in promising private goods and therefore turn to policy to compensate. Thus, incumbents like to reward supporters with private goods, all else being equal, and challengers like to promise improvements in public policy, all else being equal. Of course, all else is rarely equal, and that is at the heart of the matter.

The Value of Being Needed when *W/S* Is Large

One important way that all else may not be equal concerns the size of the winning coalition and the size of the selectorate. The sizes of these two institutions vary dramatically from state to state and also from one political system to another. The incumbent's advantage in allocating private goods diminishes rapidly as the size of the winning coalition increases or as

the size of the selectorate decreases. Let's take our example a little further. Suppose that the selectorate consists of 1 million people rather than 100,000 people and that the winning coalition requires a simple majority of 500,001 members. These conditions are more like what we would find in a democracy. The average member of the winning coalition could then expect, at most, $2,000 of the $1 billion that the leader has to

TRY THIS

One of the ways things are not equal is that not all promises or assurances are credible. What actions might a prospective leader take to provide would-be supporters with a credible promise that they will share in private goods if the prospective leader does, in fact, come to power? In answering this question, be sure to consider whether and why the recipients of the promise would or would not believe it. (*Hint:* Think in terms of how costly or cheap it is for the would-be leader to make the promise.)

spend in private benefits. This, of course, is way below the maximum expectation under the terms of our first example. What is more, the incumbent in the second example does not have to promise even this much because even in a directly elected presidential democracy there still exists a 50 percent risk that a defector will not make it into the successor winning coalition.[‡] And the most the challenger can credibly promise to provide has an expected value of only about $1,000 per coalition member. The upper bound of $2,000 per supporter in the second example compares very poorly with the upper bound of $1 million per supporter in the first example. Even the lower bounds are not as attractive; the autocratic leader must provide at least $10,000 per supporter, whereas the democratic leader need provide

---

[‡] Of course, the United States does not have a directly elected presidential system. Because of the way that the electoral college works and given the variation in population across congressional districts, a person could be elected president of the United States with significantly less than 30 percent of the popular vote.

only $1,000 per supporter. The private goods deal certainly looks a lot better for supporters of an autocrat than it does for supporters of a democratic leader.[§]

The general principle is straightforward. When the winning coalition gets bigger, private goods are spread more thinly and so can less easily make up for failed public policies. As the selectorate shrinks, the risks of defection drop off, making the incumbent's advantage in using private rewards smaller and smaller. Thus, the greatest incumbency advantage in using private goods to satisfy constituents belongs to the leaders of political systems that have small winning coalitions and large selectorates. This makes the value of current private goods high for the average supporter and makes the expected value of private goods following a political defection small. It also means that the incumbent can, if so inclined, skim much of the private goods budget for his or her own ends.

Supporters in a large-coalition public-goods-oriented setting receive the benefits of public goods even if their leader is replaced by a challenger, such as after an election. This means that they can support a challenger with little consequence. When a leader answers to a small winning coalition, he or she predominantly uses private benefits to hold the loyalty of his or her supporters. If a supporter defects to a challenger, he or she faces the possible loss of those private benefits afterward. Further, the larger the selectorate is, the greater the risk of exclusion if the challenger should come to power. A larger selectorate means more choices about whom the challenger will include in his or her new support coalition. Supporters then should be particularly loyal to a leader who answers to a small winning coalition with a large selectorate from which to draw that coalition. Such leaders can offer fewer private benefits than a challenger offers and still hold the loyalty of his or her supporters. In fact, how loyal supporters are to an incumbent is determined by the size of W relative to S.

The Loyalty Norm (W/S) and Conventional Regime Types

The ratio W/S is large in states that people normally refer to as democracies. It is miniscule in places, such as North Korea or Egypt, that operate on the basis of rigged elections. When W/S is large, coalition members have a relatively high probability of being in any future coalition because W/S indexes the odds that they will be selected. A leader needs W people out of S choices. The larger W is relative to S, the more likely an individual is to be chosen. When W is small and S is large, the leader has many substitutes available for any member of the coalition. Therefore, when W is small and S is large, coalition members face a higher risk of being excluded from a future coalition even if they successfully help a new leader come to power. This risk makes them loyal to the current incumbent. That loyalty is further reinforced by the fact that, when W is small, the leader emphasizes private rewards. These rewards are valuable, making defection potentially costly as well as risky. But when W is absolutely large and is relatively large compared to S, switching loyalty to a rival politician is neither particularly

---

[§] Private-goods payments are usually subtler in democracies than in autocracies. In democracies, leaders promote tax policies or other redistributive programs that benefit their supporters, whereas in autocracies leaders often distribute the right to be corrupt to their cronies.

risky nor costly. It is not risky because the odds of being required in a future winning coalition (*W/S*) are good, and it is not especially costly because, when *W* is large, most rewards are paid in the form of public goods that everyone enjoys, whether in the coalition or not, rather than private goods that go only to coalition members. In fact, we can think loosely about the cost of private goods as being dependent on the size of the coalition. As the coalition gets bigger, as we have seen in our two examples, the expected value of private rewards, given a fixed budget, shrink just as if they cost more. Naturally, as their value decreases, the prospect that public benefits (in the form of effective policies) will be worth as much or more to the recipient increases. Thus, for a given level of revenue, there is a coalition size at which it is more efficient for leaders to switch to emphasizing public goods over private rewards. The observed emphasis on public benefits is not the product of civic mindedness but, rather, is simply the rational response by leaders who want to keep their jobs. This means that small-coalition leaders are compelled by their political circumstances to emphasize inefficient governance as part of the reward package for their cronies, while large-coalition leaders are compelled to emphasize effective public policy to keep their coalition's loyalty.

Leader Survival

In fact, the ratio *W/S* is the single biggest factor shaping a leader's survival prospects. When the support coalition must be large, we know the leader puts more emphasis on public goods; when it is small, private goods dominate. But that just speaks to the portion of a government's policies that help everyone or the few; it does not speak to how much is spent on these benefits.

The ratio *W/S*, the loyalty norm, determines how much a leader must spend to maintain coalition loyalty and, therefore, how much can be held back for the incumbent's discretionary use. When loyalty is weak, as in a democratic, large *W*-to-*S* system, more must be spent to keep the coalition members from switching to a rival. When *W/S* is small, the risks of defection are too high and the costs too great to abandon the incumbent; hence, loyalty is stronger. This translates, as intimated in the numerical autocratic example, to more money under the leader's control. That, in turn, means that the incumbent that has a small coalition and a large selectorate (for example, in Syria in Figure 1.4) has more money for a rainy-day fund or for pet projects. So, the leader could use the pot of discretionary money to swell a Swiss bank account or to try to improve the lot of his subjects.

Examples of leaders who put discretionary funs to good, civic-minded use include the late Deng Xiaoping of China and Lee Kwan Yew of Singapore. It might also include Mao Zedong and Fidel Castro, neither of whom seems to have stolen substantial amounts of money. These leaders, however, had poor ideas about how to improve quality of life, reminding us that, when people must rely on the good intentions of their leaders rather than the pressures of accountability, they are likely to have poorer odds of getting effective policy. The law of large numbers is on the side of effective policy in large-coalition systems but not in small-coalition settings. Examples of kleptocrats who use their discretion to enrich themselves are vastly more numerous than those who try to make people better off. No one would mistake Kim Jong-il of worrying about the people of North Korea. You might try your hand at putting together a list of current leaders in small-coalition settings who you think are trying to help their people and of those who just seem to be thieves.

Autocracy and democracy, according to selectorate theory, are fundamentally different in their consequences even though all leaders are assumed to want the same thing—to keep their jobs and have discretion over as many resources as possible. Democratic politics in selectorate theory is a competition in competence to produce public goods; autocratic politics centers on the purchase of the loyalty of key supporters.

These patterns are not absolutes; they are central tendencies. Even a system with a large winning coalition will have those who receive private benefits. Leaders who answer to a small winning coalition do provide some public goods in response to coalition demands and may provide additional public goods with the resources at their discretion, that is, resources they do not need to spend on maintaining coalition loyalty. All else being equal, however, large winning coalitions induce leaders to shift public policy away from private benefits and toward the provision of public goods.

The selectorate theory logically implies several basic principles of politics that are applied repeatedly throughout this book. The most important of these principles are:

1. Regimes with large winning coalitions focus on effective successful policies, including foreign policies. When leaders' policies do poorly, they either switch them or pour more resources into trying to make them succeed.

2. Regimes with small winning coalitions tolerate failed domestic and foreign policies better than do regimes with large coalitions because in small-coalition settings loyalty to a leader depends more on receiving private rewards than public benefits. As a consequence, leaders mostly continue on their policy course even when their policies are failing. They do not change course as quickly as large-coalition leaders, and they do not put extra resources into trying to make the policies succeed under most circumstances.

3. The likelihood that a leader survives in office despite failed policies increases as W/S decreases (so that the polity becomes more autocratic) and decreases as W/S increases (so that the polity becomes more democratic).

4. As W/S increases, leaders must spend more revenue to maintain loyalty among their coalition members and, as a result, these leaders have proportionately fewer revenue sources at their discretionary use than do those who depend on a small coalition drawn from a large selectorate.

5. Corruption and kleptocracy (governing by theft) increase in prominence as W gets smaller, especially when S also gets larger.

6. When leaders can change political arrangements, they prefer to decrease the size of their coalition and increase the size of the selectorate.

7. When coalition members can change institutions (e.g., through coups), they always prefer to increase the ratio W/S and may, depending on circumstances, prefer to do so by increasing W more quickly than S or decreasing W more slowly than S.

8. When people who are not in the coalition have the opportunity to change institutions of government (e.g., through revolution or civil war), they always prefer to increase W and to increase W/S.

These eight principles form the backbone of the choices about how best to conduct foreign policy and how best to use resources (such as foreign aid) to influence governance and government policies, both foreign and domestic. They form the foundation of the assessment of international affairs throughout this book, sometimes with surprising implications, often with depressing ones. They also help point the way to how we might go about solving difficult international problems, including even problems that may lead to war.

SUMMARY

This chapter introduces a strategic perspective model of domestic institutions and foreign policy. Leaders who are intent on retaining power and authority must satisfy core constituents, identified as the winning coalition. The winning coalition is drawn from the selectorate, the set of people with a legitimate say in the selection of the government leadership. Leaders distribute a mix of benefits in the form of public policies that all enjoy and private goods that only members of the winning coalition enjoy.

We have seen that from a leader's point of view the optimal political arrangement is to have a small winning coalition and a large selectorate, as is common in systems with rigged elections. Under such arrangements, supporters receive valuable private benefits that foster loyalty to their leaders even in the face of policy failure. Furthermore, loyalty is reinforced by the high political risks associated with defection to a political rival. Those risks increase as the size of the selectorate increases and as the size of the winning coalition decreases.

A monarchy or military junta is often the optimal political arrangement from the point of view of members of the winning coalition (that is, the aristocracy). In a monarchy and military government, both of which have a small winning coalition and a small selectorate, the current value of private goods is high. This is true as well in autocracies. However, in monarchies and juntas, winning coalition members benefit from the fact that the risks associated with defection are not as great as they are in autocracies. This follows from the fact that the ratio of the winning coalition size to the selectorate size is larger in monarchies and juntas than it is in autocracies with rigged elections.

Democracy is the optimal form of government from the perspective of ordinary citizens. Relatively few private goods are doled out; instead, public policy is the focus of leadership decisions. Because good public policy benefits all people in the polity, even those not in the winning coalition are likely to fare reasonably well. Consequently, the broad mass of the population derives its greatest benefits under democracy. This is in marked contrast to monarchies, juntas, and autocracies, in which the logical focus of leaders is to provide private goods, generally at the expense of seeking out successful public policies.

We have seen hints that several principles of international politics follow from the selectorate theory. These relate to resource allocations and their impact on foreign policy and even warfare. In the remainder of this book, we explore those principles to see how they can help us better understand and perhaps engineer international affairs.

KEY CONCEPTS

constituents   25
international relations   24
politics   27
private goods   32
public goods   32

public policies   36
selectorate   31
selectorate theory   31
winning coalition   32

2 Tools for Analyzing International Affairs

OVERVIEW

- People's perceptions of reality—rather than reality itself—shape decisions in international relations. In this chapter, we develop three tools that enable us to account for the role of perceptions in decision making. Together, these help us pinpoint the ways that strategic interactions might be resolved.

- Spatial models such as the median voter theorem allow us to plot leaders' policy preferences along a line, allowing us to see, as a logical continuum, which policy option a leader prefers most and which he or she prefers least. Similarly, we can plot different leaders' policy preferences in relation to one another, allowing us to see how close or how far apart their preferences are.

- Win sets, which allow us to determine where leaders' preferences most overlap, help us identify the possible winning coalitions and policy agreements across linked or multi-dimensional issues.

- Expected utilities help us see how leaders will evaluate the costs and benefits to them of alternative courses of action and how they weight those costs and benefits according to the probability of their arising. By comparing the expected utility associated with alternative courses of action, we can predict which path a decision maker is likely to take.

This chapter offers an introduction to the toolbox of analytic techniques that are especially useful for understanding—and eventually engineering—policy choices in international affairs. It provides the foundations for understanding why leaders and followers do what they do. You may want to refer back to this and the next chapter from time to time to refresh your memory about how particular analytic tools work and when they are likely to be useful in deriving insights into international politics. You can think of the instruction here as a policymaker's or social engineer's "how to" manual that provides a structured way to think about how to solve problems and advance policy goals.

Intuition, gut feelings, opinion, and ideology may shape beliefs, but they are a poor basis for making decisions that influence whether people enjoy peace and prosperity or suffer from war and poverty. This book relies on a different way to tackle foreign policy problems. The approach to solving policy problems taken here relies on logic and evidence rather than cherry-picked anecdotes or clever rhetoric. Anecdotes can be informative, but they can also blind us to whether they reflect the typical or expected situation or, instead, reflect an odd, even unique circumstance that is unlikely to recur. Rhetoric always has a part to play in persuading the public or politicians to support (or oppose) particular policies. Rhetoric, supported by anecdotal examples, is always employed by competing politicians and interest groups to argue for or against war, to argue for negotiations or for sanctions, and to vilify or to empathize with adversaries in the hope that the one choice or the other will encourage conflict resolution. As important as the instruments of persuasion are, neither anecdotes nor rhetoric provides a sound basis for choosing between policies that influence life and death, as so many foreign policies do.

The possibility of Iran obtaining nuclear weapons capabilities has been a topic of much concern for world leaders for some time. International efforts to persuade Iran's rulers to set aside their nuclear ambitions have brought together individuals who otherwise share few interests. In this image the Supreme Leader of Iran Ayatollah Ali Khamenei (right) speaks with Russia's then president Vladimir Putin (center) as Iranian president Mahmoud Ahmadinejad listens at an official meeting in Tehran, October 16, 2007.

This chapter will help you evaluate the connections between government actions and foreign policy goals so that you can form carefully reasoned judgments about whether the actions being taken are the best way to progress toward achieving the desired ends. To do that, we need to be careful that our arguments are logically consistent rather than just clever rhetoric and that our evidence is relevant and representative rather than selected just to support our preferred point of view. The best way to ensure that our arguments and policy conclusions are grounded in sound logic and evidence and are not just dressed-up personal opinion is to rely on precise and transparent reasoning. Mathematics—primarily algebra here—reinforced with numerical examples is a good starting place. The purpose behind the use of basic mathematics is threefold: to provide a simplified view of the much more complex, albeit less explicit, calculations that real decision makers go through to decide on the actions they take; to avoid ambiguity in the inferences or conclusions we draw; and to see how careful reasoning can help identify practical solutions to important policy problems, solutions that often get overlooked when policy choices are made in a more casual way.

This and the next chapter progress from relatively simple but powerful insights to more complex and intricate modes of analysis. Of course, this is an introduction, so much is left out. Later chapters expand on some of the tools introduced here, but most of the essential tools are found in this and the next chapter. We begin with spatial models of decision making and develop the median voter theorem and some of the insights it provides. From there, we examine win sets, which identify the possible winning coalitions and policy agreements across linked or multidimensional issues, and then move on to the introduction of expected utility calculations. The next chapter shifts gear, providing an introduction to game theory, including how to solve some strategic problems in international relations when there is uncertainty about an important characteristic of the situation. For the sake of continuity, these ideas are developed in this chapter and the next in the context of a single ongoing example: the Iranian government's approach to the development of that country's nuclear potential. Before introducing various modeling approaches to strategic choice, I digress briefly to introduce the example.

THE EXAMPLE: IRAN'S NUCLEAR PURSUIT

One of the most pressing foreign policy matters currently facing the United States, the United Nations, and indeed, the entire international community, concerns Iran's intentions in the nuclear arena. The Iranian government acknowledges that it is working on enriching uranium and has been doing so for several years. It contends that its intention is to develop a civilian nuclear energy industry to help meet Iran's energy needs in the future. In support of this contention, the country's leaders note that, although Iran is a major petroleum producer and exporter, gasoline is rationed in Iran. Iran exports almost all the oil it produces and so suffers from shortages at home. Furthermore, they note that, as signatories to the Nuclear Non-Proliferation Treaty (NPT; an international agreement designed to induce members not to develop nuclear weapons), they have the right to pursue peaceful uses of nuclear energy. Thus, the Iranian government's position is that it is doing no more than pursuing its rights under the NPT.

Many in the international community are skeptical about Iran's stated intention. This skepticism has several foundations. First, Iran is the world's fourth largest producer and exporter of crude oil. Its current domestic petroleum shortages are seen as being artificially constructed by the government. What is more, Iran ranks fifth in the world in known oil reserves and second in known natural gas reserves, so for the foreseeable future it is hard to imagine that Iran's leaders expect that their populace will face real energy shortages. Second, although it is true that uranium enrichment can be used for civilian energy purposes, uranium enrichment is not required for that use; however, it is required to build a nuclear weapon. In fact, many countries have used alternative technology to develop civilian nuclear energy. Third, Iran's leadership declined a Russian offer to enrich uranium for them in Russia so that Iran can have the fuel required for its ostensible civilian nuclear energy industry without enriching uranium itself. The Iranian government's response to the offer was that it will never give up its right to enrich uranium and will never cease doing so. Fourth, the international community fears that Iran actually seeks to develop nuclear weapons. There are several motivations for the Iranian government to do so:

1. To deter the United States from making a military intervention to topple the regime
2. To deter Israel from using its military capabilities to threaten the Iranian regime or, more likely, its allies, such as Hezbollah in Lebanon and elsewhere in the Middle East
3. To reassert Iranian dominance as the leading force behind the exportation of Islamic fundamentalism in the world, recapturing that position from the terrorist organization Al Qaeda
4. To gain increased popularity among Iranian domestic political constituents who want to promote Iranian/Persian pride
5. To regain Iran's international leadership position in the Middle East region, currently seemingly possessed by Egypt or Saudi Arabia

Of course, these are only a few of the possible motivations for Iran's alleged pursuit of a nuclear weapons capability.

It is noteworthy that the international community is fairly unified in its opposition to Iran's enrichment of uranium. The United Nations Security Council, for example, has passed resolutions threatening economic sanctions on Iran for defying the international community's efforts to curb Iran's nuclear pursuits. It is also noteworthy that the Iranian government has responded to the threatened economic sanctions by hardening its position and reasserting its right to pursue nuclear energy uses. Although the UN resolutions are relatively modest, the United States in October 2007 unilaterally imposed stiff economic sanctions on Iran, banning U.S. businesses from doing business with Iran's largest banks or with firms controlled by the Iranian army's elite units, known as the Revolutionary Guard.

With this information in mind, we can begin to understand how contending views are likely to get sorted out. By investigating the logic of how decisions are made, taking people's power, preferences, and perceptions into account, we can come to grasp with, for instance, why it is so difficult to work out a compromise that satisfies both U.S. and Iranian domestic and international interests, and we can see how various threats are likely to influence policy choices by Iranian and American political leaders.

THE MEDIAN VOTER THEOREM: A SPATIAL MODEL

One of the central contentions about international relations is that states or the people who lead them are interested in enhancing **national security.** Unfortunately, as important as that idea is, there are few clear and explicit definitions of this concept. Often national security is thought to be equivalent to how much military might a state has amassed; more military power is often equated with more security (Kissinger 1979; Morgenthau 1978). This idea stems from the notion that every state is on its own, living in a world where no international body can be relied on to enforce treaties or peace between states; this notion is sometimes called **anarchy** (Waltz 1979; Milner 1998; Powell 1994). One of the central puzzles among some who investigate international politics is how cooperation or compromise ever emerges in an anarchic, dog-eat-dog world.

Yet, even if we accept the idea that the international system of states is a self-help system in which each state can count only on itself to sustain its security against outside aggression, we can easily see that it is not necessary to accumulate a large amount of military might to be secure. Spatial models provide a way for us to think about security, especially in the context of the median voter theorem for issues that can be depicted on a line. **Spatial models** are a class of abstract perspectives that assume that we can locate decision makers and their policy preferences either on a line or continuum or in a space that includes more than one dimension. With a few basic assumptions, we can identify ways to predict how those decision makers will respond to any proposed solution to a policy question, including questions that affect national security.

We can begin our exploration of analytic tools by addressing the question of what makes a state secure, doing so first in the context of a one-dimensional spatial model. I define *national security* to mean that the state has adopted policies to minimize the likelihood that any group of other states can and will coalesce against it and defeat it, in the process depriving the vanquished state of its resources, the lives of some of its citizens, and perhaps its very existence. This view of security is in keeping with the way the concept is generally used in international politics by realists or neorealists (Waltz 1979). Later, I modify this view to focus attention on the political security of individual leaders rather than on the nation's security; then I draw out a distinction between conditions that might make the state secure but the leader insecure or make the leader secure at the expense of national security. For now, however, let's just think about security as referring to the ability of the state to prevent its defeat at the hands of any other state or coalition of states.

One way to evaluate national security is to invoke a principle of politics that is common in the study of voting and legislative policymaking but is all but ignored in international relations; I have the median voter theorem in mind. The **median voter theorem** says that, if issues are one-dimensional, preferences are single-peaked, and it takes a majority to win, then the median voter's position is the winning outcome. In the international context (with a bit of clarification provided shortly), this means that, keeping the theorem's assumptions in mind, a policy position exists—the median state's policy position—that maximizes national security. The median state's position under the theorem's restrictions represents a policy stance that cannot be defeated, hence optimizing the security of any state that has endorsed the policy position supported by the median voter. This is a theorem, which means that its conclusions follow logically from its assumptions and, therefore, are logically true and empirically useful if the assumptions accurately depict the situation. When the assumptions hold, then, the median voter theorem can form the basis for predicting policy outcomes and for identifying how secure each state is. As we will see, this theorem has significant applications in international relations. That makes it a good starting point for thinking about how policy disputes get resolved.

Assumption 1: Unidimensionality

Let's take the median voter theorem apart so that we understand the exact meaning of each of its components; then, we can apply it to issues concerning security, such as the issue of Iran's nuclear ambitions. The first component of the theorem stipulates that we are investigating a unidimensional issue (or, equivalently, a one-dimensional issue). An issue is **unidimensional** if the possible ways to resolve the issue can be displayed meaningfully on a straight line. To display choices in this way, it is useful to consider that each participant in the issue's resolution has a most preferred outcome, sometimes referred to as the participant's **ideal point,** and that it is the set of these ideal points that can be placed on a single straight line. When I say that a party or decision maker has a preference, I mean that the decision maker can compare different ways to resolve the issue and can say, "I like this way better than that way" or "I like that way better than this way" or "I like these two ways equally" or "I like either of them better than some third possibility," and so forth.

Suppose, for instance, that during his administration President George W. Bush had to try to resolve what his preferences were regarding Iran's nuclear program, as surely he had to do. He might say, "I prefer that Iran have no nuclear program at all to Iran's doing research on civilian nuclear energy, but I prefer that Iran do research on civilian nuclear energy to Iran's developing a nuclear weapon." That seems consistent with President Obama's position as well as Bush's. Another concerned party, such as Iran's student leaders, has a different preference ordering. They seem to have indicated, "We prefer that Iran develop a civilian nuclear energy industry to Iran's having no nuclear program at all, but we prefer that Iran have no nuclear program at all to Iran's developing a nuclear weapon." The Iranian foreign minister seems to have expressed still a different point of view. He seems to be saying, "I prefer that Iran have a civilian nuclear energy industry to Iran's building a weapon, but I prefer that Iran build a nuclear weapon to Iran's having no nuclear program at all."

We might locate all key Iranian decision makers and their constituents, as well as a variety of international actors interested in weighing in on what Iran does on the nuclear front, along a one-dimensional line segment whose end points and specific points in between are defined to reflect progressively more (or less) extreme positions on the question of what nuclear capacity, if any, Iran should seek. Figure 2.1 illustrates this idea by assigning numeric

FIGURE 2.1	Iranian Nuclear Capacity Policy Continuum

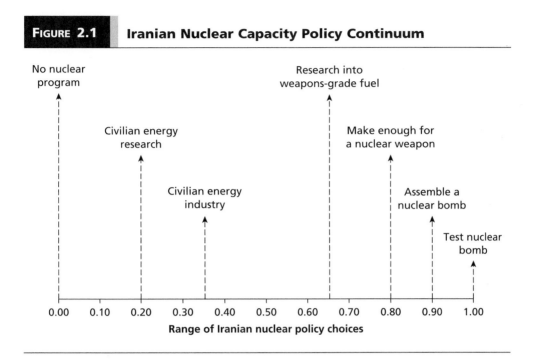

Range of Iranian nuclear policy choices

values to different points along a line and defining the meaning of those different numeric values in terms of the nuclear policy they represent. As I have defined it, positions farther to the left on the line segment reflect greater opposition to Iran's developing a nuclear capacity and points farther to the right reflect support for more and more extreme versions of the potential Iranian nuclear policy. I have defined the range of values on the nuclear policy scale in Figure 2.1 to fall between 0 and 1. The choice of range is, of course, arbitrary. I could just as easily have chosen a range of values from 0 to 100 or from −32 to 15 or anything else. The scale's range does not matter. What does matter for working out the median voter position and other features of the spatial model is the relative distance between points. So, for instance, on a scale from 0 to 1, position 0.35 is 35 percent of the way up the scale from 0 and position 0.50 is 50 percent of the way and position 0.75 is 75 percent of the way across the scale. So we know that position 0.50 is closer to the policy represented at position 0.35 than it is to the policy at 0.75. That is, the distance between numbers that define the scale are important. For any range, we can find a point that is 35 percent or 50 percent or any other percentage from one or the other end of the scale.

As it happens, position 0.35 on the scale is defined here as the policy in support of Iran's development of a civilian nuclear energy industry. This is the official policy stance of the Iranian government but may not be the true policy preference of some of Iran's leaders. The

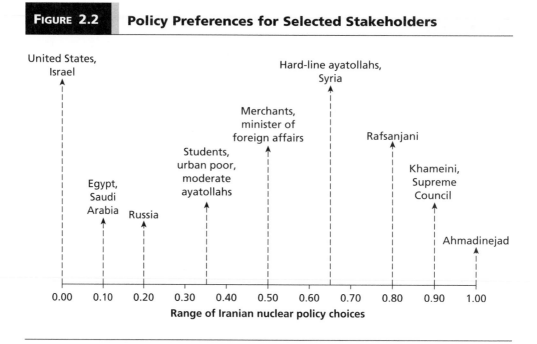

FIGURE 2.2   **Policy Preferences for Selected Stakeholders**

position of the U.S. government is at 0 on this scale; that is, the ideal outcome from the U.S. government's perspective is that Iran should have no nuclear program. Russia's government's ideal point—its most desired policy—is closer to 0.20 on the scale; Russia's leadership does not oppose Iran's research into nuclear energy but does not want Iran to go beyond research. To accommodate this view, the Russian government has offered to enrich uranium on Iran's behalf. That is precisely the policy endorsed at position 0.20 on the scale. As we can see in Figure 2.1, several other policy positions are defined on the nuclear policy scale, and these positions are spaced closer to or farther from one another to reflect their relative extremism (from left to right or right to left).

Figure 2.2 illustrates the idea that we can locate the policy position (that is, the preferred policy) of different decision makers or other interested parties on the continuum defined in Figure 2.1. Figure 2.2 does so for a selected group of Iranian political leaders and domestic interests as well as some of the more potentially influential outside sources of pressure on Iran. I base these data on my discussions with area experts who study Iran's nuclear intentions. A fairly comprehensive enumeration of those trying to influence Iran's nuclear policy includes more than eighty interested parties. For now, however, we work with a more manageable set of key players to illustrate some central ideas.

The information in Figure 2.2 would not be sufficient to determine the outcome—the median voter's position—even if the figure showed all the eighty interested parties, which, of course, it does not. For purposes of illustration, however, let's assume that everyone with an interest in influencing Iran's nuclear policy is included in the figure. To work out who the median voter is and why that interested party is the crucial decision maker, we need to understand the meaning of the other assumptions behind the median voter theorem.

Assumption 2: Single-Peaked Preferences

The assumption of **single-peaked preferences** means that any choice farther from the most preferred outcome of an interested party is less desired by that stakeholder than choices closer to its most preferred policy.* So, for example, the Israeli government does not like Iranian civilian energy research as much as it likes Iran's having no nuclear program, but it likes Iranian civilian energy research more than it likes the idea of Iran's having a civilian nuclear energy industry. The Israeli government is more in favor of (or, equivalently, less opposed to) a civilian nuclear energy industry for Iran than it is of Iran's researching weapons-grade fuel, and so forth. Similarly, we can say that Syria most favors Iranian research on weapons-grade fuel and that for Syria it is preferable that Iran makes enough weapons-grade fuel for a nuclear weapon than that Iran restricts itself to just developing a civilian nuclear energy industry. Single-peaked preferences tell us that this is Syria's desire because the distance between Syria's most preferred position (numerically 0.65 on the scale) and Iran's making weapons-grade fuel in sufficient quantity to have the capacity to assemble a weapon (position 0.80 on the line) is smaller than the distance between Syria's most preferred policy (position 0.65) and Iran's development of a civilian nuclear energy industry (position 0.35 on the scale). We can use the distance from a stakeholder's most preferred policy outcome—its ideal point—and any other possible policy outcomes to determine the order in which choices are desired by the stakeholder. The shorter the absolute distance an alternative is from the actor's ideal point, the more that stakeholder desires it.[†] This follows directly from the assumption that preferences are single-peaked.

Not all issues or all stakeholders necessarily have single-peaked preferences. We ignore certain possible preference orderings when we assume that preferences are single-peaked. To be clear about what is ruled out by this assumption, let us consider some logically possible preference orderings that are not single-peaked. Suppose, for instance, we want to know how Mahmoud Ahmadinejad, Iran's president, feels about having no nuclear program, limiting Iran to a civilian nuclear energy program, or building a nuclear weapon. It is logically possible for Ahmadinejad to order these three choices in six different ways, ignoring the possibility that he is indifferent among any pair of them. Of course, with more choices there are many more possible preference orderings. If we use the "greater than" sign (>) to denote preference, so that A > B is read "A is preferred to B," he could, in principle, hold any of the following preferences:

---

* I refer to interested parties interchangeably as *players, actors, decision makers,* or *stakeholders.*

[†] The distance between points does not depend on the direction of movement. That is, distance is always expressed as a positive value.

1. No nuclear program > civilian energy industry > make a weapon
2. No nuclear program > make a weapon > civilian energy industry
3. Civilian energy industry > no nuclear program > make a weapon
4. Civilian energy industry > make a weapon > no nuclear program
5. Make a weapon > civilian energy industry > no nuclear program
6. Make a weapon > no nuclear program > civilian energy industry

Of these six possible ways to order the preferences (ignoring indifference) among the three choices we are focused on at the moment, the assumption of single-peaked preferences rules out preference orderings 2 and 6 for anyone, no matter what their ideal point. Ahmadinejad's policy stance on this matter is believed by the experts I surveyed to favor making and testing a weapon, so his ordering, given single-peaked preferences, can be assumed to be number 5. We see in more detail in a moment why orderings 2 and 6 are ruled out by the assumption of single-peaked preferences.

Let's review the rules that are dictated by the assumption of single-peaked preferences so that we can work out anyone's presumed priorities about different policy choices if we just know their most preferred outcome, as in this case. The assumption that preferences are single-peaked tells us that the farther a choice is from an individual's most desired choice, the less that choice is valued. This establishes that the individual has a transitive preference ordering, meaning that if choice A is preferred to choice B and choice B is preferred to choice C, then choice A is preferred to choice C. Consider what this tells us about Ahmadinejad. His most desired nuclear policy is at the extreme upper end of the issue continuum depicted in Figure 2.1. This means that the more we move to lower values on the continuum, the less desirable the policy options become for Ahmadinejad. One way to represent this decline in preference is to create a measure of how intensely he likes or dislikes different policies. Using that measure, called utility (and discussed in more detail later in this chapter), we can draw a line whose slope shows how much or how little he prefers alternative nuclear policies. If we drew such a line of how intensely he likes or dislikes policy alternatives, it would have one peak and that highest point would occur at the policy Ahmadinejad most prefers—building and testing a nuclear weapon. The line showing how intensely he favors the alternatives would decline steadily as we moved farther and farther from his most preferred approach to Iran's nuclear capacity. If the line were flat across some range of points on the line, so that across those points the line was parallel to the policy scale (x axis in Figure 2.1), then that would tell us that the set of policies reflected by that part of the measure of intensity of preference reflects policies about which the decision maker is indifferent. Figure 2.3a illustrates examples of single-peaked preferences with and without indifference.

No matter where a stakeholder's most preferred policy falls on the issue continuum, the assumption of single-peaked preferences means that we can draw a line from its ideal point, with the height of the line representing its intensity of preference for the outcome at each point on the continuum, and that this line measuring intensity of preference will have one peak and will

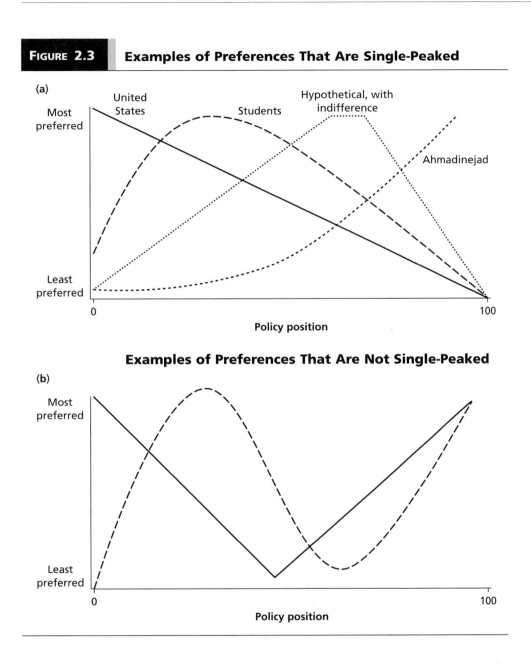

FIGURE 2.3 **Examples of Preferences That Are Single-Peaked**

decline steadily the farther we move from that actor's ideal point whether we were moving to the left or to the right. Syria's preferences, for instance, decline as we move to the left or to the right of its most preferred policy, research into weapons-grade fuel. The choices closer to weapons-grade fuel research are liked more intensely by Syria than are the policy choices farther away.

But if we plotted the preferences of a stakeholder in Figure 2.2 that had the preference order 2 or 6 from our list, we would see that the line had two peaks (see Figure 2.3b for examples of non-single-peaked preferences). Any preference ordering that leads to more than one high point (one peak) is ruled out by the assumption of single-peaked preferences.

Of course, just because we assume that no stakeholder has preferences that produce multiple peaks does not mean that no one actually has these preferences. It is possible that a stakeholder could have preferences like those in preference orders 2 and 6 despite our assumption that preferences are single-peaked. If we are mistaken in ruling out such preference orderings, then any predictions we make based on this assumption may prove to be wrong. Assumptions, after all, restrict how we think about the world. However, without them we could say that anything is possible, and so we could not choose among competing explanations of how international politics works. Assumptions are an important part of constructing expectations and give us a basis for making predictions, but we must always be clear and explicit about what we are assuming so that everyone can tell on what basis we arrived at our predictions.

TRY THIS

Draw the preference intensity lines for preference order number 2 or number 6. Can these preferences be drawn with a single peak?

The assumption of single-peaked preferences provides us with a basis for predicting which policy each stakeholder will choose if confronted with a choice between any two alternatives. For example, which policy will Egypt and Saudi Arabia, Iran's students, the Iranian minister of foreign affairs, Akbar Hashemi Rafsanjani, Iranian President Ahmadinejad, and Supreme Leader Ali Khameini choose if compelled to decide between assembling a nuclear weapon (0.90 on the scale) and having no nuclear capacity at all (position 0 on the scale)? We know how to answer this question if preferences are single-peaked.

Egypt and Saudi Arabia most desire the policy at position 0.10, but they are being asked to choose between 0.90 and 0. Their preferred policy at 0.10 is closer to 0 than to 0.90, so according to the assumption of single-peaked preferences, they will favor no nuclear capacity over a policy that endorses Iran's assembling a weapon. So will Iran's students, whose position is at 0.35.[‡] For the Iranian minister of foreign affairs, deciding between the two options currently being considered would be a closer call. His position is in between support for research into weapons-grade fuel and development of a civilian nuclear energy industry; specifically, he is at 0.50 on the scale. But the choices we have put forward are at 0 and 0.90. Building a weapon is only a little closer to his preferred policy than is having no program at all ($|0.50 - 0| > |0.50 - 0.90|$). With the assumption of single-peaked preferences, we can infer that, of the two choices, he will favor, probably reluctantly, building a nuclear weapon.

[‡] This is because the absolute value of $(0.35 - 0)$ is less than the absolute value of $(0.35 - 0.90)$; $|0.35 - 0| = 0.35$ and $|0.35 - 0.90| = 0.55$. (The symbol $| \ |$ denotes absolute value.)

Rafsanjani, Ahmadinejad, and Khameini will each elect to back the development of a nuclear weapon if faced with a stark choice between doing so and doing nothing on the nuclear front. When we compare each Iranian leader's position to the proposed alternatives, for Rafsanjani, $|0.80 - 0.90| < |0 - 0.90|$, so he would support weapons development; for Ahmadinejad $|1.00 - 0.90| < |1.00 - 0|$, so building a weapon implies less of a policy concession; and for Khameini $|0.90 - 0.90| < |0.90 - 0|$ and building a weapon is exactly what he wants. Thus, for any comparison of policy choices on the issue continuum, single-peaked preferences allow us to say who favors what.

Assumption 3: Majority Rule

Finally, the median voter theorem tells us that, with single-peaked preferences and a one-dimensional issue, the median voter—the middle voter—holds the winning position if a majority is required. This idea that the median voter wins raises two questions. First, what is special about the middle or median voter that makes that voter's position the predicted winner? Second, just what does *majority rule* mean in the context of international affairs, where there is no voting in the normal sense?

The median voter is said to be the winning position because under the assumptions of the median voter theorem (that we are examining a one-dimensional issue, that stakeholders have single-peaked preferences, and that the majority rules) we can calculate how each and every voter will vote in a comparison of any pair of choices represented on the issue continuum. The median voter has the special property that, in a head-to-head contest with any other position on the continuum, single-peaked preferences dictate that more voters—that is, more choosers—will prefer the median voter's position than any other position. To see this, consider how everyone would vote if the contest were between the median voter's position and an alternative slightly to its left. All the choosers at the median voter's position or to its right, according to the assumption of single-peaked preferences, prefer the median voter's position to the position slightly to the median player's left because their positions are closer to the median position than to the one to its left. By the definition of *median,* no more than one-half of all voters minus 1 can be to its left (or its right). Thus, at most, the position just to the left will always get one fewer vote than the median voter's position, and so, by majority rule, the median voter's position wins. Of course, the same is true if we pick a choice just to the right of the median voter's position, only then the median voter's coalition of support includes everyone to the left of the median voter's position and, together with the median voter, that coalition is at least a simple majority. Clearly, picking choices farther away from the median can only add to the median voter's support, so it always wins at least a simple majority of votes under the theorem's assumptions.

This still leaves the question of what we mean by *majority rule* in the international context, a world in which for most matters it certainly is not true that each nation has one vote. For now, I take a *majority* to refer to a majority of the power that each of the stakeholders controls in the context of the issue, and **majority rule** to mean that the position accruing the majority of this power is the chosen position. We can think of power as the ability of a stake-holder to persuade others to do what it wants them to do even when they would rather do something else. Power, or the ability to persuade others, depends on different criteria in different contexts. Power might be based on military might or economic clout or expertise or some other dimension of influence, depending on what is relevant for the issue at hand (Keohane and Nye 1977). On trade issues, for instance, military power rarely is as germane as economic might, while in a military confrontation military power typically takes precedent over other sources of influence or persuasion.

On the Iranian nuclear issue, power reflects a complex combination of conditions that give decision makers more or less ability to persuade or coerce relative to others. Some power relationships are based on military threats, others on economic influence, still others on domestic political popularity, and yet others on shared cultural or religious values. The critical thing to recognize is that power is not distributed evenly among the stakeholders—this is not a case of one-person, one-vote. Ayatollah Khameini and the Supreme Council, for instance, have vastly more power to shape Iran's nuclear policy than, say, the United States or Iran's urban poor. Khameini can mobilize the Iranian military, its politicians and citizens, and many supporters in the Shiite Muslim world. In fact, he has a formal veto right over any policy adopted by Iran.

For convenience, I divide the more than eighty stakeholders trying to influence the Iranian government into four groups, each of which is itself divided into stakeholders that hold different policy preferences: the Iranian government's leaders; Iran's nonleadership domestic political interests; other Middle Eastern governments with an interest in what Iran does on the nuclear front; and the rest of the international community, referred to here as foreign interests. For example, the United States is one of the foreign interests; Egypt is one of the Middle East players; Iranian students are a domestic interest; and Khameini, the supreme leader, is an Iranian government leader.

If we array the stakeholders along the policy scale, as in Figure 2.4, plotting how much power is located at each potential policy outcome on the scale, we can see the landscape of political influence over Iranian nuclear capacity. It is evident when we look at this figure that there is more power behind the idea of having no nuclear program whatsoever than there is behind any other single nuclear policy proposal. In that sense, we might believe that this is the most powerful proposal and that it will dominate Iran's choice, taking domestic and international pressure into account. But this position does not control a majority of power—it is not the median voter's position. It could not garner the support of a coalition that controls most of the influence in this context.

Figure 2.5 takes the values at each policy position depicted in Figure 2.4 and adds them up so that we can see the cumulative total amount of power (or, so to speak, votes) as we move from left to right on the continuum. Of course, the position of the median voter would not change if the accumulation of power were done from right to left. As is evident in Figure 2.5, the median voter's position, the position that commands a bare majority of power at just above 50 percent, is located at the policy stance that favors Iran's development of a civilian nuclear

FIGURE 2.4	**The Power and Preferences of Four Key Groups of Stakeholders**

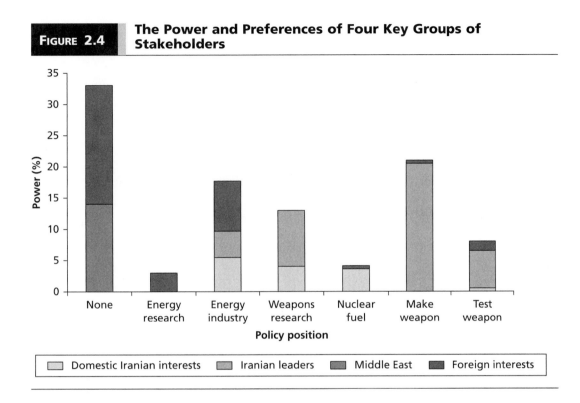

energy industry. This, then, is the predicted outcome based on the median voter theorem; that is, this is the policy we expect that the international community and the Iranians will agree to if the issue has been properly defined and the set of relevant stakeholders has been properly identified and rated accurately according to their preferences and their power.

The previous paragraph tells us two things: (1) it tells us that we can use the median voter's position as a preliminary basis for predicting the policy outcome, and (2) it draws our attention to some possible reasons that the prediction might be wrong. Let's explore these to see what we can learn. Looking back at Figure 2.4 we can see a striking pattern that raises a concern about the calibration of the median voter prediction in this case—are all these actors relevant to the Iranian government's ultimate decision or do only a subset of them actually matter?

Not a single Iranian stakeholder supports anything short of a civilian nuclear energy industry. All of the support for less than a civilian nuclear energy industry comes from foreign interests and the interests of non-Iranian Middle Easterners. What is more, the Iranian government leadership strongly favors making a nuclear weapon according to my survey of experts. If we ignore domestic politics, as is done too often in the study of international affairs, then the dictates of power politics tells us that Iran will maximize its national security against external threats by adopting the posture that it has, in fact, taken in public. That is,

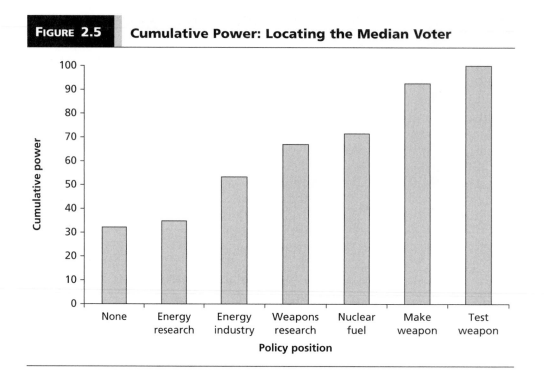

FIGURE 2.5 **Cumulative Power: Locating the Median Voter**

Iran will do no more than pursue the development of its capacity to build and operate a civilian nuclear energy industry. But we are left with the gnawing concern that Iran's official posture and its true objectives are not the same. What if Iran's policy is not dictated by international pressure but, rather, is dominated by domestic political concerns?

In fact, if we locate the median voter based just on those with a seat at the decision-making table in Iran—that is, Iran's leaders—then building a weapon is the Iranian median voter's position and international fears seem justified. So, to work out how best to address Iran's nuclear ambitions, we need to sort out whether Iran's leaders choose their policies exclusively on their own, they choose their policies taking domestic political interests into account as well, or they pay attention to international interests in addition to their domestic political audience. This is a fundamental problem that arises in almost every issue in international affairs—foreign policy may be about resolving external pressures, it may be about what works best at home, or it may be a mix of the two. This involves questions about what the relevant strategic environment is, what issues have to be resolved, and what the political consequences are in ignoring or weighting the foreign audience or the domestic audience too much (Fearon 1994; Smith 1996; Schultz 2001). Much of the rest of this book is about how to resolve that concern.

WIN SETS: THE MEDIAN VOTER AND ISSUE LINKAGE

The international community is well aware of Iranian domestic political sentiment in favor of that country's pursuit of at least a civilian nuclear energy capacity. This pursuit is a matter of national pride and reflects Iran's exercise of its sovereign rights under the NPT. As we have seen, the domestic Iranian median voter is likely to favor the pursuit of much more than just a nuclear energy capability. This is what worries much of the international community. What sorts of political maneuvers are open to the international community to try to alter the policies adopted by Iran's leaders so that the security-maximizing median voter viewpoint includes the persuasive power of non-Iranian interests? One possibility is to link Iran's nuclear program to a second, international dimension that is not reflected in the unidimensional issue continuum that we examine in the previous section; by creating a second, international dimension we may heighten sensibilities both to Iran's domestic considerations and to the wishes of the international community. That is, we can see what happens if we relax the median voter theorem's first assumption, the assumption of unidimensionality, while retaining the assumptions of single-peaked preferences and majority rules. Of course, once we relax an assumption of the theorem, the theorem no longer applies. (Later, we explore the mean voter theorem as an appropriate substitute for making predictions about multidimiensional issues.)

There is, in fact, considerable debate in the international community about what is the best approach toward Iran. Some argue in favor of negotiations, increased diplomatic contacts, and other positive cooperative efforts to encourage Iran's leaders to see that they will be rewarded if they adopt a nuclear posture more in keeping with what the international community wants. Many speculate, for instance, that Condoleezza Rice, George Bush's secretary of state, holds this view and that Egyptian President Hosni Mubarak does also. Certainly this is the view held by senior foreign policy advisors appointed by Barack Obama. Others disagree with this perspective. They believe that Iran's leaders will only harden their position if they are rewarded for what some see as Iran's uncooperative behavior. This group advocates taking a tougher stance, imposing severe economic sanctions on Iran unless that country's government verifiably abandons its efforts to enrich uranium. This group seems to have prevailed during the Bush years because the United States unilaterally imposed stiff sanctions in October 2007. Some advocate going even further, threatening the use of force to disable or dismantle Iran's enrichment facilities. Among those reported to be in the harder-line camp that advocates imposing high costs were Richard Cheney, Bush's vice president, and some in the Israeli government. Because the data for our running Iran analysis were collected during 2007, let's continue our analysis mindful that it reflects an assessment in the context of the Bush presidency and not the Obama presidency.

Each approach, and the various shadings in between, is plausible. None should be rejected out of hand based on personal taste or ideological beliefs about what works best; that is not the path to effective foreign policy. Logic and evidence should dictate the policy that is adopted, not such rhetoric as "give peace a chance" or "all they (for example, the Iranians) understand is force."

Briefly, we can summarize the logic behind each approach. Each approach addresses the incentives that people have to alter their actions, either by being rewarded for certain changes or being punished for failing to change. The approach that favors punishment is supported by a long history of effective deterrence, but there are also numerous examples of the failure of deterrence. Raising the costliness of action, just like raising prices at the grocery store, changes what people do. If the benefits from a nuclear program remain the same for Iran but the costs of such a policy become greater, then fewer people will continue to endorse the policy. They will be deterred by the desire to avoid the costs and so will moderate their policy stance. Conversely, raising the rewards for improving behavior is also a plausible approach with a long history of successes and failures. Gas stations discount the cost of gasoline for people who pump their own gas because this small effort helps the gas station save money; that is, some of these savings are passed on to the customer. Likewise, governments are likely to moderate their policies when they are given some valuable benefits—such as foreign aid—in compensation for their concessions. So, greater diplomatic ties with the United States and less international opprobrium might encourage Iran's leaders to be more responsive to international wishes. As the rhetoric of persuasion sometimes suggests, you catch more flies with honey than with vinegar. That is especially likely to be true during times of economic contraction, when the price of oil drops, making the Iranian government more vulnerable to political opposition at home and to economic assistance from abroad.

Which approach is best is not a matter of opinion or of clever phrases. Which works best depends on the rate at which the various decision makers are willing to trade costs or benefits in exchange for policy concessions. We can estimate the rate of such trade-offs, called the marginal rate of substitution by economists, by taking the salience or relative importance of the costs and benefits into account.

The costs approach and the rewards approach are part of the repertoire of international actions taken toward Iran. The United Nations Security Council, which requires unanimity among its five permanent members (the United States, Britain, France, Russia, and China), has approved in principle economic sanctions against Iran; Russia and China have made overtures to persuade the Iranian government to be more cooperative; and Condoleezza Rice had several meetings with Iranian diplomats in the context of negotiations surrounding the influence that the United States and Iran have over Iraq's government. Reportedly, the Egyptian and Saudi Arabian governments have declined to act as mediators on behalf of the United States, although each seems to desire a less bellicose approach to Iran. This still leaves open the question of whether either approach is likely to moderate Iran's alleged desire to develop a nuclear weapons capability, an allegation that finds support in the information provided in my survey of experts and shown in Figures 2.3 and 2.4.

Suppose that we locate stakeholders on this second dimension in which the choices range from increasing rewards given to Iran to increasing the costs imposed on the Iranian government under its current nuclear approach. We can link this dimension to the position each stakeholder takes regarding Iranian nuclear policy. Figure 2.6 does just this for four crucial

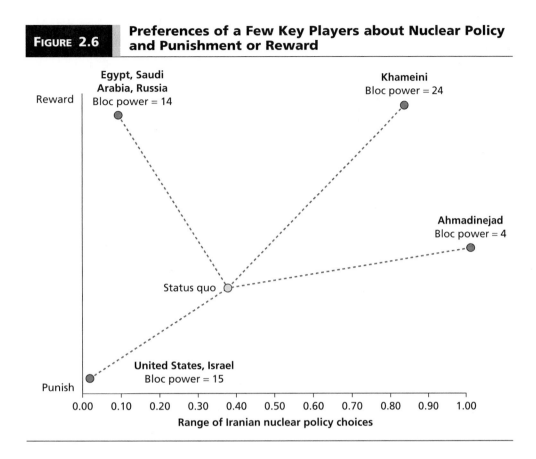

FIGURE 2.6 | **Preferences of a Few Key Players about Nuclear Policy and Punishment or Reward**

groups or interest blocs: (1) the Egyptians, Russians, and Saudis, who favor rewarding Iran for not pursuing its nuclear potential; (2) the governments of the United States and Israel, which favor imposing significant costs on Iran unless it agrees to abandon its nuclear program; (3) Iran's Supreme Leader Ali Khameini and the Supreme Council, which seek benefits for Iran from the international community and which have a veto over Iran's policy; and (4) President Ahmadinejad, who is indifferent to the view of Iran held by the international community and so seeks neither rewards nor fears punishments and who is thought to endorse building and testing a nuclear weapon.

In addition to these four crucial blocs, Figure 2.6 depicts the location of the current status quo on these two dimensions. On the dimension of reward/punishment, the status quo reflects considerably more punishment of Iran than Russia, for instance, feels is best but less punishment than is favored by the Bush administration in the United States. The status quo reflects the compromise struck between these two permanent members of the United Nations Security Council and so represents an estimate of the costliness of UN-approved sanctions. On the dimension of Iranian nuclear policy preferences, the status quo is the global median voter position that we identified with Figure 2.5. Even though Figure 2.5 is based on an assessment of more than eighty stakeholders, I show only four blocs in Figure 2.6 to keep the analysis manageable without grossly distorting the view that follows from a more nuanced, comprehensive approach to the question.

To understand how linking these two dimensions might influence Iran's policy, we need two additional assumptions beyond those used to derive the winning position based on the median voter's policy stance. We retain the assumptions that preferences are single-peaked and that a majority of the power in this group of four blocs is needed to formulate a winning strategy. In addition, since Ayatollah Khameini has a veto over Iranian policy, he must agree to the policy that is supported by a majority of power in order for it to become Iranian policy; that is, the international community may be able to gain his support through cooperative gestures or coerce his support through punishment strategies, but if it fails to win him over one way or the other, then the international community cannot impose a policy on Iran short of going to war and overthrowing the Khameini regime (Tsebelis 2002). Finally, I add the assumption that any new policy on these two dimensions must be better for the whole Iranian government, represented here by Ahmadinejad plus Khameini, than the status quo or else Iran will live with the existing situation. This is a modest enough assumption in that it stipulates that change will be agreed to only if Iran's government and the international community are aligned in favor of the change relative to the situation as it currently stands.

The assumption of single-peaked preferences allows us to discern exactly what combinations of nuclear policy and international rewards or punishments each stakeholder prefers to the status quo. For example, any combination of reward/punishment and nuclear policies that is closer to Khameini's ideal point (the policy combination that he most wants, depicted by a solid dot next to his name) will be preferred by him to the status quo, and any policy combination farther from his ideal point than the status quo will be unacceptable to him. That is exactly what is implied by the assumption of single-peaked preferences. The dotted lines in Figure 2.6, then, show the maximal policy distance that each crucial stakeholder is willing to go in forging a compromise that is, from its perspective, an improvement over the status quo.

Although Figure 2.6 shows how far each actor will go to compromise, it does not show all the policy directions each will go to find an improvement over the status quo. The assumption of single-peaked preferences tells us that any points closer to a decision maker's ideal point are preferred to points farther away. Thus, any set of points on the circumference of a circle whose center is the ideal point of a decision maker represents a set of policies about which the decision maker is indifferent when these policies are compared to one another; they are all equally good or bad because they are all equidistant from the stakeholder's ideal point.[§] The **circular indifference curve** at any distance from the ideal point of a decision maker can be

---

[§] This discussion assumes the two dimensions are equally salient or important to the stakeholders. If the salience for the two dimensions is not equal for any stakeholder, then that stakeholder will have an elliptical, not circular, indifference curve. To keep the calculations from getting too complex, I ignore this possibility here.

thought of as a ring around a mountain whose summit—the single peak—is the location of the actor's two-dimensional ideal point. The larger the radius of a circular indifference curve, the farther it is from the stakeholder's ideal point, so concentric circles that are smaller (whose points are closer to the ideal point) reflect policies preferred by the decision maker over those reflected by larger circular indifference curves (whose points are farther from the actor's ideal point). In this way, the indifference curves might be thought of as creating a topological map of the mountain slope, the larger and larger circles representing preferences that are farther and farther from the summit—the decision maker's ideal point. Of all these possible circular indifference curves, one is of particular interest. That indifference curve has a radius that is equal to the distance from the decision maker's ideal point to the point that represents the status quo because the status quo policy is the policy to beat.

Each dotted line in Figure 2.6 can be viewed as the length of the radius of a circle of points centered on each actor's ideal point such that the circumference of the circle passes through (that is, is tangent to) the status quo. The circumference of this circle describes the policies that the stakeholder values as equal to the status quo; that is, the player is indifferent between each of the policy combinations on the circumference of the circle and the policy combination that constitutes the status quo (because it is just another point on that circumference). And all the points inside the circle defined by this two-dimensional circular indifference curve are preferred by the stakeholder over the status quo because all the points inside this circle are closer to the decision maker's ideal point than is the status quo. Figure 2.7 shows this set of preferred points for each actor; the points inside the circular curves represent all the policy combinations that each individual player likes better than the current status-quo level of reward/punishment combined with the current policy about pursuing a nuclear energy capacity. Khameini's circular indifference curve that includes the status quo is shown in thick dark lines, as are three of the radii from his ideal point to the curve. The dotted lines are the equivalents from Ahmadinejad's perspective. Each arc in Figure 2.7 depicts the portion of a player's circular indifference curve that falls within the two-dimensional policy space.

Areas of shared preference between stakeholders are shown by the regions of overlap among these indifference curves and the preferred-to-status-quo sets that fall within them. That is, the areas of intersection reflect policies that two or more players prefer to the current status quo. When any two (or more) decision makers share a preference for some set of policies over the status quo, they can form a coalition to back one of those policies as a compromise replacement for the status quo. If enough decision makers agree on a policy mix they like better than the status quo, then they can replace the status quo with their preferred new policy.

The large shaded area in Figure 2.8 shows a combination of policies that are preferred to the status quo by the Egyptian-Saudi-Russian bloc, Ayatollah Khameini and the Supreme Council, and President Ahmadinejad. This shaded area includes a majority of the power among the stakeholders in Figure 2.6 and also includes the supreme leader, who has, as noted

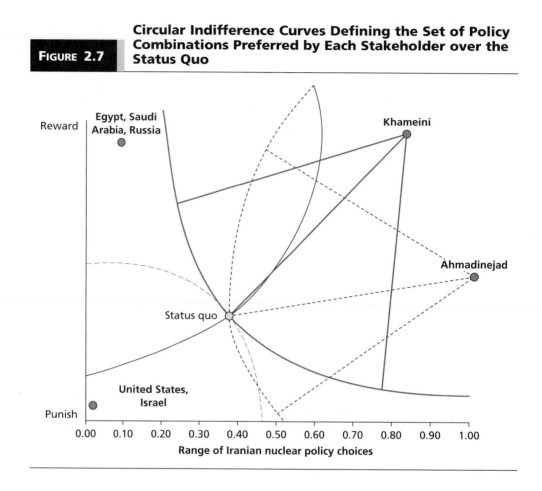

FIGURE 2.7 **Circular Indifference Curves Defining the Set of Policy Combinations Preferred by Each Stakeholder over the Status Quo**

earlier, a veto over any policy adopted in Iran. Thus, the shaded area depicts a range of compromises that could be worked out with Iran. This shaded area is known as a **win set** to indicate that it is a set of policies that can win relative to the point of comparison, in this case, the status quo. If you look closely at Figure 2.8, you will see that there is a second, politically interesting overlap in positions that (while not winning) indicates a possible compromise between the United States and Iran's president Ahmadinejad. This nonwinning set of policy preferences does not include a majority of power and it also excludes Khameini, who has a policy veto.

The win set supports a much more cooperative approach toward Iran than the status quo coupled with tolerating modest nuclear research pursuits beyond the development of a civilian nuclear energy industry. It tilts slightly to the right, indicating that the Egyptians, Russians, and Saudis would accept some Iranian nuclear research beyond that required for a civilian energy industry provided that Khameini and Ahmadinejad agreed to go no further than doing research on weapons-grade fuel. The win set indicates that these Iranian leaders would

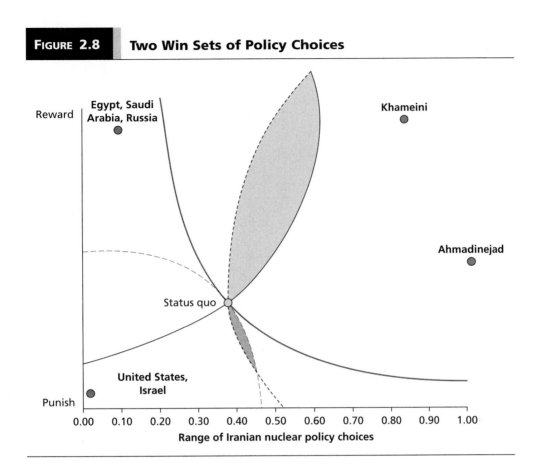

FIGURE 2.8 | **Two Win Sets of Policy Choices**

agree to this arrangement—this is what it means to say that they are in the win set and so are better off with this deal than with the existing status quo. This win set does not include the United States, suggesting that a resolution is possible outside of the UN Security Council framework; the win set could not be approved within the Security Council because the United States has a veto in that context.

The overlap between the preferences held by Ahmadinejad and the United States seen in Figure 2.8 can help us think more expansively about shaping improved policy outcomes. This region of overlapping interests implies that there is a feasible private deal available between Presidents Obama and Ahmadinejad. That compromise arrangement could relocate the status quo to a future position in which the United States would, say, resume normal diplomatic contacts with Iran (contacts that have been suspended since Iran held U.S. diplomats and embassy staff hostage in 1979) while still holding out for elimination of Iran's nuclear program in exchange for Ahmadinejad agreeing to advocate within Iran's leadership circle that his government limit its nuclear program only to include research on peaceful uses of nuclear energy. Such a compromise between the United States and Ahmadinejad, by shifting the status quo up and to the right a bit, would create a new win set that includes Russia, Saudi Arabia, Egypt, the United States, Ahmadinejad and, crucially, Khameini. Thus, the proposed private agreement between Ahmadinejad and the United States government would create the possibility of a broadly endorsed winning arrangement involving very limited Iranian research on weapons grade fuel in exchange for normalized relations with the government of the United States.

The win set analysis shows us how linking issues can sometimes break an impasse and produce multiple compromise solutions to a policy problem. It shows us something else as well. You may have wondered why it makes sense to look at these two dimensions or two issues linked together in a single graph. Why not just find the median voter on each and declare the two median voter positions to be the likely resolution of the two questions: How far should Iran go in developing its nuclear capacity, and how far should the international community go in rewarding Iran for better behavior or punishing Iran for pursuit of its nuclear ambitions? Figure 2.9 shows us the implications of such a simple approach. Figure 2.9 replicates Figure 2.8, adding one element. The gray dot above and to the left of the large win set shows the location of the median voter (based on power) on each issue dimension. On the nuclear dimension, as we know, the median is in favor of Iran's developing a nuclear energy industry; on the international reward/punishment dimension, the median position favors much more cooperation with Iran, rewarding it as the means to induce good behavior. These two median positions lie outside of the win set, and so they fail to be an improvement over the status quo in the eyes of stakeholders with sufficient power to supplant the status quo. That is, the compromise represented by the two median positions could not be implemented or relied on as credible policy commitments by either Ahmadinejad or the United States. It is a deal that Khameini and the Egyptian-Russian-Saudi bloc could accept, but these two sets of actors together do not include the elected Iranian government and so preclude reaching a credible and sustainable agreement.

This provides an important lesson. The median voter theorem is true under the conditions that it assumes. Those conditions include the restriction that issues are resolved one at a time, that is, that issues are unidimensional and fully separable—that they are not linked. Figures 2.5–2.8 illustrate what happens when issues are linked so that we cannot resolve one without also resolving the other. Many outcomes become possible, and the median voter position may or may not be among the policies that defeat the reference point (in this case, the status quo). It is important to remember that assumptions matter and that different predicted issue resolutions follow from different assumptions. If the two issues are kept separate, Iran will extract much more cooperation from the international environment, and it will build a civilian nuclear energy industry. If the issues are linked, it is possible to get Iran to trade away some of its nuclear ambitions for greater international cooperation and respect; the size of that trade-off will depend crucially on whether the United States can veto cooperation with Iran. If The United States cannot do this, then the large win set is likely to

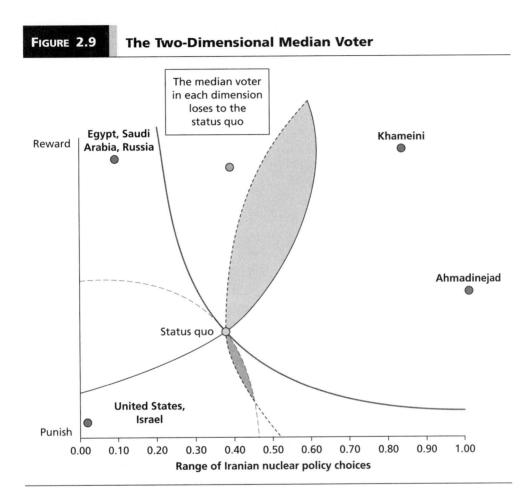

FIGURE 2.9 **The Two-Dimensional Median Voter**

The median voter in each dimension loses to the status quo

Reward

Egypt, Saudi Arabia, Russia

Khameini

Ahmadinejad

Status quo

United States, Israel

Punish

0.00 0.10 0.20 0.30 0.40 0.50 0.60 0.70 0.80 0.90 1.00

Range of Iranian nuclear policy choices

prevail. If the United States, through its leverage in the UN Security Council or through its foreign aid to Egypt and its security understandings with Saudi Arabia, can veto their reaching a separate agreement with Iran, then the feasible path to a successful compromise is for the United States and Ahmadinejad to make a private deal. So, knowing who has a veto and who does not can be critical, and for linked issues, knowing what the median voter position is may not be crucial.

In the spatial analysis, the attractiveness of different possible policy outcomes is dictated by their proximity to each stakeholder's most desired result. This notion certainly helped us sort out choices, but it did not provide much insight into the strategies that participants could adopt that might lead to one coalition forming as opposed to another. And it gave us no way to gauge the risks as well as the costs and benefits of alternative ways of solving the issue. Instead, spatial models provide just one way to pursue goals—form coalitions with like-minded actors to shape the policy outcome. Cooperating with others is certainly a useful approach to achieving objectives, but it is not the only approach. Sometimes issues get resolved by using coercion as well as cooperation. Certainly, the nuclear dispute between the United States and Iran is a candidate for either cooperation or coercion.

TRY THIS

Construct an example with two issues and three players in which two of the three players can improve how well they do by linking choices together on the two issues rather than solving them one at a time. Then construct an example with two issues and three players for which linkage appears unlikely.

When disagreements appear to be highly susceptible to cooperative outcomes—as is surely true for disagreements within the European Union or between the United States and Great Britain, for example—then one-dimensional and multidimensional spatial models are powerful tools that can be helpfully applied.

Of course, even in a fairly cooperative setting, we must be attentive to whether issues are to be negotiated one at a time, whether they are naturally linked, or whether some decision makers have an interest in linking them even if doing so does not seem natural. That is how we can sort out whether a one-dimensional or multidimensional analysis is more appropriate.

EXPECTED UTILITY

What are some of the key factors that enter into foreign policy decisions such as the ones confronting the United States and Iran over Iranian nuclear capacity? When making foreign policy decisions, policymakers typically assess the **probability,**[**] the likelihood that an outcome will arise, of policy success or failure given different approaches to a problem, and they estimate the expected **costs** (the losses in utility resulting from spending resources or forgoing opportunities to make different choices) and **benefits** (the gains in utility from the outcome of a decision) associated with different approaches. They do not do so by writing down equations as we will do here, but they act as if that is what they do. In fact, there is a substantial track record of evidence that suggests that we can predict the choices that real policymakers make on the basis of the equations and tools discussed here (Feder 1995, 2002; Ray and Russett 1996; McGurn 1996). Even more important, the evidence supports the idea that, by writing down and solving the equations that represent, in simplified form, what real decision makers contemplate, we can also use the power of the computer to improve on their decisions. We can help engineer better choices that lead to better results because with explicit calculations and computer memory we can keep track of many more players and their likely responses to alternative actions than decision makers can by themselves.

_____

[**] Taking all possible outcomes into account, the sum of the probabilities associated with each of the outcomes must be 1.

Consider, for instance, that for a problem involving just five decision makers (say, President Bush, Russia's President Putin, Iran's President Ahmadinejad, Supreme Leader Ali Khameini, and Iran's Supreme Council) there are 120 different possible conversations and exchanges of ideas that can take place each and every time these stakeholders have an opportunity to interact. We arrive at that figure by solving the factorial: $5! = 5 \times 4 \times 3 \times 2 \times 1 = 120.$[††] Bush can send proposals or signals, such as economic sanctions, to be interpreted and responded to directly by Putin, Ahmadinejad, Khameini, and the Supreme Council. Just as he can send messages to these stakeholders, so too can each of them send messages. These messages can be nuanced. For instance, instead of asking Prime Minister (formerly President) Putin to support American policy, President Bush (or now President Obama) might ask him to help convince Ahmadinejad, Khameini, and the Supreme Council to be more responsive to American concerns. And each of the other players can use his or its good relations with another stakeholder to ask that stakeholder to convey ideas to others, and so forth, leading to a possible 120 pathways of interaction among these five stakeholders. Some of these pathways involve direct exchanges, some involve third-party missions, and still others involve what in diplomacy is called a back channel. There are many ways to get a message across to the other side.

Typical real-world decision makers simplify their lives by focusing on not much more than five or six key decision makers because that is about all that they can keep track of in their heads. But many problems involve many more participants than five or six. Bush, for instance, seeks inputs into solving the Iranian nuclear issue from Putin and tries to persuade Khameini, Ahmadinejad, and the Supreme Council, but Bush also listens to the approaches suggested by his secretary of state and secretary of defense, Iran experts in various parts of the government, Egyptian President Hosni Mubarak, the Israeli prime minister, and on and on. Recall that the experts I consulted identified more than eighty decision makers and interested parties whose inputs they felt vitally influence the course of events between the United States and Iran. But imagine that the number was far fewer than that. If we just double the number of important decision makers from five to ten, we have already increased the possible paths of exchange from $5!$ $(= 120)$ to $10!$. Doing this does not merely double the number of possible pathways. In fact, the number is not even merely 10 times or 100 times larger than $5!$; $10!$ equals 3,628,800 possible interactive pathways (Bush's making a proposal directly to Putin for him to accept or reject, Bush's asking Putin to pass on a proposal to Mubarak for Mubarak to endorse or oppose, Bush's asking Putin to ask Mubarak to pass a message to Khameini, and so forth). Decision makers have no prospect of keeping all of that straight by themselves, but the computer does not get tired or bored, and it does not forget. So, by writing down the equations that represent, in simplified form, what goes on in real people's heads, we have a prospect of accurately predicting their actions and possibly even seeing ways to improve on them.

[††] The symbol ! denotes factorial. The factorial is the product of the sequence of whole numbers from 1 to the specified number.

To achieve accurate assessments and to create useful ideas about helping engineer better decisions, we need to find a way to make use of the core components of any decision: probabilities, costs, and benefits. One way of doing this that seems to enjoy considerable success is to combine this information into estimates of the expected utilities associated with alternative ways of pursuing goals. **Expected utility** calculations look at the different consequences, in terms of benefits minus costs, that can arise from a specified action; multiply each possible consequence by the probability that it will arise; and then add up these quantities across all the various consequences that have a chance of occurring given the chosen action. The resulting value is the expected utility of the action, a value that can be calculated before the action is taken and that can be compared to the expected utility of alternative actions that could be chosen so that the decision maker can pick the one that yields the greatest expected net gain. Let's see what this means in concrete terms.

Computing Expected Utilities

In our discussion of win sets, we considered how much different decision makers might value reward or punishment as an approach toward Iran, linking reward or punishment to the policy adopted on nuclear development. Now let us explore reward and punishment as strategies rather than as a positive or negative value to be given to Iran in response to its nuclear undertakings. We know that there are at least three strategies being considered by the U.S. government in its approach to Iran: (1) impose severe economic sanctions on Iran unless Iran abandons its nuclear pursuits, (2) use military force to destroy Iran's nuclear research facilities, and (3) negotiate with Iran to find a compromise resolution acceptable to all key decision makers (as, for example, we tried to do with win sets). The imposition of mild sanctions has been approved by the United Nations, and stiffer sanctions have been put into place by the United States. Sanctions, then, constitute part of the current status quo approach to Iran. Thus far, sanctions do not seem to have prompted a break in the impasse between the U.S. and Iranian governments. With that in mind, I focus first on the alternative approaches, and I then look at all three strategies simultaneously.

The United States might propose a compromise with Iran. For instance, it might offer to persuade the international community to agree to Iran's development of a civilian nuclear energy industry with suitable safeguards to ensure that Iran does not go beyond civilian energy uses of nuclear fuel. This would be a significant departure from the current American position in favor of no nuclear capability for Iran. If the Iranian government agreed to such a compromise (which allows them to do just what they say they intend to do), it would represent a major concession by those leaders who privately favor the development of an Iranian nuclear weapon.

We can use estimates of probabilities, costs, and benefits to identify the conditions under which such a compromise or some other compromise would prove acceptable to the United States and to Iran. Recall that we identified an issue continuum with the U.S. government located at position 0 and Iran's President Ahmadinejad at 1.00 (see Figure 2.2). As an alternative to offering a compromise deal, the United States might use military force to impose its will on Iran. Here are three possible outcomes of the Iran nuclear issue:

1. Iran abandons its nuclear program.
2. Iran and the United States agree on a compromise (such as nuclear development in Iran limited to the construction of a civilian nuclear energy industry; we will see what range of compromises is feasible).
3. Iran builds and tests a nuclear weapon.

We know from the assumption of single-peaked preferences that the U.S. government prefers outcome 1 to outcome 2 and prefers outcome 2 to outcome 3. Ahmadinejad's preference is exactly the opposite—3 is better than 2 and 2 is better than 1.

Let us place values on these three possible outcomes. Earlier, I talked about placing a measure of intensity of preference on such orderings as these—**utility.** Utility values have several important characteristics. Their actual numerical value is not important because they can be placed on any scale as long as their relative magnitudes do not change as a consequence of a linear transformation of values (such as adding a constant or multiplying by a constant). What is important about utility numbers is their relative values. Even whether the scale is all positive, all negative, or varies between positive and negative numbers does not matter. It is not possible to interpret a single utility value. The utility value becomes meaningful only when it is compared to another utility for a different outcome (or to the same outcome with a different strategy for achieving it) for the same stakeholder. Also, utilities cannot be meaningfully compared across stakeholders. My utility for some policy X might be 0.7, and yours might be 70. Because we do not know whether you define your utilities on the same scale that I do, we do not know whether 0.7 is bigger than, less than, or equal to 70. After all, I can transform 0.7 without changing its meaning for me by multiplying all of my utilities by 100 or by 10,000 or by whatever number I like. I have not changed how much I like policy X by doing so; I have just changed the scale on which I have defined my utility values, my measure of intensity of preference.

What we want to know from utility scores is how much more a person likes one outcome compared to another. A numeric value can be used to reflect the relative strength of a preference. Often, for computational reasons, it is convenient to attribute a utility value of 1 to a stakeholder's most desired outcome and a utility value of 0 to its least preferred outcome. Then all outcomes that are better than the worst outcome and that are inferior to the best outcome from a stakeholder's point of view have utility values that are greater than 0 and less than 1. Of course, how much better or worse they are than an alternative outcome depends on how close to or far from that outcome they are and on the rate at which the utility function declines as we move farther and farther from a decision maker's ideal point.

How quickly or slowly utility values decline determines how willingly a decision maker will gamble on a sure thing compared to a risky or probabilistic outcome. For instance, we are interested in how willing the U.S. government is and also how willing Ahmadinejad is to gamble on the consequences of a U.S. attack against Iran's nuclear facilities compared to a compromise that each side could have for sure. How willing each side is to gamble on a military attack depends on how attractive the sure thing is—that is, how much utility each attaches to the compromise—and on how high the probability of success or failure is through a military attack. I return to this idea of **risk taking** after working out the range of feasible compromises under the assumption of risk-neutral decision making. A **risk-neutral** decision maker is indifferent between a sure thing and a risky gamble if the expected value (the sum of the product of probable outcomes times the worth of each of those outcomes) of the gamble, known as a lottery, and the utility of the sure outcome are equal.

Let us say the U.S. government's utility for Iran's having no nuclear capability (position 0 on the scale) is 1. I denote this as $U_{US}(0) = 1$, where the value in parentheses denotes the U.S. position on the policy preference scale in Figure 2.2. The U.S. government's utility for position 1.00 on the scale, in which Iran builds and tests a nuclear weapon, is 0 and can be written as $U_{US}(1.00) = 0$. Let us pick a policy compromise that the United States or Iran's Ahmadinejad might propose, but for now let us not be specific about the exact content of that compromise or its exact location on the policy scale. Instead, we use some simple calculations to identify a range of compromises that both the U.S. government and Ahmadinejad could agree to. And because no Iranian leader's position is more extreme than Ahmadinejad's, we can be pretty confident that a deal he would accept would also be acceptable to the rest of the Iranian leadership. Let us call the compromise position X, knowing that $0 < U_{US}(X) < 1$. And let us stipulate, consistent with the U.S. preference for an outcome closer to 0 rather than farther from it, that $U_{US}(X) = 1 - X$; that is, the U.S. derives 0 utility if X, the proposed compromise, is at position 1.00 on the policy scale, the United States gains maximal benefit (utility = 1) if the compromise X is located at 0 on the policy scale, and the closer the proposed compromise is to 0 the more utility it brings to the United States. Conversely, Ahmadinejad's utility from some compromise position X can be thought of simply as $U_{Iran}(X) = X$. This means that the closer X is to position 1 on the issue dimension, the more utility Ahmadinejad derives from X.

Suppose the United States chose to use military force to impose its will on Iran instead of seeking a compromise solution. If the United States prevailed, it would eliminate Iran's nuclear potential, and so the United States would derive the utility associated with getting what it wants, $U_{US}(0) = 1$, but it would also pay some costs in terms of lost lives, the financial costs of an attack, and perhaps international and domestic political costs associated with initiating aggression against Iran. Let us stipulate that the costs of fighting equals some quantity k. Of course, attacking Iran does not guarantee the elimination of its nuclear capability. An attack might fail, might be defeated, and might prompt an acceleration of Iran's nuclear undertakings, resulting in that country's developing and testing a nuclear bomb. Such an outcome implies the worst result for the United States. Under that scenario, the U.S. utility for attacking and failing is equivalent to that of Ahmadinejad's nuclear ambitions prevailing; and so U.S. utility would be $U_{US}(1.00) = 0$ and the cost k would still have been paid in the unsuccessful use of force. So, if the United States launches a military strike and prevails, its net gain (benefits minus costs) is $1 - k$, and if it attacks and fails, its net gain is $0 - k$, or simply $-k$.

Probability

We know what the value for success or failure would be for the United States, but what the United States can expect to derive from a military strike depends on whether that action succeeds or not. We can say that there is some probability that the United States would prevail if it used force, and there is some probability it would lose. Probabilities always fall between 0 and 1 by definition. What is more, if we list all of the possible outcomes (such as persuading Iran to abandon its nuclear pursuits and failing to alter Iran's efforts on the nuclear front, keeping our example simple enough to involve only two possible outcomes) that could arise given a particular action (such as using military force), then the sum of the probabilities associated with that action must equal 1. That means that we are certain that one of the outcomes must occur, although we do not know which one. That is why the action is risky. As a convenient space-saving device, let us say that the value p represents the probability of U.S. success in getting Iran to abandon its nuclear program in response to a military strike against its known nuclear facilities. Then $1 - p$ represents the probability that an attack fails and that Ahmadinejad gets his way so that Iran develops and tests a nuclear weapon. Notice that we are assuming that one of these outcomes must arise following a military attack against Iran's nuclear facilities. We can see that this is so because $p + (1 - p) = 1$, leaving no room in this simple analysis for any other outcome.

Combining Probability, Costs, and Benefits

Before deciding whether to launch a military strike against Iran, American decision makers presumably would evaluate the likely consequences of their action. Such an evaluation can be made by using the notion of expected utility. Expected utility calculations consider the utility, or intensity of preference, associated with alternative outcomes and weights those utilities by the probability that each will arise. Expected utility estimates allow leaders, in essence, to make calculated risks. By assessing the alternative consequences that might arise from a course of action, decision makers can compare the expected costs and benefits of those consequences with the expected costs and benefits associated with alternative courses of action. Because costs and benefits are multiplied by their probability of occurring, the resulting value equals a stakeholder's best guess as to how much it values right now what it will end up with by pursuing this or that course of action. In our example, this is equivalent to the following expected utility calculation, with the U.S. expected utility from striking Iran's nuclear facilities denoted as EU(U.S.|Strike):[‡‡]

[‡‡] The symbol | is read "given."

$$EU(\text{U.S.}|\text{Strike}) = p(U_{US}(0) - k) + (1 - p)(U_{US}(1.00) - k).$$

That is, the U.S. expected utility given that it strikes Iran's nuclear facilities is equal to the probability that the United States prevails times the benefit of prevailing minus the costs of the strike plus the probability that the strike fails times the utility of a failed outcome minus the costs of the strike. Substituting the utility values 1 and 0 for the two outcomes, we can rewrite this expression as:

$$EU(\text{U.S.}|\text{Strike}) = p(1 - k) + (1 - p)(0 - k).$$

Expanding this expression and then simplifying gives:

$$EU(\text{U.S.}|\text{Strike}) = p - pk - k + pk = p - k.$$

Rational decision makers choose among actions based on what they believe will yield the best results. That means that they must be able to connect alternative outcomes by a relation of preference (I like outcome X better than Y or I like Y better than X or I am indifferent between X and Y), their preferences must be transitive (if X > Y and Y > Z, then X > Z, as noted earlier), and they act on their preferences while also taking their beliefs or perceptions about probabilities and other constraints into account. Ignoring for the moment Ahmadinejad's calculations, we can see that the choice of a rational American policymaker between attacking and offering a compromise will depend on the utility to the United States of the compromise and the utility expected from attacking. Recall that the utility for the United States of a compromise at position X on the policy scale is equal to $U_{US}(X) = 1 - X$ and that the United States will accept a compromise if its expected net benefit from a compromise $(1 - X)$ is at least as large as the expected utility from attacking.

The United States should compromise if $1 - X \geq p - k$; remember that the closer the proposal X is to 0 (the smaller X is), the better it is for the United States. If $1 - X < p - k$, then the United States expects to be better off by attacking.[§§] Rearranging terms to isolate the magnitude of position X that will prompt the U.S. pursuit of a compromise settlement, we see that the United States prefers a compromise to an attack provided that:

$$1 - p + k \geq X.$$

Here we can see that the simple expected utility calculation has given us a way to predict American action. We see that a compromise proposal X can be chosen to ensure that the United States prefers the compromise to attacking. For instance, Ahmadinejad could put a

---

[§§] I have assumed that if the value of attacking and the value of a compromise were equal, then the United States would choose to avoid any uncertainty about the size of war costs by offering a compromise.

compromise on the table that takes into account his subjective belief about the probability that Iran would prevail $(1 - p)$ or that the United States would win (p) if the United States chose to attack Iran's nuclear facilities and that also takes into account his best judgment as to the costs Iran could inflict on the United States as a consequence of such an attack (k). The larger the costs, the smaller the compromise he would need to offer, so as k increases, the location of the compromise, position X, can be closer to Ahmadinejad's preferred outcome of 1.00 on the policy scale. Conversely, the greater the American prospect of success in an attack (p), the larger the compromise he would need to put forward to get the United States to choose it over attacking; that is, the closer X must be to 0.

For example, suppose the U.S. probability of success is 0.75 and the expected cost of a military strike (k) is 0.20. Then the U.S. expected utility from the use of military force is 0.75 $(1 - 0.20) + (0.25)(0 - 0.20)$, which equals 0.55. To decide not to attack in this case, a compromise would have to be worth at least 0.55 to the United States. Because the U.S. utility is equal to $1 - X$, that means that the compromise would have to be at position 0.45 or less on the policy scale for the United States to select compromise over attack.

We can see how the policy compromise that would be acceptable to the United States changes as the probability of success changes or as the expected costs associated with an attack change. Suppose the U.S. chance of success is 0.50 instead of 0.75. Then the expected utility from a military strike is $(0.50)(1 - 0.20) + (0.50)(0 - 0.20) = 0.30$, and so in this case the U.S. would take a deal at position 0.70 on the policy scale rather than gamble on a military strike. An outcome at position 0.70 on the scale is not nearly as good for the United States as the outcome at 0.45 in the previous example. If the probability of victory is 0.75, the United States would reject a compromise at, say, 0.50 on the policy scale, but that is a compromise the United States would accept if it thought the chances for success with a military strike were only 0.50, holding the costs constant at 0.20.

But what if the costs were expected to be much higher? Suppose the United States believes its chances for success with a military strike is 0.75 but that success will come at a high price, say, 0.80. Then the expected utility from the use of force is $(0.75)(1 - 0.80) + (0.25)(0 - 0.80) = -0.05$. In this case, no matter how bad an offered compromise is, because it must fall on the policy scale whose boundary utilities are 0 and 1, the United States would prefer any compromise over attacking. After all, the worst outcome for the United States has a utility of 0—that can be higher than the expected utility from an

> **TRY THIS**
>
> Find the probability of success at which the United States would be indifferent between compromising and attacking if the costs of an attack are expected to be 0.80 and the compromise available is known to be located at 0.2 on the scale. Do the calculation again if the compromise is known to be at 0.6 on the scale.

attack, as it is in this example. Even with a high probability of success, the United States would cave in to Ahmadinejad's position in this hypothetical last example because of the very high expected costs of fighting. We can see from these examples that the choice of actions of American political leaders is likely to be highly responsive to their perception of the chances of success and also of the anticipated costs associated with an attack.

Of course, it takes two parties to make a deal. What does Ahmadinejad's calculation look like? If the U.S. attacks, then with the same probability with which the United States succeeds, Iran loses from Ahmadinejad's point of view. If the United States prevails in an attack, Ahmadinejad's utility is 0 ($U_{Iran}(0) = 0$), and Iran will pay a cost which, to keep calculations simple, I denote again as k, that is, the same level of cost as the United States will pay. If the United States fails (with probability $1 - p$), then Ahmadinejad's utility is 1 ($U_{Iran}(1.00) = 1$), and Iran again pays the war cost of k. We can write the expected utility expression for Ahmadinejad if the United States attacks as:

$$EU(Ahmadinejad|U.S. \; Strike) = p(U_{Iran}(0) - k) + (1 - p)(U_{Iran}(1.00) - k)$$
$$= p(0 - k) + (1 - p)(1 - k) = 1 - p - k.$$

Ahmadinejad will agree to a proposed compromise at position X if:

$$X \geq 1 - p - k.$$

We now know that the United States will choose to compromise if $1 - p + k \geq X$ and that Ahmadinejad, and therefore Iran, will also opt for compromise provided that $X \geq 1 - p - k$. Figure 2.10a depicts the points on the policy scale at which the United States will accept or reject a compromise offer; Figure 2.10b does the same for Ahmadinejad and Iran. Finally, Figure 2.10c puts the two together, showing the range of outcomes at which each party will agree to compromise. We can see that a range of points in fact exists that would produce an agreement. We can also see that there are possible compromise offers that will be agreeable to one party but not to both; in these cases, an attack seems likely.

Beliefs about the relative size of the probabilities will certainly help influence the choices made by the Iranian leadership. Notice that I said *beliefs* about the relative size of each of these probabilities, not some objective determination of their true value. The true probability of success or failure under the various strategies we are discussing cannot be known in advance. This is because how Iran's leaders will respond depends on so many factors that we cannot know about them all. For example, are Iran's leaders the sort of people who respond better to rewards or to punishments? Are they prone to gambling on their country's future, or are they likely to be cautious when it comes to engaging the United States in a fight? Do they believe the American president cannot muster the domestic political support that would be needed to launch a military strike, making them think that the U.S. subjective probability of success, given political constraints, is low or that the threat just is not credible? Or do they believe that a lame-duck president would risk a strong negative domestic reaction or that a new president, with years to recover from the possible electoral consequences of an unpopular action, would act boldly (Gaubatz 1991; Fordham 1998, 2002; Smith 2004)?

FIGURE 2.10 Compromises Acceptable or Unacceptable to the United States

(a)   U.S. government accepts compromise X if and only if $X \geq 1-p+k$

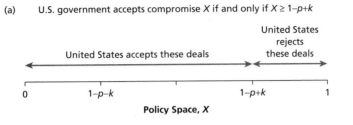

Compromises Acceptable or Unacceptable to Ahmadinejad in Iran

(b)   Iran/Ahmadinejad accepts compromise X if and only if $X \geq 1-p-k$

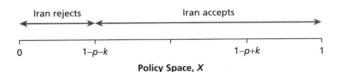

Compromises Acceptable or Unacceptable to the United States and Ahmadinejad in Iran

(c)

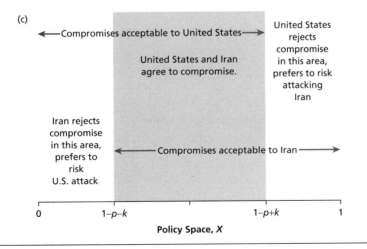

Compromises acceptable to both are in the gray area.

The reason there is a debate over how best to approach Iran is that different decision makers hold different views about the likely answers to these questions. No one knows for sure how Iran's leaders or the American electorate will respond, perhaps not even those who must make the decisions. It is one thing to say that you will or will not back down under pressure, and it is quite another to face the actual pressure and then have to choose what to do. Although relative power or influence may help shape probabilities, probabilities are subjective, and therefore their estimation reflects prior beliefs or perceptions about people and circumstances. Those whose life experiences, for instance, have taught them that people respond more positively to avoiding costs than to gaining benefits will be likely to believe that Iran's leaders will respond to coercive pressure, whether through sanctions or military force (Kahneman and Tversky 1984, 1986). Conversely, those who have observed that "you catch more flies with honey than with vinegar" will want to extend a cooperative hand to the Iranian leadership in the hope and expectation that this will induce them to reassess their nuclear program and agree to cooperate as well. Or, put differently, what a U.S. president thinks the chances of success are may be entirely different from what Iran's president thinks the U.S. chances are.

Whichever action is chosen—compromise or military force—we can be confident that the choice will be made after carefully thinking about the odds of success, the value of success and failure, and the costs of any action. Indeed, you can make just such estimates yourself, and that way you can be your own intelligence agency. The precise values for which compromise is feasible are not known, but you might try approximating these values based on, for example, the relative military might of the two countries or of each country plus its allies, or the relative size of their economies or government tax revenues or some other indicator that you believe accurately reflects the odds of victory and the factors that impact costs in lives, property, and political fallout. With such estimates, you could specify an exact range of feasible settlements and then see how your calculations match up with each side's rhetoric.***

RISK TAKING AND EXPECTED UTILITY

What does it mean to say that a given leader or government will risk war or will prefer to avoid war and take a negotiated compromise instead? Later we explore questions of war and peace in much more detail, but for now, let us just try to answer this question by reflecting on the idea of risk taking. In Figure 2.10, we looked at the utility for each possible outcome on the policy scale as simply equal to $1 - X$ for the United States and as X for Ahmadinejad. This is equivalent to treating utilities as increasing in a linear fashion the closer an outcome gets to a decision maker's ideal point. The concept of utility as a measure of intensity of preference, however, does not require that utilities change in this linear fashion. Given the

---

*** Data on relative military capabilities can be found on the Correlates of War Project Web site (www.corelatesofwar.org) and at the EUGene Web site (www.eugenesoftware.org). Gross national product (GNP) data can be found at the Web site for Penn World Tables (http://pwt.econ.upenn.edu/) and the World Bank (http://web.worldbank.org/WBSITE/EXTERNAL/DATASTATISTICS/0,menuPK:232599~pagePK:64133170~piPK:64133498~theSitePK:239419,00.html), where you can also find data on government tax revenues and many other indicators.

TABLE 2.1	Ahmadinejad's Utility for Different Policy Outcomes: Three Alternative Utility Functions		
Position on scale: X	$U_{Iran}(X) = X^2$	$U_{Iran}(X) = X$	$U_{Iran}(X) = X^{1/2}$
0 (abandon nuclear program)	0.00	0.00	0.00
0.20	0.04	0.20	0.45
0.40	0.16	0.40	0.63
0.60	0.36	0.60	0.77
0.80	0.64	0.80	0.89
1.00 (test nuclear weapon)	1.00	1.00	1.00

restriction of single-peaked preferences, our use of utility does require that a decision maker's utility decrease as some policy position X gets farther from the stakeholder's ideal point. We have defined utility in our calculations as $1 -$ (Distance from the player's ideal point). Many different functions, however, meet the single-peaked condition we have imposed. Suppose, for instance, that the utility function for Ahmadinejad is $U_{Iran}(X) = X^2$ or $U_{Iran}(X) = X^{1/2}$ or some other steadily increasing or decreasing function. Let us consider what these different utility functions imply about utilities for different positions between 0 and 1 on the policy scale and for decisions about risky lotteries compared to taking a sure-thing outcome. Table 2.1 shows Ahmadinejad's utilities for selected positions on the policy scale under different assumptions about the shape of his utility function.

Table 2.1 helps us see two important points. First, each of the utility functions illustrated here meets the single-peaked assumption in that the intensity of preference is declining steadily as we move farther from Ahmadinejad's ideal point (located at position 1.00). Second, the rate at which his utility declines depends on the function we assume or estimate for him. This second point allows us to address how willing he is to take risks, with that willingness reflected in the shape of his utility function. Figure 2.11 plots Ahmadinejad's utility relative to policy positions based on the three utility functions represented in Table 2.1.

Suppose the U.S. government offered a compromise at position 0.40 on the policy scale. That is about equal to agreement to tolerate Iran's development of a civilian nuclear energy industry. Let us suppose that Ahmadinejad is confident that Iran's military has a fifty-fifty chance of thwarting an American attack. He could easily be this confident if he reflected back on Jimmy Carter's effort in 1980 to use an air strike to rescue American diplomats being held hostage by Iranian students in the American embassy in Tehran. That air strike failed to reach its target; a sandstorm led to helicopter engine problems and to an aborted effort. Further, let us suppose that Ahmadinejad believes that the cost of such an attack would be equal to 0.10 (that is, equivalent by itself to a 10 percent premium in favor of a compromise). Then, for Ahmadinejad, gambling on an American attack has an expected utility of 0.5 $(0 - 0.1) + 0.5(1 - 0.1) = 0.40$. If his utility function is $U_{Iran}(X) = X^2$, then a compromise at

FIGURE 2.11	**Risk Taking: An Illustration**

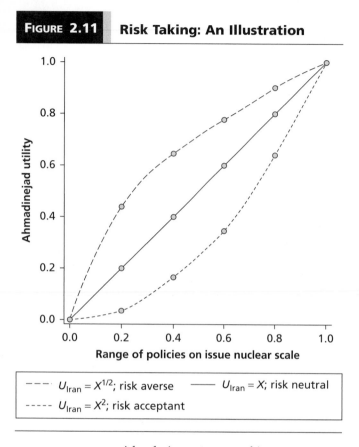

Range of policies on issue nuclear scale

- - - $U_{Iran} = X^{1/2}$; risk averse   ——— $U_{Iran} = X$; risk neutral
- - - - $U_{Iran} = X^2$; risk acceptant

position 0.40 on the policy scale is worth just 0.16 to him (see Table 2.1). He prefers to gamble on an air strike because the expected utility of the risky gamble is 0.40 and the sure-thing compromise has a utility of only 0.16. If, however, his utility function is $U_{Iran}(X) = X^{1/2}$, then the utility from the sure-thing compromise that allows Iran to pursue the development of a civilian nuclear energy industry is worth 0.63 to him (that is, 0.63 is the square root of 0.40), far more than what he expects to get out of chancing an American military attack. He will be indifferent between the sure-thing compromise and the gamble if his utility function is $U_{Iran}(X) = X$. In that case, both the risky lottery and the sure-thing compromise are valued at 0.40 and, given that we have assumed ties go to the sure thing, he will accept the compromise. So we can see that, depending on the shape of his utility function, Ahmadinejad might elect to take his chances or accept the compromise. In fact, we can say that, when his utility function looks like $U_{Iran}(X) = X^\alpha$ for any $\alpha > 1$, he is at least somewhat **risk acceptant**; that is, he favors a risky choice over a sure-thing outcome even when the sure thing and the risky choice would have the same exact expected value if $\alpha = 1$. Finally, we can say that, if $\alpha < 1$, the decision maker is **risk averse**; that is, he or she prefers to take the sure thing over the gamble even if the gamble would be just as attractive as the sure thing if $\alpha = 1$ (the risk-neutral value).

In economics, it is generally assumed that people are risk averse. This is probably a sensible assumption in that context. It means that the marginal return of the next added dollar or the next added utile (a unit of utility) is smaller than the previous dollar's value to the recipient. That is the same as assuming marginally decreasing returns in which each succeeding return is worth more than the previous return but at a decreasing rate. In international politics when we consider choices by national leaders, there is probably more variation in risk-proneness than is true in, for instance, studies of consumer behavior. People who rise to positions of national leadership take enormous risks to attain high office, and this is all the more true when they seek high office in nondemocratic societies. That does not necessarily mean that they are big risk takers; they might have optimistic views about their probability of success. Still, when we analyze international affairs, we probably should be open to the possibility that at least some decision makers are more risk acceptant (or less risk averse) than others, and so we should minimize the restrictions we impose on this aspect of utility functions.

SUMMARY

We have examined in this chapter decision making regarding Iran's nuclear program. In doing so, we have seen that the distribution of power and preferences can shape policy outcomes and that security can be conceived of in terms of proximity to the median voter position. This gives us a way to think about security-maximizing neorealist outlooks in a rigorous way that does not ignore the possibility that states have preferences about outcomes beyond their national security or power.

The median voter theorem provides a powerful tool for examining prospective foreign policy decisions when issues are one-dimensional. It is a less helpful tool when issues involve two or more linked dimensions or when two or more issues are inextricably linked together. In such cases, spatial models provide a way to think about how issues might be resolved through coalition formation. Win sets are a way to model the proximity of policy preferences among contending decision makers across dimensions. We have seen that the median voter position on each dimensions need not be in a win set, that is, be part of a winning coalition. A range of outcomes is possible. Thus, we have devised a way to predict the likely policy outcome when issues are treated separately and when they are linked together.

Finally, this chapter introduces expected utility calculations. By comparing the expected utility associated with alternative courses of action, we can predict which path a decision maker is likely to take. As we have seen, this depends not only on the value of this or that approach to a problem but also on the probability of various outcomes arising and on their costs and benefits. These are the fundamental building blocks of a strategic approach to international affairs.

KEY CONCEPTS

3 An Introduction to Game Theory

OVERVIEW

- Game theory is a powerful form of mathematics that allows us to estimate how stakeholders are likely to interact strategically in the arena of international and domestic politics. We look at two kinds of games: cooperative and noncooperative.

- We focus especially on noncooperative games because international interactions often mirror the conditions of such games. The prisoner's dilemma game demonstrates a type of interaction in which either the sequence of play is unknown or the players move simultaneously.

- Extensive form games are a way to represent noncooperative games. They allow us to highlight the sequence of action. By examining best choices that each player has at each step in the decision-making process, we can learn to solve these games and find out what is expected to happen. The tool we use to do that is called backward induction, which allows us to arrive at the subgame perfect Nash equilibrium.

Spatial models provide a powerful way to think about international problems, especially in regard to identifying policy agreements that are secure and may be stable. Spatial models, however, are static. They do not consider that players negotiate and engage in strategic behavior. It is very hard to know any player's true ideal point on issues. When issues are multidimensional, for example, as in Figure 2.6 in the previous chapter, stakeholders have an incentive to misrepresent their wishes, pretending to be more extreme than they may actually be. If you go back to Figure 2.8, you will see what I mean. Khameini, for example, takes a very extreme position relative to the status quo. His desires are apparently very far from the current conditions. By staking out an extreme position, he helps create a very large preferred-to set. This means that there are many more compromises he can agree to than if his presumed ideal point were closer to the status quo. By appearing extreme, he gives himself more bargaining leverage, more room to maneuver. Others may look at his position and consider that it may have been chosen by him to gain a strategic advantage. This suggests that his policy posture is not his sincere desire but, rather, has been determined endogenously, meaning it was chosen by him strategically, based on the logic of the situation, to influence how others negotiate with him.

Just as spatial models provide a helpful, but often incomplete, perspective on foreign affairs, so too do expected utility calculations by themselves. As intimated in the earlier discussion, we can say something about what the United States prefers to do—use military force or reach a compromise agreement—based on the utility that is expected to be derived from a military strike and based on the value of any given compromise, but the president of the United States alone cannot determine whether a given compromise is acceptable not only to him but also to the various key decision makers in Iran. Expected utility calculations by themselves provide a way for us to place values on different feasible outcomes, but they are insufficient to solve the pattern of strategic behavior that the various parties to a dispute are likely to adopt to influence the choices of others.

The best way to sort out strategic choices is neither just through the use of spatial models nor just by using a powerful decision theory tool such as expected utility calculations, although each of these

Iran's president Mahmoud Ahmadinejad has stated that his country has just as much right as any other to possess nuclear capabilities, especially to meet the country's energy needs. Others say that the government's actions speak louder than words, as in this image in which Ahmadinejad (left) welcomes Iraq's national security adviser Mowaffaq al-Rubaie (right) as Iran's chief nuclear negotiator Saeed Jalili looks on during an official meeting in Tehran in January 2009.

tools can help and each can play a part in analyzing strategic situations in a game theory context. **Game theory** is, I believe, the best available tool for working out how stakeholders are likely to interact strategically in the international and domestic politics arena; it is a form of mathematics designed specifically to sort out strategic interactions, and strategic interactions are the stuff of almost all international politics.

Game theory comes in two major forms: cooperative and noncooperative game theory. **Cooperative game theory** assumes that promises made between actors are binding, meaning they will be kept. Cooperative game theory is especially useful for working with problems in which no player has an incentive to renege on promises or in which contracts are assured of being enforced. This is, alas, not the reality for most international problems. **Noncooperative game theory** certainly allows the possibility that decision makers will cooperate with one another but only when it is in their self-interest to do so. In noncooperative games, promises are not inherently binding. The credibility of commitments depends on their being of sufficient value to stakeholders to be honored at the time that a choice must be made between honoring what the actor has said he or she will do or reneging on promises and doing something that is more beneficial. Thus, noncooperative games rivet our attention on player incentives (how are things of value going to be distributed as a function of strategic choices), including incentives to say one thing and do another (that is, bluff). So these games typically draw attention to the likely punishments for lying (the frank term for bluffing) and also sometimes for the ease or difficulty of working out whether a player cheated, made an honest mistake, or tried to do what that player said he or she would do (the problem of monitoring).

PRISONER'S DILEMMA: ILLUSTRATING A SIMPLE GAME

The distinction between cooperative and noncooperative game theory is easily illustrated by describing how rational actors interact in the situation known as the **prisoner's dilemma.** This classic two-player game is played out almost any night of the week on just about any television police show. The story is that two confederates in crime have been arrested. Each is held in a separate cell, with no communication between them. The police and the district attorney do not have enough evidence to convict both of them of the serious crime they allegedly committed. But the authorities do have enough evidence to convict them of a lesser offense. If the prisoners cooperate with one another and both remain silent, they will each be charged and convicted of the lesser crime. If they both confess, they will each receive a stiff sentence. However, if one confesses and the other does not, then the former will get off with only a light sentence (as part of a plea bargain), whereas the latter will be put away for a very long time.

Let's call the payoff that each prisoner receives when neither confesses (that is, when they cooperate with one another) the Reward (R) and the payoff that each receives if they both confess (that is, when they both defect) the Punishment (P). If one prisoner cooperates by remaining silent while the other defects by confessing, then we say that the cooperator gets the Sucker's Payoff (S) and the defector gets a payoff called the Temptation (T).

TABLE 3.1	**The Prisoner's Dilemma**	
	Player B cooperates	**Player B defects**
Player A cooperates	R, R	S, T
Player A defects	T, S	P, P

Note: T > R > P > S. P, Punishment; *R,* Reward; *S,* Sucker's Payoff; *T,* Temptation.

In the game of the prisoner's dilemma, T is worth more than R, which is worth more than P, which is worth more than S ($T > R > P > S$). Later, when we consider repeated play in the prisoner's dilemma, we will need an additional assumption; for now, I focus on just a single play of the game. Table 3.1 displays the possible outcomes of the prisoner's dilemma. Notice it does not specify the order of play. This is because, under the rules of the game, the players (A and B) each must make his or her choices without knowing what the other player's choice will be. (Remember, they are being held in separate cells with no communication possible.)

There is no dilemma if the game in Table 3.1 is cooperative. For example, if before being captured the two criminals have promised one another that, in the event they are caught, they will cooperate with one another and not with the police. Each has promised not to turn state's evidence against the other. The result is that each receives the payoff of R, a relatively light sentence. What if they have made this promise to one another but each criminal, A and B, doubts the sincerity of his or her colleague? After all, each knows that the district attorney is willing to let him or her plead to a lesser offense (worth $T > R$) for turning on his or her confederate if his or her confederate fails to confess as well. How do we solve the game under these conditions—when promises are not binding so that they matter only if they advance the player's individual interests?

The game can be solved by finding the Nash equilibrium. A **Nash equilibrium** is the set of strategies from which no player has a unilateral incentive to switch to some other strategy. A strategy is a complete plan of action for playing the game; that is, it reflects what each player will do, conditional on every possible move by the other player or players including moves that eventually do not get made. For example, the prisoner's dilemma when played once offers only two possible actions to each player: cooperate with your confederate in crime or defect. This leads to four possible combinations of action: (1) cooperate if you think the other player will cooperate, (2) cooperate if you think the other player will defect, (3) defect if you think the other player will cooperate, and (4) defect if you think the other player will defect.

The idea of a Nash equilibrium does not apply to cooperative game theory. In that version of game theory, players may have an incentive to switch strategies, but they are not permitted to once they promise not to. The idea of a Nash equilibrium was developed exactly for the purpose of finding a way to solve noncooperative games in which players can break their promises if that is best for them. This is fundamental because rational actors do what they believe is in their own best interests and they realize that all other players will act that way too. Rational actors do not do what they think is in the collective interest if they think that doing so will harm them relative to some other action they could choose. This is true in part because rational actors anticipate that no one will select a strategy that leaves that person worse off than he or she would have expected to be by choosing a different strategy. Collusion among players is, of course, possible but only if each of those colluding or cooperating expects to benefit from doing so at the time he or she decides to cooperate. In the end, after the game is over, especially when decisions must be made under uncertainty or when players must choose among risky actions, some player might be worse off than would have been true if he or she had acted differently. That does not matter. Play proceeds based on what decision makers know and believe at the time they choose and not with the 20-20 hindsight that comes from reevaluating choices after the fact, when it is too late. In the jargon of rational choice theory, people act **ex ante,** before they know the consequences, and not **ex post,** with hindsight.

To find the Nash equilibrium, player A (for example) can start by considering what the best move to make is if player B chooses to cooperate and what the best move is if B chooses to defect. By examining the payoff implications of B's potential choices, player A can determine which move will be most advantageous (although A cannot know what B will ultimately choose to do). Of course, A can also calculate from B's viewpoint, seeing what would be best for B if A cooperates or defects. In this way, both players can formulate their complete plan of action—their strategy—for the game provided they are right in assuming that the other player will do what he or she believes is best for him or her; that is, that the other player is rationally self-interested.

The prisoner's dilemma is an interesting way to look at problems of cooperation and conflict because it has a surprising implication. Notice that whatever choice A assumes that B makes, A is better off defecting than cooperating. If B cooperates, A will earn T by defecting and only R by cooperating. Because T is more valuable to A than R, it is in A's self-interest to defect. If A assumes that B will defect, then A earns P by defecting, which is not very good but still better than choosing to cooperate and thereby only earning S (the worst result). Thus, by defecting A is guaranteed either a stiff prison sentence (P) or a chance to get off with only a light sentence (T) and A avoids altogether the possibility of receiving a very long prison sentence (S).

The same logic holds for player B. Whichever action A chooses, B is better off defecting. Defection is each player's **dominant strategy.** It is dominant because defection produces the best result for the player compared to cooperating regardless of which choice the other player makes. This is true even if they promised beforehand that they would cooperate. This is precisely the limiting feature of cooperative game theory and the advantage of looking at problems through the lens of noncooperative games. When push comes to shove, decision makers are likely to do what they think is best for them even if it is different from what they promised they would do earlier on.

The source of the dilemma in the prisoner's dilemma follows from what happens when each player pursues his or her best interests. In consequence of that pursuit, each player ends up with the second-worst outcome (P), a stiff prison term. Had they been able to coordinate their choices and cooperate with one another, they could have guaranteed themselves a lighter sentence, the second-best outcome (R). By choosing rationally, they each suffer an outcome that is worse than what they would have gotten if they had cooperated. The trouble is that if either had cooperated in the hope that the other player would also cooperate, ensuring each a payoff of R, that cooperating player probably would be in for a rude awakening. The other player does not have an incentive to cooperate as well. Yes, it is true that if they both cooperate they are both better off than if neither cooperates, but the player who cheats on any promise to cooperate benefits from cheating ($T > R$) and so can be expected to exploit the good intentions of his or her confederate in crime. This type of outcome, in which players could have been better off if they could find a way to coordinate their choices, is said to be **Pareto inferior.** There is no rational change in action that leaves no one worse off. In contrast, in a **Pareto efficient** outcome, no player is made worse off and at least one player is made better off. Joint cooperation is Pareto efficient, but the players do not seem to have a rational path to get there because, no matter what the other player is expected to do, each finds that defecting dominates cooperating because it earns a bigger reward. This is the dilemma. If international politics frequently involves situations like this, then it seems that conflict rather than cooperation would prevail. This is, in fact, exactly the meaning of one of the most common assumptions about international affairs; namely that the international environment is anarchic.

The notion of anarchy is exactly equivalent to the idea that each nation (or leader) operates in a self-help environment in which there is no supranational authority that can enforce agreements between states. That is a pretty good description of the definition of noncooperative games. Anarchy implies that, as useful as the United Nations, the World Trade Organization, the International Court of Justice, and other such international institutions may be, they cannot guarantee that governments will follow through on their commitments if those governments conclude that doing so will do them more harm than some alternative course of action. (In a later chapter, we see what this implies about the design of international institutions.) In short, international interactions typically mirror the conditions of a noncooperative game, although often it is a game different from the prisoner's dilemma.

A Simple Iranian-U.S. Nuclear Game

The prisoner's dilemma is but one of an infinite variety of possible games. There are seventy-eight games just involving a choice between two actions for each of two players. These two by two games—and they are just the tip of the iceberg—provide a rich array of ways to think about international affairs, including such well-known games as Chicken, Stag Hunt, and

Battle of the Sexes, as well, of course, as the prisoner's dilemma. The prisoner's dilemma has a dominant strategy, but many other games do not. Some have **multiple equilibria,** which means that there are different ways to play the game. I will have more to say about that later when several of these other games will crop up from time to time in our examination of international politics. For now, I want to draw attention to noncooperative games that are presented not in a matrix form or, as it is sometimes referred to, **normal form** as in Table 3.1 but, rather, in what is called **extensive form.** Extensive form games highlight the sequence of play, whereas normal form games assume that the sequence of play is either unknown or that the players move simultaneously. Much of our examination of international relations depends on extensive form games.

Extensive form games follow a few basic structural rules. Laid out like a tree, an extensive form game consists of **choice nodes,** which are points in the game at which a player must choose an action. The choice nodes are linked to other choices (or to outcomes) via **branches.** Any number of branches (including an infinite number) can emerge from a choice node, but only one branch can lead into a choice node. That means that each of the branches extending out from a choice node leads to a different place in the game. That place is either another choice node or a **terminal node,** that is, a place where the game ends. This means that each specific path or sequence of possible actions in a game is unique. In this way, game theory reflects some of the ideas of **path dependence,** an argument sometimes made by historians or historically oriented students of international politics that suggests that the sequence of history is unique. Game theory provides one useful way to address this assumed uniqueness while preserving the idea that there are logical and predictable bases for how international affairs unfold.

Figures 3.1a and 3.1b depict an extensive form game in which the United States moves first, choosing either to propose a compromise to Iran or to initiate stiff economic sanctions to try to coerce Iran into giving up its nuclear program. If the United States elects to sanction Iran, then Ayatollah Khameini, Iran's key decision maker, with the assumed agreement of Ahmadinejad, Iran's elected president, either retaliates by diminishing American access to oil or backs down, acquiescing to the U.S. demand. If, however, the United States offers a compromise, then Khameini either agrees to the compromise proposal or he ignores it and pushes to accelerate Iran's nuclear weapons development. If he pushes Iran's nuclear program ahead,

TRY THIS

Look on the Web or elsewhere, and find out what the payoffs are in Stag Hunt, Battle of the Sexes, and Chicken. Do these games have a dominant strategy the way the prisoner's dilemma does? Can you see how a player in Battle of the Sexes can choose actions that will make the other player just as happy to choose one action as the other? Here's a hint: doing so is called a mixed strategy and is another Nash equilibrium for Battle of the Sexes. Perhaps you can work out yourself what that strategy looks like (pick a probability of choosing actions that makes the other player indifferent across his or her choices), or look up mixed strategies on the Web to work out what they look like.

FIGURE 3.1   **An Iranian-U.S. Strategic Interaction**

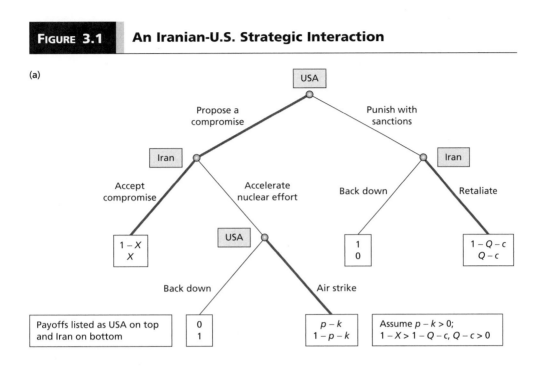

(a)

Payoffs listed as USA on top and Iran on bottom

Assume $p - k > 0$;
$1 - X > 1 - Q - c$, $Q - c > 0$

Alternative View of an Iranian-U.S. Strategic Interaction

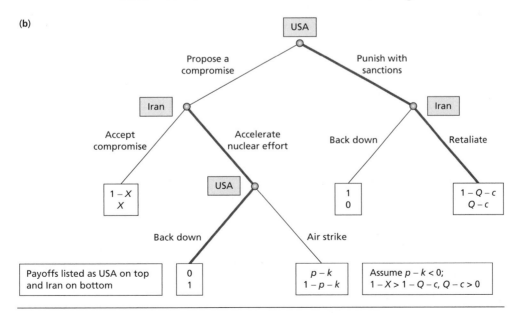

(b)

Payoffs listed as USA on top and Iran on bottom

Assume $p - k < 0$;
$1 - X > 1 - Q - c$, $Q - c > 0$

the United States responds either by imposing severe punishment, such as a military strike against Iran's nuclear facilities, or it backs down, acquiescing to the new status quo in which Iran develops weapons. This game reflects in simplified form the current debate over how best to approach Iran.

Some former candidates for the presidency, for example, Rudolph Giuliani, contended that they would never allow Iran to obtain a nuclear weapon; that efforts at diplomacy have gone on for four years without success, all the while with Iran moving ahead to enrich uranium; and that the United States must be prepared to bomb Iran to prevent that country from becoming a nuclear power. Others, for example, Barack Obama, argued during the 2008 campaign that this is a time to let diplomacy work rather than to engage in reckless threats of war, noting that Iran is still far from having a nuclear capability so that we have time to work out a negotiated settlement. Still others, for example, Hillary Rodham Clinton, supported senatorial action to declare Iran's Revolutionary Guard (the elite of its army) to be terrorists, thus paving the way for severe economic sanctions against that country.

Focusing on candidates for office for a moment allows us to see some important ways in which the game introduced here differs from and simplifies the real situation. One of those differences is extremely important and forms the nucleus of the strategic perspective used in this book—the positions staked out by presidential candidates surely partially reflect their sincerely held beliefs about the best way to deal with Iran, but we should not lose sight that their positions are also designed to appeal to voters. Candidates need backers to win office, and they are prone to saying what they think voters want to hear so that they can assemble a winning coalition. I put aside this important domestic consideration until later, but we should not forget that it is an important part of the game. I also put aside for later consideration how the Iran situation or other games play out when they are expected to be played repeatedly, not just once. Here, again for the sake of simplicity, we look only at a single-shot play of the Iranian-U.S. nuclear game.

To work out what the United States and Iran are expected to do, we must estimate the expected utility that each player attaches to each of the possible outcomes. There are five outcomes possible in this simple game:

1. The United States and Iran reach a negotiated compromise.
2. The United States backs down after Iran accelerates its nuclear effort.
3. The United States launches a military strike to punish Iran for accelerating its nuclear program.
4. Iran backs down in the face of costly economic sanctions imposed by the United States.
5. Iran retaliates with economic sanctions of its own to punish the United States for imposing sanctions on it.

We know from our expected utility analysis in Chapter 2 that the United States can offer a compromise that it values at $1 - X$ provided that X, the policy position of the compromise, is no greater than $1 - p + k$. Khameini's expected utility for a compromise agreement is equivalent to a utility of X as long as that position X is no lower on the policy scale than $1 - p - k$. That means that the United States would like to select a compromise worth the equivalent of $1 - p - k$, the best deal for the United States that is also the minimally acceptable deal for Khameini, compared to a decision to risk a military strike against Iran's nuclear facilities.

If Iran backs down after the United States institutes sanctions (outcome 4), then the United States gets the policy outcome it desires, but it pays a cost in forgone economic activity that results from its freeze on business with Iran. Let us say the cost of sanctions if Iran does not back down is c and that this cost is smaller than the cost of a military strike against Iran ($c < k$). The U.S. expected utility from launching sanctions if Iran chooses to back down is 1. Let us assume Iran also pays a cost c resulting from sanctions if it retaliates, so that the sanctions remain in force but Iran can escape the economic costs by backing down, although at the expense of giving up its nuclear ambitions. Then if Iran gives in to sanctions, its expected utility (that is, its expected payoff from backing down) is 0, its utility for giving in to the United States on nuclear policy. If, however, the United States sanctions Iran and the Iranian government launches retaliatory economic sanctions against the United States, then the outcome of prolonged sanctions for the United States is the continuation of Iran's current policy minus the cost of the sanctions. Let us stipulate that the status quo utility is $1 - Q$ for the United States and Q for Iran. Then retaliatory sanctions lead the United States to expect a payoff of $1 - Q - c$ and Khameini, on behalf of Iran, to expect $Q - c$. Although I have not yet explained how to solve the game, it should be evident that, if $0 > Q - c$ for Khameini, so he prefers to back down rather than retaliate, then the United States will certainly impose sanctions. This should be apparent because in that case Iran prefers to give in rather than resist and the United States gets its most preferred outcome cost-free—Iran's abandoning its efforts at nuclear weapons development. Therefore, to keep the problem realistic and interesting, I assume that, as is true of most economic sanction regimes, the sanctions will be resisted; this means that for Khameini $Q - c > 0$.

In the event that the United States offers a compromise and Iran still moves forward to develop a nuclear weapon, then the U.S. expected utility from launching a military strike is $p - k$; that is, $p(1 - k) + (1 - p)(0 - k) = p - k$. Khameini's expected utility following a U.S. military strike in punishment for his decision to accelerate Iran's nuclear program is $p(0 - k) + (1 - p)(1 - k) = 1 - p - k$. Finally, if the United States backs down on its demands after it learns that Iran has successfully accelerated its nuclear program, then the U.S. expected utility is 0. Iran in this circumstance gets the policy outcome that Khameini desires, so his expected payoff from successfully pursuing nuclear development and getting the United States to back down is 1.

SUBGAME PERFECTION AND BACKWARD INDUCTION

Returning to Figure 3.1a, how do we solve the game to predict what is expected to happen? We solve by backward induction to find the subgame perfect Nash equilibrium. These terms make it sound more complicated than it is. *Subgame perfection* means that at each choice node the player with a decision to make looks ahead and considers his or her options and the choices that other players will subsequently have in the game. At each choice node, the player chooses his or her best reply—his or her best move—given what he or she expects the other player or players will do from that point in the game onward. How the player got to the choice node, then, is not the critical consideration at that point. (Of course, the answer to how the players got to their current position in the game is that each player chose his or her best reply at each prior step in the game by calculating what will happen from that step forward down the tree to the terminal nodes, working out the choice each player will make from the terminal nodes back up to the top of the tree.) In this way, game theory differs from historical analyses that rely on path dependence. Although the game does identify the path of prior moves and countermoves and although that path is fundamental both in reality and in the game to understanding which choices must now be made and why certain choices were not made, in game theory it is what is expected to happen from this point forward that is critical to current choices, not how the players got to the current situation. This is akin to the economist's notion that sunk costs are sunk; they cannot be recovered, so the concern now is about what is expected to happen in the future.

For example, if the United States offers a compromise, Iran's supreme leader, Ali Khameini, arrives at a choice node in which he must decide to agree to the compromise or to accelerate Iran's nuclear program in pursuit of a nuclear weapon. To decide what to do, he must compare what he expects will happen if he compromises and if he accelerates his nuclear program. Although in the simple game in Figure 3.1a the United States does not have a further action to take if a compromise agreement is reached, it does have a further move to make if Iran is seen to have pushed forward to try to develop a nuclear weapon. Khameini chooses the action that he expects to give him the highest payoff, the greatest benefit at the smallest cost, conditional on what he thinks the U.S. response would be if he chooses to reject the compromise and instead pursues an accelerated nuclear program. For example, if Khameini believes the United States will back down (so that he believes for the United States $0 > p - k$, meaning that he believes the utility of the costs that the United States will bear from striking Iran, k, is larger than the U.S. chance of success, p), then he surely will accelerate his nuclear program rather than compromise (his payoff for accelerating the program if the United States backs down is 1 and for compromising is X; and $1 > X$). If, however, he expects that the United States will choose to strike Iran's nuclear facilities and wipe them out (he believes for the United States $p - k > 0$; that is, $k < p$), then his choice is either to agree to the proposed compromise worth X or endure a military strike against Iran with an expected utility of $1 - p - k$. If $X \geq 1 - p - k$, he will compromise.

We know from our earlier analysis that $X = (1 - p - k)$ is in the range of offers acceptable to both the United States and Iran and, in fact, is the best compromise the United States can hope to get. This means that it is likely, barring uncertainty about the size of p or of k, that the U.S. compromise offer meets the conditions required for acceptance. In short, what

Khameini will choose to do if the United States offers a compromise depends on what he believes the U.S. response will be if he accelerates Iran's nuclear program. To ensure that his response is part of a subgame perfect Nash equilibrium, he must choose his best reply given his expectations about subsequent U.S. actions. In this way, he ensures that he will not have a unilateral incentive to switch to a different strategy at each choice point in the game; likewise, the United States will choose on this basis, so it too will have no unilateral incentive to deviate from its strategy at any choice point in the game.

Subgame perfect Nash equilibrium is an important improvement over the basic Nash equilibrium concept. This is because, by looking ahead at the sequence of moves, subgame perfection eliminates any Nash equilibria that involve incredible commitments or incredible threats. For example, suppose Iran knows that the United States anticipates very high political as well as material costs from attacking Iran. Suppose it knows those costs are so high that for the United States $0 > p - k$. Then the United States might say it will attack Iran if Iran accelerates its nuclear program, but Iran knows this threat by the United States is not credible because it is not in the best interests of the United States to do so according to the U.S. expectation of payoffs (that is what it means to say that $0 > p - k$). Subgame perfection, by focusing on the best replies, dismisses this threat from the United States if, in fact, for the United States $0 > p - k$. The key is that while all subgame perfect Nash equilibria meet the definition of a Nash equilibrium, not all Nash equilibria are subgame perfect. Those that involve threats that are not credible cannot be sustained as equilibria when we consider subgame perfection.

Backward induction is the process we use to solve **complete and perfect information** extensive form games. These games tell us the sequence of moves, and this is important information in working out how best to play the game. Chess is a useful analogy here. Chess is a very complicated game. Nevertheless, it is a complete information game, which means that both players know the entire history of play—all the prior moves—in any chess game they are playing and that they know the expected payoff for each player at every terminal node of the game (that is what is meant by *perfect information*), in which, in the end, they either win, lose, or draw. The game in Figure 3.1a has exactly these same characteristics, although it is much simpler than chess. The United States knows any prior moves and, therefore, always knows which choice node it has arrived at; the same is true for Khameini. Therefore, both the United States (that is, its leaders) and Iran (that is, Khameini and his leadership team) have complete information. Also, the game assumes that each player has perfect information so that each player knows the payoff expected by him- or herself and by the other player at each terminal node of the game. The players know what each possible outcome is worth to them and to their rival. Perfect information, for instance, means that Khameini knows whether the United States expects that punishing Iran for accelerating its nuclear program is better or worse than backing down, so he knows whether the United States expects that $0 > p - k$ or $p - k > 0$. Just like chess, then, the key to playing the game well is to look ahead and think about what the other player will do in response to each and every move you can make, knowing that the other player will choose what he or she thinks is the best move now to structure the rest of the game as favorably as possible for him or her. To work this out, the easiest thing to do is to start by looking at each choice node that leads only to terminal nodes. That is, start at the bottom of the game tree and work out what choices will be made in the end, and then work your way up the tree, backward, to work out each best choice along the way after having already calculated what the consequences are of all choices closer to the end of the game.

We see, for example, that if the United States initiates stiff sanctions against Iran, then Khameini is at a choice node that leads only to terminal nodes. He has to choose to retaliate or to back down, giving up his nuclear program to escape further sanctions. If Iran retaliates, the game ends, and if Iran backs down, the game ends. So, Iran's choice at that point does not depend on what it thinks will happen afterward because there is no afterward. We see that if Iran retaliates, its expected payoff is $Q - c$, where Q represents the utility Iran attaches to its status quo nuclear policy. We know that this utility falls somewhere between the end points of the nuclear policy scale we are considering, so we know that $0 < Q < 1$. We also know that Iran's expected reward (or really punishment, in this case) if it backs down is the abandonment of its nuclear program. Then we can see that Khameini's choice is between a payoff of $Q - c$ or 0, and we can see that $Q - c > 0$ by assumption, so if the United States introduces stiff sanctions, Iran will retaliate.

Continuing with our backward induction—working from the bottom of the game up to the top—we can see that the United States has a choice node that also leads only to terminal nodes; that is, it leads to the end of the game. If the United States offers a compromise and if Iran rejects the offer, accelerating its nuclear development instead, then the United States will arrive at the choice node at which it must decide between backing down or striking Iran. As we have noted earlier, the United States will strike if $p - k > 0$ and it will back down if $0 > p - k$. For the moment, let us assume that $p - k > 0$. Later I will reverse this assumption to see what happens, and then I will introduce a way to solve the game if Iran is uncertain whether $p - k > 0$ or $0 > p - k$.

If $p - k > 0$ for the United States, then if it offers a compromise and Iran accelerates its nuclear program, the United States will attack. Notice that we have not said that the United States will attack Iran. What the United States is expected to do is contingent on whether the United States chooses to sanction Iran or to offer a compromise, and it also is contingent on what Iran chooses to do if the United States offers a compromise settlement. We are using backward induction to determine which contingencies will arise, and we are doing so exactly as in chess, by thinking ahead, "What if I do this?" or "What if I do that?" What we know is that the United States will attack if the contingencies play out, so the United States actually faces the choice of backing down or attacking.

OK, so far we know that Khameini will order retaliatory sanctions if the United States sanctions Iran and that the United States will attack if Iran accelerates its nuclear program in response to an offer of compromise by the United States, but if the United States offers a compromise, will Khameini accept the deal or will he use the opportunity to propel Iran's nuclear program forward? Now we can answer this question because we have worked out what will happen at every choice node from that point in the game forward to the terminal nodes. We know that if Iran accelerates its program, the United States will strike Iran's nuclear facilities. That tells us that Khameini gets a payoff of $1 - p - k$ if Iran accelerates its nuclear program. He cannot get the payoff of 1 associated with the United States backing down because that will not happen given the U.S. payoffs. If Khameini agrees to the compromise deal offered by the United States, the payoff is X. From our earlier analysis, we know that $X = 1 - p - k$. We have assumed that a tie in payoffs is broken in favor of the less risky, more peaceful solution—in this case, for Iran to accept the compromise. So now we know that if the United States sanctions Iran, Khameini will order retaliatory sanctions against the United States, resulting in a payoff to the United States of $1 - Q - c$. We also know that if the United States offers a compromise at policy position X on the policy choices scale, Iran will accept and the U.S. payoff will be $1 - X$. We are now at the first choice node of the game. The United States is deciding whether to sanction Iran or propose a compromise. U.S. decision makers have used backward induction to look ahead at what they expect will happen at each choice node, starting at the end of the game and working back to the beginning. They have assumed that Khameini will make his best move at each point in the game, looking ahead to the consequences of his alternative moves. The U.S. decision makers are at the beginning of the game now and are ready to act. They know what the consequences will be for each move they can make.

If $1 - X \geq 1 - Q - c$, the United States will propose a compromise. If $1 - Q - c > 1 - X$, the United States will institute economic sanctions against Iran. This reduces to a simple comparison, remembering that the larger X or Q is, the worse the policy is from the U.S. perspective (U.S. utility in each case is equal to $1 - X$ and $1 - Q$). Rearranging the terms, we can see that the choice comes down to a comparison of the trade-off between costs and policy results. If $c \geq X - Q$, that is, if the costs of sanctions are greater than the policy gain to be had through compromise compared to the current Iranian policy, then a compromise will be struck. If the compromise is closer to the desired U.S. position than is the status quo policy ($X < Q$), compromise will happen regardless of how large or small the costs of sanctions are expected to be (provided $c > 0$; that is, they are costs and not benefits). If the status quo policy is superior for the United States to the compromise ($Q < X$), it is still possible that the United States will agree to compromise provided that the costs of sanctions for the United States are sufficiently high. But if the status quo policy is better for the United States than a compromise policy and the costs to the United States of sanctions is thought to be relatively small ($c < X - Q$; $Q < X$), then, even though the Iranians would agree to the compromise deal, the United States would choose sanctions instead. Phew, that's a lot of different possibilities.

Figure 3.1a shows the choices at each choice node by highlighting the chosen action with a heavy dark line. The identification of choices is based on the assumptions that $c \geq X - Q$

and that $p - k > 0$. Although the game in Figure 3.1a is fairly simple, we can already see that there is a rich array of possible interactions between the U.S. government and the Khameini-led Iranian government. How those interactions play out depends on estimates of costs, benefits, and probabilities. These are, of course, exactly the ingredients that go into expected utility calculations. Preferences over choices are determined by core desires (the U.S. leadership, for instance, strictly prefers policies closer to 0 on the nuclear policy scale to policies farther from 0) but also by constraints such as the costs or probability of achieving them. This means that rational actors who, by definition, do what they *believe* is in their best interests, may elect to pursue a second-best or even lesser policy outcome rather than their most preferred outcome because they do not think they can achieve their most preferred outcome with a high-enough probability (it is too risky) or at an acceptable cost. We have seen, for example, that the United States might agree to a compromise deal with Iran that allows Iran to do more on the nuclear front than either the United States desires or even than Iran is currently doing. This can happen if the U.S. economic and political costs for unilaterally sanctioning Iran are thought to be too high ($c > X - Q$ even when $Q < X$, meaning $1 - Q > 1 - X$ for the United States). Rational actors work out when to sacrifice what they really want and what to substitute in its place. They do the best they can, and that is not necessarily as good as they would like.

Let us now focus on the game in Figure 3.1b and see what happens if the United States anticipates paying particularly high political and material costs for a military strike against Iran's nuclear facilities. Let us assume that the costs (k) for the United States are so high that the expected payoff from a military strike ($p - k$) is worse than backing down ($0 > p - k$). This could happen, for instance, if the United States was convinced that Iran would retaliate by launching a massive military invasion of Iraq aimed at expelling American and allied forces from that country, perhaps aided by Shiite insurgents in Iraq. Given that the American military is already stretched thin in Iraq, coping with hundreds of thousands of Iranian soldiers as well as the ongoing insurgency might be so costly that the United States would choose to back down and pull out rather than sustain the costs of a war with Iran in Iraq. Certainly, it would be the ambition of Iran's leaders to persuade the American public that such a costly circumstance would follow if the United States struck at Iran's nuclear facilities.

Solving the game in Figure 3.1b by backward induction, we find that Iran's choice is the same as in Figure 3.1a in the event the United States institutes economic sanctions. The U.S. choice, however, is different if Iran accelerates its nuclear program following an American offer to compromise. Assuming that for the United States $0 > p - k$, we see that the United States will back down to avoid a war in Iraq with Iran. This changes Khameini's calculation. Now, if the United States offers to compromise, his government faces a choice between agreeing to a compromise, worth X, or seizing the initiative following a signal of "weakness" by the United States by accelerating the program and gaining a utility of 1 ($1 > X$). Under complete and perfect information, the United States will correctly anticipate this reaction by Iran's leaders and will, therefore, have to choose between initiating sanctions, with a payoff of $1 - Q - c$, or capitulating, with a payoff of 0. If $1 - Q - c$ is a sufficiently bad outcome ($1 - Q - c < 0$), the United States will forgo sanctions and offer to compromise, only to face having to capitulate to Iran's development of nuclear weapons. But if the status quo policy is not so bad (that is, if $1 - Q > c$) or the cost of sanctions is sufficiently low, the United States will opt for sanctions against Iran even though that means retaliatory sanctions by Iran. In Figure 3.1b, I assume that $1 - Q - c > 0$, so the United States opts for sanctions.

Counterfactual Reasoning

Figures 3.1a and 3.1b help us see a few important general principles. Each figure has a set of heavy black lines that denote each player's choice at each choice node. In each figure, one set of heavy black lines forms a continuous path from the start of the game to a terminal node that signifies the end of the game. The actions chosen along this continuous set of heavy black lines constitutes the actions that the game leads us to predict we will observe in the world if the specified conditions of the game are correct. But there also are heavy black lines associated with choices leading to other terminal nodes; in those cases, the heavy lines are not continuous from the start of the game to the end. These lines reflect part of the complete plan of action for the game. They are part of the equilibrium strategy of one or the other player. Unlike the lines that are continuously linked from the start of the game to a terminal node, these lines are said to be **off the equilibrium path.** The continuous lines show the equilibrium path; the choices off the equilibrium path reflect expectations about what would happen if those choice nodes were reached. The choice nodes that are not on the equilibrium path are not reached exactly because what a player, at an earlier choice node, anticipates will happen there is inferior and so the player avoids this inferior outcome by making a choice that produces a better result from that point forward. That is exactly the point of looking ahead in a game to figure out the consequences of alternative actions, the very information that results from undertaking a backward induction to identify the subgame perfect Nash equilibrium outcome. Thus, off-the-equilibrium-path expectations are crucial to shaping which choices people make.

In a complete and perfect information environment, we never observe these off-the-equilibrium-path actions because, well, as the name indicates, they are off the equilibrium path, so they are not actions that get taken. These potential choices reflect a hypothetical, counterfactual world, a world of actions that have not occurred because of their anticipated poor consequences and that yet, because of their counterfactual implications, help shape what we do observe. This alerts us that understanding what we observe in the world requires more than just looking at what happens. It also requires sorting out what decision makers expected would happen if they chose differently. All game theory models emphasize the importance of counterfactual reasoning and, in that way, tend to differ from more standard accounts by historians, many case study analysts, and many quantitative statistical analysts, whose attention tends to be riveted on what did happen and not on why something else didn't occur.

Counterfactual reasoning, as we see in more detail in later chapters, leads to important considerations that are often overlooked in other forms of research on international affairs. For instance, we know that a significant percentage of allied nations fail to come to their alliance partner's aid when their ally is attacked. Many people look at this fact and infer that many alliances are worth no more than the paper on which they are written. They conclude that many alliances, maybe even most alliances, are unreliable. Yet this inference is questionable if we undertake a game theoretic analysis and examine which actions are on or off the equilibrium path. For instance, if Iran contemplates attacking Israel, knowing that Israel is allied with a powerful country, the United States, then Iran may decide not to attack even though Iran's current president has declared that he wants Israel to cease to exist. An attack does not occur, perhaps because of the anticipation that it would precipitate a retaliatory strike by Israel with U.S. support. But if Iran believes that the U.S. commitment to Israel is shaky, then Iran might attack Israel thinking that it can win even if it does not believe it could defeat the joint power of the United States and Israel. If we look only at cases in which attacks take place, we are selecting cases in which the attacker expects that the target's ally probably will not participate because either it is not sufficiently committed or it is not strong enough to make a difference in the outcome. We might then infer, as many have, that alliances are unreliable because most of the time, when attacks against allied states take place, the allies of the target of attack failed to help their partner. But if we did this, we would be ignoring the times when the attack was placed off the equilibrium path by the expectation that the target's ally was a reliable and powerful partner. so the would-be attacker chose not to act in the first place rather than risk having to fight the combined forces of its target and the target's allies. These cases reflect reliable alliance ties that succeeded in deterring the would-be aggressor. Game theory, with its emphasis on off-the-equilibrium-path expectations, forces us to notice the **selection effect** that leads the data on the reliability of allied nations to be biased against the conclusion that they are reliable. Statistical methods and most case study methods are more likely than game theory reasoning to lead us to neglect this insight into selection effects and, therefore, to draw the wrong inference about alliances or many other factors in politics.

TRY THIS

Find data on ten countries that belonged to alliances and that were not attacked and on ten countries that belonged to alliances and that were attacked. Are there differences in the nature of the alliance agreements (did they call for mutual defense? consultation? less?) or in the amount of military power that the allies potentially could have brought to bear if there were an attack? Does it look like the states that were attacked had a strong enough deterrent to prevent a nearby adversary from attacking?

Solving the Iranian-U.S. Game with Uncertainty

Figure 3.2 takes a final look at the strategic problem confronted by American leaders and Ali Khameini in Figures 3.1a and 3.1b. Figure 3.2 differs from the earlier analyses by relaxing the assumption that the decision makers know one another's expected payoffs at the

FIGURE 3.2 — Choosing Actions under Uncertainty: Converting Incomplete Information into Imperfect Information

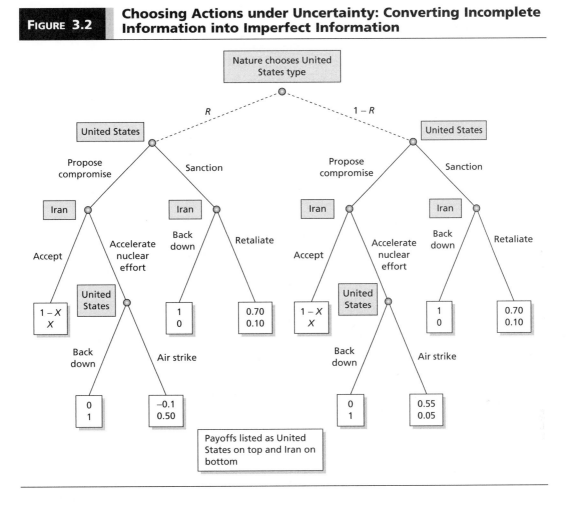

terminal nodes of the game. Suppose, for instance, that Khameini is unsure whether the United States will retaliate with a military strike or back down if Iran accelerates its nuclear program. He may not know how confident the U.S. leadership is of success (that is, he may be uncertain about the size of p, the probability that the United States succeeds in eliminating Iran's nuclear facilities) or how small the United States believes the costs of a fight with Iran would be. This means that he does not know whether $0 > p - k$ or $p - k > 0$. What the United States will choose to do if Iran accelerates its nuclear program is, as we have seen, crucially dependent on whether the U.S. leaders believe $p - k > 0$ or $0 > p - k$. The problem Khameini faces with this uncertainty is equivalent to his being uncertain whether he is playing the game in Figure 3.1a or the one in Figure 3.1b. Figure 3.2 shows a way to cope with this uncertainty so that he (and we) can solve the game. To keep the algebra behind the example relatively simple, I use numerical values here (and non-numerical calculations in footnotes) to work out Khameini's actions given his uncertainty.

Let us imagine that before the United States must choose between sanctions and offering a compromise settlement, nature makes a move. By this I mean that some process outside the player's immediate control has determined the likelihood that the United States is the tough type that will retaliate with military strikes if Iran moves to build a nuclear weapon or that it is the weak type that will capitulate to avoid a war. That move by nature might reflect the electoral preferences of American voters or a chance electoral result on this dimension with voters choosing on some completely different basis, such as the state of the economy. Let's say the move by nature assigns a probability R to the U.S. president's being the sort of player that will risk backing down if Iran accelerates its nuclear program rather than choosing to launch a military strike against Iran's nuclear facilities. Then, there is a probability $1 - R$ that the U.S. president is the type for whom launching a military strike is better than backing down. We want to evaluate how large $1 - R$ has to be to induce Khameini to prefer to accept a compromise rather than risk a military strike. We can think about R and $1 - R$ as a measure of Khameini's belief or perception about the toughness of the U.S. president.

The United States (that is, the president), of course, knows which type it is; that is, the U.S. decision makers know whether they believe that $p - k > 0$ or $0 > p - k$, but Ali Khameini does not know this information about the United States. Let us say, then, that he thinks there is a probability R that $p - k = -0.1$ for the United States. This could be true, for example, if he believes that the United States has only a 20 percent chance of prevailing in a war that would follow from a U.S. strike against Iran's nuclear program ($p = 0.20$) and that the costs (k) of the ensuing war will be 0.30 or any other combination of values for p and k such that $p - k < 0$. On the other hand, with probability $1 - R$, Khameini believes that the United States thinks its chance of prevailing with a military strike is 0.75 and that the United States can contain costs with a quick success so that the expected costs (k) will be only 0.20. In that case, with probability $1 - R$, $p - k = 0.55$, which is, of course, better than the expected payoff to the United States of 0 from backing down. With this information in hand, we can determine how big Khameini has to believe the probability R is for him to gamble on building nuclear weapons rather than accepting the compromise offered by the United States, and we can also work out what the compromise offered by the United States is likely to be so that the United States chooses it over initiating severe economic sanctions given Khameini's uncertainty about how the United States will respond if he accelerates Iran's nuclear development program. To make these calculations, we must assume, as is standard in game theory, that beliefs are common knowledge. By **common knowledge,** I mean that Khameini knows his belief about the United States (that is, the size of R) and the United States knows what Khameini believes the probability is that the United States is tough or weak (that is, R is known to the United States), and Khameini knows that the United States knows and the United States knows that Khameini knows that the United States knows, and so forth.

What Khameini knows is that if he is offered a compromise and he uses the bargaining setting to accelerate Iran's nuclear program, there is a chance the United States will attack Iran and there is a chance that the United States will back down in the face of a nuclear fait accompli. Which action the United States will select depends on whether the United States is the weak type or the tough type. Khameini's best way to work out whether to accept or reject a compromise offer is to calculate his expected payoff if he accelerates Iran's nuclear program and compare that to his expected utility from agreeing to a compromise settlement. We already know that he values a compromise at X. How does he value accelerating Iran's nuclear endeavors? We know that with probability $1 - R$ the United States will retaliate and he will end up with a payoff of $1 - p - k = 1 - 0.75 - 0.20 = 0.05$; and we know that with probability R, the United States will back down and Iran will get a payoff of 1. Thus, Khameini's expected payoff from accelerating Iran's nuclear program is $R(1) + (1 - R)(0.05)$. He will accelerate the nuclear program if the United States offers a compromise X provided that $R(1) + (1 - R)(0.05) > X$; if that is not true, then he will accept the compromise offered by the United States.

Solving this expected utility comparison is quite informative and will help us see the significance of choosing the magnitude of a compromise offer **endogenously.** By that I mean that the U.S. government, if it wishes to avoid finding it necessary either to attack Iran or to impose sanctions, will pick the best compromise, from its perspective, that Khameini will prefer to accept rather than accelerating Iran's progress toward the development of a nuclear weapon and that the United States will prefer over sanctioning Iran. This idea of endogenous choices alerts us to be attentive to reverse causality. For instance, in this example, the proposed compromise will not be the cause of there being no attack; instead, the contents of the proposed compromise are *caused* by expectations about the consequences of an attack. That's getting to be a bit complicated, but questions of war and peace are not simple. To recap, we are working out the probability that Khameini will risk accelerating Iran's nuclear program, and with that information solved, we will work out which is the best compromise offer for the United States to make and for Iran to accept that will cost the United States as little as possible.

The size of the compromise in this game will be dictated by calculations solely in Iran and the United States. Of course, a more comprehensive view would consider the expected strategic behavior of all interested parties, both international and domestic. We, however, will stick to this simpler game for now. As we will see in a moment, if X, the compromise policy, is chosen in accordance with the calculations laid out in Figure 2.10c, this could ensure in an environment without uncertainty that Khameini would accept a negotiated compromise, but it ensures in the uncertain environment we are examining now that he will accelerate Iran's nuclear program. That is, when Khameini's utility for the compromise policy X is the same as his utility for a military strike $(1 - p - k)$, he will, under uncertainty, never agree to a compromise, no matter how large or small he believes p and k really are, as long as neither equals 0. In other words, he needs a better deal in the face of uncertainty. Let's see why this is true.

As we have seen, Khameini's expected utility if he accelerates his country's nuclear development is equal to $R(1) + (1 - R)(0.05)$. If X, the compromise, is chosen by the United States to reflect the minimum deal that Khameini will accept if he is certain the United States will retaliate ($R = 0$), then the compromise is worth 0.05 to Khameini. What happens if the United States offers this minimum compromise to him? His payoff from choosing to accelerate Iran's nuclear program, $R(1) + (1 - R)(0.05)$ must be larger than 0.05, the expected utility that Khameini gets from the offered compromise. How confident does he have to be that the United States will back down (that is, how big must R be) for him to reject a compromise and accelerate Iran's nuclear program instead? We can rearrange the expression $R(1) + (1 - R)(0.05) > 0.05$ to solve for R. When we do so, we find that he will risk a military strike rather than accept a compromise provided that:*

$$R > \frac{0.05 + 0.75 + 0.20 - 1}{0.75 + 0.20} = \frac{0}{0.95} = 0$$

This expression simplifies to $R > 0$.[†] If the United States chooses X, in accordance with Figure 2.10c, to be the smallest compromise acceptable to Khameini under complete and perfect information (and, therefore, the best possible compromise settlement from the U.S. point of view; that is, $1 - p - k$) when there is no chance of the United States backing down ($R = 0$), then Khameini will never accept the compromise if there is any chance that the United States will back down, that is, if $R > 0$. To see this, let us work out what Khameini's expected payoffs are for the compromise compared to accelerating his nuclear effort.

Khameini believes with probability R that accelerating his nuclear program will result in the U.S. backing down (because the U.S. payoff in this case is 0 for backing down and −0.1 for launching an air strike), giving Iran a payoff of 1. With probability $1 - R$ he thinks that the United States is the tough type that will launch air strikes (worth 0.55 to the tough United States, while backing down is worth 0) in retaliation for Iran's accelerating its nuclear program. In that $(1 - R)$ case Iran's payoff would be 0.05. Iran's payoff for accepting the U.S. endogenously chosen, cheapest compromise when there is no uncertainty about the U.S. type is $1 - p - k = 1 - 0.75 - 0.20 = 0.05$. So, Khameini accelerates his nuclear program if $R(1) + (1 - R)0.05 > 0.05$. Because we know that $R > 0$, we know that a U.S. compromise offer of $X = 0.05$ cannot be as valuable to Khameini as accelerating Iran's nuclear program. To convince Khameini to compromise when he believes that there is some prospect that the United States will back down, the United States has to offer more.

---

* The general case is equivalent to:

$$R > \frac{X + p + k - 1}{p + k} = \frac{1 - p - k + p - k - 1}{p + k} = \frac{0}{p + k} \quad \text{if } X = 1 - p\text{-}k.$$

[†] Satisfy yourself that this expression also equals 0 if we assume any other values for p and k.

For Khameini to agree to a compromise, the compromise has to be more attractive from Iran's point of view than is required under certainty about the U.S. response. So, to avoid the risks associated with Iran's rejecting a compromise offer, the United States has to be prepared to offer a policy outcome that is less attractive from its point of view and more attractive from Iran's perspective than when there is no uncertainty about U.S. preparedness to be tough. This means that the United States has a strong incentive to remove any uncertainty by making it clear that it is prepared to use force to prevent Iran from acquiring a nuclear weapon. Doing so improves the prospects of reaching a compromise agreement that minimizes the size of the required U.S. concessions, provided, of course, that the United States does believe that its payoff from retaliation $(p - k)$ is better than its payoff from backing down (0).

Removing uncertainty is difficult because Khameini knows that the U.S. leadership has an incentive to pretend to be tougher than it really is. Just like in poker, foreign policy leaders have incentives to bluff to try to get a better result than their actual situation warrants. One way to clarify a U.S. commitment to use force as a last resort is to make a public declaration of that intention. Such a declaration undoubtedly would prompt domestic political opposition, both in the Congress and among the public. Showing a willingness to bear the political costs of such a declaration is a way of demonstrating resolve on the part of U.S. leaders exactly because the unpopularity of such a step is likely to cost the party in power votes in the next election. Such a costly declaration is known as a **costly signal.** It helps a rival calibrate the sincerity of a declaration. The costlier the declaration is and the harder, or costlier, it is to back down from, the more likely it is that the declarer means what he or she says (Fearon 1995).

Conversely, a threat to use force made strictly through private diplomatic or military channels is more likely to be seen as just so much **cheap talk.** After all, a benefit from making a military threat only in private is that the threatening party avoids triggering the domestic political opposition that would arise if the declared intent were made in public. Cheap talk imposes no cost on the actor sending the signal and so provides no information that an opponent can use to update his or her belief about the threatening party's sincerity. Cheap talk is just babbling; it adds no information that changes the mind or expectations of its target.[‡]

Whatever offer the United States might put together is constrained by how much uncertainty the Iranians have about U.S. resolve; that is, Khameini's uncertainty about U.S. toughness means that the United States has to make a more generous offer to get him to agree to it. But there is another constraint pulling the United States in a different direction—the United States also has to like any compromise it offers better than it likes the consequences of economic sanctions; otherwise, it will not make the offer.[§]

[‡] The exception to this statement is when cheap talk is sent to someone who shares the signaler's objectives. Then the cheap talk provides a way for the actors to coordinate their actions (see Sartori 2006). For example, U.S. private declarations to NATO allies about the rules of engagement in Afghanistan are cheap talk signals that are likely to be effective because all involved parties want to avoid friendly fire incidents.

[§] That is, for the United States to offer a compromise and for Khameini to accept it, the following must be true: $1 - Q - c < 1 - X$ for the United States; $X > 1 - p - k$ for Khameini; and $(X - p - k - 1)/(p + k) > R$ for Khameini.

Now, let's again substitute numbers from our earlier examples to get an idea of what compromise offer the United States would have to make to get Khameini to agree to it and for it still to be sufficiently attractive that the U.S. leadership prefers the compromise to imposing economic sanctions. We do so in the context of the real environment in which the United States has not sent a particularly costly signal of a commitment to use force. Rather, U.S. public declarations on that front are cautious, asserting that all options remain on the table. A costly signal would be, for example, an explicit declaration, such as "the United States will use force to destroy Iran's nuclear enrichment facilities if Iran does not stop enriching uranium by the end of the week" accompanied, for instance, by daily violations of Iranian airspace in which U.S. military aircraft fly over Iran's uranium-enrichment facilities. Such a provocative declaration and action certainly show resolve, but they also certainly are likely to prompt a domestic political backlash. This means that there are powerful political reasons not to make such a declaration or take such action. Sending a costly signal is costly at home and not sending one is costly in terms of leverage with Iran. Foreign policy leaders really do not have an easy job.

We are assuming that the United States knows its probability of success in striking Iran's nuclear facilities, and we set that probability at 0.75 for this discussion. We also assume that this strike could be done at a cost guesstimated to be equivalent to a utility loss of about 0.20 (on a 0–1 scale). This means, as noted earlier, that the maximum compromise Khameini could agree to $(1 - p - k)$ is equivalent to a policy outcome (utility) at 0.05 if he is certain that the United States will take out his nuclear facilities if he rejects the compromise (see Figures 2.10b and 2.10c). That is substantively equivalent to Iran all but abandoning its nuclear program. We know that such an offer will not be sufficient if Khameini is at all uncertain about whether the United States actually will use military force to eliminate Iran's nuclear capabilities $(1 - R)$. The largest concession that the United States is prepared to contemplate, (putting aside sanctions as an option for the moment) is equivalent to a utility of $1 - X = 1 - p + k$, as seen in Figures 2.10a and 2.10c; $1 - 0.75 + 0.20 = 0.45$ utility for the United States. The policy X for which U.S. utility $(1 - X)$ is worth 0.45 occurs when $X = 0.55$. As we can see in Figure 2.1, that is akin to agreeing to continued Iranian research into the production of weapons-grade fuel but without actually making such fuel.

So, a compromise apparently resides somewhere between Iran's nearly total abandonment of research even into civilian energy uses and Iran's pursuit of research into weapons-grade fuel (around 0.55). But we must also consider that the United States can further limit what it is prepared to do and what Iran can choose by deciding how severe any proposed sanctions would be and by affecting how certain or uncertain Iran's leaders are of the American determination to launch a strike against Iran's nuclear facilities if Iran ignores a compromise and accelerates its quest for nuclear weapons.

To be preferred to sanctioning Iran, a compromise must be sufficiently attractive that the United States expects to be better off with the compromise policy than with sanctions. This means that $1 - X > 1 - Q - c$. This requires that we estimate two factors: Q (the status quo) and c (the cost of sanctions). Iran claims that it seeks no more than the development of a civilian nuclear energy industry. That is equivalent to position 0.35 on the policy scale. Iran has not yet attained that capability, so 0.35 is the worst case for our estimate of the current status quo. It is more likely, however, that the current status quo reflects research into the development of that capability but falls short of it, so that it is somewhere around 0.20. Therefore, I believe it makes sense here to assume that $Q = 0.20$. We also know that $c < k$. Because we have assumed that k is known to be 0.20 by the United States, let us assume that c is approximately 0.10. Of course, if we were advising policymakers on this question, we would want to make the estimates of these values as precise as possible. That is one of the purposes behind the existence of intelligence services such as the Central intelligence Agency and military intelligence, and it is also one of the reasons that the State Department employs diplomats in the field and country desk officers in Washington, D.C., who can provide expert information about what is happening in any country.

For the United States to choose to offer a compromise rather than impose economic sanctions on Iran, it must be true that $1 - X \geq 1 - Q - c$; that is, $1 - X \geq 1 - 0.20 - 0.10$, provided the United States is confident that the Iranians will not reject a compromise and accelerate their development of a nuclear weapon. We have not assumed uncertainty on this front, and to keep the example manageable, we will not. Again, if we were advising decision makers, this would be a critical factor to consider. So now we see that the United States will prefer to compromise if $1 - X \geq 1 - 0.20 - 0.10 = 0.70$, so that compromise policy $X = 0.30$. This suggests that the United States will agree to a deal in which Iran pursues the development of a civilian nuclear energy industry (approximately position 0.30 on the policy scale), presumably with safeguards against its secretly going further to develop a nuclear weapons capability.

Will Khameini also agree to this deal? For Khameini to agree, his expected utility from the deal must be at least as good as his expected utility from accelerating Iran's nuclear program, thereby risking an American military strike. That is, for Khameini to agree to the U.S. compromise offer at 0.30 on the policy scale, the following must be true:

$$0.30 \geq R(1) + (1 - R)(1 - 0.75 - 0.20),$$

or, equivalently, $0.25/0.95 \geq R$. To take the compromise offer, Khameini must believe that the chance of the United States backing down (rather than striking) if Iran accelerates its nuclear weapons development is less than 0.263 (that is, 0.25/0.95), or about 26 percent. So, in other words, if Khameini and his fellow Iranian leaders believe that the chance of a U.S. strike is less than approximately 74 percent, they will reject the compromise that the United States is willing to make and, in anticipation of that rejection, the United States will choose to impose economic sanctions on Iran.

Since at least 2006, the U.S. government has repeatedly called for UN-approved and European Union–backed economic sanctions against Iran and has imposed some significant unilateral sanctions on Iran. In addition, during this same period President Bush, Vice

President Cheney, and others repeatedly have intimated, but not absolutely declared, that they would use military force if necessary to prevent Iran from obtaining a nuclear weapon. In September 2007, Israel bombed a nuclear research facility in Syria, and the Syrian government admitted that the building bombed by the Israelis was being used for that purpose. Israel seems to have believed that the facility was part of the early stages of Syria's pursuit of a nuclear weapon. The Iranian government remained silent on the subject of this Israeli attack, and President Bush declined to comment on it as well. One possibility is that the Israelis, with implicit if not explicit U.S. approval, raised the credibility of a threat against nuclear research facilities in the region. After all, the Israelis had destroyed Iraq's nuclear research facility at Osiraq in 1981 when Saddam Hussein's government was thought to be progressing toward the development of a nuclear bomb. By striking against Syria, it may be that the Israelis were helping to raise the expectation in the minds of Iran's leaders that there was a high probability that they would experience such a strike—from the Israelis, the United States, or both—if they continued their nuclear efforts. Certainly the Israeli act was a costly signal by Israeli leaders, at least in that it invited their own domestic opposition to rise up against the government; it also invited Middle Eastern and other governments to chastise Israel in the United Nations or to impose economic sanctions on Israel. Nevertheless, this Israeli action may have reinforced U.S. veiled threats against Iran, thereby helping to increase Khameini's belief that the probability of a U.S. strike under the contingency we have been considering is, in fact, pretty high. The higher Khameini thinks the risk of such a strike is (that is, the greater $1 - R$ is), the more likely he is to agree to a policy compromise with the United States (falling, for instance, somewhere between 0.20 and 0.30 on the policy scale). Thus, we can see how military threats from the United States can help promote a compromise settlement with Iran.**

SUMMARY

The analysis of spatial models in Chapter 2 left us without a way to think about strategic behavior. Spatial models generally assume that everyone acts on his or her preferences in a sincere manner. The concept of subgame perfect Nash equilibrium, however, alerts us that adopting sincere behavior at each step in a decision process can lead to an inferior outcome for a decision maker. Instead, decision makers have strong incentives to be strategic. They choose their actions by taking their preferences into account to be sure. But they also consider the constraints they operate under, such as how much power they have compared to a rival, how confident they are about what their rival really wants, and how willing they are to take risks in pursuit of the policy results they desire. We have seen that game theory can be a very useful tool for sorting out the complexity of international interactions and that it can

---

** Indeed, the imposition of severe sanctions can do the same if the game is not one-shot as portrayed here but, instead, repeated over time, as is certainly closer to the real situation. Here, however, my purpose has been to introduce the basics of game theory, and so we will leave for later a consideration of what might happen if this is a repeated game.

be useful in informing policy choices and in predicting what actions people are likely to take and what offers they are likely to make to try to resolve problems. These issues are the essence of international affairs.

The rest of this book applies the tools introduced here to situations involving conflict and situations involving cooperation in international relations. The objective is to elucidate why things work the way they do and also to facilitate our ability to predict what is likely to happen in specific situations and develop the skills and knowledge to provide useful advice to leaders charged with the responsibility for making life and death decisions in the international arena.

KEY CONCEPTS

backward induction   93
branches   88
cheap talk   103
choice nodes   88
common knowledge   100
complete and perfect information   93
cooperative game theory   84
costly signal   103
dominant strategy   86
endogenously   101
ex ante   86
ex post   86
extensive form   88

game theory   84
multiple equilibria   88
Nash equilibrium   85
noncooperative game theory   84
normal form   88
off the equilibrium path   97
Pareto efficient   87
Pareto inferior   87
path dependence   88
prisoner's dilemma   84
selection effect   98
subgame perfect Nash equilibrium   93
terminal nodes   88

4 | Two Structural Theories of War

OVERVIEW

- This chapter investigates the major structural theories of war: neorealism and the power transition school of thought.

- War is generally inefficient compared to reaching a negotiated settlement. The risks of war may be exacerbated by uncertainty, by problems with making credible commitments, or when the issue in dispute involves a winner-takes-all situation.

- Some important neorealist hypotheses about international peace and stability do not flow logically from that theory's core assumptions. Other important neorealist hypotheses are falsified by the empirical record.

- The link between power transition theory's assumptions and hypotheses is more clear-cut than is true in the case of neorealism.

- Some core power transition hypotheses follow from the theory's logic and are supported by evidence; others either do not follow logically or are not borne out by evidence.

- The power transition theory outperforms neorealism when it comes to offering a structural explanation for war, but its weaknesses point to a need to reconsider its approach to domestic politics.

Warfare represents the most egregious breakdown of international cooperation. Yet even during wars there are numerous examples of cooperative behavior. Of course, allies sometimes assist one another in defeating a foe. But even enemies engage in cooperation. The Geneva Conventions, for example, establish rules of war. Although not always obeyed, these rules do help control wartime excesses; they proscribe the unnecessary and wanton killing of innocent civilians, provide rules for handling prisoners of war, and impose limits on the uses of certain types of weapons (for example, poison chemicals and gases).

International agreements discipline behavior in wartime. This is accomplished by creating clear expectations about what is not acceptable and by reinforcing the expectation that the loser will be held accountable for wartime misconduct (Ash 1997; Morrow 1998, 2007). Proscribed behavior reflects rules or institutions that limit leaders' freedom of action. This, in fact, is the purpose behind such institutions. Thus, even at the height of war, some international cooperation is evident between adversaries. Still, the fundamental feature of warfare is the breakdown of cooperation and its replacement with violence and destruction.

Because war is so destructive, its causes have occupied generations of researchers. Many theories persist as plausible explanations of warfare. The most prominent of these occupy our attention here.

WAR VERSUS NEGOTIATION: INDIVISIBILITY, UNCERTAINTY, AND COMMITMENT

It is reasonable to ask why war ever occurs. One possibility is that emotions overpower people's ability to reason. Hatred, envy, and ideology may so cloud judgment that leaders blindly plunge their nations into horrifically costly and destructive wars. There may be some truth to this contention, but there is also significant evidence that raises doubts about this psychological perspective on war. For instance, if judgments are clouded and war is the product of unrestrained emotion or other seemingly nonstrategic choices, then how do we explain the strong association between who starts wars and who wins them? If, as I argue here, initiating war is a purposive act, then we should expect the initiators to be advantaged as,

The age-old conflict between Israelis and Palestinians was exacerbated by the establishment of the state of Israel following World War II, and a peaceful resolution seems unlikely to many worldwide. Evidence of the violence, such as these buildings destroyed in Israeli airstrikes in the Rafah refugee camp in the southern Gaza Strip in January 2009, is apparent throughout the region, and although the UN and other international organizations have called for a cease fire, neither side appears willing to step back.

indeed, it turns out they are. If wars arose out of some momentary emotional pique, then who wins, loses, or draws (Stam 1999) should be unassociated with who initiates fighting.

Over 60 percent of war initiators win according to data from the highly regarded Correlates of War Project. In contrast, over 54 percent of defenders in war either lose outright (43 percent) or end up with a draw (11 percent). For reasons explained later, the odds of winning for initiators are even greater when the initiator is a democracy. According to Dani Reiter and Allan Stam (2002), democratic nations win 93 percent of the wars they start. Yet we might reasonably think that democracy is a form of governance that is particularly susceptible to the passions of the masses and so especially prone to fight wars against the odds. But given the victorious track record of war initiators, a good starting place to think about such conflicts is that they are the product of rational, purposive, calculations by attackers and defenders.

This, however, leaves us with a puzzle. Why do defenders, given that they are likely to lose, not look for a way to make a deal before enduring the costs of war? This question is another way of saying that war is always ex post (that is, after the fact) inefficient. What this means is that, once adversaries know what outcome a war has produced, they also know a negotiated deal they could have struck ex ante (that is, before the fact) that would have left them at least as well off, and possibly better off, than they are after fighting a war. This is so because war involves **transaction costs** in lost life and property, costs that in principle could be avoided beforehand by the adversaries' agreeing to whatever outcome the war subsequently reveals as the resolution of the issues between them. The ex ante problems that seem to lead to war can be reduced to three main factors: (1) uncertainty, (2) commitment problems, and (3) indivisibility of issues. Each of these factors can cloud what the optimal deal might be (Fearon 1995; Slantchev 2003).

As James Fearon (1995) makes clear, **asymmetric information** or, in common parlance, **uncertainty** can lead entirely rational actors to different conclusions about what they can expect to gain or lose in war (as the Iranian-U.S. example in Chapter 3 illustrates) and, therefore, can make negotiated agreements difficult to construct. It is true, for instance, that defenders are more likely to lose than are initiators, but they are far from certain of losing. They do win a fair amount of the time. Likewise, it is important to recognize that the absence of **credible commitments** between the sides, or, loosely speaking, a lack of trust, can make agreeing on a settlement difficult because of inadequate confidence that what is agreed to will be faithfully acted on. Promises of mercy, for example, may help encourage a peace agreement, but how can any country be certain that once its soldiers lay down their arms it will not be taken advantage of. We'll see how difficult this problem can be when we look at some of the issues that surround terrorism in Chapter 7. Promises can and, all too often, are broken. Finally, the risk of war can be exacerbated by the dispute being over an indivisible objective, such as keeping or losing sovereignty. This can stand in the way of agreement because the circumstance dictates that the winner gets everything and the loser gets nothing.

To understand these conditions better, I offer an illustration of how a negotiated compromise can be reached and then consider how any one of these three conditions makes compromise difficult. Let us consider the dispute between Israelis and Palestinians over land. The Palestinians desire control over some of the territory controlled by the Israelis and the Israelis do not want to cede control of this land to the Palestinians. Suppose that through victory in war the Palestinians gain control over all of the disputed land. Is there a deal that could have been worked out beforehand that would have left both the Palestinian and the Israeli governments better off than they are after fighting? As we will see by calculating expected utilities, the answer is yes; a compromise could have been struck.

Let us consider the value of victory and defeat in war for the Palestinians and for the Israelis compared to the value of some compromise. A Palestinian victory has a utility of 1 for the Palestinians. Remember that a victory means they get to control all of the disputed land. You could think loosely, then, of a utility of 1 as being equivalent to control-

ling 100 percent of the land following victory in war. Suppose that they lose a war over the same land. Their utility for defeat is 0. We can think of a utility of 0 as signifying that they control none of the land—0 percent—after losing a war.

Likewise, victory for the Israelis (keeping the land) is worth 1, and defeat (losing the land) is worth 0. Win, lose, or draw, in our equation each combatant pays a price equal to k for fighting. Suppose Palestine's chance of winning is p and Israel's chance of victory is $1 - p$. That is, Israel's probability of winning is equal to Palestine's probability of losing $(1 - p)$, and Palestine's probability of winning is equal to Israel's probability of losing (p). We can use the idea of expected utility introduced in Chapter 2 to work out a negotiated compromise about the allocation of the disputed land that would be better for the Palestinians than fighting a war. To do so, we use the information just set out so that we know what each side *expects* to get out of a war. Then we can find the value of a division of the land—a compromise—that is Pareto efficient so that both sides are at least as well off, and perhaps better off, making a deal rather than fighting.

Palestine's expected utility for a war must reflect its probability of winning (p); its utility for winning and controlling all of the disputed land (1); its probability of losing $(1 - p)$; its utility for losing and, therefore, not controlling any of the disputed land (0); and the costs its pays for fighting a war (k). Putting these pieces together, we find that Palestine's expected utility from risking defeat in a costly war to have the chance to win control over the disputed land is worth $p(1 - k) + (1 - p)(0 - k)$. We can simplify this expression; $p(1 - k) + (1 - p)(0 - k)$ is exactly the same as $p - k$. Of course, we can also use our information to work out Israel's expected utility from risking defeat in a war over disputed land in order to have a chance to secure its control over the land. For the Israelis, the expected utility from fighting a war is $p(0 - k) + (1 - p)(1 - k)$ or, equivalently, $1 - p - k$.

To avoid a war between Israel and Palestine over disputed land, it is necessary to find a compromise both can accept. A compromise will be acceptable to Israel if the deal gives Israel control over an amount of land worth enough to it so that it prefers to agree to the compromise rather than gamble on the outcome of a war. Likewise a compromise must give Palestine control over enough land that it won't risk a war. We can find that value now because we know what each side expects a war to be worth. That is, we can work out in a compromise deal the amount of land that is *equivalent* to what each side expects to get out of a war.

Suppose the Palestinians propose a compromise in which they get control of x of the disputed land, where x is a percentage between none and all (that is, between 0 and 1.00) of the disputed land. Then, assuming risk-neutral decision makers on both sides, the Palestinian utility for the compromise (x of the land for them and the remainder, $1 - x$, for Israel) is equal to x (they benefit from gaining more of the land occupied by the Israelis) and the Israeli utility for the proposed settlement x is $1 - x$ (the amount of the disputed land that the Israelis would have if they agreed to give x of the land to the Palestinians).

The Palestinians will agree to a compromise rather than fight if x (the percentage of land they get through negotiations) is at least worth $p - k$, their expected utility from fighting a war over the land. That is, they will accept a compromise if $x \geq p - k$. Likewise, the Israelis will accept a settlement if $1 - x \geq 1 - p - k$, or (when we rearrange terms) Israel will accept a compromise provided that $p + k \geq x$. You may recognize this setup as being exactly the same as the discussion of negotiations between the United States and the Khamenei government in Iran presented in Chapter 3. This is a useful generic way to think about bargaining. Figure 4.1 depicts the bargaining situation in the face of the threat of war in this simplified representation of a Palestinian-Israeli dispute over land. The figure shows how the expected consequences of war shape the range of possible land agreements that could be negotiated between the Israelis and the Palestinians, with three provisions. The total territory in dispute must be dividable in a way that falls in the range of possible agreements, each side must be trusted to make no further territorial demands once the bargain is finalized, and each side must agree about its respective probabilities of victory (p and $1 - p$) and costs (k) in a war, as well as the value of the land (x) proposed in the settlement. That is, a deal can be struck if the land is divisible, there is no question about each side's commitment to an agreement, and there is no uncertainty about the expectations about the land allocation following war. As should be clear, avoiding war can mean satisfying some pretty demanding conditions.

Seeking Compromise when a Dispute Is about an Indivisible Good: Winner-Takes-All

Imagine that the Palestinian demand for land is in accordance with the stated objective of the Palestinian group Hamas. This group does not recognize Israel's right to exist. Therefore,

FIGURE 4.1	A Hypothetical Palestinian-Israeli Compromise over Land

Percentage of land given to the Palestinians

it demands control over all of the land that is Israel. If control over all the land currently held by Israel is truly its irreducible objective, then the land is viewed as indivisible by Hamas—it is an **indivisible good.** Hamas's leaders, in fact, say that this is the case, although, of course, they may just be posturing to try to extract as much as possible in exchange for peace with the Israelis. That is, we are uncertain of their true expectations. Similarly, some Israeli settlers claim that all of the land was given to their ancestors in a covenant with God and so is indivisible. They also contend that giving even an inch is unacceptable.

In that case, for Hamas $x = 1$ and, as we can see in Figure 4.1, that is more than the Israelis will accept. And if the settlers controlled the Israeli government, their proposed settlement is $x = 0$, which is unacceptable to the Palestinians. No settlement can produce a compromise in this case of indivisibility, and so there is a severe risk of war.

One important source of division between the two main political parties in the Palestinian Authority—Fatah and Hamas—is over Israel's right to exist. Fatah takes a more pragmatic approach than Hamas. For instance, Fatah's leader, Mahmoud Abbas, participated in an international conference held in Annapolis, Maryland, in November 2007 to try to make progress toward the establishment of an independent Palestinian state that would include some, but certainly not all, land held by Israel. Hamas was not invited to the conference. Hamas's leaders held their own conference rejecting the idea of ceding, as they put it, even 1 centimeter of land that was Palestinian before the creation of Israel in 1948. Abbas has continued to negotiate with the Israeli leadership while Hamas has been excluded from the discussions exactly because it refuses to agree that Israel has a right to exist. There is no point to negotiating if the prospective negotiating partner really denies the possibility that there is any acceptable compromise.

War, Compromise, and Uncertainty

A peaceful settlement can also be made difficult or impossible by uncertainty or by a commitment problem. Imagine that the Israelis think their probability of victory $(1 - p)$ is 0.8 (so that they think their chance of losing, p, equals 0.2) and that the cost of war (k) is 0.1. Then they will accept any deal (x) involving their giving up no more than 0.3 worth of land. Now suppose that the Palestinians think their own chance of victory is 0.5 and they agree with the Israelis that the cost of war is 0.1. Then the Palestinians will compromise if $x \geq p - k$ or, equivalently, $x \geq 0.4$. Because of the differences in their beliefs about their chances of victory, the two sides cannot agree on a compromise; the deals acceptable to one side are unacceptable to the other. This uncertainty about the true probability of victory or defeat might arise out of private information about the morale of their fighting forces, about knowledge of outside help, about the quality of their war plans, or a host of other possible factors. In this case, uncertainty makes war likely. Without the disagreement about the probability of victory, there could have been a mutually acceptable negotiated settlement.

War, Compromise, and Commitment Problems

Now let's consider two different issues that might create a commitment problem that makes it difficult for either side to trust that the other will do whatever it promises to do through negotiations. First, let us imagine that the Palestinians have a first-strike advantage, so that their chance of winning is made greater by striking first than by attacking simultaneously or waiting to retaliate in a second strike after being attacked by the Israelis. Let us label the chance of victory for the Palestinians, given that they strike first, as $p_{(first)}$. If both sides attack simultaneously, then, as before, the probability of a Palestinian victory is p, and if the Palestinians wait to strike second, it is $p_{(second)}$. Suppose $p_{(first)} > p > p_{(second)}$. The Palestinians would negotiate rather than attack if $p_{(first)} - k < x$. Similarly, the Israelis do not attack if $1 - p_{(second)} - k < 1 - x$ or, equivalently, $x < p_{(second)} + k$. We can reorganize these two calculations to say, equivalently, that $p_{(first)} - k < x < p_{(second)} + k$, from which it follows that negotiations will occur if $p_{(first)} - k < p_{(second)} + k$. This means that whether the sides can credibly commit to negotiate depends on the expected costs of war. If $p_{(first)} - p_{(second)} < 2k$, negotiations are feasible. If the costs of war are sufficiently small, then the rivals cannot credibly commit to negotiate.

Let's suppose that $p_{(first)} = 0.7$, $p_{(second)} = 0.4$, and $k = 0.1$ as before. Then, $p_{(first)} - k = 0.6$ and $p_{(second)} + k = 0.5$, so $p_{(first)} - k$ is not less than $p_{(second)} + k$. In this circumstance, the Israelis will not trust the Palestinians to negotiate in good faith because the land the Palestinians could extract by force, taking advantage of their first-strike option, exceeds the deals the Israelis are willing to make. The same is true the other way around. That is, the Palestinians will not trust an Israeli promise not to exploit its first-strike advantage because that advantage can produce benefits that cannot be achieved through negotiation. Thus, once a first-strike advantage is introduced, each side has a problem making a credible commitment to negotiate in good faith and a prisoner's dilemma situation emerges in which each side ends up living with a worse outcome than could have been achieved by negotiating without fear of exploitation at the hands of an adversary with a first-strike advantage. Here the inability to commit to negotiating patiently rather than seizing the first-strike advantage exacerbates the risk of war (Powell 1999; Slantchev 2003).

Now let's think about a different commitment problem. The most common approach among negotiators dealing with the Israeli-Palestinian dispute is to seek a land-for-peace formula. That was the approach agreed to in Oslo in 1993, for example, and pursued for several years until the Oslo land-for-peace formula failed. The idea is that the Israelis give up some land in exchange for a guarantee of peace. An alternative formulation reverses the sequence of concessions—the Palestinian Authority disarms its factions that engage in violence against Israel in return for land concessions. Either approach is likely to fail because each induces a fundamental commitment problem. Here I illustrate the problem in the case of land for peace. In Chapter 7, when we examine terrorism, I more fully assess the problem of committing to peace first to get concessions later.

Land for peace suffers from what in game theory is sometimes called a **time inconsistency** problem. That is, one party (the Israelis in this case) gives an irreversible benefit—such as a land concession—to the other party (the Palestinians in this example) today in the hope that the other side will reciprocate by assuring peace tomorrow. Almost certainly, the party that gets the irreversible benefit today will exploit it to seek still more concessions before it says it will deliver on its promises. We can easily look at this in the context of our present example. Suppose the Israelis and Palestinians strike a negotiated compromise in which Israel transfers x of its land holdings to the Palestinians. Suppose the probability of the Palestinians' defeating Israel in a war increases as the amount of land and resources controlled by the Palestinians increases. Whereas before we stipulated that their chance of victory in war was p, it now becomes $p + \Delta$, where Δ is the incremental improvement in the Palestinians' war chances as a result of their gaining control of x of the land held before by the Israelis. Then, the land that the Palestinians could gain through war is the remaining part that they didn't get in the previous deal—that is, the remaining $1 - x$ of the original land in dispute. That is what they stand to gain by winning a war following a partial land concession. The Palestinians' expected utility from fighting a war with the Israelis, then, is $(p + \Delta)(1 - x - k) + (1 - p + \Delta)(0 - k)$. Israel, having ceded x of the land to the Palestinians, now holds $1 - x$ of the land still in dispute. Suppose the Palestinians propose a new deal in which they would receive y, a percentage of the remaining $1 - x$ of the land originally in dispute in exchange for a promise of peace ($y \leq 1 - x$). They will prefer the proposed compromise to going to war if

$$y \geq (p + \Delta)(1 - x) - k$$

The new demand, y, is positive; that is, it involves an additional land transfer, provided that the costs of war k are smaller than the expected gain from war $(p + \Delta)(1 - x)$. This means that, under most circumstances, the Palestinians, having gained land before, are now in a stronger position to demand additional land in exchange for peace. We could repeat this process many times over until there is no land left for the Israelis to concede. Here is the commitment problem in the form of time inconsistency. A concession today emboldens the recipient to make a further demand tomorrow and tomorrow and tomorrow until, through what Robert Powell (1999) has termed salami tactics—cutting the sausage into thinner and thinner slices—eventually there is nothing left. As we will see, a similar commitment problem occurs if we reverse the process, seeking the disarmament of terrorists now in exchange for land concessions later.

TRY THIS

Redraw Figure 4.1 to show the range of land deals that the Palestinians will accept and the range that the Israelis will accept if the Palestinians have a first-strike advantage and $p_{(first)} - k > p_{(second)} + k$. Substitute actual values for $p_{(first)}$ and $p_{(second)}$, and compare the results to the possibilities if there is no first-strike advantage.

We have now seen how uncertainty, commitment issues, or a dispute over an indivisible good can increase the risk of war. In showing how these conditions can lead to war, I have assumed that each party to the dispute has one unified set of expected utility values by which to compare alternative approaches (such as fight or compromise). Our example here involves Israel and Palestine, but this analysis will work for any situation in which each party's choices can be represented by the calculations of a single actor. That is, I have looked at the question of war by assuming that each party is a unitary actor so that there are disputes between the opposing sides but not among decision makers on the same side.

With this discussion in hand, and recognizing that it implicitly assumes that states are rational unitary actors, let us now consider some specific theories about the causes of war. I explore the logic and evidence for two theories in depth: neorealism and power transition theory. The first looks at international affairs and war in particular, completely outside the context of domestic political considerations. The second focuses primarily on international considerations, but gives some attention to domestic factors. I also introduce the international interaction game as a variation of neorealism (the game is considered in more detail in Chapter 5).

REALIST THEORIES OF WAR

Neorealist theorists believe that the distribution of power in the international system is a major factor in determining whether international affairs are stable or unstable. **Stability** refers to circumstances in which the sovereignty of key states is preserved (Gulick 1955). **Instability** refers to changes in the composition of the international system, especially changes involving the disappearance or emergence of "key" states following large wars. Key states are those whose assistance might be necessary to counteract a threat from a rival coalition of states. Sometimes I refer to these states as **essential actors** to highlight their ability to turn a potentially losing situation into a winning one or, at least, into one that blocks adversaries from victory (Niou, Ordeshook, and Rose 1989).

Because war represents a potential threat to sovereignty, neorealist theorists are concerned with its causes, especially those of big wars capable of jeopardizing the survival of great powers. In addressing war and instability, neorealist theories start with the following four assumptions:

1. International politics is anarchic.
2. States, as rational unitary entities, are the central actors in international politics.
3. States seek to maximize their security above all else and consider other factors only after security is assured.
4. States seek to increase their power as long as doing so does not place their security at risk.

Anarchy, you recall, means that there is no supranational authority that can enforce agreements between states. Consequently, in the international arena every state must look out for its own well-being; international politics involves self-help above all else. The second assumption means that domestic politics is irrelevant to international politics. International politics is the interplay among states and that interplay does not depend on who the leaders of a country are or what form of government it has. We see in Chapter 6, when we look closely at the phenomenon known as the democratic peace, that this contention is false and that, therefore, theories that make this assumption provide insight into a more limited range of real-world circumstances than many international relations researchers acknowledge. The third assumption establishes the primacy of security. It also establishes that states are not willing to trade away their security for other benefits. Other possible goals, such as wealth, are pursued only after security has been assured. This assumption should lend considerable predictability to states' behavior.

The final assumption tells us that states are interested in increasing their influence over other states. No state is content to be weak, but states accept being weaker than they might otherwise be if the pursuit of greater power would place their security at risk. This assumption places restrictions on the actions that states take in pursuit of power. For example, if a state becomes sufficiently powerful that other states foresee the possibility that their security will be threatened by it in the future, then they are expected to join together to deprive the growing state of the power to threaten them. Thus, an increase in a state's power can actually make the state weaker in the long run. This happens if the increase in power alarms rivals and mobilizes them to form an opposition alliance. A coalition or alliance of states will come together to beat back a growing state if that state's power threatens to become large enough that others face a possible loss of sovereignty. This phenomenon is sometimes known as the **security dilemma** (Jervis 1978; Nalebuff 1991).

These four assumptions provide a parsimonious and potentially powerful view of international politics. Several important hypotheses are said to follow from them. The most important neorealist hypotheses about the threat of war or instability are:

1. Bipolar systems are more stable than multipolar systems.
2. States engage in balancing behavior so that power becomes more or less equally divided among states over time.
3. States mimic, or echo, one another's behavior.

How Well Does Neorealism Do in Explaining War and Instability?

Our examination of neorealist theory and the risk of war proceeds in stages. First, we investigate whether the three primary neorealist hypotheses are logically implied by the four assumptions of neorealist theory. Then we examine how well those hypotheses describe historical circumstances. In this way, we can assess the logical and historical significance of the neorealist view of war and international politics.

If the neorealist hypotheses are not accurate descriptions of international affairs, then their logical status is unimportant. Hypotheses may be logically implied by the assumptions of a theory, but if the predictions are inconsistent with observed behavior even more so than the predictions of other theories, then the theory's predictions are falsified. If the neorealist hypotheses are consistent with observed behavior but do not follow from its assumptions, then we need to alter the assumptions to account for the observed facts. In this case, an additional, new set of implications will probably follow from these new assumptions. We will also want to know whether those new implications are consistent with the facts. It is through this process of evaluation and alteration that theories grow and we achieve a better understanding of how the world works. Finally, if the hypotheses follow logically from the assumptions and the hypotheses accurately account for observed behavior, then neorealist theory is a powerful tool for understanding international politics.

Bipolarity and Stability

A **bipolar** international system is dominated by two very powerful states, with weaker nations clustered around each of the two power poles. A **multipolar** system consists of more than two very powerful states. The great powers in a multipolar environment may also attract the support of other, lesser states. In a multipolar system, there are more than two such concentrations of power.

TRY THIS

What do you consider to be the important poles or blocs of nations today? How do you decide which states are part of a particular bloc or pole and which are not? Might looking at the similarity in their military alliance commitments help sort out bloc memberships?

The argument that bipolar structures are more stable than multipolar ones is built on the claim that there is more uncertainty in a multipolar system than in a bipolar one. In a multipolar world, it is difficult to anticipate how nations will organize themselves in the event of a threat by one nation against another. There are so many possible linkages between different blocs of nations that the commitments of third parties not directly involved in a confrontation become difficult to predict. So, bipolarity is thought to alleviate two of the conditions we have discussed that are thought to increase the risk of war: uncertainty and commitment problems.

Suppose the international system consists of five powerful nations, A, B, C, D, and E, each of which is the leader of a bloc. If A and B get into a squabble, each will be relatively uncertain about what C, D, and E will do. In contrast, if the international system consists of only two big

| **FIGURE 4.2** | **European Great Power Alliance Commitments, 1914** |

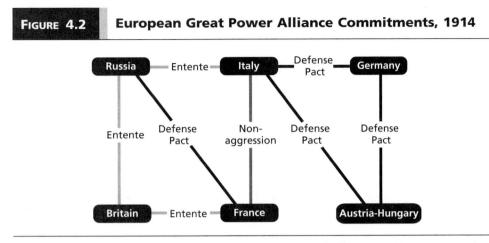

After World War I was over, many experts maintained that rigid alliance commitments created a trip wire that allowed the 1914 crisis between Austria-Hungary and Serbia to escalate into a global conflict. However, a look at the great power alliance ties in June 1914, just before World War I erupted, suggests that in fact the boundaries demarcating commitments were far from clear.

powers, A and B, then there must be less uncertainty. Each is the adversary of the other, and neither needs to worry about anyone else. Neorealists conclude that because there is less uncertainty in a bipolar world, fewer errors are made by the leaders of states in bipolar international politics. Therefore, they claim, bipolar systems are more stable than multipolar systems.

We can see how this argument about polarity and uncertainty works by considering the configuration of international military commitments shown in Figures 4.2 and 4.3. Figure 4.2 displays the military commitments of the major powers on the eve of World War I. Six major powers were actively engaged in European diplomacy in 1914. They included Austria-Hungary, Britain, France, Germany, Italy, and Russia. The United States and Japan were also great powers at that time, but their foreign policies, although actively promoting trade, generally reflected a desire to stay out of European security questions.

It is evident from Figure 4.2 that there was considerable uncertainty about how the great powers would respond to hostilities between Austria-Hungary and Russia over the future of Serbia, the immediate issue that led to World War I. It is notable that the combinations of states that eventually formed the two sides in World War I did not make up obviously distinct sets of interests before the war. England, France, and Russia stuck together in fighting against Austria-Hungary and Germany, but that they would do so was neither inevitable nor obvious before the war. Italy, with ties to both camps, held back, declaring its neutrality on the eve of the beginning of fighting. Italy finally came in on the side of the Triple Entente in April 1915. Figure 4.2 reminds us that explanations of World War I that say that the alliances worked like trip wires, making a massive war inevitable, rely more on hindsight than on the actual prewar facts.

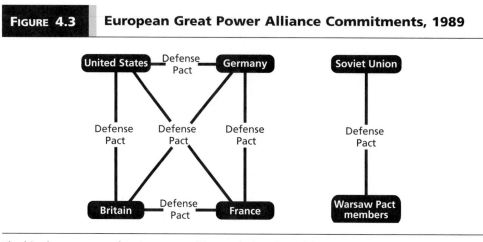

FIGURE 4.3   **European Great Power Alliance Commitments, 1989**

The bipolar structure of major power alliances during the cold war contained little ambiguity.

England had revealed itself to have weak ties to France and Russia, promising only to consult with them and no more. We might have readily imagined from this that Britain would stay out of the war altogether; in fact, that's just what the Germans thought the British would do. France, for its part, was closely aligned with Russia but also had a neutrality pact with Italy. Italy, in turn, was strongly associated with Austria-Hungary and Germany through an alliance that promised mutual defense. The sides that appeared to be polar opposites after the war began were intricately intertwined before. Certainly, the war would have been much more limited had Britain stayed out of it and had France participated only half-heartedly.

The ambiguous alliance commitments of 1914 stand in sharp contrast to the structure of the major power commitments in European affairs during the cold war. As shown in Figure 4.3, European security affairs were dominated by five major powers: Britain, France, Germany, the Soviet Union, and the United States.* China had emerged as a great Asian power, but it was involved very little in European security questions. Likewise, Japan was a great economic power but not a major player on the European or world security stage.

The major power system during the cold war years was unambiguous. The United States led the NATO alliance, which included all the European great powers except the Soviet Union, and the Soviets led the Warsaw Pact countries. No alliance commitments ran from one bloc to the other to create ambiguities about who was committed to whom. The cold war bipolar structure contained very little uncertainty indeed.

We can see that a system in which two states are dominant is unlikely to contain much uncertainty and that a multipolar system with more than two important centers of power can

---

* Germany's primary strategic importance during the cold war lay in the fact that both the United States and the Soviet Union had stationed large numbers of troops on German soil. Germany was the point at which a war between the United States and the Soviet Union was most likely to begin.

easily contain uncertainty. It appears that neorealists are correct in their contention that in multipolar systems decisions are made under greater uncertainty than in bipolar systems. But there is a considerable logical leap from the association of uncertainty with multipolarity to the association of multipolarity with instability and bipolarity with stability. Indeed, some have argued that multipolar systems are more stable than bipolar systems precisely because multipolarity produces uncertainty (Deutsch and Singer 1964). Others have argued that there may be no relationship at all between polarity and stability (Bueno de Mesquita 1978).

Neorealism's Bipolarity Hypothesis Does Not Follow from the Theory's Assumptions

There are several problems with the argument that because bipolar systems encompass less uncertainty than multipolar systems they yield greater stability. To start with, this argument is not implied logically by the four key assumptions of neorealism. In fact, those assumptions say nothing at all about uncertainty or how uncertainty affects stability. To conclude that there is a relationship between uncertainty and the stability of the international system, we would need to make additional assumptions.

In particular, we would need to make some assumption about how states (or decision makers) respond to uncertainty. Here we run into disagreement about what uncertainty implies about decision making and stability. For example, uncertainty may prompt states (or their leaders) to behave especially cautiously. At the same time, powerful nations may attempt to eliminate or diminish a rival precisely because greater certainty makes evident the opportunity to do so. If uncertainty promotes caution and certainty encourages opportunism, then bipolarity encourages instability. This is essentially the argument that led Karl Deutsch and J. David Singer (1964) to conclude that multipolar systems are more stable than bipolar ones.

To support the argument that bipolarity fosters stability, then, we might assume that certainty makes states more cautious, whereas multipolarity and uncertainty make states somewhat reckless, less cautious and maybe even risk-seeking. That is, we must logically exclude the possibility that uncertainty breeds more caution than certainty. If this is true, then all states are particularly (and perhaps even equally) risk averse in the face of certainty. Although this is a strong assumption, it does solve the logical dilemma we face, and it is consistent with the third neorealist hypothesis, which holds that states echo one another's actions. Whether it solves the logical problem we are confronted with at the price of departing too much from reality is an empirical question to be resolved by examining evidence rather than making a judgment about whether we think the assumption is realistic or not.

The fix I have just proposed precludes the possibility that different leaders or different states respond in different ways to uncertainty, and it is consistent with the system-level view of neorealism. Yet the notion that states (or their leaders) react to uncertainty each in its own way presents three immediate problems. First, it violates the unitary rational actor assumption, which contends that important choices in international politics are driven by structural factors, not by considerations internal to the state. Second, if different decision makers respond to uncertainty in different ways, then there is no reason to expect any empirical relationship between bipolarity and stability at all. Some leaders might be particularly cautious when faced with an uncertain situation, whereas others might be more reckless. If there is a roughly equal mix of states (or leaders) with reckless and with cautious reactions, then, on average, uncertainty would not have any systematic effect on stability. Half the time uncertainty would prompt cautious, stability-enhancing actions, and the rest of the time it would prompt reckless, instability-producing actions. Third, if leaders differ in how they respond to uncertainty, then the third hypothesis (that states mimic one another) does not hold up. Clearly, neorealist theory's equating bipolarity with stability cannot tolerate the possibility that individual decision makers vary in their responses to uncertainty.

The bipolarity argument is problematic even if we ignore the fact that it offers no explanation of how uncertainty or certainty affects international stability. The deeper problem is that the hypothesis that stability is fostered by bipolarity is inconsistent with the four assumptions of neorealism. In fact, taking the neorealist assumptions into account, we can show that it is logically true that more distributions of power are stable in a multipolar world than in a bipolar world.

To prove this claim, let's suppose that there are 300 units of power in the international system. Two distributions of power are of interest when it comes to a bipolar world. If the distribution of power for bloc or nation A and bloc or nation B is exactly 150-150, then neither state can destabilize the system by trying to take power away from the other bloc. Each is exactly powerful enough to prevent a victory by its rival. Such a bipolar **balance-of-power** system would be very stable indeed, as hypothesized by neorealist thinkers. If, however, the distribution of power differs at all from that perfect 150-150 split, then the system must be unstable according to neorealist assumptions, if not neorealist conclusions (Niou, Ordeshook, and Rose 1989).

Suppose, for example, that nation A has 151 units of power but nation B has 149. The system is practically balanced, but not quite. According to assumption 3, nation A wants more power but, per assumption 4, it will not seek more power if doing so puts nation A's security at risk. Because power is the ability to make a rival do something it otherwise would not want to do, A has the absolute ability to force B to give up all of its resources (that is, the 149 units of power). A is stronger than B. If B does not willingly give up its resources, A can just take them. In a bipolar world, nation B cannot turn to anyone else for help because there is no one else. By taking B's resources, A increases its own power and does

TRY THIS

I have been careful to say that the distribution of power is precisely equal, or is perceived to be precisely equal, when bipolarity implies stability. What if the real distribution of power in a bipolar setting is 120–180, but the perceived distribution is 150–150? Is this system likely to foment an attempt by one bloc to take power from another? What if the real distribution of power is 150–150, but the perceived distribution is 120–180? In this case, is one bloc likely to try to take power away from the other? Think about the answers to these questions strictly in regard to the assumptions of neorealism. What does the theory logically imply? What does the theory say about perceptions? Are the implications consistent or inconsistent with the hypothesis that bipolarity leads to stability?

not place its sovereignty or its security at risk because it knows that it can beat B. This is what it means to say that A is more powerful than B in the terms of a structural perspective such as neorealism. Therefore, except in the unlikely event that power is perfectly balanced or is perceived to be so, bipolar systems are unstable according to neorealist logic.

Unbalanced bipolarity results in the destruction of one big state or bloc of states by the other, bigger state or bloc. This argument holds even after we introduce uncertainty about the exact distribution of power or account for a range of costs associated with war. The introduction of uncertainty in the bipolar setting, in fact, turns the argument for the stability of bipolar systems on its head. Remember, bipolar systems are supposed to be less uncertain than multipolar systems.

Now let's consider two different multipolar systems. Each system consists of five nations (or blocs of nations): A, B, C, D, and E. System I contains the following possible power distributions: A = 75, B = 74, C = 75, D = 74, and E = 2. System II's power distribution differs slightly: A = 78, B = 74, C = 73, D = 73, and E = 2. According to the assumptions of neorealism, what can we say about the stability of these systems?

System I (75, 74, 75, 74, 2) is a stable system. No state can be eliminated from the international system given the current distribution of power—not even state E, although E holds only 2/300 of the total power. In fact, state E is an important stabilizing element in this system because it can join with states B and D, building a coalition strong enough to protect itself from the remaining combination of rivals, A and C. State E helps itself and other states enhance their security.

According to neorealism, any combination of states with power totaling more than half the available capabilities can defeat any combination of opponents. For hypothetical systems with 300 units of power, then, any combination of states that controls more than 150 units of power can defeat the remaining states. As such, in accordance with the fourth neorealist assumption, each state has an incentive to prevent the formation of such a coalition if the alliance excludes that state. By forging a **blocking coalition** that itself holds 150 units of power, states can ensure their security. Viewed mathematically, we can say that, where R = resources (that is, power), the blocking coalition must equal $R/2$. Recall that in our earlier bipolar system, stability was achieved when each pole formed a blocking coalition with $R/2$ units of power (that is, 150 each).

In System I, as previously noted, nation E might align with nations B and D (74 + 74 + 2 = 150 = $R/2$) against A and C. This arrangement is stable in that neither side is strong enough to eliminate any one state. Each state in the system is essential because each state can turn a losing coalition into a winning coalition or a blocking coalition. Notice that if A attacks E, other states will join to defend E and defeat A. They will do so because if they do not their own security will be diminished by the lost opportunity to form a blocking coalition with E or a subsequent winning coalition against A. By ignoring E's plight, C and D place their own future security at risk. This is something they would not do according to the assumptions of neorealist theory. Less obviously, B's security also will be at risk. Under the assumptions of neorealism, there is no sustainable additional benefit in regard to security for B (or anyone else) once a coalition with $R/2$ resources has formed. The power distribution may or may not remain stable, but all the states will survive because they all play a crucial role in helping to preserve someone else's security and so they can credibly commit to ensure one another's survival. There is no need to redistribute power to ensure security, although security could be ensured even if the power were to be redistributed. For example, a redistribution of power to 75, 75, 70, 70, 10 would also engender stability, as would a redistribution that gave any one state 150 units of power.

But notice that in System II (78, 74, 73, 73, 2) there is no combination of states that cares to ensure the survival of nation E because no state requires E's assistance to form a blocking or winning coalition. E cannot extract a credible alliance commitment from any other state. Nation A can form a winning coalition just by joining with B, or, if B is not willing, by aligning with C or D. Adding E to any of these coalitions is superfluous. B, likewise, can forge winning coalitions by aligning with A or with C and D. No winning or blocking coalition can form from an otherwise losing coalition by adding nation E to it. Consequently, E is expendable. Should any of the remaining states (or all of the remaining states) defeat and seize E's two units of power, this will not change their ability to form winning coalitions. Thus, A, B, C, and D have ensured security for themselves by being an essential component of at least one blocking or winning coalition; in contrast, E is an **inessential actor.**

We can see how System II might evolve by applying to it the rules of neorealism. States A and D might threaten to gobble up states B, C, and E, provided that A and D can credibly commit to one another to evenly split all available resources at the war's end. If no power is dissipated in war costs, each would acquire 150 units of power at the end of the fighting. If either accepted anything less, it would quickly succumb to its erstwhile ally. States B, C, and E would obviously be unhappy with this state of affairs. States B and C might therefore head off such a threat to their security by approaching A and offering it a deal that is at least as good for A as the one it could have by forming an alliance with D to destroy B, C, and E. B and C might suggest to A that it destroy E and thereby gain E's 2 units of power (so it now has 80 units of power instead of just 78) and, in addition, take 35 units each from B and C, each of whom would give it willingly—say, by transferring territory or some other tangible source of power—so that A will end up with 150 units of power without ever having to fight a big war against B, C, and E and without having to take the risk that D might come out ahead of A in the war. Under this arrangement, although B and C sacrifice power, they ensure their survival because once A has 150 units of power ($R/2 = 150$), the surviving states are all essential and so can credibly commit to one another's defense. The new distribution of power might be A = 150, B = 39, C = 38, and D = 73; or, perhaps, A = 150, B = 74, C = 3, and D = 73; or any of a number of other possibilities.

In summary, state E is an essential actor in the first hypothetical multipolar system. In System I, no one can afford to see state E eliminated. Its demise would needlessly place someone else's future security at risk, in direct violation of neorealist assumption 4. In this system, for any winning alliance that could form, some other state can offer a better deal (that is, more security) to some member of the winning combination in exchange for its support in a blocking coalition. Because of the possibility of switching alliances to get a better deal, no state is expendable in this system. Thus, System I is stable, although the distribution of power may be subject to change.

The second hypothetical multipolar system, although similar to the first, is not stable according to neorealism because there is no circumstance in which E can survive that is consistent with neorealist assumptions. Other states can increase their power by destroying E without placing their own security at risk. The key to stability, at least in regard to the survival of states, is that each state be essential to the formation of at least one winning or blocking coalition. Although some states remain essential through a transfer of power to rival states, they at least survive. But states that are inessential cannot survive. As such, any system containing an inessential state must be unstable (Niou, Ordeshook, and Rose 1989).

It should be evident that many different distributions of power in a multipolar system can be stable and that just as many others cannot. Among potentially stable multipolar systems—one in which every state can survive—are those in which power is perfectly evenly distributed among the member states. Such a system, however, is subject to power redistributions that shift the equilibrium away from perfect equality. This is so because a blocking coalition with power equivalent to $R/2$ that ensures the survival of all states can be formed without redistributing resources only if the system is multipolar, has an even number of members, and has resources that initially are equally distributed between two camps.

Stability in a multipolar world is not limited to the situation of exact power equality. This is in marked contrast to the bipolar world, in which stability can be achieved only through a perfectly equal division of

> ### TRY THIS
>
> A survey of systems over the past five hundred years makes clear that, contrary to the claims of neorealists and other structural theorists, the bipolar major power system that began in 1945 and ended in 1989 was not especially long-lived. Construct ten hypothetical multipolar systems of five blocs each that are stable according to neorealist criteria. Does this come close to exhausting the number of possible stable multipolar power configurations? If power is equally distributed in a multipolar system, how might a blocking coalition be formed? Does an exactly equal distribution of power ensure the survival of all states? Does it prevent any redistribution of resources?

resources between two blocs. Thus, it appears that the first neorealist hypothesis, that bipolarity promotes stability and multipolarity promotes instability, is logically false given the assumptions of the theory. Further, it seems that a true balance of power is essential for stability in a bipolar world, but not in a multipolar one, contradicting the second hypothesis. A vast array of power distributions produce stability. In a multipolar environment, an exact balance of power is irrelevant. Either the balance of power does not matter in multipolarity or the term is defined to mean any system in which each actor is essential. In the latter case, the concept becomes so broad as to be vacuous—too many systems would then qualify as a balance-of-power system to give the concept much meaning in our search for answers.

Bipolarity and Stability: A Second Look

You might object that the portrayal of the relationship between polarity and stability is too simple. After all, war or any other means of taking away a rival's power and threatening its sovereignty is a risky business. Success is not a certainty. More powerful states or alliances of states cannot be sure of their advantage unless that advantage is very large indeed (Morgenthau 1978). The risk associated with war may mean that a bipolar system will still be stable even though power is not divided exactly equally between the rival camps. Indeed, Figure 4.1 illustrates such a situation.

Although this argument seems appealing, it cannot be used to salvage neorealism's argument that bipolarity is stable because it actually contradicts fundamental aspects of neorealist theory. We will return to the bipolar example of instability to see why this is so, but before doing so, let me remind you again that the basis for the claim that bipolar systems are more stable than multipolar systems hinges on the contention that multipolarity encompasses greater uncertainty than does bipolarity. In an effort to save the logical foundation of this hypothesis, I now turn this contention on its head by asserting that uncertainty is especially a problem in bipolar systems.

Suppose nation A thinks there is some chance, p, that it can defeat nation B. If this is so, then there is also a chance, equal to $1 - p$, that A will be defeated by B. For convenience, we can define p so that it equals the ratio of A's power to the sum of A's and B's power. A will not try to take advantage of B if it perceives that:

$$p(U_{A \text{ winning}}) + (1 - p)(U_{A \text{ losing}}) < U_{A \text{ status quo}},$$

where $U_{A \text{ winning}}$ is the utility for A of capturing B's power, $U_{A \text{ losing}}$ is the utility for A of losing its sovereignty to B, and $U_{A \text{ status quo}}$ is the utility for A of maintaining the status quo in terms of its level of security.

Suppose that A attaches a utility of 1 to capturing all of B's power and a utility of 0 to losing its sovereignty. In addition, we know that in accordance with neorealist assumptions A prefers capturing B's power to losing its own sovereignty or maintaining the status quo and that A prefers the status quo to losing its sovereignty. With these conditions in mind, we can develop rules for A that will guide its decision on whether or not to go after B's power. First, we need to rearrange the terms in our expression:

$$p > (U_{A \text{ status quo}} - U_{A \text{ losing}})/(U_{A \text{ winning}} - U_{A \text{ losing}}),$$

and then substitute our given values:

$$p > (U_{A \text{ status quo}} - 0)/(1 - 0),$$

to establish that

if $p > U_{A \text{ status quo}}$, then A will attack B　　　　　　　　　　(Rule 1) and

$$\text{if } p \le U_{A \text{ status quo}}, \text{ then A will not attack B.} \qquad \text{(Rule 2)}$$

It is clear that the decision A makes depends on how much it likes or dislikes the status quo in regard to its security. States that are very unhappy with the status quo might, under rules 1 and 2, attack the rival pole in a bipolar system even though the rival pole is much stronger. That is, p could be quite small and still be bigger than the value such states attach to the status quo. Imagine, for example, that the value of the status quo is 0.1. This is more than the value of losing sovereignty (0) and less than the value of gaining B's power (1). If p is 0.2, then Rule 1, A attacks B, is satisfied. This is equivalent to saying that it is possible in a bipolar world for nation A to attack nation B when A's power is 60 and B's power is 240; that is, p = A's power/(A's power + B's power) = 60/(60 + 240) = 0.2. This is what is implied by the measurement of p based on the power of A compared to B and by a utility for the status quo equal to 0.1. So in this example, A attacks B even though A's chance of success in gaining power is very small.

A state that is relatively happy with the status quo might not attack B in a bipolar system, even if B is much weaker. That is, p could be very large and still be smaller than the value this state attaches to the status quo. For example, suppose that the value of the status quo is 0.9. Even if p is equal to 0.8, Rule 1 would not be satisfied, and A would not attack B. Even though A's power equals 240 and B's power only totals 60, A still would not feel confident enough to seize B's capabilities, given the high value of the status quo for A relative to a potentially disastrous defeat.

Such conclusions make a lot of intuitive sense. The problem is that they contradict neorealist assumptions. The fourth neorealist assumption limits the pursuit of increased power to just those situations in which national security is not at risk. As Kenneth Waltz, the creator of neorealist theory, has aptly noted in explaining neorealism,

> In anarchy, security is the highest end. Only if survival is *assured* can states safely seek such other goals as tranquility, profit, and power. Because power is a means and not an end, states prefer to join the weaker of two coalitions. They cannot let power, a possibly useful means, become the end they pursue. The goal the system encourages them to seek is security. Increased power may or may not serve that end.... The first concern of states is not to maximize power but to maintain their positions in the system. (1979, 126 [emphasis added])

Because an anarchic world almost never ensures survival, it is rarely possible from the neorealist point of view for states to trade between security and other desirable goals. Yet, by assuming that the outcome of a contest for power is probabilistic, we necessarily introduce trade-offs between security (that is, the preservation of sovereignty) and the quest for power. With probabilistic outcomes we can imagine a probability of success large enough to warrant putting security at risk (recall the example in which the probability of success is quite low). In doing so, we violate assumptions 3 and 4 and so are no longer examining the logic of neorealist theory but, rather, the logic of some other theory in which security need not take precedence.

The hypothesis that bipolarity leads to stability does not follow from the stated assumptions of neorealism. Although it is perfectly acceptable to develop additional assumptions to rescue a theory, no theory can be rescued by contradicting its own basic assumptions. Therefore, we cannot maintain the neorealist argument by acknowledging that leaders might make different choices about whether to try to gain power at the possible expense of security. Calculations concerning the value of the status quo versus the risks inherent in pursuing more power fly in the face of neorealist views about how states behave.

History and Neorealist Empirical Claims

Is it worth our while to try to save the bipolarity argument of neorealism? That is, is the record of history sufficiently consistent with the hypothesis that we should find some logical explanation for the stability produced by bipolarity? There are many ways to go about figuring out whether a strong historical relationship exists between the international system's level of polarity and its stability. I address several of these now, mindful of Kenneth Waltz's admonition that all theory, including neorealism, should be subjected to distinct and demanding tests (1979, 13).

One method that seems to make sense in light of neorealist arguments is to evaluate how long the structure of the international system remained unchanged under different configurations. According to neorealists, the modern international system began in 1648 with the end of the Thirty Years War. The international system was multipolar in structure from 1648 until the defeat of Germany in 1945. Thus, between 1648 and 1945 there were many major powers, with no one or two predominating. The multipolar system lasted for 297 years, although many internal changes took place during that time, with great powers rising and falling along the way. The bipolar system began in 1945 and lasted until about 1989, when the Berlin Wall was torn down, symbolizing the end of the bipolar cold war. That is, the bipolar system lasted just forty-four years. The international system has now entered a new phase of multipolarity (the United States as one pole, perhaps the European Union as another, China as a third, and Russia as a fourth) or, perhaps, **unipolarity** (with the United States as the globally predominant state). Of course, we do not know how long this will last. It is evident, however, that the first multipolar period lasted much longer than the first bipolar system. In this sense, it appears that multipolarity is more stable than bipolarity.

Neorealists, however, might object that this assessment is not correct. We have already noted that many internal changes occurred during the 297 years associated with the multipolar system. Spain, for example, was one of the great powers during the sixteenth and seventeenth centuries, but it certainly was not among this elite group of states in the nineteenth or twentieth centuries. The United States is the most powerful state in the world today, but it did not even exist in 1648 and remained a sleepy backwater at least until the Spanish-American War in 1898. If stability requires that the set of great powers remain unaltered, then each time the list of major powers changes, we can say that a new system has emerged.

| FIGURE 4.4 | **Stability of International Systems** |

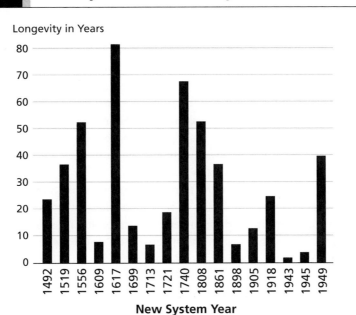

A survey of systems over the past five hundred years makes clear that, contrary to the claims of neorealists and other structural theorists, the bipolar major power system that began in 1945 and ended in 1989 was not especially long lived.

Using Jack Levy's (1983) classification of great powers since 1492, we can determine whether the longevity of the bipolar system was comparatively long or short.

Figure 4.4 shows the longevity of each system defined as the period during which the makeup of the major powers remained unaltered. It is evident that the forty or so years of the bipolar international system were neither unusually long nor unusually short. Many multipolar great power systems lasted longer; many lasted a shorter time. We cannot conclude on the basis of the longevity of the major power system that multipolarity produces less stability than the one instance of bipolarity.

Of course, the longevity of a given international structure is not the only way to think about system stability. Another way to evaluate the stability of the international system is to examine the frequency of wars among the most influential states in the world, the major powers. During the bipolar years, there were two dominant powers: the United States and the Soviet Union. It is noteworthy that no war erupted between these two dominant states during those years. Still, although the superpowers never engaged in battle against one another, both fought several wars against other states, and there was at least one war between a major power and a superpower during the bipolar years. The Korean War (1950–1953) saw combat between the United States and China. In addition, China and the Soviet Union fought sporadically along their extensive border. Although many casualties and deaths resulted from this, the Sino-Soviet conflict is rarely elevated to the status of war.

The peace between the two superpowers has been described by the historian John Gaddis (1987) as "the long peace." Just how long it was and whether or not it was due to bipolarity are both tricky questions. Numerous changes in international affairs can be singled out to explain the long peace. Bipolarity is one, but there is no reason to think it a more or less plausible factor than several other possibilities. Consider, for example, the advent of nuclear deterrence. Nuclear deterrence tends to push the international system toward multipolarity, especially when several well-endowed nuclear powers make the costs of an attack excessive relative to the prospective benefits. Nuclear weapons may have raised the anticipated costs of war well beyond the level of any foreseeable benefits.

Some might point to the creation of the United Nations as a significant improvement over its prewar predecessor, the League of Nations, in helping to limit superpower warfare. Certainly the United Nations has been involved in numerous peacekeeping missions that have helped contain and resolve disputes that might have otherwise entangled the great powers (Fortna 2004). The most powerful arm of the United Nations is the Security Council. Each of its five permanent members—Britain, China, France, Russia, and the United States (sometimes called the P-5)—can veto any resolution brought before the Council, and pretty much all major security issues not directly involving these P-5 states do come before it. The UN Security Council, then, by institutionalizing a multipolar decision-making structure, has provided a counterweight to bipolarity. This too may be an explanation for the long peace.

TRY THIS

Russia rolled tanks and thousands of Russian soldiers into the Republic of Georgia during summer 2008. The United States and the members of the European Union strenuously objected to Russia's use of military force. Why didn't this go to the UN Security Council? What could the Security Council have done to compel the Russians and Georgians to negotiate to find a solution to their differences?

Numerous other explanations for the long peace between the great powers have been put forth (Mueller 1989). The advent of commercial television and the increasing frequency of intercontinental air travel, for example, have both been claimed as pacifying developments because each brings people closer together and fosters greater cultural understanding. Of course, it also could be said that familiarity breeds contempt. We should not leap too quickly to endorse these or the many other explanations of the long peace because each has counterarguments. Still, we have already seen that bipolarity as an explanation of stability has counterarguments that are at least as persuasive as the arguments in its favor.

Just how long has the long peace really lasted? The most obvious answer is that during all forty-four of the years between the end of World War II and the tearing down of the Berlin Wall there was no war between the superpowers; there was peace in a limited but important sense. But only thirty-six years passed without a war between two major powers (excluding the Sino-Soviet border fighting), and there was barely a moment without some smaller war going on, wars often involving a major power. Recall that the Korean War pitted the United States against China. In addition, the French fought in Indochina in the early 1950s; the French and the British fought in Egypt in the Suez War in 1956; the United States fought in the Dominican Republic, Grenada, Panama, Vietnam, and elsewhere; the Chinese fought in India and Vietnam, among other countries, and along the Soviet border; and the Soviet Union engaged in combat in Afghanistan, Czechoslovakia, Hungary, and along the Chinese border. It is reasonable to ask whether forty-four years or even thirty-six years (or less) is really an unusually long time without a war between major powers.

Again, we can turn to Levy's compilation to assess whether the long peace was really all that long. Levy's data show that thirty-eight years passed without a war between major powers from the end of the Napoleonic Wars (1815) to the beginning of the Crimean War (1853). Forty-three years passed between the end of the Franco-Prussian War (1871) and the beginning of World War I (1914).[†] Other lengthy intervals between major power wars can be found scattered throughout the past several centuries. Levy identifies seven general wars since the Treaty of Westphalia: the Dutch War of Louis XIV (1672–1678), the War of the League of Augsburg (1688–1697), the War of the Spanish Succession (1701–1713), the Seven Years War (1755–1763), the French Revolution and Napoleonic Wars (1792–1815), World War I (1914–1918), and World War II (1939–1945). The average interval between general wars is thirty-four years; the longest interval is ninety-nine years, much longer than the so-called long peace. It appears, then, that the long peace cannot be considered unusually long after all.

> **TRY THIS**
>
> These calculations underestimate the weakness of the long-peace argument by counting intervals between any great power wars, whereas the bipolarity argument draws our attention to the two most powerful states and their allies. The more major powers there are, the higher the probability of a war between them if war is randomly distributed with regard to power (which it is not). Look at the post–Thirty Years War world in terms of intervals without war between the two strongest states in each international system. How long are the intervals between wars when only the two most powerful states are counted?

OTHER NEOREALIST HYPOTHESES AND THE HISTORICAL RECORD

Another way to assess the predictive accuracy of the neorealist structural perspective involves the careful examination of what does follow logically from neorealist assumptions. We can then determine whether or not the hypotheses that follow logically from the theory are historically accurate. Several careful studies of the logic of neorealism have been conducted. Emerson Niou, Peter Ordeshook, and Gregory Rose (1989) carefully trace out the logic of

---

[†] We might object that the Russo-Japanese War qualifies as a war between major powers. Japan's status as a potential factor in global power politics, however, was established by its performance in that war and did not predate the event. Still, in some respects Japan had already attained great power status. If we include it among our list of great power wars, then the interval between the Franco-Prussian War and the Russo-Japanese War was thirty-three years.

neorealism and reach four central conclusions based on neorealist assumptions. These implications of neorealism, proven as theorems within a neorealist framework, are:

1. Essential states never become inessential.
2. Essential states are never eliminated from the international system.
3. Inessential states never become essential states.
4. Inessential states are always eliminated from the international system.

An essential state, you will recall, is any state that can join a losing coalition and, by dint of its membership and the power it can bring to bear, turn that coalition into a blocking coalition or a winning coalition. Inessential states are states that are unable to turn even one losing alliance into a winning or blocking coalition.

The Survival of Essential and Inessential States

Each of these propositions is historically false. Austria-Hungary was an essential state at the outset of World War I. By the war's end, it had not only become inessential but was completely eliminated from the international system. Likewise, the Soviet Union was an essential state throughout the cold war—indeed, it was a superpower. Today, it does not exist. In fact, the Soviet Union willingly and peacefully gave up its sphere of influence and its status as a great power. It is not yet clear whether any of its successor states have willingly reduced their power to ensure their survival or are themselves inessential and possibly doomed to extinction. It is clear from Russia's incursion into Georgia in 2008 that the Russian government is reasserting Russia's place among the great powers. After all, it chose to solve its dispute with Georgia by force rather than, for instance, seeking UN approval to impose economic sanctions on Georgia or negotiating directly with the Georgian government. Whether a global economic decline and the accompanying fall in oil prices will upset Russia's efforts to establish itself as a great power remains an open and important question.

The United States in the nineteenth century was an inessential state. Obviously, today it is an essential player; it is arguably the lone remaining superpower. This cannot happen according to neorealist logic. Many other examples can be given to show that the four hypotheses identified by Niou, Ordeshook, and Rose from neorealist logic are simply not consistent with history.

TRY THIS

Add to the list of once-essential states that are now inessential or that no longer exist. Identify some once-inessential states that are now essential or that still exist but remain inessential. If possible, list states in each of these categories over the span of the past three or four centuries.

Uncertainty and War

David Lalman and I have also constructed a formalized version of neorealist theory (Bueno de Mesquita and Lalman 1992). We focus attention on the competing demands of states.

These demands form the core of international disputes. According to neorealist logic, a state makes demands based on its need to protect its security and enhance its power. Therefore, what is demanded (and what is not) depends on the structure of the situation in which the state finds itself. Demands in the international arena are the result of strategic choices—that is, they are endogenous. Because demands are developed based on the logic of the situation at hand, nations would never knowingly choose actions that lead to war and risk their survival. Lalman and I demonstrate this within the context of the neorealist version of our international interaction game (IIG). In the IIG, rival heads of state choose whether or not to make foreign policy demands; whether or not to respond with counterdemands; and whether or not to negotiate, fight, or appease adversaries.

Numerous other game theoretic examinations of war (Powell 1990, 1999; Fearon 1995; Morrow 1997) within a structural perspective indicate that war does not arise without uncertainty. These findings appear to support the neorealist claim equating bipolarity with peace produced by stability. (Remember, bipolarity is really a surrogate for the absence of uncertainty, and multipolarity is really a surrogate for the presence of uncertainty.) In fact, if states lived within a neorealist world and were faced with no uncertainty, they would knowingly choose only those actions that protected the status quo or that led to a negotiated resolution of differences.[‡] Three hypotheses follow directly from the neorealist version of the IIG:

1. Uncertainty promotes war and certainty promotes negotiations or the status quo.
2. Regardless of information circumstances (uncertainty or certainty), no nation will ever acquiesce peacefully to the demands of another state (that is, no appeasement).
3. A necessary, but not sufficient, condition for war is that both parties to the war believe their chances of winning are better than 50 percent.

The record of history does not support any of these hypotheses either. Figure 4.5 shows that there is no straightforward historical relationship between uncertainty and the risk of war. At low levels of uncertainty there is a statistically significant increase in the likelihood of war as uncertainty itself increases. This is followed by a significant decrease in the risk of war at moderate to high levels of uncertainty. At extremely high levels of uncertainty, the probability that disputes will turn into war turns sharply upward. For most of the range of degrees of uncertainty, the probability of war stays well below 20 percent, rising above that level only under truly extreme conditions. The two periods during which the level of uncertainty was so high that it predicted war with near certainty are 1866, when Prussia, Austria, and several smaller German states fought the Seven Weeks War, and 1966–1968, when

---

[‡] Lalman and I measured uncertainty in several different ways. One measure indicates that uncertainty increases as the variation in risk-taking inclinations of state leaders increases. In the neorealist view, remember, bipolar systems have little uncertainty and everyone responds to risks by being cautious. A second measure of uncertainty compares the probability of victory for side A and the probability of victory for side B in any dispute. The more unequal the distribution of power between sides A and B (and therefore the more likely one side is to win rather than the other), the less uncertainty there is about the outcome of a dispute.

| FIGURE 4.5 | War and Uncertainty |

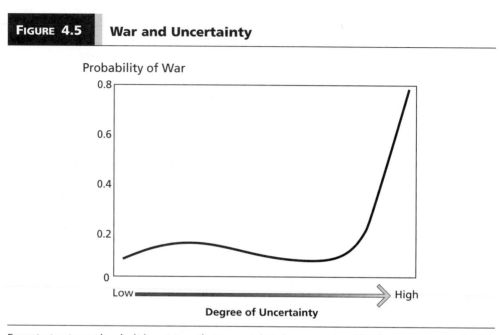

Except at extreme levels, it is not true that uncertainty increases the risk of war. Moderate levels of uncertainty actually produce less war than do low levels of uncertainty.

mounting cold war tensions culminated in the Soviet invasion of Czechoslovakia. In the mid-1860s, as in the mid-1960s, long-established ties among nations were under great strain, making leaders more uncertain than usual about who they could count on. In both of these general instances of extremely high uncertainty, it is interesting to note that the associated conflicts were among states allied to one another. The states involved in the Seven Weeks War were all members of the same mutual defense pact. This was also true in the cases of tension under high uncertainty during the period 1966–1968. Because allies typically share similar foreign policy commitments, it is difficult to discern how states will line up behind belligerents. This difficulty reflects uncertainty in the international system.

Lalman and I examined the role of uncertainty in promoting peaceful dispute resolutions using data from 1816 to 1974. Our neorealist deduction—that diminished uncertainty should increase the odds of peaceful dispute resolutions—is a more general form of Waltz's contention that bipolarity reduces the threat of instability and presages Fearon's rationalist explanations of war. The failure of Lalman's and my neorealist proposition to find support in the historical record is quite troubling for the neorealist perspective, especially in light of all the other evidence against the hypothesis that bipolarity promotes stability. (We see further evidence in this regard in the next chapter, when we separate the conditions under which uncertainty is expected to increase the threat of war from other conditions under which it is expected to reduce that threat.)

Acquiescence and Neorealism

The second hypothesis derived from the realpolitik variant of the IIG contends that a state will never choose to just give in to the demands of another state rather than trying to negotiate a compromise or fighting to protect its interests. This hypothesis is also historically false. That nations do acquiesce to the demands of others is evident. During the Fashoda Crisis between Britain and France in 1898, for example, Britain sought control of as much of the Upper Nile as possible. The French-held town of Fashoda in the Sudan lay exactly in the path of British ambitions. The British were unyielding in their demands. They wanted nothing less than a full acquiescence by the French and were prepared to go to war to pursue their ends. The French were in a militarily weak position. What's more, domestic dissatisfaction with the French cabinet left the government in a vulnerable political position. Rather than resisting and provoking a British attack that would almost certainly lead to a humiliating military defeat and most probably to the downfall of the government as well, France's leaders gave in to British demands. They recognized that they were better off acquiescing in this case than adding fuel to domestic political dissatisfaction with an international crisis. [§]

In late 2003, the Libyan government acquiesced to American demands regarding Libya's nuclear research and potential weapons development programs. After admitting that Libya had a weapons development program despite being signatories to the Nuclear Nonproliferation Treaty (NPT), the government agreed to allow American and British experts to come in and dismantle their facilities with the supervision of the International Atomic Energy Agency (IAEA). This action is another example of acquiescence that contradicts the implicit logic of neorealism. Contrary to that logic, acquiescence is not impossible; in fact, it happens quite often in international affairs.

Balance of Power and Neorealism

Perhaps the most common claim among neorealist theorists is that war occurs only when both sides believe that their chance of winning is greater than 50 percent. This is a partial statement of what has come to be known as the balance-of-power theory. It invokes the idea that war is the product of mutual optimism by rival states, meaning that they overestimate their chances of victory so that their subjective probabilities of victory sum to more than 1. From a game theoretic point of view, there is controversy over whether such a state of affairs can be logically consistent or indicates that one or another party to a dispute is ignoring important information that would force it to adjust its view of its chances of victory, taking into account the observed actions of its rival (Ramsey and Fey 2006).

Many eminent scholars and statesmen have suggested that, when power is fairly evenly distributed, peace is likely to prevail; however, they contend that, when power is unevenly distributed, the risk of war increases. Still, these scholars and statesmen sometimes disagree on exactly what is meant by an even, or balanced, distribution of power. Some emphasize the

---

[§] Although the government did avoid adding fuel to the fire, it was not enough. The French government fell soon after in the face of overwhelming domestic opposition.

TABLE 4.1	The Major Powers' Balance of Power in 1896		
Country	Power (%)	Blocs formed	Power (%)
Germany	21.4	Germany, Austria-Hungary, and Italy	34.9
Austria-Hungary	8.4		
Italy	5.1		
Russia	17.3	Russia, Japan, and France	36.9
Japan	4.6		
France	15.0		
Britain	28.2	Britain[a]	28.2
Total	100.0		100.0

a. Britain did not form a bloc with other nations.

effects of the distribution of power among influential states; others emphasize the effects of the distribution of power among coalitions or blocs of states. These two emphases can mean two very different things.

Consider the estimates of national power depicted in Table 4.1. The table shows estimates of the national capabilities of the seven states that were major powers in 1896. It also shows the capabilities of these powers based on their aggregation into military blocs (with Britain remaining sufficiently distinct in its foreign policies to be considered a bloc unto itself) in 1896, based on calculations of similarity in their military alliance commitments. The data are drawn from the Correlates of War project. The list of capabilities of each of the major powers presents quite a different picture from that of the three major power blocs. The individual states were quite unequal in their relative power. Britain alone controlled over more than 28 percent of the capabilities of the major powers. Japan controlled less than 5 percent, and Italy controlled just barely more than 5 percent of the major power capabilities. Yet the bloc that Italy belonged to, which included Germany and Austria-Hungary, possessed almost 35 percent of the total capabilities of the major powers. A second bloc, composed of Russia, Japan, and France, controlled a little less than 37 percent of total capabilities. Britain, in a bloc by itself, possessed the remaining 28 percent.

One way to measure the extent to which power is unequally divided is to add up the absolute differences between the power of the average nation (or coalition of nations) and the power of each individual nation (or coalition of nations).* If every unit has exactly the same

---

* That is,

$$\text{Balance of power} = \frac{\sum_{i=1}^{n} |C_i - \frac{1}{n}|}{1 - \frac{1}{n}}$$

where C_i = Capabilities of state i, and n = the total number of states (or blocs) being evaluated.

TABLE 4.2	Is a Greater than 50-50 Chance of Victory a Necessary Condition for War?	
Did war occur?	Initiator's probability of victory > 50 percent	Initiator's probability of victory < 50 percent
Yes	52 (13.1%)	37 (11.9%)
No	345 (86.9%)	273 (88.1%)

Source: Bueno de Mesquita and Lalman (1992, 70).

amount of power, then our measure of the balance of power will equal 0 (that is, the total absolute deviation from the mean equals 0 percent). If one state (or coalition) has all the power and the others have none (the most unbalanced system possible), then the balance-of-power measure will be 100 (that is, the total absolute deviation from the mean equals 100 percent). If we focus on the individual major powers in Table 4.1, we find that the balance-of-power measure equals 49.5, which reflects a great inequality in the distribution of power among the major states in 1896. In contrast, if we focus on the major power alliance blocs of 1896, we find a more balanced system. In fact, the sum of the absolute deviations from the mean for each bloc is only 15.3 percent. Clearly, the manner in which we group power (that is, by states or by blocs) profoundly influences whether or not we define a system as balanced. Whichever measure we use, however, it turns out that there is no systematic relationship between the likelihood of war and the balance of power (Singer, Bremer, and Stuckey 1972; Organski and Kugler 1980; Bueno de Mesquita and Lalman 1988).

Nor is there a significant association between estimates of the probability of victory for either side in a war and the likelihood that there will be a war, as shown in Table 4.2. The evidence fails to support the neorealist hypothesis that it is necessary (but not sufficient) that each side in a dispute think its chance of victory is greater than 50 percent before war will occur. If the neorealist hypothesis were correct, then the entry in the cell that corresponds with the row labeled "Yes" and the column labeled "Initiator's probability of victory < 50 percent" would be zero because that cell violates the hypothesized necessary condition for war. Not only is it not zero, but it is not meaningfully closer to zero than the cell that corresponds to the row labeled "Yes" and the column labeled "Initiator's probability of victory > 50 percent." The data in Table 4.2 take into account all disputes within Europe between 1816 and 1974. As such, the table presents a broad-based test of this neorealist claim.

THE POWER TRANSITION: A STRUCTURAL ALTERNATIVE TO NEOREALISM

Building on the work of Edward Carr (1939, 1945), A. F. K. Organski (1958) constructed what was perhaps the first challenge to realism that was neither idealistic nor normative. Organski's **power transition theory** shares with realism a focus on the importance of power

FIGURE 4.6   **The Power Hierarchy in Power Transition Theory**

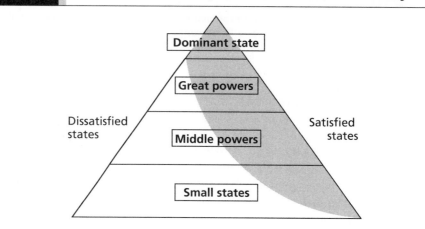

Power transition theory divides the world into two coalitions: satisfied states and dissatisfied states. The stronger a state is, the more likely that it is satisfied with the organization of the international system and the status quo that reflects that system's rules. Weaker states are more likely to be dissatisfied.

in international affairs. However, it breaks with the balance-of-power realism of Morgenthau and Waltz, most notably by maintaining that the international system is not anarchic. Instead, foreshadowing the later development of neoliberal theory (Keohane and Nye 1977) and the study of international political economy, Organski suggests that the international system is hierarchically organized. Figure 4.6 depicts the power triangle that Organski suggests captures fundamental elements of international affairs. The triangular shape reflects the observation that the more powerful and influential a category of states is, the fewer the states in that category. Many nations are small, with few resources with which to influence international relations. Some examples of such states include Chad, Haiti, Laos, and Liechtenstein. Middle powers are less numerous, as reflected by the smaller area of the power triangle given over to them, but they are generally more influential than the small states. Examples of middle powers include Mexico, the Netherlands, Nigeria, and Pakistan. The great powers, such as Britain, China, France, and Russia, exert substantial influence over international affairs. The dominant state throughout the post–World War II years has been the United States. Its position at the pinnacle of the power triangle is ensured by a combination of great national wealth, great per capita wealth, and overwhelming military prowess. According to Organski's power transition viewpoint, there is only one dominant state at any given time. That state establishes the fundamental rules and **norms** of behavior in the international arena.

Figure 4.6 also hints at another assumption of Organski's power transition theory and also of Robert Gilpin's similar theory of hegemonic stability (1981). The shaded area in the power triangle indicates that there is a set of satisfied states, content with the international order. However, the larger, unshaded area indicates that most states are dissatisfied with the international order. In this view of the world, rather than wishing to maximize security or power, nations are interested in maximizing their control over the rules and customs that govern international interactions so that they can define the status quo according to their interests. Dissatisfaction, then, is most prevalent among those least content with the existing status quo. However, it is the more powerful dissatisfied states that represent the biggest threat to international peace and stability. If they have the wherewithal, they will, according to power transition theory, try to alter the hierarchy to put themselves at the top.

The rules of the international system are selected by the dominant state and enforced by that state and other members of the satisfied coalition. System-transforming conflicts occur when a dissatisfied state gains sufficient power to challenge the existing order. Thus, we can see that the focus of hierarchical theories such as the power transition theory is very much on the rules and norms that govern behavior rather than on the distribution of power or state security per se.

The supposition that the dominant state determines rules and norms of action is an important departure from neorealist thinking. Although power transition theorists share the neorealists' view of the state as the central actor in international affairs, they disagree with the assumption that all nations are trying to maximize power and security (Organski 1958; Organski and Kugler 1980; Kim and Morrow 1992; Lemke 2002;). Rather, power transition theorists argue that states have policy objectives that they wish to impose on other states. These goals or objectives can best be imposed by establishing rules and norms that govern international interactions. Control over the rules and norms, then, is tantamount to control over the course of international politics.

The very fact that a dominant state can impose rules suggests that it has the means at its disposal to enforce those rules. Enforcement depends on power. As such, power transition and hegemonic stability theorists consider power to be the essential instrument of international affairs. In this way they differ markedly from the idealists, who dominated thinking about international relations before World War II. For idealists, ethics, morality, and maximizing collective welfare, rather than individual national well-being, were the normative guideposts for international intercourse. Their views are currently enjoying a renaissance in more sophisticated constructivist theories about the role that ideas play in international affairs (Katzenstein 1985; Goldstein and Keohane 1993; Wendt 1999). For power transition theorists, however, normative concerns or social constructions are not central to understanding international relations.

Examples of International Rules and Norms

What are the rules and norms governing international politics? Examples abound both in the domain of international economic exchange and in that of security. After World War II, the United States promoted a currency regime known as the **Bretton Woods Agreement.** At

Bretton Woods, the U.S. dollar became the currency against which the value of all other currencies was pegged. Before Bretton Woods, much of the world was on the gold standard, meaning that the price of an ounce of gold was fixed but the amount of a given currency that was needed to purchase that ounce of gold fluctuated. The gold standard began to crumble during the interwar years, with international financial interests looking for a substitute (Simmons 1994).

Under the Bretton Woods Agreement, the U.S. dollar took over the role of gold, becoming the fixed standard against which other money was valued. This meant that the dollar became the most desired means of exchange in international markets and, hence, that the United States was at center stage in economic dealings. The abandonment of the Bretton Woods Agreement by President Richard Nixon led some observers to speak of a decline in American hegemony (Keohane 1984; Kennedy 1987). Whether there was a decline in American hegemony or not (Russett 1985; Strange 1987; Kugler and Organski 1989), what is important to recognize here is that the Bretton Woods Agreement represented a new set of rules imposed on the international community after World War II by the hegemonic United States.

Over the past several decades, the United States has been the world leader in pressing for the establishment of a free-trade regime, first through the General Agreement on Tariffs and Trade (GATT) from 1947 to 1995 and then through the World Trade Organization (WTO). Although, as we see later in Chapter 10, the United States has not always practiced free trade itself, it has steadfastly promoted free trade among other nations. Whether it will continue to do so following the financial crisis of 2008 is an interesting question. If past behavior is a good predictor of future policy, despite U.S. deviations—such as taking over the big financial house of Bear, Stearns, bailing out the giant insurance company AIG, and buying up bad mortgage loans that were freezing credit markets—from a market orientation, it is likely to continue to promote market solutions to most economic problems in the poorer parts of the world.

The free-trade regime enforced by the GATT and now the WTO and other trade arrangements such as the North American Free Trade Agreement (NAFTA) establishes rules for judging whether or not specific trade practices are protectionist. Even though their enforcement powers are limited, these agreements still maintain a rule-based and normative influence on the trading practices of their members. For example, tariff levels are today less than one-tenth of what they were in 1947, when the GATT first began to operate, and they appear to continue to be dropping under the supervision of the WTO. This is the direct consequence of the trading rules promoted by the United States.

Perhaps the most visible norm engendered by the U.S. international leadership has been arguing in favor of the promotion of democratic institutions and the protection of human rights. These ideas are clearly embedded in the American perception of what constitutes an appropriate basis on which people should be governed. Long before the United States emerged as a hegemonic power, it was touting the benefits of democratic practices. Most visible among its early efforts was the inclusion of self-determination as one of Woodrow Wilson's famous fourteen points, articulated at the end of World War I.

Although the United States has from time to time collaborated with nondemocratic and even antidemocratic states, its closest ties have always been reserved for like-minded governments. It is unlikely that the North Atlantic Treaty Organization (NATO), for example, would have remained as cohesive as it did throughout the cold war if the members had shared only a common fear of the Soviet Union. Surely, if that were the only glue holding NATO together, some members would have defected and made separate arrangements with the Soviets. All the members of NATO, however, shared a common commitment to democracy and human rights, at least on their own turf. Indeed, some western European states, such as Spain and Portugal, were prohibited from joining NATO or the European Community until their dictatorships (under Gen. Francisco Franco in Spain and Antonio de Oliveira Salazar in Portugal) were replaced by democratic systems. Likewise, NATO expansion to include Eastern European states formerly in the Warsaw Pact has depended in part on the ability of those states to demonstrate a commitment to democratic norms of conduct. Yet, as we see in Chapter 8, there are few examples in which the United States successfully exported democracy to other countries, and there are good reasons that few examples exist.

On the security front, the United States was a prime mover behind the establishment of the United Nations as an institution designed to promote peace throughout the world. Although the UN General Assembly has frequently voted in support of points of view opposed by the United States, the United States remains an active UN participant. The United States, especially during the presidencies of George H. W. Bush and Bill Clinton, steadfastly looked to the United Nations to provide legal, political, and moral support for major international military interventions. It has relied on UN coalitions to justify wars against Iraq and Afghanistan and military actions against Somalia, Haiti, and others. To be sure, U.S. political and financial support of the United Nations has waxed and waned, as during the build-up to the 2003 war against Iraq, but the United States today remains a promoter of a peacekeeping, security-providing role for the United Nations. Indeed, under President Obama it is likely that the United States will become more supportive of an expanded role for the UN in peacekeeping and other international security issues.

> **TRY THIS**
>
> What rules or norms of international conduct did Britain try to enforce around the world during its time as the hegemonic power of the nineteenth century? Provide examples of changes in conduct imposed by the French under Napoleon on their far-flung empire. Had Germany won World War II, what might it have introduced as the norms and rules of international relations? In less recent times, did the Catholic Church impose rules of behavior on other states when it was Europe's hegemonic power? How was the Church's hegemony challenged and ultimately defeated? Look back still further to ancient Rome or Greece. What rules did they impose? Examine Edward Creasy's *Fifteen Decisive Battles of the World* (1960). He chose his "decisive" battles precisely because they represented turning points in international norms and rules.

It is not difficult to imagine that many of the rules and norms promoted by the United States would have been discarded had the Soviet Union won in the competition to become world hegemon. Certainly, the Soviets were interested in promoting socialist economic systems rather than the free-trade, market-oriented regime espoused by the United States. The Soviets would have promoted authoritarian governments, as they did throughout their sphere of influence, to protect and enhance the control of communist parties around the world. And they probably would not have supported the United Nations politically if it routinely opposed their point of view.

Dissatisfaction, the Status Quo, and War

When their perspectives on the rules governing international interactions differ markedly, dominant states and those in the groupings below them in the power triangle may clash. **Dissatisfaction** with the status quo becomes the principal source of international tension. Conflict arises when a powerful, dissatisfied state grows strong enough to challenge the authority of the hegemon. Because such a challenge concerns the very way in which international affairs are conducted, the ensuing conflict is fierce and costly. Wars over changes in the rules have the potential for transforming the international system.

But when do such wars occur? The dominant state will not sit by and permit the challenger to pass it by in terms of power. It will not peacefully concede control to the upstart. At the same time, the challenger is reluctant to start a fight before it has enough power to give it a credible chance of defeating the hegemon. The conjunction of these conditions arises, according to power transition theorists, when the two rivals are just about equal in power. This time period during which the challenger roughly comes to equal and then surpass the dominant state in power is known as the power transition. It is the time when the threat of a major war is hypothesized to be at its peak.

Contrary to the balance-of-power perspective, power transition and hegemonic stability theorists believe that major wars are most likely to occur when the power of the opposed states is about equal. According to these theorists, a balance of power promotes war. They maintain that system-transforming wars—that is, wars that lead to a new power hierarchy and to new rules and norms—will occur only when the power of a challenger and the dominant state are about equal and the power of the challenger is increasing faster than that of the dominant state. These claims have been extended and shown to have empirical bite at the regional as well as the global level, so that regional hegemons apparently face the same pressures and the same sources of war as their global counterparts (Lemke 1996, 2002).

How does a threatening balance of power develop in the first place? It should be evident from the power triangle that it is virtually impossible for transition-inducing conflict to emerge as a result of alliances. After all, satisfied states are concentrated at the upper reaches of the power triangle; they are not likely to join forces with a powerful dissatisfied state intent on challenging the hegemon because satisfied states, by their very definition, prefer the rules and norms of the existing status quo to those of a potential hegemonic rival. Thus, we must look elsewhere for the source of the shifts in power that create a transition-inducing balance of power.

For power transition and hegemonic stability theorists, a threatening balance of power emerges as a result of differing rates of internal growth between a dominant state and a

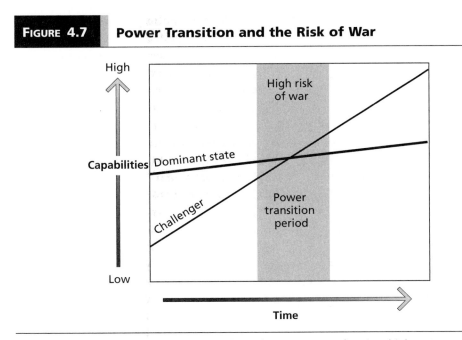

| FIGURE 4.7 | **Power Transition and the Risk of War** |

Power transition theory leads to the hypothesis that system-transforming, high-cost wars are especially likely when a dissatisfied challenger state achieves approximate power parity with the dominant, status quo–defending state.

challenger state. These theories still give little attention to domestic politics per se, but they do recognize that internal factors shape rates of growth. In fact, power transition theory defines domestic affairs as those issues pertaining to economic matters, such as the skills of the population; the quality of infrastructure; and the value of national resources such as labor, capital, and natural assets. Domestic politics affects these matters only in that each polity varies in its ability to mobilize its society's wealth for foreign (or domestic) policy purposes. Growth rates themselves are not viewed as a product of strategic decision making or internal politics, in contrast to the selectorate theory introduced in Chapter 1. Quite the contrary, the leading power transition theorists maintain that the long-term rate of economic growth is inevitable and cannot be altered, even by such massive shocks as national defeat in war (Organski and Kugler 1980; Kugler and Lemke 1995), even if such a defeat results in altered domestic political institutions.

The likelihood of war, as predicted by the power transition and hegemonic stability theories, is summarized in Figure 4.7. When a dissatisfied state lags far behind the dominant state in power, war is not expected to occur. Likewise, if the rising challenger state overtakes the dominant state by a substantial margin of power, war again is unlikely. In this case, a peaceful transition takes place. But when the challenger's power rises quickly, first to equal and

TABLE 4.3	Empirical Evidence for the Power Transition Theory, 1815–1980		
Does war occur?	Power is unequal	Power is equal and challenger is not overtaking hegemon	Power is equal and challenger is overtaking hegemon
No	4	6	5
Yes	0	0	5

Source: Adapted from Organski and Kugler (1980, 52, Table 1.7).

Note: The table shows the results of a τ_c statistical test, which is a test of correlation for ordinal data that evaluates the magnitude of deviations in an asymmetric matrix for the data from the diagonal running from the upper left cell to the lower right cell. Here, $\tau_c = 0.5$ and probability < 0.05. Cell entries represent the number of great power–hegemon pairings satisfying the conditions specified in the cell's column and row headings. For instance, Organski and Kugler's data include four instances of pairings of a great power and the dominant state (hegemon) with unequal power between them and no instance of war.

then to overtake the dominant state, a wrenching, system-transforming power transition war is predicted to be likely to occur.

Organski and Jacek Kugler (1980) subject the power transition theory's core war hypothesis to empirical testing. They note that there are three different types of power distributions that can arise between states: (1) the challenger can be significantly weaker than the dominant state, (2) the challenger can be about equal in power to the dominant state but not growing so fast as to appear to be overtaking the hegemon, or (3) the challenger can be about equal in power to the dominant state and be growing so fast that it appears to equal and then overtake the dominant power. Organski and Kugler hypothesize that major wars can occur only in the third circumstance. Table 4.3 shows the results of their examination of interactions between major powers from 1815 to 1980. The table indicates that there is a statistically significant probability that the power transition theory's main war hypothesis is accurate, although some critics have raised important questions about the method of case selection (Siverson and Sullivan 1983).

The power transition argument has been formalized to tease out its precise logical implications. Woosang Kim and James Morrow (1992), for example, show that although some of the core hypotheses stated by Organski and Kugler are in fact borne out by precise formal logic, other important hypotheses are not and must be modified. Kim and Morrow show that there is a critical time during which the risk of war is at a maximum. This occurs when the challenger feels that the costs of deferring an effort to defeat the existing status quo are equal to the benefits that would be obtained from proceeding with such an effort and when the dominant state believes that the costs of fighting are less than the costs of granting concessions to the challenger. However, the emergence of that critical interval during which both states are prepared to fight does not depend on an equal or approximately equal distribution of power (Kim and Morrow 1992; Powell 1996), in contradiction to the main power transition claim.

Kim and Morrow have shown that the distribution of power at which the rivals will fight depends on their willingness to take the risks of waiting. The longer the challenger waits to attack, the higher is its probability of victory. This is true because the challenger's power is growing faster than the dominant state's power. Thus, the longer the challenger puts off a war, the greater will be the odds in its favor. However, the longer it waits, the longer it must endure the rules of international intercourse with which it is dissatisfied. The challenger's decision about whether or not to attack the dominant state, then, depends on its inclination to take risks, on how quickly it is growing in power, on how costly the war is expected to be, and on how unhappy it is with the status quo. Kim and Morrow have shown that the interval during which the challenger is willing to fight expands as the expected costs of the war increase, as the challenger's dissatisfaction with the status quo increases, as the challenger's relative growth rate declines, and as the challenger becomes more risk acceptant.

Conversely, the longer the dominant state waits, the worse its political and military prospects will be. The difference in their respective growth rates places the dominant state increasingly at a disadvantage relative to the challenger. For the hegemon, then, waiting is risky business. But it does forestall the day when the hegemon may lose control over the rules of the game, making it impossible for the hegemon to credibly commit to altering the international rules and norms by peaceful means before it absolutely has to. The dominant state's willingness to fight is postponed, making war less likely to be tied to the period of the power transition, if there is a war at all, as the expected costs of war decrease and as the growth rate of the challenger increases. Under these circumstances, the hegemon becomes increasingly risk averse. How long the challenger and the dominant states will wait before fighting, then, depends on their respective responses to risk, their relative rates of growth, the expected costs of the war, and their respective degrees of satisfaction with the status quo.

TRY THIS

Table 4.3 shows a statistical test, called τ_c (tau-c), which assesses the correlation between the conditions of the power transition theory and the likelihood of war. It is statistically significant and so lends consequential support to the power transition theory's most important hypothesis. However, there is another way to look at the table. We generally want to know how much better a theory does at predicting events (in this case, whether specific great powers will wage war or not) than the naïve prediction that the most frequently occurring outcome will happen in every case. That is, we want to know what percentage of the predictive errors made with the naïve approach are eliminated by the theory being tested. This is known as the proportionate reduction in error (PRE). The PRE equals the sum of the maximum cell value in each column of the table minus the maximum row total (that row total being the number of cases we get right just using the naïve prediction) divided by the number of observations in the table minus the maximum row total. The denominator tells us how many additional cases we *could* get right with our theory that we miss with the naïve prediction. The numerator tells us how many additional cases we *actually* got right with our theory compared to the naïve prediction. What is the PRE gained from the power transition theory, as indicated by the evidence in Table 4.3? What should we infer when different statistical tests legitimately lead to different conclusions about a theory's explanatory and predictive potential?

The empirical evidence supports some claims of power transition theory, but other important power transition hypotheses fail the empirical test. For example, differences in growth rates turn out not to be crucial empirically. Critically, power transitions need not occur at the time of approximate equality in power. Indeed, power transitions per se cannot explain especially costly wars. As Paul Huth has observed, "no state initiates war if it expects the war to be long and bloody" (1988, 74). In fact, although there is a critical time during which wars are more likely to occur, that period of time is not a function of the distribution of power and can fluctuate widely to either side of a power balance, depending on the specific risk-taking proclivities of the relevant leaders, the magnitude of dissatisfaction with the status quo, the anticipated costs of war, and the precise growth-rate differential between the challenger and the hegemon.

SUMMARY

In this chapter we have seen that war is ex post inefficient and can—but need not—arise because of uncertainty, commitment problems, or a dispute over an indivisible objective. We have also examined the central hypotheses of two major structural theories of the causes of war: neorealism and power transition theory. Neorealism's claims that bipolarity promotes stability, that uncertainty provokes instability, that states routinely mimic one another, and that a balance of power fosters stability are logically flawed and unsupported by the historical record. The alternative structural explanation presented here, the power transition theory, is consistent with the historical facts with regard to some of its core predictions but not others. Neither theory seems to provide a sufficiently robust explanation of why or when war is likely.

Scientific progress in understanding how the world works is made by building progressively on the ideas that we inherit and discarding those parts that clearly fail us in exchange for superior alternatives. Much valuable debate has been stimulated by structural theories, and many useful insights have been gleaned from these approaches. However, as we see in Chapter 5, strategic game theory treatments of war provide alternative accounts that explain what structural theories explain and also explain things not accounted for by structural approaches such as neorealism or power transition theory.

KEY CONCEPTS

asymmetric information (or uncertainty)   110
balance of power   122
bipolarity   118
blocking coalition   123
Bretton Woods Agreement   139
credible commitments   110
dissatisfaction   142
essential actors   116
indivisible goods   113
inessential actors   124

instability   116
multipolarity   118
norms   138
power transition theory   137
security dilemma   117
stability   116
time inconsistency   115
transaction costs   110
unipolarity   128

5 | Strategic Theories of War

OVERVIEW

- War is correctly viewed as ex post inefficient from the perspective of national welfare; however, it can be efficient for leaders, especially those who head a small-coalition, autocratic government.

- When domestic politics plays a part in shaping demands for war, uncertainty can increase or decrease the probability of war, thereby contradicting a fundamental prediction from structural theories.

- The evidence supports the contention that the likelihood of war is reduced by uncertainty under specific preference conditions and is increased under others.

- Although realism associates aggression and war with power, the strategic perspective highlights contingent conditions under which the weak are especially likely to initiate the use of violence.

- Terrorism may be an instance in which otherwise peacefully inclined people become unusually aggressive because they are weak relative to their opponents and so can bring few bargaining chips to the negotiating table.

In March 1999, NATO forces, including American, British, Dutch, and German troops, among others, began a bombing campaign against Serbia in the heart of Europe. The purpose of this action was to force Serbian president Slobodan Milosevic to abandon his push to drive the Albanian population, of which 90 percent were Muslims, out of Christian Serbia's Kosovo province. President Milosevic's policy of ethnic cleansing was, and is, abhorrent.

The military campaign against Serbia was not motivated by any concerns for the general security of the United States or even of the European NATO countries. Although it is true that conflict in Serbia, and in the Balkans in general, was at the root of World War I and that the area remains a tinderbox today, few observers believed that by driving the Albanian Kosovars out of Kosovo and into Albania, Macedonia, and other neighboring states, the Serbs would destabilize Europe, although the flow of refugees certainly posed an immense burden on the surrounding states. If security concerns were not a major issue, how can we explain the willingness of the NATO countries to wage war against Serbia? For that matter, how can we explain NATO's Operation Deliberate Force in 1995, designed to put an end to Serbia's foray into ethnic cleansing in Bosnia or efforts by the United States and the United Nations to put an end to the rule of warlords in Somalia in the early 1990s? By the same token, how do we explain the U.S. decision to participate in World War I, a case in which there was a clear threat to American commerce but little prospect of a fundamental threat to homeland security?*

A decade after NATO forces first entered Serbia, regional conflict has necessitated their continued presence. In March 2008, French NATO peacekeeping vehicles were set on fire and NATO troops came under fire during riots in the ethnically divided city of Mitrovia.

---

* The threat of German submarines to American commerce and passenger ships was the centerpiece of Woodrow Wilson's decision in 1917 to seek a congressional declaration of war against Germany. The submarine threat was neatly captured in the slogan, "Remember the *Lusitania*," an American ship sunk by German submarines in May 1915, resulting in the death of 128 Americans. In addition to passengers, the Lusitania also carried munitions for Britain's use in World War I. Although the national security threat from German submarine warfare was very real, this account of the U.S. entry into World War I cannot be the whole story. The Lusitania was sunk nearly two years before the United States declared war. In addition, President Wilson won reelection in 1916 on the slogan, "He kept us out of war." After securing a second term, however, he pointed to Germany's submarine warfare threat (which had been renewed after a period of relative quiescence) to mobilize public opinion. The German threat was primarily against ships approaching ports in England or Ireland, the likely destinations for ships carrying munitions and other material of significance in the allied war effort. The German effort to forge an alliance with Mexico against the United States (as revealed in the infamous Zimmerman telegram), which included promises to return to Mexico territories lost to the United States (such as Texas) was unlikely to have been taken seriously except as a propaganda tool. What the balance was between Wilson's concern that American security was at grave risk due to Germany's submarine warfare policy and his conclusion that U.S. interests lay with Britain cannot be known for certain. What is clear, however, is that he weighed carefully the domestic implications of his choices (hence his campaign slogan) and their national security consequences.

The proposed answer to these questions is that the political leaders in NATO in 1999, leaders in other countries on earlier occasions, and, more recently, leaders of the war on terrorism calculated that the domestic and international repercussions of doing nothing were worse than the expected consequences of going to war. At the same time, leaders such as Milosevic calculated that such foes did not have the resolve to endure the high human and political costs that came with fighting. They believed that if they just stood firm, their rivals would ultimately seek a negotiated means to bringing the war to a close. Thus, in these cases, domestic and foreign strategic factors, not global considerations such as the balance of power, came together to create a conflict that culminated in war. Here we have examples in which, as Fearon (1995) suggests, war might be ex post inefficient for the countries involved but might not be inefficient for the individual leaders choosing between war and the peace of appeasement (Chiozza and Goemans 2004).

To explore in a readily digestible form the logic behind war fighting against the backdrop of domestic political considerations, I examine the domestic version of the international interaction game developed by David Lalman and me (Bueno de Mesquita and Lalman 1992) and contrast it to a realist variant. Realism, as you know, contends that what goes on inside states is not relevant to international politics. Rather, according to realism, or really its current incarnation, neorealism, states try to maximize their security and their national survival. In contrast, in the strategic perspective embodied in the domestic version of the IIG, states pursue foreign policies based on the choices their leaders make taking domestic and international political conditions into account.

By comparing the neorealist version of the IIG discussed in Chapter 4 to the domestic version, we have a general way to look at the relationship between uncertainty and war as well as the relationship between power and aggression. In this chapter, we also examine two hypotheses, the resurrection hypothesis and the pacific dove hypothesis, that suggest that weakness and domestic considerations can, under special circumstances, encourage aggression. In addition, we evaluate theories that link arms races to war and theories that explain war as a diversion from domestic difficulties. In each case, we examine the logic and the evidence behind the arguments.

THE INTERNATIONAL INTERACTION GAME AND WAR

According to the domestic version of the **international interaction game** (IIG), policy demands and threats are motivated by domestic political considerations, whereas choices of action are shaped by the international context. Figure 5.1 shows the sequence of interactions in international relations according to the IIG. The game indicates that international interactions have eight possible generic outcomes:

1. The status quo prevails.
2. The contending sides (let's call them A and B) reach a negotiated settlement.
3. A acquiesces (that is, gives in to a demand without offering armed resistance or facing an armed attack).

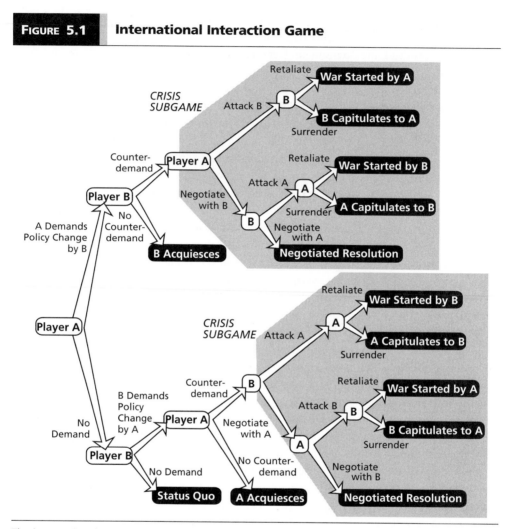

FIGURE 5.1   **International Interaction Game**

The international interaction game offers a scaffolding from which to investigate international interactions. The game identifies eight generic outcomes of international interactions and emphasizes both international and domestic factors that influence the course of international events.

4. B acquiesces.
5. A capitulates (that is, gives in to a demand immediately after sustaining an armed attack).
6. B capitulates.
7. A initiates a war (the mutual use of force in pursuit of fulfillment of a demand).
8. B initiates a war.

The domestic version of the IIG has seven behavioral assumptions. These assumptions define restrictions over the possible ordering of preferences for each decision maker across the eight possible outcomes. The seven assumptions of the domestic version of the IIG are:

1. Each decision maker is rational in the sense that he or she chooses actions so that the strategies played are subgame perfect Nash equilibria. (Recall that a subgame perfect Nash equilibrium is a Nash equilibrium for every subgame of the larger game so that each player selects a best reply to the anticipated actions of the other from that stage of the game forward.)
2. The outcome of any acquiescence or capitulation is known with certainty so that the probability of success in these instances is $p = 0$ or $p = 1$, depending on whether a state is giving in or being given in to. The acquiescing or capitulating state loses and the state that is acquiesced or capitulated to gains its demand for certain. The status quo also does not have a probabilistic outcome.
3. Disputes that are resolved through negotiations or through war involve a lottery in which each player has a chance of gaining his or her objective (p_A and p_B for players A and B, respectively) and a chance of losing ($1 - p_A$ and $1 - p_B$, respectively), with $0 < p < 1$.
4. Each state prefers to resolve disputes through negotiation rather than through war, and this preference for negotiation over war is common knowledge.
5. Violent disputes involve costs not involved in negotiations. In war, a would-be attacker expects to lose fewer lives and less property if it attacks rather than if it is attacked; that is, there is a first-strike advantage. A capitulation involves being attacked and then giving in without retaliating; the state that gives in absorbs the costs inflicted in the initial attack. Any state using violence pays a domestic political cost for failing to resolve the dispute through peaceful means. This cost is a way of recognizing that war is ex post inefficient.
6. Each decision maker prefers to gain any policy change he or she has demanded from the rival rather than have the status quo persist; at the same time, each decision maker prefers that the status quo persist rather than he or she acquiesce to the policy demanded by the rival.
7. Foreign policy demands are shaped by domestic political considerations that may (but need not) take into account international constraints.

This theory models international relations as a process of strategic interaction involving external and domestic considerations, with domestic considerations treated in a greatly simplified way. Without the seven assumptions, it would be logically possible for each of the two players in the IIG to prefer the eight possible outcomes of the game in any order. For example, without the restrictions imposed by the assumptions, a state might prefer capitulating to its adversary over the status quo, the status quo over a war it starts, a war it starts over negotiating, negotiating over acquiescing to its adversary, acquiescing to its adversary over having

TABLE 5.1	Restrictions on Preferences for Decision Maker *i* in the International Interaction Game	
Outcome	Restriction on ordering	Possible preference rank[a]
Status quo	> Acquiescence by *i*, capitulation by *i*	7 to 3
Acquiescence by *j*	> All other outcomes	8
Acquiescence by *i*	> Capitulation by *i*	5 to 2
Negotiation	> Acquiescence by *i*, capitulation by *i*, war started by *i*, war started by *j*	7 to 5
Capitulation by *j*	> War started by *i*, war started by *j*	7 to 3
War started by *i*	> War started by *j*	5 to 2
Capitulation by *i*	> None assured	4 to 1
War started by *j*	> None assured	4 to 1

a. Rank order runs from 1 (least preferred) to 8 (most preferred). We see, then, that the assumptions restrict how valued or disliked given outcomes can be. For instance, having the other guy (*j*) acquiesce to you (*i*) is always the best result (preference rank 8). Acquiescing to the other guy, however, can fall anywhere between being the fourth-best outcome (preference rank 5) and being the second-worst outcome (preference rank 2) for you. You always prefer acquiescing yourself to capitulating (that's why it cannot be preference rank 1—the worst outcome), and you always prefer that the other guy acquiesce to you, that the status quo continue, or that there be a negotiated compromise between you and the other guy (so your acquiescing cannot be preferences rank 6, 7, or 8 because there are three outcomes that are always better for you than acquiescing). Hence, your acquiescence cannot be better than fifth-worst or worse than second-worst among possible outcomes.

its adversary acquiesce to it, having its adversary acquiesce to it over fighting a war started by its adversary, and fighting a war started by its adversary over having its adversary capitulate to it. Obviously, some of these are very strange preferences indeed and, given the game's assumptions, they are ruled out from consideration. Without the seven assumptions, there are 8! possible ways to order the game's outcomes for each player, or $(8!)^2$ possible pairs of preferences for the two players. This equals 1,625,702,400 possible pairs of preference orderings. By making these seven assumptions, we reduce the logically permitted set of preference orderings to 52^2, or 2,704; we consider only a small number of this still large, but greatly reduced, set. Table 5.1 summarizes the limitations imposed by the assumptions of the domestic IIG in regard to how preferences about the possible outcomes are restricted. Clearly, the assumptions greatly simplify the world; they eliminate 99.9998 percent of all possible pairs of preference orders. Perhaps this is too drastic a reduction, and perhaps it is not. This can be determined only by seeing what follows logically from the theory and then testing the theoretical results against the empirical evidence. Despite the huge reduction in possible pairs of preference orders, the theory remains rich (more than 2,700 pairs of preference orderings) in possible combinations of player interactions.

The domestic version of the IIG assumes that leaders select policy demands for their state based on domestic political pressures—that is, on the needs of those key domestic supporters who maintain them in office. This produces one fundamental difference between the IIG's neorealist version and its domestic variant. The neorealist version differs in only one assumption; in the neorealist version, we assume that it is not possible for a decision maker to prefer to compel a rival to capitulate rather than to negotiate with that rival. This is not because adversaries are nicer but, rather, because demands are assumed to be shaped by the structure of the international situation, without regard to domestic politics. That is, after all, an essential feature of neorealist thinking. By assumption, states seek to minimize any risk to their security. Because capitulation following an attack reduces a state's security by compelling it to give in to whatever its adversary has demanded and to bear costs in lost lives and property, each state structures its response to its adversary's demand in a way that allows it to avoid such losses. This is accomplished by offering the rival just enough in concessions to make the would-be aggressor prefer to negotiate a compromise settlement, given the concessions that are put on the table, rather than use force. In effect, each state hones its demands to steer its adversary toward indifference between a peaceful settlement and the use of force. By negotiating, the would-be attacker gains less of whatever it demanded (such as territorial or policy concessions from the foe) than it might have had it used force, but it conserves resources by avoiding the costs it would have endured as a consequence of its attack. As long as the expected utility from negotiating is at least as large as the expected utility from attacking, the rival will negotiate rather than attack.[†] This leaves the would-be attacker no worse off and the would-be target better off.

By contrast, in the domestic version of the IIG, although it is possible for one side to persuade the other side to negotiate rather than attack, the assumptions of the theory do not preclude the possibility that one state's leaders will prefer to force a capitulation rather than negotiate. The domestic constituents' passions of the moment, for example, may demand extracting a pound of flesh for a perceived misdeed by the rival, and a leader who ignores that demand does so at his or her political peril. Therefore, the domestic IIG allows some preference orderings that the neorealist version does not—namely, any orderings in which forcing a capitulation is preferred to negotiating.

Be careful not to get confused here. In either version of the IIG, any state prefers to negotiate rather than be compelled to capitulate. The difference is not in choosing to capitulate or to negotiate. The difference is that in the domestic version a state can try to make another state capitulate, whereas in the neorealist variant, in which demands are chosen only in response to the external dispute, it cannot. In the neorealist version of the IIG, negotiation always wins out over a forced capitulation because players choose demands to make sure of that. In the domestic IIG, actors that prefer to negotiate with a rival rather than forcing the rival to capitulate are labeled doves; actors that prefer to force a rival to capitulate rather than negotiating are labeled hawks.

[†] The procedure for identifying endogenously chosen demands is explained in Bueno de Mesquita and Lalman (1992, Chap. 3).

The existence of hawks as well as doves in the domestic version of the IIG produces predictions about war that are fundamentally different from those produced by the neorealist version. Lalman and I prove what we call the IIG's basic war theorem. This theorem, or logical implication of the game, shows that the game contains conditions that are both necessary and sufficient for war under complete and perfect information. In other words, when there is no uncertainty, war can occur if and only if these conditions hold true. In the absence of uncertainty, war cannot occur at any other time. The complete and perfect information conditions that lead to war reflect an inherent commitment problem that emerges from the structure of the IIG. That commitment problem has to do with the risks inherent in offering to negotiate with someone who is a hawk and who, therefore, will be inclined to seize a first-strike advantage if the opportunity presents itself. In the game tree (Figure 5.1), we can see exactly where this opportunity arises. If player A, for instance, offers a compromise in the hopes of reaching a negotiated settlement and player B is known to be a hawk, A can anticipate that B will attack rather than continue negotiating provided that A is in a weak enough situation that it will not retaliate if attacked. In anticipation of such an attack, A may be better off not trying to negotiate in the first place, choosing instead to get the first-strike advantage for itself. B's inability to commit to negotiating lies at the heart of the problem. Let's see how we prove this.

Basic war theorem of the domestic IIG: War is the complete and perfect information equilibrium outcome if there is no uncertainty about the other players preferences and four preference conditions are fulfilled:

1. Player A prefers to initiate a war rather than acquiesce to the demands of player B.
2. Player A prefers to capitulate if attacked rather than retaliate and fight a war in which player B has gained the advantages of a first strike.
3. Player B prefers to fight a war started by player A rather than acquiesce to the demands of A.
4. Player B prefers to force player A to capitulate rather than negotiate with A (that is, player B is a hawk).

The fourth preference condition cannot arise in the realist version of the IIG. In that game, B and A each picks its demand to minimize threats to its security. Each rival can always find a demand that is more modest than what it really wants and that makes its opponent just as happy to negotiate as to try to force a capitulation. When demands are chosen strategically within the international framework, the fourth preference condition is the preference that each actor worries about most and so takes action to offset. Negotiation is always better for the state that otherwise would have to capitulate. Negotiation not only allows that state to avoid the physical costs of being attacked but also provides it with some chance (remember, $0 < p < 1$) of getting at least part of what it wants. When a state is compelled to capitulate, there is no such chance.

The second preference condition establishes a first-strike advantage sufficiently large that B cannot credibly commit to negotiate rather than take advantage of A if given the chance and

A is unwilling to give up the first-strike advantage to B rather than capitalize on it itself. A simple way to think about how such a situation could arise is to think of a situation similar to a prisoner's dilemma occurring in one of the "Crisis subgame" parts of Figure 5.1. What happens, in essence, is that the threat of being forced to capitulate can lead a state to initiate war if it has a large enough first-strike advantage. Knowing that its rival will take advantage and force a capitulation if it offers to negotiate, a state that has a valuable first-strike advantage of its own may decide to initiate a fight rather than cede the first-strike advantage to a foe. Even if the prospective target of the preemptive strike professes that it will negotiate in good faith, the existence of a first-strike advantage prevents the professed commitment to negotiate from being credible. We have seen an example of just this problem in Chapter 4 in the commitment problem that makes peace between the Israelis and the Palestinians difficult to achieve.

> ### TRY THIS
>
> Use Figure 5.1 to satisfy yourself that the basic war theorem leads to war in the IIG. To do so, start at any terminal node, identify the choice of each player at each terminal node, and work your way up the game tree. Be sure not to violate any of the theory's assumptions when determining the choice of moves at each node in the game, and be sure to adhere to the theorem's conditions. Note that if a player prefers to capitulate rather than retaliate, then it must also prefer to acquiesce rather than retaliate because the latter involves the same policy outcome as capitulation but with no loss of life or property; that is, with lower costs.

The derivation of conditions under which war is logically possible with complete and perfect information also implies important differences between the domestic IIG and neorealism (the most widely used way of thinking about international affairs). Neorealist theory says that uncertainty increases the risk of instability (and war is often both a source and symptom of instability). It looks at how states organize themselves into alliance blocs or poles, noting that when there are just two poles there is very little uncertainty about which side each state is on; however, when there is multipolarity there is a lot of uncertainty. Thus, neorealist thinking indicates that bipolar international politics (such as dominated during the cold war between the United States and the Soviet Union) is stable and that multipolar politics (which preceded the cold war and perhaps reflects current conditions) is unstable and war prone.

If the IIG's logically necessary and sufficient conditions for war are met, then war is expected to take place. That is, if preferences and payoffs are common knowledge and the four basic preference conditions of the basic war theorem are met, then the conditions for war are satisfied. Suppose, however, that, because of uncertainty, rivals do not know the preferences of their adversaries (that is, there is imperfect information). This uncertainty reduces the likelihood that the choices that are made will lead to war. If at least one leader mistakenly perceives that a rival's preferences are anything other than what is stated in the basic war theorem, then the risk of war is reduced by uncertainty. This must be true if the theorem is correct because, by definition, the probability that an action will be taken when its necessary and sufficient conditions are met is 1. The theorem, of course, stipulates complete and perfect information. If perfect information is absent but the rest of the theorem's conditions hold, the necessary and sufficient conditions for war are no longer satisfied. In such cases, the probability of the relevant event or action occurring can only decrease as a result of the decision maker's uncertainty.

For example, player A might mistakenly believe that B is a dove that prefers to negotiate rather than exploit its first-strike advantage to attack A. Consequently, A might offer to negotiate rather than grab the military initiative. If B really is a hawk and knows that A will capitulate if attacked, then B will attack and A will find it necessary to capitulate. But if B mistakenly believes A is the type who will retaliate if attacked so that B thinks its choice is between negotiation and war, then B will respond to A's offer to negotiate by negotiating as well. In this instance, uncertainty about the preferences of the adversary can avert a war that would have occurred if the players had better information about their rival's preference ordering of the outcomes. More perfect information would have made the risk of war greater, not smaller.

Similarly, it is possible for decision makers to mistakenly perceive that the conditions for war are met so that their interaction is ripe for war. If the conditions for war under complete and perfect information are not met but, because of uncertainty, leaders believe that those conditions have been met, then uncertainty increases the risk of war because without uncertainty there would be no chance of war at all. Thus, uncertainty does not always have the same effect on the instability created by the risk of war in the international system. In effect, uncertainty can both increase the risks of a destabilizing conflict and decrease that risk, each under specific, identifiable circumstances.‡

TRY THIS

Construct an example in which uncertainty about player preferences results in war when, if there had been certainty, there would not have been a war. Be sure that the preference orderings and the sources of uncertainty about them are consistent with the general assumptions behind the domestic IIG.

War and Uncertainty: The International Interaction Game and Neorealism

The results of the domestic IIG can be compared directly with the hypotheses of neorealism. In neorealism, uncertainty makes war (and other sources of instability) more likely, and certainty makes war less likely. Put more broadly, according to neorealist thinking the greater the degree of uncertainty, the higher the probability of destabilizing events such as war. By contrast, the domestic IIG identifies conditions under which increases in uncertainty make war more likely (that is, at least one of the four conditions is not met, but decision makers mistakenly perceive that all four are satisfied because each decision maker has imperfect information about the preferences of the other) and conditions under which increases in

‡ This general result does not depend on which theory is used to identify the necessary and sufficient conditions for war. The result depends only on the existence of necessary and sufficient conditions under which an action or event is certain to happen and the existence of uncertainty.

TABLE 5.2	**Predictions about the Risk of War: The Domestic International Interaction Game and Neorealism**		

		Information condition	
		No uncertainty	Uncertainty
Domestic IIG preference conditions	War preferences satisfied	Circumstance 1	Circumstance 2
		IIG: $p_{war} = 1$	IIG: $p_{war} < 1$
		NR: $p_{war} = 0$	NR: $p_{war} \leq 1$
	War preferences not satisfied	Circumstance 3	Circumstance 4
		IIG: $p_{war} = 0$	IIG: $0 \leq p_{war} \leq 1$
		NR: $p_{war} = 0$	NR: $p_{war} \leq 1$

Notes: The first probability in each box is the domestic IIG prediction; the second is the neorealism prediction. IIG, international interaction game; NR neorealism; p_{war}, probability of war.

uncertainty make war less likely (that is, the four conditions are met but uncertainty about the preferences of an opponent leads to choices that do not result in war).

Table 5.2 shows the predictions from the domestic IIG and from neorealism about the likelihood of war under four different circumstances:

1. The domestic IIG's preference conditions for war are met, and there is no uncertainty.
2. The domestic IIG's preference conditions for war are met, but A or B or both are uncertain about the other's preferences over the game's outcomes.
3. The domestic IIG's preference conditions for war are not met, and there is no uncertainty.
4. The domestic IIG's preference conditions for war are not met, but A or B or both are uncertain about the other's preferences over the games outcomes.

In circumstance 1, the IIG predicts war for sure and neorealist thinking predicts that there will not be war. Here we have a major parting of the ways of the two theoretical approaches to international conflict. This difference provides an opportunity for a demanding test of the contending hypotheses and the assumptions from which they are derived. In addition, the domestic version of the IIG sees uncertainty as generally increasing the risk of war in circumstance 4 and as decreasing it in circumstance 2, whereas neorealism makes no distinction between these circumstances.

We see from Table 5.2 that sometimes neorealism and the domestic IIG make the same predictions about the likelihood of war (or other forms of instability) and that other times they make opposite predictions. Of course, we cannot choose between theories on the basis of cases that make the same predictions (for such cases, they are either both right or both wrong). But when two different theories make different predictions, we have an opportunity to conduct a critical test of the relative accuracy of the alternative explanations of instability and conflict.

FIGURE 5.2   **War, IIG Conditions Met, and Uncertainty**

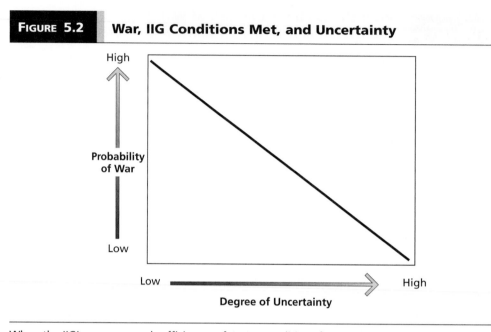

When the IIG's necessary and sufficient preference conditions for war are met, but there is uncertainty about the preferences of rivals, then war is less likely to occur than in the case where there is no uncertainty. This result contradicts the predictions of liberal and neorealist theory, which contend that increases in uncertainty always increase the risk of instability. The IIG accounts for cases not explained by structural theories.

Let us go back to the historical record. Evidence from European disputes since 1816 supports the domestic IIG's hypotheses about war and uncertainty and contradicts those of neorealism. Figures 5.2 and 5.3 show the relationship between the probability of war and the level of uncertainty in the European system for all disputes in that part of the world between 1816 and 1974. In Figure 5.2, the IIG's necessary and sufficient conditions for war under complete and perfect information are met, and in Figure 5.3 they are not. In both figures, uncertainty varies from very low levels to very high levels.[§] If neorealist predictions are supported, then both graphs should slope upward; as we have discussed, this theory predicts that uncertainty is destabilizing and that less uncertainty produces greater stability. If the IIG is supported, then the first graph should slope downward and the second graph should slope upward, showing the differences caused by the status of the preference conditions. As we can see, in contradiction to neorealist thinking the two figures clearly support the expectations deduced from the domestic IIG. Reevaluations of the claims of the IIG that

---

[§] The figures are based on a statistical test called Logit analysis, which estimates the likelihood of a binary dependent variable (in this case, "War" or "No war") as a function of a set of independent variables. The actual statistical test used here as well as a more demanding version of the test can be found in Bueno de Mesquita and Lalman (1992, 77, 216). All relevant variables are statistically significant and in the direction predicted by the domestic version of the IIG.

FIGURE 5.3	**War, IIG Conditions Not Met, and Uncertainty**

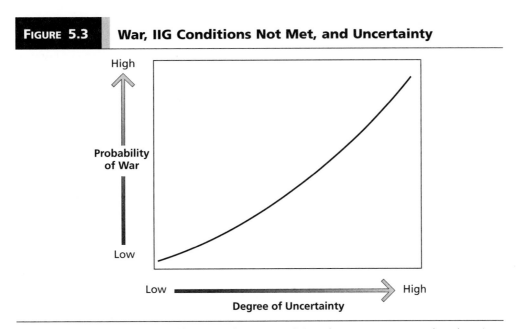

When the IIG's necessary and sufficient preference conditions for war are not met, but there is uncertainty about the preferences of rivals, then war is more likely than in the case where there is no uncertainty. This result also supports the predictions of liberal and neorealist theory, which contend that increases in uncertainty always increase the risk of instability. The IIG accounts for cases also explained by structural theories.

use more advanced statistical methods or control for more potentially confounding factors (but unfortunately with inadequate consideration of uncertainty) and that are conducted on a larger sample of countries generally reinforce these findings, although in some cases with significant qualifications and modifications (Gelpi and Grieco 1998; Signorino 1999; Smith 1999; Bennett and Stam 2000a, 2000b).

Weakness and War: Resurrection and Pacific Doves

Before leaving the domestic IIG, two other results are worth discussing. Belligerence is often thought to increase as a state becomes more powerful. As Henry Kissinger, secretary of state under Richard Nixon, has written: "In the final reckoning weakness has invariably tempted aggression and impotence brings abdication of policy in its train" (1979, 195). Kissinger's view that aggressiveness increases irreversibly with power is widely shared—yet it is probably incorrect. There are several reasons why a weak state or nonstate actor such as a terrorist group might, because of its weakness, be more aggressive than a stronger counterpart. Let me suggest two.

The Resurrection Hypothesis. George W. Downs and David M. Rocke (1995) develop what they call the resurrection hypothesis. This hypothesis begins with the now familiar premise that leaders want to keep their jobs. Downs and Rocke show that when leaders face a military defeat and anticipate being ousted as a result, they have a strong incentive to fight on in the hope that good fortune will turn events in their favor; that is, their only hope of political resurrection is to fight on despite great military disadvantage. In essence, the **resurrection hypothesis** says that the extreme efforts of apparently defeated leaders do not reflect a loss of rationality under extreme stress, which has been the more common explanation of such efforts among psychologically oriented arguments (Gurr 1970). To the contrary, extreme efforts in the face of defeat are actually a rational response. Such leaders lose nothing by fighting on and stand to gain much if luck should turn their way.

For example, Adolf Hitler launched the Battle of the Bulge after the rapid advance of the Allied armies toward Germany following the invasion of Normandy in June 1944. Hitler's action appears to have been an instance of the resurrection hypothesis at work. The Battle of the Bulge was a desperate attempt to save Germany from an Allied invasion. Although Germany lost the battle, the Germans were able to mount a much tougher campaign than the Allies believed was still possible.

The Tet offensive undertaken by the North Vietnamese on January 31, 1968, is another example of the resurrection hypothesis put into practice. U.S. military and political leaders believed that they had already punished the North Vietnamese to such an extent that they were no longer capable of launching a military offensive. Likewise, the American public had become convinced that the war in Vietnam was virtually won. And, in fact, the Tet offensive was a considerable military rout—of the North Vietnamese by the Americans. But just by the very fact that they were able to launch the offensive at all, the North Vietnamese pulled off a stunning political and propaganda victory that resurrected their hopes and led, ultimately, to a negotiated resolution of the Vietnam War that was very favorable to the North Vietnamese side.

The resurrection hypothesis provides an important lesson about foreign policy. During wartime, and during the diplomatic negotiations preceding a war, leaders commonly demonize their foes. George H. W. Bush, for example, referred to Saddam Hussein of Iraq in 1990 and 1991 as another Hitler, thereby casting Hussein in the eyes of the American public as a major menace to world peace. Bush may well have been right about Hussein. Whether he was right or not, demonizing Hussein may have actually had the effect of making him even more dangerous to his own people, if not to the United States, than he already was, thus helping to ensure his political survival for another twelve years before he was ousted in the 2003 U.S.-Iraqi war. If Hussein believed, rightly or wrongly, that the United States was committed to marching into Baghdad and overthrowing him—a threat resurrected in 2002 and carried out in 2003 by George W. Bush—then this might have encouraged Hussein to take great risks to resurrect himself politically.

What were those risks? In the run-up to the 2003 war between the United States and Iraq, the United Nations made repeated efforts to inspect Iraqi sites that were thought possibly to be storage facilities or manufacturing facilities for weapons of mass destruction, including chemical, biological, and possibly even radiological weapons. Today we are confident that Saddam Hussein did not possess such weapons, but in 2003 many believed that he did. He helped reinforce that belief by first resisting and then obstructing UN inspections. Many reasoned that if he did not have these weapons he had no reason to impede the UN inspection effort. But if he did have weapons of mass destruction, in contravention to the terms that ended the 1991 Gulf War, then he surely had an incentive to hide the fact by making inspections difficult. There was, however, a third possibility: Hussein did not have such weapons, but he believed that acting as if he did by obstructing inspections might diminish the chances that the United States would invade Iraq. His reasoning could have been that by seeming to have such weapons he could raise the specter of tens of thousands of American casualties, with that fear being sufficient to deter the United States from invading. This was a significant calculated risk. Saddam Hussein may well have decreased the odds of an invasion—indeed, the United Nations did not go along with the U.S. decision to use force and neither did many U.S. allies—by raising the specter of an unconventional war. In the process, he increased the prospect that he would be deposed if the United States attacked while he simultaneously maneuvered to reduce the probability of such an attack. In 1991 during the first Iraq War, he signaled that he might use chemical or biological weapons against Israel, and according to the insightful account provided by Avigdor Haselkorn (1999), he succeeded in deterring the coalition forces from marching into Baghdad. In 2003, he seems to have tried a similar gambit, but this time he failed and was deposed.

By demonizing Saddam Hussein, both George H. W. Bush and later George W. Bush gave up the possibility of successfully negotiating an agreement for Hussein to go into exile because he could no longer believe that the United States would honor a commitment to leave him alone once he was out of Iraq and no longer had a viable military threat. Pushing leaders to the point where they need to gamble on resurrecting themselves, leaving them no graceful way out of a dispute, increases the risk of carnage and the prospects of watching such leaders snatch victory from the jaws of defeat. The resurrection hypothesis highlights a difficult political trade-off. When a country demonizes an adversary, this helps mobilize domestic political support

TRY THIS

War crime tribunals have commenced under the aegis of the United Nations to punish those guilty of atrocities during the Bosnian-Serbian conflict and the Kosovo conflict in the former Yugoslavia. Such trials provide an opportunity to obtain justice, although at the expense of possibly triggering more intense fighting as nearly defeated leaders attempt to resurrect themselves. Consider the circumstances under which the threat of such trials might prevent atrocities in the first place and the extent to which they might provoke war criminals to commit additional atrocities to gain sufficient leverage to negotiate their way out of punishment. What policies strike the right balance between the desire for justice and the desire to avoid further carnage?

for the use of force, thereby increasing the chances of victory against the adversary. But demonizing an enemy also motivates that adversary to try harder to win, raising the risk of increased loss of life. The tactic also makes it harder for the country to sell at home the idea of negotiating with the "evil" foe.

The Pacific Dove Hypothesis. The IIG has its own brand of the resurrection hypothesis called the **pacific dove hypothesis.** This hypothesis states that under certain circumstances a weak state—or terrorist group—has incentives to initiate a war or other violent dispute against a stronger state even if the weak initiator strongly prefers a negotiated compromise to resolve their differences. As in the resurrection hypothesis, such a circumstance arises when conditions become so extreme as to compel a state, in desperation, to act in an unexpected, some would even say seemingly irrational, manner.

As noted earlier, a dove is a player that prefers to negotiate with a rival rather than force that rival to capitulate. Lalman and I identify a special type of dove we call a pacific dove. Not only does a pacific dove prefer to negotiate rather than force its opponents to capitulate, but a pacific dove itself also prefers to capitulate if attacked rather than retaliate. If a state—or nonstate actor such as a terrorist group—is a pacific dove and it is uncertain of its foe's type, then the weaker the pacific dove is relative to its opponent, the higher the probability is that it will launch a preemptive attack in an effort to extract a capitulation from that opponent.

The intuition undergirding this phenomenon is similar to that undergirding the resurrection hypothesis. In the IIG, when a dispute arises between a weak state and a strong state, the strong state's advantage in negotiations is proportional to its relative strength. The weaker a state is relative to its opponent, the less attractive negotiation is precisely because the weaker state does not bring much leverage in the form of power to the negotiating table. Still, a pacific dove prefers to negotiate rather than force the rival to capitulate, even if that rival is itself willing to give in. The trouble is, if the initiator in any dispute tries to negotiate, there is a danger of being attacked by the foe if that foe turns out to be a hawk. Thus, the extra leverage that a weak state gains from seizing a first-strike advantage may, for it, be well worth the attendant risk of severe defeat by its more powerful adversary.

Consider the thought processes of a weak pacific dove if it is uncertain whether its opponent is a hawk or a dove and also whether the opponent is the type that will retaliate if attacked or will view the issue as not worth the costs of a fight. The weak pacific dove simply does not know what will happen if it does not attack. It chooses not to attack in the hope that its foe will also do nothing and allow the status quo to persist. Perhaps there will be a negotiated settlement with the foe or perhaps the weak pacific dove will be forced to cave in following an attack by a hawkish adversary. As it turns out, these are two fairly poor choices. Negotiations do not look that attractive to the weak pacific dove because its weakness means it lacks leverage; in diplomatic parlance, it lacks bargaining chips. Giving up the first-strike advantage and facing the danger of being forced to cave in looks bad too. For the weak pacific dove, then, the best prospect, although not a good prospect, is to attack and hope that its stronger rival is not motivated to fight back. This is the only way that a weak pacific dove can derive benefits from the situation.

A numeric example may help make the intuition behind this claim clear. Let me stipulate the payoffs for A in the crisis subgame depicted in Figure 5.1. Consistent with the idea of A's being a dove, let A's payoff for negotiation equal 5 and A's payoff for making B capitulate equal 4. In addition, let A's payoff for starting a war against B equal 3, capitulating to B equal 2, and retaliating if B attacks A equal 1. Because A prefers capitulating to retaliating (2 is better than 1), A is pacific as well as being a dove. Suppose A is uncertain of B's preferences. Let Q equal the probability with which A believes B is a dove (that is, that B prefers negotiation to forcing A to capitulate) so that $1 - Q$ is the probability that, if A offers to negotiate, B will attack, forcing A to capitulate. To keep the example relatively simple, assume that A—which prefers to negotiate rather than forcing B to capitulate (5 is better than 4)—is certain B will capitulate if attacked. Then A will attack B if the expected utility from offering to negotiate is worse than the expected utility from attacking. In this case, that means that $5Q + 2 \times (1 - Q) < 3$. That is, A will attack B if $Q < \frac{1}{3}$ and will offer to negotiate if $Q > \frac{1}{3}$.

Now, suppose some state A′ is in the same situation but is considerably more powerful than A, so that A′ expects to gain 20 from negotiation, whereas the weaker player A expected only 5. Because A′ is also certain that B will capitulate if attacked (a condition not required for the generalization about pacific doves but that is convenient to keep the example simple) nothing else of relevance changes when A′ calculates its expected utility for negotiating versus attacking B. A′ attacks B if $20Q + 2 \times (1 - Q) < 3$. That is, A′ attacks if $Q < 1/18$ and offers to negotiate if $Q > 1/18$. In plain English, A is weaker than A′. As a result, A expects fewer benefits from a negotiated settlement than does A′. Therefore, A attacks under more circumstances than does A′. If A′ believes that there is only a one-eighteenth chance that B is a dove, that is sufficient for it to gamble on negotiation, but A must be more confident that B is a dove to undertake the gamble. Weak A attacks unless there is at least a one-third chance that B is a dove and thus will, by definition, negotiate rather that attack A.

Let's illustrate this using our European sample. Although there are just forty instances of pacific doves in Lalman's and my analysis, we can see clearly in Figure 5.4 that they behaved as predicted by the IIG. The figure depicts the significant statistical relationship between the probability of victory, estimated as the initiator's capabilities divided by the sum of capabilities of the initiator and the target (that is, an odds ratio), and the likelihood that a pacific dove will initiate violence. As we can see, there is a greater probability that pacific doves will attack when the possibility of victory is low (that is, they are weak). Contrast Figure 5.4 with Figure 5.5. The latter shows the same statistical analysis for initiators of violent disputes that were not pacific doves. The difference is stark and completely in line with the domestic IIG. This result, like the earlier results regarding uncertainty, illustrates the importance of identifying the contingent conditions under which one or another relationship is expected to hold. Although the standard view that more powerful states are also more violent states is often true, it is not always true. For pacific doves, grabbing the initiative and engaging in violence helps make their demands more credible in a negotiation, but it also makes getting negotiations under way more difficult.

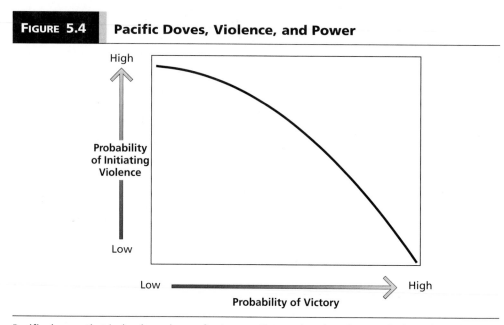

FIGURE 5.4   **Pacific Doves, Violence, and Power**

Pacific doves—that is, leaders who prefer to negotiate rather than force a rival to give in but who would themselves give in rather than retaliate if attacked—are especially likely to initiate violence when their chances of winning are low. Here, then, is a case in which weakness fosters violence in otherwise peace-loving leaders.

That pacific doves are more likely to engage in violence when they are weak rather than strong raises difficult questions about conflict resolution. Terrorist organizations, for example, typically are small and weak compared with the military might of their enemies. We observe terrorists as terrorists only when they engage in violent action. In such circumstances, we cannot tell them apart from hawks. Both hawks and weak pacific doves (but not powerful pacific doves) behave in the same way when they are sufficiently uncertain of the response they can expect if they pursue peaceful solutions to their disputes. A fundamental problem in crises is that it is dangerous for weak parties to gamble on trying to negotiate if the foe is a hawk that will seize the initiative and try to destroy them. Gambling on negotiation can be fatal (a point highlighted in Chapter 7 on terrorism), yet failing to gamble on negotiation can mean giving up the opportunity for a peaceful and successful end to the dispute. In thinking about conflict resolution, we must always be careful not to underestimate the risks associated both with aggression and with gambling on peace. Either can be deadly.

ARMS RACE, DETERRENCE, AND WAR

One of the great debates among foreign policy leaders and scholars is whether arming to the hilt increases the prospects of peace or the prospects of war. The fourth-century Roman

| FIGURE 5.5 | **Types Other than Pacific Doves, Violence, and Power** |

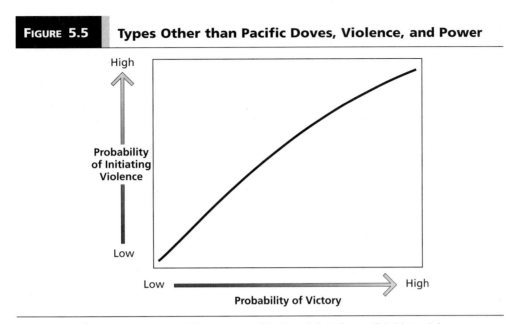

For those leaders who are not pacific doves, the likelihood that they will initiate violence increases as their power increases relative to that of their opponents.

military expert Vegetius said that those who desire peace must prepare for war. In our own time, Albert Einstein argued that you cannot simultaneously prepare for war and make peace. For those who share Einstein's view, vigilant efforts at arms control; prevention of the proliferation of nuclear, biological, and chemical (sometimes known as NBC) weapons; and, ultimately, disarmament are the surest paths to peace. For those who take Vegetius's view, peace is promoted by developing weapons that are so destructive as to keep foes from seeking an advantage through the use of force, encouraging them to look instead for ways to resolve differences through negotiations; this is called **deterrence.** These two perspectives are so different that they define a political divide. Often, political liberals, or doves, are associated with the perspective that promotes arms control and fears the consequences of **arms races,** competitions between rivals to buy, produce, and stockpile weapons, whereas political conservatives, or hawks, are associated with the perspective that promotes deterrence and fears a lack of military preparedness. How these alternative outlooks are linked to war is the subject we now examine.

After World War I, Lewis Fry Richardson, a brilliant meteorologist by trade, set out to understand arms races and their relationship to war. As a scientist, he was eager to construct and test a logically rigorous theory of arms races. He argues that nations acquire arms in response to the hostility they perceive in a foreign adversary, the rate at which that adversary is arming, and the "fatigue" that a nation feels in devoting economic resources to arms rather than to goods for domestic use. The "fatigue" that Richardson has in mind is the degree that the domestic population eventually grows tired of postponing material improvements so that the government can buy more weapons. For example, in the 1980s, the leader of the Soviet Union, Mikhail Gorbachev, sought an arms-control agreement with the United States. He may have been motivated by his concern that the Soviet citizenry was tired of paying for weapons and wanted more consumer goods instead. In Richardson's model (1960/1949), which is based on differential equations, fatigue slows arms races, whereas a rival's hostility and acquisition of arms accelerate arms purchases. He describes an arms race as a situation in which the fatigue factor is weak relative to the accelerating purchasing of weapons to offset the perceived threat implied by an opponent's choices. Richardson concludes that, if hostility intensifies to the point where it overcomes the fatigue factor, then arms purchases will spiral out of control, with each side buying more and more arms until a war erupts (Siverson and Diehl 1989).

Richardson's model fits brilliantly with the data he amassed about World War I. His theory, however, fails to predict or account well for the advent of World War II. One possible reason lies in an intellectual leap of faith in Richardson's argument. The **dependent variable**—the outcomes to be explained—in what has come to be known as the Richardson model is the change in arms expenditures of each participant in the alleged arms race. However, his argument that war results when the arms race spirals out of control is not grounded in the mathematical structure or logic of the theory. Also, why nations do not eventually become exhausted from this behavior is not evident in the theory either. Nor is it evident why states, fearing exhaustion but not yet exhausted, turn to war rather than to some other means of redressing their frustration and concern over being outspent by the other side. Finally, because the Richardson model contains no uncertainty, it is not evident why the parties to an arms race cannot foresee the consequences of their spending and find a solution short of war before the situation spirals out of control.

The argument for an arms spiral is, in the parlance of mathematical modelers, a hand wave. That is, it seems like a sensible conclusion and it might be true, but it does not follow from the theory. In fact, the Richardson model assumes a knee-jerk, stimulus-response, action-reaction environment, with no strategic interaction at all, no effort by either party in the race to try to improve the situation. His arms racers do not select their actions strategically; neither side is assumed to consider the effects of its own actions on the subsequent decisions of its adversary. Consequently, the participants in a Richardson arms race have no basis on which to look ahead, consider the consequences of their decisions, and avoid having circumstances spiral out of control. They show no signs of being rational.

Richardson is not to be faulted for this. After all, he developed his arms race model two decades before the first formal inklings of game theory were set down and five decades before game theory was capable of dealing with the complex strategic interactions involving uncertainty that characterize efforts at deterrence. Furthermore, as a physical scientist, he was trained to think about interaction among particles, not about strategic interaction. This, after all, is one of the major differences between the physical sciences and the social sciences. In the purely physical world, particles—whether molecular, atomic, or subatomic—are not sentient.

They do not prepare themselves for collisions or attempt to maneuver away from or toward collisions. But people and other sentient agents do, and so they interact strategically.

Despite the nonstrategic foundations of Richardson's model, the idea of arms races as sources of war persists, and considerable effort has been expended to refine Richardson's core ideas. The notion that each side in a pair of adversarial states is arming in reaction to the arms decisions of the other immediately raises a problem in that there is an **observationally equivalent explanation,** that is, another explanation that also fits the data, for escalating arms expenditure.

For example, consider the difficulty of distinguishing an arms race from a situation in which two national defense establishments are each arguing on a domestic level for greater budgetary authority. Organizational theorists have noted that bureaucracies and their leaders measure their success in part by the size of their budgets (Niskanen 1973; Wildavsky 1979). The more they have to spend, the more sway they have over people and policies. This means that leaders of organizations, including those in the military who argue for ever-expanding defense and weapons-procurement budgets, have an incentive other than concern for the national well-being to seek more resources. Military leaders may be agents of the national government, but they often pursue their own interests, especially in light of the legitimate basis for debate over whether arms acquisition or arms control is in the national interest.

Figure 5.6 depicts two alternative causal relationships that account for the arms possessed by two nations at different moments in time. Because the length of the observed intervals between periods of weapons acquisitions is arbitrary, we cannot tell which of the time intervals in the figure represent budgetary growth for weapons through bureaucratic competition within each state (and possibly involving complicity by bureaucrats in "competing" states) and which signify the series of actions and reactions that characterizes arms races between states. No wonder there is so much rhetoric and so little solid evidence about whether arms-acquisition programs are motivated by national security concerns or by everyday bureaucratic and interest group infighting that takes seriously the domestic strategic setting.

> **TRY THIS**
>
> Can you think of other aspects of international relations theory that might be subject to observational equivalence, making it difficult to distinguish between alternative explanations? Think about how to devise a test to separate the accounts of contending theories that face the problem of observational equivalence.

> **TRY THIS**
>
> Identifying arms races is difficult. How might you go about identifying an arms race without relying on hindsight? What criteria might you look for? Make a list of criteria, and then look at the historical record to see if your criteria separate arms races from domestic bureaucratic efforts by militaries to expand their budgets. See if your criteria help predict whether a violent conflict subsequently arose between the racing states or not.

| FIGURE 5.6 | **Arms Race or Growing Organizational Budgets?** |

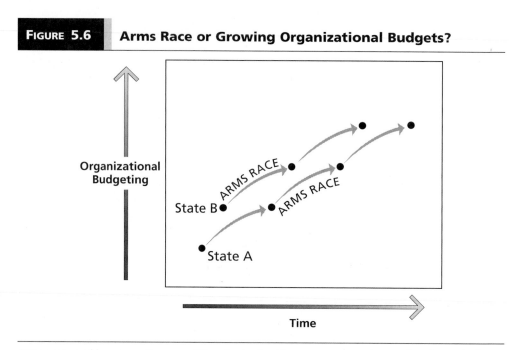

Arms races and bureaucratic competition for budget increases create observationally equivalent predictions about the trajectory of arms expenditures. This means that it is difficult to tell arms races apart from ordinary internal budget competition.

Figure 5.6 alerts us to the concern expressed by President Dwight Eisenhower on the occasion of his farewell to the American people. Eisenhower warned of the growing influence of what he termed the "military-industrial complex." The *military-industrial complex* refers to the shared interests that weapons manufacturers and military leaders have in expanding their respective budgets by persuading Congress to spend more on weapons and defense. Thus, the military-industrial complex had an interest during the cold war in promoting the belief that the Soviet Union was accelerating its weapons capabilities while the United States was falling farther and farther behind.

During the 1960 presidential campaign between Richard M. Nixon and John F. Kennedy, one of the most hotly debated topics was the alleged missile gap. Kennedy argued that the United States lagged far behind the Soviets; Nixon was confident that American military capabilities were ahead of those of the Soviets. We know today that there was no missile gap. It was a political perspective that served the defense establishment well but that did not reflect reality. We now know that the Central Intelligence Agency (CIA), for example, routinely and systematically overestimated Soviet capabilities. These overestimates helped fuel congressional willingness to invest large sums in expensive defense projects. That doesn't mean that the CIA intentionally overstated Soviet military might; Soviet leaders certainly had a strategic interest in encouraging Americans to think the Soviet Union was mightier than it was. More recently, as previously discussed, the Bush administration argued that Saddam Hussein's government had weapons of mass destruction that we now know they did not have. The threat of these weapons was an important part of the justification for the U.S. going to war in Iraq. Can we conclude that the president and his advisors intentionally misled us? Perhaps, and perhaps not! We know that it was also in Saddam Hussein's interest to promote the idea that he had such weapons as a way to deter the United States from invading his country. These examples remind us that we, as citizens, have an interest in finding ways to sort out the incentives that our leaders have, their bureaucratic agents have, and our rivals have in shaping our beliefs about foreign affairs.

Today, it continues to be commonplace for the military-industrial complex to argue that the United States needs to produce more new submarines and massively expensive aircraft such as Stealth bombers or even more expensive antimissile systems so that it will be prepared for as-yet unforeseen enemies and threats. Such arguments might, should a real threat emerge swiftly and menacingly, seem prescient. Based on what we know about the military capabilities of other states around the world, however, they only serve to underscore the contemporary relevance of Eisenhower's decades-old warning. These arguments are consonant with the strategic perspective, which favors a domestic explanation of the growing arms budgets and compels us to ask what the incentives are behind declarations of potential military threat. Such declarations should never be dismissed out of hand—doing so could risk disaster. Nor should they be accepted on their face—that could risk massive wastes of taxpayer dollars. They should be scrutinized to understand the alternative incentives that lead to their being made, including the possibility that they are sincere reflections of what leaders believe is true; that they reflect what is in fact true (which can be hard to know ex ante); or that they reflect bluffs designed to extract benefits for political leaders at the expense either of ourselves or of our foes.

Even if we ignore the confusion with budgeting raised in Figure 5.6 and the incentives some leaders or bureaucrats have to exaggerate the need for more weapons, there are other problems with the logic of arms-race models. There is the problem of **reverse causality,** or endogeneity, introduced in Chapter 3. That is, there is the problem that an apparent arms race may represent a buildup of weapons during a prolonged period of tension between states in anticipation of the need to be prepared to fight. In this case, the arms buildup does not cause war; the buildup is caused by the high risk of war. The causality runs opposite to the notion of an arms race that has spiraled out of control. That is, in game theory parlance, the arms buildup is endogenous to the threat of war, not the cause of it as in arms-race models.

Arguments in favor of arms control to prevent war represent the flip side of arguments that favor deterrence. The idea behind arms control is that the risk of war is reduced if adversaries have fewer weapons. Little systematic empirical research has been done to evaluate the actual impact that arms-control agreements have on conflict. One substantial investigation of this subject, by Vasiliki Koubi (1993), shows that arms-control agreements, such as the

Washington Naval Conferences of the 1920s that restricted the number of battleships in the fleets of the world's key naval powers, reduce hostility briefly but have no consequential effect in diminishing the threat of war beyond a brief period after signing. Indeed, many arms-control agreements either codify decisions to limit the pursuit of an already obsolete technology or, by limiting known technologies, push countries in the direction of spending on weapons innovation. The Washington Naval Conference, for example, actually produced an agreement by which participants sank some of their own battleships (or dreadnaughts as they were then known). It did not limit the construction of aircraft carriers or submarines, the two new technologies that were rapidly making the battleship a highly vulnerable, largely obsolete weapon, suggesting that the actual agreement was shallow in what it demanded of the signatories. That is, it did not call for a meaningful, costly change in behavior from what the signatory states were already doing. (We look at international organizations and agreements in light of the possibility that they are shallow in more detail in Chapter 11.)

Negotiations between the United States and the Soviet Union in the late 1960s and early 1970s to limit the number of missiles available to deliver nuclear weapons led to the introduction of multiple independent reentry vehicles (MIRV) technology. In effect, the agreement resulted in the greatly improved efficiency of individual missiles to deliver warheads. Before the first Strategic Arms Limitation Talks (SALT I) and the resultant Antiballistic Missile (ABM) Treaty, each missile carried only one warhead. Afterward, with the number of missiles allowed to each side limited by treaty, a single missile could carry multiple warheads.

In 2002, the United States and Russian governments agreed to massive reductions in nuclear warheads, with each side free to choose which particular warheads or weapons systems to curtail and which to maintain. This arms-reduction agreement was reached with relative ease and reflected more the fact that relations between the United States and Russia had changed than the notion that they were trying to diminish the then very low level of threat between them. That is, this latest arms-control agreement seems designed more to codify the improved relations that were emerging, with fits and starts, between these former enemies than to mute the remaining tensions. Still, it also helps pave the way for the American effort to develop antimissile defenses while abandoning the cold war–inspired ABM Treaty.

TRY THIS

The abandonment of the ABM Treaty is a source of controversy between the United States and Russia. George W. Bush wanted to scrap the treaty, and Russia's Vladimir Putin preferred to keep it. Draw up lists of advantages and disadvantages that are likely to result from the abandonment of the treaty from the U.S. perspective and from the Russian point of view. Would these lists have looked different during the cold war?

An interesting question to reflect on is whether the rise in tensions between the United States and Russia in the past few years, and especially since the invasion by Russia of Georgia in 2008, will lead to greater efforts at arms negotiations or less. Another interesting question is whether Russia's greater assertiveness is the result of U.S. antimissile defense efforts and other such efforts that weaken Russia's ability to defend itself against a future U.S. attack, whether the United States continues to pursue antimissile defenses in Europe out of fear of a resurgent Russia, or whether other fears spur on the United States while exacerbating relations with Russia. Addressing these issues is one of the most important foreign policy challenges facing American and Russian leaders at least for next several years.

Arms control is an idea with great public appeal. James Morrow (1991b), for example, has demonstrated that when American presidents were at risk of losing their reelection campaigns during the cold war, they were likely to make extra concessions to the Soviets in order to get an arms-control agreement. These agreements boosted their popularity, helping improve their reelection prospects. But what should we logically expect the consequence of an arms-control agreement to be in regard to the risk of war? Arms-reduction agreements never roll arms back to zero. Even if they did, we should remember that ancient humans managed to fight one another with sticks and stones before the invention of the spear, hammer, bow and arrow, catapult, crossbow, canon, repeating rifle, machine gun, bomber, and so forth. Of course, cruder weapons meant fewer deaths, a very good thing indeed. The question is, however, did fewer or lesser-advanced weapons mean less war?

We know that as the centuries have unfolded, war has become less frequent but more deadly (Levy 1982; Levy, Walker, and Edwards 1999; Wayman, Sarkees, and Singer 2003). When rivals reduce their arms, they reduce the expected costs of war. If they do not simultaneously resolve the issues creating tension between them, then arms control creates a situation in which the prospective benefits from war remain unaltered while the anticipated costs go down. In such circumstances, arms control acts like a sale on war. The price has been lowered, although the value of victory to the belligerents remains unaltered. The reduction in expected costs seems to be precisely the feature that makes such wars less deadly but also more likely.

> ## TRY THIS
>
> How do arms-control agreements influence the price of war in terms of expected losses of life and property? What does this suggest about the expected frequency of war among signatories to arms-control agreements? Do higher or lower war costs make war more or less likely? How would you design a study to see whether arms-control agreements influence the risk of war, keeping in mind possible endogenous links between such agreements and the risk of war?

The logic in support of deterrence is stronger than that in support of arms control. With deterrence, vast amounts of money may be wasted on building defensive military capabilities in response to a perceived threat that may not be real. The problem is, of course, to differentiate real threats from imagined ones before the fact. After all, real threats of war that are deterred never get to be observed as wars because deterrence places war off the equilibrium path. That means we cannot just look at what happens and conclude that arms buildups or arms control increase or decrease the risk of war.

Logic, however, can serve to help guide policy choices. For instance, trust in promises made by rivals is difficult to sustain when survival is at stake, as we have seen in the analysis of the behavior of pacific doves. This is the problem of credible commitment that we examine in Chapter 4 and that has occupied much research on international security (Fearon 1994; Gaubatz 1996; Reed 1997; Morrow 1999). Although deterrence does raise the expected costs to an adversary of undertaking an attack, deterrence does not remove the issues in dispute. Like arms control, deterrence does not reduce or resolve the benefits side of the war-making calculation. It does, however, make war more costly. By doing so, it reduces the incidence of war and thereby reduces overall deaths by warfare. After all, had deterrence not been in place during the cold war years, war (and all that it entails) would likely have occurred more often and with deadly consequences. The benefits of deterrence come at a price, however. Should the deterrent threat prove inadequate and war ensue, then the level of bloodshed is likely to be elevated by the greater stock and quality of weapons available to the belligerents.

The empirical evidence supports the notion that deterrence decreases the likelihood of war relative to arms control. Alastair Smith (1995) has shown that cases in which attacks did not take place were those in which alliance reliability was high, serving as an effective deterrent against aggression. William H. Riker and I have shown that the probability that a dispute will escalate to include violence and death increases as we move down the deterrence ladder in the nuclear age (Bueno de Mesquita and Riker 1982). We find that, although nuclear powers were involved with one another in many disputes, they did not engage in war with one another. Rivals that were protected under nuclear umbrellas but that lacked nuclear deterrents of their own were only slightly more likely to engage in war. Rivals with only conventional weapons at their disposal were the most likely to engage in war. A recent update of the data shows that this same pattern of successful nuclear deterrence continues. Despite the widespread fear of nuclear weapons, they seem to be an effective, relatively inexpensive means of diminishing the risk of war exactly because they raise war's costs so high.

OTHER HYPOTHESES ABOUT WAR

I have touched on some of the most prominent perspectives on the causes of war. There are, however, many other interesting approaches to this important topic. I mention some briefly here, but I leave their detailed exploration to you.

The Scapegoat Hypothesis

One of the most enduring claims about the causes of war is the **scapegoat hypothesis.** When a leader is in domestic political trouble—because of a bad economy, a scandal, or what have you—he or she may precipitate an international conflict, perhaps even a small war, to command the nation's attention and thereby divert it from the leadership's domestic failings. It is certainly well documented, at least for American presidents, that an international crisis creates a "rally-'round-the-flag" effect that boosts a leader's popularity for a short while (Mueller 1973; Brody 1992; Morgan and Bickers 1992). Whether or not the increase in popularity helps with reelection, however, has not been ascertained. Note that the rally-'round-the-flag effect is not necessarily tied to the creation of a bogus dispute to gain popularity. The scapegoat hypothesis, by contrast, is focused exclusively on the initiation of a dispute to gain political security.

A case that drew attention as a possible effort at scapegoating should help make the hypothesis clear. In August 1998, President Bill Clinton was compelled to give testimony before a grand jury investigating his personal conduct. Following his testimony, he gave an address to the American people in which he apologized for having had an illicit affair in the White House. A few days later, while discussions of possible impeachment swirled around Washington, D.C., the president returned from his vacation retreat to oversee a U.S. military attack on alleged terrorist targets in Afghanistan and the Sudan.

There was immediate speculation about whether the missile attacks were an effort to divert attention from the president's personal and political problems or whether these were legitimate retaliatory strikes for the bombing by terrorists of the American embassies in Kenya and Tanzania a few weeks before. The speculation was heightened by the president's declaration that he had "convincing evidence" that the selected targets were, in the first instance, a terrorist training camp and, in the second, a factory manufacturing precursor chemicals for use in chemical weapons.

Clinton's failure to provide details about whatever evidence he had fueled talk that the attacks were an effort to use terrorism as a scapegoat, or diversion, to draw attention away from the president's problems. American presidents had in the past displayed the evidence they had gathered to justify their tough reactions to foreign events. President Kennedy's ambassador to the United Nations during the Cuban Missile Crisis, Adlai Stevenson, showed satellite photographs of Soviet missile installations in Cuba to prove that Russian denials were false. President Ronald Reagan ordered the release of air-to-air recordings of conversations among Soviet pilots before they shot down a Korean commercial airliner that had strayed over Soviet territory. It was not widely known prior to the release of the recordings that the United States was able to monitor such conversations. The president compromised this intelligence source to prove convincingly that Soviet denials were false.

Whether the American attacks in Afghanistan and Sudan were motivated primarily by legitimate foreign policy objectives or by a president seeking to divert attention from his difficulties, we will probably never know. In any event, Clinton's antiterrorist actions had little sustained effect on foreign or domestic opinion about the president. In addition, it seems, in light of the tragic events of September 11, 2001, that the antiterrorist actions had little beneficial effect on reducing the risk of terrorism. But it is just these types of questions that are at the heart of the scapegoat hypothesis.

The scapegoat argument finds mixed empirical support. Although many people subscribe to the idea, no convincing evidence exists, beyond anecdotes of the sort just reviewed, to support the claim (Levy 1989; Leeds and Davis 1997) and there is mounting evidence against the hypothesis (Chiozza and Goemans 2003). This is not too surprising. In essence, the scapegoat hypothesis relies on an argument that politicians are clever, that their constituents and domestic opponents are naïve, and that observers (such as social scientists) are smart. Politicians are clever because they figure out how to use foreign policy to promote their popularity. They do this without jeopardizing their welfare because the concocted conflict is one they do not expect to lose. Their adversaries, apparently, are not so clever because they willingly engage in a dispute or small war that is designed specifically to end in their defeat. The citizens are naïve because they cannot figure out that the little dispute their country is involved in is meaningless and trumped up. And it would have to be pretty meaningless and easy to resolve or else the leader might land in deeper political trouble—after all, the whole idea behind a scapegoat is to focus blame elsewhere. We must also wonder why citizens and the political opponents of the incumbent cannot figure out that the dispute is being used to deflect attention from the leader's very real domestic problems. Game theoretic reasoning compels us to ask these questions, to put ourselves in the target's shoes, and to see the strategic weaknesses in standard scapegoat accounts.

In effect, the scapegoat dispute must be important enough that people will set aside their concerns about the leader's domestic failings but not so important as to represent a real domestic or international threat to the leader's well-being. This is a very tall order. Still more remarkable, even though political opponents and citizens cannot figure out what is going on, apparently social scientists looking at the same information are smart enough to recognize scapegoating when they see it. It is generally a good idea to be skeptical of arguments that require the assumption that one or another key participant in decision making is just plain stupid. There is too much evidence that even seemingly inattentive citizens are quite savvy about the most complex issues once those issues impinge on their well-being.

Status Inconsistency

A variety of **psychological theories** draw attention to the well-documented psychological link between frustration and aggression. One common claim in this literature is that **status inconsistency** leads nations to fight wars (Galtung 1964; Wallace 1973; Ray 1974; Midlarsky 1975). The core of this argument is that frustrated leaders become aggressive; one source of frustration arises when a state has considerable power but low international status. The powerful, low-status state believes that it should receive rewards and recognition in international affairs that are commensurate with its power, yet others treat it in accordance with its low status. Some argue that this was a major factor that drove Adolf Hitler to initiate World War II. Germany became powerful through Hitler's rearmament program, yet continued to be treated as a pariah state, forced to pay war reparations for its role in World War I and denied an influential part in determining international norms of conduct.

But the theory runs into empirical problems. Some point to China before Richard Nixon's overture in 1972 as a country suffering from status inconsistency. Although powerful by dint of its huge population and massive economy, China, albeit poor on a per capita basis, had one of the world's largest economies in the 1890s and still does today; nevertheless, it was treated as a pariah by the United States. Yet, contrary to the status inconsistency claim, China did not engage in warfare to gain greater stature in the world. On the opposite side of the ledger, Britain and Switzerland are accorded high status in international circles despite their lack of real power. Britain, despite apparently being accorded too much status, has put its position at risk by waging war (for example, against Egypt in 1956); Switzerland has not.

As with so many other theories of war, the status inconsistency argument, although appearing to make sense, musters little evidence in support of its predictions. Upon reflection, it is not too difficult to discern the reasons for its failure to explain events. The hypothesis that frustration breeds aggression and that status inconsistency is an important source of frustration is well demonstrated by psychologists who study individuals. The hypothesis that frustration foments war, however, requires several huge leaps in logic. Nations do not have psychological states. We may speak metaphorically of a nation's psyche, but metaphor is not reality. Leaders, like all individuals, do have psychological states—they may feel frustrated, and they may become aggressive. It is entirely possible, although it has not been demonstrated, that the status inconsistency of a particular nation may be a source of frustration for that nation's leader. But why should we expect leaders to act out their frustration through international aggression? Is there any more reason to believe that leaders will manifest their frustration through warfare than by hitting their heads against a wall, yelling at their spouses or children, beating their underlings, or hitting their golf balls too hard?

Geoffrey Best (1994, 362) reports having seen covert footage of senior Iraqi officers hitting helpless prisoners

> ### TRY THIS
>
> Name other states with high prestige but low power or with high power but low prestige. Are there any discernible patterns in the behavior of these states that make them different from other states? How might such inconsistency between power and prestige arise? Looking back over the past couple of centuries, can any generalizations be drawn about status inconsistency and involvement in foreign conflict?

captured during Saddam Hussein's campaign to recover control of southern Iraq, which was lost in the wake of his massive defeat in the Gulf War of 1991. The U.S. general George S. Patton famously struck one of his own soldiers during World War II. Such acts are clearly aggressive, and they are just as clearly linked to frustration. Yet they did not lead the generals involved or their political leaders to go out and redress their personal frustration through warfare. Is there any more logical reason to expect frustrated leaders to wage war than to expect them to try harder to implement successful policies that remove the source of frustration or that shift their own attention to other challenges, suppressing their frustration over their nation's status inconsistency? The obvious answer to these questions is that all of these psychological responses are plausible. The empirical record simply does not support the contention that leaders systematically respond to status inconsistency with frustration and international aggression.

War in Cycles

A substantial literature contends that war comes in cycles. These cycles are typically long, varying from about fifty years to well over a century (Doran and Parsons 1980; Thompson 1986; Modelski 1987; Goldstein 1988; Modelski and Thompson 1994). In the most sophisticated accounts of **war cycles,** states rise, reach a power peak when their influence is at a maximum, and then gradually decline as others rise to supplant them. War is most likely to occur at turning points in this cycle of growth and decay. At these junctures, leaders hold mistaken views about their prospects. The state that was on the upswing but that has now in fact reached its apex (that is, the high point or turning point, after which its power declines) remains convinced of its growth in power and fails to adjust to its new reality. It continues to expect to be accorded more respect (that is, influence) than other states are willing to give it (Doran and Parsons 1980). This misperception of the leading state's relative power becomes an important source of war, providing an alternative account to that in the power transition theory (discussed in Chapter 4) about why the relative decline of a dominant state's power might provoke war. Here aggression is the product of failing to recognize decline, whereas in the power transition war results from the anticipation of the consequences of such decline.

Much of the war cycle literature is empirically driven. It relies on the examination of long series of data, trying to discern patterns and then fitting an explanation to those patterns. But the length of a cycle is often within the eyes of the beholder. Some systematic tests for the presence of cycles of recurring length fail to support the claims (Singer and Cusack 1990). Charles Doran and Wes Parsons's (1980) thesis, however, is theoretically grounded and seems to find some empirical support. Still, their argument leaves open some important puzzles for future investigation. For example, why can the rest of the countries in the world tell when a state has reached its downturn inflection point, but the leaders in that country cannot? It is understandable that they might not recognize their changed circumstances right away, but as more and more unsuccessful interactions take place, why doesn't the theory allow for the possibility that leaders will learn from their failures, adjust their expectations, and thereby avert disastrous mistakes? Indeed, some innovative organizational theory research by Scott Gartner (1997) shows that leaders do make these types of adjustments as they figure out which of their strategies and tactics are successful and which are not.

SUMMARY

In this chapter, we have seen that uncertainty can promote international instability but that it can promote international stability as well. We have tested the logic undergirding these claims and found them to be consistent with the historical record. We have also seen that conditions exist in which weak stakeholders are expected to be belligerent, perhaps even more belligerent than strong ones. The resurrection hypothesis helps explain why leaders who face severe military defeat fight on in the hope that luck will turn the tide their way. We have also seen that demonizing an enemy leader may encourage his or her efforts at resurrection through accelerated violence, thereby possibly creating a worse situation than might otherwise have materialized. In addition, pacific doves, a particular type of actor (state or terrorist group) are especially likely to initiate violence when they are much weaker than their foes; the likelihood that pacific doves will be peaceful increases as their relative power increases. Each of these observations (as well as the findings regarding the democratic peace reported in the next chapter) would be considered false under structural, unitary actor explanations of international affairs. This is because each of these observations involves looking inside the state, breaking the unitary actor assumption, and allowing an important part of the action in international affairs to arise from factors that differ from state to state and from regime type to regime type.

In this chapter, we have also examined several theories linking arms levels to war and found them wanting either in logical rigor, empirical support, or both. The record indicating that arms races are a cause of war is weak at best. The claim that arms-control treaties reduce the threat of war is mistaken. Although arms control does reduce the deadliness of war, it appears to increase—or at least not to decrease—its frequency. Deterrence, for its part, does reduce the likelihood that disputes will escalate into violence; however, when deterrence fails, the ensuing conflict is likely to be much bloodier than would otherwise have been the case.

War is so terrible a feature of international relations that I cannot leave the subject without emphasizing the importance to all of us of improving our understanding of this deadly phenomenon. The last few decades have seen real progress in our theoretical and empirical understanding of the logic behind warfare; most of that progress arises from shifting our focus to the incentives and constraints faced by national leaders and away from treating the state as a unitary actor. Much, of course, remains to be done.

KEY CONCEPTS

6 Domestic Origins of Foreign Policy: Exploring the Democratic Peace

OVERVIEW

- Democratic peace regularities should not exist if structural or realist theories are correct.

- The evidence strongly supports the ideas that democracies tend not to fight wars with one another but do fight with nondemocracies; that democracies try harder to win when a war proves difficult and so have a much greater tendency to emerge victorious from war than do nondemocracies; and that, in the process, because they try harder, democracies fight relatively short wars with relatively few democratic battle fatalities.

- All in all, the democratic peace can be thought of as twelve empirical regularities in search of an explanation. The selectorate theory (the strategic perspective developed in Chapter 1) provides an explanation for all the relevant empirical patterns. In doing so, it also suggests why efforts to export democracy (the topic of Chapter 8) are almost certainly doomed to failure.

Structural theories and strategic theories of war sometimes lead to comparable predictions and other times lead to diametrically opposed predictions.* Of course, the relative reliability of plausible explanations can only be judged based on the differences in their predictions, not their areas of agreement. As we have seen in Chapter 5, when these perspectives diverge, strategic theories that consider domestic politics as well as international circumstances fit the facts of history better. Nowhere is this truer than in the exploration of what has come to be known as the democratic peace.

The central contention of the **democratic peace** is that democracies rarely, if ever, fight wars with one another even though they are not particularly reluctant to fight wars against nondemocratic or illiberal regimes (Babst 1964; Doyle 1986; Morgan and Campbell 1991; Bremer 1993; Maoz and Russett 1993; Mintz and Geva 1993; Russett 1993; Ray 1995; Ward and Gleditsch 1998). This observation about the pacific interactions of democracies, and the philosophical perspective that underlies it (Kant 1983), is so important and influential that Bill Clinton and George W. Bush made the promotion of democratic institutions a cornerstone of their foreign policy. Probably Barack Obama will as well. American leaders do so, in part, because they believe democratization is one of the surest paths to a more peaceful world. As we discuss in Chapters 8 and 9, it is unlikely that any president will succeed in spreading democracy, and it is even questionable whether doing so is itself a democratic act. But that does not obviate the importance of understanding why democracies live in peace with one another even though they do not live in peace with others.

It is also critical to note that the democratic peace is much more than just a statement about pacific democratic behavior. That is not the totality of what I want to discuss under the rubric of the democratic peace. In this chapter, we explore the variety of observations that collectively constitute what might be more broadly thought

U.S. troops entered Somalia in mid-1993 to assist in making the country safe for the distribution of humanitarian aid. Drawn into the middle of a political and military quagmire, the troops became the target of a local drug lord. The resulting encounter became the basis for the movie *Black Hawk Down*. In early 1995, this U.S. soldier and others guarded the UN compound in Mogadishu while assisting in the withdrawal of peacekeepers from the country.

of as the democratic peace. Our primary task is to provide an explanation for the observed patterns of behavior. Doing so will help inform our thinking about the policy consequences of democratization and will also help guide our discussion later in Chapters 8 and 9 about

---

* Significant sections of this chapter are taken from or rely on Bueno de Mesquita et al. (1999, 2004).

the benefits and liabilities of a more democratic world. I begin, however, by enumerating the collection of fairly well-established facts behind the democratic peace and then exploring how they are tied to domestic political institutions.

THE FACTS THAT MAKE UP THE DEMOCRATIC PEACE

Most of the time, when people speak of a *democratic peace* they have in mind the important, although much debated, claim that there have been no wars between democracies—or hardly any, depending on how we define *war* and *democracy*—at least during the past two hundred years and perhaps for much longer. For those who think of international politics in terms of power and the competition for it, this is a startling discovery. If war and international stability are about the distribution of power or the polarity of the international system, what can possibly explain the discovery that a country's internal governance style matters in its most fundamental, life and death choices about war and peace? This internal feature of states simply is not supposed to matter, yet, as we will see, it surely does.

The democratic peace goes well beyond even the important discovery that democracies do not seem to fight with one another. Just as that fact runs contrary to realist perspectives, so too do many of the other empirical regularities that make up the evidence for the democratic peace and for the important role that domestic institutions play in shaping foreign affairs.

Here is a list of what I think of as the central empirical regularities that collectively constitute the democratic peace. I follow the list with a brief presentation of some critical evidence that justifies the belief that the democratic peace approaches being a law of politics (Levy 1988). My list is grouped according to findings that I argue are closely intertwined; it starts with what I see as the most important empirical discoveries and progresses to the lesser ones from my point of view. I do not intend to say anything significant by my choice of order so please feel entirely free to disagree with it. The list does, after all, have to come in some sequence.

> **TRY THIS**
>
> Provide a definition of *democracy* and a definition of *war*. Can you think of examples of wars between two or more democracies that satisfy your definition? List them, and explain briefly what you think the causes of the war were. If you cannot think of examples within your definitions, then consider the following cases of violent conflict between two apparent democracies: the United States and the Confederate States during the American Civil War, the U.S. invasion of the Dominican Republic in 1965, and the fighting between Iceland and the United Kingdom over fishing rights during the 1960s. Are there characteristics that make it straightforward to explain these events in light of the democratic peace? What are they?

1. Democracies tend not to fight wars with one another (Maoz and Abdolali 1989; Russett 1993; Ray 1995).
   a. Democracies tend to reach peaceful settlements when disputes arise with other democracies (Dixon 1994).

b. Democracies are more likely to fight with one another when they are in transition to democracy than when they are mature democracies (Mansfield and Snyder 1995).

2. Democracies do fight wars with nondemocracies with considerable regularity (Maoz and Abdolali 1989).

3. Democracies make an extra effort to win when they discover that a war is more challenging than they anticipated, while nondemocracies do not (Bueno de Mesquita et al. 2003, 2004).

   a. Democracies overwhelmingly emerge victorious in war (Lake 1992; Reiter and Stam 1996, 2002).

   b. Democracies are more likely to fight shorter wars than are autocracies (Bennett and Stam 1996, 1998c).

   c. Democracies are no more reluctant than nondemocracies to fight with weak rivals, but they are more reluctant to be weak rivals themselves (Bueno de Mesquita et al. 2003, 2004).

4. Democracies are more likely to initiate war against autocracies than autocracies are to initiate wars against democracies (Bennett and Stam 1998b).

5. Democracies experience fewer battle deaths in the wars that they initiate (Siverson 1995).

6. Democracies spend more to enforce the peace following military victory than do nondemocracies (Bueno de Mesquita et al. 2003, 2004).

7. Democracies are more constrained as major powers and are therefore less likely to engage in war than are minor powers (Morgan and Campbell 1991).

Some Evidence

Before turning to explanations, let me add a few bits and pieces of evidence about some of these regularities to help put some flesh on them. The two biggest contentions are that democracies don't fight one another but that they do fight others. It is easily demonstrated just how strong this peaceful tendency among democracies is. For instance, if we define a country as a full-fledged democracy by the standard that it achieved the highest rating on the **Polity Index,** which measures, loosely speaking, the extent to which a government assures competitive participation in the leader-selection process (with competitive recruitment of leaders), constrains leaders, and makes the process open to a broad segment of the population, then no pair of democracies has fought a war with one another at least since the end of the Napoleonic era in 1815.[†] That fact stands in sharp contrast to the pattern demonstrated by other kinds of governments even after we correct for the relative scarcity of democracies for most of the past two centuries.

[†] See Marshall and Jaggers (2007). The Polity Index ranges between + 10 for the most democratic governments and −10 for the most autocratic governments.

TABLE 6.1	Is There a Democratic Peace?	
	Not a democratic pair	Democratic pair
Dispute does not become a war	2,409 (94.8%)	132 (5.2%)
Dispute becomes a war	125 (98.4%)	2 (1.6%)

We do not need to limit ourselves to a demanding, high standard of democracy to see that there is a democratic peace. Using the much weaker standard that a country is a democracy if it scores at least 7 out of 10 on the Polity Index, then only 2 of the 127 wars fought since 1816 have been between two democracies. These two conflicts were between Turkey and Cyprus in 1974 and between Pakistan and India in 1993.

Table 6.1 shows the distribution of cases of war and of conflicts short of war for pairs of countries engaged in militarized disputes against one another between 1816 and 2001.[‡] Here I am applying a rather tough test because I am ignoring the vast number of opportunities for democracies to have disputes with one another that they ignored by living in harmony with one another. In the table, the pairs of countries are divided by whether both members of the dyad in conflict were democracies or not (using the standard that they each scored above 6 on the Polity Index). The odds of there being as few as just two wars between democratic pairs, even using this weak standard for defining democracy, is so low that it is highly unlikely to have arisen by chance (the probability it occurred by chance is 0.035).

Let's expand Table 6.1 by dividing pairs of disputants into three groups instead of two. The first group contains two nondemocratic states, the second contains one democratic and the other not, and the third contains two democracies. So, in essence, Table 6.2 divides the first column of Table 6.1 into two groups.

Table 6.2 highlights interesting patterns, including the identification of evidence for the second important empirical regularity associated with the democratic peace. First, it is evident that nondemocratic rivals (such as autocracies, monarchies, and military juntas) are "oversubscribed" to war. Although they make up 61.5 percent of all disputing pairs, they represent 71.7 percent of wars. If disputes led to war by chance, only 78 of the 127 wars (rather than the 91 we observe) should have occurred between autocratic rivals given the frequency of such rivalries in these data. Disputes involving a nondemocrat and a democrat are more pacific than anticipated by chance but still far more common than between a pair of democracies; the number of mixed-pair wars arising by chance is forty-three, as opposed to the thirty-four we actually observe. Of course, the difference between expectations (forty-three wars) and actual wars (thirty-four) among democratic-nondemocratic pairs is not vast, being an undersubscription of just 20 percent. In contrast, the expected number of wars between democracies is six (or 6.37 to be excessively precise) given that democratic pairs make up 5 percent of the rivalries instead of the two

TABLE 6.2	**Are Democrats Generally Peaceful?**		
	Two nondemocracies	**One democracy and one nondemocracy**	**Two democracies**
Dispute does not become a war	1,549 (61%)	860 (33.8%)	132 (5.2%)
Dispute becomes a war	91 (71.7%)	34 (26.8 %)	2 (1.6%)
Total	1,640 (61.5%)	894 (33.5%)	134 (5.0%)

wars that we observe. So war among democrats is underrepresented by about a factor of 3. We can readily see the second regularity—that democracies are not reluctant to fight with nondemocracies—in the data while also seeing a hint that democracies may be more pacific than autocracies in general. The broader evidence for that latter claim is somewhat uneven and, because it is not fundamental to the democratic peace discussion, I ignore that debate here.

The third empirical regularity relates to how hard democratic governments try to win when a war proves difficult and why it is that they win far more often than their foes. We already know from Chapter 4 that democratic governments win about 93 percent of the wars they initiate; autocratic governments win only about 60 percent of the wars they start (Reiter and Stam 2002). That's barely more than a flip of the coin for autocratic initiators, but it is an overwhelming edge for democracies. Of course, this might be due to several factors that we explore later. For now, I just shed some light on factors contributing to the overwhelming propensity of democracies to win their wars.

Table 6.3 shows that a major reason that democrats do so well in war is that they are highly selective about the wars they fight, choosing to negotiate when the odds of victory in war are not substantial. For this table, I have selected all the disputes in which the initiating side (that is, the dispute

> **TRY THIS**
>
> Combine the last two columns of Table 6.2 so that you have a table that contrasts the incidence of war among autocracies and among rivals for which it is true that at least one is a democracy. How can you figure out the expected number of wars and nonwar disputes that belong in each of the four cells of the table you have constructed if war is randomly distributed with regard to the involvement or noninvolvement of democracies? What do you find?

initiator and its allies) could reasonably believe that they would have a tough time winning the dispute. I show here the cases for which the ex ante probability of winning, based on the capabilities controlled by the side in question relative to all the capabilities expected to be devoted to the dispute by the belligerents and their allies on both sides, was less than 70 percent.[§] The

---

[§] Comparable results are found for lower or higher thresholds.

TABLE 6.3	**Winning Coalition Size and Likelihood of War Given a Dispute**					
	Extremely autocratic ($W = 0$)	**Autocratic** ($W = 0.25$)	**Quasi-autocratic** ($W = 0.50$)	**Quasi-democratic** ($W = 0.75$)	**Mature democracy** ($W = 1.00$)	**Total**
No war	44 (33.3%)	78 (42.4%)	74 (44.3%)	79 (59.0%)	57 (85.1%)	332 (48.5%)
War	88 (66.7%)	106 (57.6%)	93 (55.7%)	55 (41.0%)	10 (14.9%)	352 (51.5%)
Total	132	184	167	134	67	684

Source: Bueno de Mesquita et al. (2004).

Notes: Ex ante probability of winning < 0.70. W is the winning coalition size.

columns measure how democratic the initiator was and the rows show whether the dispute became a war or not.** One reason democrats might win almost all the wars they start is that they avoid fighting when their odds of victory are not overwhelming, say at least as large as 70 percent.

As we can see, the most democratic states, shown in the last column of Table 6.3, are most unlikely to fight when their odds of victory going into the dispute are not larger than 70 percent. Eighty-five percent of the time under these relatively difficult conditions, democratic states don't fight. Instead, they choose to find a negotiated settlement (regularity 1a), or acquiesce to the demands of their opponent or (especially when both parties are democracies) manage to get their opponent to acquiesce to their demands. In contrast, two-thirds of the most autocratic disputants fight when their odds of wining are poorer than 70 percent. They don't seem as worried about defeat. This selection bias, the democratic preference for low-risk wars, may be why democracies are so likely to win, as reported by Reiter and Stam (2002). It may also go a long way to explaining regularity 3c, which tells us that democracies, like autocracies, are not particularly hesitant to fight against weak foes but are reluctant to be the weak side in a fight. That may be why democracies are far from immune from engaging in wars of colonial or imperial expansion. The adversaries in such conflicts are typically very weak and easily beaten. The same goes for what may seem like odd-ball wars, such as the U.S. fight against the tiny island state of Grenada in 1983.

We have seen significant evidence that provides a foundation for understanding why democracies win so often, the focus of the regularities clustered together as number 3 on my list. But we have not seen evidence for the main heading under 3 on the list—that democracies win because they make an exceptional effort to do so while autocracies do not.

** I use the selectorate theory's measure of winning coalition size, W, to assess how democratic or autocratic the dispute initiator was. Details on how this is measured are found in Bueno de Mesquita et al. (2003, 137).

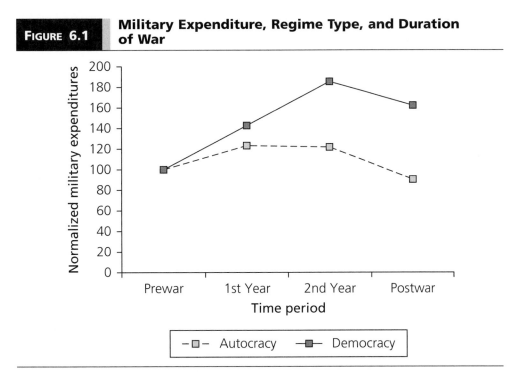

FIGURE 6.1 | **Military Expenditure, Regime Type, and Duration of War**

Source: Bueno de Mesquita et al. (2004).

Figure 6.1 helps establish that this claim is true, opening the door for this regularity, like all of the others, to be explained later in this chapter.

Figure 6.1 shows the **war effort**, measured as military expenditures, for autocracies (or, more precisely, regimes whose winning coalition size score = 0 on a 0–1 scale) and democracies (coalition size = 1) in the run-up to, during, and after war. The lines in the figure reflect the military spending levels that best fit the data on military expenditures for the average mature democracy and the average hard-line autocracy during different war stages. These differences are highly significant in a statistical as well as substantive sense, so the figure tells a fundamental and robust story about regime type and war effort.[††] Both autocracies and democracies are normalized in the figure to a baseline military expenditure value of 100 before war so that we can easily compare the percentage changes in effort once war is underway. For instance, a score of 110 means a 10 percent increase over the baseline prewar expenditure. A score of 85 means a 15 percent drop in military expenditures compared to the prewar level.

As we can see, both kinds of countries spend more on the military when a war begins than they were spending beforehand. Autocrats increase their relative effort by about 20 percent once a war gets going, while democrats increase theirs by more than 40 percent. Even more

[††] Those interested in a more detailed breakdown of the evidence should see Bueno de Mesquita et al. (2004, esp. Table 2).

striking is what happens if the war is prolonged, lasting more than one year. A prolonged war is an indication that things are not proving especially easy for either side. Democrats, as we already have seen, expect their wars to be won easily or they do not fight. Autocrats do not have the same expectation for reasons explained later. Thus, by the end of the first year of fighting, autocrats have geared up about as much as they ever will (provided the war does not turn into a war for political survival, a relatively rare event, especially when the fighting does not involve at least one powerful democracy). They are not surprised by the difficulty they are having winning because they are not terribly selective about the wars they fight. In the second and subsequent years (if any), their effort remains no different from what it was in the first year of fighting.

Democrats, unlike autocrats, are surprised when victory proves elusive. By the second year, they have discovered that the war is harder to win than they thought beforehand. They chose to fight (rather that settle) on the expectation of an easy, cheap victory. So, having learned that victory is tough they have two choices: bail out or try harder. We see shortly that bailing out is rarely an option for democratic leaders. Figure 6.1 shows us is that democrats facing a prolonged war increase their effort tremendously. They spend nearly twice as much on the military as they were spending before the war began, and they also spend vastly more than they were during the first year of fighting when they still thought victory would prove relatively easy.

Figure 6.1 also shows us what happens after the war is over. Democrats cut back modestly on military spending, while autocrats return to their baseline level or even below. We see later why this is so.

We now have some evidence under our belts that helps justify the belief in the democratic peace. Many theories prove able to explain one, two, or three of the twelve regularities I have listed, but then these theories turn out to be inconsistent with others. The selectorate approach to the strategic perspective (introduced in Chapter 1) provides a theoretical explanation for all of these regularities and others besides. Before pulling these disparate observations about regime type and war together within the selectorate's strategic approach, however, let us consider prominent alternative explanations for aspects of the democratic peace. We can begin with the skeptics who argue that the idea of a democratic peace is a chimera.

THE REALIST DEMOCRATIC-PEACE NAYSAYERS

It should come as no surprise that not everyone readily accepts even the evidence for the most prominent claim about a democratic peace, let alone the explanations for it (Small and Singer 1976; Farber and Gowa 1995; Gates, Knutsen, and Moses 1996). Some reject the notion of a democratic peace out of hand. They do not deny that the above patterns exist; instead, they question whether these patterns, or at least the first few in the list, are coincidentally correlated with democracy with the true explanation lying in standard realist accounts. For instance, democracy was a rare form of government before the mid-twentieth century. That means that the odds of a war between democracies had to be very low in those times. Think of the odds back then as the probability of drawing two aces out of a well-shuffled deck of cards. That is, imagine a world with just fifty-two countries, only four of which are democracies (the aces). The odds of drawing the first ace (a democracy) are 4 in 52. The odds of drawing the second ace (a second democracy) are 3 in 51. The chance that two aces are drawn, then, is (4/52) · (3/51) or about 1 in 221. War is a fairly rare event to begin with. If the world were made up of fifty-two countries, only four of which were democracies, the random chance of a war between any two given democrats is tiny. If that is all that's going on, then the democratic peace—at least the absence of war between democracies—might just be due to chance.

Wait a minute. What about in the twentieth and twenty-first centuries? Democracy is no longer a rare form of government. In fact, it is now quite common. Yet war between democracies still remains rare. Remember Tables 6.1 and 6.2? We have already seen that the actual odds of a war between democracies over the past couple of centuries is three times higher than the incidence of such wars, contradicting this naysayer claim that the democratic peace is just dumb luck.

The absence of democratic wars is all the more compelling because the geographical distribution of democracies ought to favor their having a particularly high risk of war with one another. One of the other important facts we know about war is that countries with shared borders are far more likely to fight with one another than are countries that do not abut one another (Senese and Vasquez 2008; Huth and Allee 2003). Democratic states tend to cluster geographically. In fact, one explanation for their clustering—that they follow "nice" strategies, cooperating in response to cooperation and being tough only in response to toughness by others—is consistent with the normative explanation of the democratic peace (detailed in the next section) (Axelrod 1984). Despite their war-provoking geographical proximity and shared borders, they still do not fight even though the odds favor their doing so.

Realists offer other reasons for the democratic peace "coincidence" (as they see it). They note that democratic states tend to be wealthy and powerful. This makes them unattractive targets for aggressors and so may explain their relative peacefulness. This explanation, however, utterly fails to account for the fact that democracies have been involved in lots of wars with nondemocracies. It is consistent with the propensity for democrats to be the initiators rather than defenders in disputes, but then that still leaves us with the puzzle of why the very same European states that used to fight with one another no longer do. Germany and France fought wars with one another in 1870–1871, 1914–1918, and 1939–1945. During none of those years were they both democratic, although they were relatively wealthy. They have not fought since World War II, and, perhaps coincidentally and perhaps not, both have been democracies since the end of that war. The United States has fought with plenty of governments since 1945 but never with Canada. Yet Canada, also of course a democracy, is not a great power, is a major economic competitor, and shares a tremendous border with the U.S. It ought to be an easy target. Realists just don't have a good explanation for these and countless other facts associated with the democratic peace.

THE NORMATIVE EXPLANATION

Among the vast majority who agree that there is a democratic peace, the debate revolves around whether a normative or an institutional explanation best accounts for the known facts. Both the normative and the institutional frameworks are within the spirit of strategic approaches that recognize that domestic politics helps shape international interactions and that war and peace choices are made taking into account expectations about how others will respond to different decisions. The two perspectives, however, differ fundamentally in how they account for the prevalence of peaceful relations among democracies.

The **normative perspective** sees political interaction as depending on the internalization of patterns of behavior, whether these patterns serve an actor's interests or not and whether they are subject to enforcement and punishment for violations or not. In doing this it focuses on several different presumptions about democracies. One such presumption is that democratic regimes share a common value system, including respect for individual liberties and for competition. William Dixon has articulated this view especially clearly:

> international disputes of democratic states are in the hands of individuals who have experienced the politics of competing values and interests and who have consistently responded within the normative guidelines of bounded competition. In situations where both parties to a dispute are democracies, not only do both sides subscribe to these norms, but the leaders of both are also fully cognizant that bounded competition is the norm, both for themselves and their opponents. (1994, 17)

A closely related argument is that citizens in democracies abhor violence (they being the ones who bear the brunt of the burdens of war) and so constrain their leaders from pursuing violent foreign policies. As Clifton Morgan and Sally Campbell have argued, "the key feature of democracy is government by the people and … the people, who must bear the costs of war, are usually unwilling to fight" (1991, 189). That, in fact, is a succinct statement of Immanuel Kant's famous original contention that democracies (or republics, in his terms) would not fight with one another.

Adherents of the normative perspective also argue that democracies are willing to set aside their abhorrence of violence or their respect for the points of view of others when they come up against authoritarian states because the latter do not share these common values. Zeev Maoz and Bruce Russett are most prominently associated with this argument. They contend, "when a democratic state confronts a nondemocratic one, it may be forced to adapt to the norms of international conflict of the latter lest it be exploited or eliminated by the nondemocratic state that takes advantage of the inherent moderation of democracies" (Maoz and Russett 1993, 625).

The normative argument says, in short, that democracies (really democratically elected leaders) are used to negotiating, competing, and compromising because that is the nature of democratic politics. Therefore, when they have disputes with one another they follow these familiar courses of action, thereby avoiding war. But, when they have a dispute with a nondemocracy, they adopt the mode of conduct of the nondemocracy because that is the best way, under those conditions, to ensure their own state's political survival. This is a variant of the golden rule; the main normative argument seems to be, "Do unto others as you expect they will do unto you." This view is consistent with the two most important facts about the democratic peace. It offers a parsimonious explanation for the absence of wars between democracies and for the existence of many such wars between democratic and nondemocratic states. It also provides an account of the fact that democracies are especially likely to resolve disputes with one another through negotiation (1a on my list). It is harder to see how the normative explanation accounts for the other empirical differences between the actions of democracies and nondemocracies in the diplomacy leading up to, the tactics during, and the effort following war. Still, getting several of the more important empirical relations right is nothing to sneeze at, or is it?

The normative explanation for the democratic peace suffers from at least two huge problems. One is logical and the other empirical.

Let's examine the logical limitation first. What does the normative account really imply as distinct from what it assumes? As the passages quoted before make clear, the normative theory assumes that democracies have a shared willingness to compromise in an effort to settle disputes peacefully. But when democracies confront nondemocratic states—that, by assumption, do not share this compromising approach to disputes—democracies adopt the expected confrontational pattern of nondemocracies. In other words, democracies don't fight with one another because, the theory assumes, they prefer negotiation. This assumption is actually a statement of two of the three facts that the theory purports to explain. The theory *assumes* that democracies negotiate with one another (regularity 1a on my list) and, therefore, don't fight with one another (regularity 1). So, the theory has not led to these critical conclusions; it has not explained them—it has assumed them! Because they are not a logical consequence of the theory, we must look elsewhere for regularities that the normative account actually explains. I am afraid that quest is in vain.

The flip side of the normative coin relates to the logical and empirical inadequacy of the normative explanation in addressing the second empirical regularity—that democracies are not reluctant to fight with nondemocratic states because the democracy's survival dictates that it must adopt the pattern of interaction common in those states. That democracies are willing to abandon their normative commitment to the peaceful resolution of disputes in the face of a threat to their survival by another state that does not adhere to those norms is entirely plausible. However, that assertion must be derived independently of the observation, either from prior axioms or from unrelated empirical evidence, in order to qualify as an explanation of the observation. That is not the case. The theory is, instead, as we have seen with the other two regularities it purportedly explains, a restatement of the observed patterns of behavior. The theory does not derive those, or any other, expectations against which it can be evaluated.

In fact, the normative account leaves us with several troubling empirical puzzles to explain. For instance, what does the normative explanation tell us about important, seemingly contradictory patterns of evidence? Studies of international covert operations seem to contradict the idea that democracies welcome opportunities for compromise with one another. Studies by Patrick James and Glenn E. Mitchell (1995) and David P. Forsythe (1992), for example, suggest that, providing they can escape public scrutiny, democratic leaders often undertake violent acts against other democracies. Does such evidence contradict a norms-based argument, or do the norms apply only to interstate conflict at the level of crises and war? And if only at that level, why?

The empirical problems do not end with research on covert operations. There are other, perhaps even more troubling empirical patterns that seem to refute the normative explanation of the democratic peace. The historical record is replete with democratic states that followed policies at variance with the norms argument, perhaps sufficiently so that we can say that the norms argument is falsified. Let's see why I suggest such a strong course of action (one that we should be willing to take cautiously when we are confident that doing so will correctly whittle down the number of theories that might actually explain what we see).

If we define a country whose score is 7 or greater on the Polity Index as democratic, then we discover that there have been more than eighty violent international disputes between pairs of democracies, at least according to the records in the Dyadic Militarized Interstate Disputes data, the most widely used source for investigating international conflict.[‡‡] Although these disputes between democracies did not rise to the standard threshold of 1,000 battle-related fatalities that is used to distinguish lesser disputes from wars, still they involved the active use of force between pairs of democratic states, something that cannot happen according to the norms argument. Even if we take the tougher standard that to qualify as a democracy, states must achieve the highest rating accorded by the Polity Index—that is, 10 on their scale—still there are twenty-four violent disputes between pairs of democracies. For instance, Iceland and the United Kingdom, both indisputably democracies, have engaged one another in military exchanges at sea over fishing rights in 1958, 1960, 1972, and 1975. The United States invaded and overthrew a democratically elected government in the Dominican Republic in 1965, apparently because the then newly elected president, Juan Bosch, was interested in friendly relations with Fidel Castro's pro-Soviet Cuba.

So, mature democracies are not immune from fighting with one another short of war, contrary to the normative theory. The problems do not end there. At least as challenging for that perspective is another set of facts that we cannot ignore. Democratic states routinely pursued (and still pursue) imperialistic policies and, in the process of building their empires, engaged in numerous wars that were about subjugation rather than self-protection. It may be correct to argue that democratic states resort to realist strategies in the face of a powerful nondemocratic opponent that threatens their existence, but too many democratic wars have been against significantly weaker states for this argument to be sustained as an explanation for the democratic peace. It is difficult to see how weak governments in places that were conquered and made colonies could have been a threat to the survival of such powerful democratic colonizers as the United States (for example, the Philippines and Cuba), the United Kingdom (on whose global empire the sun never set), France (whose empire included what is now Vietnam, Laos, Cambodia, and vast areas of Africa), Belgium (for example, the

---

[‡‡] Available at www.correlatesofwar.org/COW2%20Data/MIDs/MID310.html.

Congo), and the Netherlands (Indonesia). It seems impossible to reconcile such a pattern of imperial and colonial expansion with the upbeat view of democratic political culture espoused by the theorists who adopt the normative perspective.

INSTITUTIONAL EXPLANATIONS

The **institutional perspective** sees political interaction as depending on actors pursuing actions that are compatible with their interests and that are constrained by the structure of the situation in which they find themselves, especially the structure of political institutions. Institutional arguments intended to explain the democratic peace come in numerous guises. One prominent perspective holds that democracies are more deliberate in their decision making because their procedures preclude unilateral action by leaders. This is thought to make participation in violent acts difficult by imposing constraints on decision making and especially on the speed with which democracies can respond to challenges. As Maoz and Russett have contended, "due to the complexity of the democratic process and the require-ment of securing a broad base of support for risky policies, democratic leaders are reluctant to wage wars, except in cases wherein war seems a necessity or when the war aims are seen as justifying the mobilization costs" (1993, 626).[§§]

This argument suffers from some rather significant problems. If the complexity of democratic processes makes war unattractive, then this should apply equally well whether the adversary is a democracy or not, contradicting the second regularity on my list as the price for explaining why democracies might tend to negotiate with one another rather than fight (regularities 1 and 1a). The argument for complexity might favor the idea that wars between democracies and nondemocracies are especially likely to arise if the democracy is the dispute initiator; this could be true if initiation follows a long preparatory period during which the democracy works through its complex decision-making process. Yet such a con-tention offers no explanation for why the autocratic target sits by idly waiting for its demo-cratic adversary to ready itself to attack. We must wonder why the autocratic rival does not exploit its alleged organizational advantage by moving quickly, before the democracy has made its war preparations. Thus, complexity is weakly consistent with regularity 4 on my list. It is also consistent with regularity 7, that democratic major powers are especially con-strained (or, anyway, that all democracies are constrained, although by assumption rather than by being an implication of the argument). But it does not fit much else. The empirical record offers little to encourage those who assume that democratic decision-making pro-cesses are especially complex and slow, and that this slowness helps avert war.

Another institutional argument on behalf of the alleged peacefulness of democracies points to how cheap opposition is in such systems. The idea is that, because democracy

---

[§§] The last phrase in this quoted passage is unfortunate. Without some specification of war aims and mobilization costs, the last phrase allows anything with respect to democratic war behavior.

encourages outspoken opposition to policies that the voters think are foolish, it makes leaders reluctant to fight. Kenneth Schultz (2001) makes the best case for this point of view. He explains why democracies rarely lose the wars they fight (regularity 3a) based on a selection effect. When the opposition thinks that a foreign policy will be a failure, they speak out against it. The incumbent, not wishing to be tarred with the costs of a failed policy, takes notice that the opposition politicians will resist a war policy only if they have good reason to think there are votes to be gained in opposition. This disciplines the incumbent to be cautious about war, choosing to fight only when there is a high probability of winning. This is consistent with the observed record of military victories mentioned earlier. Given that democracies must believe they have a high probability of winning (or else their opposition politicians will speak out against war), this means that it is especially hard for a pair of democracies to satisfy this condition. It is difficult for each to believe it has a really good chance of winning, a constraint not as strongly felt by nondemocratic leaders, who do not face an electoral opposition. Thus, the low-costs argument is consistent with the main empirical facts of the democratic peace (regularities 1, 1a, and 2; 3, 3a, 3b, and 3c; and possibly 5), but it says nothing about regularities 1b, 4, 6, or 7.

The argument based on the cheapness of expressing opposition seems stronger than the other putative institutional explanations, but it too has shortcomings, one of which is that it fails to account for the well-known "rally-'round-the-flag" effect observed in democracies at the outset of crises and wars (Mueller 1973; Norpoth 1987). This effect suggests that there is not an inherent abhorrence of violence in democracies; rather, there seems to be an abhorrence of enduring high costs on the part of citizens who can hold their leaders accountable. That, in essence, is the foundation of Immanuel Kant's (1983/1795) contention in the eighteenth century that republics (that is, loosely what we mean today by *democracies*) are more pacific than monarchies. When the people must bear the cost of fighting and the people have a say in selecting their leaders, the leaders will be hesitant to inflict great costs on them. We see shortly, when we turn to the selectorate explanation of the democratic peace, that it derives this inference rather than assuming it.

Bueno de Mesquita and Lalman (1992) offer a signaling explanation for the democratic peace. In their account, democracies endure higher political costs for using force. This makes them reluctant to threaten the use of force if they will not follow through and so, when they do threaten to use force, others can readily anticipate the credibility of the threat. That is, democracies are less able than nondemocracies to bluff by making threats they are not serious about carrying out. This signaling explanation in the IIG is consistent with the most widely accepted democratic-peace regularities (1, 1a, and 2). It also provides an explanation of the major power constraint argument (regularity 7) and the propensity for democracies to be war initiators (4). But this theory, which assumes democracies pay a higher domestic political cost for using force than do autocracies, offers no insight into why democracies try harder during difficult wars (regularity 3), why they win a disproportionate share of their wars (3a), or why their costs in lost life and property are lower (3b and 6). The theory also does not address the preparedness of democratic regimes to take on much weaker adversaries (3c) or to accept high costs for enforcing postwar settlements (6).

Like the normative account, the complexity argument, and the cheap opposition explanation, Bueno de Mesquita and Lalman's signaling explanation assumes that democracies are more constrained than autocracies. Although for the last three theories (complexity, cheap opposition, and signaling), this assumption alone is not sufficient to account for the many second-tier regularities that they seek to explain, still it is far preferable that the constraints faced by different types of regimes be a deductive result of a general model than an assumption. As we know from Chapter 1, the selectorate approach demonstrates that institutional arrangements produce different levels of constraint in different political systems and what effect those institutional arrangements have on behavioral incentives. Next we see how that theory also leads to all the empirical regularities that I have listed as making up the body of knowledge known as the democratic peace.

THE SELECTORATE DEMOCRATIC PEACE

The selectorate explanation, as you know (see Chapter 1), draws our attention to how the size of a leader's winning coalition and selectorate shapes how much government revenue the incumbent spends on satisfying coalition demands and on the mix of public and private goods that are purchased with the revenue spent on the coalition.*** It makes no assumptions about the citizens' abhorrence of violence or even the ease with which they might protest governmental policies. In fact, it assumes that political leaders in democracies, autocracies, military juntas, monarchies, and any other form of government all are motivated by the same universal interest—they desire to remain in office. The selectorate approach also does not make normative assumptions about differences in the values or goals of democratic leaders or their followers compared to authoritarian leaders or their followers. Instead, all the democratic peace regularities, and many other aspects of foreign policy as well, can be derived from—and are not assumed by—the selectorate theory.

As we examine the selectorate account of the democratic peace, it is important to remember that leaders have only a scarce amount of resources to allocate to different policy goals and to help keep them in office. They can put everything into public policy that benefits everyone in the polity, put everything into private goods that are consumed only by members of the winning coalition, or (as is more usual) allocate government spending to reflect some mix of public- and private-goods provision.

Naturally, if leaders spend resources on, for instance, providing defense for the citizenry, they cannot use those same resources to provide special privileges to the members of their winning coalition. If they buy national defense only from cronies in the winning coalition, then the reduced competition to provide defense will probably result in an inefficient provision of that public good while cronies skim money off the top for their personal gain. Thus, scarcity necessarily requires

---

*** Much of the material in this section is derived from Bueno de Mesquita et al. (2003).

leaders to make choices about just how much to focus their limited resources on providing generally beneficial public policies and how much to focus on just satisfying the wants of their core supporters. The central concern in applying selectorate theory to the democratic peace revolves around identifying how scarce resources are allocated during an international dispute, given variations in institutional arrangements; identifying whatever dependencies exist between regime type and war participation and outcomes; and evaluating the prospects that leaders are retained in office as a function of their institutional arrangements. These issues, as we see shortly, influence whether leaders concentrate resources on pursuing national goals or conserve their resources to benefit key domestic constituents. In showing how this is true, we account for the empirical regularities that constitute the democratic peace.

Let's assume that two nations, called A and B, are engaged in a dispute. The national leaders must decide whether they are prepared to start a war in the hope of achieving their objectives or to rely instead on a negotiated settlement. If one side initiates a war, then both leaders must decide how much of an effort they are prepared to make to achieve military victory—by this I mean, what proportion of available resources a leader is prepared to allocate to the war effort rather than to other purposes. Obviously, leaders who dedicate large quantities of resources to the war are more likely to win but at the cost of not having those resources available to reward their supporters. Money spent on one objective is no longer available for some other purpose.

The citizens receive payoffs based on the outcome of the crisis—be it a war or a negotiated settlement—and based on the rewards that accrue to them from resources that are not consumed in the war effort. Given these payoffs, the winning coalition decides whether to retain its current leader or whether it will be better off replacing him or her with someone expected to provide more benefits. A polity's institutional arrangements shape the selection criteria that supporters use to determine whether to retain the incumbent. Hence, political institutions determine which outcomes allow a leader to keep his or her job and which do not. As we will see, these differences profoundly influence the policies that leaders choose in disputes and in wars, as well as in peace.

Citizens, in general, enjoy the benefits of public policies whether they belong to the winning coalition or not. The advantage that members of the winning coalition have is that they also enjoy a share of whatever private goods are allocated by the leadership. At most, the average member of the winning coalition receives a share of private goods equal to R/W, where R is the available pool of resources (such as government tax revenue) and W, as you know, is the size of the winning coalition.

Each member's share of private goods decreases as the winning coalition gets larger, if we hold the available budget (R) constant. This makes public policy benefits loom larger in the overall utility assessment of members of the winning coalition in more democratic polities compared to autocracies simply because winning coalitions (W) are larger in democracies than in other forms of government. One consequence of this is that democratic leaders, being just as eager to retain office as their authoritarian counterparts, must be especially concerned about policy failure. To reduce the risk of policy failure and the associated risk that they will be deposed from office, democratic leaders make a larger effort to succeed in disputes (empirical regularity 3) while keeping the costs for their constituents as low as possible (3b and 5). This means that they are willing to spend more resources on the war effort and engage only in fights they anticipate winning. In contrast, leaders with small winning coalitions reserve more resources for distribution to their supporters in the form of private goods. As long as they can provide substantial private goods, they are not at such a high risk of being deposed as are their democratic counterparts, who, exactly because R/W shrinks as W increases, cannot give a large amount of such benefits to each member of their winning coalition.

Democratic leaders are more likely to try hard to win their wars than are autocrats if they are engaged in war. When do they avoid being engaged in war? If they do not expect to win (regularities 3 and 3a), they try to avoid fighting (1a). This implies that they pick and choose their fights more carefully (3a, 3b, 3c, and 5). This has several consequences. Democrats are more likely to win wars than autocrats for two reasons. First, if they need to, democrats try hard, spending resources on the war to advance their public policy goals (Reiter and Stam 1998; Bueno de Mesquita et al. 2004). Second, fearing public policy failure, democrats try to avoid those contests they do not think they can win. Because two democrats in a dispute both try hard, both can anticipate that, if they go to war, each will spend lots of resources in a risky situation where they are not disproportionately advantaged by their great effort. This inclines democracies generally to negotiate with one another rather than fight (regularity 1a; Lake 1992; Stam 1996, 176–178). By contrast, autocrats typically reserve their resources for domestic uses because their political survival depends more on satisfying a few key constituents through the distribution of private goods than it does on military victory. Autocrats do not have a great need to produce successful public policies. Consequently, autocrats try less hard than democrats in war (regularity 3), but still sometimes fight in wars where their chances are poor because defeat does not affect so greatly their prospects of political survival at home (3a, 3b, and 6). Democrats, by their superior level of effort, more often defeat autocratic foes and achieve successful policy outcomes (3 and 6); this helps enhance their reelection.

We can see that these claims follow from the selectorate theory with a simple computational example.[†††] Imagine that two nations find themselves involved in a dispute. They might pursue negotiations, or they might use force to achieve their objectives. If they negotiate, they are likely to resolve their argument by striking a compromise that approximates the observable balance of power between them. That is, the existing military balance is likely to give shape to the bargaining leverage of the two sides. If the adversaries fight, the outcome of their war depends in part on this military balance. But it also depends on the diversion of national resources to the war effort.

Leaders may choose to reallocate available resources to tilt the balance of power and, therefore, the expected outcome of the dispute or war in their favor. Depending on how much of such

---

[†††] Of course, those who want to see a full mathematical proof of these claims can do so in the original publications from which the argument is drawn (Bueno de Mesquita et al. 1999, 2003).

resources a leader diverts to the war effort, he or she demonstrates a larger (or smaller) commitment to winning the war. One obvious source of additional resources is the pot of money normally given out as private benefits to members of the winning coalition. In autocracies, where the winning coalition is small and the share of private goods per member is large, coalition members benefit less from the quality of public policy—and therefore from the national welfare and winning a war—than they do from safeguarding their own personal, private benefits except in an extreme and unusual foreign policy situation where the very survival of the regime they support is at serious risk. Barring such a risk, autocratic leaders are unlikely to reallocate the resources spent on personal benefits to enhance the national welfare. Doing so would alienate the leader's key supporters and thereby jeopardize his or her hold on power.

In contrast, democratic leaders search out additional resources to bolster their war efforts. They do so because their hold on political power depends much more on policy success than on the allocation of private goods. Democratic leaders shift resources into the war effort by taking them away from private-goods payments or by taking them out of less important policy pursuits without suffering a marked loss of support from the winning coalition. This idea is readily shown using a simple example based on the limiting case in which all available resources are either devoted to the war effort or to private goods for members of the winning coalition.

Suppose a leader chooses between putting all the available revenue (R) into fighting a war or retaining all the revenue to distribute as private rewards to the W members of his or her winning coalition. Further, assume that the utility derived from victory (V) is assured if all revenue is put into the war effort and that defeat in the war (the utility of which is 0) is assured if all revenue is retained for use as private rewards to coalition members. Suppose $V = v + r$, where v is the public-goods component of victory enjoyed by everyone in the society and r is the additional resources that can be extracted from the vanquished state (the spoils of war) and allocated to the leader's coalition members following victory. That is, V is the total value of the public and private benefits that are gained by winning a war. Let the per capita cost of waging war be k whether the war is won or lost.

We now are ready to see the conditions under which a leader can be better off losing for sure than winning for sure. If a leader makes an all-out effort to ensure victory, then the public and private benefits of winning are worth $v + (r/W) - k$ for each member of the coalition. Note that the spoils of war, r, are divided by W to signify that each member of the coalition gets his or her share of these gains. In contrast, v is the public-goods portion of victory and as such is indivisible; everyone shares in victory's public goods benefit (such as a safer homeland). Alternatively, if the leader chooses to retain resources for use as private benefits for coalition members at the expense of losing the war for sure, then the payoff to his or her coalition members is $R/W - k$.

With this simple setup, we can now see that as W gets smaller; that is, as a regime becomes more autocratic rather than democratic, leaders increasingly prefer losing a war if that means keeping their coalition's loyalty. Don't misunderstand—all else being equal, leaders always prefer winning to losing, but all else is not equal. Winning against a tough adversary is expensive. So, the choice to allocate extra resources to victory when fighting a weak foe may not be difficult (regularity 3c), but the decision to do so when the opponent is tough enough that victory is not assured is a real and difficult one.

TRY THIS

Construct a numerical example in which victory is preferred to war by both a small-coalition regime and a large-coalition regime. Try to construct an example in which the small-coalition leader chooses victory over defeat and the large-coalition leader does not.

Domestic institutional arrangements shape the extent to which political survival hinges more on winning than on losing. A political survival–oriented leader will choose to lose rather than win a war if:

$$R/W - k > v + (r/W) - k.$$

Rearranging the terms, we can solve for how valuable the public good of victory must be for a leader to prefer winning to losing or, conversely, how big the private gains have to be for a leader to choose losing the war for sure over winning for sure. The leader prefers to make an additional effort to win when:

$$v > (R - r)/W.$$

Of course, the quantity $(R - r)/W$ decreases as the size of the coalition, W, increases, provided that $R > r$. That is, when national resources (R) exceed the value of postwar spoils (r), as is virtually always true, v is more likely to be bigger than $(R - r)/W$, and it is more likely to be smaller as W gets smaller. We see, then, that small-coalition (small-W) systems (such as autocracies and juntas) are more likely to induce leaders to choose to make relatively little extra effort to win a war and that large-coalition systems (such as democracies) are relatively more likely to induce leaders to give up paying their coalition private rewards to put relatively more extra effort into achieving victory in war (Bueno de Mesquita et al. 1999, 2004).

In sum, autocratic polities put forth less effort than democratic polities toward winning (especially competitive) wars (Lamborn 1991; Levi 1998; Rosenthal 1998). The extra effort made by democracies gives them, on average, a military advantage over autocracies in war. This difference in effort directly implies the empirical regularities associated with the democratic peace.

Because democratic leaders try harder to win wars than their autocratic counterparts, democracies make relatively unattractive military targets. In addition, democrats are more selective than autocrats in their choice of targets. Because defeat typically leads to their domestic replacement, democratic leaders fight only those wars that they expect to win. If they do not expect to win, they negotiate.

To go to war, an autocrat does not require a huge military advantage because victory is not as important (except, as mentioned, under special circumstances involving an all-out war for political survival) as is reserving funds to provide future private benefits. Democratic leaders compensate for any initial military disadvantage by devoting additional resources to the war effort; autocratic leaders do not. Democracies typically overwhelm autocracies because they are willing to mobilize more of their resources for the war effort rather than reserving them to reward domestic backers. Wars between democracies and autocracies are generally short in duration and relatively low in cost to the democracy (Bennett and Stam 1996, 1998c) because democracies tip the power balance strongly in their own favor. Likewise, they are more likely to be war initiators because they see an attractive payoff when fighting autocracies.

Autocracies, unlike democratic rivals, are less likely to back away from a fight by negotiating their way to a settlement because they can afford the risk of military defeat. Unless the autocratic leader believes that the democracy plans to depose him or her, the leader has little to fear from military defeat per se. Indeed, substantial evidence supports the contention that autocrats are unlikely to be deposed internally following defeat, while democratic leaders are overwhelmingly likely to be ousted from office after losing a war (Chiozza and Goemans 2000, 2003), something that, as we know, democrats rarely do.

As we have already noted, democracies find it difficult to overwhelm other democracies. This is, within selectorate logic, true because both democracies try hard to win the war.[‡‡‡] This makes democracies particularly unattractive targets for other democracies. Hence, democratic states rarely attack other democratic states.[§§§]

The costs that a nation endures in war are inversely related to its military dominance (Bueno de Mesquita 1983). Consequently, nations that make a greater effort gain an added military advantage that helps reduce the costs they suffer—democracies make this greater effort. Therefore, on average, we expect to find that democracies suffer fewer casualties in war than autocracies. In fact, the empirical record supports this expectation.

There are two exceptions to the theoretical claim that democracies try harder in war than autocracies, both of which have already been alluded to. First, all leaders will commit as many resources as they can in pursuit of victory if they believe they are fighting a war that will result in their being deposed by the foreign adversary if it wins. The second exception arises when the adversary is so weak or lacking in motivation compared to the attacker that no extra effort is required whether the attacker is an autocrat or a democrat. Wars of colonial and imperial expansion were typically waged by powerful states against extremely weak, poorly armed opponents that had virtually no prospect of victory. In these cases, the aggressor did not need to put in any extra effort to ensure victory. Indeed, a characteristic of all the military engagements mentioned

---

[‡‡‡] There is a noteworthy exception. Powerful democracies do not hesitate to fight against weak democracies because the odds of victory are high and small democracies are reluctant to fight back. Thus, the United States could invade the Dominican Republic in 1965 and overthrow its democratically elected government. The Dominicans were not in a position to fight back, so such events do not constitute cases of war; they are cases of military intervention. Small autocracies, however, are less reluctant than small democracies to fight back against democracies, large or small. The example of the Somalis under Gen. Mohammed Farah Aidid against the United States in the early 1990s is a case in point.

[§§§] It is worth noting that the selectorate logic does not say that it is impossible for democracies to fight one another, only that such conflicts are less likely than those between other polity pairs. The conditions under which democracies will fight one another are particularly difficult to satisfy.

earlier between pairs of democratic states is that one party to the dispute was much more power-ful than the other. None of the mentioned events concerning full-fledged democracies reached the threshold of battle-related deaths to be called wars, and this is exactly as we expect within the logic just laid out. The weaker party may test the waters a bit to see if the more powerful state is serious about its objectives. If the stronger party uses force, the weaker democratic state is expected to back down exactly because defeat in war is an even worse policy outcome than granting conces-sions to reach a settlement. Thus, democracies are not immune from using force against one another, but the weaker party is unlikely to put up a big enough fight to produce a war.

Thus far, all but three of the twelve regularities I have listed for the democratic peace have been explained by selectorate logic. I now turn to the remainder. To examine the democrat-ic-transition regularity, we must first ask what it means to be a state in a democratic tran-sition. Essentially, states in a democratic transition are situated somewhere in between democracies and autocracies in the size of their selectorates and the size of their winning coalitions. These states have selectorates that are proportionately larger than their winning coalitions when compared with those of full-fledged democracies. As such, their behavioral patterns should fall somewhere between that of a full-fledged democracy and that of an autocracy. That is, we expect to find that transitional democracies are more likely to fight than are mature, long-standing democracies (regularity 1b). This, in fact, is entirely consis-tent with empirical observation, as embodied in the democratic peace.

The empirical observation that large democracies are more constrained not to fight than are small democracies (regularity 7) is the only regularity that does not relate to the character-istics of a pair of rivals. As such, it is a bit more difficult to fit within the framework used here. Still, it is consistent with the strategic approach in that major power democracies are generally large countries. In absolute magnitude, they have very large winning coalitions. Consequently, their leaders are especially dependent on successful policy performance to retain their jobs, and they therefore strongly manifest the expected behavior of democracies (Morgan and Campbell 1991). They avoid fighting unless they are exceptionally confident of victory. Being great pow-ers, this confidence is present for most of the disputes they engage in, but it means that they avoid fighting with other great powers. As we know, wars between the major powers are rare, especially wars initiated against a major power by a democratic great power.

That leaves one more important regularity to explain—that democrats spend more enforcing the postwar peace than do autocrats (regularity 6). As Bueno de Mesquita and colleagues (2003, 2004) argue theoretically and show empirically, democrats tend to fight over policy issues, while autocrats tend to fight over extracting resources (that is, the spoils of war). The tribute extracted following an autocratic victory is transported back to the homeland or, indeed, large swathes of vanquished territory are annexed by the nondemocratic victor. Although there are no absolutes when it comes to war or to governance, the empirical record supports the theoretical claim that democrats are more likely to depose the leaders in defeated states and impose **puppet govern-ments** that will do their bidding. Their bidding usually has to do with extracting policy compli-ance that serves as a public good for the democratic victor's constituents back home. These benefits may take the form of trade concessions, security guarantees, or a host of other policy concessions. The difficulty with such agreements is that once the victor withdraws there is little reason to believe that those who oppose the concessions in the previously vanquished state will willingly continue to pay the political and economic price that the concessions imply. Thus, unless the democracy stays behind as an occupying force or bolsters its imposed puppet leadership with substantial financial assistance, the value from victory will quickly dissipate. Democrats must enforce their victories because their victories are much less about taking wealth home than about extracting a flow of concessions, a flow that is likely to stop in the absence of enforcement—hence, the regularity that democrats spend more on enforcing the peace than do autocrats.

TRY THIS

Identify three or four examples of puppet governments imposed by democratic victors. Do democratic victors commonly establish democratic governments in the places they defeat? What conditions might explain whether the imposed government is democratic or not?

This is a rather good description, for instance, of U.S. policy toward Iraq since the 2003 war. The United States maintains troops in Iraq, pressed the Iraqi government to choose as prime minister the person the United States wanted, and pours a fortune into that country (rather than compelling it to pay the costs of the American occupation with Iraqi oil revenue, which would surely be seen as a form of tribute). In exchange, the Iraqi government maintains a much more pro-American policy than it did under Saddam Hussein.

SUMMARY

In this chapter, we have examined the democratic peace. Twelve empirical regularities were identified, and evidence was shown for the most important among them. There have been numerous efforts to explain why these particular empirical patterns arise. Normative explanations and many institutional explanations assume the key results rather than deriving them from initial conditions. The selectorate theory, in contrast, implies all the empirical regularities identified with the democratic peace. As such, this example of the strategic perspective seems to offer the most comprehensive explanation of the democratic peace currently available.

The democratic peace is a crucial challenge to theories outside the strategic perspective for the simple reason that other theories dismiss the role that domestic institutions and individual incentives play in shaping decisions about war and peace. The democratic peace is not about some grand strategy, it is about the grand consequences of individual leaders' being interested in keeping their jobs.

KEY CONCEPTS

democratic peace   179
institutional perspective   191
normative perspective   188

Polity Index   181
puppet governments   199
war effort   185

7 Can Terrorism Be Rational?

OVERVIEW

- Democracies are likelier to be targets of terrorism than nondemocracies. We look at the logic of terrorism to explore its causes, as well as the difficulties, opportunities, and consequences of efforts to resolve terrorist threats and to foster peace.

- We can think of terrorism as a problem of perceptions and the associated difficulties with credible commitments.

- Perceptions can promote policies that produce unintended consequences.

- The only way to break or diminish the cycle of terrorist violence is through changes in behavior. The risks and costs associated with such changes include one side's reneging on its commitments or, if counterterrorism efforts fail, an increase in violence implemented by the remaining, more extreme terrorists who gain additional resources when more moderate factions compromise with government.

We have seen why democracies are less likely to fight wars with one another. This is an appealing feature of democracy, but not all democratic features are so nice. Democracies are, for instance, especially likely to be the targets of terrorists. This may be the result of the public-goods orientation of democrats that includes a relatively strong commitment to the rule of law. Due process, in particular, acts to constrain democracies from using tactics similar to those adopted by terrorists. Democracy also leads to declaratory policies about dealing with terrorists—such as not negotiating with them—that may increase the risk of terrorist attacks. We see why this is so in this chapter as we explore a bit about the logic of terrorism.

Let me start by relating a personal experience I had many years ago that shows that terrorism and terrorists are much more complicated matters than we sometimes realize. In spring 1970, I interviewed an elderly gentleman in Calcutta. A leading politician in one of India's many political parties, the gentleman was eager to be helpful, responding thoroughly to each of my questions about politics in India. He was a gentle soul who expressed deep revulsion toward the political and religious violence occurring in India at that time. I formed the opinion that he must have been a follower of Mahatma Gandhi during India's independence movement. From about 1920 to 1947, Gandhi's strategy of nonviolent resistance to British colonial rule moved India successfully to independence. I couldn't have been more wrong.

When asked about his activities before independence, this soft-spoken elderly gentleman revealed that he had served many hard years in a penal colony operated by the British on the Andaman Islands. His offense had been blowing up a civilian train during World War II that was also carrying British troops. He had been a member of the violent anti-British Indian underground that opposed Gandhi's strategy of nonviolent resistance. He was, in modern parlance, a terrorist or a liberation fighter, depending on which side one is on. How could such a gentle grandfatherly figure have engaged in acts of wanton violence?

A masked activist of Palestine's ruling Fatah Party raises a poster showing the late Palestinian leader Yasser Arafat and President Mahmoud Abbas during a demonstration supporting President Abbas in the West Bank city of Ramallah in February 2009. Political leaders often utilize the intense convictions of hard-liners to further their ambitions and justify their actions domestically and internationally.

We might similarly ask how the nineteen terrorists who attacked the United States on September 11, 2001, and their backers in Al Qaeda could have justified to themselves the murder of so many innocent people. What beliefs could they have held about the United States or about American citizens that led to such heinous and desperate acts of terror?

In this chapter, I offer an answer to these questions. The answer will probably surprise you; it will certainly help you to better understand the pitfalls of adopting a too simple view of international affairs and give you a broader view of terrorism in the contemporary world. The answer rests on the fact that policy declarations often shape perceptions in such a way that the policies themselves encourage the very outcomes they are designed to avoid.

BELIEFS ABOUT TERRORISM

What is a terrorist, and what characteristics does such a person display? If I were writing a treatise on terrorism, I might take up dozens of pages arguing about the definition of the term. Certainly it is a controversial concept. As is frequently observed, one person's terrorist may be another person's freedom fighter. Because I am not writing a treatise on terrorism, I offer a straightforward, fairly intuitive working definition of the concept. By **terrorism** I mean any act of violence that is undertaken for the purpose of altering a government's political policies or actions and that targets those who do not actually have the personal authority to alter or enforce governmental policy. The attacks on the United States on September 11, 2001, for instance, clearly meet this definition of terrorism. Suicide bombings in crowded markets, in cafés, and on buses meet this definition.

Terrorism encompasses all violent acts that are not motivated by a desire to injure the specific individuals who are actually victimized by the act but that, rather, are designed to influence the behavior of others (typically policymakers). An attack on a military target in wartime is not terrorism. Such an attack is aimed at an organization (the military) that could directly change its policy by, for example, surrendering. In contrast, an attack on random citizens on a busy street targets individuals who do not have direct control over policy. The goal of terrorism is to spread fear and anxiety (terror) through a population so that it will, in turn, put pressure on its leaders to change policies in a way favored by terrorists. Al Qaeda terrorists, for example, seem to want the United States to withdraw its support for the Saudi regime and to get out of the Middle East. By attacking civilians, they hope to create so much fear that ordinary citizens in democratic countries will pressure their leaders to abandon policies because of Al Qaeda attacks.

Many people think that terrorists are crazy, irrational fanatics with no sense of morality or decency. Because of this outlook, it is common for people to believe that governments should never negotiate with terrorists. Indeed, the governments of many countries, including Britain, Israel, and the United States, have frequently and openly declared that they will never enter such negotiations with terrorists. The belief that terrorists are unusual types of people with cruel and unbending inclinations is probably behind this particular response to terrorist groups. Yet it may be that it is this very attitude that precipitates some (although certainly not all) terrorist acts in the first place. There is evidence that retaliation against terrorists has no long-term deterrent effect (Brophy-Baermann and Conybeare 1994). To see how this might be so, let's consider a simple framework based on perceptions that may help us think about terrorism in a new way.

Suppose there are two different types of people, distinguished by their preference for negotiations or for violence, who become terrorists. We call one type **true believers**; these are the unbending, fanatical sort of people most of us commonly think of when we think about terrorists. Probably Al Qaeda is made up mostly of true believers. We call the other type **reluctant terrorists**; these are people who would prefer to employ traditional means of being recognized, such as negotiations and diplomacy. Probably most members of the Palestine Liberation Organization (PLO; or Fatah, its political successor) are this type. Both types must make a choice. They can either initiate a terrorist action or try to influence political leaders to change policy through the normal channels of political give and take. True believers prefer to take terrorist actions regardless of how they think the government might respond to their proposals (unless, of course, the government would simply acquiesce to anything they demanded, a possibility so remote that we can ignore it here). Reluctant terrorists, on the other hand, want to use normal political channels to reach a negotiated compromise rather than engage in terrorism. It is their assumed desire to negotiate in normal ways that encourages me to call them "reluctant" terrorists when they are observed to engage in seemingly wanton violence.

How might a government respond to an agitator's proposal for political change? This, of course, is a fundamental question that those who are unhappy with government policy must ask themselves before choosing their approach to promoting their own interests. Governments typically take seriously powerful individuals or groups for the obvious reason that powerful adversaries have a lot of leverage with any government. Terrorist organizations just about always start out as very small, weak collections of disaffected people with little influence over government. Such people are usually ignored by governments; if these individuals want to see big changes take place in society, and if they are sufficiently weak, it is possible that government leaders will institute repressive policies to thwart them. Thus, governments can be one of at least two types as well. Government leaders might be the sort that prefer to bargain in good faith with weak political opponents, taking their wishes into account despite their weakness, or government leaders might be the sort that prefer to ignore or even repress weak adversaries, calculating that they probably cannot really threaten the interests of the leaders in any significant way. Remember pacific doves from Chapter 5. They choose violence over negotiations exactly because they fear being exploited by a stronger rival, and they increase their odds of making gains by seizing any first-strike advantage and attacking before their adversary can repress them. The concept of pacific doves matches the notion of reluctant terrorists but not true believers.

With these possibilities in mind, let's consider a third type of government adversary, a type we designate complacent opponents. **Complacent opponents** are individuals or groups that would rather tolerate being taken advantage of by the government than engage in terrorist action. Of course, complacent opponents also would prefer to have the government bargain with them in good faith rather than take advantage of them. Table 7.1 spells out the preference orderings of our three types of government adversaries and our two types of governments.

Consider the problem any government adversary faces. The adversary might choose to ask the government's leaders for some political concession, or the adversary might launch a

TABLE 7.1	Preference Orderings for a Terrorism Game
Player type	**Player preference ordering**
Government adversary	
True believer	Terrorist act > good faith negotiations > being repressed
Reluctant terrorist	Good faith negotiations > terrorist act > being repressed
Complacent opponent	Good faith negotiations > being repressed > terrorist act
Government	
Responsive	Good faith negotiations > repression > terrorist target
Repressive	Repression > good faith negotiations > terrorist target

terrorist act in the hope of forcing the government to notice its plight. If the latter course is chosen, then the adversary is, by definition, a terrorist. If the former course of action is chosen, then the adversary risks the possibility that the government will choose repression and punishment rather than bargaining in good faith.

No matter how true believers think the government might respond to an offer to negotiate, they prefer to engage in acts of terrorism. For them, a total victory is preferred to negotiated concessions. Clearly, when a government confronts such an adversary there is no point in trying to negotiate in good faith or in suggesting that such negotiations are a feasible alternative. True believers want everything even if it means getting nothing. They seek an indivisible outcome of the sort we discuss in Chapter 4 when we identify the rationalist causes of war. When an issue is truly indivisible (probably a relatively rare phenomenon), the only choice is to give in or to fight. That is how most people see the question of terrorism, yet, as I have said, truly indivisible issue disputes are infrequent.

As already noted, the posture of non-negotiation is the declared policy of the United States and many other governments toward terrorists. Such opponents are perceived to be unbending and fanatical, which is precisely the case of true believers. Sadly, probably the only way to deal with such people is to punish them whenever the opportunity presents itself, as in the war on terrorism against Al Qaeda. For true believers, then, perceptions about whether the government is responsive or repressive are simply irrelevant. They want to either get everything they are after or go out in a blaze of glory. The only approach that can be taken in such circumstances is, as I said, to fight them to the finish.

A complacent opponent, regardless of the government's type, prefers negotiation to engaging in terrorist acts. Indeed, there is no circumstance under which a complacent opponent will choose terrorism over trying to bargain with the government. For complacent opponents, then, it is also true that their perceptions of the government's type—responsive or repressive—are irrelevant.

For reluctant terrorists, however, the story is entirely different. Suppose that reluctant terrorists attach a utility of 1 to negotiations with the government, a utility of 0.40 to engaging in terrorism, and a utility of 0 to submitting to government repression. Reluctant terrorists, just like everyone else, will do what they perceive to be in their best interests. They know that they can obtain an outcome worth 0.40 with certainty by engaging in terrorist acts. If they offer to negotiate, then they might achieve a much better outcome, an outcome worth 1, if the government is the fair-minded type. If the government is the repressive type, however, then they will suffer a worse outcome, one worth nothing at all. What reluctant terrorists decide to do depends entirely on their perceptions of the government and the probability that it will choose to repress them. So government choices of action help shape the acts of reluctant terrorists (but not the acts of true believers).

TRY THIS

Construct a game that reflects the possible moves described here for the three types of government opponents and the two types of governments. You may be surprised at how complicated this seemingly simple problem actually is.

If past experiences have taught the reluctant terrorists that the government leaders are fair-minded with a probability of 0.50 ($p = 0.50$) and are repressive with a probability of 0.50 ($1 - p = 0.50$), then the reluctant terrorists are better off trying to negotiate and so will not engage in terrorism. We reach this conclusion by calculating the reluctant terrorists' expected utility for trying to negotiate.

$$EU_{negotiation} = (0.50)(1) + (0.50)(0) = 0.50.$$

That is, for reluctant terrorists the expected utility for trying to negotiate is equal to the probability the government is fair-minded (0.50) times the value of dealing with a fair-minded government (1) plus the probability that the government is the nasty type (0.50) times the value of being repressed (0). The expected utility for offering to negotiate for the reluctant terrorists, therefore, is 0.50. When we calculate the expected utility for engaging in terrorist acts for the reluctant terrorists, we find it equal to only 0.40. Thus, offering to negotiate is clearly the best choice in this case. Under these circumstances, the reluctant terrorists will not commit terrorist acts and so will never be explicitly identified as terrorists of any sort.

But what happens if our probabilities are slightly different? For example, what happens if the reluctant terrorists perceive that the probability the government is repressive is 0.65? By refiguring their expected utility, we find that terrorism becomes the preferred action.

$$EU_{negotiation} = (0.35)(1) + (0.65)(0) = 0.35.$$

In this instance, reluctant terrorists will commit terrorist acts.

And significantly, in this case we cannot differentiate between the reluctant terrorists and true believer terrorists because both kinds are engaging in the same activities. That is, the equilibria for true believers and reluctant terrorists in this example are the same. We call such a situation a pooling equilibrium in game theoretic terms. Of course, we would like to separate out the reluctant terrorists from true believers because there is only one way to resolve matters with the latter, whereas the former can be persuaded by a more flexible government to give up their threat of terror. Notice also that the government does not have to be all sweetness and cream toward these reluctant terrorists, who, after all, may have done horrendous things in the past. In our numerical example, a 50-50 chance that such people will be repressed is sufficient to get them to give up terror. In fact, the odds that the government is repressive versus being oriented toward compromise could even go up to 59:41 without precipitating a terrorist response. So the government could actually be perceived as pretty repressive and still not trigger terrorism. But a 65 percent chance of repression and a 35 percent chance of not being repressed is insufficient for reluctant terrorists to abandon their terrorist tactics. So picking how punishing to be and how forgiving to be can help a government to figure out which terrorists are true believers (they will continue to attack regardless of the odds that the government will not repress them) and which can be pacified without wiping them out.

When a government declares that it will not negotiate with terrorists, how does this affect the perceptions that would-be terrorists have about the best way to deal with that government? The government is sending the following message: "If the opportunity presents itself, we will punish anyone who has engaged in terrorist actions." This message produces a negative consequence for the government. The reluctant terrorists' beliefs about the government's type are probably being influenced by the government's declaration that it will not negotiate with terrorists. If the government's statement is credible, then in the minds of the reluctant terrorists the probability that the government is the repressive type is likely to increase. The more credible the government's declaration, the greater the potential it has to turn reluctant terrorists down the path of violence rather than down the path of negotiation toward a normal political resolution of differences.

Of course, we want to be cautious before advising any government to abandon its declaratory policy against negotiating with terrorists even as we recognize that sometimes such declarations are not credible. Many governments have negotiated with terrorist groups even after saying they would not. Israel has declared it does not negotiate with terrorists, and in the past it has labeled the PLO as a terrorist group. Still, they did negotiate with each other. There is, however, a good reason for being cautious about a wholesale abandonment of the antinegotiation position. Dropping such a policy may encourage more groups of people to pretend to be terrorists (of the reluctant type) so that they can extract concessions from the government. My personal belief is that there are not many willing to engage in that extremely risky bluff, so I think it is unlikely many groups will pretend to be terrorists when doing so might get them some concessions but might also get them killed. But we really do not know how responsive people are to the opportunity to extract concessions from the government if the cost in expected repression is reduced, or, in economic terms, how elastic the demand for acting like a terrorist is as the price for being a terrorist drops.

So, how responsive are terrorists' beliefs to a change in a government's declaration about negotiating or not negotiating with terrorists? We can solve for the changed belief induced by the government declaration by using Bayes's rule. Bayes's rule allows us to answer the question: What is the probability that a stakeholder is of a particular type given that it says or does something specific? For example, what is the probability that a government is the repressive type given that it says it will not negotiate with terrorists? To answer this question, we must solve the following calculation. Let P stand for probability, R for repressive type, S for the statement against negotiation, and $\sim R$ for the government type that will negotiate rather than repress.* Then,

$$P(R|S) = \frac{P(S|R)P(R)}{P(S|R)P(R) + P(S|\sim R)P(\sim R)}$$

Suppose that before the government makes a statement, a reluctant terrorist believes the government is the repressive type with probability 0.5 (that is, $P(R) = 0.5$; this means that $P(\sim R)$, the probability the government is not the repressive type, is also 0.5). This value is the same as in our earlier example in which the reluctant terrorist group will not actually engage in terror but will instead try to persuade the government to grant it concessions.

Suppose a repressive government will always declare that it will never negotiate with terrorists so that $P(S \mid R) = 1$. Suppose further that there is a 50-50 chance that the government will make the statement against negotiation even if it is not the repressive type; that is, $P(S \mid \sim R) = 0.5$. It would do this in the hope of deterring terrorists, as seems to be the motivation behind the U.S., Israeli, and British declarations. After the government makes the statement, the terrorist group no longer thinks there is just a 0.50 chance that the government is repressive. Solving Bayes's equation for the updated belief after the government's statement, we discover:

$$P(R|S) = \frac{(1)(0.5)}{(1)(0.5) + (0.5)(0.5)} = \frac{0.05}{0.75} = 0.67$$

Whereas before the government's statement the reluctant terrorist group will not engage in acts of terror, following the government's declaration, as we know from our earlier numerical example, the reluctant terrorists now view the risk (and associated costs) of trying to negotiate as too great and so will choose terror over negotiating for a peaceful resolution of differences. (Remember their expected utility from terror is 0.40, so if $P(R \mid S) = 0.67$, trying to negotiate yields them $0.33(1) + 0.67(0) = 0.33$, which of course is less than their utility of 0.40 from terror.)

As we have seen, if the reluctant terrorists believe with sufficient confidence that their government adversary will treat them fairly in negotiations, then they, like the complacent government opponents, will choose to pursue peaceful solutions to their problems. They will not actually engage in terrorism, and we will never know that they have the potential to commit horrible acts of violence. If, however, the reluctant terrorists are not sufficiently confident of

---

* Remember that the vertical line symbol | is read "given"; the symbol ~ is read "not."

the government's intentions, then depending on just how great their belief is that the government is the repressive type, the reluctant terrorists might choose to negotiate or might choose to use terrorist tactics. The more confident the reluctant terrorists are that the government is the repressive type, the more likely they are to commit violent acts. From the government's side, if violent acts occur, the government might infer that the perpetrators are true believers, thereby reinforcing its inclination to convey the message that terrorists will be repressed.

Thus, a cycle of reinforced beliefs takes hold. The government's recalcitrance prompts an increase in the frequency of terrorist acts, which in turn reinforces the government's stand on not negotiating, which in turn prompts further terrorist acts, and so forth. This type of situation arises even though both the government and the reluctant terrorists started out with fair-minded intentions. The government just wanted to deter terrorists, and the reluctant terrorists just wanted to find a way to get some concessions (of course, those concessions may be too great for it to be worth the government's granting them, as we see later). Each has simply perceived incorrectly the true desires of the other.

Our discussion of terrorism highlights several important points related to perceptions. Perceptions can lead people to make choices that in retrospect turn out to be bad. But because we cannot distinguish them from the true intentions of the decision makers (that is, the types pool, in game theoretic terms), we cannot always tell when bad decisions have been made. An act of terrorism might actually be the work of a reluctant terrorist, but we cannot tell from that act alone whether we are dealing with a true believer or a reluctant terrorist (although we can be certain we are not dealing with a complacent opponent). As a consequence of this uncertainty, we might choose an improper response, such as declaring that we will never negotiate when, in fact, being open to negotiations is the very thing that would help us distinguish (that is, create separating equilibria in which different types of decision makers choose different equilibrium strategies) between true believers and reluctant terrorists.

Perceptions influence behavior in many other ways. It is possible that reluctant terrorists might overestimate the likelihood that the government is fair-minded and so leave themselves open to repression and, indeed, to annihilation. In such cases, we will never know that these people have the potential to be terrorists; we might, in fact, express great sympathy for those individuals or groups so punished by the government. Yet had those individuals or that group perceived the situation more accurately and engaged in terrorism, we would probably have labeled them fanatic extremists and applauded the government's action in punishing them for their deeds. Notice how much our own response depends on the perceptions we have formed based on what we have observed. We have not adequately taken into account what might have happened had the terrorists or the government behaved differently.

The cycle of terrorism and harsh government reaction has typified the relations between the Arabs and the Israelis for decades. However, once an Israeli leader was ready to negotiate and once the leader of the PLO was ready to believe that the proposed negotiations were being entered into in good faith, it proved possible to interrupt this cycle (Bueno de Mesquita 1990). Yet terrorism has not been eliminated in the Middle East—not by a long shot. The sides swing back and forth between negotiation and exchanges of violence, with these cycles fluctuating as a function of rises and declines in trust between the competing leaders and, as we see later, because of inherent characteristics of negotiations between governments and terrorists. But just as certainly, some real and sustained progress toward peace was made with the establishment of a semi-autonomous Palestinian Authority. This progress was achieved through a reexamination of perceptions and a concomitant realization that alternative explanations of behavior were more consistent with the facts.

TERRORISM, CREDIBLE COMMITMENTS, AND STRATEGIC DILEMMAS

As the facts change, so, too, do perceptions about the intentions of the rivals, and as these change, so does the level of violence. Indeed, true believers, like many in Hamas or the Islamic Jihad, escalate violence whenever negotiations appear to progress between a government and reluctant terrorists. In the larger, multilayer terrorism environment, the true believers fear that their reluctant-terrorist compatriots will make a deal that leaves the hard-liners isolated and weakened. By increasing the violence, they may hope to spur the government to adopt repressive retaliatory measures that scuttle negotiations (and thus give credibility to extremist claims that the government is repressive) (Kydd and Walter 2002). It is also possible that an agreement between the more moderate reluctant terrorists and the government will result in more resources being channeled into the hands of extremists, making it easier for them to engage in violent acts, at least for a while (E. Bueno de Mesquita 2005a).

The evidence today indicates that Fatah's leader, Mahmoud Abbas, like his predecessor, Yasser Arafat, is not a true believer. One of his problems is to manage relations with the more extremist factions within Hamas, a rival organization with a stronger commitment to destroying Israel. Whether Abbas can effectively deliver counterterrorism assistance and whether the Israelis can deliver sufficient concessions to encourage such counterterrorism remain to be seen. These are no small tasks. To better understand the difficulties involved in reaching agreements on terms of peace, let us consider the issue of credible commitment in the face of a potential increase in violence accompanying efforts to reach a negotiated peace.[†]

Thus far, we have considered how reluctant terrorists and true believers might respond to government offers to negotiate. We have indicated that the government might be either repressive or sincere in its desire for a peace based on compromise. Now let us uncover more of the subtleties of making progress toward peace using a model of strategic interplay between a government, a reluctant-terrorist faction (referred to as the moderate), and a hard-liner faction that might, in principle, accept concessions from the government if the concessions were valuable enough (it might or might not be composed of true believers). In the model that follows, as we will see:

[†] The discussion that follows provides a considerably simplified terrorism negotiation game inspired by a more subtle and nuanced game concerned with the commitment problems and adverse selection difficulties surrounding efforts by governments and terrorists to negotiate with one another. That game was developed by Ethan Bueno de Mesquita. Those interested in a deeper examination of the issues are encouraged to read his fuller treatment of this and other issues related to terrorism (E. Bueno de Mesquita 2005a, 2005b, 2005c).

1. Governments have little or no incentive to fulfill the promises they make to terrorists unless there are multiple terrorist factions and the government needs help with counterterrorism from some of these factions to combat those with which it will not compromise.

2. It is not possible for governments to reach a negotiated settlement with all terrorists, no matter how generous the governments' offers because of governments' inability to commit themselves to implementing such a deal.

3. Terrorism can be ended by reaching a negotiated compromise with some terrorists that includes their help in wiping out all remaining terrorists through counterterrorism.

4. If the counterterrorism help fails to eliminate all the terrorists who are not part of the deal with the government, then the amount of terrorist violence is likely to increase rather than decrease after the government reaches the agreement with the less extreme terrorist factions.

Let's assume that there is ongoing terrorism by both hard-liners and moderate terrorists, so that a status quo of violence serves as our backdrop. Let us also assume that it is common knowledge who the moderate terrorists are (for example, the PLO in the Palestinian Authority and the Provisional Irish Republican Army, IRA, in Northern Ireland) and who the hard-liners are (for example, the Islamic Jihad in the Palestinian Authority and the Real IRA in Northern Ireland). We have three players: the government, a moderate terrorist faction, and a hard-liner terrorist faction. Figure 7.1 displays the strategic setting in which the government opens negotiations. Because this greatly simplified negotiation game is still pretty complicated, I suggest you write down each of the assumptions on a piece of paper as I present them. That will make it easier for you to go back and think through what is going on in this three-player game. Because this is a fairly realistic representation (in simplified form) of many of the problems and issues in resolving terrorist threats, it will pay to go through this slowly and carefully. You may be surprised by some of the implications.

The government moves first by either offering some level of concessions or continuing to fight the terrorists and thus living with the status quo, in which it struggles for an all-out victory over the terrorists. I label such a victory for the government W. Of course, the terrorists struggle for victory as well. I identify a victory by the moderates M and victory by the hard-liners H. That is, W, M, and H are the utilities associated with a government victory, a moderate terrorists' victory following their preferred level of violence (equal to m), and a hard-liner terrorists' victory with their preferred level of violence (equal to h), respectively. To minimize the notation, each player is said to get the outcome W from a victory by the government, with the utility for that victory being greatest for the government and least for the hard-liners.

The government, as noted, has the option of living with the status quo (with that outcome having utility X; the detailed equation for X appears in the note appended to Figure 7.1) or of offering a policy concession k to any terrorists. This offer, if accepted by both terrorist factions, will end all terrorist acts; that is, if both factions agree to accept the offer they disarm (or, equivalently, reveal who and where they are and where their weapons are stashed away). Then the government will either implement the agreed-on concessions (k) or renege

FIGURE 7.1   **Strategic Problems in Negotiating an End to Terrorism**

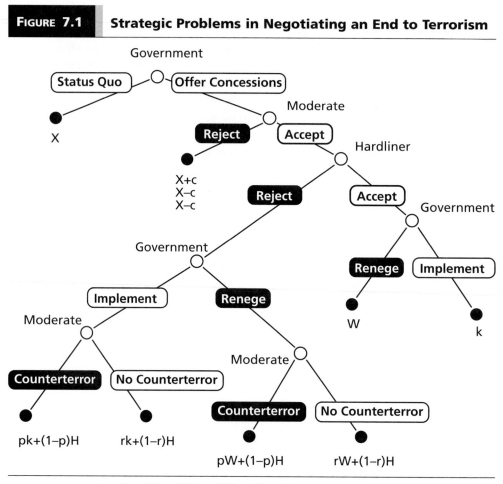

$$X = (1 - q)[(1 - s)(W) + s(H)] + (q)[1 - s)M + s(qM + sH)/q + S)].$$

$(1 - q)(1 - s)$ is the probability that the moderates lose and the hardliners lose or, in other words, the government wins. $(1 - q)(s)$ is the probability the moderates lose and the hardliners win, which also implies that the government loses. $(q)(1 - s)$ is the probability that the moderates win and the hardliners lose (as well as the government) while $(q)(s)$ is the probability that the moderates and hardliners collectively win, defeating the government and splitting their policy differences on the basis of their relative probabilities of winning on their own and the magnitude of their policy demands.

on its offer, wiping out the now-exposed and disarmed terrorist factions and gaining an outright victory (W).

Because the hard-liners are more demanding than the moderate terrorists, I assume that, if only one terrorist faction rejects the government's offer, it will be the hard-liners. If both factions reject it, then the conditions of the status quo persist, except that the government is given credit for offering concessions (+ *c*) and the terrorists pay a political price (−*c*) for rejecting the offer. Thus, making an offer that is rejected has a utility of *X* + *c* for the government and *X* − *c* for the terrorists. We can think of the credit given to the government as meaning that some people who leaned toward supporting the terrorists now support the government. Of course, the political cost to the terrorists is the loss of supporters or resources that results from their rejectionist strategy.

If the hard-liners reject and the moderates accept the offer, then the moderates disarm and the government must decide whether it will implement its offer (*k*) or renege, wiping out the moderates and leaving only the hard-liners as their adversary. Following the government's choice, the moderates either engage in counterterrorism to help the government resolve the ongoing threat from the hard-liners or they renege on the implicit promise that they will provide counterterrorism assistance in exchange for the government's concessions.

The preference orders are:

- For the government: $W > X + c > X > M > H$
- For the moderates: $M > H > X > X - c > W^{\ddagger}$
- For the hard-liners: $H > M > X > X - c > W$

The strategic problem for the government is to select *k* (given that the government prefers *W* to *k*) such that at least the government and the moderates prefer *k* to their other choices given the probability of getting *k* and counterterrorism support under different scenarios and given the risks associated with the continuation of terrorist violence by both the moderates and hard-liners or by just the hard-liners.

I assume that if the government offers concessions and the moderates implement a policy of counterterrorism, then the government's prospect of defeating the hard-liners is *p* (remember that $0 < p < 1$); however, if the moderates do not offer counterterrorism support, then the probability of defeating the hard-liners is *r*, where $p > r$ (that is, the government benefits from the counterterrorism efforts by the moderates). Before the government offers concessions, the probability of the moderates' defeating the government is *q* and probability of the hardliners' defeating the government is *s*, where $p > r > q > s$. The expected payoffs associated with each possible outcome of the game are found in Figure 7.1.

The Government's Credibility Problem

The first thing we notice is that the government has a credibility problem that makes it impossible for the interaction to end with the government and both groups of terrorists' coming to a negotiated agreement. Even if the government makes an offer that is exceptionally attractive to the terrorists, the hard-liners will reject it for sure because they realize that, once they disarm in exchange for the government's promised concessions, the government has every

---

‡ The alternative assumption is that there are moderate terrorists who support a total victory by the government more than a total victory by hard-liners. Such groups might exist, but it is hard to see why they would not simply have aligned with the government to defeat the hard-liners in the first place. Because the government's victory is better than a victory by the hard-liners for this hypothetical type, the government does not need to offer concessions to gain the moderates' support against the hard-liners. That is not a particularly interesting problem.

incentive to renege. For the government, winning outright (W) is always better than granting concessions to terrorists (k). Therefore, once all the terrorists accept the government's offer and disarm, they have no way to punish the government for cheating on its promise. This is exactly why the Provisional IRA in Northern Ireland has been reluctant to lay down all of its arms (or decommission, in the parlance of negotiations in Northern Ireland) and so too have the Protestant paramilitary groups in that country. Without arms, they have no recourse if the government does not deliver on its promises. So, if a compromise exists that is acceptable to everyone, there is no possibility of its being implemented in an environment that looks like the one depicted in Figure 7.1. This implies that, in a situation with multiple terrorist factions, all terrorism cannot be ended by negotiation. Shortly, we explore an even more troubling implication—that achieving an implemented negotiated deal to end terrorism requires the existence of hard-liners who can only be wiped out if more moderate terrorists agree to help improve the government's counterterrorism efforts. So, without hard-liners as foils, resolving terrorist disputes through negotiation may be quite difficult indeed.

Given the observation that no deal will be implemented that is acceptable to all terrorists, we might mistakenly leap to the conclusion that no deal can be struck and carried out at all. So far, we know only that the hard-liners will reject any deal that is offered, appearing to be true believers even though they might not be; they just might be convinced that the government is not really committed to the proposed deal. Still, it is possible that the moderates will accept an offer that the hard-liners reject. Let us now consider what the moderates might do following a government offer that is rejected by the hard-liners. Remember that we continue to assume that accepting the government's offer means disarming.

Solving the Credible Commitment Problem

The government is hoping for counterterrorism help from the moderates against the hard-liners. But before the financial backers and combatant members of the moderate faction spend resources on counterterrorism efforts, they will wait to see whether the government implements its promised concessions. If the government reneges, then the moderates will always prefer to withhold any counterterrorism help. That is why $p > r$. If the government reneges on its offered concessions, the moderates' expected utility for providing counterterrorism support is $pW + (1 - p)H$, and their expected utility for not providing counterterrorism support is $rW + (1 - r)H$. That is, counterterrorism support is offered under this condition provided that:

$$pW + (1 - p)H > rW + (1 - r)H$$

or, equivalently, $(p - r)W > (p - r)H$, which reduces further to $W > H$. Thus, those moderates who prefer an outright government victory to an outright victory by the hard-liners will provide counterterrorism support even if the government reneges on its offer.

But recall that we have assumed that there are no terrorists with such a peculiar interest in government success.[§] Thus, under the conditions assumed here, moderate terrorists will never

---

[§] See footnote ‡.

provide counterterrorism help to a government that has not granted them tangible, implemented concessions in exchange, especially concessions that cannot easily be withdrawn later on.

What if the government implements its promised concessions? Then the moderate terrorists must decide whether or not to provide counterterrorism assistance by comparing the following expected utilities, where the left-hand side is the utility the moderates expect to derive from assisting the government's counterterrorism efforts and the right-hand side is their expected utility if they renege on their promise to help the government with counterterrorism:

$$pk + (1 - p)H > rk + (1 - r)H.$$

This is equivalent to the simple statement that for the moderates $k > H$, or the offered (and implemented) government concessions are better than the policy objective of the hard-liners. This calculation helps the government begin to figure out just how much or how little it must offer and how to dole out the concessions over time (which I ignore here) to make a deal with the moderate terrorists. Remember, for the government $W > k$, so we have to figure out what magnitude of concessions is worthwhile for the government to offer and implement and for the moderates to accept and provide counterterrorism assistance. By solving for the right level of concessions, the government can ensure that its offer will be accepted and the moderate terrorists can ensure that the government will implement the agreed-on concessions, thereby solving the commitment problem that prevented its making a deal with the hard-liners.

If the government has made the calculations we just made, then it knows that the moderates will provide counterterrorism support if the government carries out its promised deal and that the moderates will not provide counterterrorism help if the government reneges. That is, the government must choose between implementing its offer and getting $pk + (1 - p)H$ or reneging and getting $rW + (1 - r)H$, where $p > r$ and $W > k$; that is, the government faces a trade-off between a better chance (p) of getting an acceptable outcome (k) versus a poorer chance (r) of getting a better outcome (W). When we rearrange the algebra to find the value of k that will lead the government to implement its promised concessions, we find that, if the following inequality holds, the government benefits from carrying out the concessions it offers to the moderates:

$$k \geq \frac{(p - r)H + rW}{p}$$

Recalling that H is the government's worst outcome and W is its best, we can simplify this statement by bounding the utilities between 0 and 1. In that case, we can say that for the government $W = 1$ and $H = 0$, with $0 < k < 1$. Then we can restate the value of k at which the government will implement concessions as:

$$k \geq \frac{r}{p}$$

and because $p > r$ we know that there is a value of $k < W$ that will lead the government to implement its concessions and gain the benefits of counterterrorism support. Because the government's utility (k) for concessions decreases as the concessions become more generous, the government wants to make the smallest concession it can (so that the utility k is as large as possible) that will ensure help with counterterrorism from the moderate terrorists. But, of course, the moderates, for whom the utility of concessions (k) increases as the concessions become more generous, want to extract the largest concession they can that is consistent with the government carrying out its promise. We also know that the government could make an offer (k) that is too large (that is, the government's utility for the concessions is $k < r/p$) to make the benefits of counterterrorism assistance it gets from the moderates worthwhile and that it could make an offer that is too small from the moderate terrorists' point of view to make their delivering counter-terrorism assistance worthwhile. Thus, for the government, finding the right concession to offer involves a delicate balance between not giving too much and getting enough counterterrorism in exchange, and not giving too little and getting nothing.

There always is a risk that the government will renege at this stage of the negotiations. However, because we have assumed all information is common knowledge, the moderates will not accept the offer unless the government is expected to implement its proposed compromise. Under all but rather odd circumstances, the moderates will not accept the government's proposal (which includes their help with the government's counterterrorism effort) unless the government will implement it. In fact, the moderates will accept the government's concessions provided that their expected utility from the implemented proposal (including their providing counterterrorism assistance) is superior to what they get by rejecting the offer ($X - c$) when it is initially made. As long as the offer meets the condition

$$k \geq \frac{X - c - (1-p)H}{p},$$

the moderates will take it.

We see, then, that there are always possible concessions that do not cost the government so much that it will not grant them and yet are large enough that the moderates will provide counterterrorism support to get them.** Remember, the utility of the concessions, k, is larger for the government when the concessions are smaller, and the utility of the concessions is larger for the moderates when the concessions are larger. (And remember that for the moderates the utility of a victory by the hard-liners, H, is an intermediate value between 1, getting the outcome they want, and W, a government victory.)

** An offer of concessions that is acceptable both to the government and to the moderate terrorists is equal to choosing k such that

$$\frac{(p-r)H + rW}{p} = \frac{X - c - (1-p)H}{p}.$$

I began this discussion by claiming that the model in Figure 7.1 allows me to logically derive four important empirical hypotheses. The first three have now been shown to follow from the model. That is, we have seen that:

1. Governments have little or no incentive to fulfill the promises they make to terrorists unless there are multiple terrorist factions and the government needs help with counterterrorism support from some of these factions to combat those with which it does not compromise. Once all terrorists are disarmed, the government prefers to maintain its policies rather than grant concessions.
2. It is not possible for governments to reach a negotiated settlement with all terrorists, no matter how generous the governments' offers because of governments' inability to commit themselves to implementing such a deal. If all terrorists agree to the government's terms and lay down their arms, they no longer have a credible threat to use violence if the government does not carry out its promises, which leads the government to renege on its promises and eliminate the disarmed terrorists.
3. Terrorism can be ended by reaching a negotiated compromise with some terrorists that includes their help in wiping out all the remaining terrorists through counterterrorism. Such a deal is possible provided that the government's concessions are large enough to improve the welfare of the moderate terrorists relative to their welfare from continuing with violence and provided that the concessions are not so large that the government prefers to renege rather than carry them out. That is the precise calculation of the size of the concessions that we worked out.

Now, we examine the fourth implication.

Why Violence Might Increase after Successful Negotiations

Our fourth claim is that, if counterterrorism fails to wipe out the hard-liners, then an agreement between the government and moderate terrorists will result in an increase in violence. To demonstrate this, let me construct a visual example of what can happen to the level of violence in a society after the moderate terrorist faction and the government's leaders reach an agreement. Figure 7.2 displays the support for, or resources behind, different violence policies before and after a compromise deal is struck with the moderate terrorists. In drawing this figure, I make the assumption that the more resources that hard-line terrorists control, the more violence they engage in.

Before the deal is struck with the moderate terrorist faction, people who prefer the government's zero-tolerance approach to terrorist violence provide resources to the government (probably through taxes) to advance its zero-tolerance objective. People who prefer the moderates' use of violence over the zero-tolerance advocated by government and the higher levels of violence advocated by hard-liners make resources available to the moderate terrorists to aid their efforts. That is, the backers of the moderate faction give them money through donations,

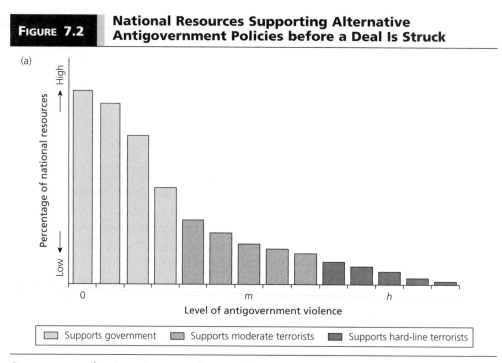

FIGURE 7.2

**National Resources Supporting Alternative
Antigovernment Policies before a Deal Is Struck**

Government prefers 0, moderates prefer *m*, and hard-liners prefer *h*; 0 < *m* < *h*.

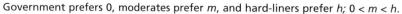

**National Resources Supporting Alternative
Antigovernment Policies after a Deal Is Struck**

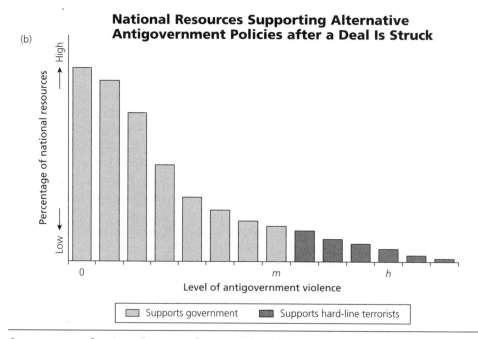

Government prefers 0, moderates prefer *m*, and hard-liners prefer *h*; 0 < *m* < *h*.

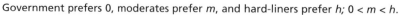

illegal business opportunities, sweat equity, and so forth, to help pay for the terrorism in which the moderates engage. Many Americans, for instance, knowingly or not, gave money to the IRA for many years, money that was used to support terrorist bombings and other such activities. All people who prefer the hard-liner terrorist faction's policy that favors high levels of terrorist violence to those of the government and moderate terrorist faction back the hard-liners. Some charities, for instance, have been found to be contributing, knowingly or not, to support Al Qaeda's efforts to promote a global jihad, or holy war.

Figure 7.2a shows the alignment of national resources (that is, the resources of the people in the society) behind the government, moderate terrorists, and hard-liners before the government makes a deal with the moderates. The positions of the three players are denoted in terms of the level of violence they favor (0, m, or h). The bars show the relative resources in the society that align with each player's position on violence. Any resources controlled by people whose attitude toward violence is closer to the government's than to the moderate terrorists' back the government. That is, anyone who is less than or exactly halfway between 0 and m (the moderate terrorists' preferred level of violence) on the horizontal axis makes resources available to the government to fight terrorism. Those whose tolerance for violence is closer to the moderates' position than the position of the government or hard-liners (h) make their resources available to the moderates. People whose view of violence is closer on the horizontal axis to the hard-liner's position (h) give support to them.

Figure 7.2b shows the alignment of national resources supporting the government and the hard-liners after the government makes a deal with the moderates. Remember that the deal, valued at k, is chosen by the government to minimize the concessions it makes while ensuring that the moderates will accept it. After the deal is struck, everyone who finds the deal acceptable takes it. Because the deal is chosen to induce the moderate terrorist faction to just barely accept it, any supporters of the moderate terrorist faction who fall between the moderate's stance on violence (m) and the hard-liner's stance (h) now shift their support to the hard-liners—the deal is not good enough from their point of view to agree to it. But offering a deal that would win this group over is too costly from the government's point of view to be worth making.

This implies the final result I said I would show—neutralizing the moderate terrorists by granting them concessions increases the government's chances of winning, but it also increases the hard-liners' ability to inflict violence on the society. Comparing the bars in Figures 7.2a and 7.2b that show who supports whom, we see that the government's clout—the resources it can call on in its fight against terrorism—increases as a result of the disarmament of the moderates and their assistance with counterterrorism activity. This is easily seen by the increased number of white bars in Figure 7.2b compared to 7.2a. These extra resources give the government's counterterrorism efforts a higher probability of success than the efforts would have without them ($p > r$).

But we also see that, if the hard-liner terrorists survive the increased pressure that they face because of counterterrorism activity, they are in a position to raise the total level of violence experienced in the society. This is most easily seen by noting that there is one more solid black bar—resources that formerly went to the moderates and that now back the hard-liners—in Figure 7.2b. As we have seen, this occurs because the more radical of the individuals who earlier backed the moderate terrorists now (because they no longer have the moderate terrorists to give money to) begin to give resources to the hard-liners. The concessions granted by the government, although acceptable to the moderate terrorists and to anyone who favored using less violence than they did, are not sufficient to satisfy those who endorsed using more violence than the now defunct moderate terrorist faction did. These people now give their resources to the hard-liners because they prefer the hard-liners' intended level of violence (h) to the government's intended level. Therefore, whenever counterterrorism efforts fail to wipe out the hard-liner faction, we should expect that a deal with the moderates will raise the level of violence, as suggested by the fourth proposition.

This result from our simplified version of Ethan Bueno de Mesquita's (2005a) model is consistent with a large body of empirical research on terrorism that reports on the frequency of increased violence after successful negotiations. That might make us think that it makes no sense to compromise even with moderate terrorists, but we must be very careful not jump to that conclusion. The increased violence occurred in those cases in which counterterrorism efforts failed to lead to the elimination of the hard-liner faction. There are many examples of hard-liner factions being completely wiped out because of the counterterrorism support granted in exchange for policy concessions. A few examples include the elimination of the Quebec separatist organization, the Front de Libération du Quebec (FLQ), in the 1980s; the intense counterterrorism efforts in Northern Ireland against the Real IRA undertaken by the Provisional IRA and the police following the deadly bombing of Omagh by the Real IRA; and the Hagannah joint effort with the British against the Irgun and Lohamei Herut Yisrael (LEHI) during the 1940s in British Mandate Palestine (see E. Bueno de Mesquita 2005a, esp.146–147).

The challenge to establishing a long-lasting peace—in the Middle East, Northern Ireland, Sri Lanka, or elsewhere—is to identify the more moderate terrorist factions and enlist their aid in eliminating or capturing hard-liners. This can be done successfully, provided the motivation and resources controlled by the relatively moderate terrorists and their newfound government allies are sufficient to punish hard-liners effectively whenever and wherever they are found. By reaching a negotiated compromise and working together, it becomes possible for all parties to separate the various types of opponents from one another so that perceptions are refined, beliefs are updated, and appropriate strategies are chosen. Members of the IRA can tell whether the British government really intends to take advantage of them and crush them or whether it intends to negotiate in good faith. The British government (as well as the British and Irish people) and others in the IRA can see who among the members of the IRA really want a negotiated peace and who will settle for peace only on their own terms. By separating types, which occurs when the government offers the correct level of concessions, the promise of peace can be turned into a reality.

LAND FOR PEACE: A CREDIBLE COMMITMENT PROBLEM

As we discuss in Chapter 4, in the Israeli-Palestinian dispute the problems are more difficult. The Israelis are asked to exchange land for peace. The difficulty here is the credibility of the commitments. Land for peace calls for sequential strategic decisions. That is, Israel gives up land now in exchange for normalized relations with the Palestinians and other Arab states later. But once the land has been given up, it is extremely costly to recover it if the Palestinians and the Arab states renege on their part of the bargain. Thus, because peace is not expected to come until the land issues are resolved, the success of such proposals relies on the perception by the Israelis that their rivals will subsequently live up to their end of the bargain. We have seen that a bargain can be struck that resolves the commitment problem for both the government and moderate terrorists, but only if they have self-interested reasons to collaborate and carry out their promises. That is, the Israelis would need to cede land (and other issues) to Mahmoud Abbas's Palestinian government and the Abbas government must use its counterterrorism capabilities to neutralize threats from hard-liners such as many in the Islamic Jihad and Hamas.

In our simple model, we relied on common knowledge to find the right offer (k). In the real world, the problem is more complicated because all the pertinent information is not common knowledge. The Israelis have learned that Mahmoud Abbas is willing to speak out against terrorist violence, but they do not yet know—although the signs so far are encouraging—whether he has the wherewithal or the will to engage in effective counterterrorism activity. Abbas, likewise cannot be certain that Israel's government will implement all the concessions that the Palestinians need in order to agree to a permanent end to terrorism in that region. There is always a risk that the Israelis will implement some concessions and renege on others.

If the Israeli leadership lacks confidence in the commitments of the Arab states, then the Israelis cannot be expected to give up land for the unenforceable promise of peace. From the Arab perspective, however, granting peace before receiving the land commitments is equally risky. Although the Arab states can retreat from peace back to war if Israel reneges on its promises of land concessions, the move back to a state of war is politically, emotionally, and materially costly. Having conceded peace, they have no assurance that Israel will yield the land. Each side is trapped in a bargaining game in which the absence of trust makes reaching a mutually beneficial outcome, a **Pareto improving** outcome, extremely difficult. Here again the problem may well be with perceptions rather than reality. It is possible that each side would behave perfectly honorably in enforcing its parts of a peace agreement. The problem is that if either did not the cost of gambling on the peace agreement may well exceed the cost of maintaining the current state of war.

SUMMARY

Terrorism is, to a significant degree, a problem of perceptions and the associated difficulties with credible commitments. Sometimes it is possible to distinguish among competing hypotheses about terrorism by changing our own behavior. This is precisely the process that led to progress toward peace in the Middle East and in Northern Ireland. Our examination of terrorism in this chapter has highlighted how perceptions can promote policies that produce unintended consequences. Only through a change in behavior—that is, through a calculated risk—is it possible to break, or at least diminish, the cycle of terrorist violence. But we cannot blithely call for such a gamble without considering the real risks and costs associated with it, including one side's reneging on its commitments and, if counterterrorism efforts fail, an increase in violence implemented by the remaining, more extreme terrorists who acquire additional resources when more moderate factions compromise with government. By improving our understanding of how perceptions and strategic conditions influence choices, we can help foster progress toward peace throughout the world.

KEY CONCEPTS

complacent opponents   204
Pareto improving   221
reluctant terrorists   204

terrorism   203
true believers   204

8 Military Intervention and Democratization

OVERVIEW

- The chances that a democratic state will succeed, through intervention, in promoting the spread of democracy abroad is slim because the citizens in target states are likely to have different policy priorities than those of the intervener's own winning coalition.

- The intervening state is less likely to establish a liberal democracy than an autocratic or rigged-election polity that it expects will be more willing to agree to implement the policies it desires. As a result, intervention does little to promote democracy and often leads to its erosion and the substitution of largely symbolic reforms for the real thing.

- Our theory suggests that the failure of nation building is indicative of a limitation of democratic institutions themselves and the nature of democratic representation.

Tyranny and corrupt rule may be defeated by coalitions of international powers, as was the case in World War II, when German high officials were ultimately forced to sign documents of surrender after Allied forces overran the Axis powers in 1945. They may also fall to domestic opposition, as was the case in November 1996, when Mobutu Sese Seko was ousted from the presidency by rebel forces in his own country of Zaire (now the Democratic Republic of the Congo).

When, on April 2, 1917, President Woodrow Wilson called on Congress to declare war against Germany, he affirmed:

> The world must be made safe for democracy. Its peace must be planted upon the tested foundations of political liberty. We have no selfish ends to serve. We desire no conquest, no dominion. We seek no indemnities for ourselves, no material compensation for the sacrifices we shall freely make. We are but one of the champions of the rights of mankind. We shall be satisfied when those rights have been made as secure as the faith and the freedom of nations can make them.*

With these few sentences, Wilson articulated his proposed solution to a problem as ancient as humanity: how to end war for all time. Like Immanuel Kant long before him, Wilson saw the solution to war in the promotion of global democracy. And yet by the war's end neither he nor the leaders in other victorious states saw in his commitment to self-determination an equal commitment to the liberation and democratization of Europe's or America's colonial

---

* For the full text of Woodrow Wilson's 1917 speech, see www.classbrain.com/artteenst/publish/article_86.shtml.

empires. Apparently the call for democracy was subdued if not completely suppressed when its spread did not serve the interests of the victors.

Self-interest, not Wilson's declaration that "We have no selfish ends," is critical to whether and when democracy can be exported to others by already democratic states. As obvious as it may be to say that leaders pursue their own (and perhaps their nation's) interests, discussions of global **democratization** fall far short of reflecting this view or of exploring its implications. Here is an arena in which a perhaps overly rosy view of domestic interests has dominated the discussion without the tough realist-like focus on whether promoting democracy is good for national security. In this chapter, we see how a realistic (as distinct from realist) view of the interplay between domestic politics and foreign policy leads to pessimism regarding the likelihood that democratic states promote the spread of democracy.

At George W. Bush's second inauguration (in 2005), he, almost certainly unintentionally, drew attention to the critical friction that exists between the optimistic view that emphasizes the benefits of democratic **nation building** and a hard-nosed view that emphasizes its downside. Bush proclaimed, "The survival of liberty in our land increasingly depends on the success of liberty in other lands. The best hope for peace in our world is the expansion of freedom in all the world.... So it is the policy of the United States to seek and support the growth of democratic movements and institutions in every nation and culture, with the ultimate goal of ending tyranny in our world." Yet in that same inaugural address he also proclaimed, "My most solemn duty is to protect this nation and its people against further attacks and emerging threats."[†]

There is great tension between the ideas contained in these few sentences—how can a nation promote democratic reform in other nations *and* protect the promoter nation and its people from foreign threats? As we have seen in Chapter 6, free, democratic societies typically live in peace with one another. They also tend to promote prosperity at home as well as between nations, making democracy seemingly attractive both as a form of governance to be exported and, we might think, as a form of government to be imported. Yet, democratic reform abroad does not always also enhance the security of Americans (or citizens elsewhere in the world) against foreign threats and may even jeopardize that security. However beneficial democracy is for peace in the long run, in the short term it can be a threat to that very peace.

Consider how much more democratic current-day Iran is (for all its tremendous democratic limitations) than it was under Shah Mohammad Reza Pahlavi (a monarch) prior to his being deposed by Iran's Islamic Revolution in 1979. Under the shah's regime, the Iranian people had no say in choosing their leaders or in removing them from power. Today, Iran has competitive political parties and elections that have real winners and losers. To be sure, no one can run for office without the approval of Iran's religious leaders in the Supreme Council (whose members are not elected), but the choices are still vastly larger than they were under the shah. Equally, consider how little the United States and other western democracies treat

---

[†] For the full text of George W. Bush's second inaugural address, see www.msnbc.msn.com/id/6848112/.

the democratically elected leaders of Hamas as legitimate spokespeople for the desires of the Palestinian people. Neither Iran's theocracy nor Palestine's (or at least Gaza's) Hamas is welcomed as a source of improvement in American security, despite their both being more (in the case of Hamas) or less (in the case of Iran's Mahmoud Ahmadinejad) democratically chosen. It is evident that the immediate concern for adverse security consequences often trumps the longer-term benefits everyone realizes through democracy. That may well be why the record for exporting and spreading democracy is as dismal and disappointing as it is.

The stirring and optimistic words of Woodrow Wilson and George W. Bush are but a pale reflection of American policy or of the policies of other democracies now or in the past. As sincere as is the belief in promoting democracy, pragmatism leads democratic leaders to reject democratic developments around the world when those developments impede the well-being of their own people. When we consider this as a strategic matter, we see that the self-interest of leaders in democratic nations generally diminishes their incentives to promote democracy. What is more, the failure to promote democracy, however lamentable it may seem, generally indicates that democratic incumbents are upholding their foremost responsibility to their own citizens. They are doing their duty; they are promoting their constituents' well-being; and, in the process, they are also promoting their own (or their party's) prospects of reelection. That is the job of all democratically elected leaders: to enhance their own reelection prospects by delivering effective policies to their own—not someone else's—voting public.

NATION BUILDING

Although it is common to contend that many military interventions are motivated by the desire to bring down an evil regime and replace it with one chosen by the people, the consequences of military intervention rarely have that effect (Bueno de Mesquita and Downs 2006; Easterly, Satyanath, and Berger, 2008). Instead, the urge by a democratic intervener to gain policy compliance that satisfies constituents at home trumps the urge to help a society become free. The U.S. intervention in Iraq in 2003 led to the overthrow of the Saddam Hussein regime. That surely was a good thing for many Iraqis. But when free elections in Iraq at the end of 2005 gave more support to the party of the transition government's prime minister, Ibrahim al-Jaafari, President Bush made it clear that Jaafari was not the American choice. The U.S. ambassador to Iraq delivered Bush's message to the leader of the largest Shiite political bloc, saying that Bush "doesn't want, doesn't support, doesn't accept" al-Jaafari as the next prime minister.[‡] Although the U.S. officially reiterated its stance that "The decisions about the choice of the prime minister are entirely up to the Iraqis," the U.S. government called for a government of national unity and strongly criticized al-Jaafari.

[‡] Quoted in Edward Wong, "Bush Opposes Iraq's Premier, Shiites Report," *New York Times*, March 29, 2008, available at www.nytimes.com/2006/03/29/international/middleeast/29iraq.html.

Al-Jaafari's interim government supported Shiite militias and drew its greatest backing from Muqtada al Sadr, an anti-American cleric with a large and powerful militia. After months of political argument and maneuvering, Nouri al-Maliki, not al-Jaafari, was chosen as prime minister. Why did Bush want al-Maliki? Because he seemed clearly more responsive to American policy interests.

Why, despite Bush's declaration in his second inaugural address, did he pressure Iraqi leaders to choose someone desired by American constituents over someone apparently preferred by Iraqi voters? The answer lies in the second passage from his inaugural address, namely his desire to improve American security, a factor critical to his constituents at home. Faced with a choice between butting out of Iraq's internal affairs at the cost of strengthening anti-American militias or butting in at the expense of interfering with democracy, the president chose the latter course. That, indeed, seems to be what many who voted for Bush over John Kerry in 2004 wanted—a president who would work to strengthen American security by being tough in Iraq and tough on Al Qaeda everywhere and anywhere.

Let's look now at how this logic extends more broadly to all interventions—military, covert, and political. The rate of democratization is rarely increased in states that have experienced intervention because it is only rarely one of the major reasons that the intervention was undertaken in the first place.[§] The focal points for an intervening state's administration are the policies of the target state that are most strongly connected with its own political success back home and continuance in office. This requires that the intervening state's leader focus on those goals rather than on the institution of democracy or any other form of government per se. In some cases, the intervener is interested in ensuring the continuance of policies that are currently being jeopardized (for example, by another claimant to power during a civil war). In other cases, the goal is to institute a policy that is different from that currently being pursued (Enterline, Balch-Lindsay, and Joyce 2008). In either case, the policies involved are more closely connected to what are regarded as domestic public goods (such as increased security) or private goods (such as increased access to natural resources) in the intervening state than they are to the more global, longer-term public good of democratization. The subordinate status of the latter is often further diminished by a belief on the part of the intervening state's administration that democratic institutions in the target country will actually reduce the likelihood that the intervening state's domestic goals will be achieved. As a consequence, intervention only occasionally leaves an improved democratic trajectory in its wake. We should never forget that politicians, especially democratically elected ones, have short time horizons. The long term for them is the next election, not some future beneficial state of the world that may help a distant successor to them at the price of costing them a reelection now.

Here, in the choice of an approach to a foreign regime following military intervention, we can see the strategic perspective in its selectorate guise at work. It turns out that a focus

---

[§] Much of the discussion that follows is drawn from Bueno de Mesquita and Downs (2006).

on domestic politics suggests that there are important differences among democratic interveners, autocratic interveners, and international institutions such as the United Nations. The domestic public-goods priorities that motivate democratic interveners and their winning coalitions could, but rarely do, have fewer negative consequences for the target state than does the private-goods orientation of autocrats and their winning coalitions. Let's see how the linkage between intervener regime type and nation building works.

DEMOCRACIES AND NATION BUILDING

We begin by asking what, according to the selectorate approach, motivates leaders to intervene in the affairs of other countries in the first place? Remember, we assume that all political leaders are motivated first and foremost by a desire to retain and, if possible, extend their political power. Any action taken by a leader must at a minimum not be expected to harm his or her prospects of political survival and will generally be designed to increase those prospects. Broadly speaking, this suggests that democratic leaders will be drawn to the strategy of intervention whenever they expect that the action will prevent them from having to absorb the electoral costs of a foreign policy failure or, conversely, enable them to reap the electoral benefits of a foreign policy success. Autocratic leaders function similarly. Although they may not have to worry about electoral costs per se, they do have to keep themselves in good standing with the constituency of wealthy and powerful individuals that enables them to continue in office, and this necessitates that they engage in similar strategic calculations.

TRY THIS

How much does the U.S. federal government spend annually promoting democracy around the world, whether through new instances of democracy-motivated military intervention or new allocations of foreign aid? How much does the government spend on national defense, health care, social security, highway maintenance, national parks, and other public goods? How high a priority does nation building seem to have in terms of spending compared to rhetoric?

Keeping political survival in mind, we need to consider where the goal of democratization is likely to rank relative to the other priorities that winning coalitions in democratic and autocratic states possess. This is an important concern because, just as it is more efficient for a democratic leader to assure his or her survival by providing public goods rather than private goods to his or her coalition members, it is also more efficient to provide the public goods that coalition members value above others.

There is no reliable theoretical guide to the relative valuation of different public goods by the citizens of democratic countries, but history strongly suggests that the democratization of other countries ranks rather low on the list. Not only is intervention an activity that democratic states spend much less on than they do on domestic public goods such as education, health care, and defense, but when they do intervene, democratization is rarely given as the major reason for doing so.

The recent American actions in Afghanistan and Iraq, although not strictly third-party interventions because the U.S. initiated the military actions against the Iraqi regime of Saddam Hussein and the Taliban regime in Afghanistan rather than intervening on behalf of one or another side in an ongoing dispute, nevertheless are probably characteristic of interventions in this regard. Although democratization has been mentioned as an ex post goal in both cases, the ex ante justifications that dominated domestic debate and presidential rhetoric were the war on terror and retaliation for the September 11, 2001, attack on the United States in the case of Afghanistan and fighting the worldwide terrorist network and eliminating weapons of mass destruction before they could fall into the hands of terrorists in the case of Iraq.

The relatively marginal status of democratization as an ex ante motivation for intervention in Afghanistan and Iraq is generally corroborated by the broader literature dealing with public opinion and foreign policy. Although there continues to be disagreement about the relative importance of domestic and international factors in determining the use of force, there is fairly compelling evidence that both the severity of the perceived threat and the condition of the U.S. domestic economy play a significant role (Behr and Iyengar 1985; Holsti and Rosenau 1990; James and Oneal 1991; Nincic 1997). Neither provides much justification for expecting that leaders of democracies who intervene are motivated primarily by a desire to establish democracy in a foreign state or will choose to do so once victory has been achieved. Severity of threat—especially high levels of threat— is a category more associated with a foreign leader's policies than with the absence of democracy in the state that he or she governs. And the establishment of democracy in a foreign state has virtually no systematic impact on the condition of the domestic economy of the potentially intervening state.** All in all, the list presented next reflects the order of priority that democratic politicians are likely to place on some common intervention goals (with the highest priority first). These goals are listed with an example of each involving the United States.††

1. Protection of lives, property, and institutions of the intervening state at home. The more immediate the threat and the greater the potential cost of not acting, the higher the priority that the mission is assigned. Example: The U.S. overthrowing of the Taliban in Afghanistan in 2001.
2. Protection of the lives and property of the intervening state's citizens abroad. Example: The U.S. intervention in Grenada following the deposition of Grenada's leader in 1983.

** Nincic (1997) attempts to directly test the impact of presidential efforts to generate public support for the goals of promoting democracy and human rights on the use of force, but the results are not significant.

†† Military interventions generally are not pure types involving only one of the five justifications for intervention. Therefore, the examples offered for each should be read as only illustrative of what we believe the primary motivation was in the specific case. It is noteworthy that after the first two items on the list it becomes more difficult to identify cases for which the listed motivation seems primary. Note that the list does not imply that the motivation listed first is necessarily the most common reason for intervention. Rather, it implies that the probability of intervention given the existence of condition 1 is higher than given the existence of condition 2, and so on.

3. Protection of the lives, property, and political institutions of allies and states with which the intervening state is tied ethnically and culturally. The required threat threshold for this goal is greater than in goal 1 or 2. Example: The U.S. short-lived intervention in Lebanon in 1958 and the longer intervention in 1982–1984.
4. Promotion of institutional stability in states that have policies that support the long-term security and economic welfare of the intervening state and its bargaining power in international institutions and destabilization of states whose policies do not. Example: The U.S. intervention in El Salvador in 1984.
5. Protection of lives and to a lesser extent property and institutions in other states. Example: The U.S. intervention in Somalia in 1992.

This list is not particularly encouraging regarding the centrality of democratization as a motivation for U.S. intervention. Not only is it not listed, but it is clear from both the descriptions of the five goals and the examples of each that the United States is often motivated to intervene in support of a nondemocratic government when doing so is likely to preserve policies that it deems to be important.

Nonetheless, granted that democratization is not the principal motivation for many interventions and granted that there are times when democracies have an incentive to prop up a sympathetic autocracy, isn't it still true that democratization often provides the best means for accomplishing many of the goals in the list? History, after all, suggests that in the long run democracies do a better job in promoting stability, providing a better quality of life, and, particularly, protecting the lives of their citizens than do autocracies. Doesn't this fact alone allow us to expect that a democratic intervener is likely to promote democracy in a target state for purely self-interested reasons even though a desire to promote democracy was not the original motivation for intervening? Alas, it seems the answer to this question is unfortunately usually no.

There are several reasons why this is the case. The first reason has to do with the cost of democratization and which states can afford it.[‡‡] The likelihood that nation building will take place is determined by the conditions on the ground as well as the wealth of the intervening state. In this sense, the nature of the target population as well as the characteristics of the intervener are "responsible" for the low rate of nation-building success in the same way that the age and physical condition of a patient pool is to some extent responsible for the success/failure rate of a health-care system. Some factors that determine the cost of democratization are a state's level of political and economic development, the level of tension among its ethnic and religious groups, the average citizen's level of education, the health of its civil society, the kind of government that its people are used to living under, the condition of its legal system, and the size and independence of its media. The worse a target state's score on each of these factors, the more difficult and the more costly the job of building a successful democracy will be.

[‡‡] An extended discussion of the role of cost in nation building and its implications can be found in Etzioni (2004).

Experience has shown us that when states intervene to defend the lives and property of their citizens, the target states often have very poor scores on many and sometimes all of these factors. More often than not, the pool of potential targets is composed of predominantly developing states that are relatively poor, are characterized by a substantial amount of internal conflict, and have had relatively little experience with democratic institutions. These are precisely the sort of states where the costs associated with the establishment of a successful enduring democracy are likely to be greatest—too great to be borne by most intervening states if there is any other means by which they can establish their principal policy goals.

If the average target state resembled the average democracy or even a relatively high-income developing state, the cost of democratization would be much less, and the ability and willingness of the average democratic intervener to assist in creating a functioning democracy in the target state in the wake of its withdrawal would probably be somewhat greater, even if that was not its primary goal. However, this is not the case. As it is, only the wealthiest states are able to afford the enormous costs associated with staying the course for the years it can take for democracy to gain a strong enough foothold that a stable party structure is developed, executive constraints are institutionalized to the point where they cannot easily be overturned, and power can realistically be expected to transfer peacefully between rival parties. Less wealthy and powerful states simply don't have the luxury of being able to afford the same level of ambition. Their limited resources ensure that their interventions will tend to be intermittent, will be short term, and will rarely if ever involve anything that looks like state building.

The second reason why intervening democracies do not elect to promote democratization in a target state is more subtle and involves the expectation on the part of even the wealthiest intervener that, in general, an autocratic administration in the target state will be more willing to adapt its policy to suit the needs of the intervening state than will a democratic administration. This is, of course, a central part of the selectorate argument on behalf of delivering benefits that coalition supporters at home value and want. To see why this is true in the realm of intervention, we need to shift our focus from the government of the intervening state to that of the target state as a means to build democracy and prosperity.

> **TRY THIS**
>
> World War II ended in 1945 and was followed by military occupations of Germany and Japan, the defeated enemy powers. When did Japan and Germany hold their first multiparty national elections free of American or Allied military supervision? Who chose Japan's and Germany's political leaders before those elections?

Implicit in the selectorate argument that democracies and autocracies emphasize the provision of different types of goods because of differences in the size of their winning coalitions is a statement about the relative prices they assign such goods. Specifically, it tells us that, all other things being equal, 1 unit of public goods has less political value to an autocratic leader than it does to the leader of a democracy because it plays a smaller role in his or her maintaining power. This means that autocracies are likely to be more accommodating than democracies when it comes to adopting policies sought by the intervener when those policies might generate substantial negative reactions at home. For example, if we have two developing states that are alike in every respect except that one state is a democracy and the other an autocracy, and a developed state offers them each the opportunity to enter into the bidding for a long-term contract that requires them to accept a substantial amount of nuclear and medical waste over the next five years, the autocratic leader is likely to charge the least for providing those services because the vast majority of the costs of the negative consequences will fall on those outside the autocrat's small winning coalition. That is, autocrats generally can be bought more cheaply because it is easy for them to sacrifice the welfare of their citizens in exchange for personal gains or gains for the members of their small coalition.

This difference in the relative pricing of public goods tells us that, except in those cases where the leader of a democratic intervener has good reason to be confident that the citizens of a target state share the same preferences as citizens of his or her own state, he or she is likely to prefer to deal with an autocracy rather than a democracy. To do otherwise is inefficient from a political standpoint and simply lessens the likelihood that the leader of the intervening state will be able to provide enough public goods to his or her own winning coalition back home to ensure political survival. The autocrat can deliver the policy concessions that the democrat desires because policy performance and domestic public goods play a relatively small role in the autocrat's political survival. Thus, the autocrat—who needs money to provide the private-good rewards that keep his or her coalition members loyal and, thereby, to help the autocrat stay in office—can credibly commit to adopting even an unpopular policy in exchange for, say, financial or military assistance. And the democratic leader paying for the policy gains makes his or her constituents happy and so help keep the democrat in office.

All of this is not to claim that the selfish preoccupations of democratic leaders are chiefly responsible for the low priority that their states place on the task of democratic state building. At bottom, a democratic incumbent's preoccupation with delivering policy benefits to core constituents—the winning coalition—is less the product of personal ambition than a consequence of the way that democratic institutions in the intervening state are designed and the value that democratic voters assign to institution building abroad relative to other priorities.

The electorate—"We, the People"—is chiefly, if not solely, interested in preventing the reappearance of whatever target state's policies provoked the intervention in the first place. Imagine, for example, the negative electoral consequences for an American president in building a democracy in a country where the voters choose a candidate who quickly implements policies protecting—even encouraging—the appropriation of American-owned property, groups funding foreign terrorism aimed at American interests, the drug trade, and nuclear proliferation. Voters are far more likely to reward a domestic candidate who helps put in office a foreign leader who adopts pro-American policies even if that person emerges from an electoral process that falls far short of the standards prevalent in most developed states. Consider, for example, how poor relations are between the United States and democratically elected Hugo Chavez, president of Venezuela, and how good relations were with

Pakistan's military dictatorship led by Gen. Pervez Musharraf. Musharraf (now deposed), who was willing to help in the war on terror; Hugo Chavez is more interested in good relations with Cuba's dictatorship than with the United States. That's not to the liking of American voters, so when push comes to shove, "We, the People" encourage our leaders to be tough on democratically elected leaders, such as Hugo Chavez, whose policies are antithetical to ours. We cannot expect democratically chosen leaders anywhere, including in the United States, to ignore what their constituents tell them to do through the ballot box.

In circumstances such as these, it is difficult to argue that it is antidemocratic from the perspective of the majority of the U.S. electorate (whether it is morally acceptable is a separate question) for the president to bypass the opportunity to help erect democratic institutions in the target state if doing so is unlikely to lead to policies that are compatible with the preferences of his or her electorate or that cost too much. Nor is this attitude likely to be restricted to American presidents. There is good reason to expect that, whenever a leader of a democratic intervening state has reason to be uncertain about the policies that are likely to emerge from the installation of traditional democratic institutions in the target state, the leader will be attracted to another option that promises more certain and favorable outcomes.

That option often involves supporting the installation of an autocrat who will back policies that the democratic intervener believes are consistent with its own preferences. In exchange for continued future policy reliability, the intervener offers a variety of goods ranging from military assistance and foreign aid to preferential trade treatment that the autocrat can use to increase his or her prospects of political survival (McGillivray and Smith, 2004, 2008). Under such circumstances, it is hardly surprising that the prospect of democratic institutions developing any time soon in the target state is very poor. Once in office, such autocratic leaders are primarily interested in consolidating their own wealth and power and those of their small circle of key supporters.

Does this mean that it is never in the interests of the leader of a democratic intervening state to construct democratic institutions? No, there are at least two circumstances in which it is in the democratic leader's interest to help another country become democratic. The first occurs when voters in the intervening state are willing to embrace the argument that the target state is so critical to their own country's long-term economic and strategic well-being that they should pay the high costs of remaining in the target country for a long time to supervise the development of stable democratic institutions. This was basically the situation in South Korea following the Korean War, when there was widespread bipartisan acceptance in the United States that South Korea would be a critical lynchpin in the cold war years, especially in the Asian theater. In this case, U.S. voters back home still placed a high priority on short-term stability, but the stakes were such that they were willing to forgo the more typical and lower-cost option of installing an autocratic agent. This was done, for example, following the **third-party intervention** (that is, the military intervention by an outside nation in a dispute usually between internal rivals) in the Congo that resulted in the overthrow of Patrice Lumumba and the eventual rise to power of Mobutu Sese Seko.

The second situation in which a democratic intervener should be willing to install democratic institutions (and already alluded to) is when there is good reason to believe that the citizenry in the target state holds policy preferences that are closely aligned with the interests of the intervener's own constituency. In that case, the risk is small of elected officials in the target state ending up pursing policies that hurt the interests of the intervening state. The reinstallation of Charles DeGaulle as the leader of France following the end of World War II, although not strictly the result of an intervention in the traditional sense of the term, illustrates this kind of situation.

Both situations are likely to be relatively rare. In the first case, this is because of the financial and political costs it entails; a long-term occupation for the purposes of state building is inconsistent with the postcolonial notion of self-determination and is at best an exorbitantly expensive enterprise that can be justified only in isolated cases in which voters of the intervening state believe that their national security is at risk. The second situation is likely to be more common than the first, but it still is likely to be rare because leaders of states, like the citizens they govern, are generally risk averse and care more about the present than the future. Only rarely are they willing to wager their own political careers on the likelihood that voters in another state will support the policies that their own domestic winning coalition believes to be undesirable.

AUTOCRACIES AND NATION BUILDING

Does the fact that democratic interveners usually do not choose to establish democratic institutions in the target country mean that their behavior is essentially equivalent to that of autocrats? Certainly the disappointing results that have followed interventions by democracies in any number of Central American and African states seem to suggest this. Nevertheless, the different relative values that incumbents in autocracies and democracies place on public and private goods provide reasons for believing that, however poorly democracies may do in this area, autocracies are likely to do no better and perhaps even worse; however, the differences in results will be hard to observe because democrats are likely to choose to intervene in states that look quite different from those in which autocrats are inclined to intervene.

The winning-coalition logic suggests that the leader of an autocratic intervener will be less interested than his or her democratic counterpart in ensuring that the target state will pursue particular policy goals and more interested in extracting rents in the form of taxes and hard resources that he or she can then subsequently use to purchase the continued loyalty of his or her much smaller winning coalition. These resources will be easier to extract if the government in the target state is also an autocracy rather than a democracy. Any significant transfer of resources to the intervening state would undermine the ability of the leader of a democratic target state to provide the expensive public goods demanded by his or her own winning coalition. As a consequence, the democratic leader would face the prospect of being voted out of office at the next election.

The leader of an autocratic target state has an easier task because his or her system is set up to be **rent-seeking,** to extract resources from the many through corruption and turn them over to the few loyal coalition members. An autocrat simply does not need to answer to the masses who bear the burden of paying tribute. He or she can maintain a loyal, small winning coalition through the provision of private goods that collectively represent a total cost that is considerably less than the cost of the public goods that would be necessary to sustain the far larger winning coalition required by a modern mass democracy. As a consequence, an autocratic ruler in a state targeted by an intervener still has sufficient resources to satisfy the demands of the intervening state. All this assumes, of course, that a stable autocracy can be established in the target state in the first place. In general, the survival rates of new autocratic leaders in developing states are generally quite low even though the form of government persists for a long time. However, postintervention, the odds of a new autocratic government surviving in the target state are significantly greater because the new regime is subsidized by the military power of the intervening state.

Finally, it is worth noting that, unlike the case of democratic interveners, there are no theoretical exceptions to the rule that autocratic interveners will establish autocratic states. No democratic administration that diverted a significant amount of public resources could survive politically against a competitor who ran on a platform of supplying more public goods to his or her coalition. Therefore, rent-seeking autocrats have every reason to prevent the installation of a democratic government in places in which autocrats intervene. This is the finding of Bueno de Mesquita and George Downs (2006); however, William Easterly, Shanker Satyanath, and Daniel Berger (2008) find, after correcting for endogeneity in the selection of places to intervene, that the United States and the Soviet Union during the cold war were equally and hugely detrimental to democratization.

THE UNITED NATIONS AND NATION BUILDING

What of the United Nations? It is commonly argued that governments should not intervene in other nations unilaterally but should rely on the UN instead. Structurally, the five permanent members of the Security Council (Britain, China, France, Russia and the United States; the P-5) are the decision makers in the UN most directly involved in authorizing an intervention. The Security Council possesses two characteristics that play an important role in determining where the UN intervenes and the effect that it is likely to have on target states: a unanimity decision rule and the fact that each of its members is an agent for a member state rather than an agent for the United Nations itself. The veto power that this structure creates, together with the agency interests of the representative of each state, operates to prevent the UN from intervening in a nation to serve the specific interests of a particular subset of the permanent members if that interest conflicts with the interests of any other member. Thus, the UN rarely intervenes for the sole purpose of changing the policy of a target state that is viewed as undesirable by a democratic member or intervenes in a state for the purpose of generating rents for an autocratic state. This reality has the beneficial effect of preventing the UN from being exploited as a tool to serve the interests of one or two of the permanent members, but it also has several less happy implications that cause the UN to be a less-effective democratic nation builder than we might expect. For instance, the UN was powerless to thwart the American decision to intervene in Iraq in 2003, and it was powerless to stop Russia from intervening in the neighboring state of Georgia in 2008.

The general disinclination to permit the UN to serve as the agent of any P-5 member and the refusal of any P-5 member to have the UN operate in a way that runs counter to its own interests mean that most UN interventions take place outside the spheres of influence of the P-5 states, in states that do not play a critical role in the political economies of only some of the P-5. This generally means that most UN interventions are concentrated in the poorest African and Asian states. An exception that proves the rule is the UN P-5 agreement to intervene to defend Kuwait against Iraq's invasion in 1990. Oil-rich Kuwait delivered political economy benefits for all of the P-5, not just some. Back in 1990, Russia was a much less important oil exporter than it is today. It is interesting to speculate whether today's Russia would support a proposal in the UN Security Council to wage war to reverse an invasion such as Iraq's into Kuwait. Reversing Iraq's invasion helped prevent the price of crude oil from rising sharply in the early 1990s; indeed, the price fell following Iraq's ouster from Kuwait. That was beneficial for Russia then, when it was an importer of high quality crude; it would not be beneficial for Russia now that it is a major exporter of such oil.

A more important implication of the P-5 veto power is financial. Given the decision rules under which the P-5 operate, UN activities will only rarely produce the high level of political-constituency benefits for the leaders of the P-5 that they are able to obtain by providing the public goods demanded by voters in their home countries. These limited domestic-constituency benefits place a corresponding limit on how much the P-5 (and other states) are willing to pay for UN activities and create a situation in which resources are a perennial problem for the international institution. It also forces the UN to continually grapple with the difficult choice of either doing what amounts to the bare minimum in the large number of countries that require assistance each year or of doing something more ambitious in only a small fraction of such states. Given the institution's mandate and composition, it is not surprising that the membership tends to choose the former course, doing little, and to focus on peacekeeping and relief efforts in many states rather than laying the foundations for a durable democracy in one or two states.

Overall, this reasoning leads to the expectation that the selection effects generated by political economy interests, the need for consensus among the P-5, and financial constraints are likely generally to prevent the UN from having a consistently positive effect on the spread of democracy (Gilligan and Stedman 2003).

WHAT DO WE EXPECT, AND WHAT DOES THE EVIDENCE SHOW?

To summarize our theorizing about nation building and focusing on domestic political calculations in their foreign policy context, we have the following hypotheses regarding military intervention and nation building:

> **Hypothesis 1:** Intervention by a democratic state will lead to no more and probably less democratic development in the target state than the counterfactual development of democracy in the absence of a military intervention.[§§]

[§§] The estimation of the counterfactual of which level of democracy would have evolved in the absence of intervention plays a major role in the analysis to follow.

Hypothesis 2: Intervention by an autocratic state will lead to less democratic development in the target state than the counterfactual development of democracy in the absence of a military intervention.

Hypothesis 3: Intervention by the United Nations will lead to no more and possibly less democratic development in the target state than the counterfactual development of democracy in the absence of a military intervention.

These propositions paint an unhappy picture for those who are optimists about the prospects of spreading democracy around the world. They fly in the face of declarations such as those of Woodrow Wilson and George W. Bush at the beginning of this chapter. Of course, just because the hypotheses follow logically from a focus on how domestic politics shapes foreign policy doesn't mean that they are statements of how things actually are. To know how things are, we must look at the evidence. That is what we do now.

Easterly, Satyanath, and Berger (2008) test propositions similar to the three listed here for the two superpowers of the cold war era. They find that the United States—a democratic superpower—decreased the degree of democracy in targeted states by about 33 percent following its political, covert, or military intervention. They find the same effect to the same degree for the Soviet Union, a nondemocratic superpower.

Bueno de Mesquita and Downs (2006) test these propositions as well but in the context of military interventions in countries that experienced civil war between 1946 and 2001. They look at institutional change in targeted countries five and ten years following intervention while controlling for baseline expected changes in democracy, that is, the pattern of institutional change in countries that were not experiencing intervention but that were otherwise comparable to countries that did.

Their examination of a large body of data regarding military interventions strongly supports the hypotheses that democracy is rarely achieved at the end of the barrel of a gun or in response to the influx of dollar bills. Table 8.1 shows the effects of different types of interveners on the prospects of democratic change in target countries a decade later.

As shown in Table 8.1, autocrats have little impact on governance in target states, whereas the United Nations diminishes democracy, as measured by the Polity Democracy-Autocracy Index*** and by the selectorate theory's indicator of coalition size. Likewise, democracies reduce the degree of democracy in states targeted for intervention by 4–5 percent. When democracies intervene along with the United Nations, the impact is even worse, leading to

---

*** The Polity Index measures how democratic or autocratic a government is on a 21-point scale ranging from −10 to + 10. Positive values are increasingly democratic. Negative values reflect increasing autocracy the smaller the value (so −10 denotes a government that is much more autocratic than one at −1). For ease of interpretation, the Polity Index values in Table 8.1 have been modified so that they range between 0 (equivalent to −10) and 1 (equivalent to + 10). This makes it easier to interpret results in terms of the proportionate shift toward or away from democracy. Polity rates every country's democracy-autocracy score every year going back to 1800. Details on how Polity scores are constructed can be found at www.systemicpeace.org/polity/polity4.htm.

TABLE 8.1	**Change in Democracy Ten Years after a Military Intervention Compared to Cases without an Intervention (%)**	
Intervener	**Polity democracy-aristocracy index predicted percentage change**[a]	**Coalition size change**
No intervention	+7.45	+2.42
Autocratic country	−0.01 ($p < 0.01$)	+2.42 (n.s.)
United Nations	−6.39 ($p < 0.05$)	−3.82 ($p < 0.10$)
Democratic country	−4.55 ($p < 0.01$)	−4.14 ($p < 0.05$)
United States	+13.01 ($p < 0.05$)	+4.82 (n.s.)
United Nations + democratic country	−10.93 ($p < 0.01$)	−10.38 ($p < 0.01$)
United Nations + United States	+6.63 (n.s.)	−1.41 (n.s.)

Notes: All predicted percentage changes include the ten-year positive gains expected due to the secular trend in democratization captured by the variable Year; that is, the baseline movement toward democracy over time in states that did not experience intervention. Percentages are rounded to the nearest tenth of a percent. Significance evaluates whether the effect of the intervention on democratic change is different from the effect of no intervention on democratic change. n.s., not significant.

a. The Polity Index ranges from +10 for the most democratic states to −10 for the most autocratic states, but for the analysis presented here it has been transformed (without any change in meaning) to range between 0 (equivalent to −10) and 100 (equivalent to +10). This makes the interpretation easier because the values in the table now refer to the percentage change in the Polity score. In typical treatments, a country is not regarded as democratic unless its Polity Index value is at least 6. On the 0 to 100 scale used here, 6 is equivalent to a value of 80.

an 11 percent decline in democracy in the targeted regimes. The figures are similar if we rely on coalition size rather than the Polity Index.

However, Table 8.1 does contain one surprise. When the United States is the intervener, it apparently increases democracy by 13 percent (based on Polity's indicator), contrary to expectation. But this positive finding for the United States is misleading. Recall that we expect democratic interveners to be motivated to create regimes in the target state that possess the trappings but not the substance of liberal democracy (because creating a true democracy is too expensive). What this means in any given instance depends on the target's starting point. This raises the possibility that the difference between the record for the United States and for other democratic interveners is the consequence of the selection of the target states. We have already suggested that wealthy states are more likely to engage in sustained interventions in particularly difficult but strategically valuable spots around the world. The United States is the world's wealthiest state. If the United States intervenes in valued, tougher cases, that is, in states that are initially more autocratic than those in which other democracies intervene, then it would have less opportunity to reduce the level of democracy that presently exists and this could explain the difference in the average levels of democracy eventually achieved by their respective target states.

To learn whether this was the case, let's consider the average level of democracy in targeted states at the time of the intervention and then again ten years later, and let's divide these targets of intervention by whether the intervener was the United States or was some other democracy. Doing so reveals that there is a huge selection effect. The average democracy scores, based either on the Polity Index or on coalition size, are significantly different for these two sets of targets. The median Polity Index (on a scale ranging from + 10 for the most democratic states to −10 for the most autocratic nations) for countries in which the United States was the intervener is only −3 (0.35 on the normalized scale from 0 to 1); that is, the United States intervenes in states that are tilted to the autocratic side of the scale. In contrast, the median Polity Index for countries in which other democracies intervene is + 4 (0.70 on the normalized scale), tilted strongly to the democratic side. This suggests that the United States has less need on average to reduce democracy in its targets to obtain policy compliance than do other intervening democracies and has comparatively more incentive to increase the symbolic trappings of democracy that are preferred (if weakly) by its winning coalition. When we correct for this, ten years after an intervention the degree of democracy in U.S. target states and in target states of other democracies is statistically the same. That is, all democratic interveners tend to restrict the extent of their targets' democratic freedoms to comparable levels (so that the level of democracy becomes symbolic but without substance) so that the interveners' policies will be carried out.

This pattern can be seen in Figure 8.1, which compares the change in democracy ten years after an intervention when the intervener is a democracy other than the United States (the dark bars) and the change when the intervener is the United States (the white bars). The figure is a little complicated, so let's go through it slowly. The vertical axis shows the change in the degree of democracy in target countries ten years after intervention. The horizontal axis shows the degree of democracy for targeted states at the time of the military intervention. So, positive scores on the vertical axis indicate an increase in democracy from the starting level and negative scores indicate a decrease in democracy. As the figure shows, whether the intervener was the United States or another democracy, targets that start in the autocratic range on the horizontal axis (scores less than 0.5) increase their degree of democracy ten years later. They are pushed modestly upward so that they end up with the symbolic trapping of democracy but not with the real thing. Targets starting in the more democratic range of the horizontal scale (scores above 0.5) tend to be pushed downward, becoming less democratic and more autocratic, as

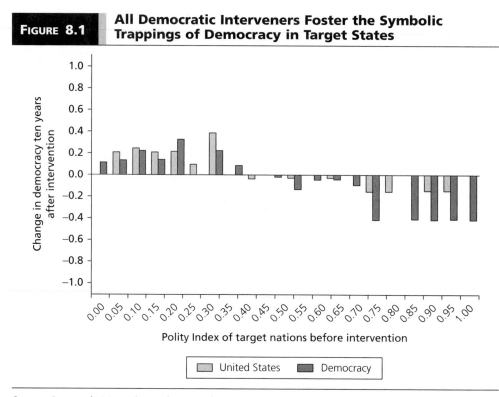

FIGURE 8.1   **All Democratic Interveners Foster the Symbolic Trappings of Democracy in Target States**

Source: Bueno de Mesquita and Downs (2006, 20).

denoted by their all falling into the negative range on the vertical axis. They, like the targets that were pushed upward, end up with only the symbolic trappings of democracy.

The absolute scores of the democratic target states are also revealing. The standard cutoff point in the literature for a democracy based on the Polity Index is 6 (on the + 10 to −10 scale). Contrast this with the mean democracy scores ten years after a democratic intervention, which are only 0.8 for U.S. targets and 1.0 for the targets of other democracies. This is well below the standard threshold for defining democracy. These two scores are essentially equal, and they are equivalent to the governance in such countries as Zambia and Liberia in the late 1990s, a far cry from democracy. So, in the end, all democratic interveners, on average, leave their targeted states looking alike, and the results do not make a pretty picture.

The statistical evidence makes the general nature of the pattern of failed democratization clear. To see how this works in a bit more focused detail, let's take a look at a few case studies of apparent success and failure in efforts to engage in nation building. These may put a bit more flesh and bone on our discussion of why democratization is so rarely achieved through outside interference.

Germany and Japan: Seemingly Hard Cases

Almost as soon as anyone proposes a policy to create democratic polities elsewhere, the post–World War II conversions of Nazi Germany and Imperial Japan are brought forth as exemplars of how this lofty goal can be attained. Newt Gingrich, the former speaker of the House, a historian by training, has argued that, "The United States has a remarkable history of helping countries grow into democracy."[†††] He goes on to mention specifically Germany and Japan (and the Republic of Korea) as evidence for America's "remarkable history of helping countries grow into democracy." Yet even these exemplars of democratization—each following a massive, bloody, and costly war—enforce rather than counter the strategic approach's cautionary tale.

Germany's Third Reich surrendered unconditionally to the Allies in 1945. Military occupation ensued immediately, along with an Allies-selected and imposed civilian government. There was no competitive, militarily unsupervised, free national election in what came to be known as West Germany until 1955, a decade after the overthrow of the Nazi regime. In the interim, the Allied powers wrote Germany's constitution and helped create its electoral system. The electoral rules imposed on Germany were rather remarkable and, therefore, worthy of close scrutiny.

We might have expected the Allies to construct an electoral system similar to that in operation in the United States or Britain, or perhaps France at the time, although France, unlike the United States and United Kingdom, had been conquered in World War II and so was itself in the process of constructing its own new electoral system. The American system was much as it is today, as was also true of the British system. But the rules imposed on Germany resembled not at all the voting rules used for elections in the United States or United Kingdom; nor did the rules resemble some complex compromise of their differences. Both the United States and Britain relied on first-past-the-post elections. This is a system that strongly encourages two-party competition by rewarding the candidate with a plurality of votes; in this system the winner takes all that is up for grabs in the election. Germany, in contrast, was given a system with an extreme form of proportional representation that virtually assures a multiparty system that relies on coalition governments. This could hardly be justified on historical grounds. It is true that Weimar Germany produced a multiparty electoral system, but that was the system that made it possible for Hitler's National Socialist Workers Party to seize control of the Reichstag and the chancellorship, and presumably the Allies had in mind the prevention of a recurrence of the twelve-year-long Thousand Year Reich.

The extreme form of proportional representation imposed by the Allies was designed, of course, to prevent a repetition of that unhappy earlier German experience, but that was surely not the sole motivation. The German electoral system ensured that coalition governments would have to form; that no party could control policy; and that, therefore, the central government would be weak and malleable. And weak and malleable it was, at least as viewed

---

[†††]Newt Gingrich, "U.S. Best Qualified to Aid Iraq," *USA Today*, April 25, 2003, available at: https://www.aei.org/publications/pubID.17051,filter.social/pub_detail.asp.

from the perspective of the occupying powers. They had an interest in the creation of a German government that was compliant with their foreign policy wishes and national security concerns, especially with regard to their policy toward the Soviet Union and its then-emerging bloc of satellite countries in the Warsaw Pact. Indeed, the political system ensured just such an outcome.

Although Germany today is certainly a democracy, it was a quarter of a century after World War II before a German chancellor adopted even a modestly independent foreign policy rather than complying precisely with the wishes of the occupying powers, the victors in the war. No German chancellor deviated from the foreign policies advocated by NATO and especially the United States until Willy Brandt introduced the idea of Ostpolitik in the 1970s. His daring departure was merely to suggest that Germany ought to pursue trade and other relations leading to rapprochement with its Eastern European neighbors, that is, Germany's natural market. Brandt's independent foreign policy irritated the U.S. leadership (and many German conservatives). It sat somewhat better with Britain, but then Brandt complied with Britain's desire at that time to enter the European Community, so the United Kingdom had a reward that was not proffered to the U.S. administration. Brandt's independent approach to Eastern Europe was anathema to an American administration keen to gain every possible advantage during the cold war. Whether by happenstance or otherwise, Brandt's political ascendancy was not long-lived. By 1974, faced with a spy scandal involving one of his closest aids, Brandt was forced from office.

Japan's story, like Germany's, is one that involves the construction of a constitution that promoted policy compliance with American foreign interests. In Japan, which was accustomed to consensual politics, the American-written constitution greatly favored representation in the Diet by the relatively thinly populated, rural agricultural constituencies. These constituencies were considerably more conservative than those in urban areas, where there were many more socialist and communist sympathizers. Japan has a one-party government, dominated for all but eighteen months of the past more than fifty years by the Liberal Democratic Party (LDP) since that party's creation and the introduction of free (non-occupier-supervised) elections in 1955. The LDP governments steadfastly supported American security policy while often proving independent-minded when it came to trade policy.

Although Japan is certainly a free society, it is noteworthy that, among such societies, Japan has a relatively controlled press because only media belonging to press clubs gain access to government sources and, in exchange, create homogeneous press accounts based on government representations of the facts. In addition, among free societies, as classified by Freedom House, Japan is one of the few wealthy countries that fails to achieve top scores for civil liberties. So this exemplar of democratization is itself limited in the extent to which opposition voices are heard and reflected in the media, in daily discourse, and in the highest circles of government. Japan is still essentially a one-party state. Even during a decade of economic downturn and deflation, creating pain that was felt by almost every Japanese citizen, the LDP managed to maintain its control over the government. It is worth noting that India and Mexico were both criticized for many years for being one-party democracies, while Japan has largely escaped this critique. That too may be because Japan, unlike Mexico or India during their periods of one-party dominance, steadfastly complied with America's foreign policy security interests.

The Usual Suspects: Iran, Congo, and Other Failed Cases

Whatever the successes are regarding Germany and Japan (or the Republic of Korea, for that matter), the United States and many of its democratic allies have a checkered record when it comes to other opportunities to promote democracy. We cannot help but question the "remarkable history" of democracy promotion attributed to the post–World War II United States

Iran's experience is an exemplar of democracies putting their own interests ahead of democratization elsewhere. Mohammad Mossadegh was the democratically chosen prime minister of Iran from 1951 until his overthrow in a British- and CIA-planned coup in 1953. Although he spent much of his life working to establish democracy in Iran, as prime minister Mossadegh irritated the United States and the United Kingdom by approving the nationalization of oil fields owned by Aramco (loosely, today's British Petroleum). Despite the British and American fervor for democracy, domestic policy concerns took precedent, resulting in Mossadegh's overthrow and his replacement by the absolute rule of Shah Mohammad Reza Pahlavi. The shah (the hereditary monarch) provided no gloss of democracy, but he certainly was compliant with the policy wishes of the U.S. and the UK governments.

The shah was overthrown in 1979 when he was known to be suffering from terminal cancer, a consideration of some significance in the selectorate theory. The new government, led by Ayatollah Ruhollah Khomeini, established a theocratic quasi-democracy. Iran, under the ayatollahs, maintains competitive, multiparty elections. There are broad enfranchisement rules that allow even fifteen-year-olds to vote (whereas the United States Constitution provides voting rights for those eighteen or older). Incumbents in Iran—even for the highest office—are often defeated at the polls and peacefully cede power to the electoral victors, as noted earlier.

There are, to be sure, serious limitations in Iran's nominal democracy. Ultimate decision-making power rests with a small number of self-selected religious leaders rather than with the voters, but even so, Iran is unquestionably more democratic under the ayatollahs than it was under the shah. The United States has not praised this progress toward democracy but, rather, has been severely critical of the Iranian regime. Certainly, Iran's leaders, starting with the seizure of the American embassy in Tehran on November 4, 1979, have maintained an unfriendly posture toward the United States and the West in general. But that is the point. The U.S. government has chosen to shape its relations with Iran based on that country's policy choices rather than on the country's political system or progress toward democracy. Faced with a choice between Iran's policy compliance (as under the shah) without democracy and some progress toward democracy without policy compliance (as under the ayatollahs), the United States and many other democratic states have chosen compliance. And that is what the leaders of these democratic states must do to be true to their democratic obligations to their constituents who elected them to advance the policy interests of those very constituents.

Let us turn now to the Democratic Republic of the Congo.[‡‡‡] In June 1960, Patrice Lumumba became the Congo's first freely elected prime minister. He was murdered on January 17, 1961, just a half year later. Lumumba ran into difficulty with western democracies because of the policies he adopted. He spoke out vehemently against the years of Belgian rule over the Congo, and he sought Soviet assistance in his efforts to remove Belgian troops and diplomats and in his fight against the secessionist movement in Katanga Province led by Moise Tchombe. The massive bulk of the evidence today points to U.S. and Belgian complicity in Lumumba's murder.

Mobutu Sese Seko assumed power in 1965 and quickly eliminated competitive elections and most of his political opponents. He received massive foreign economic assistance, especially from the United States and Belgium; unlike Lumumba, he was prepared to be anti-Soviet. Apparently Mobutu stole so much of this economic assistance that the word **kleptocracy,** meaning a form of government based on the leadership's stealing from the state, was coined to describe his form of rule. As they did in the shah's Iran, the western powers supported a government in the Congo that complied with their foreign policy interests at the expense of democracy.

Neither Iran nor the Congo is an exceptional case. The western democracies were united in their opposition to a democratically elected fundamentalist Islamic government in Algeria in 1992, supporting instead the Algerian military's refusal to let the elected government come to power. Iraq's fledgling democracy, as we have seen, is subjected to intense American pressure to select policy-compliant leaders even when the will of the voters' points in other directions. The political leaders in the United States show no eagerness to work with democratically elected governments in Latin America or elsewhere when their policies run counter to American interests, as in Venezuela. And the same has largely been true for Europe's democracies as well. In each such case, democratically elected leaders are doing what they were elected to do—delivering policies (including policy compliance from other states when possible) that benefit their constituents, even if, in doing so, they stymie democratization elsewhere.

SUMMARY

Although the leaders of states that intervene in other states frequently assert that the democratization of the target states is one of their main goals, we have seen lots of evidence suggesting that this goal is rarely achieved. More often than not, the leaders of intervening states are faced with a choice between trying to satisfy the policy interests of their own constituents to remain in office and promoting the democratic aspirations of the citizens of targeted states. Because the citizens in a transformed democratic target state are likely to have different policy priorities than those of the intervener's own winning coalition back home, the intervening state will tend to pass up the opportunity to establish a liberal democracy in

[‡‡‡] From 1971 to 1997, this country was called Zaire.

favor of establishing an autocratic or rigged-election polity that it expects will be more willing to implement the policies it desires. As a result, intervention does little to promote democracy; instead, it often leads to its erosion and the substitution of largely symbolic reforms for the real thing.

This outcome is not particularly surprising in the case of autocratic interveners, but in the case of democratic interveners, many are likely to find it disappointing. Although it is tempting to blame this outcome on a failure of the quality of leadership that exists in the intervening democratic countries, selectorate theory suggests that it is more indicative of the limitations of democratic institutions themselves and the nature of democratic representation. Democratic leaders are constitutionally charged with being the agents of their domestic constituencies and their voters' policy priorities are rarely identical with those of the citizens of target states. The fault, if there is one, lies less in the motives of the democratic executive than in the policy priorities of democratic voters and the incentives created by democratic institutions.

KEY CONCEPTS

democratization 225
kleptocracy 244
nation building 225

rent-seeking 234
third-party intervention 233

9 What Is the Problem with Foreign Aid?

OVERVIEW

- Foreign aid does little to help poor people and may actually make them worse off. Foreign aid makes threatened governments less likely to become democratic and more likely to become more autocratic, leading either to a worse dictatorship or the instability brought on by coups d'etat.

- The impact of foreign aid is pernicious. It enriches petty dictators and secures them in office. It buys policy concessions that voters in donor countries value enough to pay. It hurts those who feel want the most, the very people most of us presume are the reason foreign economic assistance is given in the first place.

- If donor states' citizens want to change this pattern of behavior they must also change their own demands. They must encourage their government leaders to believe that there are more votes to be had by helping the world's poor than by providing another small benefit at home.

Over the past several decades, foreign aid has not lived up to its presumed goal of lifting people out of poverty, ignorance, illness, inequality, and overall misery.* There is general agreement about what aid has not done, but so far there is no consensus on what the solution is.

This chapter explores foreign aid from the selectorate perspective introduced in Chapter 1. It considers foreign aid policy in the context of examining what we should expect if the alleviation of poverty is not the sole, or perhaps even the main, reason donors disperse aid. I summarize the logic and evidence for the contention that donor leaders give aid to recipient leaders in return for policy concessions. Although questionable from a normative perspective, aid-for-policy deals are a strategically rational allocation of resources and effort by recipients and donors, advancing the interests of political elites in each nation. When aid is given for these purposes, the aid is not designed primarily to relieve poverty and reduce misery. As such, we should not be surprised when it fails to fulfill normatively desirable goals. Instead, as we will see, such aid perpetuates poverty and promotes the political survival of leaders. This is not perhaps the way we wish things were, but, as I have said before, we cannot change the world if we do not first confront what motivates leaders to make the choices they make.

As we see in this chapter, American support of petty dictators through economic assistance is not some anomaly or some

Pakistani children from the Taliban-infiltrated tribal region of Bajur push a cart loaded with sacks of flour during food distribution at the Kacha Gari refugee camp in Peshawar, Pakistan, Tuesday, January 20, 2009. The camp, in Pakistan's Northwest Frontier Province, was established in the 1980s, and is among the recipients of large amounts of U.S. and international aid.

uniquely American flaw but, rather, part of an equilibrium strategy that all democratic leaders around the world follow. It is what they must do if they are to govern on behalf of "We, the People." If these policies offend us, then we should recognize that the fault, as with the use of military intervention (see Chapter 8), lies within our power to change by the simple mechanism of putting other people's interests ahead of our own. That, as it turns out, is a tough order.

FOREIGN AID: THE PROBLEM

Foreign aid is the contribution of money, goods, or services to other governments or to people or communities in foreign countries; the contributions are given for free, as heavily

---

* This chapter borrows substantially from Bueno de Mesquita and Smith (2007, 2009).

subsidized loans, or for a price well below the market price. Foreign aid is given by governments and also by nongovernmental organizations (NGOs) such as the Red Cross, Oxfam, Care, Doctors Without Borders, and countless other charities. I focus here on government-to-government foreign aid and its consequences.

With few exceptions, foreign aid programs have failed to alleviate poverty; promote social, economic, or political equality; or spread freedom or justice. Far more often than might seem proper, foreign aid is given to dictators and demagogues who steal most of it and do precious little to advance the well-being of their own citizens. Why this is so and why foreign aid has not proven effective at promoting economic growth or political freedom is the subject of a lively, sometimes heated debate. The debate is mostly among economists who are influential not only in academic circles but also in shaping foreign aid choices at the World Bank; in NGOs; and in the governments of the world's wealthiest countries, those belonging to the Organisation for Economic Cooperation and Development (OECD). The debate centers on two competing explanations for foreign aid's inadequate performance. Before turning to that debate, however, we first touch on the history of a seemingly successful aid program, the Marshall Plan, and its implications for current circumstances to help frame our understanding of what aid does and does not do, and why.

The Marshall Plan: A Model for Foreign Aid?

Probably the single most important and impressive foreign aid effort was launched by the United States after World War II. The Marshall Plan (1947–1951), named after Secretary of State George Marshall, was an enormous economic assistance program. With massive infusions of Marshall Plan money, the United States assumed responsibility to help reestablish the devastated European economies and set western Europe on its rapid rise to its current-day prosperity and freedom. Of course, this foreign aid effort was aimed at taking well-educated skilled people from the artificially induced poverty resulting from war back to their prior condition of relative prosperity. We should remember that most western European countries not only were prosperous but also had experience with democracy before the world war, so the issue was to reestablish competitive electoral politics and efficient economies, not create them for the first time. This difference between the European experience with aid and the experience of much of the rest of the world is often thought to be the key to aid's success in post–World War II Europe and to its poor record since. That explanation, however, is seriously flawed.

It is easy to argue from superficial appearances that Marshall Plan aid *caused* Europe's resurgence and so should serve as a model for rescuing the people of the world's poorest countries from misery. But, as we all know, correlation is not causation. Countries with lots of McDonald's restaurants or with many golf courses rarely fight wars with one another, but it is pretty obvious that neither golf nor hamburgers prevent war. On the plus side for the Marshall Plan, it is certainly true that countries that received Marshall Plan money generally did better economically and politically than the rest of the world. For instance, western

European economies grew much more successfully than their Eastern European counterparts. The latter, like their patron, the Soviet Union, refused Marshall Plan funds and also grew rather slowly. But why did they refuse the aid, and was it that refusal, or something else, that slowed their growth? It is in the answers to these questions that we are more likely to find out why western European economies recovered from the war more easily than Eastern European economies.

The Marshall Plan involved much more than Europe's receiving money to rebuild infrastructure and productive capacity. In fact, the plan imposed tremendous economic constraints on its recipients; there was a web of strings attached. No one was given a free ride. Recall from our discussion of the power transition theory in Chapter 4 that the United States favored, and still favors, a mostly free-trade regime pursued by market-oriented economies. Recipients of Marshall Plan dollars had to agree to pursue free-market policies. This meant that they could not nationalize private industry and still get reconstruction funds. Such a prohibition was, of course, a nonstarter for the centrally planned, socialist economies of Eastern Europe and the Soviet Union. Their governments owned virtually all business and industry operating inside their borders. They had almost no free market at all; in fact, that was the foundation of their economic and political structure. Participants in the plan also had to agree to balance their budgets, bring inflation under control, and normalize their currency exchange rates. These policies, rather than the aid dollars, are now thought by many economists to be the principal explanation for the high growth rates enjoyed by Marshall Plan participants (Milward 1984; De Long and Eichengreen 1993) and the slow growth in Eastern Europe, where these policies were ignored in favor of an ill-conceived experiment in an alternative economic model.

As further evidence that something other than aid dollars was at work, it is worth noting that much of Europe's transportation infrastructure had been reconstructed *before* aid dollars started flowing in and even before the plan was announced (De Long and Eichengreen 1993). Even tougher for the Marshall Plan case is the simple fact that there is not much of a correlation between the amount of money received by the individual countries and the differences in their growth rates (Eichengreen et al. 1992). The Netherlands, for instance, received about 5 percent of its GNP in Marshall Plan aid, while West Germany received less than half that amount; nevertheless, Germany grew between 1948 and 1951 at an annual rate well over 10 percent and the Netherlands grew well under 5 percent per year. So, the correlation between growth and aid dollars breaks down when we compare individual countries over time rather than blocs of countries that received and did not receive assistance.

So far we have seen that, although it is true that recipients of the aid grew rapidly, it is difficult to demonstrate that variations in aid made the difference. Indeed, it may be that the changes in economic policies were at the root of the growth of western Europe's economies versus the absence of comparable growth in Eastern Europe and elsewhere. These facts are a sobering reminder that correlation is not causation and that increases in aid outlays, however well-intentioned, do not necessarily lead to better economic performance by the recipients.

We should perhaps look to improved economic policies rather than increased aid as the solution to world poverty and the conflict it engenders (Burnside and Dollar 2000; Collier and Dollar 2002; Dollar and Levin 2006). Indeed, foreign aid may paradoxically be a serious impediment to improved economic and political policy.

Aid outside Europe: Not a Pretty Picture

Recognizing that much of the world lacked the **human capital** (people with productive skills and abilities derived from education and good health—that is, skilled educated people) to build successful economies, donor countries such as the United States, Britain, and France oriented some of their aid efforts outside western Europe toward improving education (rather than basic economic policies). Those efforts failed to promote significant growth, as did donor efforts oriented toward building the infrastructure that is essential for bringing skilled workers to where they were needed and facilitating the shipment of goods to market. Roads and bridges, schools and factories, ports and airports, and dams and irrigation works were built, and still people in most recipient countries languished in deepening misery, sickness, and poverty. By the 1970s, debate raged over whether the problem with foreign aid resided in the extent to which foreigners (that is, the donors), ignorant of local conditions, administered programs. It became commonplace (and still is) to argue that responsibility for deciding how best to use funds should be turned over to local officials, who understand the situation on the ground. Not surprisingly, local elites are at the forefront in making this case.

Again, to the great disappointment of aid agencies, turning control of the spending over to the recipient governments (that is, localizing decision making) seems not to produce improved economic growth, health care, educational attainment, gender equality, or any of the many other noble objectives thought to be behind foreign aid. Although there are exceptions to the generalization that foreign aid has failed, by and large the recipients of foreign aid have not improved the quality of life of their citizens and for many the quality of life has declined.

THE AID DEBATE

The average result from foreign aid has been so bad that some despair that foreign aid is making things worse rather than better. Whether aid has actually exacerbated poverty and misery or alleviated it here and there, those responsible for formulating aid policy still search for ways to make it work. This is my focus here. Those who are eager to see aid work better are divided into two camps: those who want to increase aid and those who want to improve the policies of the aid recipients. Those who apply the strategic perspective to foreign aid policy fall into neither camp, and thus form a third camp that is critical of the two perspectives that currently dominate debate among economists.

One point of view argues that the trouble with economic assistance programs is that too little is spent on foreign aid to make a difference, that aid amounts to just a drop in the bucket. For instance, U.S. foreign economic assistance (not counting money spent on the reconstruction of Iraq) only accounts for about 0.2 percent of GNP and less than 1 percent of federal budget outlays. As it happens, despite these small numbers, the United States is the largest aid donor in terms of the total amount of money given. Two-tenths of a percent of the GNP of the United States is a lot of money; it is, depending on what is counted, somewhere between $13 billion and well over $20 billion. Still, the United States more often than not is one of the smaller OECD aid donors in terms of percentage of GNP. In percentage terms, Canada is about even with the United States; Britain lags a little behind; and France, with an average outlay of about 0.4 percent of GDP, about doubles U.S. generosity. Looked at globally, foreign economic assistance has averaged around 0.3 percent of OECD economic product since 1960, and that amount has fallen in the past decade. That's not a record that inspires great pride, but it also fails to tell the whole story. Even the most generous foreign aid donors in percentage terms, such as Denmark and Norway, spend less than 1 percent of their GNP on foreign economic assistance.

With so little aid given, it is clear that one explanation for the failure of foreign aid's is how cheap donors have proven to be. For example, the economist Jeffrey Sachs (2005) looks at this record and argues vigorously that more must be given if the rich world hopes to alleviate poverty and the foreign crises likely to arise in the future between the haves and have-nots. This is a view that is easily understood and that calls for an easy solution: just spend more on foreign aid and the world will be a better place. It is a view completely aligned with the United Nations Millennium Challenge Program, which is

> **TRY THIS**
>
> Look up the economic growth rates for ten countries in Africa. Look up how much total foreign aid each of those countries received over the past decade. Are the countries that received the most aid also the ones that are now growing fastest?

intended to increase aid to an average of 0.7 percent of the donor nations' GNPs. That program, in turn, was strongly endorsed and promoted by President George W. Bush, even when the United States failed to rise to the giving level that it proposed.[†]

But things are not this simple. Indeed, one simple question clarifies what is wrong with the idea that spending more will solve the problem of world poverty. Put your game theory hat on and ask yourself: If donors are not spending enough to alleviate poverty and that is obvious to everyone, then might the explanation be that alleviating poverty is *not* the goal behind foreign aid? The key to answering this question lies in the view that the amount spent on foreign aid is part of an equilibrium, not some unilateral decision made in ignorance by

---

[†] It is worth noting, for instance, that since President George W. Bush announced in 2002 that he would give increased foreign aid to countries that use the money to promote good governance and the rule of law, invest in their citizens, and promote economic freedom relatively little additional money has actually been spent by the United States for these purposes. As noted by *The Economist*, "A much heralded shift of American aid money away from supporting governments and towards backing 'popular empowerment' has turned out to be small in scale and limited in impact" (December 11, 2003, 44).

this or that donor country.[‡] Donors know how much they are giving. They know what impact it has. And they know that aid money has not generally translated into a better quality of life for the world's poorest people. Donors did not greatly vary their inflation-adjusted giving from the late 1960s until the late 1990s. Since then, they have actually cut back in percentage terms. So with aid having very little impact and donors giving small amounts, we must consider the possibility that we are looking in the wrong place to understand what motivates foreign aid. Perhaps donors really are not motivated primarily by a desire to diminish global poverty, and perhaps the governments to which they give are not motivated by that either. Hold that thought while we look at the second side in the aid debate.

The other main perspective in the aid debate looks at the inadequacies of the recipients instead of the cheapness of donors. Craig Burnside and David Dollar (2000), for instance, note that aid helps to reduce poverty only when it is accompanied by good policies within the recipient nation. That, you recall, was the argument for why the Marshall Plan succeeded—it insisted on good economic policies as a condition for receiving assistance. Not only are poor economic policies in recipient nations seen as the culprits, but the very intentions of recipient governments have been highlighted as a problem.

Much aid is given on a government-to-government basis. Stephen Knack (2001) contends that such giving encourages corruption by leaders in the recipient nations. Because aid fosters corruption, it undermines its own beneficial potential. Easterly (2006) and others reinforce this view, focusing on the administrative and bureaucratic inefficiencies in recipient regimes. From their perspective, the central problem with aid programs lies not in how much is given, as argued by Sachs (2005), but, rather, in how it is given. According to this view, recipient governments too often either steal the money or use it ineffectively to be the right target for economic assistance. Instead, Easterly and others argue that local entrepreneurs rather than governments should be the recipients of aid. It is thought that local entrepreneurs will use the money wisely, building important local successes. Banks making small loans to individual entrepreneurs with ideas for opening a small business, a food stand, a laundry, a child-care service, may serve as a useful example.[§] Unfortunately, this perspective does not consider the political consequences that can be expected if a local entrepreneur proves successful and concentrates enough wealth to represent a potential threat to the local or national government leaders. The idea that small-scale successes can grow into a national means to alleviate poverty and misery sounds wonderful—despite there being few examples of scaling-up to national success—but it overlooks the tremendous incentives that leaders

---

[‡] Remember that a *strategy* is a complete plan of action for every contingency that can arise in a game and an *equilibrium* is the set of player strategies from which no player has a unilateral incentive to defect.

[§] Realize, however, that micro-loans, as they are known, by banks are typically at what most of us would call usurious interest rates. Not-for-profit banks making these loans average more than 30 percent in interest, way above even the extraordinary interest rates charged on credit cards. For-profit banks making micro-loans to local, poor, would-be entrepreneurs charge over 50 percent. Obviously, these are rates that cannot be easily paid, and these loans run the risk that they will help launch small mom-and-pop businesses and then crush them with debt.

have to prevent the emergence of potential rivals for power. Those who become rich are the prospective pool of just such rivals, and so they are either coopted or repressed if they grow successful enough to attract leadership attention.

So the foreign policy debate boils down to either recipient incentives and donor stinginess restricting the efficacy of aid outputs. In either case, whether the problem is with inputs, outputs, or both, the supposition behind the current debate is that donors, and perhaps recipients also, view aid primarily as an instrument to reduce poverty. But just as donors know how little they are giving and its consequences, so too do they know how much of what they give is being consumed by corrupt officials with little or no benefit to impoverished people of the world. This leaves us with the problem that the current explanations for aid's failure depend on donors not understanding what is happening

> ### TRY THIS
>
> Look up the corruption rankings of ten African governments, using Transparency International's corruption index, both for the present year and for ten years ago. Then look up how much total aid each of those ten countries received over the past decade. Did foreign aid help alleviate corruption? Are the recipients of the most aid well ranked or poorly ranked on the corruption index compared to recipients of smaller amounts, from a per capita perspective?

to their money and so blindly continuing to give it (albeit at modest levels) despite their money going down a rat hole. Again, if we adopt an equilibrium account it is hard to support the idea that donors do not know what the rest of us know—that vast amounts of aid in cash and goods are stolen or that the amounts they are giving fail to reduce poverty.

A THIRD EXPLANATION FOR AID

There is an alternative explanation for why foreign aid programs fail to solve the problems of poverty and inequality. It is an argument that contends that aid programs are quite successful at doing what they are designed for; it is just that they are not principally about alleviating poverty and they hardly ever are about promoting democracy.

Consider the possibility that neither poverty alleviation nor the promotion of freedom is the sole, or perhaps even the main, reason donors give aid. Let's think about aid more strategically and consider the implications of looking at aid programs as a way to trade dollars for policy concessions. Doing so will allow us to answer four critical questions about aid: (1) Which countries give aid, (2) how much do they give, (3) which countries get aid, and (4) how much do they get? In addressing those questions, we will also be well on the way to seeing how foreign aid gets in the way of democratization. I first summarize a game theoretic model designed to answer these questions and then review the evidence for its central hypotheses. Those interested in a fuller treatment of these questions, should see Bueno de Mesquita and Alastair Smith (2007, 2009).

The selectorate-based strategic perspective demonstrates that the answers to the four questions I just posed are all consistent with the notion that aid is not needs-based—it is policy-based. Indeed, once we look at aid that way we see that even the Marshall Plan was fully consistent with the idea that aid buys policy compliance, and we also see why it involved such a large amount of money. In the case of the Marshall Plan, recall that those who accepted U.S. assistance agreed to adopt economic policies that matched those that the U.S. government was interested in promoting. It is easy to forget that right after World War II many in the United States feared that western European governments would adopt strongly socialist policies that were friendlier to the Soviet Union than they were to the United States. Remember that the Marshall Plan was launched at the outset of the cold war. It furthered the purpose of aligning western Europe more with the interests of the U.S. government and its people than with those of the Soviet Union. Acquiring political support from democratic governments, such as existed in western Europe, comes at a high price; getting the support of nondemocratic governments, if they can live with the policy concessions being sought, typically comes at a much lower price.

Aid-for-policy deals may seem questionable from a normative perspective, but they are a rational allocation of resources and policies by recipients and by donors. In fact, aid-for-policy deals advance the interests of three out of the four groups of people affected by them. They make the constituents of the donor countries a little better off than otherwise would be true. In doing so, they improve modestly the reelection prospects of democratic leaders. They pay autocratic leaders for policy concessions, making them and their coalition of backers better off. To sell policy concessions, it is necessary that the buyer (the donor) believe that the policies it desires from another country would not be followed if aid money were not forthcoming. That means that the policies being sold are not what the people in the targeted, aid-receiving country want, and they are not policies that would be normally followed by the prospective aid recipient. Thus, the people in the targeted country are harmed in two ways by their government's acceptance of foreign aid: they get policies they don't like, and their autocratic or dictatorial leaders have extra money with which to buy their own prolonged survival in office.

Giving and Getting Aid

A good starting place for thinking about aid is to remember that small-coalition leaders survive in office primarily by providing their backers with enough private benefits to keep them loyal. Large-coalition leaders survive in office primarily by providing their supporters with enough public goods to keep them loyal. We can think of public goods broadly as national policies. Most of the time, politicians get the biggest policy bang-for-the-buck by spending money on programs at home, whether those involve building highways or schools or national defense or national parks. Constituents like to see tangible benefits from the tax dollars that their government extracts from them. Sometimes, at the margin, however, the bang-for-the-buck in terms of satisfying domestic constituents can be bigger from doing something in a far-away country than from adding another mile of highway, a public-access television station, or another soup kitchen for the homeless. Of course, the opportunity for leaders to please constituents at home by spending abroad is not nearly as prevalent as the opportunity to help their constituents directly at home. That clearly is one reason that aid outlays are so small. Even so, sometimes money spent abroad can buy more value for the dollar, making it the politically smart choice at home.

One aspect that helps make aid programs attractive, at least to some people, is that many foreign aid programs are closely tied to requirements that help constituents at home. The United States provides vast amounts of food aid to countries in Africa, for example, but only if that food is purchased from American farmers and shipped in American vessels. Naturally, we all feel good about spending a little money to combat starvation, especially when much of that money is spent on U.S.-produced products that are then shipped to far-away places using U.S.-owned transportation. As the late Representative Tom Lantos (D-Calif.) observed when President Bush suggested decoupling food aid from food produced in the United States as a way to make more food more cheaply available overseas, "It is a mistake of gigantic proportions … because support for such a program will vanish overnight, overnight." (quoted in Dugger 2007). Why? Because decoupling food aid from American farm production would cut off the domestic benefits to the small number of farmers—potentially in pivotal voting districts—who benefit from aid. When the U.S. Agency for International Development (USAID) railed against Lantos's view, it failed to consider why aid is such a small amount of money—it benefits relatively few Americans, so politicians can afford to spend little on it.**

We see similar patterns in foreign aid given by the Japanese, and even the Norwegians, Swedes, and Danes. For instance, Peter Schraeder, Steven Hook, and Bruce Taylor (1998) find that Swedish aid is strongly motivated by pro-socialist ideology and by trade benefits aimed at countries in which Sweden's impact can be large rather than in response to humanitarian need. Steven Hook and Guang Zhang similarly report that, even after the Japanese government announced that it would give aid for "democratization, human rights, and restraint in military spending" (1998, 1051), its aid giving remained dominated by self-interest, not altruism. We see this message echoed repeatedly—aid donors are looking out for what is good for them more than they are looking at what is good for poor people in poor countries.

When the bang-for-the-buck is greater by spending overseas, we do so. Because the bang-for-the-buck rarely increases through overseas spending, the total amount going to foreign aid is, as we know, the proverbial drop in the bucket. "We, the People" prefer to see our tax dollars spent on worthy projects at home such as subsidies for prescription drugs and Medicare, regulating automobile safety standards, protecting small animals from developers encroaching on their environment, and the Superfund to clean up toxic wastes than we do for it to be spent on fighting malaria in African children or digging wells in remote Indian villages. That's why our leaders spend more money on those domestic programs. If they didn't,

---

** Milner and Tingley (2006) do a nice job of showing that the likelihood of a member of Congress's voting for a foreign aid bill depends on how many of his or her constituents have close ties to recipient governments. Those whose constituents do not expect a personal benefit from aid are more likely to vote against the aid bill.

they probably wouldn't get reelected. Sure, we want to help those poor children dying needlessly from a preventable and treatable disease, but we lose sight of that goal when it starts to hit our own pocketbooks in an obvious way. If this sounds harsh, ask yourself how you would feel about the government's cutting back some domestic programs from which you benefit—say, low-interest, deferred-payment tuition loans—to help poorer people in far-away lands. Inevitably, all governments, just like all of us, face a **budget constraint,** the limit on resources that a government (or a household) can spend. There is a limit to how many good programs can be supported. Tough choices have to be made, and politicians make them with an eye on what will win the most votes or cost the fewest. As long as aid is a small amount, we don't care that the money being spent on it might instead have reduced our own health-care costs a little, little, little bit. And so, aid remains a drop in the bucket. We each spend less on aid than we spend on one month's worth of cell phone service for a modest plan.

Now, let's think about who is willing to take our aid. If it were freely given, with no strings attached, pretty much anybody and everybody would get in line to receive aid. There are far too many needy people for us to help all of them, so we have to pick and choose. The strategic perspective tells us that one major factor used by leaders in picking who to help is to think about whether giving that group aid will strengthen the support of political allies at home. When the home coalition is very large, as in a democracy, then we must pick and choose aid recipients with an eye to what the voters will support. They will support programs that give them a bigger return on the dollar through aid than they would get from the same dollar spent on domestic programs. A valued policy concession (say, allowing American military bases or providing better trade terms for U.S. goods) could be just the thing to make constituents at home happy about spending some money on aid. Governments willing to cooperate with U.S. interests are much more likely to get aid than those who are hostile to American interests. As it turns out, that is not peculiar to American aid-giving. The evidence supports that all aid-giving countries are primarily motivated by an interest in getting favorable treatment from aid-recipient governments and that that is why they give the recipients aid.

Who can most easily make policy concessions in exchange for some money? We know the answer from our examination of selectorate politics. Small-coalition leaders need money to keep their jobs. They have to have enough money on hand to pay off their few essential supporters, typically meaning they have to buy the loyalty of high-ranking military officers and senior bureaucrats and perhaps some family members too. Effective public policy is not their ticket to longevity in office. Not that they have anything against doing what is good for their people if they can, but spending money on good policies at the risk of not paying their cronies enough to keep their loyalty just is not in the cards. That would be the path to their unemployment. So, aid donors are likely to be democratic because they want policy concessions and some of those policy concessions may benefit specific constituents of theirs, helping to provide private goods (such as the overseas sales of Caterpillar tractors or American wheat) as well as public goods. Aid recipients are likely to be autocrats because they want money to help them survive in office.

Now, not all prospective recipients are equally attractive. We have seen one important way in which they differ—their ability to sell policy concessions for money. That is hard for democratic governments to do because their leaders must rely on getting lots of voter support to hold office. Selling voters out by abandoning the policies they want is no way to get reelected. But that does not mean that only autocrats get aid and that democrats never do. Let's probe the logic a bit more.

Suppose A is a leader of a democratic aid donor. We know A wants to buy policy concessions for his or her constituents. We also know that those concessions must not cost more than the price that A would pay to get a comparable improvement in his or her reelection prospects by spending the money at home. So A has to be pretty picky about how much he or she spends on aid. When can A afford to spend a lot? A can afford to spend a lot when the policy concession is really highly valued by his or her voters. When must A spend a lot? A must spend a lot when he or she really wants the concession and the policy concession that A seeks is really costly for the prospective aid recipient to give up. When is that? Well, it is hardest for democratic governments to make policy concessions, so they are least likely to be aid recipients because they are too pricey; but, if they have a valuable enough concession to give A, he or she will be willing to pay a lot for it. So, democrats, although least likely to get aid, are going to get a lot of aid if they get any. Anytime A wants a really big, salient, unpopular, and therefore costly policy concession from a prospective aid recipient, A is going to have to pay more than when he or she wants a concession that is not so hard for the recipient to grant. If a potential aid recipient wants a higher price than the concession is worth to A, then he or she either won't give that country aid or will bargain with the leaders for a smaller concession that costs less. That is easier to do with small-coalition rulers than with large-coalition leaders. They can afford to take a lower price (as we discuss in Chapter 8).

There is still more to deciding whether to give aid or accept aid. If B is a leader of a prospective aid recipient, and B's country has a large national budget (that is, the aid-recipient country is relatively well off), then B has access to that budget as revenue that can be used to buy the loyalty of his or her cronies. The richer B is, the smaller the marginal value is of the next dollar spent to keep cronies' loyalty. That is, B's utility for money is concave, which means that more money is always better than less but that the difference in the utility that B attaches to the billionth dollar compared to one dollar less than that is not as large as the utility B attaches to the first dollar or each preceding dollar. So, to buy a given policy concession from a revenue-rich leader like B is costlier than to buy the same concession from a revenue-poor leader.

This is just a quick sketch of what is, in actuality, considerably more complicated logic. Still, the gist of the case should be clear. Democrats are more likely to give aid than are autocrats. Autocrats are more likely to receive aid than are democrats. Democrats who receive aid are likely to get a larger amount of money than are autocrats who get aid. When a big policy concession is granted, more aid is received than when a small concession is granted. From the aid-giver's perspective, it is costlier to buy concessions from richer countries than from poorer

TABLE 9.1	Foreign Aid: Who Gives, Who Gets, and How Much?			
Criterion	Which countries are most likely to give aid?	Which countries are most likely to get aid?	Which countries will give the most aid?	Which countries will get the most aid?
Coalition size (democracy, nondemocracy)	Large-coalition democracies	Small-coalition autocracies	Largest-coalition donors	Large-coalition recipients
Issue salience	Those seeking politically salient concessions	Those offering politically salient concessions	Those who value the concessions most, provided the cost does not exceed the value	Those for whom the concessions are most costly to grant, provided the cost does not exceed the value for the donor
Government revenue	Those with high revenue	Those with low revenue	Those with high revenue	Those with high revenue

countries, so poorer countries are more likely to get aid than are richer countries, but a poor country is likely to get less aid than a rich country if it receives aid at all; the poor country will sell its citizens out for a lower price exactly because the next dollar is worth more to it than it is worth to someone who is richer. Table 9.1 summarizes the essential points.

Notice that, in the discussion of who gets aid, who gives aid, how much is given, and how much is received, nothing at all was said about neediness. That is not to say that donors and recipients don't care about the welfare of poor people. Perhaps they do; but they care more about aid as an instrument to help their regime stay in power. If giving to the needy doesn't interfere with that goal, then the needy will be helped. But as Table 9.1 reminds us, the poorest nations are not expected to get the largest amounts of aid. Instead, it is the relatively wealthy and relatively democratic governments that are willing to give up a highly valued policy that get the most aid if they get aid at all. This induces important selection effects. If the price of the aid is too high relative to the value of the concession that is looked for by the prospective donor, then, instead of getting lots of aid, the potential recipient will get nothing or will get much less in exchange for a lesser issue. That is why relatively well off, relatively democratic prospective recipients are less likely to get aid than are poor autocratic states; however, poor autocratic states, although highly likely to receive aid, shouldn't expect to get much. That is what we observe in the world. There are too few aid dollars compared to the vast amount of misery, but, in contrast to arguments by economists such as Sachs, this is not some oversight or error by donors and it is not inherently due to stinginess. The amount of aid given is part of an equilibrium driven by the domestic political needs and wants of citizens in donor countries. Their leaders give as much as their own constituents really want them to give.

In the same way, those who take the second perspective on foreign aid, contending that more aid is not given because too much of the money is stolen by corrupt government officials in the recipient countries, miss an essential bit of aid's logic. Corrupt officials are exactly the people who are most prepared to sell out their population by granting unpopular policy concessions to donors, whether those concessions are security-related, trade-related, or touch on other subjects. It is the small-coalition autocrats who are most likely to get aid because they can sell policy for money, which they use to buy the continued loyalty of their essential domestic allies. So, giving aid to crooked governments is also part of an equilibrium dictated by the interests of recipient leaders and their small coalition of critical supporters, and by the interests of donor leaders and their large coalition of voters. Only the poor souls in recipient countries are harmed by this arrangement, but barring a revolutionary mass movement and overthrowing their government (a topic I turn to shortly) there is nothing they can do to stop their leaders from selling them out.

Evidence for the Aid Hypotheses

The selectorate view of aid decision making is rather depressing. Of course, hypotheses should neither be accepted nor rejected based on how we feel about them. Only by examining the evidence can we ascertain whether they are consistent with what goes on in the world, and so that is what we do next. Remember that to improve outcomes in the world we first have to understand what goes on and why. Those who are unhappy with how foreign aid seems to work will have to think very hard about how it might be changed, remembering that "We, the People" are part of the problem as well as possibly part of the solution. To solve the problem, however, very large numbers of us will have to put the interests of poor people around the world ahead of our own interests, our own comforts, and our own desires for government programs that benefit us. Idealistic calls for more help for the poor won't carry much weight when those calls are accompanied by greater voter demands for subsidies at home.

Let's start with the big-picture evidence and then zoom in on some good examples of the theory at work. The big picture can be seen by looking at the pattern of aid giving by all the countries in the OECD—these countries provide the vast majority of foreign aid—and by looking at which countries get the aid and how much they get. Although the members of the OECD are the world's main foreign aid donors, they don't each give to everybody. They pick and choose to whom to give aid, just as we in the United States do.

A statistical assessment shows that large-coalition governments are vastly more likely to be donors than small-coalition regimes. They are also vastly more likely to give at least some aid to poor, dictatorial governments than they are to well-off democracies or well-off autocracies. But, when it comes to the amounts given, the picture changes in the manner predicted. Among those who get aid, larger-coalition regimes get more money and so do wealthier regimes. Those who have big policy concessions that they are willing to grant—such as trade concessions or national security concessions—get lots more money than those who just don't have a lot to offer. For instance, countries with neutral foreign policies toward the prospective donor get more than those who already strongly support the donor. Those who are geographically closer to the donor get more than those who are far away. And those who are former colonies—and therefore likely to have more active trade with the donor—get more than those who are not. Life expectancy at birth, one measure of need, turns out not to be significantly related either to the likelihood of receiving economic assistance or to the amount received. Per capita income, another indicator of need, likewise fails to explain much about aid receipts.

> **TRY THIS**
>
> Identify the countries that are the ten largest and ten smallest (but not zero) aid recipients of the United States. How do they differ in their governance and in their importance to U.S. strategic or economic interests? How do they differ in neediness (assessed as life expectancy at birth, per capita income, lack of medical care, and other indicators of quality of life)?

Looking at specific cases, we see that the big picture is reinforced. Which countries are among the largest U.S. foreign aid recipients? Israel, Egypt, and Pakistan top the list. Israel, a well-off democracy, still gets considerable support from the United States. In exchange, Israel collaborates closely with the U.S. government on major foreign policy decisions. It has given up or diminished its own desire for military action against some of its neighbors at the behest of the U.S. government. Egypt got virtually nothing from the United States before it signed the Camp David agreement in 1979, which established peace between Israel and Egypt. Even today, decades later, Egyptian schools continue to teach hatred of Israel, thereby perpetuating anti-Israeli feelings in the Egyptian population. Why? One explanation is that the huge amounts of aid that the Egyptian government gets for maintaining peace with Israel would evaporate if Egyptians chose naturally to live in peace with their neighbor. Pakistan, likewise, used to get little aid from the United States, but that changed dramatically after 9/11—Pakistan became a frontline state in the war against terrorism. It is politically costly for Pakistani leaders to take on Al Qaeda, the Taliban, and even some in Pakistan's own intelligence service (the Inter-Services Intelligence, ISI, which is thought to have planned and helped execute terrorist attacks against American interests). Such policy concessions must come at a high price, and because they are highly valued by the United States, the U.S. government pays the price.

The statistical and case study evidence shows over and over again that OECD donors look much the same as the United States: hardly anyone seems to give primarily on a needs basis, and all give primarily to advance their own political agendas. Strategic calculations about what helps incumbents remain in power seem to tell a big part of the story of who gives and who gets aid. But what about spreading democracy? Does aid at least help with that?

AID AND DEMOCRATIZATION

We know foreign aid is not doing much to alleviate poverty. That is a sad testament to the difference between the lip service that some pay to helping the neediest and the reality that we would rather help ourselves. But maybe aid helps indirectly. Maybe it helps foster more democracy. Although the evidence is mixed at best with regard to growing prosperity leading to democracy, it is pretty clear that democracy itself typically fosters growing prosperity. So, if aid programs are tied to democratic reform, as the U.S. Millennium Challenge Grants program is intended to do, then perhaps foreign aid indirectly fosters later economic success as a consequence of giving the wants of the people a greater voice in aid-receiving countries. Alas, that too is not true. In fact, the opposite tends to be true—aid inhibits democratization.

I mentioned earlier that the poor people in aid-receiving countries end up being sold out by their governments. Their leaders are willing to make policy-for-money deals to help them remain in power, and the best deals for them involve giving up policies the donor doesn't like that the recipient's citizens do like. All this mistreatment might eventually motivate people in poor countries to take to the streets, risking what little they have, on the hope and chance that by toppling their government they might get something better. Let's look now at what happens in theory and in reality when leaders face a serious threat of mass revolt.

It is hard to get enough people to take to the streets to threaten a government. After all, revolts are most likely in dictatorships, but dictators are not hesitant to imprison and even kill people who are thought to be disloyal. I do not address here the coordination problem involved in putting enough people on the streets to make for a credible threat. The easiest way to think about how this happens is that a tipping point is reached in which enough stalwart revolutionaries take the risk to encourage some others to follow suit. Then, seeing more people on the street, still others become more willing to take the risk and so on, cascading until there is a large enough number that the government feels sufficiently at risk that it has to do something (Lohmann 1994).

Just such a cascade was seen in Eastern Europe and in the Soviet Union in the late 1980s and early 1990s. First a few people protested in Poland, and then, seeing no massive response against them, more came out and then still more; eventually the government agreed to real elections and was deposed. Meanwhile, people in East Germany and elsewhere saw the possibility that they could succeed, and so they too took to the streets; and pretty soon the cold war was over, the entire Soviet empire was lost, and even the Soviet Union had collapsed. Most of the former members of that empire became democratic; a few became democratic but have since slid back into more autocratic forms of governance (including Russia); and still others never became democratic, just substituting one form of dictatorship for another. We want to be able to explain those different choices. In Kenya in December 2007 and in Zimbabwe a few months later, we also saw masses of people taking to the streets to protest what they were sure were stolen elections. These actions seem to have led to shared leadership between former rivals, but so far have not produced anything that we could reasonably describe as democracy. We want to understand what the prospects are for real democracy in places such as Kenya and Zimbabwe and how foreign aid might influence those prospects. We also saw small demonstrations in Myanmar in 2007 in which only dozens of people, many of them monks, protested against their government. The Myanmar military junta swooped in, quickly arresting the protestors and nipping the threat in the bud. The government anticipated that doing nothing would bring more protestors out, and that was something the generals were not willing to risk.

OK, so sometimes people take to the streets; more often they do not. What happens when they do? Let's address this question in terms of two diametrically opposite ways in which a government can respond: (1) increase democracy or (2) increase dictatorship. But first, let's think strategically about the factors that shape whether mass protests are feasible or even desirable.

We know from earlier chapters that governments ruled by a large coalition produce lots of public goods, including a special set of such goods that we refer to as **coordination goods,** public goods that facilitate groups of people coming together, exchanging views, and coordinating their actions; these include a free press, free speech, and freedom of assembly. These coordination goods make it much easier for a large number of people to exchange information about how they feel about their government and to express objections to any policies they don't like. This implies two effects of coordination goods that serve as fundamental assumptions in a selectorate-based game theory approach to nation building.

- The more public goods a society has, especially coordination goods, the less incentive people have to rebel against their government because they are already getting policies that they desire and demand from their government.
- The more public goods a society has, especially coordination goods, the more likely it is that a rebellion, if launched against the government, will succeed.

Put in terms of expected utility, these two assumptions say that the utility from a rebellion is relatively low in places that already produce lots of coordination goods but that the probability of a successful rebellion, if one were to occur, is relatively high. So, the expected utility from a rebellion depends on how steeply the probability of a successful rebellion increases relative to how steeply the incentive to rebel decreases in response to changes in the level of coordination goods being provided.

When people think about rebelling, they have to take several factors into account. Rebellion involves costs, so they have to sort out what it will cost them to take to the streets. They might be killed; they might be imprisoned; they might lose their jobs or homes; or the government might look the other way, treating such antigovernment demonstrations as a routine part of politics. In places such as the United States, where the Constitution guarantees the right of free assembly, free speech, and a free press and also the right to petition the government to deal with the people's grievances, demonstrations are routine politics. In the People's Republic of China, they are anything but. Still, after the disastrous earthquake in China in May 2008, many people whose children died when their schools collapsed did protest. Rather than arresting them, the government gave them payments in exchange for their signing agreements not to protest further over the possibility—indeed, the likelihood—that many children died because money that should have been spent on constructing safe school buildings was, instead, stolen by unscrupulous builders and government officials. In the Democratic People's Republic of Korea (North Korea), protests are virtually unheard of, but there people who express even mild disapproval of the government are sent off to prison and many are killed. The same was true under the leadership of Saddam Hussein in Iraq; those who disagreed with his government's policies were imprisoned, tortured, and often murdered. The absence of protests, therefore, cannot be looked at as a sign that people are happy with their government. They might be, but they might instead be deterred from protesting out of fear of the consequences. That is, the repressive nature of the regime with its poor provision of coordination goods makes the probability of successfully rebelling too low. The risk is not worth the long shot of obtaining freedom's rewards. When protests do occur, they can generate a wide range of responses, and these responses (as we see shortly) are influenced by, among other things, how much discretionary money such as foreign aid dollars the government has access to.

In the basic selectorate theory, we have considered so far only a political challenger who wants to depose the incumbent leadership and take over. Now we expand that perspective to include also the possibility that a revolutionary mass movement not only wants to topple the leadership but says it wants to change the fundamental institutions of government. It wants, as all revolutionaries claim, to turn the country into a democracy to help the poor and the downtrodden who have been abused by the current regime and the institutions under which it currently governs. Now, of course, the revolutionaries may say they want democracy, but that claim has to be taken with a grain of salt. Some successful revolutions (the American Revolution and the ones in India and South Africa) lead to democracy, but many (the revolutions in Cuba, China, and Vietnam) do not.

Let's model the threat of rebellion and the options that leaders have to diminish the threat. We start off by thinking about where government revenue comes from. One obvious source of revenue is the income tax and all the other taxes that governments levee on the labor of their citizens. Another source of revenue is money that comes to the government either because it owns and sells such natural resources as oil, diamonds, and gold or because it allows private firms to exploit those resources in exchange for a piece of the action separate from how much labor is needed to produce the revenue. A third source of income might be money given by foreign governments in the form of, speaking broadly, foreign aid. The latter two sources of revenue (from aid and from exploiting natural resources) share in common that they do not increase or decrease in direct proportion to the amount of labor used to create this revenue, whereas the first form of revenue (taxes on labor) does. That has some important implications for productivity and economic performance. When people work harder, they generate more income that can be taxed by the government. Low taxes on labor encourage people to work harder because they get to keep more of what they produce. Thus, low taxes help to increase productivity and, therefore, output, making the people richer and the government's share of that wealth smaller (although its absolute value can, of course, be quite large). So, low taxes combined with productivity-enhancing public-goods provision by the government is one way a government can generate more revenue.

As we know from the discussion of selectorate theory in Chapter 1, leaders spend money on public goods (g) and private goods (z), and anything not spent to keep their coalition loyal becomes the discretionary money controlled by the leadership. To keep straight whose public-goods provision we are looking at, let's call the public goods provided by the incumbent leader (called L) g_L and let's call the public goods promised by the revolutionary leader (called D) g_D. Public goods have a unit price of p, and private goods have an implied price of W because coalition members are the ones compensated with private benefits. Keeping in mind that public goods enhance productivity, let's define the revenue derived from taxing labor under each leader as tg_L and Tg_D, respectively, with $t > T$ (that is, the incumbent leader operates a smaller-coalition regime than that promised by the revolutionaries, who therefore promise lower tax rates on labor). The values t and T denote, respectively, the tax rate applied by the incumbent and the tax rate proposed by the would-be revolutionary to be applied to the wealth generated in their country as a consequence of the beneficial impact of any public goods (g) they provide. Assume that $T > 0$ so that total tax revenue (tg as long as the incumbent remains in power and Tg if the revolutionary comes to power and taxes at the rate he or she promised) increases with more public goods provision.[††] Let's define the (not completely) labor-free sources of revenue (natural resources and foreign aid) as R, so that the total government revenue under the incumbent regime equals $R + tg_L$. Then we stipulate that

$$R + tg_L \geq pg_L + Wz_L.$$

That is, $pg_L + Wz_L$ (the total cost of public and private goods) must not exceed the government's revenue, ($R + tg_L$), that is, its budget constraint. (We ignore the possibility of deficit spending to keep this analysis manageable.) Should the revolutionary come to power and impose the tax rate he or she promised, then the budget constraint is restated as:

$$R + Tg_D \geq pg_D + Wz_D.$$

Figure 9.1 introduces a much simplified game from that solved by Bueno de Mesquita and Smith (2009). In this game, the incumbent leader L faces a credible threat of a citizen rebellion led by the revolutionary D. The incumbent is looking for a strategy that will encourage citizens not to rebel. Two strategies immediately leap to mind for the incumbent. One approach to neutralizing the threat is to increase how many public goods, especially coordination goods, the leader distributes; the other strategy is the exact opposite—to cut back on public-goods provision, increasing the proportion of private goods that are

---

[††] For those interested in working through the analysis in a more complete way than the simplified presentation here, I suggest reading Bueno de Mesquita and Smith (2009).

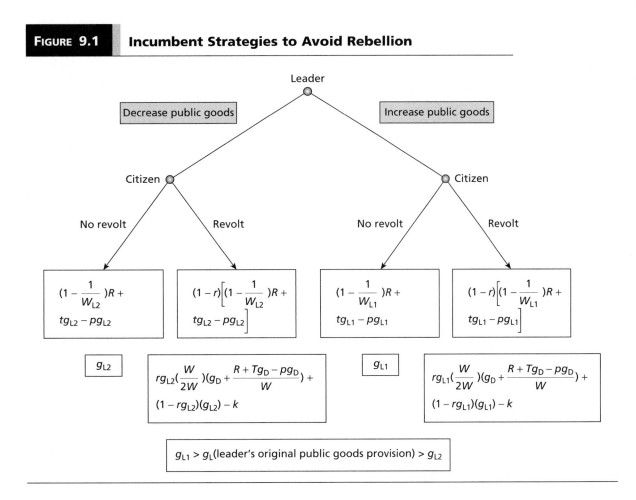

FIGURE 9.1   Incumbent Strategies to Avoid Rebellion

Leader

Decrease public goods

Increase public goods

Citizen

Citizen

No revolt | Revolt | No revolt | Revolt

$(1 - \dfrac{1}{W_{L2}})R + tg_{L2} - pg_{L2}$

$(1 - r)\left[(1 - \dfrac{1}{W_{L2}})R + tg_{L2} - pg_{L2}\right]$

$(1 - \dfrac{1}{W_{L1}})R + tg_{L1} - pg_{L1}$

$(1 - r)\left[(1 - \dfrac{1}{W_{L1}})R + tg_{L1} - pg_{L1}\right]$

g_{L2}

$rg_{L2}(\dfrac{W}{2W})(g_D + \dfrac{R + Tg_D - pg_D}{W}) + (1 - rg_{L2})(g_{L2}) - k$

g_{L1}

$rg_{L1}(\dfrac{W}{2W})(g_D + \dfrac{R + Tg_D - pg_D}{W}) + (1 - rg_{L1})(g_{L1}) - k$

$g_{L1} > g_L$(leader's original public goods provision)$> g_{L2}$

provided to his or her coalition. The first strategy is equivalent to neutralizing the threat by making people better off; the second strategy is equivalent to deterring rebellion by reducing people's confidence in their prospects of overthrowing the government by making it harder for them to come together and coordinate a mass rebellion.

In the game in Figure 9.1, leaders increase or decrease the amount they spend on public goods. Knowing the quantity of public benefits that the government is providing, citizens then choose to revolt or not to revolt. The set of people I am referring to as citizens with the potential to rebel are all people who are not in the current leader's winning coalition. This means that the only benefits they currently derive from their government are the public goods it produces. If they rebel, they have a chance of overturning the government and bringing D, the pro-democracy revolutionary leader, to power. If they overturn the incumbent regime, then, in the hardest case (for the incumbent), the revolutionary introduces democracy ($S = 2W$)[‡‡] and each citizen has a $W/2W$ (that is, 0.5) chance of getting some private benefits as well as public goods if the revolution succeeds. If the revolution fails, then the citizens continue to derive whatever public goods they were receiving before the revolt. Whether D comes to power or not, each citizen in the revolt pays a price k (which could be very high—loss of life or imprisonment—or a lower cost such as the loss of his or her job or home or friends and social standing) as a consequence of the rebellion.

Leader L, believing that he or she faces a credible threat of revolution, chooses to increase or decrease the level of public goods, especially coordination goods, being produced by his or her government. The choice is determined by three factors: (1) the rise in the level of public goods makes the citizenry sufficiently happy with their state of affairs that they will not revolt, (2) the cutback in the level of public goods makes the probability of launching a successful revolt sufficiently low that the people will not dare revolt, and (3) which one (1 or 2) leaves the incumbent better off in terms of his or her overall welfare.

Look at the payoffs in Figure 9.1, recalling that the first payoff listed at a terminal node (that is, the one on top) is the payoff for the player who moves first (that is, the incumbent leader) and the second payoff (listed below the first) is the payoff received by the citizens. Recall also that this model assumes that the probability of a successful revolution increases as the quantity of coordination goods provided by the incumbent increases. An increase in such goods (denoted g_{L1}) improves the odds of a successful revolt but diminishes the incentive of the citizens to revolt, while a decrease in such goods (denoted g_{L2}) makes the odds of a winning revolution smaller but makes the desire of the citizens to revolt greater. It is the balance between these two forces—the odds of success and the value of success—that can be manipulated by the incumbent through the mechanism of allocating fewer or more resources to public goods, especially coordination goods. That means that the citizens' expected results from rebellion are partially controlled by the incumbent regime. The regime provides the level of public goods as a strategically chosen quantity—as an endogenous factor—to minimize the risk of revolution while maximizing its own benefits.

We can find out whether citizens choose to revolt by comparing their expected benefits and costs from rebellion to their expected results from living with the status quo. In the game tree, the citizens' payoff from revolting is expressed in terms of a lengthy expected utility statement. This long expression just calculates the revolt's probability of success (rg_{L1} if public goods are increased or rg_{L2} if they are decreased) or failure, each weighted by the costs (k) and benefits (that is, public goods, denoted g_D and private goods) of a rebellion. Recall that originally I identified private goods as equal to a quantity denoted z. Now, to help tease out implications from the model, I solve for the value of z, the private goods, in terms of the budget and public goods. I do this by solving for the maximum that any government can spend, which is, of course, its budget constraint. A little bit of algebraic manipulation, solving for z, leads to the second benefit term in Figure 9.1:

[‡‡] Recall from Chapter 1 that S is the selectorate and W is the winning coalition.

$$R + Tg_\mathrm{D} \geq pg_\mathrm{D} + WZ_\mathrm{D} \Rightarrow Z_\mathrm{D} = (R + Tg_\mathrm{D} - pg_\mathrm{D})/W.$$

In deciding whether to revolt, citizens compare this to the payoff they get from sticking with the incumbent government ($g_{\mathrm{L}1}$ or $g_{\mathrm{L}2}$). If revolting is worth more, they revolt; otherwise, they stay with the incumbent regime. Solving for the case where the probability of winning a revolt (r) is large enough to render the payoff from revolting greater than the payoff from doing nothing, we find that it makes sense to revolt if:

$$r > \frac{2kW}{g_L(R - 2g_L W + Tg_D - pg_D + g_D W)} \tag{9.1}$$

Let's take a close look at inequality (9.1); note that I have suppressed the subscript that would tell us whether we are looking at the case in which the incumbent increases public goods or decreases them. Expression (9.1) looks complicated, and in fact it is. So, rather than going through the algebra, let's draw a picture based on a numeric example that follows expression (9.1) to see how increasing or decreasing public-goods provision influences the size of r that is required if citizens are to revolt; remember that r designates part of the probability of a successful revolt and that the other part—the amount of public goods provided—influences whether r is higher or lower. The incumbent's objective is to raise the right-hand side of expression (9.1) so as to diminish the odds that r is greater than the rest of the expression. This means L needs to make the right-hand side, depicted on the vertical axis in Figure 9.2, larger to avoid revolt. When r is less than or equal to the right-hand side of (9.1), it no longer pays for citizens to revolt; they are better off with the benefits they are getting now than they expect to be by taking to the streets.

Figure 9.2 shows the change in the revolt threshold (the value that r must exceed) as public goods increase or decrease. I have assumed specific values (listed below the figure), but the shape of the graph is not dependent on these specific values. The shape is, in fact, quite general. In Figure 9.2, there are two vertical lines passing through crucial points on the horizontal axis. The first, at 20, is the status-quo provision of public goods by the regime threatened with a revolt; the second vertical line is at position 93. The horizontal line that is at about 0.05 on the vertical axis shows the value at which r equals the right-hand side of expression (9.1) given our assumed specific values. If public-goods provision increases or decreases, then the threshold value of r (that is, the value at which r just exceeds the right-hand side of expression 9.1) changes. If the value goes up, the conditions to justify a revolt become harder to satisfy, and so revolt becomes less likely. If the new threshold value decreases because of a change in public-goods provision, then the conditions that must be met for the citizens to revolt become easier to satisfy, and so a revolt becomes more likely. If the threat of a revolt rises, putting the incumbent L at risk, then leader L can change policies to reduce the threat. L can increase the public-goods provision to make revolting less

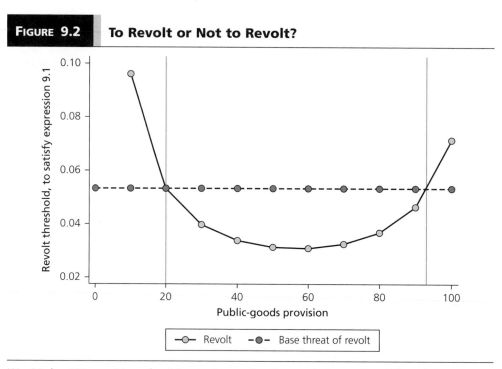

FIGURE 9.2   To Revolt or Not to Revolt?

$W = 50$, $k = 100$, provision of public goods promised by revolutionary D = 100, and the base-line public goods under the existing regime = 20. The horizontal axis depicts the range of possible public-goods provision by the existing regime (0–100). Revenue from natural resources and foreign aid (R) is set at 400, the tax rate is at 70, and the unit price of a public good (p) is at 10.

attractive, or L can decrease the public-goods provision to make the risk of revolting too great for citizens to take to the streets.

Keeping this logic in mind, let's take a close look at Figure 9.2. The curved line in Figure 9.2 shows the values of r derived from expression (9.1) under public-goods levels between 0 and 100. Note that the curve rises to the left of the vertical line at 20 as the quantity of public goods offered by the incumbent government decreases. This indicates that by decreasing the public-goods provision to below 20, the incumbent L can make the citizens more reluctant to rebel. Their threshold for gambling on revolt will rise, making it harder and harder for them to satisfy themselves that the risk of revolution is worth it. Notice that the curve rises steeply as public goods fall below 20. This means that the fewer public goods produced by the government, the more confident citizens will have to be of victory (r must be getting closer and closer to 1) before they gamble on revolution.

The curve remains above the horizontal line for public goods allocations between 0 and 20 and then falls below the status-quo baseline value for r until the quantity of public goods equals 93; then the value rises again above the baseline threshold risk of revolution. That is, between 20 and 93, increasing the public goods makes revolution even more likely than at the status quo of 20. The extra public goods help raise the probability of a successful revolution faster than they offset that probability by increasing the value to citizens of the additional benefits they receive. No leader will want to provide public goods in that interval between 20 and 93. But above 93, the value of the added public goods so satisfy people that they no longer have a reason to rebel, even though if they did so they would be in good shape to succeed.

As Figure 9.2 shows, the incumbent regime can either decrease or increase the public-goods provision to diminish the prospects of a citizen revolt. Which approach is chosen has direct implications for whether the incumbent government democratizes or becomes more autocratic. Remember that the mix or proportion of public goods provided compared to private goods is determined by the coalition size. If leader L shifts from providing 20 units of public goods to offering 93 units, then L's public-goods provision relative to private goods (holding the budget constraint fixed) will become out of whack with the size of his or her winning coalition. Twenty units of public goods was the equilibrium amount of such benefits for a small-coalition regime. Ninety-three units are appropriate for a much larger coalition. In our numeric example, a coalition equal to half the size of the selectorate (that is, the governance structure promised by D) provides 100 units of public goods. To be in equilibrium with an increase in public benefits from 20 to 93, the incumbent regime must greatly increase its coalition size—it must democratize.

Of course, we also know from Figure 9.2 that the incumbent can achieve an equivalent reduction in the threat of revolution by decreasing public goods from their initial level of 20 units to something closer to zero. But if public goods are reduced relative to private rewards (again, holding the budget constraint constant), then once again the regime's institutions will become out of whack with the allocation of resources to public and private goods. One solution to this dilemma is for the incumbent L to purge some members of the winning coalition, making the regime more autocratic. This raises the risk of a coup if coalition members get wind of the planned change before it is implemented and becomes a fait accompli. If the incumbent cannot pull off the purge before others get wind of it, then another solution is to keep the government as autocratic as before but sacrifice some personal discretionary spending by putting it toward the relative increase in private rewards that are called for in this scenario. That is never the preferred solution by an incumbent, but it is L's best bet if a purge is likely to trigger a coup.

How do leaders decide whether to solve the threat of revolution by expanding public goods (and their coalition) or contracting public goods? Let's take a look at how revenue from foreign aid and from natural resources (R) influences this choice. Figure 9.3 shows how the leader's welfare changes as the essentially labor-free revenue sources—foreign aid and natural resources—increase as a percentage of national income. Here we see plainly that leaders would rather contract public goods than expand them and that their preference is stronger

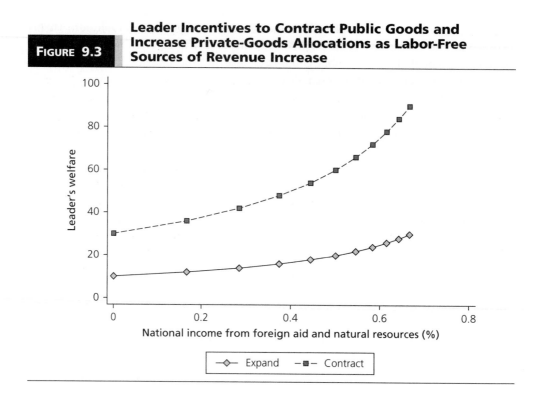

FIGURE 9.3 Leader Incentives to Contract Public Goods and Increase Private-Goods Allocations as Labor-Free Sources of Revenue Increase

when non-tax-based sources of revenue increase. This follows straightforwardly from the logic of selectorate theory. Recall that as coalition size shrinks, as is likely when leaders contract the provision of public goods, the pot of government revenue that is spent at the discretion of the leader increases. That pot of money grows with access to revenue sources such as foreign aid and, if the coalition is made smaller, it also grows because a smaller coalition means a higher tax rate. With regard to foreign aid, it is good to remember also that the odds of getting aid increase as the coalition size decreases, so this source of money is more likely to come the leader's way if he or she contracts public-goods spending.

Note in Figure 9.3 that, any leader's welfare, represented as his or her discretionary pot of money (that is, total revenue minus the coalition-driven expenditures on public and private goods), increases as the share of revenue from foreign aid and natural resources increases. Note also that the incumbent's welfare rises faster if he or she contracts public-goods provision instead of expanding it to ward off the threat of revolution. But, even though contraction is always more appealing to leaders, we also know that there is the risk of a coup if the leader tries to contract the size of the coalition to match the new mix of contracted public goods to private goods being provided. If the risk of a coup is sufficiently large, then expanding the coalition can be the more attractive choice for the incumbent.

Total revenue spent on satisfying coalition members increases as the ratio W/S increases (or the loyalty norm introduced in Chapter 1 weakens). In an unconstrained world, leaders will always choose to contract public goods provision and purge members of their coalition, giving themselves greater security in office and greater control over revenue. But the world is constrained. When faced with a revolutionary threat, we know from Figure 9.2 that leaders can secure their hold on power by either expanding or contracting public goods. We see in Figure 9.3 that, when the regime's revenue stream has little in the way of natural resource income or foreign aid income, which path is chosen to solve the revolutionary threat is a closer call, more likely to be tipped in favor of expansion to avoid instigating a coup threat. The magnitude of the difference in leader welfare gets larger when leaders have more of these resources. The greater benefit that leaders can derive by contracting public goods (and their coalition) when they have a lot of non-labor-based income makes contraction more attractive, increasing the odds that they will become more autocratic. Without those revenue sources, coup avoidance looks more important to leaders because their marginal gain from contracting the coalition (and public goods) is not so great compared to expanding both. Thus, democratization is more likely to be the response to a credible revolutionary threat when leaders have little income from natural resources or from foreign aid.

It turns out that the evidence for this model's logic strongly supports its depressing conclusions. Foreign aid and what economists call the **natural resource curse,** that a country's possession of natural resources that require relatively little labor to convert them into income-producing products (for example, having lots of revenue from oil or gold or diamonds) has the consequence of making a few people rich and many more people poor, stand in the way of democratization. For instance, in autocratic regimes that depend on a very small coalition, Bueno de Mesquita and Smith (2009) report that a 10 percent increase in GNP derived from foreign aid or oil revenue is about equivalent to an 8 percent decrease in the few freedoms that people in such a society have. This is a sad finding but one that is consistent with the logic of the strategic perspective. So, when a donor government purchases policy compliance through foreign aid from a troubled government facing serious popular unrest, it is helping to quash the movement for greater democracy and is indirectly—and probably unwittingly—helping to shore up a petty dictatorship, even helping to make it more dictatorial. This is worth thinking about when we look around the world at troubled regimes—such as those in Zimbabwe, Kenya, and Pakistan—that seek more aid and also contend that they are moving toward democracy. Giving such a regime aid is more likely to stifle any progress in governance than it is to help it.

SUMMARY

Consider what we have discovered. Foreign aid does little to help poor people and may actually make them worse off. In addition, foreign aid makes threatened governments less likely to become more democratic and more likely to become more autocratic, leading either to a worse dictatorship or the instability brought on by a series of coups d'etat. So when world leaders call on their brethren to engage in debt relief—a form of foreign aid—to offset the political instability brought on by a state's debt burden, they are decreasing the odds that the beneficiaries (that is, the petty dictators) will use the aid to improve governance and freedom.

The impact of foreign aid is pernicious. It enriches petty dictators and secures them in office. It buys policy concessions that voters in donor countries value enough to pay for them, but it hurts those who are most in need, the very people that most of us presume are the reason foreign economic assistance is given in the first place. If we want to change this pattern of behavior, we will also have to change our own demands and the incentives of foreign leaders who receive aid. We will have to encourage our government to believe that there are more votes to be had by helping the world's poor than by providing another small benefit at home, and we will need to convince aid recipients that their hold on power is better assured by expanding public-goods provision than by contracting it. That would be a noble outcome, but in a world where altruism seems infrequent, it may prove hard to come by.

KEY CONCEPTS

budget constraint   256
coordination goods   262
foreign aid   247

human capital   250
natural resource curse   271

10 The International Political Economy of Trade

OVERVIEW

- The public debate about globalization pits those who favor free trade against those who favor trade protection and those who see globalization as a way to reward the rich at the expense of the poor against those who see it as a way to narrow the gap between poor and rich.

- Public debate on globalization would be greatly improved if there were a better understanding of the economics and politics of trade.

- Every country has a comparative advantage in some aspect of production, so trade is beneficial between two countries even when one of them can produce any product more cheaply than can the other.

- As consumers, all people benefit from the increased competition and lower prices produced by free trade, but as workers or owners of businesses some people may benefit more than others from free trade and some may be harmed.

- When labor and capital are both mobile, then free trade benefits the workers in poor countries more than the managers or owners in those countries and benefits the owners and managers in rich countries more than it benefits the workers in rich countries.

- Consequently, in a world with complete labor and capital mobility, demands for protection against imports divide along class lines.

- When labor and capital are immobile or one is more mobile than the other, then the mobile factors of production benefit from free trade but the immobile factors do not. This implies that industries with little mobility (because their assets—capital and skilled labor—are not easily adapted to use in other industries) seek protection both for their labor and capital against imports, creating interindustry conflict.

- Less democratic regimes are more likely to resist free trade to protect the government's cronies from competition than are democratic polities.

W orld leaders gathered in Seattle, Washington, on November 29, 1999, for a meeting of the WTO. The purpose of the WTO meeting was to further the process of trade liberalization known as **globalization,** the international process that leads to the worldwide integration of market-driven exchanges in goods, services, and capital.

Thousands of protesters—many peaceful, some violent—also gathered in Seattle in November 1999. They made up a loose coalition of environmentalists, trade unionists, and students opposed to the idea of globalization and to what some perceive as the pro-corporation and antidemocratic processes of the WTO. They were there to stop globalization if they could. Many of these protesters also turned up in Bologna, Italy, in October 2001, once again demonstrating at a WTO meeting in an effort to thwart the discussion of trade liberalization. More recently, there have been fewer antiglobalization protests, which probably has more to do with other international developments (especially war) deflecting the attention of the antiglobalization constituency than with any diminishing concerns over free trade. In fact, with the world's economy in shambles, we probably can expect an upsurge in antiglobalization demonstrations. Certainly, trade protectionism versus free trade and job outsourcing versus keeping jobs within the United States were major themes of the 2008 presidential campaign. People who oppose outsourcing and free trade are taking fundamentally antiglobalization approaches, and people who promote free trade and noninterference with outsourcing are adopting the pro-globalization point of view.

The WTO efforts and the opposition to those efforts raise fundamental questions about trade policy as well as monetary and fiscal policy. As we turn to the issues surrounding trade and currency policies, it is important that we sort out purely the economic matters from those that are political. International trade, whether in goods, services, or money, does, after all, involve both economic and political considerations. Trade occurs between businesses or between individuals and businesses or just between individuals. Typically, governments do not themselves engage directly in much international trade, other than trade in currencies. The role of governments in the international economy involves taxing and regulating cross-border exchanges and guaranteeing contract enforcement through the legal system. In addition, governments monitor compliance with international rules, such as those

Many world leaders believe that free trade ultimately will prove beneficial to international commerce and national economies; others fail to see its upside. Here, a group of farmers cross a toll booth in the town of Tepozotlan on the outskirts of Mexico City, on January 30, 2008. Several farmers groups gathered in Mexico City to protest the lifting of import tariffs on corn and beans as agreed by the North American Free Trade Agreement (NAFTA) timetable.

accepted by the signatories to such international organizations as the WTO; the European Union; NAFTA; and Latin America's Mercosur, a common market agreement among Argentina, Brazil, Paraguay, and Uruguay. When violations are detected, governments may punish the violators. Furthermore, governments provide the essential infrastructure that supports trade.

For instance, there would be much less exchange of goods and services across borders if governments did not provide for reasonably secure and stable currencies and for well-established means to protect the transfer of payments. One common failing of many autocracies, for instance, is that their leaders gain political advantage by manipulating the value of their country's currency. Because autocrats do not provide secure and stable value for their country's money, they are limited in their attractiveness as trading partners and in their ability to entice investors. This is one of several reasons that people who live in such small-coalition regimes are, by and large, poor. Such seemingly mundane government functions as maintaining a credible currency and **currency convertibility,** and facilitating currency exchange and the repatriation of capital while providing an efficient check-clearing mechanism are essential for trade. We cannot understand trade and trade policies without understanding the foundations of economic exchange and the interplay between government and economics, known as **political economy.**

Governments even routinely influence trade over issues not ostensibly about trade. Consider how they use punishment strategies such as trade sanctions to enforce particular norms or preferences about national and international policies that may be unrelated to trade. Punishment through trade sanctions, of course, is not restricted to violations of trade agreements. The U.S. government, for example, has for nearly fifty years severely restricted the opportunity of American citizens and businesses to trade with Cuba in an effort to punish the Cuban government for policies of which many political leaders and well-organized constituents in the United States disapprove. The United States imposes economic sanctions on Iran in the hope that they will cost enough to convince the Iranian government to stop enriching uranium. The international community has also applied trade sanctions—with varying degrees of effectiveness—to Iraq, North Korea, and many other countries from time to time. As we see in the next chapter, it is difficult to use these punishment strategies effectively to alter policies disliked by many in the international community. This is one of the central arenas in which constructivist reasoning fails to account adequately for the persistence of policies adopted by some governments in contradiction to international norms.

Globalization draws our attention to the role that government plays in international trade and to the actions that can be taken to advance or retard movement toward greater trade liberalization. The WTO, established in 1995, is the successor organization to the General Agreement on Tariffs and Trade (GATT). The GATT was one of the international institutions developed in the aftermath of World War II to promote economic recovery and growth. The WTO, like the GATT, is designed to promote international trade and ensure that it flows as smoothly, freely, and predictably as possible. As such, it is the central international organization responsible for monitoring adherence to a free-trade regime, and it has important responsibilities as well regarding the enforcement of the terms of agreement. Its membership includes the vast majority of nations in the world, including the very rich, the very poor, and pretty much every nation in between.

The process of globalization promoted by the WTO and the efforts to stymie it represent fundamental puzzles about the international political economy. These puzzles revolve around the domestic political considerations that influence the degree to which different governments subscribe to globalization and the consequences of violations of or the promotion of free trade. As we go through the political economy behind trade policies, I clarify who wins and who loses if globalization progresses and who wins or loses if globalization is stopped or even reversed. To do this, I offer a brief historical account of globalization, followed by a primer on some critical insights from economics. When those two tasks are completed, we can turn to evaluating currency and trade policies and their ties to politics.

GLOBALIZATION IN HISTORICAL PERSPECTIVE

Globalization is not a new phenomenon, nor is it inevitable. To understand the current debate about globalization, it is useful to begin by considering what the world of commerce was like before the telegraph, the railroad, and perhaps even ships capable of traversing the deep water of the oceans. Strong economic incentives prompted secrecy surrounding navigation routes during the fifteenth and sixteenth centuries, just as corporations protect trade secrets today. If an individual could get goods cheaply in one place (say gold from the Americas) and simultaneously sell them for more in another place—a process called **arbitrage**—then there was a great incentive to keep pertinent information out of the hands of competitors. Arbitrage is a way to equalize prices in different places by increasing the supply of a good where it is scarce (that is, the price is high) and reducing the supply where it is cheap (that is, where supply initially is abundant). It is interesting to realize that price equalization apparently was not terribly different in Europe even in the thirteenth century from what it is today. The difference in prices between England and Holland for eight commodities (barley, butter, cheese, eggs, oats, peas, silver, and wheat) in 1273, as reported by Kenneth Froot, Michael Kim, and Kenneth Rogoff (1997), is comparable to price differences observed across the English Channel in the 1990s. Greater price differences—as in textiles, beer, and wine—provided an impetus for the burgeoning trade in the High Middle Ages. International trade is stimulated by the possibility of buying something at a low price in one place and selling it for a higher price in another. But this stimulus to trade and price equalization can be and often is stymied by government intervention.

Price differences can be sustained as long as a comparable product cannot be produced competitively in the buyer's locale. As the cost of moving goods from one location to another drops, competition from imports, if unregulated by government or by collusion among the domestic competitors of the imports, ensures that prices will fall, making access to the goods available to a broader segment of society. If the goods are significantly more expensive in one market than in another, more supply will flow to the higher-priced market. The ensuing competition—again, if unregulated by government or by collusion—brings the price down until it is comparable (controlling for differences in shipping costs and product quality) in different markets. This pressure toward comparable prices spreads farther and farther from the point of production as the costs of shipping, storage, and information about goods and services falls, provided government does not intervene to maintain a price differential. The expected price convergence is an important feature of globalization, and it is a feature we experience in our everyday lives.

Consider an example. If I know that I can buy television sets in Tokyo for much less than I can buy comparable ones in San Francisco, then I have an incentive to go to Tokyo, buy lots of television sets, and bring them to San Francisco to sell at the much higher price. That is, I export television sets from Japan and import them into the United States. As long as the San Francisco price is sufficiently high so that the cost of going to Tokyo and bringing television sets back still leaves me with a large profit margin, I will want to take advantage of the opportunity. But others who know about the price difference will also want to pursue this opportunity, and they will have an incentive to sell the television sets for less than I do so that buyers go to them instead of me. I, of course, will respond to this competition by reducing my price, as long as selling remains profitable. This process will resolve quickly at a price that is comparable to the cost of television sets in Tokyo, adjusted for the transportation costs involved in getting them to the San Francisco market and differences in the quality or reliability of service offered by different vendors. This is, in fact, exactly what has happened over the years as shipping costs have dropped and as information about prices in different parts of the world has spread and become common knowledge. Indeed, one of the most important consequences of the growth of the Internet is that information about the price of goods is available to anyone with access to the Internet. So, too, is information about the reliability of different online sellers. As a result, it is possible to purchase goods at low prices on the Web, which, in turn, forces shops to reduce their prices (subject to their advantages in providing service and in sometimes being more reliable than Internet shopping).

Innumerable examples of price convergence are readily available. Think about the availability of Hong Kong pearls, New Zealand lamb, Swedish automobiles, Mexican tomatoes, Egyptian cotton, English marmalade, French wine, clothing manufactured in Sri Lanka or China, online medical billing services in India, electronics assembled in El Salvador, movies from Italy, and other goods and services available in the American market. Think about American products, including television programming, movies, McDonald's hamburgers, Intel computer chips, Boeing airplanes, management consulting services, soybeans, wheat, Caterpillar earth moving equipment, and on and on, that are available in much of the world marketplace.

A similar story could be told about English textile exports to the European continent in the Middle Ages and the English importation of French wine, Asian spices, and so forth during the same period. When and where trade was unrestricted, goods were exported and imported, prices fell, and consumers had a greater variety of choices. As the economist John

Maynard Keynes aptly observed of the nineteenth century—a period of rapid progress toward globalization—compared to the world following the start of World War I:

> What an extraordinary episode in the progress of man that age which came to an end in August 1914! ... The inhabitant of London could order by telephone, sipping his morning tea in bed, the various products of the whole earth.... he could at the same time and by the same means adventure his wealth in the natural resources and new enterprise of any quarter of the world. (Keynes 1920, 11)

The onset of World War I led to a great expansion in protectionism. Although there certainly were many tariffs and other restrictions on free trade in the nineteenth century and before, the degree of protectionism in trade expanded mightily during the years between the two world wars. Indeed, one of the factors that exacerbated the Great Depression (which began in 1929 and did not end until the onset of World War II) was the decision by the U.S. Congress to pass the Smoot-Hawley Tariff Act in 1930. This legislation imposed the highest level of tariff protection on behalf of American industry in the history of the United States. Import duties (that is, taxes on imports) increased from 39 to 53 percent. The bill was intended to insulate American farm products and manufactured goods from stiff foreign competition. The idea was to improve the lot of American workers and business owners who were suffering from the onset of the Depression. In response to American protectionism, other countries passed retaliatory tariffs. Just as American politicians sought to protect their constituents from foreign competition, so too did foreign leaders try to protect their own constituents from American competition.

Rather than easing the economic pressures from competition, the cycle of protective tariffs severely deepened and extended the Depression, pushing unemployment to record heights. By 1932, 13 million American workers (out of a total population of about 123 million) were unemployed, up from 3 million in January 1930, six months before the passage of the Smoot-Hawley bill. American unemployment eventually rose to 30 percent of the workforce. At the same time, trade plummeted, falling about two-thirds between 1929 and 1933. Let's hope that today's politicians, facing the understandable frustration of their constituents during a long and deep economic downturn, will not make the mistakes of their Smoot-Hawley predecessors. Doing so will just prolong economic suffering on Main Street, as we will see.

Attitudes toward protectionism underwent a sea change after the end of World War II. The U.S. government gradually emerged as a proponent of free trade. To be sure, the United States tried, and still tries, to protect many of its industries, but the depth and breadth of tariff protection began to diminish. By the late 1970s and early 1980s, the degree of global freedom from tariffs had reached very high levels. Globalization, retarded from 1914 to 1945, was moving forward again. In 1950, about 7 percent of world production was exported; in 2008, about 25 percent of world production was exported. With these facts in mind, we are now ready to explore the ways in which this trend toward renewed globalization is beneficial or harmful.

AN ECONOMICS PRIMER: COMPARATIVE ADVANTAGE, SUPPLY, AND DEMAND

As mentioned, globalization depends on market-driven exchanges. By *market-driven* I mean exchanges that are determined by supply and demand for goods, services, and capital unconstrained by government regulation, with the exception of credible government commitments to the rule of law, property rights, currency guarantees, and the adjudication and enforcement of voluntary contracts between buyers and sellers. I add these caveats regarding property rights, rule of law, currency guarantees, and enforcement of contracts because without performing these fundamental functions government fails to ensure that competition is fair in the marketplace. These conditions are, in essence, the domestic analog of national security; without them, society would be run by bullies. They are among the domestic guarantors of life, liberty, and the pursuit of happiness (or, as John Locke put it, the pursuit of property).

Comparative Advantage

A good place to begin our economics primer is with a discussion of comparative advantage. This concept, first rigorously demonstrated by the English economist David Ricardo in the early nineteenth century, is fundamental to understanding trade and to understanding why a country (or a company or a worker) gains from trade even if it is not the best in making anything. To understand comparative advantage, it is necessary to see how it differs from absolute advantage. By grasping this distinction, we can gain critical insights into the fundamentals behind how and why competition works to produce economic efficiency, trade, and prosperity. We can also understand why, even if a country is not better than any other at anything, it still stands to benefit more from free trade than from trade protectionism.

Imagine two countries, say the United States and India. The United States produces airplanes at a lower cost than India does, whereas India designs computer software more cheaply than the United States. It makes sense, then, for people in America to buy computer software designed in India and for people in India to buy airplanes from the United States. In fact, India buys many airplanes from the American firm Boeing, and India is a large exporter of software programs to the American market. These countries could have an **absolute advantage** in what they produce; that is, they produce these goods and services for a price that is lower than any other country can. Trading one country's relatively cheaper good for the other country's relatively cheaper good leads to gains from trade for both the United States and India. Yet neither the United States nor India nor other countries necessarily choose to focus their efforts on making all the things in which they have an absolute advantage. What is more, not every country (or every individual) has an absolute advantage; that is, not every country (or individual) is the best at doing or making something. Absolute advantage is nice to have, but it is insufficient for us to grasp what different countries produce, buy, and sell.

Let me begin the discussion of comparative advantage with a prosaic, personal example. Then I will turn to a more careful statement of the idea. It just so happens that I type very

TABLE 10.1	Labor Productivity in Making Wine and Cloth		
Country	Available labor-hours	Hours needed to make 1 unit of wine	Hours needed to make 1 unit of cloth
Portugal	12	1	2
England	12	6	3

fast, about seventy words per minute (with just two fingers, I might add). Some professional typists do not type as quickly and accurately as I do, yet I do not choose to compete for their jobs. I do not specialize in typing because, even if I have an absolute advantage in typing skills, it is not my **comparative advantage**; it is not the activity that maximizes my income or other aspects of my well-being, and so I do not specialize in it. This is the kernel of comparative advantage. Resources are put to use in the way that maximizes their return. People specialize in what they are *comparatively* better at even if others are absolutely better than they are at the particular skill. I may be a better typist than many typists, but still they specialize in typing and I do not.

Ricardo provided a clear and useful example of comparative advantage in his book *On the Principles of Political Economy and Taxation,* published in 1817. I use his basic example here because it remains pertinent today. Imagine that England and Portugal each produce two goods, cloth and wine. Furthermore, imagine that the only input (that is, the only resource) in production is labor (ignoring for now raw materials, capital with which to process the raw materials, and so forth). Let us further assume that how much output each worker produces (that is, the productivity of labor) varies both from industry to industry (cloth vs. wine) and between England and Portugal. To make a sharp distinction between absolute advantage and comparative advantage, let us also assume—as Ricardo does—that Portugal has an absolute advantage over England in the production of both cloth and wine. Table 10.1 provides a numerical example of the assumptions that I use throughout this discussion.

It is clear from Table 10.1 that Portugal's labor productivity in making both wine and cloth is higher than England's. Fewer hours of labor are needed in Portugal to produce a unit of cloth (say, a yard of cloth) or a unit of wine (say, a bottle of wine) than in England. This is how we know that Portugal has an absolute advantage in the production of both goods. Can a wine and cloth trade still take place between England and Portugal when Portugal is better at making both cloth and wine than England is? How can England gain from trade in this circumstance? What will the Portuguese buy from England when they both can produce the same two products and Portugal produces both products more efficiently and, in this example, there are no other products? Ricardo's analysis of comparative advantage nicely shows us that trade will take place and that it makes sense for England to specialize in the production of one of the goods and for Portugal to specialize in the production of the other.

FIGURE 10.1	The Production Possibility Frontiers for Portugal and England

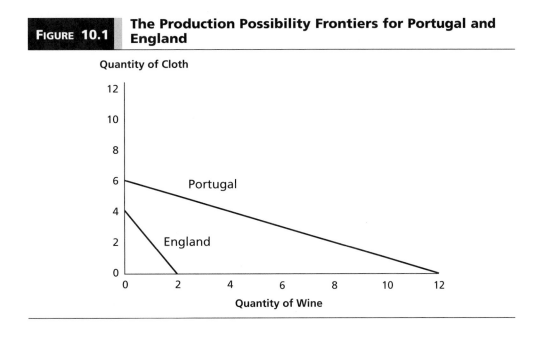

Furthermore, he shows that total world output of both goods could rise through such specialization. Indeed, he shows that with free trade and with the right terms of trade—that is, the amount of one good traded for the other—both England and Portugal could end up with more of each good through specialization than they would have in the absence of trade.

How should England and Portugal go about determining which good to specialize in? Random selection will not do. Rather, each should specialize in the good in which the country enjoys a comparative advantage in production. To figure out which good each country has a comparative advantage in, we must compare the **opportunity cost** each pays in producing cloth and in producing wine. The opportunity cost, a concept introduced briefly earlier in this book, evaluates how much of the other good is given up when a country chooses to focus its resources on the good being produced. That is, it is not how much labor or how much money it costs to produce a good that determines the good in which a country has comparative advantage in production; the opportunity costs are the key. The information in Table 10.1 is used in Figure 10.1 to discover in which good each country has a comparative advantage. Figure 10.1 plots what is called the **production possibility frontier,** that is, the maximum amount of goods that England or Portugal can produce given the available resources (labor in this case) and the cost of production. The cost of production in this case is the amount of labor needed to make a unit of cloth or a unit of wine. To calculate the production possibility frontier, we solve the following two equations:

Quantity of wine = (Available labor/Hours of labor needed to make 1 unit of wine) − [(Hours needed to make 1 unit of cloth/Hours needed to make 1 unit of wine) × Quantity of cloth];

Quantity of cloth = (Available labor/Hours of labor needed to make 1 unit of cloth) − [(Hours needed to make 1 unit of wine/Hours needed to make 1 unit of cloth) × Quantity of wine].

To solve the first equation, assume that no cloth is made (Quantity of cloth = 0). To solve the second, assume that no wine is produced (Quantity of wine = 0). Then, the production possibility frontier is the line that joins the points (Quantity of wine, 0 cloth) and (0 wine, Quantity of cloth). We find that for Portugal the solution to the first equation equals 12 units of wine (when there is no cloth produced), and the solution to the second equation is 6 units of cloth (when there is no wine produced). Of course, given the trade-off between labor and production, Portugal can produce any amount of wine and cloth that falls on or below the line graphing its production possibility frontier. The production possibility frontier, after all, specifies the maximum mix of production if all available labor is used (that is, there is full employment). For England the comparable values are 4 units of cloth (when there is no wine produced) and 2 units of wine (when there is no cloth produced).

Several factors are noteworthy in Figure 10.1. If England produces only cloth and Portugal produces only wine, then the market will have 12 units of wine and 4 units of cloth. If, instead, England specializes in wine production and Portugal specializes in cloth production, then there will be only 2 units of wine and 6 units of cloth in the marketplace. This will be better for cloth consumers—more product in general means lower prices—but it will not be in the interest of Portugal's producers to specialize in cloth by sacrificing their opportunity in the wine trade. Because they can make so much more wine than cloth, they have a greater opportunity to consume what they need at home and export the rest overseas when it comes to wine than when it comes to cloth. Thus, although cloth buyers will have more choice if Portugal specializes in cloth production, the total number of goods—cloth and wine—in the marketplace will drop, and that will make the average consumer worse off because the average consumer will want to buy a mix of goods, not just one type of good.

Suppose England and Portugal both decide to try to be self-sufficient; that is, they each produce both cloth and wine. Then, if each country applies equal labor to each product, the market will have 7 units of wine (6 Portuguese and 1 English) and 5 units of cloth (3 Portuguese and 2 English). For the market, this is a gain of 1 unit of cloth over what will be available if Portugal produces only wine and England only cloth. But to gain that 1 unit of cloth, the market (that is, consumers) pay a big price—they lose the production of 5 units of wine. The total quantity of products made (16; that is, 12 units of wine and 4 units of cloth) is greatest when England specializes in cloth production and Portugal specializes in wine production. That's the best circumstance for consumers—they have the most goods available, which, as we will see, reduces prices—and for producers.

We can see the opportunity costs from alternative production decisions by examining the slopes of the production possibility frontiers. Although Portugal has an absolute advantage in both goods, as seen by the fact that its production possibility frontier is always higher than England's (we assume equal labor pools), its slope is flatter, and England's is steeper, as we move from fewer units of wine production to more units of wine production. This tells us that Portugal has a comparative advantage in wine production and England has one in cloth production. For instance, we can see that, for England, giving up each additional unit of wine production to make cloth leads to more cloth (at a ratio of 2 units of cloth for every 1 unit of wine given up), hence the steeper slope of the line. Looking at the Portuguese production possibility frontier, we see that giving up cloth to make wine is most efficient for Portugal but that the relative gain is greater for England (that is why the slope is steeper) than it is for Portugal even though Portugal has an absolute advantage in the production of wine and cloth. By each country's specializing in the product in which it has a comparative advantage, labor is used most productively to yield the greatest quantity of goods in the global market.

As we have seen, England must calculate how much wine production it must give up to make cloth and how much cloth manufacture it must give up to make wine, the very calculation facilitated by Figure 10.1. These trade-offs between wine and cloth production are the relevant opportunity costs. Portugal must, of course, make the same calculation. England has a comparative advantage in cloth production relative to Portugal provided that the amount of wine production it must give up to make one more unit of cloth is smaller than the amount of wine production that Portugal has to give up to make an additional unit of cloth. We can see that this is true in Figure 10.1. Draw a line at a right angle to the horizontal axis at 1 unit of wine production so that it just touches the production possibility frontier for England. Draw another line at a right angle to the vertical axis so that it just touches the

TRY THIS

Construct an example in which both cloth production and wine production are greater with specialization than without it. Draw the production possibility frontiers for the example you chose. Imagine that a poor country has a comparative advantage in labor and a rich country has an absolute advantage both in labor (that is, labor has a higher productivity than in the poor country) and in capital. Does it still make sense for the rich country to import labor-intensive goods from the poor country and for the poor country to import capital-intensive goods from the rich country? Can you find examples of such exchanges between the United States and Mexico or between other relatively rich and relatively poor countries?

English production possibility frontier at the same point as the perpendicular line from the horizontal axis. Notice that producing 1 unit of wine in England is equivalent to producing 2 units of cloth. If England does not produce that 1 unit of wine, then, as its production possibility frontier shows us, it will produce 4 units of cloth (That is, when wine production = 0, cloth production in England = 4; when wine production = 1, cloth production = 2). Repeat this process for Portugal and you will see that to go from 5 units of cloth to 6, a gain of 1 as in the English example, Portugal would have to give up 2 units of wine. Thus, England has comparative advantage on cloth production even though Portugal makes both wine and cloth more cheaply than does England in terms of the cost of labor (and capital).

Each country has a comparative advantage in the production of some good or goods (or services). By pursuing its comparative advantage, each country benefits through specialization and trade. Portugal, in our example, has a comparative advantage in wine production. By specializing in wine production, it frees up resources that would have been used by it *relatively inefficiently* in making cloth. And because England has the comparative advantage in making cloth, it avoids the opportunity cost of spending resources on wine production that could be better used by it to make cloth. Both Portugal and England, then, focus their resources on the use that yields the greatest productivity—the most efficient use—thereby pursuing their comparative advantage. This is just the same as my decision to be a professor rather than a typist.

Sometimes a country (or an individual manufacturer) has both an absolute advantage and a comparative advantage in producing one good over another (as with Portugal and wine production). There is no problem or contradiction in saying that a country's absolute advantage can turn out also to be its comparative advantage, but it is not necessary for the two advantages to be the same. Some people apparently believe that to benefit from trade a country has to be the best at making something. Those who hold this view believe that an exporter cannot be competitive unless it is better than any other exporter in the production of its product or service. Those who hold this belief are confusing absolute advantage with comparative advantage.

Comparative advantage teaches a fundamental lesson about trade, a lesson that is especially pertinent in debates about globalization. It makes clear that gains from trade follow from specialization. It is not necessary to be best at anything to gain from trade. By specializing in the production of its comparative advantage (that is, the goods that reflect the lowest opportunity cost to the maker) an exporter will gain from trade even if another exporter is absolutely better at making the product. Remember, I might be better than others at typing, but I do not sell this skill in the market for typists because my comparative advantage lies elsewhere.

Every country has a comparative advantage in something even though it may not have an absolute advantage. As Figure 10.1 makes clear, by specializing in its comparative advantage, England (the absolutely disadvantaged country) benefits and so does Portugal. More English labor is employed making cloth, and more Portuguese labor produces wine. And consumers in each country have a larger supply of cloth and wine available for purchase, so they are better off.

Supply and Demand

Supply and demand together establish the **equilibrium price** for goods, services, or capital in a market. Producers seek to maximize their total profit; profit is simply the difference between the total costs of production and the price garnered for the goods (or services)

FIGURE 10.2   Supply and Demand

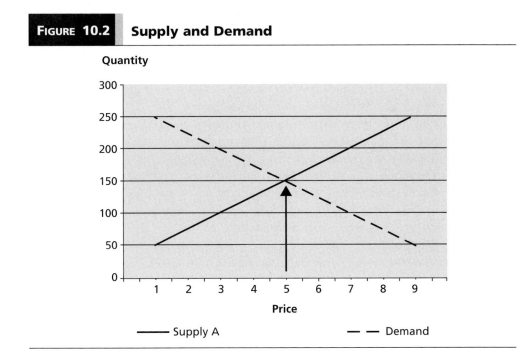

Quantity

Price

———— Supply A   — — Demand

produced. Producers produce until the additional revenue (price times quantity) from the *n*th unit just equals the cost of production for that unit; that is, until the marginal profit equals zero. This determines the amount of the good they supply. If they produce more, they start to lose money; if they produce less, they leave money in people's pockets that could have been theirs.

Producers naturally would like to charge the highest price they can for their goods, and they will stop producing when the marginal cost* exceeds the price they can get for it. The problem they face in pricing is that, as the price for goods or services (or capital and so forth) increases, demand falls. In plain English, we consumers buy less when the price is high than we do when it is low. So, producers want as high a price as they can get, but, as the Rolling Stones remind us, "You can't always get what you want." This leads to the well-known relationship between supply and demand illustrated in Figure 10.2.

In Figure 10.2 we see the relationship between the quantity of goods (or services or capital or many other things—let's call them widgets) that a producer is prepared to supply and the quantity of widgets that buyers demand (that is, are willing to purchase) at different prices.

---

* The marginal cost is the cost of making the next unit of the good given the cost of the inputs needed to make that next unit, where the inputs include factors such as fixed expenses (for example, machinery and rent) and variable costs (for example, the price of materials and labor).

The **supply curve** shows how producers respond (the quantity supplied) to changing prices, provided that the cost of additional production does not exceed the price. The **demand curve** is, equivalently, the response curve for consumers to changing prices. Each curve is assumed to be independently determined, the price of the good—widgets, in this case—being determined endogenously by the interaction of the two curves, as discussed shortly.

For convenience, let us treat the prices shown in the figure as dollars, although they could be denominated in any currency and any amount of money. As noted, producers will make widgets up to the point at which the marginal cost of producing one more widget equals the marginal gain from that one extra widget, that is, up to the point at which there is no more profit to extract from making another widget. Once the cost exceeds the benefit, producers will not want to make more widgets. A similar argument can be made for buyers. This naturally implies that more widgets can be made if they sell for a higher price than if they sell for a lower price, all else (for example, costs) being equal.

In Figure 10.2, we see that suppliers are willing to sell 200 widgets at a price of $7.00 per widget. Buyers, however, will purchase only 100 widgets if they sell for $7.00 each. There is not much point in supplying so many more widgets than the market demands because it is costly to do so. With a surplus supply (that is, the amount of supply in excess of demand) of 100 widgets (200 supplied minus 100 demanded at $7.00 per widget), widget sellers have a strong incentive to reduce the price in order to sell their inventory of unsold widgets rather than paying to store it and tying up capital. Conversely, if widgets sold for just $1.00, there would be surplus demand;. there would be demand for 250 widgets, but there would be only 50 widgets supplied in the marketplace. The shortage of widgets would lead buyers to compete for the scarce supply, pushing the price up.

By observing where the supply and demand curves cross one another, we can estimate just how many widgets will be bought and sold and at what price. The equilibrium between supply and demand arises when the quantity supplied equals the quantity demanded so that there is neither a surplus demand pushing the price up nor a surplus supply pushing the price down. The equilibrium price is the price for which widgets sell at this intersection of supply and demand. In Figure 10.2, supply equals demand for 150 widgets at a price of $5.00 per widget. The arrow shows the equilibrium price. Reading across horizontally from the top of the arrow, we see the equilibrium quantity supplied and demanded at that price.

The world of Figure 10.2 has no government intervention to alter the price of goods. In such a world, trade presumably is limited only by the cost of getting goods from one place to another. In fact, economists have constructed what is called the gravity model of trade. This model seeks to provide a baseline estimate of how much trade is expected between any pair of countries assuming no government restrictions. It says that trade is inversely related to the distance between the countries and is proportional to the product of their sizes. That is, all else being equal, countries that are far apart are less likely to trade with one another than are countries that are close together. For example, Mexico is the third largest trading partner of the United States, and Canada is the largest. Furthermore, the larger the countries

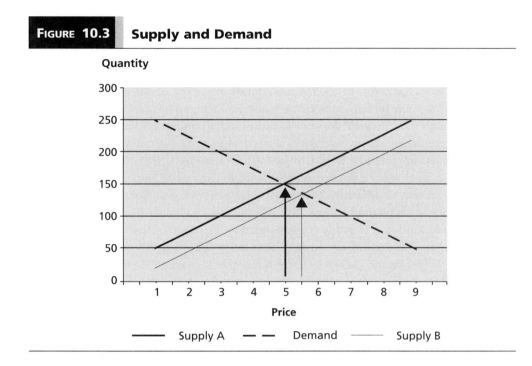

FIGURE 10.3   Supply and Demand

Quantity

Price

——— Supply A   — — Demand   ——— Supply B

are (in economic size), the greater the trade expected between them. U.S.-Chinese trade reflects this size aspect of the gravity model, with total trade between the United States and China just slightly larger than that between Mexico and the United States in 2007.

This simple apolitical model does pretty well at accounting for trade levels, but much still remains to be explained. In fact, much of what remains depends on domestic political pressure for governments to intervene in international trade. To see how politics can intrude on supply, demand, prices, and trade, let us consider what happens if the government imposes a purely domestic tax on the production of widgets. To illustrate the effect of this tax, in Figure 10.3 I have relabeled the original supply curve from Figure 10.2 Supply A and show a second supply curve, called Supply B, that shows the availability of widgets at selling prices given a government tax on production. As we can see in Figure 10.3, the supply of widgets decreases when there is a tax on their production. That is, Supply B is shifted down from the untaxed Supply A curve. Recall that producers produce up to the point at which marginal gains and marginal costs are equal. The government's tax increases the costs that the producer pays for making widgets. Because suppliers produce until the marginal cost of the nth unit equals the marginal revenue for that unit, the added cost from the tax is passed on to consumers; this leads to a higher price, which decreases demand. In Figure 10.3, we see how the cost of the tax is passed on to consumers. Without the tax (Supply A), 150 widgets cost $5.00 each, but with the tax (Supply B), the same amount cost $6.00 each.

By examining the intersections of the supply lines and the demand curve, we can see the economic consequences of the government's tax. Whereas without the tax, 150 widgets are produced and sold at a price of $5.00 each (intersection with Supply A; see the dark arrow), with the tax, about 136 widgets are made and sold for about $5.50 each (intersection with Supply B; see the lighter arrow to find the new equilibrium price). In other words, consumers are worse off. Assuming that producers are initially producing widgets at the efficient market price, then the tax must increase the price to consumers, lowering demand and forcing producers to reduce the equilibrium supply. The result is fewer widgets at a higher price than before the tax was imposed.

Suppose we now redefine the two supply curves in Figure 10.3. Let us say that the two supply curves reflect two different sets of producers, A and B (instead of the same producer with and without a tax on production). The widgets produced by both sets of producers are the same quality. Producers in group A, represented by Supply A (the darker line), can profitably produce more widgets at a given price than can producers in group B, represented by Supply B (the lighter line). That is why curve A is higher than curve B.

Imagine that A represents all foreign producers of widgets and B reflects domestic producers (or reverse the order, if you prefer). The foreign producers A apparently have lower costs of production than do the domestic suppliers B. That is, the foreign producers are more efficient in supplying widgets than are their domestic competitors. Clearly, consumers will prefer to buy the less expensive foreign-produced widgets. Up to 150 foreign widgets can be bought for just $5.00 each. To buy 150 domestic widgets, consumers will have to pay $6.00 each. As we can see in Figure 10.3, at $6.00 each, there is enough demand for only 125 domestic widgets. At the domestic equilibrium price of $5.50, only 136 widgets will be sold. As long as foreign widgets are on the market, consumers presumably will buy the cheaper, foreign-made product.

TRY THIS

Find out the cost of making shirts in Sri Lanka or China or India compared to making them in the United States? Does this help explain why so much clothing is made for American companies in foreign countries? Pick three or four other goods or services and see if you can estimate how much off-shore production is stimulated mostly by the quantity that can be supplied at a given price and how much by tax advantages derived from producing outside the United States. Would you, as a consumer, be better off if tariffs (taxes on imports) were increased or if U.S. taxes on production were increased or decreased?

Domestic producers are likely to find their situation extremely disturbing. Because of their relative inefficiency, they cannot compete as long as the imported widgets enjoy their price advantage. Domestic widget workers and manufacturers both have incentives to put pressure on the government to exclude foreign widgets from the market, especially if they cannot easily switch jobs or change their business. Even though the domestic producer does not seem to have a comparative advantage in producing widgets, the workers and owners in that industry understandably want to keep their jobs (and so do the politicians who represent them). The domestic producers and workers have votes or other forms of political support to offer government leaders in exchange for help. The government can help by providing the domestic widget industry with an equal chance to sell its widgets by imposing on foreign producers a tax, known as a **tariff.** If the tariff charged on all imported widgets is priced just right, then the domestic and foreign producers will be in the same boat. The foreign producers' supply curve (A) will shift down until it sits right on top of domestic producers' curve (B), depriving A of its efficiency advantage. Consumers will pay an average of $5.50 per widget and will be indifferent between domestic- and foreign-made widgets. If the tariff is set higher, so that the cost of foreign production plus the tax on importation is greater than the domestic cost of production without a tax, then curve A will shift down until it is below curve B. Under these conditions, consumers will buy only domestic widgets, presumably driving the foreign producers out of the domestic market. Probably the domestic widget industry will lobby for a tariff that high so that it can corner the domestic market and not have to compete with imports.

The consequence of a tariff imposed on foreign widgets is twofold: domestic consumers who buy widgets pay more than they would have paid without the tariff protection, and people employed in the domestic widget industry are insulated from the effects of competition. Insulating the industry from competition reduces the incentive for domestic suppliers to become more efficient and so heightens the risk that the industry will need long-term protection. This can have the effect of weakening still further the buyer demand in the economy if the indifference curves of supply and demand are not straight lines as in Figures 10.2 and 10.3. If buyers, for example, have a strong need for widgets—that is, they have a relatively inelastic demand—so that their demand does not drop much as the price increases, then the tariff takes dollars out of the consumer economy that might otherwise have gone to purchase other products.[†] That is, the extra money spent on tariff-protected widgets ($0.50 per widget) is money that can no longer be used to buy other goods and services. Therefore, although domestic widget makers do better, workers in other, unprotected parts of the economy suffer a loss due to the diminished purchasing power created by the tariff. So, the tariff rewards some domestic workers at the expense of other domestic workers, those who don't get protected by politicians.

> **TRY THIS**
>
> Examine Figure 10.3. How many widgets will buyers want to purchase at $3.50 per widget? How many can the suppliers in group A provide at $3.50? How many can the suppliers in group B provide at $3.50? Make the same comparisons if the price is $8.00 per widget. What will happen to supply, demand, and the equilibrium price if the government imposes a tax on buyers (such as a sales tax or a value-added tax)?

[†] It is worth noting that elasticities (of demand or supply) are evaluated as the momentary slopes of the supply and demand curves. Thus, the elasticity of demand or supply can change constantly, depending on the point on the curve at which the situation is located. Notice that, if the curve is linear, elasticities are constant and equal the slope of the curve.

The examples we have discussed so far seem rather simple. Nevertheless, taken together, they tell a fundamental story. In the first example, in which there is no government intervention in the widget industry, supply responds only to price. Likewise, there is consumer demand for widgets, and consumers who need or want widgets respond only to price. The preference of producers is to sell more widgets as long as doing so remains profitable. This means that if producers increase prices, as long as this does not result in diminishing marginal returns, they will produce more widgets. The interest of consumers is to buy widgets at a low price, so they will buy more widgets as the price drops. Thus, widgets are bought and sold at the efficient, market price.

In the second and third examples, government action is added to the story. The government imposes a tax either on all producers or on certain, more efficient producers (which, in the example, happen to be foreign producers of widgets; the tax is, then, a tariff on importation designed to nullify their comparative advantage). When the government enters the picture, consumers can end up being worse off in at least three ways: the price of widgets—but not their quality—increases; widgets become scarcer so widgets are harder to come by in shops; and fewer dollars might remain to buy other goods and services after extra money is spent on widgets, thereby harming other parts of the economy. The government's intervention in both examples leads the price to rise from $5.00 to about $5.50 and the supply to drop from 150 to about 136. This is the direct consequence of government intervention in a properly operating, competitive market.

Naturally, in the real world there sometimes are good reasons for government intervention. Some of these are discussed later in this chapter. In the example with tariffs, the reason for government intervention is to protect a domestic producer from the competition arising from more efficient foreign producers. There may be good *political* reasons for doing so. It is a greater stretch to make the case that there are good *economic* reasons. In fact, virtually all economists agree that free trade improves economic well-being in the aggregate, although, of course, for some workers and industries free trade represents a deadweight loss[‡] in personal welfare. And sometimes government interference in the market serves to protect other important political principles, such as national security, rather than just winning votes.

Still, in the aggregate—that is, on average—welfare is improved by free trade. There are, however, winners and losers. Who they are, and under what circumstances, is fundamental to understanding the arguments for and against globalization. You might make a note now of who you think gains and who you think loses from free trade. You may be surprised by the answer as it unfolds later in this chapter.

TRADE AS A PUBLIC OR PRIVATE GOOD

If we treat widget production and consumption as indicative of all production and consumption, then we can see that the absence of government intervention in trade (or, put positively, governmental assurance of free trade) is a public good. Everyone is a consumer,

---

[‡] A *deadweight loss* is essentially a loss without any offsetting benefit or compensation to those experiencing it.

and therefore everyone derives a benefit from the lower prices that arise without tariffs. Equally, it is important to note that tariffs act as private goods, benefiting (in our example) domestic widget makers (both the domestic companies and domestic workers that make widgets) at the expense of more efficient foreign competitors and of domestic consumers (and possibly the producers of other products, depending on the elasticity of supply and demand). For many years, for instance, India kept Boeing aircraft out of its domestic market to protect airplanes made by Hindustan Aeronautics, a domestic aircraft maker. Clearly, the trade protection helped the workers and owners in that company but at the expense of anyone with the resources to fly in India. Likewise, India protected its domestic aluminum industry, providing a private gain for those associated with aluminum manufacture there but at the expense of hundreds of millions of people who were compelled to buy relatively low-quality Indian aluminum cookware at inflated, tariff-protected prices.

Tariffs or **fair trade,** as such policies are sometimes labeled, are classic private goods subject to many of the political considerations discussed in the context of the selectorate theory. Unregulated trade is a public good that is likewise subject to the political considerations addressed in that same theory. It should be evident that free trade benefits many, whereas fair trade benefits only a few. For the few, of course, the benefit from tariffs may outweigh the value of the public benefit that everyone gets from free trade. Presumably, if no one benefited more from trade protection than from free trade (that is, if the public-goods benefit outweighed the private-goods component for everyone), then there would be no tariffs or other means of making imports less competitive. In this regard, we should note that tariffs arise for more than one reason. Tariffs can be used to protect domestic industries from competition, as is commonly the case, but they can also be used to punish foreign governments that do not observe free-trade policies in their own right. President George W. Bush justified his call for a tariff on certain steel products in March 2002 by alleging unfair trade practices by Japan and Europe designed to bolster their steel industries at the expense of American industry. They countered—apparently correctly, given how readily the United States negotiated a resolution favorable to Europe's and Japan's steel industries—by threatening retaliatory tariffs to compel the United States to enforce its free-trade obligations under the WTO.

In all these cases, domestic political considerations seem to be behind the use of tariffs as foreign policy maneuvers. One of the central concerns in this chapter is to answer the questions: Why do tariffs exist, and who benefits from them and who is harmed by them? Answering these questions will take us a long way to understanding why some people are enthusiastic about globalization and others remain adamantly opposed to it.

In thinking about globalization and trade policy, we should think expansively. For example, currencies are traded in much the same way that cars, apples, consulting, or other products and services are traded. The number of Japanese yen it takes to buy an American dollar or a British pound fluctuates all the time as the supply and demand for dollars, pounds, yen, and other currencies rise and fall. Globalization raises questions about fiscal and monetary policies that may influence exchange rates and the associated cost to people in developing countries who want or need to buy baby formula and drugs to treat acquired immunode-ficiency syndrome (AIDS) or to prevent polio, malaria, and the like. These concerns are certainly warranted, although the proposed solutions too often reflect an inadequate under-standing of either the economics or the politics of trade. Let me first touch on currency policy to help clarify how different national currency strategies influence globalization before turning to the consequences of free trade in general.

CURRENCY, EXCHANGE RATES, AND INTERNATIONAL POLITICAL ECONOMY

Governments can adopt a variety of methods of supplying and otherwise regulating the value of their currency. The quantity of one currency that it takes to buy a unit of another currency is the **exchange rate** of those currencies. For instance, the exchange rate for converting U.S. dollars to euros was $1.27 in February 2009. That is, it cost $1.27 to buy 1 euro. There are several ways to determine the exchange rate between currencies. One strategy is to allow a currency to **float**; that is, the exchange rate is allowed to fluctuate in response to the supply and demand for money. The American dollar, for instance, floats in the world market; the value of the American dollar relative to the British pound, the euro, the yen, the Mexican peso, the Australian dollar, and many other currencies constantly changes in response to the supply and demand for those currencies and for American dollars. You can readily find the exchange rates quoted every day on the financial pages of major newspapers or on the Internet.

The dollar has not always floated. For instance, before President Nixon abandoned the Bretton Woods agreement in 1971, the dollar was set to a fixed exchange rate linked to gold. The U.S. government guaranteed to give anyone $35 in exchange for 1 ounce of gold. This meant that the U.S. government could not print more money without having the gold on hand to back it up. Fixed exchange rates are another way to regulate and stabilize currency. When President Nixon broke the link between dollars and gold and allowed the dollar's value to fluctuate in the world market, the dollar's value sank dramatically. After a short while, it took more than $350 to buy 1 ounce of gold. What does such a devaluation mean in the context of international relations?

To address this question let us look at the relationship between the U.S. dollar and the Japanese yen. Over the past several years, the dollar and the yen have fluctuated dramatically. The range of yen needed to buy a dollar has varied, roughly, from 90 to 140 during the past decade. When more yen are needed to buy $1, the dollar is stronger—that is, it is worth more—than when fewer yen are needed to buy $1. This fluctuation influences trade and the balance of payments between countries.

Suppose a Honda made in Japan sells for ¥3 million or, equivalently, $25,000 at $1 = ¥120. If the dollar strengthens so that $1 = ¥140, then the exact same car at the exact same yen price could sell in the United States for about $21,400 without any loss in return in yen to Honda because each dollar earned by Honda can now be turned into more yen. Conversely, if the dollar becomes much weaker compared to the yen, so that $1 buys only ¥100, then the exact same Honda would have to sell for $30,000 to give Honda the same return. Reality is rather more complicated, but this is sufficient to make the fundamental point. One way that a government can manipulate trade without imposing tariffs is to flood the market with its currency by printing more money. In doing so, it weakens its currency, thereby making it harder for its citizens to buy imported goods and easier for them to export domestic goods.

Suppose an American looking for a new car is torn between a Honda and a Ford. If a Ford comparable to the Honda under consideration costs $25,000, then when the dollar is strong against the yen, the Honda looks like a very attractive buy (being $3,600 cheaper if $1 = ¥140). But when the dollar is weak, the Ford looks like a terrific buy (being $5,000 cheaper if $1 = ¥100). So, the U.S. government can protect Ford or other American car makers without imposing a tariff. It just needs to print more money to encourage more consumption of domestic goods and less consumption of imported goods.

But, of course, printing more money is inflationary, meaning that the dollar doesn't buy as much as it did before more money was printed. U.S. political leaders are constrained in their ability to manipulate the value of the currency for political gain, however, because the Federal Reserve Bank (the Fed) sets interest rates that determine how much it costs to borrow money. The Fed, like the European Union's central bank and other central banks, is largely autonomous. Its director and other officers serve long terms that extend well beyond any one president's term in office. As a result, the Fed is not easily intimidated by political pressure. When the Fed raises or lowers interest rates, it makes dollars more or less expensive, thereby influencing the demand for dollars compared, for instance, to yen or euros. The alteration of interest rates is intended to ensure that the price for a dollar—that is, how many dollars it takes to buy something—is kept in check so that inflation is kept under control and the exchange rate is maintained within desired bounds. In this way, the Fed helps control the

> **TRY THIS**
>
> Go online and get data for the past five or ten years on the average monthly dollar-euro or dollar-pound exchange rate. Then get data for the same period on the price of a barrel of crude oil. (A good price to use is the price of West Texas Intermediate Light Sweet Crude.) Plot the value of the dollar against the price of oil. Do you see a pattern? Now, add to your plot the amount of crude oil sold on average each month during the same period. How well does that indicate the price of a barrel of oil? Do you have a view of how much supply and demand shape the price and how much decisions by the Fed shape the price? How might you test that view?

inclination of politicians to use the supply of money as a way to manipulate the economy and trade (Frieden 1987; Simmons 1994; Broz and Frieden 2001; Clark 2003).

If currency manipulation for political ends is not reined in by a central bank or by some other reliable mechanism (such as a peg, explained shortly), then politicians have the flexibility to influence their economy. But this flexibility comes at a price. They may enjoy few of the benefits of a stable, predictable exchange rate for their currency and create uncertainty; uncertainty is the enemy of investors. Foreign investors with a choice of countries in which to risk their money are reluctant to put it at risk in places where unfettered government control can radically devalue their investments overnight. This is one reason that few investors seem willing to risk their money in most of Africa, in Argentina, and in many other places where inflation rates can soar to more than 1,000 percent per year or where the government can change the currency's value by fiat.

Consider, for instance, the difference between European Union currency policy in the recent past and the comparable policy in Russia. In the 1993 Maastricht Treaty, the members of the European Union agreed to the steps leading to a common European currency. They agreed that the euro would slowly be brought into use (but by a specified time) after the members met requirements to bring inflation under control and to bring the value of their currencies up to particular standards. The euro was introduced for major commercial exchanges well in advance of actual euro currency going into circulation. For several years, prices all over the European Union were listed in terms both of the local currency and in euros even though goods could not yet be purchased with or sold for euros; in this way, people became accustomed to thinking about costs in euros. Finally, in 2001, euro currency was introduced into the market to replace local currencies. People were given ample time to convert their francs, guilders, marks, lira, and so forth into euros. Currency stabilization and lots of information about what was happening and on what schedule facilitated a smooth transition. Uncertainty was kept to a minimum.

Russia also made major changes in its currency several years ago. In 1993, the Russian government removed Soviet-era rubles from circulation. They did so with only a few days advance notice, leading to panicked spending and runs on banks. Earlier, the Russian government had abolished 50-ruble and 100-ruble notes, again with little warning, leaving people with substantial economic losses and with little trust in their government. It is exactly such arbitrary currency policy by government that deters investors, thereby stifling economic growth.

Poor countries face particular difficulties in the global market. As we learned earlier, they just about always enjoy comparative advantage in some aspect of their economy—often in the price of labor—that gives them an opportunity for good terms of trade. Unfortunately, poor countries frequently pursue monetary policies that give the government tremendous flexibility in manipulating the value of their currency and, as a result, the expected terms of trade. Naturally, buyers in the market for the goods or services that these countries export recognize the risk associated with doing business under such politically volatile circumstances. There are several solutions to such problems. Sometimes contracts are negotiated in terms of a currency other than the seller's currency. In these instances, the currency chosen is one that is relatively stable so that its value at the close of the contract is predictable. The U.S. dollar is often used in this way even when neither the buyer nor the seller is American. Crude oil, for instance, is bought and sold in U.S. dollars all around the world. The British pound sterling is another currency that has been widely used for this purpose because it is deemed to have a trustworthy value.

Other times, the price negotiated between the buyer and the seller takes into account the risk that the exchange rate when the contract is fulfilled will be markedly different from what it is when the contract is entered into. This is known as a risk premium, and it is very common for contracts with businesses in developing countries to involve one. This is a sensible solution to the expectation that the seller may not fulfill his or her obligations. It is also a reasonable way to address concern that the value of payment in the local currency will be manipulated by government leaders to assist their cronies. But, if the contract is properly fulfilled and the currency was not manipulated, then the risk premium paid up front becomes a deadweight loss for the seller in the impoverished country.

Regina Baker (2002) has demonstrated that poor countries are particularly likely to peg their currency if they are subject to a high-risk premium; that is, they settle on a nearly fixed exchange rate (or one that is constrained to trade in a very narrow range) that determines the value of their currency by linking it to the value of another currency. The Hong Kong dollar and the Chinese yuan, for example, are pegged to the American dollar. It is always the case that it takes about 7.5 Hong Kong dollars or 8.6 yuan to buy 1 American dollar. So, except for small variations, when the American dollar devalues, so do the Hong Kong dollar and Chinese yuan; likewise, when the American dollar strengthens, so do the Hong Kong dollar and Chinese yuan. This helps establish as much confidence in the Hong Kong dollar and the Chinese yuan as people have in the American dollar. Even after Hong Kong was returned by Britain to the People's Republic of China on July 1, 1997, the Chinese government maintained the peg for the Hong Kong dollar to try to protect Hong Kong's economy; it had pegged its own currency to the dollar in 1995. One concern of some investors was that China would drop the peg, just as it has eroded other parts of its assurances regarding Hong Kong's economic autonomy (Bueno de Mesquita, Newman, and Rabushka 1996; Bowring 2002).

China faced lots of external political pressure to abandon the peg and allow its currency to float. The U.S. government has made the argument for a floating yuan on the basis that its peg to a weak dollar creates unfair competition for firms in the United States that try to compete with Chinese companies. In this way, the U.S. case goes, the peg exacerbates the large trade deficit between the United States and China; that is, the United States buys vastly more from China than China buys from the United States. In fact, the Chinese gave in to the pressure, depegging the yuan in July 2005. This has helped strengthen the Chinese yuan, making Chinese consumers better able to buy American goods.

Some poor countries go even further than pegging their currency to a stable currency from another country. Several countries around the world formally or informally adopt **dollarization** as a strategy. That means that they use the U.S. dollar as their currency for all or much of their exchange. Panama, Ecuador, and East Timor use the dollar as their currency. Argentina has seriously considered dollarizing its economy in addition to having had serious discussions with Brazil about forming a common currency. Still others, such as Cuba, maintain their own currency even though a large proportion of economic exchange takes place in dollars and not in the local currency. This happens because people lack confidence in the trustworthiness of their own currency and prefer the dollar.

There are several reasons for such distrust. One reason is currency manipulation, as already discussed. A second reason is that many currencies cannot be converted or can be converted only at a government-set, artificial price unrelated to the market price of the currency. Convertibility ensures that people can, on demand, exchange their money for another currency. Anyone who has traveled outside the United States knows that it is easy to buy euros or Mexican pesos or Japanese yen for dollars; that it is just as easy to buy dollars with euros, pesos, or yen; and that these currencies sell for the same price whether changed in a bank or between individuals on the street. That is, there is no problem turning one currency into the other, and there is no black-market premium one way or the other in the exchange. Equally, travelers in China, India, and many other countries know that local citizens (as distinct from import and export businesses) either cannot readily turn their money into dollars or, if they can do so legally, can convert local currency into dollars only at exchange rates that bear little relationship to the supply and demand for the currencies involved. This is one of the reasons that black markets for money develop in such societies.

Nonconvertibility is a nontariff barrier that can keep foreign products and foreign investment out of a country. When currencies are not readily converted, there is no easy way for foreign investors to repatriate their profits or for people or firms to be paid in a currency that they can use outside the country to which they are selling. These losses in flexibility for investors and manufacturers mean increases in the price of selling or investing, and so fewer people will pursue the opportunity. Naturally, this hurts not only the prospective sellers and prospective investors but also the local population, who are deprived of the opportunity to buy imported goods or to take advantage of the economic growth opportunities promoted by foreign investment.

POLITICAL ECONOMY AND TRADE

We have seen that free trade, on average, provides cheaper goods and services to consumers. It also provides more abundant goods and services both in quantity and in diversity. Yet free trade has not been the norm throughout history. I have already hinted at why this is so. Free trade is a public good, but the effects of trade involve both public- and private-goods components. Trade affects domestic producers and sellers differently from importers, exporters, and consumers, and government trade policies affect the wealth of each of these groups differently. So, the distribution of wealth in a society depends, in part, on governmental approaches to trade. If trade is unrestricted, then domestic producers for the domestic market are at a potential disadvantage and foreign exporters and domestic importers could have an advantage.

Imports can be restricted through such means as tariffs or nontariff barriers. **Nontariff barriers** are a more subtle way for governments to limit imports than imposing tariffs. Nonconvertibility has already been mentioned; other examples of nontariff barriers are exchange rate manipulation, environmental or health standards that exclude foreign-made products, quotas that restrict the quantity of an item that can be imported, and restrictions on the movement of people or capital to where they can command the highest price. They have become increasingly popular among members of the WTO as the political means to limit imports because, although the WTO (and some other regional trade organizations such as NAFTA) has strict rules about tariffs, its rules about nontariff barriers to trade are somewhat harder to enforce. Still, the use of nontariff barriers has come under increasingly close scrutiny by the WTO and other international trade organizations because these barriers have assumed a major role in keeping goods and services from flowing freely across national borders despite the absence of protective tariffs.

For instance, France makes some extraordinarily fine cheeses from raw, unpasteurized milk. These soft cheeses (for example, true Camembert) are at their peak flavor when they are less than sixty days old. France is a country with excellent health standards and a high standard of living, and the French have been enjoying these cheeses for centuries with no discernible ill effects. Nevertheless, such cheeses cannot be purchased in the United States. Among unpasteurized (raw-milk) cheeses, only those that are more than sixty days old are permitted to enter the United States. Why? Ostensibly to protect Americans from health risks. In reality, the nontariff barrier on these cheeses just protects American cheese makers and, perhaps, helps stimulate American tourism to Normandy.

Similarly, it is difficult to bring into the United States an automobile that was purchased elsewhere. Daimler-Benz offers many models in Germany that cannot be bought in the United States. These vehicles can enter the United States only if they are retrofitted with expensive equipment to protect the environment. Of course, protecting the environment may provide a public good that justifies the nontariff restrictions imposed on some foreign cars; nevertheless, we should not lose sight of the fact that these restrictions also serve to limit consumer choices and to raise prices. Here we have an instance of a trade-off between environmental concerns and consumer interests that is resolved by government restrictions in favor of the environment. This, of course, can be a very good thing. But the U.S. government fails to show an equal commitment to the environment when it comes to imposing restrictions on popular but gas-guzzling and air-polluting sports utility vehicles (SUVs) manufactured in the United States. Whether the actual trade-off adopted in the United States (or elsewhere) between the environment and free trade is motivated primarily by a desire for cleaner air or a desire for fewer imported vehicles is an issue worth close exploration.

Try This

Provide a list of ten nontariff barriers that influence whether you or your family has access to particular goods and services. Think broadly about this question. For example, does the requirement of a passport or visa to travel to or from the United States act as a nontariff barrier? What effect does the Internet have on trade barriers? In addition to the examples I give here, how do health, environmental, safety, or cultural restrictions (for example, movie ratings and censorship) create nontariff barriers? Can you give examples of such barriers imposed on U.S. goods and services by other governments?

Under the terms of NAFTA, the United States was expected to permit Mexican trucks to cross the border and proceed to their destinations within the United States. Yet the U.S.

Congress, citing environmental issues, for many years successfully restricted Mexican trucks from going more than 20 miles from the border. One effect of this nontariff barrier was that Mexican goods coming into the United States by truck had to be unloaded near the border and reloaded on to American trucks. This, of course, delayed (and therefore harmed) the delivery of perishable food stuffs, increased the cost of shipping goods to the United States, and so ultimately harmed the American consumer. It also raised the price of electronics and any other goods shipped from Mexico to the United States, again harming the consumer. Mexico reciprocated by imposing restrictions on American trucks crossing into Mexico, thereby harming Mexican consumers. So great is the political pressure from interest groups—mostly American truckers—that the U.S. Senate voted in September 2007 to ban Mexican trucks from the United States. Even the 20-mile limit apparently was not enough to satisfy many American politicians. Of course, they are not devoid of arguments favoring a ban on Mexican trucks.

Environmentalists can sensibly argue that the price distortion for Mexican products trucked into the United States is created by unfair trade practices originating in Mexico. The argument is that Mexican modes of transport, including trucks, are artificially cheap because their prices do not reflect the social cost of the pollution they generate and that the proper route to free trade would be to adjust Mexican environmental policy. Thus far, however, adjudication of claims on both sides of the border regarding obligations under NAFTA does not support this contention.

President George W. Bush pushed for greater implementation of the NAFTA requirements even as Congress pushed to maintain the restrictions on Mexican trucks. The ostensible justification for these restrictions is environmental and highway safety, although little evidence has been mustered to support the claims of those who favor the restrictions. Some American truckers, manufacturers, and growers and packers of fruits and vegetables benefit from these nontariff barriers. Despite these barriers to trade, the years between 1994 (when NAFTA went into effect) and 2007 saw a tremendous expansion in trade between Mexico and the United States, with the dollar value of imports plus exports increasing well over 300 percent. Even with nontariff barriers, Mexico has surged in a few years to become very nearly equal to China in total trade with the United States. In 2007, for instance (the most recent year with complete data), China bought goods from and sold goods to the United States worth $387 billion. The comparable figure for Mexico is $347 billion, and, of course, on a per capita basis Mexico has become a much larger trading partner than China. Japan, in contrast, represented just $208 billion in trade with the United States in 2007. Figure 10.4 depicts the change in total trade between the United States and Canada, China, Mexico, and Japan since 1985.

Before leaving the issue of nontariff barriers, we should be careful to recognize that eliminating these barriers to free trade is controversial precisely because of the difficulty of distinguishing such cynical ploys from policies sincerely aimed at protecting consumers, the environment, and workers. Consider the U.S. Environmental Protection Agency (EPA)

| FIGURE 10.4 | Growth in Mexican Trade with the United States: NAFTA at Work |

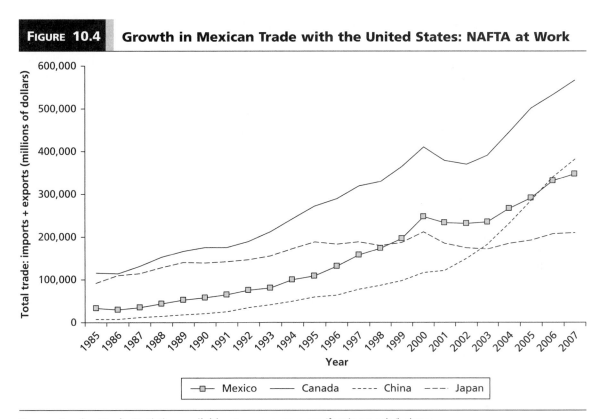

Source: Foreign Trade Statistics, available at www.census.gov/foreign-trade/balance.

prohibitions against importing foods grown with certain pesticides such as DDT. Many Latin American farmers view this restriction as an unfair trade practice. Even reasonable people can reasonably disagree about whether the price distortion induced by the ban outweighs the negative health and medical care externalities associated with the use of these pesticides. How appealing the trade-off is between higher food prices with fewer pesticides in fruits, vegetables, and meat products and lower prices with more pesticides is sure to vary from society to society and from consumer to consumer.

These and many, many other examples, involving not only the United States but also almost every country in the world, reveal a common pattern of influence over trade protectionism. Again, free trade is a public good. Yet trade restrictions create private benefits—usually income—to only a few people. Add to this the fact that public goods are generally underprovided for because people free ride (Olson 1965; Medina 2007); that is, individuals have incentives to consume the benefits from public goods while letting others bear the cost of their provision because, once they are provided, public goods benefit everyone. It is therefore difficult to motivate a large group of people—say consumers—to take action to protect their interests when their collective action will yield each one only a small gain relative to the costs of being an activist for free trade. This is a fundamental coordination problem that inhibits consumers from fully exercising their collective influence over government policies. Conversely, it is not so difficult to mobilize small groups of producers or workers whose incomes are significantly diminished if their jobs disappear because of foreign competition. For them, the stakes are high; for the average individual consumer the gain from reversing any particular trade restriction tends to be small. To summarize, private benefits arise from trade protectionism that can be distributed to certain domestic producers or workers; consumers derive public goods—not private goods—from free trade.

Therefore, the strategic problem in trade policy is a classic coordination and distribution problem. The asymmetry between diffuse collective (or public) benefits and the concentrated costs (through lost private benefits) associated with trade is a substantial factor contributing to the existence of trade protectionism. In general, the greater the private benefits from protection, the more likely are interest groups, lobbyists, and other coalitions of affected individuals to mobilize to exercise their political influence on leaders. To the extent that a leader's hold on political office requires support from those who seek protection from foreign competition, we can expect that protection will be forthcoming. As we learned earlier, less democratic political systems, in which leaders rely on a small coalition to stay in office, use private benefits to reward backers more than do more democratic systems, in which leaders require a large coalition of supporters. So, we should expect more trade protectionism in autocracies than in democracies. This is, in fact, the case. The average democratic regime is about 25 percent more open to trade than is the average autocratic regime, a difference that is extremely unlikely to be the result of chance (Bueno de Mesquita et al. 2003). Not all seekers of protection can expect to have their wishes fulfilled. They may not be essential supporters of the leadership. In that case, their appeals for protection are likely to fall on deaf ears. They may be in a relatively weak position to advance their cause, making it hard to get the attention of leaders.

In fact, Fiona McGillivray (2004) has shown that even in democracies we can trace the pattern of trade protection to the fundamentals of the political system. For instance, in polities where people vote for representatives of their district, such as the United States and Great Britain, firms with high employment in pivotal districts that can shape electoral outcomes—districts that are highly competitive between the parties—tend to get lots of trade protection if they want it. In proportional representation systems, where people vote for a list of candidates and the top vote-getters across the country win seats in parliament, this is not true. In those systems, protection tends to be less concentrated on individual firms and more concentrated on large industries across the country. So, who gets protected varies according to their political clout, and that, in turn, varies with the electoral rules that influence the size of the winning coalition.

FACTORS OF PRODUCTION

People's interests regarding trade are shaped both by their economic interests and by their political interests. Whichever our emphasis is on, we are still addressing politics. Trade policies, after all, are set by government and as such they are political.

Let us divide all people in any given country into two basic economic groups: those who provide labor and those who provide capital. Labor and capital are called **factors of production.** Let us also assume that a country has two industries, say, widgets and gadgets. Widget manufacturing is capital-intensive, whereas gadget manufacturing is labor-intensive. By this I mean that the ratio of capital to labor used for widgets is larger than it is for gadgets. In plain English, the widget business relies more heavily on capital (loosely, money) than on labor (loosely, workers) to produce its product, and the gadget industry uses labor more intensively than it does capital to make its product. We also assume that everyone has the same preferences when they are in the role of consumer so that variations in preferences are due to considerations other than the consumer's role. As a consumer, everyone wants a large selection of high-quality goods and services at low prices. By assuming that all consumers have the same preferences, we can evaluate how a tariff influences the return on labor and capital. By knowing the relative economic returns on the factors of production, we can infer how a tariff affects the interests of people based on their particular factor endowments (that is, the extent to which they offer more in the form of capital or in the form of labor).

One place to begin our analysis is by asking whether a given country is more likely to export labor-intensive products or capital-intensive products. Imagine, for example, a rich country, such as France, Germany, Japan, Singapore, or the United States, and a poor country, such as China, Ghana, India, or Peru. Can we say anything about their exports based on the relative abundance of the two factors of production, capital and labor? The Hecksher-Ohlin theorem allows us to do so. This theorem, or logically proven proposition, addresses the mix of a country's exports and imports based on the relative abundance of the factors of production in an economy. Specifically, if there are two factors of production, a country will export products that are based on the intensive use of its relatively abundant factor and will import products whose production is based on the intensive use of its relatively scarce factor. That is, countries with a relative abundance of capital, like many rich countries, will tend to export products that are capital-intensive and import labor-intensive products. Poor countries tend to have a relative abundance of labor and so use labor intensively in production. They will tend to export labor-intensive products and import capital-intensive products. The link between this idea and the concept of comparative advantage should be evident.

The dichotomy I have drawn between rich and poor countries is a bit simpler than reality, but it is essentially right. The complicating factor is the word *relative* when speaking about the abundance of different factors of production. The Hecksher-Ohlin theorem, for instance, can also be readily applied to trade between two wealthy economies or two poor economies because, in each case, one factor will be relatively more abundant in one country than in the other.

Returning to the world of widgets and gadgets, let us imagine that there are two countries, Richland and Poorland, and that capital is relatively abundant in Richland and labor is relatively abundant in Poorland. The Hecksher-Ohlin theorem leads us to expect that Richland will want to export capital-intensive widgets to Poorland and Poorland will want to export labor-intensive gadgets to Richland. I say *want* because we have not yet considered whether labor, capital, or both in some industry will seek government protection in either Richland or Poorland. If the government acts purely on the basis of a policy in favor of free trade, then we can say, based on the Hecksher-Ohlin theorem, that Richland will export widgets and import gadgets while Poorland will export gadgets and import widgets.

TRY THIS

Using the Internet or an annual yearbook, find a list of the leading exports and imports of Brazil, China, the Netherlands, Nigeria, and the United States, or select your own list of countries to look up. In each case, see if you can find out whether the exports or imports are relatively labor-intensive or capital-intensive. How open is each of these economies to free trade? What trade protection, if any, is there against foreign imports in these countries? Are the countries you selected members of the WTO?

Who will seek protection depends on several considerations. One consideration is related to the economic return on widget and gadget production. A second consideration is the preparedness of individuals to organize to press for the private benefits that could be derived from protection or to try to protect the public goods that could be derived from a free-trade policy. Still another consideration is how the institutions of government—particularly dependence on a large coalition (as in democracy) or dependence on a small coalition (as in autocracy)—influence the responsiveness of political leaders to pressure for or against protection. A good place to start our investigation of economic returns to factors of production is to think about how easily capital or labor can be shifted from one industry to another because this significantly influences who wants protection. This is the topic of the next section.

MOBILITY OF FACTORS OF PRODUCTION

Capital and labor can both be mobile. That means in the context of our hypothetical example that workers and capital can move easily from one job to another. Workers (labor), for instance, might move from producing widgets to producing gadgets or other goods within their own country, or they might even move to jobs in another country. Naturally, all else being equal, they will want to move only if they expect to be better off as a result of changing positions. Likewise, if capital is mobile, this means that capital can move freely between businesses or even across country boundaries, so that capital could shift from Richland to Poorland (or vice versa). Like labor, all else being equal, owners of capital will not move their resource unless they expect that moving it will give a better return than keeping it where it is.

To illustrate, consider why many relatively unskilled Mexican workers migrate to the United States. Their labor is mobile to the extent that they can perform unskilled jobs anywhere. Although poorly paid by U.S. standards, these Mexican workers get paid considerably more in the U.S. market than they do in the Mexican market. Consistent with the Hecksher-Ohlin theorem, Mexico exports labor-intensive products, including labor itself, to the United States. Mexican workers, when they can, exercise their **labor mobility** (workers moving from one location to another or from one business to another) by seeking a better return on their labor by coming to the United States. Many, of course, save the money they earn and return to Mexico, where they help improve the welfare of their family, local communities, and country. Many more cannot enter the United States because the U.S. government restricts the mobility of labor across the national frontier.

Consider also why many corporations, including many U.S. corporations, invest in businesses in Mexico, China, or India. These economies, starting from a low baseline and with relatively cheap labor, appear to have better growth prospects than does the United States over the next several years. Higher growth is likely to mean a better return to capital in those markets than in the United States. So, again consistent with the Hecksher-Ohlin theorem, U.S. firms export capital by investing in places with high-growth prospects when they can, moving capital to where it is expected to produce the best return. Not all governments, however, permit **capital mobility** (money and expensive equipment being moved from one location to another or from one business to another) across their frontiers. They restrict the movement of capital by limiting the ownership rights and opportunities of foreign investors seeking to enter their marketplace.

The two examples help clarify what is meant by *labor mobility* and *capital mobility,* but they also highlight two of the many reasons that labor or capital might not be mobile. In addition to the government restrictions alluded to, it is also possible that neither labor nor capital is mobile because either or both might be useful only in so specialized a way that the productive capacity in one sector does not translate into a comparable productive capacity in another sector. This is known as **asset specificity.** Skilled surgeons, for example, cannot easily move to positions as design engineers creating new automobiles, nor can automobile design engineers move easily into positions as surgeons. Neither engineers nor surgeons have the requisite specialized skills to do the other's job productively. Of course, they are not completely immobile in reality. People can and do retool, but this is expensive in time and money, and so it is done only if the expected benefits from learning new skills outweigh the expected costs. It is likely, for example, that many blacksmiths in the early twentieth century retooled to do new jobs as the automobile supplanted the horse-drawn technology of the nineteenth century. More recently, we can see that many people in the typewriter manufacturing and repair industries retooled as typewriters were supplanted by personal computers. Typewriter repair shops used to be commonplace; now there are hardly any.

Still another possible scenario is that one factor of production is substantially more mobile than the other. Whether capital is likely to be more mobile than labor, or vice versa, depends on how specialized the use of labor is in a given economy and on how specialized the use of capital is, as well as on government policies restricting the movement of one or the other.

The economic incentives to seek protection depend, in part, on whether both labor and capital are mobile, only one is mobile, or neither is mobile (Hiscox 2002). I proceed by examining these three situations in turn.

Interindustry Factor Mobility

If both labor and capital are mobile, then we know from what is called the Stolper-Samuelson theorem that a change in the price of a product is more than proportionally reflected in the return to the factor that is used (more intensively) to produce that product. This is a fairly complicated statement, so let's break it down into its important parts using our Richland and Poorland example.

The widget industry is capital-intensive. Richland is more competitive at making widgets than gadgets. As the price of widgets increases, the economic return (profit) to widget producers in Richland increases at a faster rate than does the return in Richland from making gadgets. That, however, is not all the Stolper-Samuelson theorem tells us. The proportional return to capital relative to labor increases across the entire Richland economy if the economy emphasizes the production of capital-intensive goods. Even in the gadget industry, the return to capital increases proportionally more than the return to labor in Richland. Equivalently, and this is very important in understanding the policy debate over globalization, in Poorland there is a more than proportional return to labor as the price of gadgets—the labor-intensive product—increases in Poorland's labor-intensive economy.

Now, let us suppose that for some reason (for example, a policy shift favoring free trade) the price of imports—gadgets—falls in Richland. One consequence of the drop in price is that Richland's domestic gadget producers will make fewer gadgets (see the Supply A curve in Figure 10.3) and so will need less labor. Another consequence is that the relative price of Richland's widgets, its capital-intensive export good, will rise. The rise in the relative price of widgets will lead to an increased demand for capital because any expansion in widget production is capital-intensive. This means that labor in Richland will be in relatively abundant supply following the decrease in the price of gadgets, and capital will be in relatively short supply following the increase in the price of widgets. The widget makers will not pick up the slack in labor because, after all, widget making is capital-intensive. They need relatively more capital to exploit the increased price, not more labor. In fact, because the demand for capital in Richland rises in this example while the demand for labor falls, the relative price for all labor drops, provided that both labor and capital are mobile across the economy. At the same time, the relative price of capital rises across the economy—not just in the widget business—as long as it is mobile. This is because, if there is interindustry mobility, capital will move from one industry to another to find its highest price, and labor will do the same. That, after all, is what comparative advantage is about. Because the demand for capital has grown, the only way to attract new capital is to pay more for it by giving higher returns. Because the demand for labor has dropped relative to capital, the only way for labor to be used more is to reduce its relative price so that it becomes more competitive. So, in Richland we can expect the relative return to capital to rise and the relative return to labor to fall.

In Poorland it is likely that the opposite effect will be observed under a free-trade regime. That is, the return to labor is likely to increase relatively more than the return to capital because in Poorland labor, not capital, is the more intensively used factor of production. Gadget makers, now exporting more gadgets to Richland, will need more labor and so will bid up the price of labor across their economy to attract more workers. They will not need more capital, and so capital will chase possible users and its price will drop as those who provide capital compete to find uses for their less-in-demand factor of production.

The argument thus far shows us that in a country with relatively more capital-intensive industry—like Richland—free trade makes the owners of capital winners and the owners of labor, relatively speaking, losers. But in a country where industry is relatively labor-intensive—like Poorland—free trade is a winning strategy for labor and a losing strategy for capital. So, to the extent that both factors of production are mobile, globalization of free trade has four economic effects (Magee 1978; Hill and Mendez 1983; McKeown 1984; Rogowski 1989). Generally, with interindustry **factor mobility** (the factors of production—capital and labor—being able to move from one location to another or from one business to another):

1. Workers in poor countries become wealthier.
2. Owners of capital in rich countries become wealthier.
3. Owners of capital in poor countries do relatively worse (but absolutely better) with free trade.
4. Labor in rich countries does relatively worse (but absolutely better) with free trade.

Recall that at the beginning of this chapter I listed labor unions, environmentalists, and students as being among the opponents of globalization who demonstrated in Seattle, Bologna, and elsewhere. Now we can pause to think about their opposition in the context of mobile factors of production and the economic returns from free trade versus trade protectionism.

The group of demonstrators against globalization can be described as people living in wealthy countries who share a dislike for big business. To be sure, they are right in believing that, if capital and labor are both mobile, then in countries with an abundance of capital capital-intensive big business is a winner from free trade. The losers in a capital-intensive economy—most prominently labor—are most likely to exercise their political clout to try to stop free trade and promote protection. Debate about free trade versus trade protection is extremely salient for them because its outcome directly influences their welfare. But the anti-free-trade demonstrators are mistaken about the effects on workers in poor countries that tend to emphasize labor-intensive industry. In those countries, we should expect labor's relative return to improve disproportionately as a result of free trade, while the return to capital does not. That is, rich businesspeople in poor countries with mobile factors of production can be expected to oppose free trade. And laborers and unions can be expected to support free trade in poor countries with interindustry factor mobility.

So, if both factors of production are mobile, it is incorrect to think that free trade helps the rich (or the poor) across the board and harms the other economic class. Rather, free trade allows each economy to pursue its comparative advantage in labor or capital so that it competes as efficiently as it can in the worldwide market. Where labor is the abundant factor—as in much of the developing world—protectionism as a trade policy harms workers and benefits capitalists.

In a world with perfect interindustry factor mobility, we can see that political pressure will arise for protection against foreign competition among those whose factor of production—whether it be capital or labor—is relatively disadvantaged by free trade. That is, in a world with perfect factor mobility, trade conflict will be along class lines. Either labor (workers and unions) will seek protection and capital (corporate management) will not, or capital will seek protection and labor will not. This conclusion helps us understand the opposition to globalization by labor and students in wealthy countries. Students typically are not yet significant owners of capital and, on average, they do not yet have skills that endow them with asset specificity that would allow them to command a high price as labor. They naturally identify with the relatively worse off in their rich society. Labor unions have as their mission to improve the conditions for labor in their own industry or community; they are not as interested in the welfare of laborers in other industries or in other countries. The opponents of free trade in the United States align with the interests of labor at the expense of capital; that is, they side with workers in their own country at the expense of business owners. However, they are *also* siding against poorer workers in poor, labor-intensive countries, and probably without realizing it, they are siding with the big businesses of developing countries.

The big magnates in developing countries may be disadvantaged in their ability to compete with capital-intensive goods made in wealthier countries, and so they seek protection against capital-intensive imports. In India, for example, the only available automobile for many years was the Hindustan Ambassador. It was basically a twenty-year-old model that could not compete with foreign imports. Until relatively recently, the Indian government's solution was to bow to political pressure (in the name of national self-sufficiency) to make it prohibitively expensive to import foreign cars into India. This was equally true for the availability of aluminum, many types of iron and steel, foodstuffs, and medical supplies. The upshot was a great distortion of the economy to the benefit of wealthy Indian producers and at the expense of Indian consumers, helping to make the rich very rich and the poor exceedingly poor. Since India shifted to somewhat freer trade (although it still is far from having a free-trade policy), its economic growth rate has skyrocketed, a substantial middle class has emerged, and its economy provides improved opportunities for its poor workers.

No Interindustry Factor Mobility

Perfectly mobile factors of production are an ideal. Such perfection may be achieved in the future, but it is not an accurate description of the mobility of capital or labor on the ground. Because the true adjustment of prices and returns resulting from free trade is not instantaneous without perfect factor mobility, the predictions of the Stolper-Samuelson theorem need to be examined in regard to their effects in the shorter term. In the short run, factor mobility might be quite limited. To assess the short-term effects, let's examine what happens following the introduction of a tariff when neither labor nor capital is mobile at all.

If factors are completely immobile, a new equilibrium price cannot be achieved (as it was in the Stolper-Samuelson world) by having capital and labor move from one industry to another to seek their best return—they are stuck where they are and cannot move from one industry to another. North Korea comes close to the ideal type of a society in which labor and capital are both immobile. The authoritarian government of North Korea does not permit people to move from one part of the country to another, nor does it allow people to change jobs at will. Rather, labor mobility is strictly determined by the whim of the government. Being a communist state, North Korea also does not promote capital investment by its citizens and permits capital movement by foreigners only within a narrow special economic zone. It is, in short, a society without labor or capital mobility. In such a case, if a tariff is imposed, inflating the price of one good compared with another, then price adjustments can occur only through changes in the price of the factors of production. There is no additional effect arising because of labor or capital mobility. Therefore, the effects of price changes for factors of production are localized to specific industries rather than across the economy. Without factor mobility, any effect felt from a tariff will be industry-specific.

Let us assume that factor prices are completely flexible so that they can change readily. Let us also assume that the economy has full employment prior to the introduction of a tariff (as is nominally true in North Korea). This means that there is no elasticity in the supply of either factor because both factors are fully used. With these conditions in place, the introduction of a tariff will not lead to a change in the quantity produced by either capital-intensive or labor-intensive industry. In North Korea's case, however, trade is almost completely quashed by government action. North Korea exports missiles to some Middle Eastern states, but otherwise it has no export market for any other consequential goods; it imports little as well. So let's return to the hypothetical world of widgets and gadgets so we can talk about the effects of trade.

Without factor mobility, the relative returns to factors do not change when a tariff is imposed, in contrast to the world with complete interindustry mobility. However, an important change does occur. The amount paid for capital and labor within an industry that is protected by a tariff increases relative to an unprotected industry. If a tariff is imposed on gadgets, for instance, both capital and labor in the gadget industry will benefit relative to capital and labor in the widget industry. In our previous case with factor mobility, we see that policy preferences about protection are factor-dependent. With immobile factors of production, policy pressures for trade protection arise on an industry-by-industry basis rather than on a factor-by-factor basis. So, with immobile factors, labor and capital in the gadget business will seek government protection and be pitted politically against labor and capital in the widget industry. In this case, some of the relatively well-off people and some of the relatively poor people will benefit from trade protection, just as some of each group in the unprotected industries will be losers. Thus, who tries to organize for protection differs depending on factor mobility.

In our case with full mobility we expect, all else being equal, to see class warfare over trade policy. In contrast, with immobility, we expect to see interindustry warfare. In this environment, the relatively wealthy and the relatively poor in a given industry win as a result of the imposition of a tariff, but other relatively wealthy and relatively poor people employed in other, unprotected industries suffer. Consumers, in general, of course are harmed, as are labor and capital in Poorland's export industry, becoming victims of the tariff (Alt and Gilligan 1994).

These conclusions can help us understand the political motivation behind Congress's protection of the American farming industry through the use of government price supports or subsidies. As Darin Acemoglu and James Robinson (2001) demonstrate, farmers have incentives to ensure that the farm population is protected from diminution by people shifting to other types of work. Let us take their example of farming versus manufacturing. Politicians can protect themselves and their winning coalition by using price supports rather than cash transfers to farmers because price supports depress labor mobility away from farming and toward manufacturing by artificially inflating the return on farming. Then those receiving price supports are likely to remain the loyal supporters of the politicians who protect them. Cash payments to existing farmers, in contrast, end with them; cash payments do not provide a future stream of benefits to those who might become farmers or manufacturers. Thus, politics is used to reduce labor mobility (from farming to manufacturing) and, thereby, creates exactly the sort of interindustry conflict just described. As with all such distortions, consumers—and we all are consumers—are the losers.

Specific Factor Mobility

Both perfectly immobile factors and perfectly mobile interindustry factors are the extremes and therefore unrealistic. Trade policy is completely driven neither by factor mobility nor by immobility. Rather, factor mobility appears to vary from place to place and from time to time, which may help explain the waxing and waning of trade protectionism versus free-trade policies across countries and within countries over time (Hiscox 2002).

Before turning to other considerations, let's see what happens when one factor is perfectly mobile and the other is not. In this setting, we are in the world of the Ricardo-Viner theorem. For our purposes, the important element of this theorem is the implication of asymmetric factor mobility for the politics of protectionism. As we see shortly, unlike the Stolper-Samuelson world of complete factor mobility, here we expect demands for protection to be industry-specific and supported both by labor and capital in the industry (not class-based as in the Stolper-Samuelson setting).

Under the specific factor approach, one factor of production is specific to a particular industry, that is, it cannot be moved to improve the return from it and it can be moved to another industry only at a cost, whereas the other factor is mobile. For convenience I assume that labor is perfectly mobile whereas capital is tied to its specific industry. The conclusions, however, are equally applicable if we reverse this convenience as long as we keep track of our assumptions about which factor is mobile and which is specific.

The implications of tariffs depend on whether they are applied to the specific factor's industry or to the mobile factor of production. Imagine that each person in an economy possesses only one of these two factors of production. Then, as in the immobile-factor world, those who own the specific factor will form views about tariff protection based on the circumstances in the industry in which they work. If those with the specific factor are at a competitive disadvantage with regard to foreign producers, then they will want protection from imports in their industry, although they may readily oppose tariff protection for other industries. Those who possess the mobile factor of production will form views regarding tariff protection based on the circumstances affecting their mobile factor. If this mobile factor is not intensively used in their economy, they will want protection from foreign competition; if this factor is intensively used in their economy, then they will prefer free trade to tariffs (Hillman 1982; Grossman 1983; Rogowski 1989).

Let us imagine that in Richland that capital is industry-specific, so that it is costly to move the capital used in producing widgets to the gadget industry, and vice versa. In contrast, we assume that the labor used in making widgets and gadgets is mobile across industries. We also assume comparable facts for Poorland. In Richland, gadgets are an import industry and widgets are an export industry. If Richland does not impose a tariff on Poorland's gadgets, the price of gadgets will fall as a result of import competition. The domestic production of gadgets will also fall in response to the price drop brought on by the free importation of Poorland gadgets. Labor will respond by moving away from domestic gadget production and seeking employment in the export-oriented widget business. Capital (the specific, or immobile, factor) will not be able to move. Although capital remains in the import-competing gadget business, the industry can no longer attract sufficient labor, and so the domestic gadget makers become less productive. The result is that the income from capital in the domestic gadget industry will drop with respect to both the price of Richland's export good—widgets—and the price of Poorland's gadgets imported into Richland.

Meanwhile, mobile labor in Richland will be moving from the domestic gadget industry to the export-oriented domestic widget business, where prices are rising relative to the domestic import-competing gadgets. The extra labor made available to capital in the export widget industry will improve the productivity of capital in that business. Consequently, the return on capital used to make widgets will rise relative to both the price of widgets and the price of imported gadgets.

In summary, in this scenario, the return on capital (the specific, or immobile, factor) under free trade is industry-specific. In an export-oriented industry, capital does especially well, but in an industry with import competition, capital does especially poorly. Labor (the mobile factor) moves to the industry in which it can command its highest return—that is, the export-oriented industry. Any labor that still remains in the industry facing import competition shares the desire of capital in that industry to be protected against the more competitive prices of the imported goods.

If, instead of free trade, there is government protection, naturally, the industries that face import competition and that own the industry-specific factor of production will be more inclined to pressure government to impose a tariff than will export-oriented industries that own the industry-specific factor or any industries that own the mobile factor of production. So, the owners of capital devoted to making gadgets in Richland (or aluminum, cars, or airplanes—all requiring vast commitments of hard-to-move capital—in India) will seek government protection and so will their labor force. Labor does not need protection because it can move to the more productive, export-oriented widget business; those with capital invested in making widgets in Richland (or computer software in India) likewise will not want protection. Under these circumstances, protection helps only immobile capital in the import-competing industry. This industry is a winner under government protection, whereas just about everyone else is a loser.

THE CONSEQUENCE OF FREE TRADE: SOME EVIDENCE

Logic tells us that free trade creates many more winners than losers. Trade protection distorts the economy by insulating relatively inefficient industries from competition. Trade protection arises to protect the few with political clout at the expense of the many. The few who press for protection can exercise their political influence effectively for two reasons. First, those who benefit from protection have a focused interest in persuading government to protect them. This focus makes it easier for them to overcome coordination problems. They are more likely to avoid the problem of free riding than are the many who benefit from the public good of free trade. Second, where the domestic political environment rewards leaders with long tenure in office if they compensate their backers with private goods, those seeking protection back leaders who will provide them with the protection they seek (a private good). Recall that autocrats rely on dispensing private goods to stay in office and that democrats rely more on providing public goods. I have already mentioned that autocratic governments are substantially less supportive of free trade than are democrats.

Now we can ask whether the preference for free trade translates into improved social well-being. We can think of social welfare in two distinct ways. Governments routinely must choose between policies that advance efficiency and policies that advance equity. By *efficiency* I mean that the policies do not interfere with the smooth working of a free market. In free markets, producers and consumers all seek their own comparative advantage. As a result, resources are used in the most efficient way possible, avoiding the waste and distortions that arise from regulation. But efficient markets can be cruel. Those who are less competitive suffer, sometimes through no fault of their own. Without a social safety net, such as social security, unemployment insurance, and progressive taxation, they might not be able to survive. Therefore, markets are often regulated and resources redistributed to improve equity, that is, the more equal treatment of all citizens.

Much of the debate about globalization is really a debate about equity. Opponents of globalization may accept, along with virtually all economists, that free trade promotes efficiency, but they fear that it is inequitable. We have seen that, in theory, trade protectionism creates winners and losers. Who wins and loses is not systematically related to whether they are relatively wealthy or poor but, rather, to who has incentives to press for protection and who is in a good position to overcome free-rider problems and organize to use their political clout to get protection. Let's examine some historical evidence about the equity effects of trade policy.

Governments can be evaluated in terms of their **receptivity to trade.** For example, we can assess the percentage of a country's GDP that comes from exports and imports (measured in 1985 international dollars). Penn World Tables is a data source that has just such information in a variable called Openness in current prices (OPENC).[§] Likewise, we can evaluate how evenly or unevenly income is distributed within each country. The standard way of evaluating income inequality is through a **Gini index.** The higher the value of the Gini index, the less equally distributed is income in a country. Essentially, the Gini index compares the percentage of the population, ranked from lowest income to highest, to the percentage of total income accounted for at each level. If, for instance, the top 10 percent of the population accounts for 30 percent of income while the bottom 10 percent accounts for only 1 percent, then income is pretty unevenly distributed. The closer the cumulative percentage of the population is to the cumulative percentage of income, the more equally—or equitably—income is distributed.

If receptivity to trade (OPENC) promotes inequality, then we will observe that the more open a country is to trade, on average, the larger is its Gini index score. Conversely, if openness to trade promotes more equal income distributions (by helping to lift the poor to narrow the gap with the rich), the Gini index will be closer to zero. In evaluating the relationship between trade openness and income inequality, I control for the independent impact of per capita income levels to make sure that whatever we discover is not simply a product of the differences in wealth across countries. This speaks directly to the worry of those opposed to globalization that it is just a means to make the rich richer at the expense of the poor and that the idea of free trade has been hijacked by large corporations to enrich themselves at the expense of workers. Naturally, large corporation executives, if left to their own devices (as we have seen so dramatically in the run up to the 2008 financial crisis), would try to maximize their personal welfare, just as workers, if left to their own devices, would do the same. Free trade, however, ensures competition that makes any such inefficient exploitation of resources exceedingly difficult.

With the statistical control for per capita income in place, we can see the independent impact that trade openness has on income equality. To assess this impact, I use all available

---

[§] Penn World Tables, http://pwt.econ.upenn.edu/php_site/pwt62/pwt62_form.php (accessed October 8, 2008).

data. These include data for the years 1950–1992 and for all countries for which data are available. The number of countries with the required data varies from year to year from about twenty countries to more than fifty. These countries differ markedly in income levels, with the lowest in per capita income being Ethiopia in 1984 ($318) and the highest being Switzerland in 1989 ($16,304). The United States, unfortunately, is missing from the data set.

Wealthy countries enjoy greater income equality on average than do poor countries. In fact, every doubling in per capita income is associated with 1.5 percent less income inequality on average. If, however, we investigate the magnitude, or percentage change, in income inequality looking three years ahead of when we observe the per capita income, we discover that income levels do not significantly influence changes in inequality one way or the other.

With the assessment of income levels in mind, we can now evaluate the impact on income inequality from the degree of receptivity to trade. Countries vary in their income inequality from a best-case Gini index score of about 20 to a worst-case score of about 60. Remember, the closer the Gini index is to zero, the more equally income is distributed, and the closer it is to 100, the more income is in the hands of only a small segment of the population. The trade openness measure OPENC varies from a low of about 8 (meaning that 8 percent of GDP comes from imports and exports) to a high of more than 200 (an economy that is completely dependent on trade; such an economy produces and consumes very little that is not imported or made for export). The statistical evidence tells us that a country that is closed to trade (that is, OPENC equals about 8) can expect a Gini index of 54. The evidence also tells us that an economy that is most open to trade (that is, OPENC equals about 212) can anticipate a Gini index of about 43. In other words, those who use the most trade protectionism also promote income inequality, keeping the poor poor and keeping the rich rich. The probability that this relationship arose by chance is less than 1 in 1,000. What is more, if we ask what will happen to income inequality in the future as a result of openness to trade now, we discover that strong equity effects persist.

Before closing, I think it is worthwhile to take one more statistical look at the effects of free trade. We now know that trade improves income equality, but what specifically does it do for labor and for capital? To evaluate the effect of openness to trade on labor, I assess labor's share of value-added in manufacturing as measured by the World Bank. To evaluate the effect of openness to trade on capital, I examine real gross domestic investment (private and public) as a percentage of GDP (both in 1985 international prices) using Penn World Tables data. Again, I control for the independent effect of per capita income levels.

Not surprisingly, the higher a country's average income level, the smaller the contribution that labor makes to value-added in manufacturing. This is a significant effect that is consistent with our Richland example, in which the wealthier country tends to have more capital-intensive industries. Openness to trade, however, has a huge impact on labor's contribution to the value-added through manufacturing. The significance level is so great that there is virtually no chance this result has arisen by chance. Those countries that offer the most trade protection can anticipate that labor's share of value-added in manufacturing will be only 41 percent.

Those that are most open to trade can anticipate that labor's share will be 59 percent. Clearly, a greater commitment to free trade is beneficial to labor.

Equally, a commitment to free trade is beneficial to capital. Higher-income countries have only a marginally better prospect of attracting investment than do poorer countries. The strength of the statistical relationship is weak enough that it would happen in seven out of every one hundred samples. Trade openness, in contrast, so strongly attracts foreign investment that the statistical relationship would happen by chance less than once in ten thousand samples. Those countries least open to trade have, on average, about 12 percent public and private investment as a share of GDP. Those countries most open to trade average investments equal to 18 percent of GDP, or 50 percent more than those closed to trade.

So we can see that nations that favor free-trade policies promote greater income equality (equity) and better returns to labor, and they attract more capital. Those that eschew free trade protect special domestic interests, but they foster inequity, poor returns to labor, and low investment in the society's future growth.

SUMMARY

Trade is a vital and growing area of international interaction. Efforts to promote globalization are supported by many governments around the world and, equally, are opposed by other governments and by well-organized interest groups. Free trade is good for consumers, but it can harm particular industries or those who own particular factors of production. Who is harmed by free trade depends on the mobility of labor and capital and on the ability of interested groups to overcome free-rider problems by organizing to pressure government for protection. If both labor and capital are fairly mobile, then over the long run free trade is relatively beneficial for capital in capital-intensive economies (like many wealthy countries) and is beneficial for labor in labor-intensive economies (like many poor countries). I say over the long run because, given sufficient time, both labor and capital are likely to find ways to move if they want to. In the short run, mobility is more difficult because investments are tied up, workers have family commitments, the government might restrict mobility, and so forth. In the long run, free trade is also relatively disadvantageous for the owners of capital in poor countries and for labor in rich countries. In short, free trade has the long-term prospect of being a great equalizer of income across countries and across owners of labor and owners of capital.

The evidence from our data set of countries over the past fifty years shows us the effects of different trade policies. Countries that restrict trade so that it is a small part of their economic picture tend to have relatively unequal income distributions, to provide relatively little value-added to labor, and to attract relatively small amounts of investment. Countries that have been open to trade tend to have relatively equal income distributions, to provide a relatively large value-added to labor, and to attract relatively large amounts of investment. Apparently, governments that interfere least in foreign trade produce the best outcomes, on average, for most of their citizens.

KEY CONCEPTS

absolute advantage   279
arbitrage   276
asset specificity   303
capital mobility   303
comparative advantage   280
currency convertibility   275
demand curves   286
dollarization   295
equilibrium price   284
exchange rates   292
factor mobility   305
factors of production   301

fair trade   291
float   292
Gini index   311
globalization   274
labor mobility   303
nontariff barriers   296
opportunity costs   281
political economy   275
production possibility frontier   281
receptivity to trade   311
supply curves   286
tariffs   289

11 International Organizations and International Law

- There is a proliferation of both governmental and nongovernmental international organizations. These organizations are designed to regulate international behavior, enforce international law, and create norms of conduct.

- The creation of sovereignty and the inviolability of policy within national borders is one of the most important and enduring international institutional arrangements.

- International organizations with broad membership, such as the United Nations, often are thought to be based on shallow agreements in that they can only ask for little change in behavior in order to get so many states to join.

- Smaller organizations, such as the Organization of Oil Exporting Countries (OPEC), tend to make deeper demands, but they also tend to have weak monitoring and enforcement powers.

The end of World War II produced renewed vigor and interest in promoting cooperation among the world's nations. This interest is manifest in the explosion of international organizations dedicated to creating rules designed to coordinate and regulate behavior. Such rules and regulations are prominent in almost every domain of international interaction. Some multilateral organizations or agreements and the rules they promulgate have been dedicated to conflict resolution, including, for instance, the United Nations and the Nuclear Nonproliferation Treaty. The WTO and regional organizations—including, for instance, NAFTA, Mercosur, and the European Union—regulate trade. Bodies such as the G-8,* the International Monetary Fund (IMF), the World Bank, and the Asian Development Bank help govern other forms of economic interaction. The Red Cross and the Red Crescent, Amnesty International, and other NGOs focus on a variety of social, environmental, informational, and human rights issues. These issues, likewise, are the focus of international law, multilateral agreements, and a host of other international organizations. In fact, virtually every aspect of international interactions has been the subject of the burgeoning body of international law and international institutions. The prominence of these institutions and their rules and regulations raises fundamental questions about international politics. Those questions are the subject of this chapter.

Several puzzles revolve around the proliferation—or even the existence—of international law and international organizations. Foremost among these is whether they make a difference. Certainly the events of September 11, 2001, compel us to wonder about the efficacy of international law. Do these organizations and regulations alter behavior or merely codify existing interests and actions? Are they effective in promoting cooperation when, otherwise, private interests would prevail over collective welfare? Do they undermine sovereignty to the advantage of intergovernmental organizations such as NATO and the United Nations, or of NGOs such as the World Economic Forum (which consists of 1,000 multinational corporations)? Or do they protect states against the erosion of their sovereignty by the Internet—which makes government restrictions on the flow of information difficult to enforce just as it makes collecting taxes

International organizations are an essential tool in facilitating international relations. In November 2008, heads of state of the member nations of the Asia-Pacific Economic Cooperation (APEC) organization convened for a summit in Lima, Peru.

---

* The G-8, called the G-7 before the addition of Russia, is a regularly scheduled summit of leaders from Canada, France, Germany, Italy, Japan, Russia, the United Kingdom, and the United States to coordinate economic policy.

on revenue difficult for governments to achieve—or by a few powerful predatory states or businesses? There are no generally accepted answers to any of these questions. The competing perspectives of international relations prompt different conclusions, and the body of evidence remains too incomplete to reach firm judgments.

INTERNATIONAL LAW, ORGANIZATIONS, AND REGIMES: DEFINITIONS AND DISTINCTIONS

Before turning to the specifics of international law, international organizations, and international regimes, we should be clear about how these categories differ and how they overlap. This is especially important because I sometimes treat them together and other times make sharp distinctions among the three categories.

International Law

International law consists of a body of treaty obligations that states enter into. Because they are treaties, rather than lesser agreements among states or subnational or non-national actors, they carry the force of law. This often means that independent nonstate bodies—such as certain international organizations—have the authority to adjudicate disputes and, at least in principle, to punish violations. This also often means that signatory states can press legal claims against alleged violations within the court system of the member states.

Consider the importance assigned to treaties in the U.S. Constitution. The Constitution designates treaties as special arrangements. It explicitly forbids individual states within the United States from entering into treaties or alliances. Doing this is exclusively the domain of the federal government. Within that domain, the president is given the power "by and with the advice and consent of the Senate, to make Treaties, provided two thirds of the Senators present concur" (Art. II, Sec. 2, Cl. 2). The adjudication of disputes involving treaties is also given a special place in the legal structure of the United States. The Constitution (Art. III, Sec. 2, Cl. 1) stipulates that "[t]he judicial Power shall extend to all Cases, in Law and Equity, arising under this Constitution, the Laws of the United States, and Treaties made, or which shall be made, under their Authority, ... and between a State, or the Citizens thereof, and foreign States, Citizens, or Subjects." Here the Constitution places the status of treaties on a par with the laws

> **TRY THIS**
>
> What are the implications of the Constitution's discussion of treaties for understanding the obligations of the U.S. government toward American Indian tribes as a result of peace treaties signed between these tribes and the U.S. government in the nineteenth century? Do these obligations differ legally from the obligations of the U.S. government under the Treaty of Versailles, which ended World War I, or the Paris Peace Treaty, which ended the war in Vietnam? What does the existence of such treaties with American Indian tribes indicate about their legal status as recognized by the U.S. government? Is the treatment of American Indians a purely internal affair, or is it subject to scrutiny under international law?

promulgated within the United States and on an equal footing with the Constitution itself, so treaties cannot be voided purely on the basis of a judgment that they violate other aspects of the Constitution. They become part of the core law and commitments of the nation once they are ratified in accordance with the procedures set out in the Constitution.

International law includes treaties about such diverse topics as fishing and exploration rights within the world's oceans, protection of human rights, prohibitions against torture, the treatment of prisoners of war, regulation of international commerce, copyrights and other intellectual property rights, the nonproliferation of nuclear weapons, and the use of land mines. Countries can opt out of the obligation to obey a given international law by failing to endorse the law. In this way, international law can be very different from laws within countries. People living in a given country do not have the option of picking and choosing the laws they are obligated to obey, but to a much larger degree, nations do have this choice. That is one indication that international politics is anarchic, as suggested by realists.

One central question about international law that clearly separates approaches to international relations is whether such law is binding, is not binding but alters behavior, merely codifies existing norms and beliefs, or is irrelevant to the actions of nations. Constructivists, as discussed in the Introduction to this book, see international law as reshaping the internal perception of national interests and, thereby, changing how states behave. In their view and as a central tenet of constructivism, law helps to create norms of conduct. Legalistic observers, in contrast, perceive international law as binding rather than as reflecting accepted norms of conduct. International lawyers, for example, do not think of law as reflecting strategic interactions but, rather, as a body of legally binding obligations to which signatory states have subjected themselves. The strategic perspective views treaty obligations as costly signals that constrain the range of choices that leaders can make, allowing one generation of leaders to tie the hands—that is, limit the freedom of action—of future leaders. If the restraints imposed by international law deviate too greatly from a leader's interests, then the strategic point of view

PERSPECTIVES ON INTERNATIONAL LAW

Constructivism: International law creates norms of conduct. For many governments, it alters their perception of their own national interest. Violations are expected to be infrequent.

Liberalism: International law creates norms of conduct and promotes shared values that favor cooperation among states. The norms of conduct are often promulgated and protected by a hegemonic power. Departures from the law are expected to be infrequent.

Realism: International law codifies current perceptions of the national interest, especially for powerful states. Relatively frequent violations by the powerful are expected when interests in specific circumstances are not advanced by existing international law or agreements.

Strategic approach: Acceptance of international law creates costly signals that constrain a state's future range of actions. Because the hands of future leaders are tied by international commitments, relatively few violations of international law and agreements are expected.

suggests that the leader will opt out of the law because the costs of doing so are smaller than the gains. Because such breaks with prior treaty agreements are costly, they are expected to be infrequent.

Realists consider international law largely as the codification of current interests and, therefore, as easily altered or violated when the nation's interests are no longer served by the existing treaty obligations. Realism, then, suggests there will be more frequent breaks with international law than is implied by the strategic perspective or a constructivist viewpoint. Liberal theorists perceive international law as a foundation on which nations build cooperative arrangements that facilitate coordination in the areas covered by the law. As such, they anticipate infrequent departures from such law because its purpose is to facilitate the advancement of shared national interests in creating a cooperative environment. Liberal theorists share with constructivists the conviction that international law fosters the creation of new norms of conduct among states (Keohane and Nye 1977; Goldstein and Keohane 1993; Clark 2003).

International Organizations

International law is sometimes enforced within national courts, and at other times it is enforced within bodies specifically created for that purpose. Some **international organizations** (for example, the WTO) fall into this latter category; they are institutions created by participating states for the purpose of enforcing, elaborating, and modifying international laws, much as a nation's legislature reviews and alters national law from time to time. Just as laws within a country are binding only on citizens and residents within the country, so international laws generally are enforceable only against signatories to the treaties that created the law. This means that international organizations created to enforce certain rules and regulations generally have no standing with nonsignatory states. This restriction on enforceability is itself an area of considerable discussion among students of international organizations. As we see later in this chapter, there are benefits and costs associated with making an international organization more or less inclusive in its membership.

Perhaps the most prominent international organization in today's world is the United Nations. The United Nations, with its main headquarters in New York City, was created at the end of World War II. It was designed as an organization that would be as universal in membership as possible and that would establish and enforce international law across a wide area concerned with preserving or restoring peace and protecting human rights. Its largest body, the General Assembly, includes almost every state in the world. The General Assembly passes resolutions and debates many of the fundamental international policy questions of the day.

The Security Council is the most powerful body in the United Nations. It is currently made up of fifteen countries, five, as noted earlier, of which are permanent members with veto power (the P-5). There is an ongoing discussion about expanding the Security Council and, particularly, about giving a veto to such countries as Japan, India, and Brazil. Not surprisingly, the members that currently have a veto are resisting the proposed change. The remaining ten nonpermanent, nonveto slots rotate among member states based on regional associations, such as the Arab League or the Organization of American States. All questions concerned with international security and peace are in the domain of the Security Council if it chooses to consider them. It also has the power to implement resolutions of the United Nations with force if necessary, provided the permanent members all agree to do so.

The International Court of Justice, located in The Hague, Netherlands, has responsibility for adjudicating cases involving alleged violations of member obligations under the UN Charter, with the charter being the UN's equivalent to the U.S. Constitution. That is, the charter is the fundamental law that all member states agree to abide by when they become members of the United Nations. Later in this chapter, I examine how well these and other aspects of the United Nations work in practice.

Not all international organizations exist to create or enforce laws that are, in principle, binding obligations among signatory states. Some international organizations exist to facilitate coordination and cooperation among members, although they lack the standing of law. The World Bank and the Asian Development Bank, for example, are voluntary organizations designed to facilitate economic assistance among member states. The Asian Development Bank makes loans and sometimes provides economic advice to member states so as to facilitate economic growth. The World Bank does much the same. The Organization of Oil Exporting Countries (OPEC) is designed to help member states coordinate their production and sale of petroleum to influence and stabilize the price of crude oil around the world. Members agree to produce no more than their assigned quota of oil; however, OPEC has virtually no mechanisms to enforce **compliance** with its quotas.

Probably the most significant emerging international body in the world is the European Union (EU). The EU, consists of twenty-seven European states ranging from such small countries as Malta and Cyprus to such large countries as France, Germany, and the United Kingdom. With some exceptions (the United Kingdom and Sweden), the member states have adopted a common currency (the euro) and are governed by a common central bank. The EU has established an elected parliament, many common economic and social policies, shared limits on indebtedness and other financial matters, and free movement for EU citizens across the borders of its member states.

The EU started out in 1951 as the European Coal and Steel Community (ECSC) and was designed to help Europe rebuild itself after World War II. The 1987 Single European Act promulgated much greater economic integration in Europe by creating a largely free-trade internal market, somewhat paralleling the U.S. Constitution's prohibition on tariffs and other trade limitations among the American states. In 1992, the fifteen western European nations that then made up the European Community (EC) signed the Maastricht Treaty, which expanded the domain of the EC's shared interests beyond economic matters to include political concerns and an emerging political structure. Since then, other treaties have continued to modify the structure of the European Union in an effort to forge a workable balance between local national interests and the common interests of the member states as represented in the European Parliament and European Commission.

The EU appears to be on the path to building a more or less united Europe, a federation of states with political, economic, and even military clout roughly comparable to the United States. Indeed, if European integration does not stumble over issues of relative voting weights for the member states or concerns over differential wealth and the like, the EU may well emerge as the principal international body to rival the United States for global influence. After all, Europe's gross product—not China's or India's or Japan's—is about equal to that of the United States. Its territory is smaller but still vast; its technology is cutting edge in many fields; and it possesses a well-educated, highly skilled population. Thus, the political and economic prospects of a united Europe are daunting but so too is the task of creating it. In 2005, for instance, the members of the EU voted on a constitution to further unification, but the proposed constitution failed the electoral test. The French public, for example, voted against the proposed constitution in May 2005, thereby scuttling the document. In 2008, facing a broad financial and economic crisis, the European Union tried to devise a united policy for helping to salvage struggling banks and protect assets. Germany balked, resisting the idea that Germans would not control who would be rescued with their tax euros. Whether these developments mark a major reversal in progress toward unification or a bump along the way, we will learn in the years ahead. We return to issues concerning the EU as an international organization later in this chapter.

International organizations are formally established bodies designed to facilitate coordination among member states, much as the EU is doing, or among nongovernmental actors, as is true for such NGOs as the International Red Cross, the Catholic Church, CARE, and Amnesty International. Although each of these organizations has operations based in specific countries, they normally are not operated, controlled, or organized by governments; they exist to help facilitate the promotion and fulfillment of their mission on a regional or global basis without the intervention of national governments. Of course, they are restricted to operating within the laws of the states in which they perform their services, but otherwise their members choose their own rules and regulations.

The number of international organizations, and particularly the number of NGOs, has grown tremendously over the decades since the end of World War II. There are many possible explanations for this proliferation (Lauren 1998). Constructivists and liberal theorists suggest that the growth in such bodies is the result of a shared realization that the world can avoid disaster only through better mechanisms for coordinating action, creating shared values, and promoting cooperation (Risse-Kappen, Ropp, and Sikkink 1999). The end of World War II and the subsequent decades of cold war both served to increase these concerns.

The strategic perspective, although not in disagreement with this viewpoint, also suggests that the emergence of more international organizations and NGOs was fostered by the proliferation of democratic governments after World War II and especially since the end of the cold war. Because democracies experience high rates of turnover in leaders, their governments have especially strong incentives to reduce the inherent policy uncertainty created by such turnovers. One way to do so is by limiting the freedom of action of future leaders through public, explicit, international commitments. Violating such commitments can be politically costly (as discussed shortly). Therefore, membership in international organizations helps promote compliance, especially for democratic leaders, who are vulnerable to the domestic political costs associated with rapid reversals in policy, making such organizations an attractive vehicle for reducing uncertainty and promoting stability in foreign affairs.

International Regimes

International regimes are international institutions, rules, regulations, and norms; these subsume international law and international organizations. Thus, international regimes constitute a generic category intended to promote the importance of ideas in international politics (Goldstein and Keohane 1993). States and their leaders respond not only to explicit legal obligations through law but also to informal understandings and expectations resulting from norms of conduct. Norms of behavior change, and these changes result in altered patterns of international interaction. For example, today's norms of conduct prohibit targeting specific political leaders for capture or assassination, but in the Middle Ages, capturing and ransoming foreign leaders was a legitimate aspect of warfare. Today, ransoming prisoners of war for money is widely regarded as inappropriate and inhumane, but during the Hundred Years War, in the fourteenth and fifteenth centuries, ransoming prisoners of war was not only normal conduct but the basis for the relatively humane treatment of prisoners. Today, torture, although still used frequently enough to have prompted an international treaty against torture and a subject of much concern in the United States during the George W. Bush presidency, violates contemporary norms of behavior. This is clear from the international outrage at and the embarrassment of many Americans because of the torture of Iraqi prisoners at the Abu Ghraib prison and at Guantanamo Bay and elsewhere. Torture now is seen as abominable conduct. But in the twelfth century, the Catholic Church saw torture as a means of saving souls, rescuing people from eternal damnation; in those days, it was perceived as a good thing.

When norms of conduct are insufficient to promote cooperation, then more formal arrangements become important as means to reduce international conflict. Thus, informal regimes get replaced by formal international organizations or by codified laws of conduct when norms alone prove insufficient to achieve the desired ends. When and why any of these mechanisms work is the focus of the remainder of this chapter.

CAN WE EVALUATE THE EFFECTS OF INTERNATIONAL REGIMES?

The degree of influence that international law and international organizations exert on the actions of nations is difficult to resolve, primarily because institutions, rules, and regulations are endogenous. That is, neither international law nor any specific organization arises spontaneously or by chance. They are the consequence of negotiated agreements among leaders of states. Thus, it is difficult to separate the interests that these leaders represent from the choices they make regarding the structures of international organizations and rules. Certainly it is unlikely that they would agree to structures that constrain their behavior in ways that are contrary to their interests—but if that is so, then international regimes, rather than influencing national actions, just reflect national interests. There are also counterarguments that support the opposite conclusion—that international law, organizations, rules, and regulations alter behavior rather than just reflecting national (leader or regime) interests.

The Constructivist Case

Constructivists argue that the very content of a country's national interest can be redefined by its membership in an international organization. This is hypothesized to happen as a result of three factors: legitimation, role redefinition, and reflection. The argument for regime **legitimation** maintains that, when members comply with an organization's mission, the members endow the regime's rules and regulations with authority and legitimacy. Oren Young and M.A. Levy (1999), for example, maintain that organization members do not engage in the kind of cost-benefit calculations that characterize strategic behavior because they have internalized the regime's routines and they have been socialized to accept them. Little evidence, however, is offered to bolster this claim and, as we learn in the Introduction, evidence is now emerging that challenges these predictions. Among the unanswered questions about the constructivist case is why a member of an international regime would see the regime's rules and regulations as being either legitimate or authoritative if they run counter to the interests of the state. George Downs (2000) suggests there is evidence that states do not in the case of environmental regimes, just as Feryal Cherif (2005) does in her investigation of the role women play in the political life of countries that are signatories to the 1979 United Nations Convention on the Elimination of All Forms of Discrimination Against Women (CEDAW).

Role redefinition, the creation or changing of a nation's or decision maker's identity as a function of the part the nation is assigned in an international organization or series of interactions, is also hypothesized to be a factor in redefining national interests; that is, organizations, being complex, assign different roles to different actors and these organizational roles can affect policy positions. For example, Japan was thrust into a leadership role during the environmental negotiations over what came to be called the Kyoto Protocols. The country took a stronger pro-environmental stance than it had in earlier negotiations, perhaps because its new role gave it a new identity. From a strategic perspective, Japan changed its position perhaps because it realized that U.S. opposition would defeat the Kyoto proposals anyway, and so it could safely say it supported them, collect the good press for doing so, and still get the same result it had wanted all along (nonpassage of the proposals) without having to go out on a limb by declaring itself to be opposed. In fact, contrary to constructivist expectations, the Japanese government subsequently admitted that it cannot meet the greenhouse gas emissions reductions it promised to make as part of the Kyoto Protocols.

Alexander Wendt (1994) contends that the roles a nations plays in international organizations gradually create a new identity for the state as it associates itself with the role in which it has been placed. This new identity, in turn, promotes new interests, thereby redefining the national interest. Of course, organization members agree to accept particular roles. This means that it is difficult to distinguish between a true change in national identity and the acceptance of roles as part of an endogenous, negotiated process that reflects national or individual leader interests. The idea of role redefinition is intriguing, although it has yet to be subjected to rigorous empirical scrutiny beyond selected case studies (Weiss and Jacobson 1998).

TRY THIS

The Kyoto Protocols went into effect in 2005 despite U.S. opposition. This provides a natural experiment in which we can test Japan's, or any other signatory's, commitment to changing its behavior. Find data on Japanese emissions over time of the noxious gases covered by the protocol. Are the observed results for Japanese emissions better than, the same as, or worse than they were before the Kyoto Protocols went into effect? Check whether the rate of decline (or increase) in such emissions has accelerated now that the protocol is in effect compared to before the protocol. Make this assessment again for U.S. emissions. How do the Japanese emissions compare to U.S. emissions during the same time period?

The idea that member states, through the process of interaction within an organization, learn to see themselves as others see them is called reflection. This is hypothesized to be in part a direct process and in part an indirect process. The more a country realizes that other countries perceive it as cooperative or as obstreperous, for example, the more that reflected perception leads to reinforced or changed behavior. Furthermore, the more a country behaves cooperatively, the more likely it is that other countries change their views and reflect back its new image as a cooperator. That reflected improvement in perceptions, in turn, is hypothesized to lead to or to reinforce changes in behavior and in self-definition.

Such a psychological process may go on, but we do not yet have sufficient evidence to conclude that reflection takes place and changes self-identity or interests (Wendt 1994). George Downs (2000), in fact, provides a thoughtful review and critique of the constructivist perspective about international organizations and their prospects for promoting changes in the national interest and in cooperation. He puts forward example after example in which such changes do not appear to have occurred.

Furthermore, even if such changes in outlook occur for the agent representing a given government in an organization, it is not clear why the leadership of the country would maintain the representative in office. If a representative's orientation is out of alignment with the national leadership's perception of the national interest, then it seems likely that the representative will be replaced. In such a circumstance, there is an agency problem; that is, the principal (the person or citizenry for whom the representative works) is not getting support from the agent (the subordinate or representative) that is expected. The nation's leaders will retain such a representative only if the representative's actions do not deviate so much from their own interests that they feel the cost of retaining the representative is too high. In that case, however, with only small deviations allowed, the national interest has not been materially changed. Thus, the constructivist notion of reflection could be true in influencing small, marginal changes within the confines of what the principal-agent relationship will tolerate. It cannot be true as regards a material shift away from the national interest, however the national political leadership defines that interest. It is hard to tell empirically whether any change in the national interest has taken place because reflection must fall within the presumably narrow bounds of tolerance that the principal has for any shifts in approach that his or her agent in an international organization may make. Testing whether such reflection occurs at all or whether deviations from the wishes of the leadership back home are just indicative of the routine latitude of agents with special knowledge is a daunting empirical question. In this particular instance, neither the constructivist nor the principal-agent account can be easily falsified.

The Strategic Case

The strategic perspective helps us see that what constitutes the national interest can be manipulated by individual political leaders. They build coalitions around interests and can link issues together so that many different winning coalitions can be formed. Indeed, even a supermajority of relevant constituents can be assembled in favor of widely divergent and even contradictory policy stances through skillful political maneuvering. As we know, for instance, when issues are linked together (guns and butter, trade policy and national security policy, and foreign aid to alleviate poverty and to gain policy compliance), the median voter theorem no longer holds. Winning coalitions can be formed that support virtually any change from the status quo policies, making what defines the national interest utterly manipulable. Observers might mistake the policies of any of these coalitions as being deviations from the national interest, but such deviations can arise only if the national interest is assumed to have some specific content as opposed to being viewed as a product of strategic maneuvering and bargaining.

Skillful political leaders can shape the focus of the national interest on issues and policy positions that are advantageous for them because many different majority coalitions can be assembled by using linkage politics, that is, tying choices together across multiple issues as in win set analyses (introduced in Chapter 2). This suggests both strengths and limitations to the influence that international agreements or organizations can have. Leaders come and go. Few leaders of democracies last even as long as five years; autocrats last longer, but few even among autocrats survive in office beyond a decade or two. International organizations commonly survive several generations of national leaders. NATO, for example, was formed in 1949. Each member country has undergone many, many domestic turnovers in political leadership during the more than half century since NATO's creation, yet NATO's fundamental rules remain the same. The **Treaty of Westphalia** was signed more than 350 years ago, yet many of its specifications regarding **sovereignty,** that is, the right and authority to rule within a specified, usually geographical domain, remain relevant to international interaction today. These examples remind us that international law and international organizations are not as ephemeral as are the terms in office of political leaders or as their view of the national interest.

Organizations and law are **sticky**; by this I mean that it takes large changes in the interests of member states before it is possible to make substantial changes in the structure of law and organizations. The transaction costs associated with change often exceed the expected benefits. In this way, international bodies are much like a factory. Business owners do not tear down their factories and rebuild every time there is an improvement in technology. The cost of doing so is just too high—they live with some inefficiency in their factories rather than bearing the cost of change. Only when the inefficiency becomes too costly do business owners tear down and rebuild.[†] So it is with international organizations or law. New leaders come to power and find that some of the organizations or rules that their predecessors endorsed are not optimal for their purposes. Still, the organizations may provide enough benefits that the new leaders can live with them rather than trying to make politically costly changes or withdrawing from the organizations.

The stickiness of international organizations has a deeper strategic implication. The decision to form or belong to international institutions is, as noted, endogenous. That is, political leaders make a strategic choice, presumably designed to enhance their own or their political party's prospects of remaining in office and to ensure that, should they lose their position, their policy preferences will persist. By forming or accepting the rules of an international organization or by endorsing a body of international law, current leaders impose these rules and laws as constraints on subsequent leaders. The value in imposing constraints on subsequent leaders, according to the strategic perspective, depends on the expected frequency of, intensity of, and uncertainty about deviations in the ideal points of future leaders. As we know, political leadership turns over more frequently in democracies. There are, therefore, more opportunities for someone to come to power whose coalition's interests deviate markedly from those currently in place. Autocrats, in contrast, tend to stay in office considerably longer; consequently, autocrats face less uncertainty about policy shifts because they will be in office longer and be able to sustain their own policy objectives. International organizations and international laws are arguably more valuable to the leaders of democracies because the cost of abandoning the law or organization in the future constrains future leaders to adhere to the policies, rules, and regulations already in effect (Gartzke and Gleditsch 2002).

The bureaucrats who make up the civil service of a large international organization can play an active role as well in preserving such institutions, even when the institution's reasons for existing may have ended or be greatly altered. Interested agents may inflate the expected cost of doing away with an organization to give the appearance that getting rid of it would just not be cost-effective. This possibility alerts us to the fact that international regimes can be critical sources of conflict between the bureaucrats who run them and the leaders of member states (or NGOs). The former are in the role of agents, and the latter are in the role of principals. To the extent that international regimes foster principal-agent problems, it is likely that such regimes only partially reflect national interests and so may be ineffective in

---

[†] I am indebted to Barry Weingast for this argument.

promoting the goals of the membership. If principal-agent problems are prominent in international regimes, then we may indeed observe organizations adopting policies that deviate from the national interests of some member states, as suggested by constructivists and neoliberal theorists. In such cases, if the strategic perspective is correct, the organization should prove to be unsuccessful in extracting meaningful compliance from the affected members.

The North Atlantic Treaty Organization and Organizational Inertia: An Illustrative Case

NATO was created in 1949 to provide security for Europe and North America against the threat of Soviet expansion. The organization erected a large, complex bureaucracy, currently situated primarily in Brussels, Belgium. The armies of the member states are highly integrated, using common weapons and a common command structure. This and many other complex features of NATO were designed to make it an efficient and effective fighting force against the often-superior numbers of the Soviet military.

Many credit NATO with playing a central part in maintaining peace during the cold war and probably rightly so. But NATO did not cease to exist after the Soviet Union collapsed. Now, as we approach twenty years after the Soviet Union's demise, NATO is still a large and powerful international organization. It has broadened its scope—of course, it had to do so because its original purpose no longer exists, although a related purpose seems to be looming large for the future following Russia's invasion of Georgia, a non-NATO state, in 2008—to include peacekeeping missions in, for instance, central Europe and protecting and defending the membership's shared democratic values. The mission is much broader and vaguer than it was in 1949, and the membership has been expanded to include former members of the Warsaw Pact, NATO's long-time adversary. The change in mission, indeed, is not unique to NATO. It is typical for alliances and other international organizations to persist beyond the issues for which they were formed (Bennett and Tarry 1996).

When bureaucratic inertia helps an organization survive, it is likely that the organization will become less effective in pursuing its mission. It is also likely that compliance with the new activities of the organization will diminish as members contend over exactly what their obligations are. Such divisions were evident throughout the Bosnia and Kosovo crises of the 1990s and the Iraq War of 2003. NATO's members were not of one mind with regard to whether they should or could intervene in these violent disputes. As a consequence, NATO was slow to act and failed to achieve consensus on how it ought to act. Although the organization was created to coordinate defense policies, divisions among the member states arising from its uncertain mission during the war in Kosovo and its aftermath diminished the effectiveness of the fighting forces. Edward Luttwak, a foreign policy analyst, reported on April 11, 2000, that

> [t]he Albanian terror campaign against Serb and Roma civilians started as soon as the Serb forces withdrew. General Clark and the British Kosovo Force Commander therefore urged NATO forces to deploy as quickly as possible, and to patrol intensively to stop the

mayhem. British troops maximized control of their sector by patrolling on foot in half squads by day and by night. But the U.S. Joint Chiefs insisted that the first priority was to ensure the protection and comfort of the U.S. garrison. While $36 million was being spent to erect the defenses and comfort facilities of Camp Bonesteel (complete with two PX stores, fast-food cafeterias, etc.), U.S. troops were only sent out on patrol in large detachments mounted on vehicles, which remained on the main roads. Albanian ethnic cleansing was virtually unopposed in the U.S. sector, in which no Serbs or Roma now remain. French patrol practices at first resembled those of the British. Once the French realized that the other NATO forces were avoiding effort and risk, they too stopped their intensive patrols. The phenomenon of "multi-national troop degradation" had set in.

The circumstances described by Luttwak highlight a crucial issue for all international organizations. International regimes are erected to coordinate cooperation among members, especially when individual interests dictate that some members are better off not cooperating. Yet, as the example of U.S. and then French forces makes clear, the member states of NATO faced the prisoners' dilemma in the aftermath of the Kosovo war. The objective of NATO's forces was to act aggressively to stop ethnic cleansing. All members would benefit if the ethnic cleansing ended and the situation were stabilized. But members would also benefit by free riding on the efforts of others, avoiding the risks inherent in aggressive military patrols. As we know, if the prisoners' dilemma is not indefinitely repeated, players are most likely to choose to defect; that is, in this case, they are likely not to patrol. The United States engaged in lax patrols while the British and French (for a time) took greater risks. Realizing that the Americans were avoiding circumstances that put them in harm's way, France reciprocated by also choosing a low-risk patrol strategy. The consequence was that NATO was poorly positioned to implement its objective effectively. Thus, NATO did not, in this case, enforce its desired actions when those actions were contrary to the interests of some of its members. Let us now turn to an example of a successfully implemented set of treaty obligations.

TRY THIS

I describe the actions of France and the United States in their patrols in Kosovo as a prisoners' dilemma game. Can you make the case that this is the wrong game to represent that situation? Might the Battle of the Sexes game better reflect the situation? Design your own simple game to capture the dynamics of the military patrol problem discussed by Luttwak. Consider a three-player game, consisting of the British, French, and Americans, or even a four-player game that expands the set to include the Albanians engaged in ethnic cleansing.

SOVEREIGNTY: A SUCCESSFUL INTERNATIONAL INSTITUTION

In earlier chapters we have seen some of the important aspects of the Treaty of Westphalia and noted that this treaty established many elements of international law regarding sovereignty. Let us examine two articles of that treaty. Article 64 states:

And to prevent for the future any Differences arising in the Politick State, all and every one of the Electors, Princes and States of the Roman Empire, are so establish'd and confirm'd in their antient, Prerogatives, Libertys, Privileges, free exercise of Territorial Right, as well Ecclesiastick, as Politick Lordships, Regales, by virtue of this present Transaction: that they never can or ought to be molested therein by any whomsoever upon any manner of pretence.

Article 67 states:

That as well as general as particular Diets, the free Towns, and other States of the Empire, shall have decisive Votes; they shall, without molestation, keep their Regales, Customs, annual Revenues, Libertys, Privileges to confiscate, to raise Taxes, and other Rights, lawfully obtain'd from the Emperor and Empire, or enjoy'd long before these Commotions, with a full Jurisdiction within the inclosure of their Walls, and their Territorys: making void at the same time, annulling and for the future prohibiting all Things, which by Reprisals, Arrests, stopping of Passages, and other prejudicial Acts, either during the War, under what pretext soever they have been done and attempted hitherto by private Authority, or may hereafter without any preceding formality of Right be enterpris'd. As for the rest, all laudable Customs of the sacred Roman Empire, the fundamental Constitutions and Laws, shall for the future be strictly observ'd, all the Confusions which time of War have, or could introduce, being remov'd and laid aside.

These two articles provide, in modern parlance, for states to be secure within their borders. The sovereign government within a state is free to make its own rules and regulations regarding virtually every aspect of its citizens' lives. Some of the examples enumerated in these articles are the rights of the sovereign—that is, the governing authority—to establish religious practices within the bounds of his or her territory and to raise taxes to advance the policies and programs to which the sovereign subscribes.

Regardless of how repugnant these internal activities may be to outsiders, the expectation established in these articles is that outsiders have no right to interfere in the domestic affairs of other states. What are the consequences, if any, of these stipulations? How have they shaped international politics? Is it likely that international politics would have looked the same whether or not these two articles of the Treaty of Westphalia had been formally written down?

International Borders as Institutions

The two articles of the treaty establish essential principles of international law and practice that are still observed to this day. Article 64 is intended to bar foreign rivals from interfering in the sovereign's rights within his or her territory. Article 67 reinforces this point, emphasizing that the sovereign has full jurisdiction over all matters within the borders of the state. In this way, territorial borders are created as an institution of international politics, an institution with standing in international law. That law, of course, is the treaty itself. States are granted the right to defend their actions and privileges within their borders. Other states do not have the right to cross a country's border and impose their will on the sovereign territory of another government and people.

Even today, more than three and a half centuries after the Treaty of Westphalia was signed, this has profound implications. There are, of course, the obvious implications regarding war and aggression. The Treaty of Westphalia set out rules and regulations restricting the rights of states to use force against one another. These rules are generally obeyed. Aggression is regarded in principle as unacceptable conduct in international affairs, and it is relatively rare. The relations among few states can long be characterized as aggressive. Yet territorial issues, especially the location of borders, are the most frequent sources of war (Vasquez 1995; Huth 1996). That certainly was, for instance, a major factor in Russia's invasion of Georgia in summer 2008. Among Georgia's provinces, two—Abkhazia and South Ossetia—are ethnically predominantly Russian and border on Russia. Russia's government shares the view of most people who live in South Ossetia and Abkhazia, that these provinces should be part of Russia, not Georgia. The Georgian government understandably disagrees. The result, unfortunately, was a territorial war of the sort that the Treaty of Westphalia was designed to avoid.

The body of international law that has grown up around the enforcement of territorial sovereignty accurately characterizes most international relationships most (but not all) of the time. Whether the enforcement of or respect for borders is a consequence of the restrictions imposed by international law or the restrictions of international law reflect the interests of powerful states is difficult to sort out. Doing so requires that we assess how frequent territorial disputes would be in a counterfactual world (or a pre-Westphalian world) in which international laws and regulations regarding borders did not exist. Whatever effect international law has had on the sanctity of borders, it is clear that most people most of the time oppose on principled, normative grounds the use of aggression to violate sovereignty. In this way, the law has created a norm of conduct. So strong is the normative belief that the citizens of a state have the right to be secure within its borders that the violation of such borders is perceived generally as unwarranted aggression. Yet the law regarding sovereign rights within borders has a less obvious and perhaps morally reprehensible consequence, a consequence that suggests that the norms surrounding the sanctity of borders are gradually changing.

Consider the case of ethnic genocide. Under the leadership of Pol Pot (1976–1979), the Cambodian government engaged in genocide against its own people. Nearly 2 million Cambodians were killed during Pol Pot's reign of terror. Neither the United Nations nor the United States nor anyone else other than Vietnam intervened against Pol Pot's genocide, ostensibly because there was no basis in international law to do so. The reasoning was as simple as it was troubling. The Pol Pot regime was exercising its right to do whatever it chose within its own borders. The Cambodian government, in keeping with Article 67 of the Treaty of Westphalia, was acting with "full Jurisdiction within the inclosure of their Walls, and their Territorys." The United Nations, then, seemingly had no jurisdiction. Just as the law gave Pol Pot his rights in Cambodia, the law denied to the nations of the world the right to intervene to save the people of that country. Vietnam eventually did intervene, deposing Pol Pot in the process and receiving a condemnation from the United States and other countries for violating the sovereign territory of Cambodia.

The United Nations, however, could have provided a legal basis to intervene in Cambodia had it been willing to interpret its authority a bit more broadly. The UN Convention on the Prevention and Punishment of the Crime of Genocide was approved by a vote of 55 to 0 in December 1948. The convention defines *genocide* as the commission of certain acts with the intent to destroy, wholly or in part, a national, ethnic, racial, or religious group, and it deems it a crime under international law, whether committed in war or in peace. Here, then, we have another difficulty with international law—the legal status of sovereignty protects states from foreign intervention in their domestic affairs, yet since 1948 the law regarding genocide has theoretically empowered states to intervene in the domestic affairs of another state to prevent or stop genocide.[‡] In fact, this contradiction was much on the mind of U.S. senators who were responsible for ratifying the convention. Although President Harry Truman signed the convention on December 12, 1948, the U.S. Senate did not ratify it until 1988. The Senate's hesitation was precisely due to concern over the convention's prospects of leading to interference in U.S. domestic affairs and the erosion of sovereignty.

The right of foreign governmental and nongovernmental interests to interfere in the internal actions of sovereign states, then, can change to reflect changing interests, sensibilities, and power. Perhaps, as constructivists argue, experience and reflection led participants in the convention against genocide to internalize stronger norms about the value of human life, norms sufficiently strong that they could overcome the earlier norm against intervention in the internal policies of a state.

Why one norm usurps another is a question unanswered by constructivism, but this question may be answered by the strategic perspective. Constructivism, as discussed earlier, is about the formation of preferences and not about the actions that are expected given those preferences. The strategic perspective does not explain where preferences come from, but it offers an equilibrium basis for thinking about how people act on their preferences. Together, the two approaches may provide a coherent explanation of changing values and actions in international affairs.

As the world becomes more democratic, it may be that it is harder to sustain the old norms that favored thinking of states as unitary sovereigns. The more we think about state policies as the aggregation of individual interests, the more likely we are to elevate the importance of individuals over collective ideas such as "the state." Thus, newly constructed values in favor of individual welfare over the collective national welfare might gain greater importance. Democratic practices place great emphasis on individual interests, whereas authoritarian arrangements compress the state and the dictator into a single actor. When the

---

[‡] I say, "theoretically empowers states to intervene in the domestic affairs of another state" because when the convention on genocide was established the members had the Holocaust of World War II in mind. It is not evident that they envisioned a circumstance in which a government committed genocide exclusively against its own people.

state is seen as a unitary actor, it is difficult to sustain a norm that addresses the welfare of individual constituents. If we consider state policies to reflect aggregated individual preferences, then the constructivist focus suggests that norms and values are likely to be reshaped, becoming attentive to individual welfare. The strategic perspective, then, identifies the circumstances under which those governments that are so inclined can act to enforce these reshaped norms that place value on individual welfare. The genocide convention, of course, is illustrative of just such a set of normative values.

International law has frequently been changed and its domain expanded. The convention on genocide, although signed by the vast majority of the world's nations, was not actually used as a basis for an international legal action until September 1998 when Rwanda's Hutu leaders were charged with genocide in connection with their actions against Rwanda's Tutsi population. This marked an important shift in the use of international law to deal with gross misconduct within a nation's borders.

The Expansion of International Law: The Example of Helsinki

There is another example that may be even more significant because it shows the use of international regimes to alter the behavior of a great power. Consider how the **Helsinki Final Act** of 1975 expanded international law to permit governmental and nongovernmental interference in the face of human rights violations in any of the signatory states, including the Soviet Union.

The Soviet Union agreed, along with thirty-four other states, to the Helsinki Final Act to ensure the recognition of the independence of its ally, the German Democratic Republic (also known as East Germany). In exchange for this recognition, the Soviets (probably unwittingly) set the stage for tremendous international pressure designed to foster democratization and the spread of freedom across the Soviet empire. Without the agreement in Helsinki, it would have been difficult—as it had been for decades prior to the Helsinki Final Act—to speak out authoritatively against the internal policies of the Soviet Union and its Eastern European satellites.

The thirty-five signatories to the Helsinki Final Act reached seemingly innocuous agreements stipulating that:

> [t]he participating States will respect human rights and fundamental freedoms, including the freedom of thought, conscience, religion or belief, for all without distinction as to race, sex, language, or religion.
>
> They will promote and encourage the effective exercise of civil, political, economic, social, cultural, and other rights and freedoms all of which derive from the inherent dignity of the human person and are essential for his free and full development....
>
> The participating States recognize the universal significance of human rights and fundamental freedoms, respect for which is an essential factor for the peace, justice and well-being necessary to ensure the development of friendly relations and co-operation among themselves as among all States.[§]

[§] See www.civnet.org/resources/historic/helsinki.htm.

Through these seemingly innocent terms, the Helsinki Final Act permitted western states and NGOs such as Amnesty International to assert something approximating a right to oversee and to influence domestic policies regarding human rights in any or all of the signatory states (Clark 2003). The act authorized them "to promote and encourage the effective exercise of civil, political, economic, social, cultural, and other rights and freedoms," and so they promoted and encouraged these rights and freedoms with vigor. Because the Soviet Union and its allies in the Warsaw Pact had agreed to the Helsinki Final Act, the other signatories had a legitimate basis to question the human rights policies in those states without being accused of infringing on the internal sovereign rights of the Soviets and their allies in Europe. After all, the Soviets and their allies agreed to these conditions by signing the act. Signing the act, then, proved to be a costly action for the Soviets (Thomas 2001).

Human rights watchdog groups (mostly NGOs) sprang up almost immediately within the Warsaw Pact countries and in the West. Both the former and the latter groups reported on human rights violations in the Soviet Union and especially in its allied states. They fomented government-to-government pressures to improve human rights conditions. Movements such as Solidarity in Poland and equivalent forces for free expression throughout Eastern Europe were bolstered by intense legitimate scrutiny from the outside world, scrutiny fostered by the Helsinki Final Act. Whereas the Soviets had easily argued against foreign intervention during similar efforts to promote freedom in Hungary in 1956 and in Czechoslovakia in 1968, their signature on the Helsinki Final Act made such arguments hollow in the late 1970s and early 1980s. Thus, the Helsinki Final Act established the foundation for international pressure to see democratic principles spread to the Soviet Union and Eastern Europe in a manner fully consistent with the constructivist perspective. Just how successful these pressures were perhaps can be gleaned by looking at how the world has changed since 1975. Of course, many other considerations contributed to the downfall of the Soviet Union and to the end of the cold war. Still, the Helsinki Final Act stands out as an example of international regulations and agreements, coupled with international pressure, influencing significantly the course of international relations in a manner not easily accounted for by a neorealist focus on international power and bipolar structure. Nor is it easily explained by liberal theory's emphasis on hegemony. Indeed, at the time of the Helsinki Act, liberal scholars were arguing that American hegemony was in decline (Keohane 1984).

From the strategic perspective, we can infer that the Soviets either were willing to make a costly commitment regarding human rights oversight in exchange for the recognition of East German sovereignty or that they believed that once such sovereignty was granted it would be costly for the western democracies to renege. They may have believed it would be less costly for them to renege on their side of the bargain. Soviet and East European leaders ruled in autocracies, which were not subject to severe internal political sanction—such as the loss of reelection—if they violated agreements, so they may have believed they were free to continue business as usual in their approach to human rights. That the West was prepared to make it costly for Soviet regimes to back down on their commitment may not have been adequately foreseen or may have been a price that the Soviets and their allies were prepared to pay. That is, they may have perceived the benefits of East German recognition as larger than the costs of permitting greater external intervention in internal affairs.

This calculation may have been correct as far as it went. Of course, other developments, such as the incredibly poor performance of the Soviet economy, may have soaked up any surplus benefits the Soviets anticipated from the Helsinki Final Act. Poor economic performance by the Soviets and their client states during the last decade or so of the cold war may have left them more vulnerable to external pressure than would have been the case had their own and their client states' economies been doing better. The United States, in particular, had the leverage to compel the Soviets to comply with their end of the agreement. This leverage came from contracts to sell large quantities of agricultural products—essentially subsidies—to the Soviet Union to help prevent serious shortfalls in grains. The Soviets needed help, and the West wanted compliance in return for it.

The Helsinki Final Act is an exemplar for those, like constructivists, who believe that international law makes a difference on important matters. For those more focused on a strategic perspective, it is an example of how international law can be used to create trade-offs and gambles that can prove highly productive or that can backfire. It is likely that the United States and its allies at Helsinki agreed to recognize East Germany because doing so had little cost and because they attached great value to the possibilities created by the right to challenge Eastern European and Soviet human rights practices. Soviet leaders may have gone along because they thought the human rights elements would prove harmless and they could diminish their spending on the defense of East Germany against the threat of a western European or American incursion while gaining a propaganda coup. In the end, the Soviet leaders proved to have made a bad choice, but of course they could not have known that at the time. The Helsinki Final Act, coupled with declining Soviet economic strength and the U.S. military expansion under President Reagan a few years later, led to the Soviet leaders' struggling on so many fronts that they could no longer resist the pressures for change (Gorbachev 1996; Skinner et al. 2007).

With the examples of Westphalia and Helsinki in mind, we can now examine more closely the purposes of international law and international organizations. We can also investigate the conditions under which international rules and regulations are likely to matter.

THE PURPOSE OF INTERNATIONAL RULES AND INSTITUTIONS

We now return to discussing coordination and distribution problems and how they might be solved through international rules and institutions. Sometimes it is politically beneficial for leaders of different countries to find a way to coordinate their activities. When issues involve only coordination, without any differences in the benefits to be derived from cooperating with others, then reaching international agreements to regulate behavior is rather easy. Air traffic control is a good example of an international agreement that no one has a strong incentive to violate. By agreeing to a common language—English—for commercial air traffic communications around the world, everyone helps minimize the risk of a tragic accident resulting from misunderstanding. Cooperation is easily achieved when it is in everyone's interest and when no one has an incentive to cheat—that is, when no one can get extra benefits by free riding or by secretly breaking the agreement. The interesting challenge for those who hope to promote international cooperation is to design agreements and institutions to enforce them when incentives do exist to cheat or to free ride.

The Soviet Union, for instance, had strong incentives to renege on its promise to promote and respect human rights even though it wanted other nations that signed the Helsinki Final Act to respect East German sovereignty. Iraq's invasion of Kuwait in 1990 to gain control of some Kuwaiti oil fields apparently reflected Saddam Hussein's incentives to violate borders and the international laws and norms that grew up around the Treaty of Westphalia. Members of OPEC want to coordinate in increasing the price of oil by keeping supply down, but inevitably some members (such as Nigeria) cheat by producing more than their quota in order to reap the economic advantages that follow from gaining more market share. They rarely incur punishment for cheating.

International organizations can help solve some of these problems. To see how, let's pause to look at what happens when the same players interact repeatedly in a prisoner's dilemma setting. We know that one-time interactions fail to lead to cooperation because it does not serve either player's interests to do so. Can repeated interaction, such as is often established through membership in an ongoing international organization, change the dominance of the defection strategy? You may be surprised to learn that it can!

Cooperation through Repeated Interaction

Even in a tough situation such as the prisoner's dilemma, self-interest can promote cooperation in the long run. We know that short-term interests favor conflict in the prisoner's dilemma and that, in fact, players have a dominant strategy—defect. But when the game is repeated an indefinite number of times, it turns out players can find a self-interested path to cooperation. This is a point heavily emphasized in liberal theory. It relies on a concept called the **shadow of the future.** This concept states that, under certain circumstances, decision makers who benefit in the short run from noncooperation can be persuaded to engage in cooperative relationships if they are shown that to do so would garner them a long-term stream of benefits (Taylor 1976; Axelrod 1984).

The logic for promoting cooperation when short-term interests encourage noncooperative behavior is readily explained in the context of the prisoner's dilemma. Recall that the payoffs are T (for Temptation) for a player who does not cooperate when the other player does, S (Sucker) for a player who cooperates when the other does not, R (Reward) when both players cooperate, and P (Punishment) when neither player cooperates. The game assumes that $T > R > P > S$. To induce cooperation when the game is repeated without the players knowing when it will end, it must also be true that the value of the reward payoff is larger than the average of the values of the sucker and temptation payoffs ($R > (T + S)/2$). This added condition means that it is better for the players to cooperate than it is for them to alternate between one defecting (being nasty) and the other cooperating (being nice) and then switching roles.

Recall that the game is solved by finding the Nash equilibrium, the set of strategies from which no player has a unilateral incentive to switch. Those strategies in one-shot play are, as we know, for each to defect. But with repeated play, joint cooperation proves to be one of the many possible Nash equilibria. Let's see why that is true.

International players may find themselves involved in the troubling circumstances of a prisoner's dilemma over and over again across an indefinite period of time. For example, during the cold war years, the United States and the Soviet Union faced off repeatedly in situations where mutual cooperation would have benefited both but mutual distrust prevented (potentially costly) attempts at cooperation. After all, if one trusted that the other was well intentioned when it wasn't that could have led to a disaster such as war! Distrust, in fact, is at the heart of the prisoner's dilemma and at the heart of arms races. Because the prisoner's dilemma is a noncooperative game, promises made by either player or both players to cooperate with the other mean nothing. Whatever agreement might have been reached previously, each should recognize that the other player could exploit the situation by defecting. Neither player can count on any promise given by the other. This is a perennial problem when competitor nations unilaterally agree to reduce arms or to accept oil-production quotas within OPEC or agree to free trade across borders in NAFTA. The promise is not binding, nor is it credible, and if one state honors its promise and the other does not, the one that cheats gains a significant advantage.

The dilemma can be escaped provided that the sucker's payoff is bad but not fatal. That is, suppose it is something from which the player can recover over time. If the game is played an indefinite number of times, then it makes sense to experiment by starting out by cooperating. If the other player also cooperates, both are better off ($R > P$). If the other player does not cooperate, he or she can be punished by the first player, who chooses not to cooperate again. Over an indefinite period of repetition, the one-time loss from that initial sucker's payoff becomes trivial—provided it was not game-ending, such as the destruction of one state by the other—against the possible benefit if the other player subsequently cooperates, provided enough value is attached to future payoffs. If this is the case, then each player can credibly declare that his or her strategy will be to make the move the other player made in the previous round of interaction. This strategy is called **tit-for-tat** (do unto the other what the other just did to you—defect if the other defected; cooperate if the other cooperated). If one player defects, then both players will get caught up in a cycle of repeated defection; if a player cooperates, however, a cycle of cooperation can continue indefinitely.

Deciding whether to risk getting the sucker's payoff by cooperating depends on how easy it will be to recover from the costly one-time loss. This is the notion of the shadow of the future. It is a straightforward economic concept. Suppose someone offers to give me $100 today or that person agrees to put aside some money so that he or she will give me $200 in a year's time. How do I decide whether to take the $100 today or the $200 in a year? Well, it depends on how much I value money in a year compared to money now; it depends on my shadow of the future. For sure, I would rather have $100 today than $100 in a year. Inflation will erode the value of the $100 a year from now so it won't buy quite as much as it does now. If I get $100 now, I could put it in an interest-bearing bank account, say at 4 percent. Then I'll have $104 in a year, which obviously is worth more to me than getting the $100 a year from now. But if 4 percent interest is the best I can expect to do, then $100 today is exactly equal to $104 to me in a year. Following this logic, we can say that I discount tomorrow's money relative to today's, in this case by 96 percent ($104 · 0.96 = $100).

How much money would I need to get today for it to be worth the same to me as collecting some larger amount in two years? To answer this let's do a little algebra. I am going to label the rate at which I discount future money δ (the Greek lowercase delta is the standard way to denote discounted values), and for this example I continue to stipulate that $\delta = 0.96$. We know that $(\$104)\delta = \$100$. Earlier I expressed this as meaning that I value $100 today the same as $104 in a year, but I can express this differently. What I really want to know is how much is some benefit today worth to me compared to the same benefit in a year, in two years, in three years, or after an infinite amount of time. In this example, I want to know what $100 is worth to me in one year, in two years, and so forth. We can say that today $100 is worth $100 to me. Next year, $100 is worth 100δ, that is (rounding to the nearest dollar), $96. Getting $100 in two years is worth $(100\delta)\delta$ or, more simply $(100\delta^2)$, that is, its value in one year discounted by the same percentage for the next year. I can express this more generally. If I specify that t refers to the number of years (0, 1, 2, 3, out to infinity), then the value I will attach to $100 given to me in t years is $\$100\delta^t$.

If I am playing the prisoner's dilemma over and over again and I am cooperating and so is the other player, then my reward and the other player's reward (assuming for convenience we both discount benefits at the same rate) if the game goes on forever is $R + \delta R + \delta^2 R + \delta^3 R + \cdots + \delta^\infty R$. As it happens, this infinitely repeated summation has a known value: $R[1/(1 - \delta)]$. Returning to our numerical example, in which $R = 100$ and $\delta = 0.96$, the sum of the cumulative benefits of $100 every year forever is equivalent to being paid $2,500 today: $100 \cdot (1/1 - 0.96) = 100 \cdot (1/0.04) = \$2,500$. Now, if I cooperate at the outset and the other player defects, leading me to defect in the future (playing tit-for-tat, or "I do to you tomorrow what you did to me today"), then the other player's total payoff equals $T + P[\delta/(1 - \delta)]$, that is, whatever T is worth right away (say a gain of $150) and then the next year and each year thereafter the punishment payoff (P, we both defect). Let's say P is worth $50. So, by cheating on the first move—getting T, the big payoff, when it is most valuable—the other player ends up with $150 + 50 \cdot (0.96/1 - 0.96) = \$150 + 50 \cdot (0.96/0.04) = \$1,350$. It just didn't pay for that person not to cooperate.

Why can players be induced to cooperate with one another when they are involved in an indefinitely repeating prisoner's dilemma? Because it turns out, as we have seen, that they can be made better off! The key is to communicate to the other player how you plan to play the game and establish a credible scheme for punishing cheaters. The NAFTA among the United States, Canada, and Mexico is, in essence, a declaration of each country's strategy for dealing with trade relations in the future. Each player promises to keep its market open to the others largely unfettered by tariffs and nontariff barriers. Although there are areas where nontariff barriers exist within NAFTA (for example, U.S. environmental requirements imposed on Mexico), these are part of the agreement and so do not represent cheating. NAFTA has rules and procedures for mediating disputes over alleged cheating.

But even without an international regime such as NAFTA, it is possible for mutual self-interest to be effective in designing a strategy that leads to cooperation between states engaged in an indefinitely repeated prisoner's dilemma. It just requires a simple mechanism such as tit-for-tat (Axelrod 1984). As we has seen in the numerical example, under tit-for-tat, if one player defects in any round of play, then the other player will defect in the next round. In this way, the second player punishes the first for cheating. If one actor cooperates in any round, then the other will cooperate in the next round. This is the way each can reward the other for cooperating rather than seizing the chance to exploit cooperation for a short-term gain. Such a cooperative move by either player would not be rational if the game were played a known number of times, but it is rational when the game is played indefinitely with a large shadow of the future so that there is a big cumulative impact on each decision maker's welfare from cooperating. Tit-for-tat is a "nice" strategy (Axelrod 1984). It is quick to forgive and quick to punish; it is also easy for each decision maker to observe the emerging pattern of play.

However, tit-for-tat cannot succeed in making cooperation an equilibrium strategy if the repetitions of the prisoner's dilemma are for a known number of times. In fact, in such a situation, the dilemma cannot be escaped. The reason is simple. Suppose you and I were to play this game five times. We might each promise to cooperate at the outset. We might even play a nastier strategy than tit-for-tat that increases the cost of punishment. We might follow a punishment strategy called a **grim trigger.** Under this punishment strategy, I declare that if you defect even once—even by accident—I will never cooperate again. It is easy to see that tit-for-tat becomes indistinguishable from the grim trigger once someone has defected. Now, it is straightforward for me to calculate that I cannot punish you if you defect the fifth time we play the game because there will not be a sixth repetition. Of course, you realize that the same holds for me. So, we each have an incentive to defect in the fifth round because at that point the game is not going to be repeated and there can be no punishment for defecting. That means that the fourth round of play really seems like the last part of the repeated game. Further, I already know that you have a dominant strategy in the fifth round and that strategy is to defect. As such, the fourth round really is now like the last repetition because I will have no subsequent opportunity to punish you for defecting. Therefore, because each of us will defect in the fourth round, round three will become like the last repetition, and so on down to round one. When the number of repetitions are known, the chance to cooperate unravels, pushing us to defect even in round one because there will be no opportunity to recover from the sucker's payoff in the future by avoiding the punishment payoff and obtaining the reward payoff.

It is important to recognize that with a large enough shadow of the future, and with indefinite repetition, cooperation can be an equilibrium strategy and that therefore the prisoner's dilemma can be escaped. But we must also realize that cooperation is not the only equilibrium strategy, even with infinite repetition. Defection and just about every mix of moves in between always defecting and always cooperating are other possible equilibrium strategies. In fact, a well-known result in game theory, called a Folk Theorem, is that almost any combination of moves can be an equilibrium if a game is repeated an infinite (or indefinite) number of times. It is also important to note that tit-for-tat is an effective, but not foolproof, way to encourage cooperation in the indefinitely repeated prisoner's dilemma. As the examples here show, there can be incentives to cheat from time to time provided that a switch back to temporary cooperation can be negotiated quickly enough. What is more, valuing the future a lot does not always guarantee an increased incentive to cooperate. That depends on the structure of the situation. Depending on the temporal sequence of costs and benefits, a large shadow of the future can actually make cooperation less likely if costs are borne today to get a stream of benefits tomorrow, as in a one-sided arms buildup (Powell 1999).

INTERNATIONAL ORGANIZATIONS AS A WAY TO PROMOTE REPEATED COOPERATIVE INTERACTION

International institutions are sometimes established to resolve problems in which individual interests lead to inefficient outcomes. They can help solve the Pareto-inferior payoffs that result from one-time prisoner's dilemma interaction. Consider the difference between markets and situations regulated by an international organization. Markets provide an efficient means of solving many forms of competition in international affairs. For instance, as we have seen in Chapter 10, free trade generally leads to efficient pricing and an efficient supply of goods. The problem that confronts the marketplace for trade is that politicians often protect domestic businesses and labor from competition so as to gain domestic political advantage. One potential solution to that problem is for politicians to limit their own freedom of action by joining international organizations that promote free trade and that punish states for violating international rules that favor free trade. They can, through the international organization, tie their own hands, improving the odds that they will follow a cooperative, or tit-for-tat, strategy over time because the organization establishes a framework for repeated interaction.

The marketplace differs from a free-trade international organization in that the market is not capable of restraining a politician's temptation to gain political advantage from protectionism; an international organization may have that capability. I illustrate this point by reflecting on how NAFTA may serve this purpose.

Because the United States belongs to NAFTA, American presidents might successfully shift responsibility away from themselves for the free-trade policies they apply to Canada and Mexico as dictated by NAFTA. The president can reasonably argue that it would be costly to the **national reputation** (that is, beliefs about how a nation will respond to situations based on its past pattern of responses to similar situations) of the United States as a country that respects the rule of law if it were to withdraw from NAFTA or if it were to selectively enforce or violate the terms of NAFTA. Thus, the presidents can insulate themselves from political accountability for free trade with Mexico or Canada by pointing to their predecessors who signed and abided by NAFTA. Their actions created precedents that now are part of U.S. practice and that, if violated, could jeopardize the nation's reputation and its ability to invoke NAFTA if another signatory violates its terms. In this way, the international agreement will have altered the short-term actions of these presidents by providing a way for them to liberate themselves from political accountability for what might be an unpopular policy. The same, of course, also holds true for the president of Mexico and the prime minister of Canada. Each can point to how they are making their constituents better off by sustaining a cooperative equilibrium, avoiding the costs of protectionist tariffs countered by protectionist tariffs from the other NAFTA members.

Leaders, however, are unlikely to concern themselves with matters of national reputation if the costs for maintaining such a reputation are high, that is, if the shadow of their future is small. Having his or her hands tied through precedent is unlikely to carry much weight when doing so harms the leader's political interests more than it benefits them. The reputation of the United States for cooperation in NAFTA may carry weight in influencing how other countries think about the United States when it comes to trade agreements in other arenas, such as the WTO. However, it is unlikely that a reputation in one arena will carry over as a generalized national reputation. This is so for several reasons.

National civil service bureaucracies tend to have a slow turnover in personnel. As a result, it is likely that the same people will help shape and implement policy in a particular bureaucracy's arena for many years. Therefore, each bureaucracy is likely to form a reputation that is tied to a set of people that changes only slowly. But there is no special reason to think that the policies formed in the trade arena and the policies formed, say, in the national security arena are made by the same people with the same interests at stake. Thus, it is unlikely that a nation has an overall reputation for cooperation or for anything else. Tit-for-tat, or any policy and strategy is likely to be issue-specific, a factor emphasized in liberal theory.

Furthermore, the turnover for leaders at the national level is more rapid on average than for civil servants. This is especially true in democratic polities. As a consequence, some portion of what is thought of as national reputation adheres to the individual leader rather than the state—and that part of the national reputation changes when leaders change (Guisinger and Smith 2002; McGillivray and Smith 2008). It is unlikely, for instance, that the reputation of the United States in foreign policy was the same under George W. Bush as it was under Bill Clinton or any earlier president or that it is the same under Barack Obama as it was under Bush. Of course, all presidents inherit treaty commitments that tie their hands, but they also have latitude to negotiate changes in prior agreements, much as George W. Bush decided that the United States ought not to adhere to the ABM Treaty that was promulgated during the cold war. Creating a national reputation is a weak foundation on which to build organizational commitments. Reputations limited to specific agencies of government, however, may provide a sounder basis for influencing national decisions about organizational regulations in specific circumscribed issue areas.

I have mentioned that the president's hands can be tied by the prior actions of past presidents. This is especially true when foreign policies are enshrined as law by signing a treaty. The president (or other executive) is legally bound to enforce the terms of treaties. In fact, as noted earlier, in the United States, treaty obligations take precedence over other restrictions in the U.S. Constitution. Interests that benefit from NAFTA, for example, can bring suit in U.S. courts if they believe that the executive branch is not properly following the law. This means that the executive branch must convince the judicial branch that its actions do not violate the law. At the same time, if any president wants to change the law, he or she has to renegotiate the treaty with a foreign power and, if successful in doing so, he or she must then get the modified treaty ratified by the Senate. These are difficult time-consuming steps. Consequently, executives are likely to enforce the current provisions of a treaty to the degree that their—or their constituents'—ideal point does not differ dramatically from the treaty's obligations and to the degree that they expect to be challenged in court for failing to do so.

International organizations are sometimes formed to promote efficient market outcomes where individual incentives would otherwise lead to less efficient solutions. Not all problems, however, have a market solution as the alternative. Consider the problem of war. International conflict is always inefficient ex post, as we learn in Chapter 4. That, however, does not easily fit into a market-oriented account of the world. States go to war presumably because the leaders in the belligerent countries believe that it serves their best interests to fight rather than give in to the other side. That is, before the fact they expect that conflict or even war will prove to be an effective way to reduce uncertainty about what the resolution of a dispute should be.

Yet it is likely that each potential belligerent also realizes that there are better ways to solve problems. Imagine, for instance, that Israel and the Palestinian Authority are on the verge of war over their respective territorial claims in Jerusalem, an all-too-common occurrence. Each side surely recognizes that reaching whatever settlement they may ultimately agree to after decades of violence is not as good as reaching the exact same agreement right now without violence. One problem faced by each side is that there is insufficient trust to make transparent the information needed to determine what the contents of such an agreement might be. Neither side can credibly commit to revealing reliable information to the other side. Another problem is that neither side seems willing to trust the role of an international organization such as the United Nations to help discover and enforce the as yet undiscovered prospective agreement.

The Palestinian Authority's leaders might want to appeal to the United Nations General Assembly for its judgment on the contents of an agreement. That body makes decisions based on a majority vote of the member states, and it can pass resolutions that specify expected conduct. Also, a majority of General Assembly members seem sympathetic to the plight of the Palestinians. So, too, do many members of the Security Council, although that body is more guarded in what it is prepared to approve (for reasons explained shortly).

Therefore, a problem arises for the Palestinians if they turn to the United Nations for help—the issue is unlikely to remain before the General Assembly, and the Palestinian leaders are much less confident of a supportive outcome in the Security Council.

Let us consider as an example of UN decision making regarding the dispute between Israel and the Palestinians—the oft-invoked and never enforced Resolution 242 passed on November 22, 1967. It states:

> The Security Council,
>
> Expressing its continuing concern with the grave situation in the Middle East,
>
> Emphasizing the inadmissibility of the acquisition of territory by war and the need to work for a just and lasting peace in which every State in the area can live in security,
>
> Emphasizing further that all Member States in their acceptance of the Charter of the United Nations have undertaken a commitment to act in accordance with Article 2 of the Charter,
>
> 1. Affirms that the fulfillment of Charter principles requires the establishment of a just and lasting peace in the Middle East which should include the application of both the following principles:
>   (i) Withdrawal of Israel armed forces from territories occupied in the recent conflict;
>   (ii) Termination of all claims or states of belligerency and respect for and acknowledgment of the sovereignty, territorial integrity and political independence of every State in the area and their right to live in peace within secure and recognized boundaries free from threats or acts of force;
>
> 2. Affirms further the necessity
>   (a) For guaranteeing freedom of navigation through international waterways in the area;
>   (b) For achieving a just settlement of the refugee problem;
>   (c) For guaranteeing the territorial inviolability and political independence of every State in the area, through measures including the establishment of demilitarized zones;
>
> 3. Requests the Secretary-General to designate a Special Representative to proceed to the Middle East to establish and maintain contacts with the States concerned in order to promote agreement and assist efforts to achieve a peaceful and accepted settlement in accordance with the provisions and principles in this resolution;
>
> 4. Requests the Secretary-General to report to the Security Council on the progress of the efforts of the Special Representative as soon as possible.
>
> Adopted unanimously at the 1382nd meeting.

This resolution provides the foundation in international law for the idea that the Israeli-Palestinian conflict can be resolved through a deal of land for peace. The resolution specifies that Israel must return to its borders as they were before the 1967 War, or Six-Day

War, fought between Arabs and Israelis in 1967, when Israel was a much smaller country (with not only less territory but also far fewer people), but it also specifies other conditions, such as an end to belligerency, that thus far have not been met. Israel seems unwilling to abide by Resolution 242's call for a return to the pre-1967 borders (condition 1.i) because each of its governments since 1967 has thus far concluded that some of the territory captured by Israel during the 1967 War—such as the Golan Heights between Israel and Syria—is vital to providing Israel's citizens with secure borders (condition 1.ii). Further, it remains unconvinced that a promise of peace in exchange for land reflects a credible commitment for peace from the Arab states, as discussed earlier. Israel's government points to the many occasions on which, from its perspective, Palestinian leaders reneged on promises and infers from these occasions that they and their Arab backers do not value a reputation for reliability in fulfilling international commitments. The United Nations membership and its secretary-general are powerless to enforce this or any resolution if enforcement does not have the support of the five permanent members of the Security Council. Thus, although the UN—especially the General Assembly—provides an opportunity for deliberations and a place where world leaders can exchange views, it lacks the teeth to enforce its judgments.

Israel might be willing to refer its grievances to the Security Council provided that it is confident the United States (or some other permanent member) will veto any action called for by that body that is contrary to Israel's interests. The United States did not veto Resolution 242, but then, neither has it taken action to enforce Israeli withdrawal from the territories captured during the 1967 War. Nor, for that matter, does the resolution speak clearly with regard to another fundamental issue in dispute—the Palestinian Authority's leader's claim of a "right of return" for all Palestinian refugees. The Israelis refuse to recognize this claim because it could mean that Israel would be deluged by millions of Palestinians, the majority of whom never actually lived in what is today's Israel.

The Palestinian Authority might be reluctant to rely on the Security Council, where it has no staunch friends among the permanent members. Its leaders might point to the failure of the United Nations to enforce Resolution 242's condition 1.i as evidence that the Security Council's permanent members—especially the United States—are not serious in their claim to seek peace. For the Palestinians (or the Israelis), the Security Council's decisions seem more important as propaganda tools in their conflict than as genuine means of resolving the dispute.

As described earlier, the Security Council includes rotating membership from each region of the world plus five permanent members. The rotating members are selected by regional organizations of countries; this means, in effect, that Israel is the only country in the world with no prospect of selection for a term of membership. The Arab states constitute the geographical region that Israel naturally falls in, but they do not collectively recognize Israel's existence and so never select Israel for membership in the Security Council. Any one of the five permanent members—China, France, Russia, the United Kingdom, and the United States—can veto any proposal before the Security Council. Israel, of course, might choose to resist an action approved by the Security Council. Even if a majority of the council, including the five permanent members, voted to enforce Resolution 242 (as they did), Israel could still balk and refuse to turn over any territory to, for instance, Syria, pointing to the absence of assurances that 242's condition 1.ii will be fulfilled. Ultimately, the ability of the United Nations to enforce its will depends on the preparedness of each of the five permanent members to support the mobilization of a military force under United Nations command to enforce the council's decisions.

Thus, the Security Council's effectiveness is seriously limited by its structure. These limitations, of course, are by design; they are not an accident. The right of each permanent member to veto any Security Council decision ensures that such decisions can be meaningful only if they serve the interests of each permanent member. This suggests that national interests (that is, the interests of the leaders of the moment) and national power, and not the United Nations itself, are the mechanism by which international policies are enforced. But if that is the case, then why bother to have an international organization in the first place? This is the most crucial question regarding international organizations and international law when issues involve more than just coordination. The Palestinian-Israeli case highlights how cooperation can break down when cooperation requires that one or both sides in a dispute also sacrifice individual gains. The purpose of international rules and regulations and the organizations that promulgate them is to promote international cooperation, sometimes by acting as an impartial mediator and sometimes by acting as an interested party with authority to mete out punishment to violators. Cooperation is difficult to achieve when distributive issues crop up that make the benefits from cooperation greater for some than for others. In such cases, as may be true of the commitment of the Security Council's permanent members to Resolution 242, rules and regulations may be little more than cheap talk.

Because cooperation is difficult to achieve when organizations face distribution issues, an organization's design must reflect at the outset the best judgments of the members regarding how to address the problems that are likely to arise, keeping in mind that their best judgment reflects what is best for each of them within the organization rather that what is best for everyone. That is, in designing the structure of an international organization, members must be strategic about the choices they make. In particular, there are five primary questions that must be considered when designing an international organization:

1. How inclusive is the organization's membership?
2. How are decisions made?
3. How likely is compliance with the organization's decisions?
4. How is punishment imposed for noncompliance?
5. How effective are the rules and regulations established by the organization?

Let us now address each of these concerns.

MEMBERSHIP INCLUSIVENESS: TRADE-OFFS BETWEEN REGIME EFFICIENCY AND EFFECTIVENESS

How inclusive should an international regime be? Some international organizations, such as the United Nations, are extraordinarily **inclusive**; almost every state in the world is a member of the UN, although the Republic of China on Taiwan, for instance, is not because the People's Republic of China claims it as a breakaway province. Other organizations, such as NAFTA, have an **exclusive** membership consisting of very few participants. Still others fall everywhere and anywhere in between. The WTO is very large; OPEC is of moderate size, as are NATO, the Organization of American States, and the European Union, all of which are significantly larger than NAFTA or Mercosur.

Larger organizations leave less leeway for states to avoid punishment if they are caught cheating, but they also make it more difficult to establish rules that effectively alter behavior than do smaller organizations. In general, organizations achieve high levels of compliance when their decisions are shallow (Downs, Rocke, and Barsoom 1996). By *shallow* I mean that the decisions do not constrain actions by the member states much, so the problem addressed by the rule or regulation is not effectively resolved. Larger organizations are more likely to make shallow decisions than are smaller, more selective organizations. It is easy to comply with rules that do not demand a costly change in behavior, and it is difficult to get many states to agree to rules that require significant and costly changes in behavior. Likewise, we generally can expect that decision rules are easier to satisfy when decisions are less likely to be enforced than when they are more likely to be enforced or when, even with enforcement, the decisions are not particularly effective. Let us consider each of these factors in turn.

The inclusiveness or exclusiveness of an international organization is a design issue that turns out to be controversial. Consider the implications for decision making that arise as the size of the decision-making body increases. An international organization with a small membership, such as NAFTA, limits participation to governments or private organizations with little diversity in their preferences for organizational policy. As more members are added to an organization, the diversity that we can expect in policy preferences increases. Indeed, there is a real risk as an organization becomes larger that new members with preferences far from those of the founding members will block progress toward cooperation that might more easily have been achieved if the organization had stayed with just a few members (E. Bueno de Mesquita and Stephenson 2006). Larger membership, then, diminishes the chances that the participants will reach agreement on rules and regulations to promote meaningful steps toward international cooperation.

Consider the exclusion of Britain from the original European Coal and Steel Agreement that served as the forerunner to the European Union. Britain was opposed to virtually every important decision made by the ECSC and, later, by the EC during the first twenty or so years of the existence of these organizations. Had Britain been brought in as a member at the outset in 1951, it is likely that the British—because of domestic political concerns about their coal and steel industries—would have disrupted progress toward European integration. It is difficult to imagine that the 1957 Treaty of Rome, signed by Belgium, France, Germany, Italy, Luxembourg, and the Netherlands, could have gained British approval. The Treaty of Rome propelled European integration forward, adding the European Atomic Energy Community (Euratom) and the European Economic Community (EEC) to the ECSC. Furthermore, the treaty explicitly promoted the idea of closer integration across European states and singled out national exchange rate policies as a matter to be worked on, presumably with an eye toward the creation of a single currency (as occurred finally in 2002).

Even after Britain joined the EC in 1972, it acted against the policy wishes of a significant number of member states and probably diminished the effectiveness of the organization on important decisions, especially those regarding currency integration. Indeed, currency integration was a major issue that split the British Conservative Party in the early 1990s and contributed to the party's decision to oust Prime Minister Margaret Thatcher—who opposed currency integration—in favor of John Major. Even today, Britain maintains its own currency—the pound sterling—rather than adopting the euro.

Whether larger or smaller organizations are preferable is openly debated. A constructivist perspective differs sharply from the realist view that a large membership in an organization reduces effectiveness. Realists maintain that inclusiveness waters down decisions by allowing too much diversity in policy preferences. After all, from the realist perspective, states act on their national interests, and the more states that are included in an organization, the less likely it is that the organization can reflect the national interests of its member states. Constructivists, in contrast, maintain that cooperation is stimulated by participation in international organizations. From this perspective, inclusiveness is a highly desirable property of international organizations. Constructivism suggests that preferences are not exogenous to the situation in which decision makers find themselves; rather, preferences are shaped and reshaped by participation in and deliberation with alternative viewpoints, as suggested earlier in the discussion of identity formation and the redefinition of the national interest. Alexander Wendt (1994), you recall, suggests that members of an international organization learn to see themselves as others see them through the process of interaction such as that promoted by an inclusive international organization. The effect of such interactions on self-perception is strongest in situations involving dependence on the views of other actors, again as can be true in large international organizations. From this point of view, organizations such as the UN General Assembly might be expected to be especially effective in fostering cooperation by exposing representatives from so many states to the perspectives of others. Although constructivists and realists each muster case studies to support their own point of view, neither the hypothesis in favor of inclusiveness nor that in favor of exclusiveness has been subjected to rigorous analysis.

At first blush we might infer that the strategic perspective favors inclusive organizations. As we have seen earlier, systems that rely on a large coalition drawn from a large selectorate tend to produce more public welfare. In the international context, it is sometimes true that cooperation among member states is a public good for all the participants in an international organization. But that claim assumes that members of an organization agree on which policies contribute public goods. That is, it assumes that the preferences of the median voter are the goals that leaders must fulfill. This makes perfectly good sense in settings in which members of the selectorate cannot easily withdraw and cannot freely violate the policy decisions made by their leaders. However, states can and do sometimes withdraw from international organizations, and they decidedly can and do violate the policies of those organizations. Violations of the law probably are more easily detected within a state than they are among the members of an international organization. This is true because the amount that an organization spends on detecting violations is likely to be smaller the more diverse the interests of its membership. Punishment is also difficult to mete out in international organizations, as discussed later.

On balance, then, the strategic perspective favors inclusiveness of membership (the selectorate) only if the rules also ensure inclusiveness in the coalition of members whose support is needed to keep the leadership of the organization in office (the winning coalition). The United Nations, for example, fails to meet these requirements. Its leadership in the Secretariat requires broad support among the membership, but as a practical matter, no one can be effective as secretary-general without the support of the oligarchy of permanent members of the Security Council. Thus, it has characteristics similar to those of an autocracy, in which many have a chance to join a winning coalition but a small group is essential and is guaranteed a primary role in choosing leaders and, therefore, policies. In such an environment, the organization is likely to be ineffective in promoting policies that are contrary to the interests of the oligarchs who occupy a privileged position. As Ethan Bueno de Mesquita and Matthew Stephenson (2006) show, informal networks or formal organizations bound by costly contract rules have an optimal size. If they are too large, the costs of monitoring and punishing deviant behavior become large as the expectation of deviant behavior increases with the variability in preferences. If they are too small, then there are few gains from trade or economies of scale in coordinating cooperative behavior, so the benefits are inadequate to sustain cooperation. What constitutes the optimal size of an organization depends in an identifiable way on the trade-offs among the costs, benefits, and risks created by the organization.

ORGANIZATIONAL DECISION-MAKING RULES

In any international regime, decision rules are likely to be chosen strategically. The more consequential the policy being regulated, the more stringent the decision rule is likely to be. Let's consider once again the example of decision making in the UN General Assembly and in the Security Council and then move on to the European Union.

The United Nations and Decision-Making Rules

A simple majority of member states in the General Assembly can pass resolutions on any policy question that comes before them. The secretary-general of the United Nations might point to these resolutions as demonstrations of the UN's ability to form international policy regarding human rights, the environment, security issues, or just about anything else. Yet we have also seen that the General Assembly is not endowed with the means to enforce its resolutions, so achieving compliance could be a difficult problem in the case of resolutions that demand significant changes in behavior by member states. As a result, we can expect that most resolutions passed by the General Assembly are shallow, are passed by a huge margin, and experience a high degree of compliance or that they are deep, important policy statements with no teeth behind them to ensure compliance. The vast majority of General Assembly resolutions are unlikely to be effective either because they do not call for a substantial change in behavior from what individual national political calculations already call for or because they are unenforceable. These claims imply that the decision rule is endogenous; that is, it is strategically chosen, taking into account the depth of the issues to which it is likely to be applied.

The decision rule in the Security Council is much more demanding than that used by the General Assembly. The Charter of the United Nations gives the Security Council primary responsibility for maintaining international peace and security. It therefore has the right to order economic sanctions, send peacekeepers, or take other actions to protect or restore peace. Because of its primary responsibility for promoting peace and security, the United Nations requires that a representative from each of the Security Council's member states be present at all times at UN headquarters in case the council is compelled to meet unexpectedly in response to a crisis. Because the issues that come before the council often have profound consequences, its rules are constructed to ensure that its actions are based on a strong consensus.

The United Nations Security Council: Great Power Interests and the P-5 Veto. If a simple majority were all that was required for decisions in the Security Council, then it would operate the way the General Assembly operates. The Security Council, however, has the opportunity to make much more consequential decisions. If it votes to enforce its decisions, then the UN can raise an army of peacekeepers or peacemakers and put them in harm's way in combat situations. It has done so in Kosovo to try to maintain peace in that embattled land. It also has done so in numerous disputes in Africa, Asia, and elsewhere around the world. Most notably, it did so in Korea during the Korean War (1950–1953) in a successful effort to push the North Koreans back to the prewar boundary between North and South Korea—that is, to the 38th parallel.

Security Council decisions require the support of a majority of all its voting members and no dissent among the P-5 (its five permanent members). This means that fourteen of the fifteen members at any one time could vote for an action and the action could still be defeated if one permanent member voted against it. Because it can be difficult to get unanimous approval (or abstention) among the five permanent members, we can expect that considerable horse-trading takes place before a vote, watering down proposals until no permanent member will exercise a veto. The unanimity rule for the P-5 ensures that Security Council decisions have teeth behind them and, therefore, on controversial matters its decisions are likely to be shallow; they will enjoy compliance among the members but prove ineffective.

When Security Council decisions are not shallow, they can be effective. If the permanent members are genuinely behind a UN resolution and the resolution is not the product of a substantial compromise, then compliance with the resolution is likely and the resolution itself is likely to be effective. Of course, in such cases, the decision of the council is in the interest of the P-5; otherwise, it would be vetoed. This suggests that the Security Council can effectively perform a coordination/facilitation function but that it is unlikely to redefine the policies of the permanent members.

Consider the UN Security Council decision in June 1950 to mount a force to engage in what was called a "police action" in Korea. This action constituted the UN's first consequential multilateral military mission. As such, it is an important case to understand because it both set precedent and created a deeper awareness among member states about how to use and how not to use the Security Council.

We might well wonder how the Security Council could approve this use of force when at that time the Soviet Union—a permanent member with a veto—was allied with China, the key backer of the North Korean invasion of South Korea. At the time, China's seat as a permanent member was occupied by the Republic of China on Taiwan and not by the People's Republic of China (PRC; then sometimes referred to as Mainland China or Red China).** Had the PRC been a permanent member in 1950, it certainly would have vetoed the United Nation's use of military force to counter the invasion of South Korea by North Korea, an invasion fully supported by the PRC. The only friend that communist North Korea had at the time among the Security Council's permanent members was the Soviet Union. In a remarkable blunder, the Soviet delegate was under orders to boycott meetings of the council to protest the exclusion of the PRC and the inclusion of Taiwan. Apparently the Soviets believed that a failure to vote carried the same weight as a veto. The absence of the Soviet delegate opened the door for a vote without a Soviet veto, a mistake the Soviets did not make again. Because of the Soviet ambassador's error, the Security Council was able to put a policy in force that had real teeth, and because any other permanent member could subsequently veto any Soviet effort to undo its error, the UN could sustain its "police action." In essence, the Security Council resolution made it possible for the United States and its allies to wage a war against North Korea to restore the status quo prior to the North Korean invasion of South Korea and to do so under the UN's umbrella.

Even here, we must question the effectiveness of the Security Council's action. Had it failed to support military action in defense of South Korea, the United States probably would have committed its own troops anyway, just as it did in Iraq in 2003. The UN provided greater

---

** The PRC was not admitted to membership in the United Nations until 1971, at which time it displaced the government on Taiwan as China's permanent UN member.

apparent legitimacy to the U.S. action, but it probably did not alter what the United States and its allies did. In that sense, the Security Council did not alter behavior so much as provide a gloss of international legitimacy to the an action that would have been taken in any case.

We have seen that the decision rules in different parts of the UN are different and that they almost certainly represent negotiated deals among the members. That the rules are endogenous seems a certainty. That this means they cannot influence future behavior is less clear. Let us now consider some of the ways that organizational decision rules influence action and how they can be more than just a codification of the intentions of an organization's powerful members.

The Chernobyl Disaster and Structure-Induced Equilibrium

Realists maintain that the rules and regulations promulgated by international organizations reflect the distribution of power among member states. If an organization calls for an action contrary to a powerful member's interests, then, according to realists, the organization either will be changed or ignored. Liberals disagree. They contend that such organizations are developed to facilitate coordination among member states, with the most powerful member—the hegemon—providing the public good of assuming the costs of coordination. If that is right, international organizations at least can promote cooperation when their most powerful members bear the costs of coordinating behavior. In this view, the role of the hegemon can help alter the expected utility calculations of member states, making the expected utility from cooperation larger than it would be in the absence of a coordinator. Constructivism contends that the very preferences or interests of member states are reshaped by their participation in an international organization. The organization reconstitutes the initially divergent interests of members, creating a desire for cooperation even in situations in which, left to their own devices, individual states would be in contention with one another. Organizations achieve cooperation in this view not just by altering the probability that cooperation can be achieved, as is argued by liberals, but by changing the desire for cooperation among the members. Each of these arguments sounds plausible, although the evidence for each is scattered and tentative, depending generally on case studies selected to reinforce a particular point of view rather than selected with an eye to falsifying a perspective's claims. Still, let us see how rules might help to reshape behavior. To do so, I take an example from an environmental policy decision made by the EC in the wake of the nuclear accident in Chernobyl, Ukraine, in 1986. The decision concerns limitations on the level and type of radioactive contaminants in food that would be tolerated by the EC (now the European Union).

In April 1986, a combination of staff members' conducting an unauthorized experiment, poor reactor design, and poor emergency-preparedness training of the on-site staff led to a near-meltdown of the nuclear reactor in Chernobyl. The result was an explosion and an improper shutdown that sent a cloud of radioactive dust across most of Europe. Although the United Nations now attributes about fifty to sixty deaths to the Chernobyl accident and general opinion seems to be that thousands died, the UN Scientific Committee on the Effects of Atomic Radiation reported the following on June 6, 2000:

There is no scientific evidence of increases in overall cancer incidence or mortality or in non-malignant disorders that could be related to radiation exposure. The risk of leukaemia, one of the main concerns owing to its short latency time, does not appear to be elevated, not even among the recovery operation workers. Although those most highly exposed individuals are at an increased risk of radiation associated effects, the great majority of the population are not likely to experience serious health consequences from radiation from the Chernobyl accident.[††]

The specter of nuclear disaster understandably heightened concern in Europe about the risks of radioactively contaminated food products being imported from Eastern Europe and the Soviet Union. It took the then twelve members of the EC—Belgium, Denmark, France, West Germany, Greece, Ireland, Italy, Luxembourg, the Netherlands, Portugal, Spain, and the United Kingdom—just one month to reach an interim agreement in the EC's Commission on how much radioactive contamination they would tolerate. This agreement called for tolerance of not more than 370 becquerels of cesium radioactive contamination per liter of milk or kilogram of children's food and 600 becquerels per kilogram of other foods (Van den Bos 1994). Although this compromise was to be in effect only until November 1986, agreement on a long-term policy took nineteen more months to resolve.

The case of limitations on radioactive contaminants in food products raises several fundamental issues about international organizations and the specific decision rules they use to choose policies. For instance, the EC Commission, consisting of delegates from each of the twelve member states, required unanimity to extend the temporary agreement beyond November 1986. The French viewed the temporary regulation as too restrictive, whereas the Dutch wanted not only to continue the temporary approach but as tough a permanent arrangement as possible. A tough policy would have calmed concerns over environmental consequences in the Netherlands and would have helped protect Dutch farmers from Eastern European competition. The extension of the temporary agreement was achieved only after the French agreed to abstain. What might have happened had the decision rule been less demanding than unanimity?

Table 11.1 displays data on the voting power of each member state in the European Community other than Belgium as of December 1987, when this issue was resolved. The Belgians did not stake out a position on this question.[‡‡] The voting power levels are precisely the weighted voting scheme used by the EC and its successor, the European Union, to determine the relative influence over policy choices exercised through voting by each member state. The table also shows the policy, or position, supported by each member state at the outset of the deliberations. The policy scale has been calibrated so that the lower numbers reflect lower tolerance for radioactive contaminants (that is, higher standards) and the

---

[††] For the full text of the UN report, see www.un.org/ha/chernobyl/docs/unsceare.htm.

[‡‡] Belgium had a statutory right to a weighted vote equal to 5.

TABLE 11.1	European Community Preferences Regarding Tolerable Radiation Levels, December 22, 1987		
Stakeholder	Voting power	Position[a]	Salience[b]
France	10	100.0	100
United Kingdom	10	100.0	75
Spain	5	100.0	50
Italy	10	81.3	60
Greece	5	81.3	10
Denmark	3	25.0	100
Portugal	5	10.8	25
Ireland	3	10.8	70
Luxembourg	2	10.8	80
West Germany	10	10.0	100

Source: Bueno de Mesquita and Stokman (1994, Tables 3.4, 3.7).

a. Lower numbers reflect lower tolerance for radioactive contaminants (and therefore a higher standard) and the higher numbers reflect higher tolerance (and therefore a lower standard).

b. Salience measures the degree to which the issue was a high priority (values closer to 100) or a low priority (values closer to 0) of the member states.

higher numbers reflect higher tolerance (and, therefore, lower standards). Finally, the table shows the level of salience attached to the question of tolerable radioactive contaminants for each member state. This variable estimates how high or low a priority the decision makers representing the member states attached to this issue compared to all other matters before them. The salience and position values were estimated through expert interviews conducted by Frans Stokman and his collaborators on a large project studying decision making in the European Community, as explained in Bueno de Mesquita and Stokman (1994).

As is evident from Table 11.1, France, the United Kingdom, and Spain favored lax standards. West Germany, with its proximity to Eastern Europe and presumed heightened exposure to radiation, supported especially tough standards against radioactive contaminants in agricultural products. Italy and Greece were prepared to live with weak standards, whereas the Netherlands, Portugal, Ireland, and Luxembourg were almost as tough-minded as the Germans. Surprisingly, the Danish government—normally a country with extremely pro-environmental policies—took a somewhat middle-of-the-road position. This was possibly because Denmark's own large agricultural industry might have been adversely affected by tougher regulations.[§§]

[§§] Whatever the reasons for the relatively moderate position of Denmark, it is worth noting that Danish policies in the European Union are generally more sensitive to domestic political considerations—especially on environmental issues—than are those of any of the other member states. Of course, domestic political considerations play a part in the policies adopted by each and every member state. The Danish referendum procedures to ratify or reject EC decisions at the time, however, gave unusually large weight to domestic Danish politics in determining whether Denmark would agree to and comply with policy choices.

With the information from Table 11.1 in hand, we can see how the EC's decision rules influenced policy by asking what the emissions standards probably would have been under different rules. We can see how the rules actually chosen might have influenced the outcome, creating a **structure-induced equilibrium,** constraints on Nash equilibria established by the institutional or other structural factors in a situation (Shepsle and Weingast 1981).

Comparing the Effects of Voting Rules. Suppose preferences regarding radioactive contamination were single-peaked, as is likely, and that the decision about contaminants was not linked to any other policy decision in the EC. If the rule was that a plurality of votes was needed for the EC Commission to adopt one standard over another, then the standard associated with the most votes would have been chosen. If that were the case, then the lowest standard—100 on the position scale—would have been chosen. It had the backing of twenty-five votes, whereas the moderately lax standard (81.3 on the position scale), backed by Italy and Greece, and the pretty tough standard (10.8 on the scale), backed by the Netherlands, Portugal, Ireland, and Luxembourg, would have tied for second place with fifteen votes each. The seemingly weakest position was that endorsed by Denmark (25.0 on the position scale). It had only Denmark's three votes. Yet, as we will see, under the rule actually used, the policy chosen came closer to Denmark's position than to any other state's expressed preference.

If, instead of plurality voting, the rule was that the simple majority prevailed, the final choice would not have been the most lax radioactive contamination standard. Rather, the median voter position would have carried the day among the eleven members engaged on this issue. The median voter in this case was in favor of the somewhat tougher standard equal to 81.3 on the policy position scale.

In actuality, neither plurality voting nor simple majority rule was in use in the EC Commission at the time. The commission had two voting rules, each invoked under different circumstances. One called for a *qualified majority,* defined by the European Community as 71 percent of the weighted votes, with that 71 percent representing 58 percent of the population of the EC Commission's member states.*** The other rule called for unanimity.

The eleven members voting on radioactive contamination had a combined total of sixty-eight votes. Under the qualified majority voting rule (and assuming Belgium abstained), for a policy to win it needed forty-eight of the sixty-eight votes. Looking at Table 11.1, and remembering that we are assuming single-peaked preferences, we can see that none of the initially stated positions readily attracts a qualified majority. To get a qualified majority, it would be necessary to draw at least one of the states supporting 10.8 into a coalition that included Denmark and the members supporting a standard of either 81.3 or 100.0. Portugal,

---

*** An EC policy established that it would revisit the definition of a *qualified majority* once its membership exceeded twenty to adjust the weighted voting to represent its new reality. The twelve original members of the EC (now European Union) are Belgium, Denmark, France, Germany, Greece, Ireland, Italy, Luxembourg, the Netherlands, Portugal, Spain, and the United Kingdom. In January 1995, Austria and Sweden (with four votes each) and Finland (with three votes) joined. In May 2004, Cyprus, the Czech Republic, Estonia, Hungary, Latvia, Lithuania, Malta, Poland, the Slovak Republic, and Slovenia were incorporated, and the conditions for achieving a qualified majority were redefined. In January 2007, Bulgaria and Romania joined. Current candidate nations are Croatia, Macedonia, and Turkey.

with enough votes and very low salience, might have seemed like the best target among those supporting 10.8 to be attracted to a compromise.

Assuming that Portugal (or any other vote combination in the 10.8 coalition that could produce five votes in favor of a compromise) was willing to compromise, what might the agreement have looked like? To answer this question, we must think about the swing voters. The status quo going into the deliberations was 10.8, the temporary measure that the Netherlands wanted to see maintained. France had allowed this temporary measure for a while but was unlikely to continue to do so. The coalition in favor of the weakest standard would have to remain united, however, in order to deprive all the other members of the opportunity to combine in a compromise that controlled a qualified majority. Assuming that France, the United Kingdom, and Spain remained united (possibly a strong assumption), they could exert considerable bargaining power in constructing a compromise. By the same token, without Denmark and a five-vote combination from the 10.8 coalition, a qualified majority could not be assembled. The most likely deal lay somewhere between Denmark's position and the Italian and Greek position. If the two sides split the difference, they would have compromised somewhere around 54 on the scale. Assuming that such a resolution was better than no resolution for the groups at the extremes of this compromise (that is, a weighted vote worth five from the 10.8 coalition plus the votes of all members of the 100.0 coalition and everyone in between), a qualified majority could be assembled toward the middle of the scale. This analysis indicates that a shift from simple majority rule to the qualified majority would have produced a change in standards from 81.3 (the median voter position) to somewhere between 25.0 and 81.3, perhaps in the neighborhood of 54. But when the issue was finally resolved, the agreement was to tolerate a more modest level of radiation contamination equal to 35.6 on the position scale.

> **TRY THIS**
>
> It is likely that members of the European Community lobbied one another over standards for radioactive contaminants. Imagine that the influence they exerted over one another depended not only on how many votes each member had but also on the salience or focus each member brought to this issue. One way to reflect that focus is to discount the total number of votes—or leverage—that could be exercised by the willingness to focus time and effort on this issue rather than other issues. You can estimate this leverage by multiplying voting power times salience and then dividing by 100. Do that using the data in Table 11.1, and recalculate the plurality policy position, the simple majority policy position, and the qualified majority policy positions that could win.

If the unanimity rule had been invoked, then it appears that France, Denmark, and West Germany—with their intense salience for this environmental issue—might have rejected any policy far from their preferred outcomes. The unanimity rule could have provoked a severe problem. France favored the weakest radioactivity contamination standard, and West Germany supported the toughest standard. They were as far apart as possible, making the likelihood that they would come to an agreement fairly small. It is unclear whether, given the salience of the other decision makers, any felt strong enough to veto a compromise standard if it were proposed under the unanimity rule. For many EC members, other issues were more important than the concerns over radioactive contaminants in agricultural products, despite the initial alarm following the Chernobyl accident. Perhaps the scientific evidence that was emerging helped quell their fears. Whatever the reasons, it is apparent from the data in Table 11.1 that Greece and Portugal cared little about this question and that Spain and Italy gave it only modest attention. Belgium, as we have noted, did not even involve itself in the debate.

We have now seen that different decision rules could have had a dramatic impact on Europe's decision about tolerance for radioactive contaminants in food products. The EC commissioners really had a choice only between two voting rules: the qualified majority and unanimity. Which of these two rules would be applicable to the particular decision we are examining surely was itself a matter for negotiation and strategic maneuvering. For the West German government, for instance, passage of anything other than a stringent standard might have alienated its environmentally sensitive constituents at home, perhaps even jeopardizing the political survival of the incumbent West German government in the face of Green Party swing votes. The Germans, then, would have had strong reasons to press for the unanimity decision rule. If, however, they and other like-minded members thwarted all decisions with which they disagreed, they could have anticipated the collapse of the EC as an organization. In that case, they would have had essentially no influence over the domestic environmental policies of any other member state in the future. This calculation about future consequences for the organization may help restrain the use of the unanimity rule or the exercise of vetoes except under extreme circumstances. In that sense, the expected cost of losing the benefits that for member states follow from the existence of the EC as a functioning organization may have been sufficient for them to tolerate some decisions that they opposed. If that is the case, then the institution's rules can be expected to be sticky, as suggested earlier. The cost of constantly altering the rules could easily exceed the benefits derived from the EC/European Union as a body that coordinates policy across many countries and many issue areas.

COMPLIANCE, PUNISHMENT, AND EFFECTIVENESS

In actuality, the European Community adopted 35.6 as the radioactive contaminants standard for agricultural products. This is a less demanding standard than was proposed by half the members. It is also a far more stringent standard than was favored by three of the four most powerful member states. Obviously the decision was a compromise designed to mollify the opposition on both sides of the issue. Such compromises often are constructed to ensure a high level of compliance (Bueno de Mesquita and Stokman 1994; Thomson et al. 2006). That is, members of the organization can be expected to adhere to the chosen policy. That does not mean, however, that the policy is effective in reducing radioactive contamination of foods. Consider the post-Chernobyl experience in Europe.

The United Nations Food and Agriculture Organization sponsored a study that evaluated the risks to the food chain from post-Chernobyl radioactive fallout (see Winteringham

1989). The study also compared these effects with those resulting from atmospheric nuclear tests. Among the key findings were claims that the radioactive fallout from Chernobyl was likely to have little impact on crops—possibly no higher than background radiation levels— and also little impact on grazing animals or other elements of the land-based food chain. It was possible, however, that the fallout might have some debilitating consequences for foods that were part of the aquatic food chain (Winteringham 1989). With that in mind, it is evident that the high temporary standard adopted by the EC immediately after Chernobyl was important and effective in reducing a risk commonly agreed on by the members of the European Union. However, it is also evident from this report that the monitoring infrastructure was already in place within the individual member countries. In that sense, it also seems apparent that the negotiated compromise standard that was subsequently passed to replace the temporary standard was weaker and made little difference in the actual behavior of members of the European Union.

An international regime faces many obstacles to achieving compliance when countries find it costly to cooperate with its rules and regulations. A good rule of thumb when examining international organizations is that the more effective an agreement is in addressing costly distribution issues, the harder it is to get compliance. The reason for this is easily seen.

Two tasks that confront international organizations are monitoring and punishing behavior that deviates from agreed principles. Several difficulties surround efforts to detect cheating or deviations. Naturally, cheaters have an incentive to hide their behavior. Because it is not out in the open, it can be difficult to prove that a member has cheated. For instance, OPEC assigns oil production quotas to the member states. Nigeria is believed to sell more oil than is permitted under its quota. Following oil from the wellhead to a pipeline to a tanker and then to the marketplace can be very difficult, and OPEC does not have monitors who can go to Nigeria and count how many barrels are produced or sold each day. The organization's Saudi leaders have been wise enough to avoid such heavy-handed monitoring practices. If they had not been so wise, they would face stiff resistance from Nigeria (and from other member states that allegedly cheat). The Nigerian government probably would not allow inspectors to monitor oil production and sales so closely. That is one reason Saudi Arabia and other OPEC members are wise not to insist too strongly on compliance with the assigned quotas. To do so would just invite some members to leave the organization, further weakening its already limited long-term ability to influence world oil prices.

Effective monitoring and punishment confront a host of information problems. A member may be thought to be cheating, but the member may deny this, claiming instead that its seemingly aberrant behavior was an error on its part or that the claim that its behavior is aberrant is a misinterpretation of the situation. The problems of monitoring behavior and doling out punishment for cheating were at the heart of the dispute between the United States and other members of the United Nations Security Council regarding whether Iraq was hiding weapons of mass destruction or was truly cooperating with UN inspectors in the run up to the 2003 war. As we have seen earlier, Iraq may have had incentives to mislead inspectors about its capability for weapons of mass destruction when, in fact, it had none. The United States misled other members of the Security Council when Secretary of State Colin Powell left them with the impression that the United States knew where the weapons were. What the truth was and what to do about it were irresolvable questions for the Security Council.

Even if behavior that deviates from international agreements is detected, designing effective punishment strategies can be difficult. One solution, which we have discussed before as the grim trigger strategy, is to have members agree that they will never again cooperate with anyone who cheats. This policy, if implemented, certainly makes deviant behavior potentially very costly—but, then, it also makes punishing the culprit costly for the punishers. Imagine two trading partners. Trade often arises under conditions very much like those in the prisoner's dilemma. If both parties adopt free trade, then both benefit from the jointly cooperative outcome. But each player knows that, if it persists in cooperating by not adopting tariffs while the other cheats, then it is suffering a severe loss. This was the exact issue before the WTO in 2002 when the United States imposed steel tariffs on Europe and Japan, tariffs it eventually removed following a ruling by the WTO that the U.S. policy violated WTO rules. Cutting off trade forever with the cheater, however, means that both the buyer and the seller will suffer. Eventually the cost of maintaining the punishment exceeds the benefit, and the punisher seeks to renegotiate the relationship with the cheater. A cheater, of course, can calculate how much cost the enforcer will tolerate before renegotiating away from the grim trigger. As a consequence, the grim trigger is not a credible punishment strategy.

An alternative to the grim trigger as applied to nations is to restrict the imposition of the punishment strategy to leaders. Fiona McGillivray and Alastair Smith (2000, 2008) demonstrate that international interests can influence the domestic affairs of a target state by determining not to cooperate with a leader who previously violated the rules of the international organization or agreement to which they all belong. In this way, the coalition backing the leader who has violated the agreement knows that they can restore their access to the benefits of the international regime if they depose their leader. This creates an incentive for them to punish their leader for violations and induces better behavior by leaders by making the threat of their overthrow more credible. We can see examples of tying punishment to leaders in the cases of the ending of sanctions against South Africa's apartheid regime once it was replaced by the government of Nelson Mandela in 1994 and, more recently, of removing sanctions against Iraq once Saddam Hussein was overthrown in 2003.

The Temptation to Cheat

Temptation is generally the root cause of cheating on an agreement, but it is not evident that an organizational structure is essential to control cheating. Consider a frequent source of difficulty—problems surrounding common pool resources (Ostrom 1999). Common pool resources, such as fisheries, grazing land, and water energy, have in common with public goods that they are nonexcludable, and they have in common with private goods that they are divisible and consumable and, therefore, can be depleted. Imagine a fishing area in international waters. Fish come into and go out of the waterway. The resources of the waterway represent a common pool. Anyone has the right to fish in the waters. If the waterway is overfished, too few fish will remain to replenish the supply and everyone will lose out. However, if a fisherman exceeds the permitted quota, he or she has more fish to sell and so makes more money in the short run. But in the long run, the fisherman's overfishing means that he or she, like everyone else, can no longer catch fish economically and so suffers a loss. This is a problem known as the **tragedy of the commons.** All will benefit from using restraint, but if everyone else uses restraint, then cheating is attractive. But if everyone (or many) cheats, then everyone loses.

As Elinor Ostrom (1999) and her collaborators have demonstrated, it is not essential to have a complex organization to monitor and punish cheating. Often, if the group of fishers (or other users of a common pool resource) is not too large, it is perfectly capable of arriving at a cooperative norm that minimizes, but usually does not fully eliminate, cheating. The problem is solved, in essence, by the anticipation of market forces. When the magnitude of cheating is high, the supply of the common pool resource is large and so commands a relatively low price. This makes excessive exploitation of the common pool resource relatively unattractive compared with fishers' investing their time and resources in other income-generating opportunities. The more people who divert their energy and time away from exploiting the common pool resource, the less of it finds its way to market. With the supply to the market reduced, the price rises, making it attractive for more time and energy to be devoted to using the resource than to putting time and energy into some other activity. Thus, there is a long-term equilibrium use of the resource that stabilizes price and supply, provided that people have relatively attractive next-best alternative uses of their time and energy (that is, their factors of production are mobile). What this means is that the users of a common pool resource have a good prospect of avoiding the tragedy of the commons even without developing an elaborate oversight organization. This is akin to the observation that if people are engaged in an indefinitely repeated prisoner's dilemma situation, there are cooperative equilibria that emerge and can be sustained by individual actions without the benefit—or costs—of introducing organizational structure into the mix.

SUMMARY

The central theme of this chapter has been that international rules, regulations, and organizations may help induce cooperative behavior, but they cannot be counted on to do so. Rules, regulations, and structure are likely to be the product of strategic maneuvering. As such, they are more likely to reflect national or individual interests as defined at a given moment than they are to be the factor that shapes national or individual interests. Still, organizations are sticky. Once created, they are hard to get rid of, so they can help tie the hands of leaders or increase the costs of deviant behavior.

A high level of compliance with an organization's rules and regulations should not be mistaken for evidence that the organization is effective in altering behavior. The level of compliance is likely to be endogenous. Organizations are unlikely to pass rules that members are unwilling to follow unless the organization does not bother with effective means to monitor compliance and punish deviant behavior. As a consequence, many organizational decisions are likely to be shallow, making compliance easy. Decisions that would effectively alter behavior undoubtedly exist, but they may be relatively rare.

Compliance may be seen as a way to establish a national reputation. A reputation for cooperative behavior may make it easier for a state to reach cooperative arrangements with other states in the future. However, reputation should be thought of as being divided into at least three important constituent parts: general, executive, and bureaucratic. Nations may have reputations in general, but it is more likely that individual leaders will develop reputations and that those reputations will not adhere to the state and will not survive after they are gone from office. Individual government agencies with persistent civil service bureaucracies may develop reputations that are issue- or area-specific. These are likely to matter and to continue over time, but they are unlikely to carry over into arenas outside the purview of the particular government organization or agency.

KEY CONCEPTS

compliance 320	**national reputation** 339
exclusive 345	**role redefinition** 323
grim trigger 338	**shadow of the future** 335
Helsinki Final Act 332	**sovereignty** 325
inclusive 345	**sticky** 326
international law 317	**structure-induced equilibrium** 353
international organizations 319	**tit-for-tat** 336
international regimes 322	**tragedy of the commons** 358
legitimation 323	**Treaty of Westphalia** 325

Appendix A

Modern Political Economic History and International Politics

OVERVIEW

- What has occurred in the past and what will in the future are not due to happenstance but, rather, depend on choices about alternative paths that can be taken.

- To understand international affairs, we need to know the facts of history and we need theories to organize these facts.

- A common background in essential facts from the past five hundred years will provide a common ground to explore the present and future.

- The past several hundred years of history provide a natural experiment in the alternative forms of governance that shape our world.

The events of history are sometimes described as a sequence of chance (path dependent) developments. Such a view leads to the memorization of key dates and names rather than an appreciation of how intertwined the events of history really are. If we think of historical developments and change as arising by chance, then we have no reason to believe that lessons for the future can be learned from a study of the past. This book rejects that viewpoint and maintains that lessons can be learned from history. Although we can readily imagine alternative courses that history might have taken, we should not infer that the actual flow of events was due to happenstance in the past or that it is likely to be due to happenstance in the future. What actually happened is largely dependent on the anticipated consequences of alternative courses of action that were not chosen. Why, for example, did the United States launch a war on terror after Al Qaeda's attacks on September 11, 2001? Because the leaders of the American government thought that the consequences of not retaliating would be worse than the consequences of retaliating. These alternative courses—sometimes called counterfactual histories—are what did *not* happen. History can teach us lessons for the future by allowing us to understand both why particular choices were made and why other choices, leading to alternative histories, were not made. To examine decisions in an informed way, we need to know something about what decision makers knew or believed at the time they made their choices.

The distinction between what is known when a decision is made and what is known later is an important element in judging the past and in the evaluation of arguments about the future. Decisions can only be made before their consequences are known, so knowing the prior flow of events and its causes often is instrumental in shaping the views of decision makers about what to do next. Of course, using information that is known afterward when evaluating the decisions that leaders made is both unfair and misleading when developing explanations or causal arguments. Historians and political scientists studying international relations commonly confuse what was known before the fact with what is known after the fact. For example, many scholars who are interested in determining the causes of large-scale, destructive wars such as World War I focus their research only on big wars (Organski and Kugler 1980; Gilpin 1981; Kennedy 1987). Yet the decision makers of

Armed conflict is as much an element of international relations as is diplomacy, and the two are often inextricably entwined. A series of treaties and secret pacts among the powers of Europe catapulted the continent into World War I. By the time the United States entered on the side of Great Britain and its allies in 1917, the countries of Europe had fought themselves to a stalemate of attrition that would earn the conflict the title "the war to end all wars."

the time did not know they were entering into an extraordinarily long, widespread, and costly war. Had they known how devastating these wars would be, at least some of them probably would have been more inclined to settle their differences without resorting to violence and its attendant costs. For example, we know now that the German invasion of Poland on September 1, 1939, led to World War II. But the leaders of the time did not know that; in fact, contemporary newspaper accounts referred to the invasion as the "German-Polish War."*

The making of foreign policy decisions, the shaping of international politics, and our understanding of arguments and evidence depend on two basic but fundamentally different components: facts and theoretical perspective. This appendix looks at some important facts of history to establish a basic shared knowledge. Appendix B examines the tools for evaluating facts in light of logic and evidence.

I begin with essential facts about the political and economic history of the past 550 years. Of course, in a short appendix, I can offer only a rudimentary review of history. Therefore, I draw attention especially to the development of different forms of governance over the centuries and to the conflicts that were crucial in determining which sets of ideas about government institutions prevailed and which fell by the wayside. Naturally, there are many other ways to retell the history of the centuries I cover here, so even in choosing how to relate facts, we must already impose guiding assumptions. Those who want a more in-depth or a different treatment should consult any of the numerous excellent book-length accounts of world history. A suggested list of such readings can be found at the Web site for this book, http://college.cqpress.com/bdm.

THE FIFTEENTH CENTURY

The years 1452–1453 produced a host of important developments. For example, 1453 marked the collapse of the Byzantine Empire; this successor to the ancient Roman Empire fell when Islamic Ottoman Turkey took control of Constantinople. For many historians, the end of the Byzantine Empire also marks the end of the Middle Ages and the beginning of the modern era. The argument that 1453 ends the Middle Ages is closely tied to the economic consequences of the fall of Constantinople and, incidentally, the implications of those economic consequences for Columbus's later voyages of discovery. The victory by the Turks meant that they could keep European traders from directly exploiting land routes to the spice trade with India and beyond. The increased costs and risks of the overland routes to Asia contributed to the search by the European powers for a sea route to India, China, and Japan. Thus, Spain's decision to back Columbus in his quest for such a path to Asian trade followed directly from the heightened costs of overland trade brought about by the defeat of the Byzantine Empire by the Ottoman Turks. Spain was motivated by Ferdinand and Isabella's interest in securing their personal hold on power and by their desire to enrich and strengthen themselves by enriching and strengthening their kingdom.

---

* For example, my mother, who fled Belgium when it was bombed by the Nazis on May 10, 1940, always said that World War II started on May 10, 1940. When I pressed her about the German invasion of Poland eight months earlier, she responded, "Oh, that was the German-Polish War."

MAP A.1 | Holy Roman, Ottoman, and Russian Empires, 1400s–1500s

Russian Empire 1400s
Russian Empire 1500s
Holy Roman Empire 1400s
Holy Roman Empire 1500s
Ottoman Empire 1400s
Ottoman Empire 1500s

Competition for control of Europe is evident in the expansion of the Holy Roman, Ottoman, and Russian Empires during the 1400s and 1500s.

Other events in Europe at the time set the stage for future developments and conflicts over the next several centuries and even into our own time. Germany—then a loose confederation of principalities—had been ruled by the Habsburg dynasty since 1273. Habsburg rule, however, took a great leap forward in power when Frederick III became the holy Roman emperor in 1452. The Holy Roman Empire was probably the most powerful secular authority in Europe at the time, with only the Catholic Church being at least as powerful. The Habsburgs maintained their control over the Holy Roman Empire until 1806, when it ceased to exist. In the intervening centuries, German political, cultural, and military influence waned and waxed, helping to set the stage for German ambitions in the First and Second World Wars. Perhaps even contemporary Germany's great influence within the European Union today can be traced back to Frederick III in the fifteenth century.

The years 1452–1453, then, witnessed the emergence of critical new powers in northern Europe and the development of southeastern Europe's ties to Asia through Turkey. Still other events were unfolding that helped redefine the political map and interests of Europe's leading powers. In the west, England and France finally resolved the Hundred Years War (1337–1453). At the war's outset, England had held vast territories in what today is called France. English kings claimed the French throne just as French kings—harking back to France's William, Duke of Normandy, who as William the Conqueror took control of England in 1066 and became its ruler—made claims on the English crown. The French emerged victorious from the Hundred Years War, expelling England from almost all of its continental territories and helping to solidify France's borders along lines close to those of modern France. The French victory also helped define the French nationality and **nationalism,** a process already under way by 1302, when the French king, Philip the Fair, launched a war against Pope Boniface VIII and called on the people of France to die for their country (*pro patria mori*). Similar consequences for England emerged from the Hundred Years War; in the process of losing the war, modern England began to take form.

None expressed the profound change in national self-awareness in England better than did William Shakespeare in writing two centuries later about Henry V and the English success in the Battle of Agincourt (2002/1415):

This day is called the feast of Crispian:

He that outlives this day, and comes safe home,

Will stand a-tiptoe when this day is named,

And rouse him at the name of Crispian....

And gentlemen in England now a-bed

Shall think themselves accursed they were not here,

And hold their manhoods cheap whiles any speaks

That fought with us upon Saint Crispin's day. (*Henry V,* Act IV, Scene 3, lines 41–68)

The Hundred Years War secured English national consciousness and the gradual development of an English culture that is distinctly different from that of France. Although England was already well on the way to establishing its common law and parliamentary government, 1453 and its aftermath mark a crucial turning point in English and French history. The emerging political institutions in England served to strengthen the Crown both at the expense of external interests, especially the Catholic Church, and internal rivals, most notably the wealthiest earls and dukes. These institutional developments were, in other words, the product not of chance ideas but of strategic maneuvers by England's king (and France's as well) to make secure his own political position.

In the northeastern part of Europe, equally momentous events unfolded only a quarter of a century later. Modern Russia was born in 1480 when Ivan III, having defeated Asia's Mongols (the heirs of Genghis Khan), created an independent Russian state. His successor, Ivan the Terrible, then set about building a Russian empire that made the country a major competitor for political influence throughout Europe, a position Russia maintains to this day.

Halfway across the world, other pivotal events were taking place. Developments in modern-day Mexico in 1430 helped set the stage for some of the most significant events in the sixteenth century. During the eleventh and twelfth centuries, the then nomadic Aztecs encountered and eventually overtook the Toltec civilization in the Valley of Mexico. The Aztecs elected their first king, Tenoch, in 1349. He ruled for more than forty years. During this time, control of Mexico was divided among numerous competing tribes, but in 1430 a league of three Aztec cities formed—Tenochtitlan, Texcuco, and Tlacopén—to build an empire. The three-city league fought wars with its political rivals and fairly quickly established Aztec control over an empire that ranged from the Pacific Ocean to the Gulf of Mexico. In less than a century, this empire and the imperial pursuits of Spain clashed, leading to the conquest of Mexico.

As the fifteenth century drew to a close, Spain was united, schisms that had divided the papacy appeared to be resolved, England and France were emerging from decades of war, and European monarchs seemed poised to expand their influence throughout the New World. Yet other events were taking place that challenged the fundamental world order inherited at the turn of the century.

THE SIXTEENTH CENTURY

The fifteen hundreds witnessed the flowering of the Protestant Reformation with its attendant implications for the secularization of Europe. Habsburg control over the Holy Roman Empire provided a crucial backdrop for the success of the Protestant Reformation. Martin Luther posted his ninety-five theses in 1517, challenging the legitimacy of the Catholic Church's religious and political hegemony in Europe. The monarchs of northern Europe saw this and a slew of other anti-Church protests and declarations as a political opportunity to undermine the pope's authority and to weaken the influence of the Catholic Church as a competitor for political influence. Protests against the Church leadership's apparent venality and corruption served the political interests of the monarchs. The Reformation gave them an opportunity to foster loyalty both by promoting nationalism and by encouraging new Protestant religions as an alternative to Roman Catholicism. By fostering the legitimacy of Protestant religious principles, monarchs could deprive the Church of the power inherent in its ability to excommunicate individuals or to deprive whole communities of the sacraments (through interdiction). Prior to the Protestant Reformation, western Europeans who failed to subscribe to the teachings of Roman Catholicism exposed themselves to severe prejudice and extreme risks. Earlier efforts to reform the Catholic hierarchy had met with disaster, as experienced, for instance, by the monk Girolamo Savonarola, who was burned at the stake on May 23, 1498, for condemning Church practices and the lavish lifestyle of the Church's leaders.

What Savonarola could not do successfully from his base in Florence—right in the papacy's backyard—Martin Luther and others did from their more remote outposts in northern Europe. With the advent of the Reformation, those who no longer subscribed to Catholicism did not need the Church hierarchy to serve as intermediaries between them and God. People could practice new forms of Christianity, knowing that their leaders supported these practices, and in this way the Church was weakened. The changing perception of the Catholic Church played an important part in increasing the apparent power and influence of secular political institutions throughout Europe. Because many people no longer believed that their salvation depended on the Church's approval or on confession to a Catholic priest, local rulers were strengthened in their ability to assert sovereign authority. Thus, changes in beliefs resulted in fundamental changes in the authority of states as opposed to the supernational Church.

The Catholic leadership, of course, did not stand by idly while its power was eroded. A counterreformation was launched that was part reform and part oppression of the Protestant dissenters. By the seventeenth century these political-religious disputes in Europe came to a head, culminating in the Thirty Years War (1618–1648).

While the struggle for national emergence and sovereignty continued in sixteenth-century Europe, Suleiman the Magnificent (1520–1566) built on the successes of the Ottomans in the previous century. He turned Ottoman Turkey into the Ottoman Empire, exercising significant political and economic control from Asia Minor to North Africa and spreading into Europe. In the last great battle in Europe between Islamic and Christian adherents until our own time, Suleiman laid siege to Vienna in 1529. The Ottoman Empire was defeated, and the Ottoman Empire and the influence of Islam were gradually forced to retreat from most of Europe. (A similar clash in Europe between Christians and Muslims did not arise again until the end of the cold war, when the collapse of the Soviet Union led Yugoslavia to unravel into its constituent parts, producing wars in Bosnia and Kosovo—wars that involved disputes between European Christians and Muslims. The current conflict between Muslim extremists and the United States and its allies can be seen in a similar light.[†])

The search for a sea route from Europe to Asia in the fifteenth century had failed, but in the process of searching, Columbus and others after him made European leaders aware of the vast resources of the Americas. In 1518, Hernán Cortés fought and defeated the Aztecs in his quest for wealth for himself and his Spanish sovereign. Francisco Pizarro had much the same motivations when he overthrew the Inca Empire, in what is today Peru, in 1533. By the last two decades of the sixteenth century, tremendous amounts of wealth were being extracted from the Americas and shipped to Europe. Piracy became a critical source of private and national wealth. Indeed, Spain was losing a substantial portion of the wealth it took from the Americas because of theft on the high seas by English pirates (called privateers), many of whom were handsomely rewarded by the English Crown. This led in 1588 to the Spanish monarch's decision to mount a fierce naval armada designed to destroy the English threat at sea. The Spanish Armada, however, was soundly defeated by a combination of bad weather and the more mobile, faster ships of England, marking the decline of Spain and the ascent of England as a great naval power.

[†] Although not strictly a war between Christian and Islamic cultures, our own time has produced the war on terror begun in 2001 by the United States and its allies against Muslim extremists in Afghanistan known as the Taliban and their partner Al Qaeda; in addition the American-led war against Iraq began in 2003. These wars and terrorist attacks against western-influenced countries have created such intense feelings that in 2004 a prominent German leader in the European Union argued against eventually allowing Turkey to join the EU. He maintained that this would advance the Islamization of Europe and would undo the gains made in Europe since the final defeat of Suleiman at the gates of Vienna in 1683.

MAP A.2   Europe in 1648

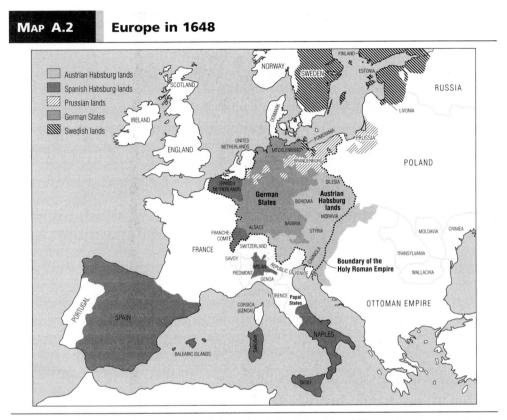

The Treaty of Westphalia, which marked the end of the Thirty Years' War and an important step in the evolution of sovereignty, redrew the map of Europe and redefined the norms and rules of international law that states were expected to obey. The influence of the Catholic Church in political affairs was greatly diminished, and new alignments emerged. It is interesting to note that no defeated monarch was overthrown by the victors in the Thirty Years' War.

By the close of the fifteen hundreds, Spain and Portugal, the two great naval powers of that century, were in decline. Islam had been turned back from much of Europe (though its major defeat at the gates of Vienna remained nearly a century into the future), although it had secured its hold in North Africa and Asia Minor. The exploitation of America's wealth stimulated colonization, leading eventually to the establishment of permanent European settlements and holdings in North and South America. The world of international competition and commerce had become much larger than it had been one hundred years earlier. We might say that this marked the beginning of the modern movement toward globalization in **trade,** the exchange of goods, services, knowledge, and even culture across vast expanses of geography. The greatest power in Europe—the Catholic Church—faced its last battle for domination, a battle it lost as the Protestant Reformation spread across northern Europe.

THE SEVENTEENTH CENTURY

Much of Europe was enveloped in war from 1618 to 1648. The Thirty Years War was partially a religious conflict and partially a struggle to eliminate the supremacy of the Holy Roman Empire, replacing it with numerous sovereign nation-states. It ended with the Treaty of Westphalia, which marks for many the defining moment of transition to the modern state-dominated international system. The new international order following the Thirty Years War consisted of a system in which territorial, sovereign governments lived securely within what were usually well-defined borders and exercised control over the political, military, economic, and social life within those borders. Today, we give little thought to a world without states. Yet the state as we understand it has not always existed and may not always exist in the future.

The Treaty of Westphalia contains more than one hundred specific articles laying out the terms and conditions of the war's end. Most of these articles deal with the allocation or restoration of valuable resources among the participants. A few articles, however, pertain directly to the establishment of territorial sovereignty and to the specific rights and privileges of states. Article 64 establishes territoriality and the right of the state to choose its own religion, as well as the right to noninterference by other states in any of these matters. This article codifies the end of Roman Catholicism's hegemony in Europe. Article 65 spells out the rights of sovereign authority with regard to foreign policy. For example, it establishes that no supernational authority (at that time, the Catholic Church or the Holy Roman Empire) can make or negate alliances made between sovereigns for the purpose of protecting each nation's security. Similarly, Article 67 establishes that sovereign states can determine their own domestic policies, free from external pressures and "with full Jurisdiction within the inclosure of their Walls and their Territorys").[‡]

The Westphalian System unquestionably marks a crucial point in international affairs, but it would be a mistake to think that the modern state sprang up suddenly and completely as a result of the Thirty Years War. Competition between the Church and monarchies, starting with the papacy of Gregory VII in the late eleventh century, had already put changes into motion, with the Treaty of Westphalia codifying the changes that were taking place.

By the end of the Thirty Years War, Europe's balance of power had fundamentally changed. Not only had the Catholic Church declined in influence, but also political power had shifted to France. The war killed about half of all Germans, and France's monarch emerged as the new dominant power in Europe. The ascent of France marked the pinnacle of absolute monarchy, as captured by the French king Louis XIV's famous phrase, "L'état c'est moi" ("I am the state"). Louis was an innovator in government and in national security. He was one of the first sovereigns to maintain a permanent standing army rather than rely on hiring mercenary soldiers to fight when needed. The adoption of a permanent standing army was accompanied by great technological improvements in drill, fighting skill, and

---

[‡] For the full text, including, of course, the language for article LXVII (67), see http://fletcher.tufts.edu/multi/texts/historical/westphalia.txt.

weaponry, all of which contributed to strengthening the central authority of the state ruled by an absolute, hereditary monarch.

The Thirty Years War finished a change in monarchy that had been gradually emerging for some time. Throughout much of the Middle Ages and even before the Norman Conquest of Britain in 1066, monarchy was elective rather than strictly hereditary. Noble birth was a requirement for kingship, and being the child and heir to the previous monarch was a great advantage in gaining the crown, but one still had to be elected. The election of monarchs sometimes led to the selection of someone other than the immediate heir apparent to the throne. The change to heredity as the fundamental means of choosing kings carried important implications for foreign policy. Kings never have to answer to many people, but hereditary kings usually have to answer to even fewer than elected kings. As explained by the selectorate theory, when leaders require the support of very few people, they have incentives to promote their own wealth and that of the few at whose pleasure they serve rather than to promote the welfare of the many who live in their society. So it was for the monarchs who were now less beholden than they had been. Their relative independence from the well-being of their subjects unleashed foreign policy adventures oriented toward securing wealth and power—wealth and power that did not devolve to the people. This meant that war changed in its intensity. The pressure to fight in unpopular wars and the burden of paying for such adventures through heavy taxation eventually destroyed the political advantages of the new monarchism over its older feudal form. By the eighteenth century the failings of absolute, hereditary monarchy gave rise to revolution and to dramatic changes in political institutions, leading to the emergence of the two dominant forms of modern government: rigged-election autocracy and liberal democracy. The first stirrings of threats to monarchy, however, arose even before the Thirty Years War ended.

The English Civil War (1642–1648) saw the commoner, Oliver Cromwell, rise to power as he succeeded temporarily in overthrowing the British monarchy. The English king, Charles I, was beheaded in 1649, suggesting a move away from monarchy to either dictatorship or possibly even a nascent democracy. But Cromwell's efforts against monarchy failed to survive him. Cromwell died in 1658; the monarchy was restored in 1660. Still, the power of the Parliament increased as the monarchy became more and more dependent on the financial backing of Parliament to pursue its policies.

Experiments with republican government had occurred throughout the centuries. The Italian republics had flourished during the Renaissance, only to decline as they lost their quasi-republican forms of governance and were taken over by oligarchs. In the Netherlands, great wealth accompanied the move to a semi-republican form of government led by city magistrates. As in England, this shift toward a partially representative government was accompanied by a tremendous outpouring of entrepreneurial activity and great economic prosperity.

The new ideas and debates about government, including the ideas of Thomas Hobbes in *The Leviathan* (2009/1651) and of John Locke in his *Two Treatises of Civil Government* (1690), unleashed a wealth of views about government as a social contract between the ruler and the ruled. These and other ideas, coupled with the religious consequences of the Thirty Years War, contributed to a wave of new settlers in the New World, settlers who seemed committed to experimenting with innovative forms of government designed to escape the oppressive burdens of monarchy. Whereas the early forays into the Americas by Europeans had focused on limited stays designed to extract tradable goods (for example, furs, lumber, new foodstuffs, and other crops) and mineral wealth, the new European arrivals were more interested in permanent settlements.

The Danes, English, French, and Dutch colonized the Caribbean, building slave-based economies around, particularly, the growth and export of sugarcane. Dutch-settled Nieuw Amsterdam (later New York) became a central source of commerce. Peter Stuyvesant, the governor of Nieuw Amsterdam, faced continual political challenges from Adrian Van der Donk, a Dutch lawyer and colonist. Thanks to van der Donk, one of the most important yet little known figures in American history, Nieuw Amsterdam became the source of new ideas about governance, including freedom of religion, freedom to come and go as one pleased, and freedom of speech. Even today, the governing charter that van der Donk wrote remains the core of New York City's charter and, perhaps, the foundation of American liberties.

The Pilgrims and other dissenting groups settled up and down the east coast of North America in search of religious freedom and economic opportunity. It should be understood that their quest for religious freedom often meant freedom to practice their own religious views and not freedom for people to practice other dissenting views. The Mayflower Compact, an agreement on governance signed by the Pilgrims aboard the *Mayflower*, served as an early model for a self-governing community and helped pave the way for reforms in governing institutions that pervade American history and that represented a departure from the confiscatory economic policies that monarchs often pursued toward their subjects.

The latter half of the seventeenth century presaged other dramatic changes in international politics. By the end of the century, William and Mary sat on the throne in England, but political parties had emerged as a critical source of influence in Parliament. The English prime minister became a figure of considerable political consequence rather than merely a spokesman for the Crown. In science, the discoveries of Francis Bacon, René Descartes, Isaac Newton, Robert Boyle, and others began to change how educated people understood the world. Laws of nature were discovered and the scientific method of experimentation and empirical evaluation began to supplant religious conviction as the basis for reasoned arguments. This, too, weakened the claim of monarchs to rule by divine right (that is, by the will of God). The world was again on the verge of tremendous changes in attitudes and of significant shifts in political and economic factors governing international relations.

THE EIGHTEENTH CENTURY

Spain had entered a long period of decline by the end of the sixteenth century. The opening of the eighteenth century turned the country into a crucial source of political struggle in

Europe. The War of the Spanish Succession (1701–1714) might reasonably be called a world war. It not only involved many European powers, including Spain, Italy, Prussia (a German principality), Holland, France, and England, fighting in military theaters throughout Europe, it also involved extensive naval engagements at sea. The immediate cause of the war was the death of Spain's Charles II, without an heir of direct descent. Charles had willed the crown to Philip of Anjou, the grandson of France's Louis XIV. The French and the Spaniards agreed to make Philip king and to unite France and Spain. Such a union represented a threat to the security of virtually all other European monarchs.

The intention to make Philip of Anjou the king of a united Spain and France prompted an alliance among England, Holland, Prussia, and Austria. This alliance backed the Archduke Charles of Austria for the Spanish crown. War followed and with it numerous French defeats. However, in 1711, the Austrian emperor Joseph I died and Archduke Charles of Austria succeeded him as the new holy Roman emperor. With Charles now holy Roman emperor, the alliance became concerned that, if Charles also secured the throne in Spain, Austria would hold too much power. With Charles in his new position, the threat that the Habsburgs would once again secure their domination over European politics led the other alliance partners to reach a compromise with the French.

The Treaty of Utrecht (1713) ended the war. Philip became king of Spain; the French and Spaniards agreed never to unite; and Great Britain secured control over Gibraltar, Newfoundland, Nova Scotia, the Hudson Bay Territories and a monopoly over the slave trade in Latin America. The Treaty of Utrecht imposed limitations on France's designs for greater power in Europe, prevented the further expansion of Habsburg influence, and greatly improved Britain's prospects for political ascendancy.

Almost inevitably, the aftermath of the War of the Spanish Succession saw an increase in tensions between France and Great Britain. These two powers fought one another in the Seven Years War in Europe and in the associated British-French War (1754–1763; also called the French and Indian War) in the Americas. The British-French War culminated in England's taking control of the Ohio Valley and forging close ties with American Indian tribes. Recognition by Britain of these tribes as sovereign nations threatened the interests in land speculation in the Ohio Valley by American colonists. The aftermath of the war contributed to tensions between the American colonists and England, even as it promoted closer ties between the colonists and France. It was also in this war that George Washington first attracted attention as a military leader.

Although the war in the Americas later turned out to have profound consequences for world history, the main action in the Seven Years War at the time was perceived to be in Europe. That is, the decision makers of the day did not foresee—how could they?—that the "sideshow" in the Americas would eventually become fundamental to world events. This is a good reminder that decisions can be judged based only on what decision makers know and believe at the time they choose, and not on what we come to know later. In Europe, France, Austria, and Russia fought against Britain and Prussia. Among its many consequences, the

Seven Years War led to the emergence of Prussia as a major European power under Frederick the Great. It also was instrumental in establishing the United Kingdom (created from England, Wales, and Scotland in 1707) as the leader in global colonization. Prussia, of course, remained a major force in European affairs, eventually defeating Austria in the Seven Weeks War (1866), which gave rise to the modern conception of Germany.

The Seven Years War and its accompanying battles in North America cost the British government dearly. In an effort to recoup its costs, the English Crown launched new aggressive tax policies, including the infamous Stamp Tax, in the American colonies. Once again, monarchy led to an effort to make people pay for policies they had not endorsed. Harking back to a principle established by England's Edward I in 1297 when he signed *Confirmatio Cartarum* to gain economic support for a war he wanted to fight in Gascony (France), the colonists cried out against taxation without representation, a refrain then also in common use among anti-English factions in Ireland. All English subjects, in principle, had the right to refuse a tax levied by the Crown. Gradually, colonial resentment and British ineptitude escalated into an urge for American sovereignty, leading to the Declaration of Independence in 1776. War followed, with the colonists performing poorly against the better-trained and better-equipped British troops. However, the war took a favorable turn for the would-be Americans when a large French fleet aided them in defeating the British. The British accepted American independence when they signed the Treaty of Paris in 1783.

The leaders of the newly independent American state floundered as they struggled to formulate a workable government among the original colonies while also finding a way to capitalize on international trade in a world in which the British kept American ships out of British-controlled ports. From this early stage of development, when America was still a poor, dependent, third-world backwater, its potential as a seafaring power and growing opportunities for trade encouraged a strong free-trade, antiprotectionism attitude in some of its early leaders, particularly Alexander Hamilton and George Washington (in opposition to the attitudes of Thomas Jefferson, James Madison, and other founders). Building on the writings of Locke, Hume, and others, the new country's founders—particularly Madison and Hamilton, with an assist from earlier efforts by John Adams of Massachusetts—crafted the U.S. Constitution and with it a dramatic new experiment in democratic republican rule in which merit rather than aristocracy was to be the cornerstone of a person's progress through life. To be sure, reality was much more checkered than the rhetoric of the day; still, the American experiment in governance reflected a dramatic departure from absolute hereditary monarchy and its confiscatory tax policies. Slavery remained an issue of contention and became a crucial factor that led to the creation of a compromise federal structure of government. Eventually the federal bargain unraveled, leading to the American Civil War (1861–1865) nearly a century later.

Not long after the success of the American revolutionaries, Europe itself experienced a major assault on the dominance of monarchy as the primary means of government. England was already well on its way to a form of constitutional monarchy when the French Revolution shook the world. French revolutionaries overthrew the monarchy and proclaimed a republic based on the ideas of liberty, fraternity, and equality—that is, just the opposite orientation to monarchic institutions. The Reign of Terror followed in which thousands of French aristocrats and ordinary French citizens were beheaded as the new leadership sought to remove the vestiges of nobility and inequality from French rule. The movement was doomed because the revolutionaries fought one another, failed to put together a well-structured government, and led the country into chaos. In 1795, Napoleon succeeded in seizing political control, and France drifted from republic to imperial power.

THE NINETEENTH CENTURY

After Napoleon took control of France, he set his sights on other parts of Europe. The continent became embroiled in the Napoleonic Wars from 1795 to 1815, with Napoleon declaring himself emperor in 1804. Napoleon's army—using the first universal military training system—swept across Europe and North Africa. In 1802, he agreed to the Peace of Amiens, in which Great Britain surrendered many of its colonial holdings to France in exchange for the French agreeing to withdraw from Egypt. By 1805, Napoleon suffered a serious setback when his navy was defeated at the Battle of Trafalgar, marking the end of France's threat to invade England. A year later, in 1806, the Prussians were defeated at the Battle of Jena, resulting in Prussia's loss of its Polish territories, a matter that later became a fundamental issue for Hitler's Germany at the outset of World War II. Napoleon himself was finally defeated at the Battle of Waterloo in 1815 and sent into exile, where he apparently was murdered by poisoning.

Napoleon's conquests left an indelible mark. He helped rationalize governance in much of Europe by imposing the Napoleonic code of law. Even today, we can find the influence of French law in significant parts of Europe and in Louisiana in the United States (the state was once a French territory). Following his defeat, the victors, including Austria, Great Britain, Prussia, and Russia, created the Concert of Europe (forged at the Congress of Vienna) to coordinate foreign policy among the great powers in the hopes of preventing a future Napoleon from jeopardizing sovereign control in Europe's states. Among the more dramatic actions taken by the Concert of Europe was that the victors agreed to restore the French monarchy and bring France back in as one of the great powers.

Meanwhile, the revolutionary storm unleashed in France at the end of the seventeen hundreds continued largely unabated. Efforts to topple monarchy and establish a more popular government arose in 1830 and again in 1848 as dissident youths and others took to the barricades. Although these movements failed, they planted the seeds for sharp changes in the years to come.

In England, the monarch was becoming increasingly a constitutional figurehead, and the prime minister and Parliament were the growing seats of power. By 1835, Britain had adopted a voting rights act that clearly made it into a constitutional monarchy—a new form of government—in which the House of Commons was the source of political power. During this same period, English domination of the seas was unquestioned, and British banking was fundamental to the colonial and other ambitions of much of Europe. The nineteenth century marked the peak of British **colonial power,** that is, the domination of a people and territory by occupation or governance by an external power, especially in India, elsewhere in Asia, and in Africa.

England surged far ahead of its competitors for several reasons. Britain, as an island nation, had developed superior naval capabilities to foster and support its colonial holdings and to secure its borders against foreign threats. In addition, the industrial revolution took place in Britain earlier than on the European continent, in large measure because of the greater responsiveness to entrepreneurial ideas and land enclosures that rationalized agriculture in England. Also, England had a stronger orientation toward relatively free trade than did France and others. This orientation promoted greater competitiveness in English industry, promoting efficiency and rapid economic growth.

The English quest for new goods and new markets helped fuel its imperial ambitions. Between 1839 and 1842, for instance, Britain fought China in the Opium War, which arose from China's efforts to prevent Britain from importing opium into China from Britain's colony in India. The British won the war, which was ended by the unequal Treaty of Nanking. Under the terms of this treaty, Britain obtained control over several Chinese ports, including Hong Kong (which it returned to China on July 1, 1997, on the expiration of its lease over the territory). The English also gained special privileges and legal protections in China. The Chinese received little in return. Unequal French and American treaties with China followed soon thereafter, solidifying the era of imperial expansion.

As part of American **expansionism,** the United States fought Mexico in the Mexican-American War (1846–1848). The United States established the Rio Grande as its border with Mexico and claimed Texas and California. It secured ownership over vast territories through purchase (the Louisiana Purchase) and through conquest, including the present-day plains states. These states were taken from the sovereign Indian tribes of those areas. Many of the treaties signed with Indian nations in the 1800s are the legal basis today for the proliferation of Indian-operated casinos on tribal lands, which are, because of the treaties, exempt from taxation.

American expansionist designs were not confined, however, to the North American continent. In 1854, U.S. naval ships forced the shogun-led Japanese military government to open Japan's ports to trade with the United States. By 1867, internal dissent led to the resignation of the shogun, the end of the shogunate's more than 250-year rule, and the reassertion of the emperor's role as the primary leader of Japan. The Meiji Restoration of 1868 allowed Emperor Mutsuhito to reassert the emperor's traditional powers, which had lapsed during the shogun period. This led for a time to a more pro-western orientation and an effort in Japan to adapt to western ideas and business practices. However, the military party gained substantial influence in Japan's newly created parliament in 1878. The military opposed European ideas, favoring instead Japan's own role as an expansionist, imperial power. The party encouraged Japan to pursue expansion on to the Asian continent. This, in turn, led to the Sino-Japanese War of 1894 and the Russo-Japanese War a decade later. With these two wars, Japan established itself as a significant political power in Asia, taking control of substantial portions of China and Korea. Japanese expansionist ambitions in Asia continued until its defeat in World War II.

Meanwhile, on the European continent, the struggle to control Europe's destiny continued. Otto von Bismarck first succeeded in unifying Prussia and several smaller German principalities during the Seven Weeks War (1866), in which, to the surprise of most European leaders, he quickly and easily defeated Austria. This war marked the end of the Concert of Europe system that had been forged half a century earlier in the wake of Napoleon's defeat. Austria, at risk of losing its status as a major power, was forced to accept an arrangement with Hungary that resulted in the creation of the Austro-Hungarian Empire. This new alliance was an attempt by Austria to shore up its declining political position relative to Prussia's. Just four years later, Bismarck went to war against France, defeating Napoleon III in the Franco-Prussian War of 1870–1871. With France's defeat, Bismarck succeeded in unifying the remaining German principalities, creating modern-day Germany. He also established Prussia/Germany as the rising power of Europe and France as a state in decline. This set the stage for the two world wars of the twentieth century.

The nineteenth century was not only a time of continental expansion for the United States and a time when it began to spread its influence abroad, it was also a period of rapid economic growth and the establishment of the country as a transcontinental power. Following the American Civil War, the United States incorporated vast territories as new states. With the building of the transcontinental railroad, the U.S. government made it possible to control its continental territory and provided a cheap and fast means to transport people and goods across the continent. Likewise, the construction of the Panama Canal greatly stimulated commerce between the east coast of the United States and the west coast and beyond, shortening the time and cost of shipping goods between ports on the Atlantic and Pacific Oceans. By the end of the nineteenth century, the United States was actively engaged as a colonial power, gaining influence in the Philippines and Cuba as a result of America's defeat of Spain in the Spanish-American War. The United States was well on the way to supplanting Britain as the richest country in the world.

THE TWENTIETH CENTURY

The fifteenth to seventeenth centuries witnessed the consolidation and gradual decline of monarchy. The eighteenth and nineteenth centuries were, broadly speaking, a period in which those who adopted more democratic forms of government and more capitalist modes of economics enjoyed burgeoning wealth and influence in the world. Some changes were to the good—as in the expansion of rule of law and improvement in living conditions—and some involved the imposition of colonial rule on people who fought for and preferred to

MAP A.3   **U.S., British, and Japanese Colonialism, circa 1900**

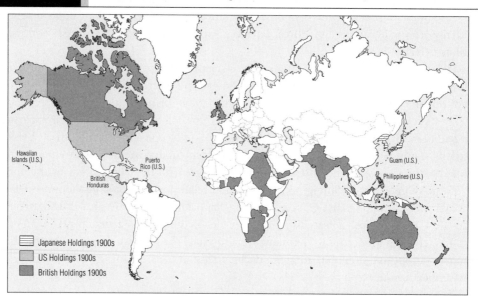

Japanese Holdings 1900s
US Holdings 1900s
British Holdings 1900s

The impulse for colonial expansion was especially strong in the eighteenth and nineteenth centuries. By the beginning of the twentieth century, colonialism was starting to wane, with the Americas almost completely liberated from their eighteenth-century rulers. Nevertheless, colonialism remained an important feature of foreign policy and economic expansion until the end of World War II. Although old colonial ties remain strong indicators of current economic relations among European and non-European states, little of the world remains under the control of foreign "hosts" today.

pursue their own destinies. Many of these centuries-old patterns culminated in dramatic global changes during the twentieth century.

The World through the First World War

Revolutions against monarchy and oligarchy arose in Russia in 1905 and China in 1911. Mexico likewise gave birth to a popular revolution seeking to overthrow oligarchy. By 1914, tensions between the expansionist designs of the Austro-Hungarian Empire in Europe and Serbian nationalism led to a seemingly minor tragic event, the assassination of the prospective heir to the Austro-Hungarian throne, Archduke Franz Ferdinand, in Sarajevo, Serbia. Following the assassination, Austria issued an ultimatum to the Serbian government that essentially called for the Serbs to give up their sovereignty. As tensions mounted, Europe's great powers chose sides in the dispute. Russia sided with the Serbs. Under the terms of the Triple Entente, an alliance between Russia, France, and England, France and England also sided with the Serbs. Under the terms of the Dual Alliance between Germany and Austria, those two great powers backed one another, with additional support coming from Romania, Turkey, and elsewhere. Fearing an aggressive move by Germany, the Russians mobilized, prompting a similar mobilization by Germany. In a short time, the conflict over Serbia had escalated to involve all of the great powers on the continent. The Great War (later called World War I) had begun.

Fought between 1914 and 1918, the war greatly accelerated political change in Europe and fundamentally altered international relations. By the end of the war, the world had experienced its first truly modern trench warfare. Mustard gas (a chemical weapon) had been used effectively, raising the specter that future wars would be nonconventional. Modern weapons had greatly increased the war's carnage, prompting intense efforts to find ways to avert future cataclysms.

The war ended with the Treaty of Versailles, which imposed harsh terms on Germany, including the tremendous economic burden of reparation payments to help France and other nations recuperate the costs of the war. One consequence of the war's end was that the map of Europe was redrawn. The Austro-Hungarian Empire ceased to exist, replaced by independent countries carved out of its territory. Germany was greatly weakened, but so too were the victors, especially England, France, and Russia. The United States, under President Woodrow Wilson, emerged as the most powerful nation in the world. Wilson's Fourteen Points called for a major transformation in international politics. In an effort to prevent a future Great War, the victors built on Wilson's ideas to create the League of Nations to maintain peace through collective security. The United States, however, seeking to return to a policy of isolation, did not join the League, which ensured that this international body lacked the teeth necessary to play a major peacekeeping role.

One of the tenets promoted by Wilson in his Fourteen Points was that people should be free to choose their own government, thereby helping seal the terminal fate of monarchy and advancing Wilson's objective of making the world safe for democracy. Unfortunately, Wilson did not endorse the idea that self-determination should necessarily carry over right away to colonial areas. One of those dejected by that failure of the Treaty of Versailles was a young man named Ho Chi Minh, who later emerged as the leader of North Vietnam. He led the Vietnamese wars against the French and then the Americans in Indochina and Vietnam throughout the 1950s, 1960s, and into the 1970s, in part for that right of self-determination. Regrettably, in the process he imposed communist rule in Vietnam with its attendant dictatorship and oppression of the very principle of self-determination that he had at one time advocated. To this day, the Vietnamese people do not have the right to freely elect their own government.

World War I imposed extreme costs on the tsarist regime in Russia. By 1917, the tsar's government faced revolution. The Russian Revolution succeeded in overthrowing the monarchy and led briefly to a liberal, democratic government. That government, however, was weak and unable to consolidate its power when faced with a challenge by Vladimir Ilyich

Lenin's Bolsheviks. Between 1917 and 1922, Lenin converted Russia into a Soviet Republic with a socialist government led by the Communist Party. This meant that ordinary people had little, if any, say in the government because (according to the communist regime) they were susceptible to bourgeois influence and suffered from a trade-union mentality that did not allow them to see the big picture—the hypothesized shared self-interest of working people everywhere. Therefore, decisions were centered in the hands of the elite in the Communist Party because they were the vanguard of the proletariat (common laborers) who supposedly understood the proper path to socialism.

The Interregnum between World Wars

The Russian Revolution launched a bold experiment in the application of Karl Marx's and Friedrich Engel's ideas of communism as an alternative to capitalism. In **communism,** the economic ideal is that each individual would contribute to society according to his or her ability and each would receive whatever he or she needed from society in return. In **capitalism,** the economic ideal is that the "hidden hand" of market forces would produce efficient growth and prosperity; that is, no individual or firm could be big enough to control the price at which goods and services were bought or sold.

Many people saw the ideas of communism as the likely long-term successor to monarchy—then in its final death throes—and to liberal democracy. Communism seemed to integrate economics and politics in a way that promoted equality on both fronts. As appealing as the ideal may have seemed, in practice it was an utter failure as a basis for economics or politics. Faced with few incentives to be productive—because what people received from the state was not supposed to depend on what they produced—people shirked their jobs, trying to benefit from the labor of others while doing little themselves (called free riding). Like monarchy before it, communism/socialism unintentionally discouraged people from hard, productive labor because they were not rewarded in proportion to what they produced. Those who did work hard were, in essence, subjected to the confiscation of their earnings to support others who did not work hard. Thus, communism, like monarchy, hampered economic growth and prosperity for the common people.

The communist political system was grounded in beliefs such as the existence of common interests among all workers. It assumed that this entire class of people shared the same preferences about domestic and foreign policies. For this reason, dissent could not be tolerated. When Lenin observed that the proletariat did not act as if all of its members shared this core set of preferences, it became necessary to stifle their opportunity to express dissent. Thus, he established the Communist Party to protect against the risk that ignorant and impressionable workers would undermine his revolutionary objectives.

The result was that the political system naturally lapsed into dictatorship as the economy languished in the absence of individual incentives to produce. These problems, already manifest by the early 1920s, became much worse following Lenin's death. Joseph Stalin replaced Lenin and gradually converted the Soviet system into a personal dictatorship. He did so by purging anyone and everyone he even suspected of disagreeing with him. Almost all the top political leaders were branded enemies of the people and executed during the latter part of the 1930s. Stalin likewise intentionally created a famine in the Ukraine, leading to the deaths of millions of people he feared were disloyal to him. Like absolute monarchs before him, Stalin became answerable to only a handful of people whose support he needed to maintain him in power.

While the communist movement took hold in Russia after World War I, **fascism,** a system of totalitarian government in which the government controls all aspects of economic and political activity (unlike communism in which the people, in theory, control the means of production), rose as another alternative to monarchy, starting in Italy under Mussolini in 1922 and in Germany under Hitler from 1933 onward. Fascism, like communism, gave rise to harsh dictatorships with no respect for rule of law or individual rights. The extreme economic circumstances in Germany after World War I provided the impetus for a dictatorship to replace Germany's democratic but weak Weimar Republic. The onset of the Great Depression in North America and across Europe in 1929 sent the global economy into a tailspin. When global trade collapsed, Germany's currency became all but worthless, and it was unable to make war-reparation payments. Millions of its citizens were out of work. In this atmosphere, Adolf Hitler and his followers gained popularity, winning seats in the Reichstag (the German parliament). Hitler quickly converted his early electoral success into burgeoning political influence and, through shrewd maneuvering, was elevated to the post of chancellor of Germany. Once he reached this position, Hitler suspended democratic elections and never again allowed himself or his National Socialist Workers Party (the Nazi Party) to face the will of the people. He might as well have done so, however, because by all appearances he was incredibly popular as he rebuilt Germany's military might and standing in Europe.

The World War II Years

Germany had been banned from rebuilding its military after World War I under the terms of the Treaty of Versailles. Nevertheless, Hitler went ahead and did so in the 1930s and then used this military to reoccupy the land given up at the end of the war. Because he got away with his first actions, he became emboldened. At Munich in 1938, Hitler struck a deal with Britain's prime minister, Neville Chamberlain, in which Hitler was allowed to take over parts of Czechoslovakia but nothing else. Chamberlain's appeasement of Hitler was warmly welcomed in Britain at the time. However, when Hitler then attacked Poland on September 1, 1939, the British realized that Hitler's declaration that he had "no more territorial claims in Europe" was a lie. England declared war on Germany immediately following Germany's invasion of Poland, and Winston Churchill emerged as the new British prime minister. The French and others quickly joined in the war against Germany.

Russia, however, was not among the Allied powers that declared war on Germany. Under the terms of the Molotov-Ribbentrop Pact, signed in summer 1939, Stalin's Soviet Union and Hitler's Germany were allies. They had agreed to partition Poland, with some parts of Poland going to Germany and others to Russia. Remarkably, anticommunist Germany and ostensibly antifascist Russia joined in a common cause. That common interest, however, was broken when Hitler later invaded the Soviet Union, pushing Stalin into a wartime alliance with the British, French, and Americans.

Although there is speculation that President Franklin D. Roosevelt wanted to enter the war on Britain's side almost from the outset, the United States remained militarily aloof from the war in Europe, working on its own domestic economic problems until Japan bombed the U.S. naval base at Pearl Harbor, Hawaii, on December 7, 1941. Before that moment, U.S. war policy largely consisted of providing substantial economic assistance to England (called lend-lease) but no military contingents or commitment. Winston Churchill, in one eloquent speech after another during those dark days of 1940 and 1941 that followed the defeat of France, Belgium, and the Netherlands by Germany, reiterated at every opportunity that England stood alone in defense of freedom and democracy. By the beginning of 1942, however, the United States was fully committed to the war effort in Europe and Asia.

Prior to the attack on Pearl Harbor, Japan's expansionist ambitions in Asia were being thwarted by a U.S. trade embargo imposed by President Roosevelt. In a daring decision, the Japanese leaders concluded that their best chance of prevailing in Asia depended on removing the latent threat that the United States would enter the war to stop them. They concluded that if they could cripple the U.S. Navy, then they could take control of essential areas in Asia before the United States could rebuild and mount a counterattack. The Japanese leaders' hope was that if they realized their ambitions, the United States would see it as a fait accompli and live with the consequences rather than fight a costly, protracted war. By bombing Pearl Harbor, the Japanese hoped to wipe out the American Pacific Fleet and achieve their objectives. They failed and, as they themselves anticipated, the consequence of that failure was a high probability of subsequent defeat in the war.

With the United States fully committed to the war effort, its economy began to expand rapidly. The Great Depression began to fade into the past. America's industrial capacity was unmatched by Japan or by Germany and its ally Italy, even after taking into account the resources of the huge areas conquered by the German army or the millions of slave workers and prisoners forced to labor on behalf of Germany's war effort. With intense military pressure from the Russians in the east and from the Americans, British, Free French, Polish expatriates, and others in the west, the tide of battle turned against Germany. Likewise, in the Pacific, the U.S. naval victory at Midway destroyed so much of the Japanese fleet that the war in Asia also turned in favor of U.S. interests. In June 1945, Hitler's Germany lay in ruins and surrendered unconditionally. Mussolini's Italy had been beaten earlier when the Italian people themselves overthrew their dictator and joined the Allied side. In August 1945, Japan, which continued to fight, was compelled to surrender following the atomic bombings of Hiroshima and Nagasaki by the United States; these acts announced the arrival of the nuclear age. Japan's surrender, unlike Germany's, was not unconditional. Japan was allowed to retain its emperor.

World War II was the deadliest conflict in all of history. Tens of millions died, including 20 million Russians. Approximately 6 million Jews were murdered in Germany's concentration camps, eliminating almost all of Europe's Jewry. In addition, the Nazis singled out gypsies, homosexuals, communists, Slavs, and other groups for extermination. Despite overwhelming evidence that such exterminations were taking place, few countries willingly provided homes for those seeking refuge from Nazi-dominated Europe—only Mexico and the Dominican Republic unconditionally opened their doors to Jews fleeing Europe. The United States maintained its strict immigration quotas, even turning ships of refugees back to Europe and to certain death. The Swiss government, ostensibly neutral throughout the war, likewise refused to provide a safe haven for those fleeing the murderous policies of the Nazi regime.

The Cold War Years

By 1945, it was evident that the Nazis would lose and so planning for the postwar world began. The negotiations among the British, Americans, and Russians at Yalta and then at Potsdam as the European war drew to a close established some principles that were intended to guide the postwar world. Most of Eastern Europe, having been liberated from the Nazis by the Soviet army, fell under Soviet control. Stalin's government quickly imposed communist dictatorships. Germany was partitioned, with portions controlled by the United States, France, England, and the Soviet Union. Sovereignty was restored in western Europe to all the countries that had been subjugated by Germany during the war, and these states went about the business of holding competitive elections to choose their own leaders. In the parts of Germany not controlled by the Soviet Union (that is, in what came to be called West Germany), a new constitution was written by the victors, creating a pro-American democratic government with competitive elections, civil liberties, rule of law, and the like. The United States similarly helped write a democratic constitution for Japan and helped put that country on the way to becoming a liberal democratic society that would strongly support U.S. foreign policy for decades after the war ended.

At the end of World War II, the United States was by far the most powerful and richest country in the world. While much of the rest of the world's economy lay in the ruins of war, the U.S. economy was thriving. In an effort to resuscitate the global economy, the United States launched the Marshall Plan in 1948. The plan's economic policy requirements plus money helped rebuild Europe and helped forge closer ties between the United States and the governments it aided. Although such assistance was also offered to the Soviet Union, the Soviets refused.

Through the establishment of the Bretton Woods monetary system, which established the U. S. dollar as the bulwark of international economic transactions, and the creation of the United Nations, the United States, with the support of its allies, attempted to erect a favorable economic and security framework for the postwar world. The United Nations was designed with two main bodies for dealing with fundamental matters: the General Assembly and the Security Council. The former contains representation from every member country. The latter is a smaller body that is the key United Nations instrument for addressing threats to peace. The Security Council is made up of rotating seats and five permanent seats. The permanent members—the United States, Russia, France, England, and China—each has a veto. This means that the United Nations cannot intervene in a security matter if intervention is opposed by even one of these five states.

Severe cracks in cooperation among the war's victors emerged within two years of the end of the war. By 1947, it was evident that the Soviet Union would not continue as a cooperative ally working with the United States, Britain, France, and others. In 1946, Soviet tanks gathered on Iran's border, threatening to overrun that country. A quick response by the United States prevented the spread of Soviet influence to that oil-rich and strategically located country. Two years later, in 1948, Stalin stopped allowing Allied trucks to enter the western sector of Berlin, thereby cutting the city off from supplies. This was possible because the city of Berlin itself, in addition to the country of Germany, had been partitioned at the war's end; Berlin, however, was situated in East Germany and thus West Berlin became an enclave surrounded by East Germany. President Harry S. Truman stood up to the Soviet threat by creating an airlift that provided the people of West Berlin with supplies. The Soviets backed down and once again allowed truck traffic from the West into Berlin. By now it was clear that a cold war (which lasted approximately from 1947 to 1989) had emerged between the United States and its western European allies, on the one hand, and the Soviet Union and its allies, on the other.

The rift between communism and capitalism, between dictatorship and democracy, grew worse with the victory of China's communists under Mao Zedong over the autocratic Kuomintang government. The latter retreated from China's mainland to Taiwan, where it created the Republic of China and where, after decades of autocratic rule, it has now created a democracy with a thriving economy. The People's Republic of China, for its part, continues to claim Taiwan as a rebellious province and does not recognize the government on Taiwan as a sovereign state. Mainland China is far behind Taiwan in economic performance, although its economy has grown at an impressive annual rate since about 1979, when Deng Xiaoping, then China's leader, introduced economic reforms. The country, however, persists as one of the world's more autocratic regimes, remaining far behind Taiwan in the development of democratic government and economic well-being for its citizens.

The cold war turned hot between 1950 and 1953 following North Korea's invasion of South Korea. Korea had been divided between communist North Korea and autocratic, anti-communist South Korea following World War II. China pitched in to help the North Koreans. The United States and others, under the auspices of the United Nations, intervened to push the North Koreans and China back above the 38th parallel, the previously established line of partition. The Korean War ended in 1953 with the reestablishment of the prewar line of partition, but U.S. troops have remained stationed in South Korea ever since to help ensure that the North does not again attempt to invade the South. In the meantime, North Korea has grown into one of the most reclusive, secretive, and heavily militarized regimes in the world, while South Korea has moved from autocracy to democracy and has experienced extraordinary economic growth. The North and South Korean people had comparable per capita incomes in the 1950s, but today the people of the South enjoy a per capita income that is about twenty-five to thirty times larger than that in the North.

MAP A.4 Divided Germany

Partially in response to pressures unleashed by World War II and partially because of political pressure brought to bear by the anticolonial rhetoric of the Soviet Union, the years following the war experienced a tremendous proliferation in national liberation and decolonization. Britain agreed to quit India and create independent Indian and Pakistani states at the end of the 1940s. Likewise, under extreme pressure from fighters within Palestine, Britain gave up its control in that part of the world, leading to the creation of the state of Israel. The bloody war that followed between Israelis and Palestinians persists as one of the most dangerous unresolved conflicts in the world.

The 1950s and early 1960s saw much of Africa freed of its colonial "masters." Tragically, few of the liberated colonies, following their struggles against colonialism, have emerged as successful states that promote the welfare of their own citizens. Instead, most have become petty dictatorships dominated by corrupt bureaucrats and kleptocratic leaders who seem more inclined to take national wealth and foreign aid and channel it into their personal bank accounts than to spend it on national programs to stimulate economic and social well-being. South Africa over the past decade or so and Botswana for most of its independent history since 1966 are two exceptions, reflecting democratic governments that seem committed to improving the lot of their citizens. Over the past five to ten years, Africa in general seems to have moved in a positive direction and now enjoys modest economic growth rather than decline.

By the 1960s, the United States and the Soviet Union seemed to be making progress toward a long-term means of living with one another. The development of nuclear weapons and intercontinental missiles had created an environment of mutually assured destruction (MAD) in which each side feared that a conflict with the other could expand into a war that would leave the Earth in ruins. Probably the major turning point toward a *modus vivendi* followed the Cuban Missile Crisis in October 1962. With Soviet influence having spread to Cuba through Fidel Castro's successful communist revolution, the United States under President John F. Kennedy made an effort to topple the Cuban regime. The American-planned and American-sponsored Bay of Pigs invasion was intended as a Cuban expatriate invasion of the island country that would foment a popular uprising. It failed to do so, but it did prompt the Soviet government of Nikita Khrushchev to further strengthen its ties to Castro. One manifestation of those strengthened ties was that the Soviet Union sought to place missiles in Cuba to threaten the United States and countries in Latin America (from the American point of view) or to deter the United States from again trying to overthrow the Castro regime in Cuba (from the Soviet point of view). Once the Soviet missiles in Cuba were uncovered by reconnaissance photographs, Kennedy called for their removal and emphasized that there was a grave danger of nuclear war if the missiles were not removed. After two weeks of severe tension, including a U.S. naval blockade of Cuba, the Soviet Union agreed to remove the missiles, and Kennedy promised not to invade Cuba and secretly agreed to remove American missiles from Turkey. After the crisis was resolved, it became apparent that the two nuclear superpowers needed to find a way to coexist.

The prospects of peaceful coexistence improved during Richard M. Nixon's presidency when the United States and the Soviet Union adopted a policy of détente toward one another. Arms control agreements were negotiated. The Vietnam War (1965–1973) between the United States and South Vietnam, on one side, and communist North Vietnam, on the other, ended in an American withdrawal and the subsequent defeat of South Vietnam by North Vietnam, but at least Vietnam was removed as a source of tension in Soviet-American relations. Meanwhile, President Nixon and Henry Kissinger, his secretary of state, began a dialog with China that eventually led to renewed contacts and diplomatic relations after decades of estrangement following the post–World War II Chinese Revolution.

Likewise, after the 1967 and 1973 Arab-Israeli wars, Nixon and Kissinger helped encourage Egypt's president Anwar Sadat to make a significant peace overture to Israel. Sadat offered to visit Jerusalem and make peace with Israel. Menachem Begin, then the Israeli prime minister, and Sadat took courageous steps that culminated in the Camp David Accord brokered with the help of President Jimmy Carter in 1979. Since then, the Israelis and Egyptians have maintained diplomatic relations, and Egypt, along with Israel, receives substantial U.S. foreign aid. Despite the peace agreement between the two, however, relations between Israel and Egypt are cool because the successor to the assassinated Anwar Sadat, Hosni Mubarak, has done little to promote improved relations between his country and Israel. Indeed, for reasons explained in Chapter 9, Mubarak might lose U.S. aid if he promoted genuine friendship between Israel and Egypt.

At roughly the same time that the United States was helping build a peace settlement between Israel and Egypt, the Soviet Union broke with détente by invading Afghanistan in 1979. President Carter, declaring himself surprised by the Soviet move, reduced trade with the Soviet Union and cooled relations. The year 1979 saw other momentous events, including the overthrow of the shah of Iran by a fundamentalist Muslim movement led by the Ayatollah Ruhollah Khomeini. Near the end of 1979, the American embassy staff in Tehran, Iran, was taken hostage in a gross breach of international law and diplomatic conduct. The Americans were held hostage for more than a year and were released at the time of Ronald Reagan's inauguration as president of the United States. Relations between the United States and Iran have remained strained since then. The Iranian revolution marked the beginning of the current era of fundamentalist Islamic contention throughout the Muslim world. This continues to be one of the central sources of international dispute and friction in the Middle East and in Asia Minor, western China, Indonesia, Malaysia, and elsewhere in Asia.

When Ronald Reagan became president in 1981, he implemented a massive military spending program that was intentionally designed to force the Soviet government to choose between continued competition and potential economic collapse or fundamental policy change (Skinner, Anderson, and Anderson 2001). The Strategic Defense Initiative (SDI; or Star Wars, as it came to be called) was also intended to put the Soviet Union on notice that the United States would no longer live within the confines of the old policy of MAD. Rather, the United States under Reagan sought the means to keep the American people secure by neutralizing the threat of a ballistic missile attack. While these pressures mounted, so too did internal pressure for change throughout Eastern Europe. The Soviets agreed to the Helsinki Final Act in 1975 by which the United States recognized the sovereignty of East Germany and acknowledged as permanent the partition of Germany that ended World War II. In exchange, the Soviets recognized West Germany and agreed to planks regarding human rights and the authority of watchdog groups to report on human rights violations throughout the Soviet Union and Eastern Europe. These groups and the legitimacy of such reportage fostered by the Helsinki Final Act paved the way for antigovernment uprisings in Eastern Europe. The Solidarity trade union movement in Poland, for instance, was emboldened by the publicity ensured through the Helsinki Final Act as well as by the positive attitude toward change supported by the Polish pope John Paul II. The Helsinki Final Act also helped undermine a fundamental principle of the 1648 Treaty of Westphalia that ensured that what sovereigns did within their own territory was not subject to rebuke by foreign powers (see Chapter 11).

The Post–Cold War World

As Leonid Brezhnev and his short-lived Soviet successors passed from the scene, the Soviet Union underwent dramatic internal changes. Mikhail Gorbachev took over the government and soon thereafter launched a program of economic reform and liberalization of the Soviet hold over its Eastern European empire. By 1988, Margaret Thatcher, the British prime minister, reacting to the dramatic changes taking place in the Soviet bloc, declared that the cold war was over. In 1989, the Berlin Wall, built in 1961 and the prime symbol of Soviet oppression in Europe, was torn down, and within two years after that the Soviet Union no longer existed. The U.S.-Soviet rivalry that had defined the years between 1945 and 1990 was replaced by a resurgence of American influence around the world, the unification of Germany, a surge in democratization all over the globe, and a rapid shift to market-based economies and away from state-planned socialism.

The last decade of the twentieth century saw efforts to define a new world order. The end of the cold war removed many of the restraints that had held smaller prospective conflicts in check out of fear of exacerbating U.S.-Soviet relations. With the Soviet Union out of the picture, war erupted in the Persian Gulf and in numerous pockets of ethnic rivalry throughout Eastern Europe, but most notably in Chechnya, Bosnia, Kosovo, and other parts of the former Yugoslavia. At this writing, these and other rivalries—most notably the war on terror, the U.S. occupation of Iraq (scheduled by a mutual U.S.-Iraqi government agreement to end in 2011), the war for Chechen independence, and the struggle for control over portions of Georgia—persist as indicators that the tectonic plates of international affairs are still shifting and feeling the aftershocks of the end of the cold war.

The 1990s also saw direct assaults on U.S. interests, with an attempted terrorist bombing of the World Trade Center in New York and the destruction of two American embassies in Africa and on the *USS Cole* in Aden, Yemen. In counterpoint to these conflicts, the cold war's end has also fostered new arenas of cooperation. Many states formerly in the Soviet sphere of influence, including Poland, Latvia, Estonia, Lithuania, and others, are now partners of the North Atlantic Treaty Organization (NATO). NATO was originally formed to help contain the Soviet Union. After developing closer ties with Russia following the end of the cold war, today NATO again has strained relations with that country, especially since Russia's invasion of Georgia in 2008.

The first decade of the twenty-first century has continued the bloody playing out of post–cold war tensions and fundamentalist Islamic ambitions. The United States experienced the most deadly attack on its shores on September 11, 2001, when Al Qaeda terrorists crashed airplanes into New York's World Trade Center buildings, into the Pentagon (home of the Department of Defense), and into a field in Pennsylvania when courageous passengers fought against the terrorist hijackers and prevented them from flying the plane they had commandeered into the White House or some other U.S. government target in Washington, D.C. The attack of September 11 killed about three thousand people, more even than the Japanese bombing of Pearl Harbor on December 7, 1941. American allies around the world have also been subjected to horrific terrorist attacks as Al Qaeda tries to promote a global jihad. Hundreds of Australians and Indonesians in Bali, Indonesia, and hundreds of Spaniards were murdered in terrorist attacks in the early years after 2000.

Following the September 11 attack, the United States, with the support of the United Nations, launched a war against the pro–Al Qaeda Taliban government of Afghanistan and overthrew it. Today, the Taliban, although no longer in control of Afghanistan, remain a serious, even resurgent threat. Its growing influence along the Afghan-Pakistani border, as well as the growing political instability within Pakistan, represents one of the most significant challenges facing the United States and its European allies in the second decade of the twenty-first century.

Not all developments around the world in the first few years of the new century have been as disheartening as the spread of terrorism. In Mexico, the election of Vicente Fox as president on July 2, 2000, marked the beginning of a new era of genuinely competitive politics. Indeed, the presidential election in 2006 was hotly contested and was a very close call between the eventual winner, Felipe Calderon, and his opponent, Andres Manuel Lopez Obrador. Although Obrador claimed the election was stolen from him and some of his supporters took to the streets, calm quickly returned as the mass of the Mexican people endorsed the electoral process as having been free and fair. With the transfer of power from one party to another, Mexico seems well on its way to a strong commitment to democracy. This promises to be good for the economy and to promote reduced corruption and a greatly improved quality of life for the citizens of Mexico. Similar stirrings of political reform have been seen in Tanzania, Kenya, Nigeria, and elsewhere in Africa. Although these reforms have been subject to backsliding, still there seem to be signs of political change for the better.

SUMMARY

This brief overview of history provides a useful backdrop against which to think about international politics. International politics is not the product of randomly emerging events. As I have tried to make clear, events are the product of patterns of choices made by decision makers responding to and creating new circumstances in the international arena. Appendix B provides some ground rules to help guide our thinking about facts and events.

KEY CONCEPTS

capitalism   378
colonial power   374
communism   378
expansionism   374

fascism   379
nationalism   364
trade   367

Appendix B

Evaluating Arguments about International Politics

OVERVIEW

- Theories are important in helping us sort out which facts are essential in understanding international affairs.

- Every theory should be susceptible to being falsified by evidence and should be evaluated in terms of its logical consistency.

- In keeping with the first principle of wing walking, a theory should not be abandoned before there is substantial evidence in favor of an alternative explanation.

- Logic and evidence, rather than personal tastes, are the key ingredients in assessing the merits of competing theories.

- The scientific method is the least subjective and most beneficial way of evaluating the merits of alternative explanations of the same phenomena.

A theory is an explanation of some empirical phenomena. For example, we might construct a theory that proposes an explanation of conditions that lead to or prevent war, that encourage or discourage economic prosperity, that govern the motion of stars and planets, or that influence changes in the weather.

The fundamental components of any theory are:

1. Assumptions
2. Logic
3. Predictions

The elements needed to evaluate a theory are:

1. Logical consistency among the theory's assumptions
2. Evidence that matches or contradicts the theory's predictions
3. Evidence that reveals whether alternative theories outperform or are outperformed by the theory being assessed

THEORIES AS SIMPLIFICATIONS OF REALITY

History provides a description of reality, whereas **theories** provide prospective explanations of reality. Theories are deductive. They consist of a set of assumptions that limits how we view reality. The assumptions can be fit together according to the rules of logic to derive predictions—also known as **hypotheses**—that represent the theory's explanation of the portion of reality with which it is concerned. Theories are not strings of facts, one seemingly leading to another, without a logical structure to guide which facts to examine or which data to collect.

All theories offer simplified representations of what we think of as the true state of the world. By making different assumptions, each theory simplifies in its own way what we know and believe. Theorizing is essential for policymakers; it is not just something pursued by academics. Policymakers must make decisions prospectively; they cannot make and implement policies with hindsight. When they act, they must do so

When wing-walking it is best to hang on tight. Whether on a plane or at the negotiation table, there is no net should you lose your grip, and a fall could be fatal.

on the basis of the information at hand and their understanding of what that information implies at the time they choose a course of action. This means that they—and we, as students of politics—need to understand how to make choices while still in the dark about how things will turn out. And that means they need to have some way to evaluate arguments and to use evidence from the past to help inform decisions before results can be known. That way is theory building and testing.

This appendix develops rules for selecting among competing explanations and evidence so that we form a shared basis for judging facts as evidence. By using the scientific guidelines set out here, you will learn to evaluate the logic and evidence for alternative explanations of international relations. We draw distinctions between assumptions and hypotheses. We distinguish between the **empirical accuracy** of hypotheses and assumptions (that is, how well facts fit with a theory's predictions) and become familiar with the first principle of wing-walking as a guideline for choosing among competing theories. The distinctions made here constitute the basis for applying the scientific method to international affairs.

As noted in Appendix A, our understanding of arguments and evidence about international relations depends both on facts and theoretical perspective. An outlook that focuses on facts alone—a purely inductive approach—is impossible; all of us select facts to look at based on the theories we carry around with us, just as how we interpret those facts is shaped by that theoretical point of view. Employing a useful set of tools—that is, an effective theoretical perspective—for making sense of facts may allow us to predict the range of actions available to policymakers in international affairs and may even help us predict how things will turn out. In doing so we may help to engineer better decisions in the future than have sometimes been made in the past.

Theorizing begins by picking and choosing what we think is important for explaining how cooperation or conflict arises. For example, should we focus on the distribution of military might across countries; the flow of trade; variations in political institutions; the personality characteristics of particular leaders; or differences in cultures, languages, or religious beliefs? What seems important is in the eye of the beholder; whether the beholder is right or not depends on how well the evidence fits the beholder's—the theorist's—point of view.

If you were asked to list the causes of Iran's program to develop a nuclear capability during the first decade of this century, you might not reflect on the invention of the internal combustion engine in the nineteenth century. Yet the principal reason the Iranian government gives for its efforts to enrich uranium (seen as a step toward developing nuclear weapons by the U.S. government and the governments of many other states) is to ensure energy self-sufficiency after its vast petroleum reserves are used up by the voracious world appetite for energy to power automobiles, heat and cool homes, and fuel world industry. Of course, without the internal combustion engine, Iran's oil reserves would last much longer. Still, many doubt Iran's claim that its uranium enrichment efforts are motivated by concerns about running out of crude oil. Consequently, the invention of the internal combustion engine is not one of the facts behind most proposed explanations of Iran's efforts or most proposed accounts of how best to manage relations with Iran so as to lead to the termination of its uranium enrichment research. If Iran's claim was believed, then efforts to address Iran's nuclear program might focus on ways to conserve crude oil reserves by developing alternative sources of energy, improving automobile fuel efficiency, and building greener homes and factories. Although these are worthy efforts that are pursued in response to theoretically derived predictions about global warming, the cost of energy, and related issues, none of those considerations is central to most explanations of or solutions to Iran's apparent nuclear ambitions.

Do we explain Iran's nuclear program as motivated by (1) the internal political and economic problems facing Iran's political leadership (such as antigovernment student demonstrations, broad-based displeasure with the influence of mullahs over civic affairs, or declining oil reserves); (2) the opportunity afforded by the high price of oil; (3) Iranian ambitions to regain its place, ahead of terrorist organizations such as Al Qaeda, as the foremost exponent of a fundamentalist, global Islamic revolution; (4) an effort to deter Israel; (5) an effort to deter the United States from further expansion in the Middle East; (6) an effort to limit Saudi influence in the Middle East; (7) some combined effect of all or part of this list of possible motivations; or (8) other factors not listed here? Each of these proposed explanations is plausible and is touched on in Chapters 2 and 3. Some are complementary, whereas others are contradictory. Making choices about matters such as these constitutes the first step in theory building.

What Is a Theory?

Theories state the expected relationships between variables. Expectations are formed by linking some variables as causes or probabilistic contributors to other variables as consequences in a series of logically connected arguments. The logical connections stipulate the relationship between the variables. A **variable** is a characteristic, event, or idea that can take on more than one value. Constants—that is, characteristics, events, ideas, and so forth that have only one value—are not variables. Consequently, theories are not about constants.

In the theory of arms races, for example, the dependent variables generally include such concepts as the arms expenditures of a country and the likelihood that a country will find itself at war. These are the phenomena that theories of arms races are designed to explain. Notice that the dependent variables are not individual events such as World War I or the 2008 U.S. defense budget. Rather, World War I might be an event that constitutes one of many events reflected by a dependent variable, such as the "likelihood of war." The 2008 U.S. defense budget, likewise, is an example of a defense expenditure decision; it is not itself a variable but, rather, a single value or single observation. A series of such values or observations creates a variable.

All theories include dependent and independent variables. A **dependent variable** is something that we hope to explain; an **independent variable** is something that we think will provide us with all or part of the explanation of the different values taken on by the dependent variable.

Statements about how independent variables relate to dependent variables constitute the propositions or, equivalently, the hypotheses of a theory. These hypotheses, in turn, provide the basis for predicting the values of the dependent variable in the past and, most important, in the future.

The relations among variables generally take one of four forms:

- Some value or values of independent variable A are necessary for some predicted value or values of dependent variable B (necessary conditions satisfy the statement: if not A, then not B).
- Some value or values of independent variable A are sufficient for some predicted value or values of dependent variable B (sufficient conditions satisfy the statement: if A, then B).
- Some value or values of independent variable A are both necessary and sufficient for some predicted value or values of dependent variable B (if not A, then not B, and if A, then B).
- Some value or values of independent variable A probabilistically give rise to some predicted value or values of dependent variable B (if A, then probably B).

Two common independent variables in theories of arms races are (1) the magnitude of the perceived threat coming from an adversary (often measured as that country's level of arms expenditure) and (2) the domestic demand for consumer goods, public services, and so forth other than defense (that is, guns vs. butter or defense vs. consumerism). Changes in the values of the independent variables are expected to lead to changes in the value of the dependent variable. For example, in a famous arms race theory developed by Lewis Fry Richardson (1960/1949), increases in the level of perceived threat and decreases in public demands for consumer goods and social services together are expected to lead to an increase in the likelihood of war. The theory of arms races states relationships between its independent variables and its dependent variable. It does not state a detailed explanation of a single event; rather, it tries to provide an explanation for at least one class of events.

Predictions follow from the propositions deduced logically in a theory. They serve as a way of **testing** a theory's explanation (Friedman 1953). Reliable explanations almost certainly suggest that at least some reliable prediction is possible, provided that the necessary tools of measurement and observation are available. Accurate predictions, however, can be achieved even without a meaningful explanation, and a meaningful explanation may lead only to limited predictive accuracy. Consider an example of accurate prediction that does not provide an explanation. Cricket chirps are highly correlated with the temperature of the air. If we know the number of cricket chirps per minute, we can predict the temperature outside quite accurately even though we may not have a clue about why crickets chirp as often as they do. It is certainly more likely that the temperature influences the chirping of crickets than that cricket chirps influence the temperature.

Constructing Theories

How is a theory constructed? In some ways, there are as many answers to this question as there are theories—or theorists. But every theory has some core features in common. For example, every theory contains a set of assumptions. The **assumptions** of a theory are its crucial building blocks; they specify the group of simplifying conditions under which the theory is expected to be a helpful tool for explaining and predicting the phenomena with which it is concerned. In the study of international politics, a researcher selects assumptions that reflect his or her views and understanding of international affairs. Consequently, different researchers adopt different assumptions as they try to explain a broad range of international events.

For instance, one well-regarded theory of international politics is called neorealism (see the Introduction). Neorealist theorists are interested in explaining when the set of states in the world and the relations between them are stable and when they are not. To do so, they assume that states are unitary actors without any internal domestic divisions or factions even though they know that in every state many individuals, often with different opinions, are involved in decisions that influence international politics. Neorealists make the implicit judgment that variations in opinions from decision maker to decision maker are not sufficient to distort the predictions made by a theory that assumes states are holistic unitary actors.

Conversely, those who theorize based on the notion that bureaucracies shape foreign policy reject the idea that states are unitary actors, preferring instead to focus on the organizational mission of specific bureaucracies and their leaders. Naturally, these researchers know that on some issues, such as the American declaration of war against Japan on December 8, 1941, there was virtual unanimity among responsible decision makers in the United States. They know that the unitary actor assumption can be a helpful convenience in some cases, but they believe it oversimplifies reality

TRY THIS

What do you think is the effect on the likelihood that country A will fight a war with country B if

1. B threatens A, and A's citizens are prepared to sacrifice consumption to support increased spending on A's military?
2. B threatens A, and A's citizens are not prepared to sacrifice consumption to support increased spending on A's military?
3. B reduces its threat against A, and A's citizens are prepared to sacrifice consumption to support increased spending on A's military?
4. B reduces its threat against A, and A's citizens are not prepared to sacrifice consumption to support increased spending on A's military?

Consider whether A's spending more on the military deters B from escalating its threat against A or leads B to believe that A is preparing to attack. Consider whether A's spending more on the military is a response to B or is a response in A to politicking by A's generals to increase their budget. Consider whether asking the citizens in A to sacrifice consumption for defense is likely to be beneficial or harmful to the reelection of a democratic leader and to the retention of an autocratic leader. These are just a few of the calculations that policymakers must go through in deciding how to respond to changes in perceived threats from abroad.

in too many cases to be of real help in structuring a reliable account of international affairs. Neorealism rejects the idea that military spending or the perception of a threat to national security reflects manipulation by generals in order to increase their defense budget, but theories about bureaucracies imply the idea that generals try to manipulate threat perceptions to increase their budgets. Thus, neorealism and bureaucratic politics theories make different predictions based on the hypothetical scenarios posed earlier about threats by country B against country A and their implications for military spending and the risk of war.

Assumptions are the principal means by which theorists simplify reality. Assumptions describe the set of conditions under which the theory's predictions are expected to hold. That means that one of the most important questions to ask about any theory is whether its assumptions limit the domain of circumstances that the theory is capable of addressing so much that the theory seems trivial. If a theory's assumptions prevent it from addressing the real-world phenomena that motivated its construction in the first place, then the theory's value is certainly limited.

If, for instance, we are interested in explaining why small wars occur, then a theory that addresses *only* the causes of global war is not very helpful. Such a theory does not provide an answer to the question that motivated the construction of the theory in the first place. In general, the more events or facts a theory can explain with a limited set of assumptions, the more useful the theory is. This is the principle of **parsimony.** Thus, a theory of war that does not require us to distinguish between big wars and little wars has greater potential value for the study of war than does a theory of nuclear war or a theory of short, low-cost, bilateral wars or a theory of trade wars. A theory of politics that also explains war is more useful still, even though it was not constructed to explain war alone.

JUDGING THEORIES

Making a judgment of any theory revolves around its logical truth or falsity and whether its predictions are trivial or useful. The logical truthfulness of a theory is a question of consistency; that is, no assumptions can contradict others contained within the same theory. The accuracy of empirical predictions about what happens in the world is the primary means we have to judge the usefulness of a theory as an explanation for the real-world events that concern us. As human beings, we often make value judgments, but we should not confuse these with the dispassionate evaluation of the logic and evidence for and against a theory. We do not have to like a theory's implications for those implications to be true. And we certainly cannot make the world a better place by ignoring unpleasant or inconvenient realities. In fact, we must confront those realities through logic and evidence so that we can think about how to improve the world without violating the laws of nature.

The Importance of Logical Consistency

A good starting place to judge a theory's value is to evaluate whether its assumptions contradict one another, that is, whether there are **internal inconsistencies.** If they do, there will be considerable confusion about exactly what the theory predicts or what its explanation is—and this confusion will be irreconcilable. The presence of internal inconsistencies means that at least part of the theory is false on logical grounds. We do not even need to look at reality to judge its usefulness. Predictions that depend on logical contradictions cannot be useful because, whatever is observed, the opposite might just as easily be a prediction that can be defended using the same theory. These predictions will be of the type "if A, then B, but also if A, then not B and, maybe, if not A, then B." Such a theory has nothing valuable to say about the relationship between independent variable A and dependent variable B.

Contradictions are sometimes unintentionally overlooked or sidestepped when scholars theorize about international affairs. We can and must guard against such oversights by insisting that assumptions be stated clearly and explicitly. Only when we know all of a theory's assumptions can we figure out the logical connections that link the independent and dependent variables in that theory. There is no room for careless reasoning because such reasoning can get us—and the world—into too much trouble. To see how much trouble imprecision can cause, consider the following assumptions from a prominent theory of international politics:

> Since the desire to attain a maximum of power is universal, all nations must always be afraid that their own miscalculations and the power increases of other nations might add up to an inferiority for themselves which they must at all costs try to avoid. Hence all nations who have gained an apparent edge over their competitors tend to consolidate that advantage and use it for changing the distribution of power permanently in their favor.... The status quo nations, which by definition are dedicated to peaceful pursuits and want only to hold what they have, will hardly be able to keep pace with the dynamic and rapid increase in power characteristic of a nation bent upon imperialistic expansion. (Morgenthau 1978, 215–217)

This statement is drawn from perhaps the most influential international relations theorist of the past several decades, Hans Morgenthau. His theory of realism focuses on power as the essential determinant of how nations relate to one another. His is a brilliantly parsimonious effort to develop a comprehensive set of generalizations, or laws, about politics among nations. Much of his theory offers keen insight and wisdom, which is why his writings are still influential with policymakers today. Yet his theory houses fundamental contradictions, as reflected in this quotation. And these contradictions make it difficult to figure out exactly what Morgenthau is arguing or what his theory predicts.

On the one hand, Morgenthau's theory of realism is about a world in which each and every nation wants power so badly that it pursues the acquisition of more and more power at any cost. On the other hand, we are told that there are at least two kinds of nations in the world: status quo powers, which are content with what they have and so do not pursue increases in their power, and imperialist powers, which are dissatisfied with the amount of power they have and so try to gain more. What, then, does the theory predict about the relationship between a nation's power and its actions? Looked at purely as a problem in logic, nations are defined as of two types, status quo–oriented and imperialist. The first part of the quotation states a universal characteristic of all nations such that, if A is a nation (that is, A is status quo–oriented or imperialist), then A tries to change the distribution of power to its advantage. So, if A is a nation and B is shorthand for "the pursuit of an advantageous change in the distribution of power," Morgenthau predicts if A, then B: being a nation is sufficient to pursue increases in power. But then, the second part of the quotation says that, if A is a status quo nation, then A does not try to change the distribution of power in its favor; that is, if A, then B, given that A is imperialist and if A, then not B, given that A is status quo–oriented. This second claim denies the universality of the first claim—both cannot be true.

Actions by an imperial power can be consistent with the theory. Actions by status quo nations always contradict some condition of the theory and are consistent with other parts of the theory. Therefore, behavior is not, in fact, predicted by the theory, and the theory cannot be proven to be wrong, even in principle. Yet consistency is a fundamental requirement of any theoretical proposition or prediction. Without logical consistency, theories or loose arguments provide no guidance in making predictions or in proffering explanations.

Truth and Falsity in Assumptions

Assumptions are not casual statements to be taken seriously when it is convenient and ignored otherwise. An assumption is a defining characteristic of a theory. A theory cannot exist outside of its assumptions because it is the logical connections among the assumptions that imply the theory's hypotheses. I emphasize the importance of consistency because it is virtually impossible to know what is being argued when theorists (or policymakers) contradict themselves. And we cannot evaluate arguments if we do not know what they are.

TRY THIS

How would the implications of Morgenthau's theory change if status quo states did not avoid an inferiority in power at all costs but, instead, were willing to tolerate an inferiority in power to reduce their costs so they were lower than in imperialist states? Could imperialist and status quo states coexist?

Because assumptions are so important, it may seem appropriate, even important, to establish whether a stated assumption is true or not. However, in my opinion this is not a fruitful basis for evaluating a theory. As I explain my view on this issue, keep in mind that my viewpoint, although quite common in the physical sciences and in much of economics, is controversial among some social scientists.

To begin with, what exactly is meant by *true* or *false*? We can distinguish between the two on purely logical grounds. A true theory is one in which the predictions follow logically from the assumptions. This is a somewhat narrow use of the term, and you may prefer to substitute the phrase *logically true* in its place in the discussion that follows. If the propositions do not follow from the assumptions, then we can say the theory is false. A theory with contradictions in it, then, is false (at least with regard to the parts influenced by the contradictory assumptions). In these terms, Morgenthau's theory, or at least part of it, is false. Note that

I have not arrived at this judgment because I disagree with any one of his assumptions. My disagreement with any of his assumptions would be a matter of taste or personal judgment. Whether two (or more) assumptions are mutually contradictory is not a matter of taste, however, it is a matter of logic.

We can distinguish true and false from the notions useful and trivial. The usefulness of a theory is an empirical question. If the theory makes predictions that reliably help us understand the questions that motivated the theory's construction, then the theory is useful. If the predictions are irrelevant or excessively inaccurate, then the theory is trivial. So while true or false refers to the internal logic of the theory, useful or trivial refers to its empirical value. False theories are inevitably trivial.* Some true theories are also trivial because they fail to account for the facts we hoped to explain. What we all seek to discover are theories that are both true and useful.

So, what is meant by *true* or *false* when it comes to assumptions? Because true and false refer to internal consistency, I do not attempt to establish whether this or that individual assumption is true or false. What I do address is whether the set of assumptions behind a theory is both true and useful. The set is true if the assumptions do not contradict one another and the predictions derived from the theory follow logically from the assumptions— that is, it has **internal consistency.** The set is useful if the assumptions lead to explanations and predictions that are consistent with reality according to some stated criteria for evaluating the theory's empirical performance. Although individual assumptions may describe a world we do not care about (and so may be trivial), a single assumption cannot contradict itself (and so is neither true nor false).

Even recognizing this, we still may object that some assumptions are not true in the sense that they misrepresent an important part of reality. Yet when people say such assumptions are not true, they really mean that they are not useful. For example, it is common among many international relations researchers to talk about the national interest (Krasner 1978) or the nation's foreign policy. The nation is treated as if it were a unitary, singular actor, almost as if it were a human being. Such a description of a nation is obviously not true in some empirical sense. No nation consists of a single person or of a large number of people who unanimously hold the same opinion about every foreign policy matter.

The unitary actor assumption seems to be at odds with reality much of the time. But does that necessarily mean that we should toss it out? Although it *may* not be a useful assumption, I am confident that such a judgment cannot be made at the time the assumption is stated. We must always keep in mind that theories inevitably simplify reality in order to make explanation and prediction feasible and practical. Assumptions are the vehicle through which

---

* Even if some of the predictions of a logically inconsistent theory are supported by the empirical record, the theory must be false. Although the empirical record suggests that it is worthwhile to construct a theory that in fact truly leads to predictions about the events supposedly "predicted" by the false theory, the falseness of the theory still cannot be in doubt. Logical inconsistency can allow us to make almost any claim or statement. Any part of a theory that is logically inconsistent is of no empirical interest per se. So, too, is any part that fails to pass the stated criteria in empirical tests of the theory's usefulness.

theorists simplify. Perhaps the unitary actor assumption simplifies too much, and perhaps it does not. We can judge the value of assumptions (apart from their internal logical consistency within a theory) only in terms of their output. What does this or that assumption contribute to the theory's explanation and prediction of events? This is the relevant question for judging its value. Tossing out the unitary actor assumption means that we must dispose of our inclination to talk about the *nation's* policy, the *state's* interests, and so forth. So embedded is the notion of the state as a meaningful concept that we should be cautious about throwing out the unitary actor assumption before demonstrating that there is a more useful, productive representation of reality.

If a set of assumptions provides many accurate predictions, then it does not simplify reality too much. If the assumptions of a theory do not provide many helpful and accurate predictions, then they do simplify too much. We can make these sorts of judgments only after we have evaluated the whole of any theory and have seen what happens as we drop each of its assumptions, one at a time. We cannot tell how valuable an assumption is going to be on philosophical grounds. The value of one or another assumption is a practical matter; if an assumption adds to the theory's predictive ability more than it takes away, then it is useful. Because the addition of assumptions increasingly restricts a theory's domain, it is important that we have only enough assumptions to deal with the circumstances of interest. The more assumptions we add, the fewer are the circumstances to which the theory can be applied. Therefore, it is useful to know exactly which assumptions from a theory are required to produce each of its hypotheses. Some hypotheses may need only a few assumptions, whereas others require the whole set. If any assumption is not required for the predictions that follow from a theory, then that assumption need not be included in the theory.

When the critics of a theory argue that an individual assumption is false, they are really saying that either they have evidence that the implications or predictions that depend on the assumption are false or they are making an argument based on taste, their personal likes and dislikes. Arguments based on differences in taste generally are not productive. Just as different people find different forms of music or painting or literature or movies or foods or clothing appealing, so too different people find different theoretical perspectives more or less appealing. The best way to deal with such differences in opinion about what are potentially fruitful assumptions is to put alternative views of the world to the test of history and to the test of the future. In this regard, it is wise to be pragmatic. None of us truly knows exactly how international relations works, just as no one truly knows how the physical world works. If we knew completely how any physical or human sphere of study really worked, then that subject would be a dead subject. No new research would be needed no matter how many new facts were accumulated nor how much time had passed. If the phenomena are fully explained, then there is nothing new to say. For example, no one is still studying the causes and cure of smallpox; a full explanation has been achieved. Perhaps a new variety of smallpox will emerge in the future (as has happened with tuberculosis), thereby creating a need for new theorizing or new empirical research, but for now the subject has nothing left to study. This is not the case with international politics. In international politics, we do not have a full explanation; instead, we must judge whether one theory or another explains more of the facts of interest without creating more confusion than clarity.

THE FIRST PRINCIPLE OF WING-WALKING

Explanations are always tentative. Theories are expected to prevail only as long as they out-perform rival explanations of the same phenomena. If a more accurate, more predictive explanation comes along, it is likely to supplant less successful theories. This may happen quickly or it may take many generations, but eventually better ideas come to prevail over inferior ones.

Sometimes theories, although capable of being proved false, can accommodate the discovery of *some* contradictory evidence. They are judged to be false only if the body of contradictory evidence grows large enough. Consider, for instance, Ptolemy's theory of mechanics, which predated Newton's theory. No one today relies on Ptolemaic theories of motion to explain the movement of planets and stars even though for most everyday purposes the Ptolemaic view does as well as Newtonian mechanics and Albert Einstein's theory of relativity. Ptolemaic theory persisted for a long time, but the ideas of Nikolaus Copernicus, Johannes Kepler, and others eventually shook scientists' confidence in it. Ptolemaic astronomy predicts fewer events correctly than does Newtonian theory. For instance, although Ptolemy's theory does rather well in predicting the motion of heavenly bodies, it does not do well in predicting the trajectory of falling objects on Earth.

Ptolemaic theory contends that planets do not follow elliptical orbits around the sun but, rather, follow epicycles (roughly, loop-the-loops) around the Earth. Such a pattern of movement is consistent with observations taken from the night sky. If we plot the location of a distant planet from night to night over the course of the year, we will not observe an orderly path of motion. The path can be made predictable, however, if we assume that the planet loops back from time to time. But once we accept Copernicus's theory that the sun, not the Earth, is at the center of the solar system, Ptolemaic astronomy no longer makes sense. Eventually, the evidence against the Ptolemaic view became too great for the theory to be sustained. Rival arguments did a better job of explaining the facts, including those the Ptolemaic perspective simply could not accommodate.

Clearly, we need some guidelines to help us judge when the evidence or the flaws in an argument are sufficient to conclude that the theory or argument in question is inadequate. In our everyday lives, we make such judgments all the time. Few of us rely on our daily horoscope to plan our activities. Reading horoscopes may be fun, but there just does not seem to be a reliable relationship between prediction and reality. We have concluded that it is not an adequate tool. It is the accumulation of evidence and counterarguments about what happens in reality that is at the heart of choosing among competing theories. We would be rather alarmed to discover that our foreign policy leaders choose their actions according to horoscope readings. In fact, false rumors that Ronald Reagan relied on astrological readings during negotiations with Mikhail Gorbachev created quite a stir and not a few jokes at Reagan's expense.

Sometimes we cling to a theory even when we know it is not reliable. Usually we do so in accordance with the **first principle of wing-walking.**[†] If you are out on the wing of an airplane in flight (and I *really* recommend against finding yourself in such a situation), don't let go of what you are holding on to unless you have something better to hold on to. Even then, you may have to think twice about letting go. Knowing that something better is available does not mean that the alternative is sufficiently attractive that you immediately want to make the switch, especially if there are associated risks or costs. This is one reason why Ptolemaic mechanics held sway for so long. However hard it was to believe that planets or stars loop back on themselves, there was no point in giving up that theory until something better (such as Newtonian mechanics) came along. Even then, switching was costly, and so people clung to the old ideas for a long time. Newtonian mechanics was not regularly taught in British schools for one hundred years after their development.

The first principle of wing-walking is particularly relevant when dealing with beliefs about how things work in the world. Giving up beliefs is costly. The benefits of a new set of beliefs had better be large enough to compensate for the costs of abandoning the old ones. One reason that international politics may be predictable is that beliefs are not easily abandoned. Because leaders stick to their beliefs until it becomes too costly to continue to do so, behavior is likely to run a predictable course.

Consider this simple example of the costs of switching from an inferior tool to a superior one. Suppose we are doing a fix-it job at home; perhaps we are assembling a new television stand or wiring a stereo. In either case, we probably will need a screwdriver. Now, perhaps we do not have the best-fitting screwdriver for the job, but we do have a screwdriver that will work, even if it wiggles around in the screw slot a bit too much. Most of us would know that a better-fitting screwdriver exists, but most of us would not spend the time and money involved in getting the better tool. After all, we probably won't need the new tool very often and the screwdriver we do have is adequate—not ideal, but adequate. So it is with the selection and the use of theories. We do not always strive to use the best tool because identifying the best tool may be too costly, or even if we know what tool to use, it may be too costly to learn how to use it. If the stakes are large enough, and errors are expected to be sufficiently costly, then we probably will spend the time and money to learn about a better tool. If, for instance, we need to repair a fighter aircraft with a screwdriver, then we will probably get the best screwdriver available for the task. The cost of an error is too great to risk using the wrong tool. Crossed stereo wires are one thing; a malfunction at 40,000 feet at twice the speed of sound is quite another.

The first principle of wing-walking was an essential (although unspoken) feature of the national security debate in the United States during the presidency of Ronald Reagan. At that time, the noted physicist (and father of the hydrogen bomb) Edward Teller proposed a defensive

---

[†] I thank Kenneth Shepsle, who first introduced me to this principle.

response to the threat of nuclear holocaust. The policy Teller proposed was to develop a defense against incoming missiles. This was known officially as the Strategic Defense Initiative (SDI); its critics dubbed it Star Wars. Teller's proposal represented a sharp departure from existing U.S. policy and a return to a military approach more commonly seen before World War II.

Before World War II, an important feature of any nation's military policy was to maintain a strong defense against foreign aggression. The emergence of a nuclear threat, however, changed this thinking in the United States. Americans introduced the idea of mutually assured destruction (MAD), in which it was thought that the best defense against nuclear war was an offense so powerful that it could ensure its possessor's ability to wreak unacceptable destruction even after an opponent had launched a successful first-strike attack. Under MAD, cities and civilian populations were the priority targets of attack rather than weapons and military installations precisely because it was thought that the fear of such devastating and demoralizing losses would curb anyone's appetite for war. SDI would have changed that by providing a protective shield against the destruction of cities, a defensive strategy. Among the many arguments made against SDI, one focused on the technical unfeasibility of the program. Another relied on the first principle of wing-walking. That is, many observed that nuclear deterrence through MAD had successfully provided peace and stability for decades. They believed that there was no good reason to switch to a different approach that might or might not prove to be a significant improvement over existing policy. They chose to live with the existing theory of nuclear security (nuclear deterrence) rather than switch to a new theory based on defense (SDI). Debate over SDI persists to this day. Some argue for the development of antimissile defense system, while opponents decry the effort as a risk to international stability.

The first principle of wing-walking forces us to pay attention to the costs as well as to the benefits of alternative ways of thinking about a problem. Weighing both costs and benefits is one of the reasons that some rather disappointing theories of international politics remain prominent long after they have been shown to be lacking in explanatory or predictive capabilities. After all, the first principle of wing-walking encourages caution in rejecting theories. It reminds us to be skeptical of new ideas while it encourages us to be open to persuasive evidence against old ideas. One threat to such openness arises because we have certain "habits of mind" that help us in thinking about things (Margolis 1993). Consider a simple example. Look around you, and make a list of some of the objects that you see that are moving and some that are not. Perhaps you have noticed that the chair you are sitting on is quite still (or are you rocking back on its legs?) but that people around you are moving about. Surely you can draw up a long list of things that are moving and things that are still. However, in fact, *no* object is still—after all, you, your chair, this book, and everything else around you is hurtling through space at tremendous speed.

One of Galileo's great intellectual triumphs was to begin his theorizing by assuming that objects can naturally be in motion unless they are brought to rest. He assumed that this was true of objects such as himself, the planet Earth, the stars, and everything else. Galileo's assumption contradicted a well-established "habit of mind" of his day and, perhaps, even of ours—people usually follow their senses. In Galileo's day, people were used to thinking that stones and trees and especially the Earth did not move. It seemed to Galileo's contemporaries that some objects moved—for example, the sun and the moon—and other objects stood still. To them, Galileo's assumption seemed absurd, and so, therefore, did the implications or predictions of his theory. Even today, the language we use to describe dawn and dusk depends on the pre-Galilean notion that the sun is moving around the Earth, rising and falling, rather than that the Earth is moving around the sun and around its own axis.

The notion that objects are naturally in motion represented a radical departure from conventional thinking in Galileo's day. It not only violated people's sense of what was true, but it also appeared to contradict Scripture and, consequently, the teachings of the Catholic Church. That, of course, got Galileo into a great deal of very serious trouble. Rather than face the consequences of his heresy, he reluctantly agreed to stop teaching that the Earth moved, but neither his recanting nor commonsense observations could change reality or the evidence that would gradually be amassed to show that Galileo was right. The resolution of the issue did not depend on whether or not people liked the assumption, nor on whether or not Galileo recanted his politically incorrect view; it depended on the predictions that followed from the assumption (in conjunction with his other, less controversial assumptions, such as a friction-free surface) and the consistency between the evidence in the world and the expectations from theories that assume objects move until stopped rather than stand still until moved. Galileo's experience teaches us to be humble about assumptions and encourages us not to be overly resistant to new ideas. We should not be too quick to dismiss a theory because we doubt its assumptions. Rather, we should wait for the evidence about the theory's predictions. The proof of the theory is in the testing, not in our judgment of the quality of its assumptions.

One final comment about assumptions and the first principle of wing-walking is in order before we move on. Sometimes people are tempted to dismiss a theory because they believe the assumptions reflect some bias. In fact, they may be right. Capitalists tend to dismiss Marxist arguments on such grounds, much as Marxists often dismiss free market–oriented theories based on ideological bias. This is just another guise by which people object to assumptions on the basis of differences in taste. Whether assumptions are selected because of a bias or not does not matter as long as the standard for evaluating the usefulness of assumptions is how well the theory performs in predicting and explaining events. If the tests are biased, then there will be a problem. However, despite the motivation behind its construction, the theory itself is best judged on the basis of whether it accounts for the facts it was constructed to explain and predict. Biased assumptions have no advantage over unbiased assumptions (whatever those may be) in regard to empirical performance.

THE CASE STUDY METHOD AND TESTING THEORIES

In international relations research, it is common to evaluate the empirical usefulness of theories by presenting one or several case histories that are consistent with a theory's predictions.

The evaluation of a theory through the close scrutiny of a single event and its associated details is often referred to as a **case study.** Case studies can be helpful tools for developing ideas about a phenomenon or for shedding light on a specific event, but when cases are selected because they are consistent with a particular claim, they are not a fair test of the accuracy of the claim.

For example, consider the following test of the claim that arms races cause war. We look at the circumstances of the relevant nations just before the Napoleonic wars, World War I, and World War II, and we see that in each case an arms race was in progress. We infer, therefore, that the claim that arms races cause war is true. But this inference is not warranted by the evidence for many reasons, one of which is that there are many other (overlooked) examples in which arms races were not followed by war. Picking cases because they are consistent with a theory leads us to miss all those cases that could refute the theory; this is a form of **selection bias.** In the example just given, the arms races were identified only after we knew that there was a war, so the selection of cases was driven by ex post knowledge of the value on the dependent variable. This is a no-no for testing a theory unless the theory predicts that A is necessary for B; then we want to know can we find an example of B (the dependent variable) that was *not* preceded by A.

Sometimes people try to justify selecting cases that are consistent with a theory by noting that they are picking a "difficult" case. Usually this just compounds the problem because the case is "difficult" in the sense that it is not representative of the class of events that the theory seeks to explain. That is, the case is "difficult" because it has some features that make it extremely unusual. Cases for investigation should be selected because they represent a wide array of variation on the independent *and* dependent variables, not because they represent a particular value on the dependent variable or because they seem "difficult" because confounding factors are in operation. This principle of random case selection has been well established among statisticians for about a century.

Remember that theories are about relationships among variables, not about constants. Yet many, many investigations of the causes of very large wars examine only the constants. There are literally thousands of studies on the causes of World War I. Many of these evaluate a theory, or at least some hypothesis, about the causes of deadly, long, multilateral wars. But these studies select facts based on a particular value of the dependent variable. In fact, the dependent variable turns out not to be a variable at all. It is a constant within the case, which leaves nothing to be explained. For instance, understanding the causes of large wars requires that we understand how those causes differ from the causes of small wars or other types of conflicts. Looking at only large wars leaves no variation in the thing to be explained— namely, the causes of large wars. If we want to know what makes them large, we must also know what factors prevent other conflicts from turning into large wars. We need cases with different scales of war that can be compared with one another.

A similar problem in selection bias is common among studies of international political economy when such studies focus on regimes and cooperation. Many researchers are interested in evaluating what impact regimes have in encouraging cooperation. *Regimes* in this context refers to organizations, institutions, or norms that regulate a pattern of behavior (Ruggie 1975; Krasner 1983; Keohane 1984; Morrow 1994a). Usually the interest behind regime studies is in explaining cooperation between states. Commonly, the researcher selects a case with a known cooperative outcome and then looks for the existence of an international regime or organization that can be said to have fostered the cooperative outcome. Perhaps the author is correct in the assessment of the role of the regime, but this does not at all tell us whether similar regimes also operated in settings that did not lead to cooperation between states. The question of whether certain regimes promote cooperation (a relationship between variables, including the presence or absence of a regime and the presence or absence of cooperation) simply cannot be evaluated without knowing more about the tendency of the regime context to produce cooperative outcomes compared with circumstances not embedded in a regime context. Are there regimes designed to foster cooperation that end up yielding conflict? Of course there are, but studies typically do not pay attention to these failures and so produce biased inferences. OPEC, which was designed to foster cooperation among oil-producing and -exporting countries, is frequently home to conflict among its members over what their oil production quota ought to be. Although widely studied by economists and others interested in cartels, there are few studies of OPEC done by regime theorists interested in international cooperation.

Are there instances of cooperation without a regime? Again the answer is yes. For decades, the U.S. government and the Israeli government have demonstrated a high degree of cooperation without relying on a formal alliance agreement. Although substantial research has been done on U.S.-Israeli relations, little of it has been conducted by international relations specialists interested in the role of regimes in fostering cooperation.

The cases of OPEC and U.S.-Israeli relations help sort out how important regimes are in fostering, or not fostering, cooperation (Downs and Rocke 1990, 1995). Selecting cases based on the dependent variable by picking only cases of cooperation in regimes introduces an analytical bias and makes use of knowledge about what ultimately happened, knowledge that the decision makers could not possibly have had before the fact. Analytical bias and hindsight are two elements that we should avoid in designing ways to assess how well alternative theories perform empirically.[‡]

Before leaving our discussion of case studies, I add one more set of thoughts to the discussion. It is possible to establish or refute certain claims of a theory unambiguously

TRY THIS

Think of other examples of international organizations in which the member states commonly fight (verbally or even violently) with one another. Now think of other examples of states that generally cooperate despite having no formal agreement between them about the conditions for cooperation.

[‡] Note that selecting cases based on the dependent variable is a problem for any argument concerned with identifying factors sufficient to cause a result, but it is not a problem when the concern is only to identify factors that are necessary for a result (see Most and Starr 1989).

through the use of even a single case study. To understand this, let us think about case studies, necessity, sufficiency, and interstate cooperation. Tables B.1, B.2, and B.3 look at whether a regime is present (the independent variable) in a set of circumstances and relate this to whether that set of circumstances culminates in cooperation or conflict (the dependent variable). The regimes literature suggests the hypothesis that regimes foster cooperation (see Chapter 11). Table B.1 shows an example with forty hypothetical observations that support the inference that the presence of a regime is necessary but not sufficient for cooperation. Table B.2 illustrates an example with forty hypothetical observations that support the claim that regimes are sufficient but not necessary for cooperation. Table B.3 depicts an example with forty hypothetical observations in which regimes are both necessary and sufficient for cooperation. Keep in mind as you read these or any other data tables that the numbers in the cells of the table represent how many cases fit the value of the row and column variables.

In Table B.1, we can see that whenever cooperation is observed (the dependent variable), we also observe that a regime is present. At the same time, it is evident that regimes do not guarantee cooperation (it is not a sufficient condition); half of the time, when a regime is present there is still conflict. But there is never cooperation without a regime; this is what we mean by a **necessary condition.** If there are no problems with assigning cases to each category in the table, then a single instance of cooperation without a regime, such as the U.S.-Israeli case, refutes the hypothesis that a regime is necessary for cooperation.

Table B.2 shows that whenever a regime is present there is cooperation, although cooperation can also occur without a regime. Thus, Table B.2 illustrates the case in which the presence of a regime is sufficient to produce cooperation—it is a **sufficient condition**—but not necessary. This is evident from the fact that there are cases of cooperation without regimes. The hypothesis that a regime is sufficient to ensure cooperation would be refuted

TABLE B.1 — **Regime and Cooperation: Necessary but Not Sufficient Condition**

Regime	Cooperation	Conflict
Yes	10	10
No	0	20

TABLE B.2 — **Regime and Cooperation: Sufficient but Not Necessary Condition**

Regime	Cooperation	Conflict
Yes	20	0
No	10	10

TABLE B.3	Regime and Cooperation: Necessary and Sufficient Condition	
Regime	Cooperation	Conflict
Yes	20	0
No	0	20

by a case in which there is a regime and instances of no cooperation (that is, conflict), such as the case of OPEC.

Table B.3 shows that cooperation occurs only if a regime is present and that conflict arises only if a regime is absent, illustrating that a regime is a **necessary and sufficient condition.** Either the U.S.-Israeli case or the OPEC case refutes the argument that regimes are both necessary and sufficient to ensure cooperation.

Suppose a theory makes a weaker prediction than that implied by necessity, sufficiency, or both. If a theory predicts that something is possible under certain conditions—not necessary or sufficient or even probable—then we can prove the claim with just one case. A single demonstration that the specified conditions have occurred and the possible outcome has arisen is adequate to prove such a weak claim. These claims are known as existence claims. Let's look at an example.

Two similar and widely held theories suggest that wars that fundamentally alter the structure of international relations, especially relations between the most powerful states, must be large costly wars.[§] An alternative view, the theory of strategic competition between states, suggests that it is possible for a system-transforming war to occur even if the war is short and costs relatively few lives. The Seven Weeks War, fought in 1866 between Prussia and Austria with participation by Italy and several small German principalities, is an example of just such a war (Bueno de Mesquita 1990). The existence claim of the strategic perspective is proved because this small, relatively low-cost war transformed how the states of Europe related to one another, as suggested by the strategic perspective but in contradiction to the other two theories. This one case does not prove that the theory from which the claim is derived is true, just that the specified phenomenon can exist in contradiction to some other theory.

But testing using a single case is usually not enough. Most theories about international relations or, for that matter, any other social phenomenon make predictions that are probabilistic. Such hypotheses typically say something like, "The more the independent variables increase in value, the more likely it is that the dependent variable will increase." For instance, a typical hypothesis might say, "The more balanced power is between rival states, the more likely they are to live peacefully with one another." A single case study cannot provide any information about the credibility of such a hypothesis. The hypothesis claims that there will be a mix of outcomes (that is what *probabilistic* means) associated with changes in the values

---

[§] These theories are discussed in Chapter 4. They are known as the theory of the power transition and the theory of hegemonic stability.

of the independent variables but that the mix of values will tend toward peaceful relations as power becomes more equal between rivals. Even two or three cases are insufficient to evaluate the accuracy of this hypothesis in a convincing way. When hypotheses are probabilistic, confidence either in a claim or its refutation improves as we observe a larger and larger number of relevant cases. That is, probabilistic hypotheses are better tested with statistical methods than with a small number of individual case histories.

A STANDARD FOR COMPARING THEORIES

How can we choose among competing theories? We can use the first principle of wing-walking. This means we choose one theory over another if it clearly outperforms the competing theory (Popper 1963; Laudan 1977; Lakatos 1978). The criteria applied here are straightforward. When two theories make predictions about the same phenomena or set of events, one is judged to be better than the other if it explains those facts accounted for by the competing theory plus some additional facts not explained by the competing theory. Furthermore, the allegedly better theory must explain these additional facts without adding a net surplus of newly unexplained circumstances. Thus, our standard of judgment is quite pragmatic. The more things a theory can explain and the fewer the errors it makes compared with alternative theories, the better it is. A theory will be abandoned only after the evidence shows that a competing theory does a superior job of accounting for the facts. It is not enough to get more things right; the theory must also not get things wrong that were previously accounted for. There must be a net improvement in prediction. There are, of course, practical difficulties in the implementation of this, or any, standard, but at least it is removed from arguments about personal tastes and embedded in criteria on which people can agree.

The Scientific Method

There are so many alternative ways to think about what is going on in international affairs that amassing facts and making decisions can be a daunting task. Fortunately, there are sensible guidelines to help us and our leaders evaluate the effectiveness of these alternative ways of thinking about international problems and to decide when a perspective is probably wrong. By using these guidelines, we can expect to make reasonable and helpful judgments about the quality of different arguments and the credibility of the evidence for or against those arguments.

What I am referring to here is use of the **scientific method,** that is, evaluating arguments in terms of their logical consistency and in terms of the extent to which observational or experimental evidence is consistent with the predictions that they logically imply. The scientific method imposes only a few basic conditions. In doing so, it guides our application of the first principle of wing-walking by helping us to see when to hold on to an old theory and when to let it go and embrace a new one. As I emphasized earlier, scientific analysis requires logical consistency. This means that we must state clearly how one set of factors implies or causes another set of factors. Competing arguments must be evaluated through experiments that control for confounding, alternative explanations. This is a much easier requirement to satisfy in the physical sciences than in the social sciences. Within the field of international politics, *controlled experiments* usually means that theoretical expectations are evaluated against historical data. The cases selected for evaluation must be representative of the class of events in which we are interested. To ensure that cases are representative, we choose randomly with regard to factors that are not part of the argument. Randomness ensures that the tests control for the possible effects of other factors. Tests must also be replicable; that is, different researchers examining the same body of observational or experimental evidence should reach the same conclusions even if they are unfamiliar with one another's investigations. The conclusions are not based on personal judgments or on personal values. Theories lead to empirical predictions. This is why both the logic and the evidence for or against a theory are so important.

Predictions are always contingent. They differ from prophecies in that scientific predictions state that if certain conditions are met, then certain results are expected to follow (Gaddis 1992; Ray and Russett 1996). When other conditions are met, then the theory may predict other outcomes. Prophecies are not concerned with the conditions from which consequences follow; they are concerned only with the consequences. Scientific predictions can be about things that have already happened or about things that have not yet happened. For example, using Newtonian mechanics we can predict the location of Mars in the night sky on any day of any year, past, present, or future. If Mars were observed to be somewhere other than the predicted location, then the theory on which the prediction was based would be called into question. This would be just as true if Mars proved to have been somewhere else on a past date or a future date. Tests of theories about international affairs also rely on predictions. Sometimes the evidence is based on how closely past events fit the expectations of a given theory. In the most demanding cases, the evidence for a theory pertains to predictions about events that have not yet happened.

The scientific method focuses our attention on the internal, logical consistency of alternative explanations of the facts and compels us to look for critical, replicable tests and evidence that allow any of us to reach theoretically and empirically defensible conclusions about competing arguments. We may disagree about the interpretation of the evidence or the weight to be given to it in assessing the strengths and weaknesses of a theory, but at least we will be able to discuss these matters based on the same criteria, even if we do not share common judgments or expectations. Careful judgments about alternative theories, grounded in the scientific method, are important because the costs of wrong decisions in international affairs can be devastating. We certainly want to avoid using wrong ideas or ideas that are inappropriate for the problem at hand.

When a Theory Is Wrong

The notion that a theory can "go wrong" does not seem terribly complicated. Most of us probably understand this phrase in pretty much the same way. For one thing, we probably would have no problem agreeing that if a theory regularly leads to predictions that are inconsistent with reality, then the theory, rather than reality, is wrong. After all, reality is what it is. Reality may be "wrong" in a moral sense—we may not like what happens—but it still incontrovertibly happens.

But some theorists argue that reality is "wrong" when what actually happens does not conform to the theorist's expectations of what should have happened. For example, Marxist theory sometimes exhibits this characteristic because it is interpreted along Marxist ideological lines. Marxism as a theory is intended to explain changes in economic and social relations over time. It is an effort to explain history and to predict the future course of events. Class conflict is presumed to be inevitable in Marxist theory. If class conflict does not arise, then Marxist theorists usually presume that something is "wrong" with people's class consciousness. The theory is presumed to be correct, and people are presumed to be mistaken.

Soviet founder Vladimir Ilyich Lenin, a theorist as well as a revolutionary leader, devised such concepts as a "trade union mentality" and the "vanguard of the proletariat" to deal with the problem of inconsistencies between predicted behavior and observed behavior. A trade union mentality is, in more modern parlance, equivalent to false consciousness. Lenin constructed the idea that, because some members of the working class might misunderstand their true interests (that is, have a trade union mentality), a group such as the Communist Party elites was needed to lead the way for the proletariat. According to Lenin, party elites, the vanguard of the proletariat, could be better trusted than workers to know what was in the true interest of the working class. Indeed, many argue that Lenin's concept of the vanguard of the proletariat ensured that Marxist theory would, if put into practice along Leninist lines, evolve into a dictatorial ideology. Lenin (1902), in fact, argued in his essay "What Is to Be Done?" against any debate regarding socialist ideology. His logic inevitably led to the conclusion that, if the observed facts contradicted socialist or Marxist predictions, then the facts were in error because they reflected a bourgeois ideology.

Marxist predictions and reality were not consistent with one another in 1914. Marxist theorists predicted that a world war could not happen because the workers of the world would recognize their common class interests and the divergence between their interests and those of the aristocratic and capitalist classes who were making war. The workers simply were not expected to agree to serve in the armies of their countries, fighting against their class fellows from other lands. Clearly Marxist theorists greatly underestimated the power of nationalist feelings to join people together, even against members of their own class. Indeed, Marxism had no room for nationalism because nationalism competes with class as an organizing principle. Marxist predictions about World War I proved wrong, but Marxist theorists dismissed the problem as being an error of the workers, who were fooled by false consciousness (that is, nationalism, trade union mentality, and the like) rather than an error of the theory. They invented auxiliary arguments to cope with the failed predictions of their theory. It took repeated failures, culminating in the early 1990s, before most Marxist theorists accepted the overwhelming evidence that their theoretical perspective was wrong as a practical approach to governance. As suggested by the first principle of wing-walking, Marxists were conservative in their unwillingness to surrender their preferred theory. They needed to be convinced by a great preponderance of evidence. They had to reach the point at which they recognized that their auxiliary arguments had become unsustainable.

Note that the addition of auxiliary arguments to a theory is not inherently problematic. If the additional arguments explain previously unexplained events without becoming wrong when applied to previously explained events, then the gains in explanation can exceed the costs in lost parsimony. A theory is more or less parsimonious depending on how many facts it explains compared with the number of assumptions it requires to make predictions. In general, the more events or facts a theory can explain with a limited set of assumptions, the greater the potential usefulness of the theory and the greater its parsimony. So, if auxiliary arguments (such as nationalism, trade union mentality, and encirclement by the bourgeois states) are added and explain only one event each, then there is no improvement in parsimony. In fact, such additions are evidence that the theory in question is degenerate—that is, the theory needs to make up a special explanation for each new circumstance and so really is no explanation at all (Lakatos 1976, 1978; Elman and Elman 1997; Vasquez 1997). In fact, a practical software tool for assessing the degree of parsimony or efficiency of theories has been developed and tested on many international relations theories (Zinnes 2004). Some of the most prominent realist theories, alas, have been shown not to be parsimonious at all. They contain no more generalizations than assumptions.

The principle of parsimony is important because it provides one benchmark by which we can choose among competing theories. When a theory, or its auxiliary statements, needs to be changed to suit many new observations—sometimes even each observation—then we should suspect that the theory is just plain wrong.

Scientific Theories Must Be Falsifiable

How we judge predictions is certainly open to some dispute. Some theories do not allow any possibility that evidence might show them to be wrong; such theories are not falsifiable. They may be true (or not), but we have no way to be confident they are true or useful (we cannot test them), short of faith. Indeed, religious beliefs can be thought of as a set of theories or tools devised to explain human behavior and phenomena in nature. They may be true (or not), but we cannot judge their veracity by normal scientific standards; we must rely on faith. Core religious beliefs, such as a belief in the existence of God, are not falsifiable, although lesser religious arguments, such as when the world is expected to come to an end, clearly can be shown to be false (although perhaps not convincingly to a believer). It is essential that a theory seeking the imprimatur of science be susceptible to possible falsification. A theory that has scientific standing is falsifiable; that is, it is one for which it is possible to imagine a test or set of tests whose results would lead us to conclude that the theory, or at least its central predictions, are just plain wrong. If no such test can be imagined, then the theory really is an article of faith, not an article of science.

Sometimes people are confused by this idea of falsifiability. They think, "Well, if a theory is true, it cannot be falsified, so how can falsifiability be helpful with true theories?" I want to be very clear. **Falsifiability** does not have to do with whether an argument is true or false; instead, it has to do with whether conditions exist in principle under which we might conclude that the argument is false. In short, true claims cannot be falsified (proved to be false), but they can be falsifiable. For example, every falling object near the Earth's surface accelerates at 32 feet per second if we assume that there is no air friction. Apparently this is an excellent approximation of the upper bound of an object's acceleration despite the fact that the simplifying assumption that there is no air friction is never precisely met. It is also a falsifiable claim. If, for instance, we let go of a rock near the Earth's surface when there is no air friction and there is nothing holding the rock back or otherwise interfering with it and it rises rather than falls, then the hypothesis would be disproved. Thus, we can state the conditions for falsification. Whether they are satisfied or not is related to falsification; that they can be stated is sufficient to establish falsifiability.

One objective throughout this book is to sort out which theories of international relations are falsifiable and which are not. We can do this by examining the logic of each theory and the evidence for and against it relative to alternative theories. We have seen earlier that an important part of Morgenthau's theory of realism is not falsifiable according to the standards of science. Those who subscribe to parts of it may be right about how the world works, but we have no way to tell. Falsifiability and the examination of logic and evidence are ways we can assess the relative merits of competing explanations while upholding the first principle of wing-walking.

> **_TRY THIS_**
>
> Think of a current foreign policy dispute in which one state is threatening another with dire consequences if the latter does not change its behavior. Has the exact nature of those consequences been made clear (for example, economic sanctions, military action, or severing of diplomatic relations)? Now think of a dispute in which a state seems to be hiding its true intentions, saying one thing but seemingly doing another. Which is more reliable information, what a state's leaders say they are doing or what they are observed to be doing?

PRACTICAL USES OF THEORIES

Someplace in today's newspaper there is a story about an international dispute, possibly over trade barriers, ethnic rivalries, border clashes, or religious differences. Perhaps Turkey and Greece are arguing over the possibility of admitting Turkey into the European Union. Maybe India and Pakistan are engaged in a dispute over their claims to Kashmir. Possibly the United States and Canada disagree about the interpretation of NAFTA. Maybe Mexico is threatening to seal its border, cutting off Central Americans who are trying to pass through Mexico to enter the United States as undocumented aliens. China, Vietnam, Malaysia, Taiwan, and others may each be claiming the rights to oil deposits near the Spratly Islands in the South China Sea. Iran and the United Nations may be quarreling over Iran's weapons-grade uranium enrichment program, or Israel and Syria may be arguing over the Golan Heights. Romanians and Moldavians may be disputing the location of the boundaries between their territories.

Whatever the headlines, it is evident that there are lots of different ways to explain each of these conflicts of interest. News accounts of ethnic rivalry, the balance of power, economic dependency, or imperialism reflect ideas about theories or organizing principles that explain international affairs. Such common ideas as "do unto others as you would have them do unto you," "an eye for an eye, a tooth for a tooth," and "turn the other cheek" are just a few ways people think about what encourages countries to resolve their differences or discourages them from doing so. Each is part of some theory of international relations that has been developed as a tool that might help us understand how nations relate to one another. Each tool directs us to focus our attention on different facts and offers a different explanation of events.

Theories about norms may turn our attention to the history of past interactions between particular states. If we focus on norms, then we are likely to be concerned about the domestic social and cultural constraints that leaders face. Perhaps the cultural or social values in some countries make using violent strategies especially costly for political leaders. In that case, norms could be a pacifying influence in foreign policy. Balance of power theory, by contrast, encourages us to seek out facts about the power resources of states and to assume that nations are inherently hostile toward one another. We are more concerned with the military might of states if we take a balance of power perspective than if we approach a rivalry from the perspective of cooperative norms. From the point of view of a theory of cooperative norms, such as liberalism or constructivism (see the Introduction), power is thought to be less consequential than, for example, the history of shared interests and cultural values.

The choice among alternative theories, or tools, and the standards for evaluating them are important not only for us as students and citizens but also for those individuals entrusted with the responsibility for making the myriad decisions that describe the relations between nations. Decision makers probably do not choose their courses of action by throwing darts at a list of options. Surely if we believed that our leaders made life and death decisions in such an irresponsible way we would throw them out of office. And that, remember, is a risk that people who are ambitious to lead do not take lightly. All leaders around the world rely, knowingly or unconsciously, on some tools or theories of international affairs to help guide their decisions. Leaders often quote the principles or hypotheses derived from such tools as the justification for their decisions. Consider two examples of principles used by leaders in critical foreign policy settings.

Admiral Isoroku Yamamoto, the architect of Japan's attack against Pearl Harbor, was fond of saying, "an efficient hawk hides his claws" (Prange 1981, 13). Here is a generalization about international affairs that helped guide the secretiveness behind Japan's planning and execution of its attack. It may or may not be a useful or helpful principle, but it certainly was an important one. After all, it was not inevitable that the Japanese would choose the secret and aggressive course of action that they chose to carry out on December 7, 1941.

The Japanese might just as readily have taken a different point of view. They might have subscribed to a hypothesis commonly argued by those who believe in the theory of deterrence. Had they accepted a deterrence point of view, the Japanese might have openly declared in 1941 that they would launch a severely punishing attack against American interests unless the United States lifted its trade embargo against Japan and stopped threatening its activities in the Pacific. Probably Japan's leaders would not have wanted to say exactly what the threatened punishment would be or exactly when it would take place. That would have put their fleet of aircraft carriers at unnecessary risk (Colaresi, Thompson, and Rasler 2008). Still, they might have chosen an open threat intended to alter America's behavior. Such an approach would have relied on an utterly different assessment of the appropriate tools for accomplishing their objectives than the tools that led to their clandestine attack. Had they believed they could deter the United States by persuading Franklin Roosevelt that the costs of his policies toward Japan outweighed the benefits, then the threat of punishment alone might have been sufficient to achieve their goals. They might never have attacked any U.S. facilities at all. Here, then, is a case where a fundamental policy choice depended on which theory of international affairs decision makers had in mind.

Leaders often talk about "maintaining the balance of power" or "promoting a favorable balance of power" (which usually means having a great imbalance in their favor) as a guideline for conducting their nations' foreign policies. Indeed, a couple of illustrations may help suggest that a concern with the theory of the balance of power is as old as history and as fresh as today's headlines. Consider the following two quotations. Each reveals a concern about the balance of power between rivals. The first comes from the New Testament Gospel according to Luke and the second from a memorandum by Sir Eyre Crowe to the British government shortly before the outbreak of World War I.

> What king, going to make war against another king, sitteth not down first and consulteth whether he be able with ten thousand to meet him that cometh against him with twenty thousand. Or else, while the other is still far away he sends a delegation and asks terms of peace. (Luke 14:31)

> History shows that the danger threatening the independence of this or that nation has generally arisen, at least in part, out of the momentary predominance of a neighboring State at once militarily powerful, economically efficient, and ambitious to extend its frontiers or spread its influence…. The only check on the abuse of political predominance derived from such a position has always consisted in the opposition of an equally formidable rival, or of a combination of several countries forming leagues of defence. The equilibrium established by such a grouping of forces is technically known as the balance of power. (Quoted in Hartmann 1978, 316)

Such examples suggest that leaders, at least some of the time, take very seriously the theories that have been used to try to make sense of history. Theories probably do not determine choices in a mechanistic way as much as they serve as signposts for leaders who must map out a foreign policy course. That is one reason why it is important to understand the tools that shape their judgments, even if those tools prove to be faulty or just plain wrong. Even if a theory is woefully inaccurate, if leaders rely on it we should strive to understand it and to understand why it goes wrong and with what consequences. I believe that the discussion in Chapters 4 and 5 will convince you that the balance of power theory is incorrect in many of its most important predictions.

Think of an explanation of foreign policy that is falsifiable. Then think of an explanation that is not falsifiable. When journalists explain clashes between ethnic groups by saying that the fighting stems from cultural differences or from the fact that the groups have hated one another for hundreds of years, are the journalists making a falsifiable claim? Is the claim false? How can you account for the periods of peaceful coexistence between such ethnic groups in light of the journalistic explanation of their clashes?

Yet it strongly influences how leaders make decisions. Surely it is as important for us to understand what consequences follow from reliance on incorrect arguments as it is to understand what consequences emerge from reliance on correct arguments? By comprehending a theory's faults, we may help prevent foreign policy errors in the future.

SUMMARY

The first principle of wing-walking establishes that we should not abandon one theory for another until the new theory proves to be a better tool for explaining the events of interest. The reliability of predictions is the primary standard for judging the relative merits of competing explanations of events. Theories provide the linkage between assumptions and empirical generalizations. They stipulate how variables relate to one another. In doing so, theories identify the causal or probabilistic association between independent and dependent variables. They provide a simplified view of reality that is believed to reduce the complexity of the real world to its essential components.

Assumptions describe the set of conditions under which a theory is expected to apply to the phenomena of interest. Hence, assumptions define a theory's relevant world of applicability. If the assumed world is too far removed from the world in which we live, then the theory's predictions will prove unreliable and we will conclude that the theory is useless or trivial. If the assumptions contradict one another on logical grounds, then the theory is logically false and so cannot provide a coherent explanation of the world in which we live. Consequently, theories are judged based on their logical consistency and empirical usefulness. Taste or aesthetic appeal are not relevant in evaluating alternative explanations of international affairs; adherence to the requirements of the scientific method is critical.

KEY CONCEPTS

Bibliography

The Bibliography contains not only all the works referenced in the book but also others to help you explore research on international relations more thoroughly. Examine the Bibliography for other readings that interest you.

Acemoglu, Daron, and James A. Robinson. 2001. "Inefficient Redistribution." *American Political Science Review* 95: 645–661.

Allison, Graham. 1972. *The Essence of Decision: Explaining the Cuban Missile Crisis.* Boston: Little, Brown.

Alt, James E., and Michael Gilligan. 1994. "The Political Economy of Trading States." *Journal of Political Philosophy* 2: 165–192.

Arrow, Kenneth. 1951. *Social Choice and Individual Values.* New York: John Wiley.

Ash, Timothy G. 1997. *The File: A Personal History.* London: HarperCollins.

Austen-Smith, David, and Jeffrey Banks. 1998. "Social Choice Theory, Game Theory, and Positive Political Theory." In *Annual Review of Political Science,* ed. Nelson Polsby. Palo Alto, Calif.: Annual Reviews.

Axelrod, Robert. 1984. *The Evolution of Cooperation.* New York: Basic Books.

Axelrod, Robert, and Robert Keohane. 1986. "Achieving Cooperation under Anarchy: Strategies and Institutions." In *Cooperation under Anarchy,* ed. Kenneth Oye. Princeton, N.J.: Princeton University Press.

Babst, Dean V. 1964. "Elective Governments—A Force for Peace." *Wisconsin Sociologist* 3(1): 9–14.

Baker, Regina. 2002. "Market Realism: Political Development, Currency Risk, and the Gains from Trade under the Liberal International Economic Order." Ph.D. dissertation, University of Michigan.

Behr, R. L., and Shanto Iyengar. 1985. "Television News, Real-World Cues, and Changes in the Public Agenda," *Public Opinion Quarterly* 49: 38–57.

Bennett, D. Scott. 1996. "Security, Bargaining, and the End of Interstate Rivalry." *International Studies Quarterly* 40: 157–183.

———. 1997a. "Democracy, Regime Change, and Rivalry Termination." *International Interactions* 22: 369–397.

———. 1997b. "Measuring Rivalry Termination, 1816–1992." *Journal of Conflict Resolution* 41: 227–254.

Bennett, D. Scott, and Alan C. Stam III. 1996. "The Duration of Interstate Wars: 1812–1985." *American Political Science Review* 90: 239–257.

———. 1998a. "Comparative Theory Testing: Expected Utility versus All Comers." Paper presented at the annual meeting of the International Studies Association, Minneapolis, Minn., March 18.

———. 1998b. "Conflict Initiation and Escalation." Pennsylvania State University, Department of Political Science.

———. 1998c. "The Declining Advantage of Democracy: A Combined Model of War Outcomes and Duration." *Journal of Conflict Resolution* 42: 344–366.

———. 2000a. "A Cross-Validation of Bueno de Mesquita and Lalman's International Interaction Game." *British Journal of Political Science* 30: 541–561.

———. 2000b. "A Universal Test of an Expected Utility Theory of War." *International Studies Quarterly* 44: 451–480.

Bennett, D. Scott, and S. E. Tarry. 1996. "Self-Perpetuation or Rational Choices?: A Model of Rationality and Hysterisis in International Alliances." Paper presented at the annual meeting of the Midwest Political Science Association, Chicago, April 18–20.

Best, Geoffrey. 1994. *War and Law since 1945.* Oxford: Clarendon Press.

Binmore, Ken. 1990. *Essays on the Foundations of Game Theory.* Cambridge, Mass.: Blackwell.

Black, Duncan. 1958. *The Theory of Committees and Elections.* Cambridge, UK: Cambridge University Press.

Bowring, Philip. 2002. "Accountability—But Not to the People," *International Herald Tribune,* May 4. Available at www.iht.com.

Brams, Steven J. 1985. *Superpower Games.* New Haven, Conn.: Yale University Press.

———. 1990. *Negotiation Games: Applying Game Theory to Bargaining and Arbitration.* New York: Routledge.

Brams, Steven J., and Alan D. Taylor. 1996. *Fair Division: From Cake-Cutting to Dispute Resolution.* Cambridge, UK: Cambridge University Press.

Brehm, John, and Scott Gates. 1997. *Working, Shirking, and Sabotage: Bureaucratic Response to a Democratic Public.* Ann Arbor, Mich.: University of Michigan Press.

Bremer, Stuart. 1993. "Democracy and Militarized Interstate Conflict, 1816–1965." *International Interactions* 18: 231–249.

Brody, Richard A. 1992. *Assessing the President: The Media, Elite Opinion, and Public Support.* Stanford, Calif.: Stanford University Press.

Brody, Richard A., and Benjamin Page. 1975. "The Impact of Events on Presidential Popularity." In *Perspectives on the Presidency,* ed. Aaron Wildavsky. Boston: Little, Brown.

Brophy-Baermann, Bryan, and John A. C. Conybeare. 1994. "Retaliating against Terrorism: Rational Expectations and the Optimality of Rules versus Discretion." *American Journal of Political Science* 38: 196–210.

Broz, Lawrence, and Jeff Frieden. 2001. "The Political Economy of International Monetary Relations." *Annual Review of Political Science,* ed. Nelson Polsby. Palo Alto, Calif.: Annual Reviews.

Bueno de Mesquita, Bruce. 1978. "Systemic Polarization and the Occurrence and Duration of War." *Journal of Conflict Resolution* 22: 241–267.

———. 1983. "The Costs of War: A Rational Expectations Approach." *American Political Science Review* 77: 347–357.

———. 1990. "Pride of Place: The Origins of German Hegemony." *World Politics* 43 (October): 28–52.

———. 1996. "Counterfactuals and International Affairs: Some Insights from Game Theory." In *Counterfactual Experiments in World Politics,* ed. P. Tetlock and A. Belkin. Princeton, N.J.: Princeton University Press.

Bueno de Mesquita, Bruce, and George W. Downs. 2006. "Intervention and Democracy." *International Organization* 60(3): 627–649.

Bueno de Mesquita, Bruce, and David Lalman. 1988. "Systemic and Dyadic Explanations of War." *World Politics* 40: 1–20.

———. 1992. *War and Reason.* New Haven, Conn.: Yale University Press.

Bueno de Mesquita, Bruce, James D. Morrow, Randolph M Siverson, and Alastair Smith. 2004. "Testing Novel Implications from the Selectorate Theory of War." *World Politics* 56 (3): 363–388.

Bueno de Mesquita, Bruce, David Newman, and Alvin Rabushka. 1996. *Red Flag over Hong Kong.* Chatham, N.J.: Chatham House.

Bueno de Mesquita, Bruce, and William H. Riker. 1982. "Assessing the Merits of Selective Nuclear Proliferation." *Journal of Conflict Resolution* 26: 283–306.

Bueno de Mesquita, Bruce, and Randolph M. Siverson. 1995. "War and the Survival of Political Leaders: A Comparative Study of Regime Types and Political Accountability." *American Political Science Review* 89: 841–855.

Bueno de Mesquita, Bruce, Randolph M. Siverson, James D. Morrow, and Alastair Smith. 1999. "An Institutional Explanation of the Democratic Peace." *American Political Science Review* 93(December): 791–807.

Bueno de Mesquita, Bruce, and Alastair Smith. 2007. "Foreign Aid and Policy Concessions," *Journal of Conflict Resolution.* 51 (April): 251–284.

———. 2009. "A Political Economy of Aid," *International Organization,*forthcoming.

Bueno de Mesquita, Bruce, Alastair Smith, Randolph M. Siverson, and James D. Morrow. 2003. *The Logic of Political Survival.* Cambridge, Mass.: MIT Press.

Bueno de Mesquita, Bruce, and Frans Stokman. 1994. *European Community Decision Making.* New Haven, Conn.: Yale University Press.

Bueno de Mesquita, Ethan. 2005a. "Conciliation, Counterterrorism, and Patterns of Terrorist Violence." *International Organization* 59(1): 145–176.

———. 2005b. "The Quality of Terror." *American Journal of Political Science* 49(3): 515–530.

———. 2005c. "The Terrorist Endgame: A Model with Moral Hazard and Learning." *Journal of Conflict Resolution* 49(2): 237–258.

Bueno de Mesquita, Ethan, and Matthew Stephenson. 2006. "Legal Institutions and Informal Networks." *Journal of Theoretical Politics* 18(1): 41–68.

Burnside, Craig, and David Dollar. 2000. "Aid, Policies, and Growth." *American Economic Review* 90(4): 847–868.

Calvert, Randall L. 1985. "The Value of Biased Information: A Rational Choice Model of Political Advice." *Journal of Politics* 47: 530–555.

Carr, Edward Hallett. 1939. *The Twenty Years' Crisis: 1919–1939.* London: Macmillan.

———. 1945. *Nationalism and After.* London: Macmillan.

Checkel, J. 2003. "'Going Native' in Europe?: Theorizing Social Interaction in European Institutions." *Comparative Political Studies* 36: 209–231.

Cherif, Feyral. 2005. "Symbol or Substance: International Institutions, Advocacy Networks, and the Status of Women." Ph.D. dissertation, New York University.

Chiozza, Giacomo, and Hein Goemans. 2000. "Fighting for Survival: The Fate of Leaders and the Duration of War." *Journal of Conflict Resolution* 44(5): 555–579.

———. 2003. "Peace through Insecurity: Tenure and International Conflict." *Journal of Conflict Resolution* 47(4): 443–467.

Chiozza, Giacomo, and Hein Goemans. 2004. "International Conflict and the Tenure of Leaders: Is War Still *Ex Post* Inefficient?" *American Journal of Political Science* 48(July): 604–619.

Chomsky, Noam. 2003. *Hegemony or Survival: America's Quest for Global Dominance.* London: Penguin.

Christensen, Thomas J., and Jack Snyder. 1990. "Chain Gangs and Passed Bucks." *International Organization* 44: 137–168.

Clark, William Roberts. 2003. *Capitalism, Not Globalism: Capital Mobility, Central Bank Independence, and the Political Control of the Economy.* Ann Arbor, Mich.: University of Michigan Press.

Colaresi, Michael P., William R. Thompson, and Karen Rasler. 2008. *Strategic Rivalries in World Politics: Position, Space and Conflict Escalation.* New York: Cambridge University Press.

Collier, Paul, and David Dollar. 2002. "Aid Allocation and Poverty Reduction." *European Economic Review* 46(8): 1475–1500.

De Long, J. Bradford, and Barry Eichengreen. 1993. "The Marshall Plan: History's Most Successful Structural Adjustment Program." In *Postwar Economic Reconstruction and Lessons for the East Today.* Ed. R. Dornbusch, W. Nolling, and R. Layard. Cambridge, Mass.: MIT Press.

De Tocqueville, Alexis. 2000. *Democracy in America.* Trans. and ed. Harvey C. Mansfield and Delba Winthrop. Chicago: University of Chicago Press.

Deutsch, Karl W., and J. David Singer. 1964. "Multipolar Power Systems and International Stability." *World Politics* 16: 390–406.

Diehl, Paul. 1985. "Contiguity and Escalation in Major Power Rivalries." *Journal of Politics* 47: 1203–1211.

Dixon, William. 1994. "Democracy and the Peaceful Settlement of International Conflict." *American Political Science Review* 88: 14–32.

Dollar, David, and Victoria Levin. 2006. "The Increasing Selectivity of Foreign Aid, 1984–2003." *World Development* 34(12): 2034–2046.

Doran, Charles, and Wes Parsons. 1980. "War and the Cycle of Relative Power." *American Political Science Review* 74: 947–965.

Downs, Anthony. 1957. *An Economic Theory of Democracy.* New York: Harper.

Downs, George W. 2000. "Constructing Effective Environmental Regimes." In *Annual Review of Political Science,* ed. Nelson W. Polsby. Palo Alto, Calif.: Annual Reviews.

Downs, George W., and David M. Rocke. 1990. *Tacit Bargaining, Arms Races, and Arms Control.* Ann Arbor, Mich.: University of Michigan Press.

———. 1995. *Optimal Imperfection?: Domestic Uncertainty and Institutions in International Relations.* Princeton, N.J.: Princeton University Press.

Downs, George W., David M. Rocke, and Peter N. Barsoom. 1996. "Is the Good News about Compliance Good News about Cooperation?" *International Organization* 50: 379–407.

Doyle, Michael. 1986. "Liberalism and World Politics." *American Political Science Review* 80: 1151–1161.

Drezner, Daniel. 1999. *The Sanctions Paradox: Economic Statecraft and International Relations.* Cambridge, UK: Cambridge University Press.

Dugger, Celia. 2007. "Even as Africa Hungers, Policy Slows Delivery of U.S. Food Aid." *New York Times,* April 7. Available at www.nytimes.com/2007/04/07/world/africa/zambia.html?_r=1&pagewanted=print.

Easterly, William. 2006. "Development, Democracy, and Mass Killings." Working paper no. 93, Center for Global Development, Washington, D.C.

Easterly, William, Shanker Satyanath, and Daniel Berger. 2008. "Superpower Interventions and their Consequences for Democracy: An Empirical Inquiry." NBER working paper no. 13992, National Bureau of Economic Research, Cambridge, Mass.

Eichengreen, Barry, Marc Uzan, Nicholas Crafts, and Martin Hellwig. 1992. "The Marshall Plan: Economic Effects and Implications for Eastern Europe and the Former USSR." *Economic Policy* 7(14): 14–75.

Elman, Colin, and Miriam Fendius Elman. 1997. "Lakatos and Neorealism: A Reply to Vasquez." *American Political Science Review* 91: 23–26.

Enterline, Andrew J., Dylan Balch-Lindsay, and Kyle Joyce. 2008. "A Competing Risks Approach to Third Parties and the Civil War Process." *Journal of Peace Research* 45: 345–363.

Etzioni, Amitai. 2004. *From Empire to Community: A New Approach to International Relations.* Basingstoke, UK: Palgrave.

Farber, Henry S., and Joanne Gowa. 1995. "Polities and Peace." *International Security* 20: 123–146.

Fearon, James D. 1994. "Domestic Political Audiences and the Escalation of International Disputes." *American Political Science Review* 88: 577–592.

———. 1995. "Rationalist Explanations for War." *International Organization* 49: 379–414.

Feder, Stanley. 1995. "Factions and Policon: New Ways to Analyze Politics." In *Inside CIA's Private World: Declassified Articles from the Agency's Internal Journal, 1955–1992,* ed. H. Bradford Westerfield. New Haven, Conn.: Yale University Press.

———. 2002. "Forecasting for Policy Making in the Post-Cold War Period." *Annual Review of Political Science* 5: 111–125.

Fordham, Benjamin O. 1998. "Partisanship, Macroeconomic Policy, and U.S. Uses of Force, 1949–94." *Journal of Conflict Resolution* 42(4): 418–439.

———. 2002. "Domestic Politics, International Pressure, and the Allocation of American Cold War Military Spending." *Journal of Politics* 64(1): 63–88.

Forsythe, David. P. 1992. "Democracy, War, and *Covert* Action." *Journal of Peace Research* 29(4): 369–376.

Fortna, Virginia Page. 2004. "Does Peacekeeping Keep Peace?: International Intervention and the Duration of Peace after Civil War," *International Studies Quarterly* 48: 269–292.

Frieden, Jeff. 1987. *Banking on the World: The Politics of American International Finance.* New York: Harper and Row.

Friedman, Milton. 1953. "The Methodology of Positive Economics." In *Essays in Positive Economics,* ed. Milton Friedman. Chicago: University of Chicago Press.

Froot, Kenneth, Michael Kim, and Kenneth Rogoff. 1997. "The Law of One Price over 700 Years." NBER working paper no. 5132. National Bureau of Economic Research, Cambridge, Mass.

Gaddis, John Lewis. 1987. *The Long Peace: Inquiries into the History of the Cold War.* New York: Oxford University Press.

———. 1992. "International Relations Theory and the End of the Cold War." *International Security* 17: 5–58.

Galtung, Johann. 1964. "A Structural Theory of Aggression." *Journal of Peace Research* 1: 95–119.

Gartner, Scott S. 1997. *Strategic Assessment in War.* New Haven, Conn.: Yale University Press.

Gartner, Scott S., and Randolph Siverson. 1996. "War Initiation and War Outcome." *Journal of Conflict Resolution* 40: 4–15.

Gartzke, Erik A., and K. Gleditsch. 2002. "Regime Type and Commitment: Why Democracies Are Actually Less Reliable Allies." Columbia University.

Gates, Scott, Torbjo L. Knutsen, and Jonathan W. Moses. 1996. "Democracy and Peace: A More Skeptical View." *Journal of Peace Research* 33: 1–10.

Gaubatz, Kurt Taylor. 1991. "Election Cycles and War." *Journal of Conflict Resolution* 35: 212–244.

————. 1996. "Democratic States and Commitment in International Relations." *International Organization* 50: 109–139.

————. 1999. *Elections and War.* Princeton, N.J.: Princeton University Press.

Gelpi, Christopher, and Joseph Grieco. 1998. "Democracy, Crisis Bargaining, and Audience Costs: Analyzing the Survival of Political Elites." Paper presented at the annual meeting of the American Political Science Association, Boston, September 3.

Gilligan, Michael, and Stephen Stedman. 2003. "Where Do the Peacekeepers Go?" *International Studies Review* 5(4): 37–54.

Gilpin, Robert. 1981. *War and Change in World Politics.* Cambridge, UK: Cambridge University Press.

Gleditsch, Nils Peter, and Havard Hegre. 1997. "Peace and Democracy: Three Levels of Analysis." *Journal of Conflict Resolution* 41: 283–310.

Goemans, Hein. 2000. *War and Punishment.* Princeton, N.J.: Princeton University Press.

Goertz, Gary, and Paul Diehl. 1995. "The Initiation and Termination of Enduring Rivalries: The Impact of Political Shocks." *American Journal of Political Science* 39: 30–52.

Goldstein, Joshua A. 1988. *Long Cycles: Prosperity and War in the Modern Age.* New Haven: Yale University Press.

Goldstein, Judith, and Robert O. Keohane, eds. 1993. *Ideas and Foreign Policy: Beliefs, Institutions, and Political Change.* Ithaca, N.Y.: Cornell University Press.

Gorbachev, Mikhail. 1996. *Memoirs.* Trans. Georges Peronansky and Tatjana Peronansky. New York: Doubleday.

Gowa, Joanne, and Edward Mansfield. 1993. "Power Politics and International Trade." *American Political Science Review* 87: 408–420.

Greif, Avner, Paul Milgrom, and Barry Weingast. 1994. "Coordination, Commitment, and Enforcement: The Case of the Merchant Guild." *Journal of Political Economy* 102: 745–776.

Grieco, Joseph M. 1988a. "Anarchy and the Limits of Cooperation: A Realist Critique of the Newest Liberal Institutionalism." *International Organization* 42: 485–507.

————. 1988b. "Realist Theory and the Problem of International Cooperation: Analysis with an Amended Prisoner's Dilemma Model." *Journal of Politics* 50: 600–624.

Grossman, Gene. 1983. "Partially Mobile Capital: A General Approach to Two-Sector Trade Theory." *Journal of International Economics* 15: 1–17.

Guisinger, Alexandra, and Alastair Smith. 2002. "Honest Threats: The Interaction of Reputation and Political Institutions in International Crises." *Journal of Conflict Resolution* 46: 175–200.

Gulick, Edward Vose. 1955. *Europe's Classical Balance of Power.* Ithaca, N.Y.: Cornell University Press.

Gurr, Ted Robert. 1970. *Why Men Rebel.* Princeton, N.J.: Princeton University Press.

Hartmann, Frederick H. 1978. *The Relations of Nations.* 5th ed. New York: Macmillan.

Haselkorn, Avigdor. 1999. *The Continuing Storm: Iraq, Poisonous Weapons, and Deterrence.* New Haven, Conn.: Yale University Press.

Hill, John, and José Mendez. 1983. "Factor Mobility and the General Equilibrium Model of Production." *Journal of International Economics* 15: 19–25.

Hillman, Ayre L. 1982. "Declining Industries and Political Support for Protectionist Motives." *American Economic Review* 72: 1180–1187.

Hiscox, Michael J. 2002. *International Trade and Political Conflict.* Princeton, N.J.: Princeton University Press.

Hobbes, Thomas. 2009/1651. *The Leviathan* ed. by J. C. A. Gaskin. Oxford: Oxford University Press.

Hollick, Ann L. 1991. *Global Commons: Can They Be Managed?* Cambridge, Mass.: Center for International Affairs, Harvard University.

Holsti, Ole R., and James N. Rosenau. 1990. "The Emerging U.S. Consensus on Foreign Policy." *Orbis* 34: 579–596.

Hook, Steven W., and Guang Zhang. 1998. "Japan's Aid Policy since the Cold War: Rhetoric and Reality." *Asian Survey* 38(11): 1051–1066.

Hufbauer, Gary Clyde, Jeffrey J. Schott, and Kimberly Ann Elliott. 1990. *Economic Sanctions Reconsidered.* 2d ed. Washington, D.C.: Institute for International Economics.

Huth, Paul K. 1988. *Extended Deterrence and the Prevention of War.* New Haven: Yale University Press.

———. 1996. *Standing Your Ground: Territorial Disputes and International Conflict.* Ann Arbor, Mich.: University of Michigan Press.

Huth, Paul K., and Todd L. Allee. 2003. *The Democratic Peace and Territorial Conflict in the Twentieth Century.* New York: Cambridge University Press.

James, Patrick, and Glenn E. Mitchell. 1995. "Targets of Covert Pressure: The Hidden Victims of the Democratic Peace." *International Interactions* 21(1): 85–107.

James, Patrick, and John Oneal. 1991. "The Influence of Domestic and International Politics on the President's Use of Force." *Journal of Conflict Resolution* 35: 307–332.

Jervis, Robert. 1978. "Cooperation under the Security Dilemma." *World Politics* 30: 167–214.

Jupille, J., J. Caporaso, and J. Checkel. 2003. "Integrating Institutions: Rationalism, Constructivism and the Study of the European Union." *Comparative Political Studies* 36(1–2): 7–40.

Kahneman, Daniel, and Amos Tversky. 1984. "Choices, Values and Frames." *American Psychologist* 39: 341–350.

———. 1986. "Rational Choice and the Framing of Decisions." *Journal of Business* 59: S252–S254.

Kant, Immanuel. 1983/1795. *Perpetual Peace, and Other Essays on Politics, History, and Morals.* Trans. Ted Humphrey. Indianapolis, Ind.: Hackett Publishing.

Katzenstein, Peter J. 1985. *Small States in World Markets.* Ithaca, N.Y.: Cornell University Press.

Keck, Margaret, and Kathryn Sikkink. 1998. *Activists beyond Borders: Advocacy Networks in International Politics.* Ithaca, N.Y.: Cornell University Press.

Kegley, Charles W., and Margaret G. Hermann. 1995. "Military Intervention and the Democratic Peace." *International Interactions* 21: 1–21.

Kennedy, Paul. 1987. *The Rise and Fall of the Great Powers: Economic Change and Military Conflict from 1500 to 2000.* New York: Random House.

Keohane, Robert O. 1984. *After Hegemony: Cooperation and Discord in the World Political Economy.* Princeton, N.J.: Princeton University Press.

———, ed. 1986. *Neorealism and Its Critics.* New York: Columbia University Press.

Keohane, Robert O., and Joseph S. Nye, eds. 1972. *Transnational Relations and World Politics.* Cambridge, Mass.: Harvard University Press.

———. 1977. *Power and Interdependence: World Politics in Transition.* Boston: Little, Brown.

Keynes, John Maynard. 1920. *The Economic Consequences of the Peace.* New York: Harcourt, Brace, and Howe.

Kilgour, D. Marc. 1992. "Domestic Structure and War: A Game Theoretic Approach." *Journal of Conflict Resolution* 35: 266–284.

Kim, Woosang, and James D. Morrow. 1992. "When Do Power Shifts Lead to War?" *American Journal of Political Science* 36: 896–922.

Kissinger, Henry. 1979. *White House Years.* Boston: Little, Brown.

———. 1992. "Balance of Power Sustained." In *Rethinking America's Security: Beyond Cold War to New World Order,* ed. Graham Allison and Gregory F. Treverton. New York: W. W. Norton.

Knack, Stephen. 2001. "Aid Dependence and the Quality of Governance: Cross-Country Empirical Tests." *Southern Economic Journal* 68(2): 310–329.

König, Thomas, and Brooke Luetgert (2005) "From Arguing to Evaluating?: An Empirical Examination of Actors' Position Change at the Nice Intergovernmental Conference." Paper presented at the First ECPR General Conference, Marburg, July 2003; updated in 2005, Department of Political Science, University of Mannheim.

Koubi, Vasiliki. 1993. "International Tensions and Arms Control Agreements." *American Journal of Political Science* 37: 148–164.

Krasner, Stephen D. 1978. *Defending the National Interest: Raw Materials Investments and U.S. Foreign Policy.* Princeton, N.J.: Princeton University Press.

———. 1983. "Structural Causes and Regime Consequences: Regimes as Intervening Variables." In *International Regimes,* ed. Stephen D. Krasner. Ithaca, N.Y.: Cornell University Press.

———. 1999. *Sovereignty: Organized Hypocrisy.* Princeton, N.J.: Princeton University Press.

Kugler, Jacek, and Douglas Lemke. 1995. *Parity and War: Evaluations and Extensions of the War Ledger.* Ann Arbor, Mich.: University of Michigan Press.

Kugler, Jacek, and A. F. K. Organski. 1989. "The End of Hegemony?" *International Interactions* 15: 113–128.

Kydd, Andrew, and Barbara F. Walter. 2002. "Sabotaging Peace: The Politics of Extremist Violence." *International Organization* 56(2): 263–296.

Lakatos, Imre. 1976. *Proofs and Refutations: The Logic of Mathematical Discovery.* Cambridge, UK: Cambridge University Press.

———. 1978. *The Methodology of Scientific Research Programmes.* Vol. I. Cambridge, UK: Cambridge University Press.

Lake, David. 1992. "Powerful Pacifists: Democratic States and War." *American Political Science Review* 86: 24–37.

Lake, David, and Matthew A. Baum. 2001. "The Invisible Hand of Democracy: Political Control and the Provision of Public Services." *Comparative Political Studies* 34(6): 587–621.

Lamborn, Alan C. 1991. *The Price of Power.* Boston: Unwin Hyman.

Laudan, Lawrence. 1977. *Progress and Its Problems.* Berkeley, Calif.: University of California Press.

Lauren, Paul G. 1998. *The Evolution of Human Rights.* Philadelphia: University of Pennsylvania Press.

Leeds, Brett Ashley, and David R. Davis. 1997. "Domestic Political Vulnerability and International Disputes." *Journal of Conflict Resolution* 41: 814–834.

Lemke, Douglas. 1996. "Small States and War: An Expansion of Power Transition Theory." In *Parity and War,* edited by Jacek Kugler and Douglas Lemke. Ann Arbor: University of Michigan Press.

———. 2002. *Regions of War and Peace.* Cambridge, UK: Cambridge University Press.

Lenin, Vladimir Ilyich. 1902. "What Is to Be Done?" Available at www.fordham.edu/halsall/mod/1902lenin.html.

Levi, Margaret. 1998. "Conscription: The Price of Citizenship." In *Analytic Narratives,* ed. Robert H. Bates, Avner Greif, Margaret Levi, and Jean-Laurent. Princeton, N.J.: Princeton University Press.

Levy, Jack S. 1982. "Historical Trends in Great Power War, 1495–1975." *International Studies Quarterly* 26: 278–301.

———. 1983. *War in the Modern Great Power System, 1495–1975.* Lexington, Ky.: University Press of Kentucky.

———. 1988. "Domestic Politics and War." *Journal of Interdisciplinary History.* 18(4): 653–673.

———. 1989. "The Diversionary Theory of War: A Critique." In *Handbook of War Studies,* ed. Manus Midlarsky. Boston: Unwin Hyman.

Levy, Jack S., Thomas C. Walker, and Martin S. Edwards. 1999. "Continuity and Change in the Evolution of War." In *War in a Changing World,* ed. Zeev Maoz. Ann Arbor, Mich.: University of Michigan Press.

Locke, John. 1690. *Two Treatises of Civil Government.* Available at www.constitution.org/jl/2ndtreat.htm.

Lohmann, Susanne. 1994. "Dynamics of Informational Cascades." *World Politics* 47: 42–101.

Lumsdaine, David H. 1993. *Moral Vision in International Politics: The Foreign Aid Regime, 1949–1989.* Princeton, N.J.: Princeton University Press.

Luttwak, Edward. 2000. "Roundtable, Atlantic Unbound: Picking a Good Fight, Round 2." *Atlantic Monthly,* April 11. Available at www.theatlantic.com/unbound/roundtable/goodfight/luttwak2.htm.

Magee, Stephen. 1978. "Three Simple Tests of the Stolper-Samuelson Theorem." In *Issues in International Economics,* ed. Peter Oppenheimer. Stocksfield, UK: Oriel.

Maliniak, Daniel, Amy Oakes, Susan Peterson, and Michael J. Tierney. 2007. "Inside the Ivory Tower II." *Foreign Policy* 159 (March–April): 62–68.

Mansfield, Edward, and Jack Snyder. 1995. "Democratization and the Danger of War." *International Security* 20: 5–38.

Maoz, Zeev. 1990. "Framing the National Interest: The Manipulation of Foreign Policy Decisions in Group Settings." *World Politics* 43: 77–110.

Maoz, Zeev, and Nazrin Abdolali. 1989. "Regime Type and International Conflict, 1816–1976." *Journal of Conflict Resolution* 33: 3–36.

Maoz, Zeev, and Bruce M. Russett. 1993. "Normative and Structural Causes of the Democratic Peace." *American Political Science Review* 87: 624–638.

Margolis, Howard. 1993. *Paradigms and Barriers: How Habits of Mind Govern Scientific Beliefs.* Chicago: University of Chicago Press.

Marshall, Monty G., and Keith Jaggers. 2007. *POLITY IV Project: Dataset Users' Manual.* Available at www.systemicpeace.org/inscr/p4manualv2006.pdf.

McGillivray, Fiona. 2004. *Privileging Industry: The Comparative Politics of Trade and Industrial Policy.* Princeton, N.J.: Princeton University Press.

McGillivray, Fiona, and Alastair Smith. 2000. "Trust and Cooperation through Agent Specific Punishments." *International Organization* 54(4): 809–824.

———. 2004. "The Impact of Leadership Turnover on Relations between States." *International Organization* 58 (summer): 567–600.

———. 2008. *Punishing the Prince: A Theory of Interstate Relations.* Princeton, N.J.: Princeton University Press.

McGurn, William. 1996. "We Warned You." *Far Eastern Economic Review,* June 13, 1968.

McKelvey, Richard. 1976. "Intransitivities in Multidimensional Voting Models and Some Implications for Agenda Control." *Journal of Economic Theory* 12: 472–482.

————. 1979. "General Conditions for Global Intransitivities in Formal Voting Models." *Econometrics* 47: 1085–1112.

McKeown, Timothy. 1984. "Firms and Tariff Change: Explaining the Demand for Protection." *World Politics* 36: 215–233.

Mearsheimer, John J., and Stephen M. Walt. 2007. *The Israel Lobby and U.S. Foreign Policy.* New York: Farrar, Strauss, and Giroux.

Medina, Luis Fernando. 2007. *A Unified Theory of Collective Action and Social Change.* Ann Arbor, Mich.: University of Michigan Press.

Midlarsky, Manus. 1975. *On War: Political Violence in the International System.* New York: Free Press.

Milner, Helen V. 1998. "Rationalizing Politics: The Emerging Synthesis of International, American, and Comparative Politics." *International Organization* 52 (autumn): 759–786.

Milner, Helen V., and Dustin H. Tingley. 2006. "The Domestic Politics of Foreign Aid: American Legislators and the Politics of Donor Countries." Paper presented at the annual meeting of the American Political Science Association, Philadelphia, September.

Milward, Alan S. 1984. *The Reconstruction of Western Europe, 1945–1951.* London: Methuen.

Mintz, Alex. 1993. "The Decision to Attack Iraq: A Noncompensatory Theory of Decision Making." *Journal of Conflict Resolution* 37: 595–618.

Mintz, Alex, and Nehemia Geva. 1993. "Why Don't Democracies Fight Each Other?: The Political Incentives Approach." *Journal of Conflict Resolution* 37: 487–503.

Modelski, George, ed. 1987. *Exploring Long Cycles.* Boulder, Colo.: Lynne Rienner.

Modelski, George, and William R. Thompson. 1994. *Innovation, Growth and War: The Co-Evolution of Global Politics and Economics.* Columbia, S.C.: University of South Carolina Press.

Morgan, T. Clifton, and Kenneth Bickers. 1992. "Domestic Discontent and the External Use of Force." *Journal of Conflict Resolution* 36: 25–52.

Morgan, T. Clifton, and Sally H. Campbell. 1991. "Domestic Structure, Decisional Constraints and War: So Why Kant Democracies Fight?" *Journal of Conflict Resolution* 35: 187–211.

Morgenthau, Hans J. 1978. *Politics among Nations.* 5th rev. ed. New York: Knopf.

Morrow, James D. 1991a. "Alliances and Asymmetry: An Alternative to the Capability Aggregation Model of Alliances." *American Journal of Political Science* 35: 904–933.

————. 1991b. "Electoral and Congressional Incentives and Arms Control." *Journal of Conflict Resolution* 35: 243–263.

————. 1994a. *Game Theory for Political Scientists.* Princeton, N.J.: Princeton University Press.

————. 1994b. "Modeling the Forms of Cooperation: Distribution versus Information." *International Organization* 48: 387–423.

————. 1997. "A Rational Choice Approach to International Conflict." In *Decision-Making on War and Peace: The Cognitive-Rational Debate,* ed. Alex Mintz and Nehemia Geva. Boulder, Colo.: Lynne Rienner.

————. 1998. "The Laws of War as an International Institution." Hoover Institution, Stanford University.

————. 1999. "The Strategic Setting of Choices: Signaling, Commitment, and Negotiation in International Politics." In *Strategic Choice and International Relations,* ed. David A. Lake and Robert Powell. Princeton, N.J.: Princeton University Press.

————. 2007. "When Do States Follow the Laws of War?" *American Political Science Review* 101(3): 559–572.

Most, Benjamin, and Harvey Starr. 1989. *Inquiry, Logic, and International Politics.* Columbia, S.C.: University of South Carolina Press.

Mueller, John E. 1973. *War, Presidents, and Public Opinion.* New York: John Wiley.

———. 1989. *Retreat from Doomsday: The Obsolescence of Major War.* New York: Basic Books.

Nalebuff, Barry. 1991. "Rational Deterrence in an Imperfect World," *World Politics* 43(April): 313–335.

Nincic, Miroslav. 1997. "Loss Aversion and the Domestic Context of Military Intervention." *Political Research Quarterly* 50: 97–120.

Niou, Emerson, Peter Ordeshook, and Gregory Rose. 1989. *The Balance of Power.* Cambridge, UK: Cambridge University Press.

Niskanen, William A. 1973. *Structural Reform of the Federal Budget Process.* Washington, D.C.: American Enterprise Institute for Public Policy Research.

Norpoth, Helmut. 1987. "Guns and Butter and Governmental Popularity in Britain." *American Political Science Review* 81: 949–959.

Olson, Mancur. 1965. *The Logic of Collective Action.* Cambridge, Mass.: Harvard University Press.

Oneal, John R., and Bruce M. Russett. 1997. "The Classical Liberals Were Right: Democracy, Interdependence, and Conflict, 1950–1985." *International Studies Quarterly* 41: 267–294.

Organski, A. F. K. 1958. *World Politics.* New York: Knopf.

Organski, A. F. K., and Jacek Kugler. 1980. *The War Ledger.* Chicago: University of Chicago Press.

Ostrom, Elinor. 1990. *Governing the Commons: The Evolution of Institutions for Collective Action.* Cambridge, UK: Cambridge University Press.

———. 1999. "Coping with Tragedies of the Commons." *Annual Review of Political Science,* ed. Nelson Polsby. Palo Alto, Calif.: Annual Reviews.

Popper, Karl. 1963. *Conjectures and Refutations: The Growth of Scientific Knowledge.* New York: Basic Books.

Powell, Robert. 1990. *Nuclear Deterrence Theory: The Search for Credibility.* Cambridge, UK: Cambridge University Press.

———. 1991. "Absolute and Relative Gains in International Relations Theory." *American Political Science Review* 85: 1303–1320.

———. 1994. "Anarchy in International Relations Theory: The Neorealist-Neoliberal Debate." *International Organization* 48(2): 313–344.

———. 1996. "Uncertainty, Shifting Power, and Appeasement." *American Political Science Review* 90: 749–764.

———. 1999. *In the Shadow of Power: States and Strategy in International Politics.* Princeton, N.J.: Princeton University Press.

Prange, Gordon W. 1981. *At Dawn We Slept.* New York: Penguin Books.

Putnam, Robert. 1988. "Diplomacy and Domestic Politics: The Logic of Two-Level Games." *International Organization* 42: 427–460.

Ramsey, Kristopher W., and Mark Fey. 2006. "The Common Priors Assumption: A Comment on Bargaining and the Nature of War." *Journal of Conflict Resolution* 50(4): 607–613.

Ray, James L. 1974. "Status Inconsistency and War Involvement of European States, 1816–1970." *Peace Science Society (International) Papers* 23: 69–80.

———. 1995. *Democracy and International Conflict.* Columbia, S.C.: University of South Carolina Press.

Ray, James L., and Bruce M. Russett. 1996. "The Future as Arbiter of Theoretical Controversies: Predictions, Explanations and the End of the Cold War." *British Journal of Political Science* 25: 1578.

Reed, William. 1997. "Alliance Duration and Democracy: An Extension and Cross-Validation of 'Democratic States and Commitment in International Relations.'" *American Journal of Political Science* 41: 1072–1078.

Reiter, Dani, and Allan Stam. 1996. "Democracy, War Initiation and Victory." *American Political Science Review* 90: 377–389.

———. 1998. "Democracy and Battlefield Military Effectiveness." *Journal of Conflict Resolution* 42(June): 259–277.

———. 2002 *Democracies at War*. Princeton, N.J.: Princeton University Press.

Richardson, Lewis Fry. 1960/1949. *Arms and Insecurity*. Chicago: Quadrangle.

Risse-Kappen, Thomas, Stephen C. Ropp, and Kathryn Sikkink. 1999. *The Power of Human Rights: International Norms and Domestic Change*. Cambridge, UK: Cambridge University Press.

Rogowski, Ronald. 1989. *Commerce and Coalitions*. Princeton, N.J.: Princeton University Press.

Rosenau, James N. 1963. *National Leadership and Foreign Policy: A Case Study in the Mobilization of Public Support*. Princeton, N.J.: Princeton University Press.

———, ed. 1969. *Linkage Politics: Essays on the Convergence of National and International Systems*. New York: Free Press.

Rosenthal, Jean-Laurent. 1998. "The Political Economy of Absolutism Reconsidered." In *Analytic Narratives*, ed. Robert H. Bates, Avner Greif, Margaret Levi, and Jean-Laurent. Princeton, N.J.: Princeton University Press.

Rueschmeyer, Dietrich, Evelyn Huber Stephens, and John Stephens. 1992. *Capitalist Development and Democracy*. Chicago: University of Chicago Press.

Ruggie, John G. 1975. "International Responses to Technology: Concepts and Trends." *International Organization* 29: 557–584.

Rummel, Rudolph J. 1983. "Libertarianism and International Violence." *Journal of Conflict Resolution* 27: 27–71.

Russell, James T., and Quincy Wright. 1933. "National Attitudes on the Far East Controversy." *American Political Science Review* 27(August): 555–576.

Russett, Bruce M. 1985. "The Mysterious Case of Vanishing Hegemony." *International Organization* 39: 207–232.

———. 1993. *Grasping the Democratic Peace*. Princeton, N.J.: Princeton University Press.

Sachs, Jeffrey D. 2005. *The End of Poverty: Economic Possibilities for Our Time*. New York: Penguin Press.

Sandler, Todd. 1992. *Collective Action: Theory and Applications*. Ann Arbor, Mich.: University of Michigan Press.

Sargent, Thomas J. 1993. *Bounded Rationality in Macroeconomics*. Oxford: Clarendon Press.

Sartori, Anne E. 2006. *Deterrence by Diplomacy*. Princeton, N.J.: Princeton University Press.

Schelling, Thomas. 1960. *Strategy of Conflict*. Cambridge, Mass.: Harvard University Press.

Schofield, Norman. 1978. "Instability of Simple Dynamic Games." *Review of Economic Studies* 45: 575–594.

Schraeder, Peter J., Steven W. Hook, and Bruce Taylor. 1998. "Clarifying the Foreign Aid Puzzle: A Comparison of American, Japanese, French, and Swedish Aid Flows." *World Politics* 50(2): 294–323.

Schultz, Kenneth A. 1998. "Domestic Opposition and Signaling in International Crises." *American Political Science Review* 92: 829–844.

———. 2001. *Democracy and Coercive Diplomacy.* Cambridge, Mass.: Cambridge University Press.

Senese, Paul D. 1995. "Militarized Interstate Dispute Escalation: The Effects of Geographical Proximity and Issue Salience." Paper presented at the meeting of the Peace Science Society, Ohio State University, Columbus, Ohio, October 13–15.

———. 1997. "Contiguity, Territory, and Their Interaction." Paper presented at the annual meeting of the International Studies Association, Toronto, March 18–22.

Senese, Paul D., and John A. Vasquez. 2008. *The Steps to War: An Empirical Study.* Princeton, N.J.: Princeton University Press.

Shakespeare, William. 2002/1415. *Henry V.* In *The Complete Pelican Shakespeare,* ed. Stephen Orgel and A. R. Braunmuller. Gretna, La.: Pelican Classics.

Shepsle, Kenneth A., and Barry R. Weingast. 1981. "Structure-Induced Equilibrium and Legislative Choice." *Public Choice* 37: 503–519.

Signorino, Curtis. 1999. "Strategic Interaction and the Statistical Analysis of International Conflict." *American Political Science Review* 93: 279–298.

Simmons, Beth A. 1994. *Who Adjusts?: Domestic Sources of Foreign Economic Policy during the Interwar Years.* Princeton, N.J.: Princeton University Press.

Singer, J. David, Stuart Bremer, and John Stuckey. 1972. "Capability Distribution, Uncertainty, and Major Power War, 1820–1965." In *Peace, War, and Numbers,* ed. Bruce M. Russett. Beverly Hills, Calif.: Sage.

Singer, J. David, and Thomas Cusack. 1990. "Periodicity, Inexorability, and Steermanship in International War." In *Models, Methods, and Progress in World Politics,* ed. J. David Singer. Boulder, Colo.: Westview Press.

Siverson, Randolph M. 1995. "Democracies and War Participation: In Defense of the Institutional Constraints Argument." *European Journal of International Relations* 1: 481–490.

Siverson, Randolph M., and Paul Diehl. 1989. "The Conflict Spiral, Arms Races, and the Outbreak of War." In *The Handbook of War Studies,* ed. Manus Midlarsky. New York: Allen and Hyman.

Siverson, Randolph M., and Michael P. Sullivan. 1983. "The Distribution of Power and the Onset of War." *Journal of Conflict Resolution* 27: 473–494.

Skinner, Kiron, Analise Anderson, and Martin Anderson, eds. 2001. *Reagan, in His Own Hand: The Writings of Ronald Reagan That Reveal His Revolutionary Vision for America.* New York: Simon & Schuster.

Skinner, Kiron, Serhiy Kudelia, Bruce Bueno de Mesquita, and Condoleezza Rice. 2007. *The Strategy of Campaigning: Lessons from Ronald Reagan and Boris Yeltsin.* Ann Arbor, Mich.: University of Michigan Press.

Slantchev, Brnaislav L. 2003. "The Power to Hurt: Costly Conflict with Completely Informed States." *American Political Science Review* 97(1): 123–133.

Small, Melvin, and J. David Singer. 1976. "The War-Proneness of Democratic Regimes." *Jerusalem Journal of International Relations* 1: 46–61.

Smith, Alastair. 1995. "Alliance Formation and War." *International Studies Quarterly* 39: 405–425.

———. 1996. "The Success and Use of Sanctions." *International Interactions* 21: 229–245.

———. 1998. "International Crises and Domestic Politics." *American Political Science Review* 92(3): 623–638.

———. 1999. "Testing Theories of Strategic Choice: The Example of Crisis Escalation." *American Journal of Political Science* 43: 1254–1283.

———. 2004. *Election Timing.* New York: Cambridge University Press.

Snidal, Duncan. 1991. "Relative Gains and the Pattern of International Cooperation." *American Political Science Review* 85: 701–726.

Spruyt, Hendrik. 1994. *The Sovereign State and Its Competitors.* Princeton, N.J.: Princeton University Press.

Stam, Allan C. 1996. *Win, Lose, or Draw: Domestic Politics and the Crucible of War.* Ann Arbor, Mich.: University of Michigan Press.

———. 1999. *Win, Lose, or Draw: Domestic Politics and the Crucible of War.* Ann Arbor, Mich.: University of Michigan Press.

Starr, Harvey. 1978. "'Opportunity' and 'Willingness' as Ordering Concepts in the Study of War." *International Interactions* 4: 363–387.

Stein, Arthur. 1990. *Why Nations Cooperate: Circumstance and Choice in International Relations.* Ithaca, N.Y.: Cornell University Press.

Strange, Susan. 1987. "The Persistent Myth of Lost Hegemony." *International Organization* 41: 551–574.

Taylor, Michael. 1976. *Anarchy and Cooperation.* New York: John Wiley.

———. 1987. *The Possibility of Cooperation.* Cambridge, UK: Cambridge University Press.

Tetlock, Philip, and Aaron Belkin, eds. 1996. *Counterfactual Thought Experiments in World Politics.* Princeton, N.J.: Princeton University Press.

Thomas, Daniel C. 2001. *The Helsinki Effect: International Norms, Human Rights, and the Demise of Communism.* Princeton, N.J.: Princeton University Press.

Thompson, William, "Polarity, the Long Cycle and Global Power Warfare." *Journal of Conflict Resolution* 30 (December): 587–615.

Thomson, Robert, Frans N. Stokman, Christopher H. Achen, and Thomas König, eds. 2006. *The European Union Decides.* New York: Cambridge University Press.

Tsebelis, George. 2002. *Veto Players: How Political Institutions Work.* Princeton, N.J.: Princeton University Press.

Tversky, Amos, and Daniel Kahneman. 1986. "Rational Choice and the Framing of Decisions." *Journal of Business* 59: S252–S254.

Van den Bos, Jan M. M. 1994. "The Policy Issues Analyzed." In *European Community Decision Making,* ed. Bruce Bueno de Mesquita and Frans Stokman. New Haven, Conn.: Yale University Press.

Vasquez, John A. 1987. "The Steps to War: Toward a Scientific Explanation of Correlates of War Findings." *World Politics* 40: 108–145.

———. 1993. *The War Puzzle.* Cambridge, Mass.: Cambridge University Press.

———. 1995. "Why Do Neighbors Fight?: Territoriality, Proximity, or Interactions." *Journal of Peace Research* 32: 277–293.

———. 1997. "The Realist Paradigm and Degenerative versus Progressive Research Programs: An Appraisal of Neotraditional Research on Waltz's Balancing Proposition." *American Political Science Review* 91: 899–913.

Wallace, Michael. 1973. *War and Rank among Nations.* Lexington, Mass.: Lexington Books.

Waltz, Kenneth N. 1979. *Theory of International Politics.* Reading, Mass.: Addison-Wesley.

Ward, Michael D., and Kristian S. Gleditsch. 1998. "Democratizing for Peace." *American Political Science Review* 92: 51–62.

Wayman, Frank W., Meredith Sarkees, and J. David Singer. 2003. "Inter-State, Intra-State, and Extra-State Wars: A Comprehensive Look at Their Distribution over Time, 1816–1997." *International Studies Quarterly* 47: 49–70.

Weiss, E. B., and Harold Jacobson, eds. 1998. *Engaging Countries: Strengthening Compliance with International Environmental Accords.* Cambridge, Mass.: MIT Press.

Wendt, Alexander. 1994. "Collective Identity Formation and the International State." *American Political Science Review* 88: 394–398.

———. 1999. *Social Theory of International Politics.* Cambridge, UK: Cambridge University Press.

Werner, Suzanne. 1996. "Absolute and Limited War: The Possibilities of Foreign Imposed Regime Change." *International Interactions* 22: 67–88.

Wildavsky, Aaron. 1979. *The Politics of the Budgetary Process.* Boston: Little, Brown.

Winteringham, F. P. W. 1989. *Radioactive Fallout in Soils, Crops, and Food.* FAO Soils Bulletin no. 61. New York: United Nations Food and Agriculture Organization.

Young, Oren, and M. A. Levy. 1999. "The Effectiveness of International Environmental Regimes." In *The Effectiveness of International Environmental Agreements,* ed. Oren Young. Cambridge, Mass.: MIT Press.

Zagare, Frank C. 1987. *The Dynamics of Deterrence.* Chicago: University of Chicago Press.

Zagare, Frank C., and D. Marc Kilgour. 1993. "Asymmetric Deterrence." *International Studies Quarterly* 37: 1–27.

Zinnes, Dina A. 2004. "Constructing Political Logic: The Democratic Peace Puzzle." *Journal of Conflict Resolution* 48: 430–454.

Glossary of Key Terms

Absolute advantage. The ability to produce a good or service at a lower cost than anyone else.

Anarchy. A structuring of the international system in which no supernational authority exists to enforce agreements between states, so that international affairs becomes a self-help system dependent on individual national interests. Anarchy is equivalent to the conditions of a noncooperative game in which promises are not binding and actions are based on self-interest.

Arbitrage. The process of buying goods cheaply in one place and simultaneously selling them in another place at a higher price. Arbitrage is a way to equalize prices in different places by increasing supply where it is scarce (that is, the price is high) and reducing supply where it is cheap (that is, where supply initially is abundant).

Arms races. Competitions between two or more states characterized by a reciprocal and ever-increasing acquisition of arms by each state in response to the arms procurement or foreign policy actions of the other state or states engaged in the competition.

Asset specificity. The specialization of an asset so that its productive capacity in one sector does not translate into comparable productive capacity in another sector.

Assumptions. The group of simplifying conditions under which the theory is expected to be a helpful tool for explaining and predicting the phenomena with which it is concerned.

Asymmetric information (or uncertainty). Information that can lead entirely rational actors to different conclusions about what they can expect to gain or lose.

Backward induction. A method for solving extensive form games. Individuals interested in solving an extensive form game through backward induction must begin at the terminal nodes and work their way back to the beginning of the game, identifying at each node the response that is the best choice at that juncture for the relevant player given what that player can anticipate about the subsequent choices of all other players.

Balance of power. The theory that an equal distribution of power influences international peace and stability.

Benefits. The things of value, both tangible and intangible, that actors receive as a consequence of their actions.

Bipolarity. A structuring of the international system in which international politics is dominated by two powerful states, with all other states associated with one of the two powers. There is general agreement that bipolar systems induce less uncertainty among states than do multipolar systems.

Blocking coalition. A coalition strong enough to prevent the formation of a winning coalition but not strong enough to win on its own. *See also* Winning coalition.

Branches. The choices in an extensive form game, such that no more than one branch can enter a choice node or terminal node, indicating that there is a unique sequence of branches to each choice point in the game.

Bretton Woods Agreement. The backbone of the international economy from the end of World War II until it was dismantled by Richard Nixon in 1971. The agreement pegged the U.S. dollar to gold so that 1 ounce of gold was fixed at $35.00. The United States guaranteed that it would exchange dollars for gold at this rate. Bretton Woods also established the International Monetary Fund and the International Bank for Reconstruction and Development, which evolved into the World Bank.

Budget constraint. The limit on resources that a government (or a household) can spend.

Capitalism. The economic ideal that the "hidden hand" of market forces produce efficient growth and prosperity.

Capital mobility. The ease with which capital can be moved from one industry or locale to another.

Case studies. Evaluations of a theory through the close scrutiny of a single event and its associated details.

Cheap talk. Actions or signals in a game that are costless.

Choice nodes. Points in a game at which a player must choose an action.

Circular indifference curves. Curves made up of all the points in a two-dimensional space that are equidistant from a player's ideal point. A circular indifference curve has the characteristic that the ideal point is located at the center so that the farther a point is from the center, the less valued it is.

Colonial power. The domination of a people and territory by occupation or governance by an external power.

Common knowledge. An information condition that says "I know something and you know something, you know that I know that something, I know that you know that I know that something, you know that I know that you know that I know," and so forth.

Communism. The economic ideal is that each individual will contribute to society according to his or her ability and each will receive whatever he or she needs from society in return.

Comparative advantage. The relative efficiency with which resources can be employed to produce goods or services (X and Y), such that A is relatively better at producing X than it is at producing Y compared to B, thereby conferring comparative advantage on A in the production of X.

Complacent opponents. Individuals or groups that would rather tolerate being taken advantage of by the government than engage in terrorist action.

Complete and perfect information. Information consisting of the history of play in a game, that is, all prior moves (complete information), and the value of the payoffs to each player at all terminal nodes of the game (perfect information).

Compliance. Acting in accordance with the terms of an agreement.

Constituents. Individuals who are represented by a government official, who needs their support to stay in office.

Constructivism. A theory of international relations based on the formation of values and preferences by nations.

Cooperative game theory. A game theory that assumes that promises made between actors are binding (meaning they will be kept). Cooperative game theory is especially useful for working with problems in which no player has an incentive to renege on promises or in which contracts are assured of being enforced.

Coordination. Collective action by two or more decision makers intended to lead to common or complementary strategic choices.

Coordination goods. Public goods that facilitate groups of people coming together, exchanging views, and coordinating their actions; these include a free press, free speech, and freedom of assembly.

Costly signal. An action or signal in a game that is costly to the player that sends it because in taking the action the sender gives up or spends something that the sender values.

Costs. The price associated with taking an action or not taking it. Costs must be subtracted from the benefits of actions to evaluate the net gain or loss. *See also* Opportunity costs; Transaction costs.

Credible commitments. Promises that the other player believes will be carried out because these promises advance the self-interests of the actor giving the promise.

Currency convertibility. The situation in which it is possible to change one country's unit of currency into another country's unit of currency without restrictions.

Demand curves. A curve showing the response of consumers to changing prices. *See also* Supply curves.

Democratic peace. A body of empirical regularities that indicates that democracies tend not to fight wars with one another but do fight with nondemocratic states.

Democratization. A process by which a nondemocratic state undergoes a transition to a democracy.

Dependent variables. Arrays of things to be explained by a theory.

Deterrence. The strategy designed to persuade an adversary not to take an action that it otherwise would take.

Dissatisfaction. The degree of displeasure a player attaches to a given state of affairs.

Distribution. The allocation of resources across individuals or groups.

Dollarization. A country's use of the U.S. dollar as its currency for all or much of its exchange.

Domestic politics. Competition over political or governmental office, ideas, policies, and allocation of resources within a nation's borders.

Dominant strategy. A strategy that a player prefers to pursue no matter what response other players are anticipated to make.

Empirical accuracy. How well the facts fit a theory's predictions.

Endogenously. Acting (for example, making a decision) based on the logic of the situation.

Equilibrium price. The price determined by the intersection of supply and demand curves for a product or service.

Essential actors. Actors with sufficient power that they can turn at least one losing coalition into a blocking coalition.

Ex ante. Before the consequences are known. This is how decisions are made in reality.

Exchange rates. The prices at which one currency can be used to purchase another currency.

Exclusive. The quality of having relatively few participants.

Expansionism. The acquisition of territory by a country through purchase or conquest.

Expected utility. The value obtained by evaluating the various consequences, in terms of benefits minus costs, that can arise from a specified action; multiplying each possible consequence by the probability that it will arise; and then adding up these quantities across all the various consequences that have a chance of occurring given the chosen action. This value can be calculated before the action is taken and can be compared to the expected utility of alternative actions that could be chosen so that the decision maker can pick the one that yields the greatest expected net gain.

Ex post. With hindsight; after the consequences are known. This is not how players make decisions; assuming that they do is a fallacy.

Extensive form. Payoffs and moves displayed as a tree. Any number of choices can emanate from any branch of the tree, but only one branch can enter a choice point or choice node. The tree ends in terminal nodes that represent end points in the game.

Factor mobility. The ease with which factors of production can be moved from one industry or locale to another.

Factors of production. The essential ingredients for production: land, labor, and capital.

Fair trade. Economic exchange between nations regulated by the principle that one nation should not sell goods to another nation at a price below the price at which the goods are sold in the producer country. Fair trade also includes the idea that countries should try to achieve a rough balance or equality in their trade with one another.

Falsifiability. That a theory is testable; that is, conditions exist in principle under which we might conclude that the argument is false.

Fascism. A system of totalitarian government in which the government controls all aspects of economic and political activity.

First principle of wing-walking. The principle that you should not let go of what you are holding on to (for example, a theory) unless you have something better to hold on to. Even then, think twice about letting go.

Float. When a currency's exchange rate fluctuates in response to supply and demand.

Foreign aid. Assistance given by one country or organization to another country, ostensibly to improve conditions in the recipient state.

Game theory. A mathematical means of evaluating strategic interaction in which the choices of any individual are contingent on expectations about the choices of other individuals. *See also* Extensive form; Normal form.

Gini index. A measure of the inequality of income distribution in a country.

Globalization. The international process that leads to the worldwide integration of market-driven exchanges in goods, services, and capital.

Grim trigger. A punishment strategy in which a player who has defected or otherwise punished a second player is itself punished by that player throughout the remainder of the game no matter what type of behavior the first player displays thereafter.

Helsinki Final Act. An agreement signed by most European powers in 1975 that recognized the sovereignty of East Germany and West Germany in exchange for oversight rights by governments and human rights groups regarding human rights in the Soviet-bloc countries.

Hierarchy. An ordering of states according to control over some relevant dimension in international affairs, such as the setting of rules or norms of international interaction.

Human capital. People with productive skills and abilities derived from education and good health—that is, skilled educated people.

Hypotheses. Predictions that represent a theory's explanation of a portion of reality.

Ideal point. The most-preferred resolution of an issue or issues for a single decision maker. The ideal point is the policy position at which a decision maker will receive the most utility.

Inclusive. The quality of having a large number of participants.

Independent variables. Arrays of things that we think will provide us with all or part of the explanation of the different values taken on by the dependent variable.

Indivisible good. Goods that cannot be divided in their consumption.

Inessential actors. Actors that cannot turn a losing coalition into a winning or blocking coalition.

Instability. Changes in the composition of the international system, especially changes involving the disappearance or emergence of key states following large wars.

Institutional perspective. A perspective that sees political interaction as depending on actors pursuing actions that are compatible with their interests and that are constrained by the structure of the situation in which they find themselves, especially the structure of political institutions.

Internal consistency. The assumptions of a theory do not contradict one another, and the predictions derived from the theory follow logically from the assumptions.

Internal inconsistencies. Assumptions in a theory that contradict one another, and predictions said to be derived from the theory that do not follow logically from the assumptions.

International interaction game. An example of the strategic perspective. A theory of international relations in which states are assumed to pursue foreign policies based on the choices that their leaders make, taking domestic and international political conditions into account.

International law. A body of law, generally codified in treaties, that applies to relations between states or between citizens in different states.

International organizations. Entities or structures, such as the United Nations or the World Trade Organization, formed by agreement among member sovereign states.

International regimes. International institutions, rules, regulations, and norms. This constitutes a generic category (subsuming international law and international organizations) intended to promote the importance of ideas in international politics.

International relations. Conventionally, the competition over political or governmental office, ideas, policies, and resources between states. Here, international relations is viewed as the process by which foreign policy leaders balance their ambition to pursue particular policy objectives vis-á-vis other states against their need to avoid internal and external threats to their political survival.

Kleptocracy. A form of government based on the leadership's stealing from the state.

Labor mobility. The ease with which labor can be moved from one industry or locale to another.

Legitimation. The process by which a norm or regime comes to be seen as authoritative by a community.

Liberalism. A theory of international relations that assumes that states can cooperate with one another through international regimes or through assurances that agreements will be enforced by a dominant (hegemonic) powers.

Majority rule. In a national context, the convention that the position with more than half of the votes wins. In an international context, the convention that the position accruing the majority of the power that each of the stakeholders controls in the context of the issue is the chosen position.

Median voter theorem. The theorem that, if preferences are single peaked, an issue is unidimensional, and a majority is required to win, then the position of the median voter is the winning position in a contest with any alternative.

Monitoring. Keeping track of a player's actions to determine whether it is in compliance with expectations.

Multiple equilibria. More than one set of strategies from which no player has a unilateral incentive to switch to some other strategy. *See also* Nash equilibrium.

Multipolarity. A structuring of the international system in which international politics is dominated by three or more powerful states, with all other states associated with one of the power poles. There is general agreement that multipolar systems induce more uncertainty among states than do bipolar systems.

Nash equilibrium. A set of strategies in a game such that no player has a unilateral incentive to switch to another strategy. Every finite game has at least one Nash equilibrium in mixed strategies and may have more than one in pure strategies and mixed strategies.

National interest. The set of objectives that enhances the welfare of the state. Usually the national interest is thought of in terms of protecting sovereignty, maximizing security or power, and improving national wealth. When two or more issues are linked together, there may be many conflicting views of the national interest.

Nationalism. A sense of national consciousness and loyalty to one's country.

National reputation. A belief about how a nation will respond to given situations based on its repeated pattern of responses to similar situations in the past.

National security. In neorealism, how much military might a state has amassed to ward off threats by other states and thereby secure its survival as a sovereign state.

Nation building. The process of altering a country's form of governance, usually with the intention of making the country more democratic and economically more prosperous.

Natural resource curse. A country's possession of natural resources that require relatively little labor to convert them into income-producing products (for example, having lots of revenue from oil or gold or diamonds) has the consequence of making a few people rich and many more people poor.

Necessary and sufficient condition. If not A, then not B, and if A, then B.

Necessary condition. If not A, then not B.

Neorealism. A theory of international relations in which states are assumed to maximize their security in an anarchic, self-help world.

Noncooperative game theory. A game theory that assumes that decision makers will cooperate with one another only when it is in their self-interests to do so. In noncooperative games, promises are not inherently binding.

Nontariff barriers. Measures other than tariffs designed to reduce foreign competition.

Normal form. Payoffs displayed in a matrix, showing the costs and benefits associated with the alternative strategies of the game but not showing the sequence of moves in the game.

Normative perspective. A perspective that sees political interaction as depending on the internalization of patterns of behavior, whether these patterns serve an actor's interests or not and whether they are subject to enforcement and punishment for violations or not.

Norms. Practices widely observed by custom rather than as a matter of law.

Observationally equivalent explanations. Other explanations that also fit the data.

Off the equilibrium path. Choices of actions in a game tree that are not actually made by the players; they are not part of the equilibrium path but are part of the equilibrium strategy.

Opportunity costs. The price in terms of the forgone alternative courses of action or use of resources.

Pacific dove hypothesis. The hypothesis that, if a weak state prefers to negotiate rather than force an adversary to capitulate (that is, it is a dove) and also prefers to capitulate rather than retaliate if attacked (that is, it is pacific), then that state is especially likely to initiate violence.

Pareto efficient. A type of outcome in which no player is made worse off and at least one player is made better off.

Pareto improving. A type of outcome that is mutually beneficial.

Pareto inferior. A type of outcome in which at least one player is worse off. The prisoner's dilemma is a classic example of a game with a Pareto inferior outcome.

Parsimony. The principle that the more events or facts a theory can explain with a limited set of assumptions, the more useful the theory is.

Path dependence. The extent to which chance prior events or choices determine the future course of events or choices.

Perceptions. The subjective interpretation of events and actions; how people interpret information and their beliefs about the meaning of the actions taken by others.

Polarity. *See* Bipolarity; Multipolarity; Unipolarity.

Political economy. The study of the intersection between politics and economics.

Politics. The domain of competition among groups and individuals for special advantages, particularly over control of power and wealth. *See also* Domestic politics.

Polity Index. An index that measures the extent to which a government assures competitive participation in the leader-selection process (with competitive recruitment of leaders), constrains leaders, and makes the process open to a broad segment of the population. It can be used as a measure of democratization.

Power. The ability to make others do something they otherwise would not do.

Power transition theory. A theory of great power wars based on the idea that war is most likely when a challenger rises in power, equaling and then overtaking the dominant state. In this theory, the focus of attention is on the authority to set the rules and norms of international interactions.

Preferences. The ordering of individual desires.

Prisoner's dilemma. A game with a dominant strategy equilibrium that is Pareto inferior; that is, it will end by disadvantaging both players. The game is indicative of problems of mistrust when promises are not credible.

Private goods. Goods or things that are both divisible and excludable so that by belonging to one person they cannot also belong to another person.

Probability. The chance or likelihood that a particular action or event will take place. If all possible events or circumstances are specified, then the sum of the probabilities of the events or circumstances must be 1.

Production possibility frontier. The maximum mix of goods that can be produced given the available resources.

Psychological theories. Theories based on the human psyche.

Public goods. Government policies and programs that all people benefit from whether they are in the leader's inner circle or not.

Public policies. Governmental decisions on how to distribute public goods.

Puppet governments. Governments imposed on countries by a foreign nation so that they will follow the policies of that nation.

Rational. The quality of choosing among actions based on what is believed will yield the best results.

Receptivity to trade. The extent to which a country's policies make it open to imports from other countries.

Reluctant terrorists. People who engage in terrorism because they do not believe that the government would negotiate with them in good faith if they tried to resolve their problems through negotiation rather than through violence.

Rent-seeking. Extracting resources from the many through corruption and turning them over to the few loyal coalition members.

Resurrection hypothesis. The supposition that if an actor faces virtually certain extermination by continuing to do whatever it is doing, then it will not be reluctant to undertake some other very risky action in the hope of salvaging itself because there is very little remaining downside to its taking big risks.

Reverse causality. A situation in which the supposed effect is actually the cause, and vice versa.

Risk acceptant. Favoring the risky choice over the sure-thing outcome even when the sure thing and the risky choice have the same exact expected value.

Risk averse. Favoring the sure-thing outcome over the risky choice even if the risky choice and the sure thing have the same exact expected value.

Risk neutral. Being indifferent between a sure thing and a risky choice when the risky choice and the sure thing have the same exact expected value.

Risk taking. Being willing to gamble on a risky outcome.

Role redefinition. The re-creation of a decision maker's or nation's identity as a function of the part it is assigned in an international organization or series of interactions.

Sanctioning. The use of punishment, usually through economic means, by one or more governments in an attempt to alter the behavior of another government.

Scapegoat hypothesis. The proposition that a leader has precipitated some kind of international conflict to command the nation's attention and thereby divert it from the leadership's domestic failings. If a state's domestic economy, for instance, is performing poorly, the leader may seek an international dispute to deflect attention away from its domestic problems.

Scientific method. Evaluating arguments in terms of their logical consistency and in terms of the extent to which observational or experimental evidence is consistent with the predictions that they logically imply.

Security dilemma. An increase in a state's power can actually make the state weaker in the long run. This happens if the increase in power alarms rivals and mobilizes them to form an opposition alliance; a coalition or alliance of states will come together to beat back a growing state if that state's power threatens to become large enough that others face a possible loss of sovereignty.

Selection bias. Picking cases because they are consistent with a theory, thus eliminating cases that might refute the theory.

Selection effect. The way in which cases or observations are divided over outcomes because of off-the-equilibrium-path expectations (that is, because of counterfactual circumstances).

Selectorate. The citizens of a state with a legal say in choosing the leadership.

Selectorate theory. An example of the strategic perspective. A theory that posits that variations in the size of a polity's political institutions can explain many facets of international interactions: warfare capabilities, the uses of foreign aid and military intervention to encourage or stymie democratization, the democratic peace, and why democracies are willing to fight wars of imperial and colonial expansion and are even more prepared than autocrats to overthrow foreign rivals.

Self-interests. The interests of leaders (usually to stay in office as long as possible), as opposed to the national interest.

Shadow of the future. The value a player attaches to future benefits as compared to present benefits.

Single-peaked preferences. Preferences that decline with Euclidean distance from an actor's ideal point. The alternatives can be ordered spatially such that the farther a choice is from an actor's ideal point, the less preferred that choice is to the actor.

Sovereignty. The right and authority to rule within a specified, usually geographical domain.

Spatial models A class of abstract perspectives that assume that we can locate decision makers and their policy preferences either on a line (along a continuum) or in a space that includes more than one dimension.

Stability. The preservations of the sovereignty of key states in the international system.

State. The only political entity endowed with the sovereign authority and the absolute right to use force to enforce agreements or contracts within its borders and to protect its borders from external threats or incursions. Interchangeable with nation-state.

Status inconsistency. When a state believes that it is being treated as being less prestigious than its power warrants; this may lead to aggressive behavior on its part.

Sticky. Not easily changed. Applied to institutions and capital investments.

Strategic perspective. A theoretical approach that views individuals as choosing their actions by taking into account the anticipated actions and responses of others with the intention of maximizing their own welfare.

Structure-induced equilibrium. A Nash equilibrium constrained by institutional rules or organizational structures that restrict the array of choices or outcomes that can be sustained among members.

Subgame perfect Nash equilibrium. The Nash equilibrium found by a player's looking ahead at each choice node and considering his or her options and also the choices that other players will subsequently have in the game. At each choice node, the player chooses his or her best move given what he or she expects the other player or players to do from that point in the game onward.

Sufficient condition. If A, then B.

Supply curves. A curve showing how producers respond (the quantity supplied) to changing prices, provided that the cost of additional production does not exceed the price. *See also* Demand curves.

Tariffs. Government taxes or levies on imported goods or services that are not also applied to comparable products or services that are produced domestically.

Terminal nodes. Nodes at which the game ends.

Terrorism. Any act of violence undertaken for the purpose of altering a government's policies such that the violence targets those who do not actually have the personal authority to alter or enforce governmental policy.

Testing. Checking the hypotheses of a theory for empirical accuracy and checking its assumptions for internal consistency.

Theories. Prospective explanations of reality. They are deductive, and they consist of a set of assumptions that limits how we view reality.

Third-party intervention. The military intervention by an outside nation in a dispute, usually between internal rivals.

Time inconsistency. When one party gives an irreversible benefit (such as a land concession) to the other party today in exchange for a benefit (such as peace) in the future. Almost certainly, the party receiving the irreversible benefit today will exploits it to seek still more concessions before it will deliver on its promises (if it ever does).

Tit-for-tat. A strategy in which a player echoes whatever its opponent did in the previous move of the game.

Trade. The exchange of goods, services, knowledge, and even culture across vast expanses of geography.

Tragedy of the commons. The overconsumption of a common-pool resource (a resource that is non-excludable but is divisible).

Transaction costs. The price associated with taking actions.

Treaty of Westphalia. The treaty among European nations, signed in 1648, that laid out specifications regarding sovereignty. It remains relevant to international interactions today.

True believers. Terrorists who prefer a winner-takes-all approach over compromising, and so they have no interest in negotiating.

Uncertainty. *See* Asymmetric information.

Unidimensional. One-dimensional; able to be displayed meaningfully on a straight line in a graph.

Unipolarity. A structuring of the international system in which international politics is dominated by one powerful state.

Unitary actors. States that are treated in theories of international relations as a single actors or entities, so that their internal structures, compositions, or divisions are not relevant to their actions in international affairs.

Utility. A cardinal measure of the degree to which one choice is preferred to another as measured by risks.

Variables. Characteristics, events, or ideas that can take on more than one value. *See also* Dependent variables; Independent variables.

War cycles. The hypothesis that war, like the power of states, ebbs and flows, rising and declining as a state's power peaks and then starts to decline.

War effort. The amount of resources that a country invests in war; usually measured as military expenditures.

Westphalia. *See* Treaty of Westphalia.

Winning coalition. A group of individuals that controls sufficient resources to defeat rival combinations.

Win sets. The sets of policies that can win relative to the point of comparison, usually the status quo.

Citations
of Authors

Subject Index